Free at Last!

Tony Benn is the longest serving MP in the history of the Labour Party. He left Parliament in 2001, after more than half a century in the House of Commons, to devote more time to politics. From 2001 to 2002 he was visiting professor of government and politics at the LSE and he is now engaged on a nationwide speaking tour.

He is the author of many books, including his powerful case for constitutional change, *Common Sense* (with Andrew Hood), *Arguments for Socialism*, *Arguments for Democracy*, eight volumes of Diaries and the childhood memoir, *Dare to be a Daniel: Then and Now*.

Tony Benn has four children and ten grandchildren. He was married for 51 years to Caroline, socialist, teacher and author, who died in 2000.

Ruth Winstone has edited all the volumes of Tony Benn's Diaries and several biographies of political figures. She is associate editor of *The Times Guide to the House of Commons*; and currently works as a Library Clerk in the Commons.

By the same author

The Regeneration of Britain
Speeches
Arguments for Socialism
Arguments for Democracy
Parliament, People and Power
The Sizewell Syndrome
Fighting Back: Speaking Out for Socialism in the Eighties
A Future for Socialism
Common Sense (*with Andrew Hood*)
Dare to be a Daniel: Then and Now

Years of Hope: Diaries 1940–1962
Out of the Wilderness: Diaries 1963–1967
Office Without Power: Diaries 1968–1972
Against the Tide: Diaries 1973–1976
Conflicts of Interest: Diaries 1977–1980
The End of an Era: Diaries 1980–1990
The Benn Diaries: Single Volume Edition 1940–1990
More Time for Politics: Diaries 2001–2007

TONY BENN

Free at Last!

Diaries 1991–2001

Edited by Ruth Winstone

arrow books

Published by Arrow Books in 2003

13

First published by Hutchinson in 2002

Arrow Books
The Random House Group Limited
20 Vauxhall Bridge Road, London SW1V 2SA

www.rbooks.co.uk

Addresses for companies within The Random House Group Limited can be found at: www.randomhouse.co.uk/offices.htm

The Random House Group Limited Reg. No. 954009

A CIP catalogue record for this book is available from the British Library

ISBN 9780099415022

The Random House Group Limited supports the Forest Stewardship Council® (FSC®), the leading international forest-certification organisation. Our books carrying the FSC label are printed on FSC®-certified paper. FSC is the only forest-certification scheme supported by the leading environmental organisations, including Greenpeace. Our paper procurement policy can be found at www.randomhouse.co.uk/environment

Typeset by MATS, Southend-on-Sea, Essex
Printed and bound by CPI Group
(UK) Ltd, Croydon, CR0 4YY

This book is dedicated to Caroline, to all our grandchildren and to future generations, in the hope that they may make a better world for themselves than we have been able to make for them.

Contents

Illustrations

Tony Banks *(Nils Jorgensen/Rex Features)*
Alice Mahon *(Jago Parker)*
Lady Wilson and Tony Blair *(Benn Collection)*
Betty Boothroyd *(Rex Features)*
Michael Martin *(Rex Features)*
Tony Benn, Donald Soper and Jack Jones *(Alun Jones)*
Tony Benn's 'parliamentary cake' *(Benn Collection)*
Retiring MPs *(Jeremy Young/Sunday Times)*
Tony and Caroline Benn *(PA Photos)*

Cartoons:

page 2: © Hector Breeze/*Guardian Newspapers Ltd* (March 5 1999); page 100: John Harris; page 238: © John Kent/*Times Newspapers Ltd*, London (May 17 2000); page 410: © Peter Brookes/*Times Newspapers Ltd,* London (December 9 1997); page 671: © Nicholas Garland/*Telegraph Group Ltd 1999* (June 29 1999).

Introduction

The 1990s was a most dangerous but also a most interesting decade in politics at home and abroad, including two major wars, both led by the United States in its new imperial role. We saw the replacement, in 1997, of a Tory administration after eighteen years in power, and this volume describes these and other developments from an independent perspective.

In just over ten years the Conservative Party has had four leaders, the Labour Party three. Neil Kinnock resigned in 1992 after nine years as Labour leader and two General Election defeats; he was followed by John Smith, who died tragically soon after, and then by Tony Blair who proclaimed that New Labour was a new political party.

This book chronicles the birth and development of New Labour, of which I am not a member and which, though almost certainly the smallest party in the history of British politics, is nevertheless a very powerful organisation, since most of its members are in the Cabinet or have supported it financially.

The New Labour 'Project' was devised primarily as a way of gaining and then retaining office by abandoning socialism, distancing the Party from the trade unions, and working with the Liberal Democrats and some 'wet' Conservatives.

New Labour's overriding aims have been to build an alliance with corporate Britain, embrace the concept of a federal Europe, stand uncritically with America in all matters of foreign and defence policy, commit itself to market forces and globalisation, and seek to legitimise it all in the name of the 'Third Way', a convenient philosophy apparently espoused by many European leaders and by President Clinton.

New Labour's victory in 1997 was built on two quite contradictory pillars of strength: a desire by most electors to remove the Conservatives and an equal desire by the Establishment to retain Conservative policies, which they believed were far safer in the hands of New Labour with a popular mandate than in the hands of the divided, weak and demoralised

Conservatives. Hence the phrase recently used by one of the prophets of the Project: 'We are all Thatcherites now.'

That said, there have been considerable achievements since 1997: the greatest undoubtedly have been the progress towards peace and stability in Northern Ireland, which I followed with intense interest; the introduction of the minimum wage; and extra revenue for the public services (unfortunately linked to privatisation, a throwback to the past and now rechristened modernisation).

Britain's relations with Europe have been extensively debated over this period. The Maastricht Treaty was ratified without a referendum, and the leadership of New Labour has struggled to find a formula for persuading Britain to enter the Euro-zone against strong opposition from right across the political spectrum.

This volume of my diaries completes my final ten years as a backbench MP, after more than half a century in Parliament, and marks the end, in 1994, of thirty-four years on the National Executive Committee of the Labour Party.

Since I have argued all my life that it is issues and not personalities that should underpin political action and debate, readers may be surprised – or even shocked – by some of the very harsh and possibly unwarranted personal criticisms of individuals and colleagues. These were dictated at night, to relieve my feelings before my anger had subsided, and reflect my frustration at what was being said or done, and I must apologise unreservedly, in advance, for any hurt they might cause or offence that they give.

This is inevitably much more personal than earlier volumes, covering as it does the illness and death of my wife Caroline – my best friend and inspiration – and news of my children and grandchildren, of whom I am intensely proud.

Ruth Winstone, who has most skilfully edited this volume, as she has the whole series dating from 1940, has selected the material to be published (which amounts to no more than 20 per cent of the original) with complete independence and integrity. For the many mistakes in the diary – both political and factual – I accept full personal responsibility.

Mandy Greenfield and Robyn Karney both contributed significantly to the process of editing with their perceptive comments and meticulous work. Robyn's late suggestions were invaluable. I must also thank those who transcribed the diary so carefully from cassette recordings that were often almost inaudible and syntactically complex, including my personal secretary and good friend, Sheila Hubacher, Hilary Weeks, Ruth Hobson, Diana Martin and Alison McPherson.

I owe a special debt of gratitude to Tony Whittome of Hutchinson for his unfailing support, patience and encouragement for this project, forging a friendship over many years.

No longer in Parliament, but enjoying the 'Freedom of the House', a concept suggested by my son Joshua and generously granted me by Speaker Martin, which allows me the same rights as are enjoyed by members of the House of Lords who have been MPs, I am now free to devote more time to politics. I shall continue to campaign for all those causes to which I have long been committed, in unity with those outside whose encouragement and support over the years have greatly inspired me.

Tony Benn
August 2003

Part One
January 1991–April 1992

The year 1991 was overshadowed by war with Iraq, which had invaded Kuwait, for by then it was clear that President Bush had no intention of being diverted from a military attack. I had just returned from Baghdad where I had met the Iraqi President, Saddam Hussein, who expected this attack to come even if he withdrew his forces from Kuwait.

The Prime Minister, John Major, went along with this strategy (whatever his private doubts) and committed British forces to the war, knowing that he was able to rely upon the firm support offered him by Neil Kinnock, who had been leader of the Labour Party since 1983.

Major had been Prime Minister for only a month and had given the Conservative Government a new lease of life, though the next seven years were dogged by economic volatility and political crises largely related to arguments over the European Union. The Treaty of Maastricht, which established the framework of a European Bank and a stability pact to deal with inflation, and the question of monetary union, loomed on the horizon.

BOO! HE'S A FOREIGNER!
BOO! HE'S A CAPITALIST

Friday 4 January 1991

The Iraqi Ambassador and Mr Ibrahim, the Minister, came to see me at 2.30 and stayed for about an hour to get my assessment of the situation. I said I thought it was very dangerous and that Saddam Hussein should invite Perez de Cuellar, the Secretary General of the UN, to Baghdad, and told them I had written to Perez de Cuellar suggesting this, which they knew. In the *Guardian* this morning there was a little note saying that Perez de Cuellar would be willing to go to Baghdad, which is a slight improvement. I said I thought that if Iraq could give an indication of its support to the UN, and offer a UN peace-keeping force in the disputed areas, it would transform the situation.

I decided to give back to Mr Ibrahim the presents they had given me, although it has long been the custom for embassies to give a bottle of this and that to people they know in Government. But at the same time, it is quite impossible for me to receive a gift from the Iraqis now. They had sent me four bottles of whisky, four bottles of cognac, three bottles of wine and a carpet. So I packed them all up and said to Mr Ibrahim, 'I know you will understand, but I cannot receive a gift from Iraq at the moment.'

He said, 'It was a personal gift from the Ambassador and myself.'

I said, 'I fully understand that, and I know you won't misunderstand me.' So he very kindly drove off with them. I know the Arab countries are very friendly, but at this moment you can't have gifts passing between Iraq and a British MP who is opposed to the war, so I am really relieved to have got that out of the way.

Saturday 5 January

Went to see King Hussein and Ruth Winstone, my editor, made notes. His house is at Palace Green – millionaires' row. The Head of Protocol showed us into a beautiful room with lots of pictures of the King and his American queen, all incredible really, overlooking Kensington Palace. The King came in and thanked me very much indeed for all that I had done. He said, 'You have done a marvellous job. I am deeply indebted to you.'

He said the language used by President Bush was venomous and he wasn't sure whether it was a bluff. He said Prime Minister Major behaved like a sort of team manager. I told him that Tariq Aziz knew Major. There was a disagreement between the United States and Great Britain, he thought, on the question of whether there should be an unconditional withdrawal. He said he thought Italy was distancing itself and he was trying to define the language, because Iraq wanted a peaceful solution. He said an Iraq-Saudi dialogue was developing and Gaddafi was playing some part. I suggested he might write to Neil Kinnock.

He said he thought there would be an attack on Iraq, even after withdrawal. He believed that the fundamentalists were planning an attack on Israel via Jordan, and thought Iraq and Saudi Arabia – but not Syria – would be uneasy about this. He said Israel was occupying the Lebanon and this was a matter that was never mentioned. He talked about changes in the region and the reorganisation of governments and said, 'Do the United States want a permanent base in Jordan? Jordan have no diplomatic relations with Israel. There would have to be a withdrawal of Israeli troops from the West Bank.'

Sent a fax to Larry Whitty asking Neil to take the initiative.

Wednesday 9 January

The Labour Attaché of the Israeli Embassy came to see me, a man of about forty-two, very neat and smart. I asked what he did before, and it turned out he was a colonel in the Israeli Army, had worked with the President of Israel, then moved over to the Histadrut. So he was no more a Labour Attaché than I could be a Military Attaché. Unfortunately, I didn't discover that until the end of the talk.

I told him my mother was a Fellow of the Hebrew University and had visited Chaim Weizmann before the war. I had been in Palestine/Israel at the end of the war, had stayed in a kibbutz, danced with the settlers, given the Balfour Day lecture in Tel-Aviv, knew Golda Meir, had corresponded with David Ben Gurion and showed him a little bit of Masada, which I had been given when I went there, and so on. He was absolutely flummoxed, because I think he thought he was going to come up against a really anti-Israeli person.

He said, 'Well, at least you understand.'

I said, 'Do pass on my best wishes to your Ambassador. It must be a very difficult time for you and of course, if you are involved in the war, you will just have to be very careful.' I think I outmanoeuvred him, but I don't want bad relations with the Israeli Government. I said to him, 'All that is required is some vision. I am saying to you exactly what I said to Saddam Hussein.'

Tuesday 15 January

Eric Heffer, who is desperately ill, dying of cancer, rang today and said he wanted to come in to vote. He was as frail as anything, white as a sheet, obviously on his last legs. After we had voted, he came into the Chamber and I held his arm and he said, 'I'll sit next to you.' During the Division, masses of people came up and shook him warmly by the hand and I was sitting there just crying like a baby. I didn't try to control my tears, because it makes it worse, and the tears rolled down my cheeks. The Prime Minister came over and spoke to Eric and people clapped him. I have never, in forty years, heard anyone clapping in the House of Commons. Eric was overwhelmed and I took him out and he went home.

Wednesday 16 January

I received a call at 11.40 p.m. saying, 'Switch on ITN, the war has begun.' I switched on and there was the report from CNN staff in Baghdad describing the bombing of the city. It was quite extraordinary. They were in the Al Rashid Hotel, where I had stayed a few weeks ago, and they were looking out of the window saying, 'It's like a firework display on 4 July', while all around them people were being killed! Terrible.

War began today.

Sunday 20 January

The bombing of Baghdad is going on on a huge scale with twice the weight of the bombs dropped on Hiroshima, and there is a population of four million people so there must be massive casualties. The whole thing is so awful. Israel is getting special Patriot missiles to shoot down the Scud missiles, and so on. But the tide of opinion is, of course, shifting towards war.

The Iraqi Ambassador phoned to ask if he could come and see me, and I said 'Yes' and rang the FO to tell them. He came with Ibrahim.

He said casualties were very high, not only in Baghdad but also in villages and other populated areas, and that he would send me the names of the villages. It was just a sort of exchange of information. I did find it rather embarrassing. I was nervous of the Iraqi Ambassador coming to see me at home, because of how it might be interpreted, which is why I rang the FO. I rang the FO afterwards and told them what he said. I don't care for the Ambassador very much, but Ibrahim is a cultivated, civilised and intelligent diplomat and I had a feeling that he was really in charge. He was very distressed because his family is in Baghdad.

Parliament is no use in a conflict. As soon as there is a real conflict or pressure – miners strike, Wapping, war – the two Front Benches hunch together like anything. It is important that people realise that. You have to have a party, and it's certainly worthwhile getting rid of bad governments and it's nice to know you can substitute better ones, but basically Parliament is a place for consensus and not for confrontation.

Neil Kinnock's position is disreputable, and he and Gerald Kaufman are speaking really for the Israeli position, not even for the UN. Perez de Cuellar has disappeared completely, has done absolutely nothing. The

Americans have got control of everything. Britain is tagging along, and one day people will wake up and realise there are real casualties in this war, and God knows what they will decide to do then.

Wednesday 23 January

Yesterday the *Daily Star* had a vicious attack on the Labour MPs who voted against supporting our forces, as 'a bunch of treacherous swine'.

Wednesday 30 January

Arrived at Channel 4's headquarters in Gray's Inn Road at midnight and did a two-hour programme with an anchor man and a succession of people – Professor Norman Stone, who is a Professor of History at Oxford and writes for the *Daily Mail.* I do not consider him worthy of being called a serious person; Simon Hoggart, who is equally insubstantial; Arkady Maslennikov, who used to be the chief *Pravda* correspondent in London, then went to be chief press officer for Gorbachev and is now the chief press officer for the Soviet Parliament, an old friend whom I like very much; Admiral Whitehead, and others.

I said in the course of the discussion that I thought the Russians had made a mistake to vote with the Americans on Resolution 678, because that had committed them to the war and it was very difficult to get them back.*

Arkady Maslennikov was asked about this and said, 'I cannot comment on the policy of the Soviet Government at the Security Council.' When the discussion moved to the other side of the studio, he leaned over and in a stage whisper said, very loudly, to me, 'I agree entirely with what you have said.' So that was an insight into a lot of things and made me wonder whether perhaps Gorbachev wasn't very keen on what the Soviet Foreign Minister had done at the Security Council. I hope I might see Maslennikov while he is in London.

To the Finance and General Purposes Committee of the NEC, where there was a really extremely amusing discussion because a proposal has come forward that Littlewoods Pools should have a special scheme to raise money for the Labour Party. Then we were told that 'high-value donors' were going to be approached and a dinner was going to be held in the summer for rich people to finance the LP's campaign.

Somebody said, 'What about the ordinary party members?'

They replied, 'We could have a raffle, so some ordinary working-class people could attend the dinner with rich people to raise money.'

Julia Hobsbawm, who must be the daughter of Eric, the old Marxist

*The resolution of the Security Council authorised member states co-operating with Kuwait . . . 'to *use all necessary means* to uphold and implement' previous resolutions against Iraq.

historian, which is an indication of the state we have reached, has worked out this high-value donor scheme.

Larry Whitty said, 'Before we go ahead with this, I think we ought to discuss the politics of it, because there might be some reactions by Party members to the fact that rich people were being approached to help the Party. Also we were hoping for corporate payments from companies, but we need the money and, anyway, we accept money for exhibition stands.'

Dennis Skinner said, 'We are a trade union party.' He was against it.

Neil said, 'After all, the Mandela concert didn't compromise us and that was sponsored. Anyway, there is one member of the LP who has given £100,000 to the Party, and what's wrong with that?' I think he said it was Paul Hamlyn.

Anne Davis supported the proposal.

I said, 'Exhibitions are different, because at least the people who buy space are getting some sort of service, but if you encourage rich people to give money to the Party, they will expect favours in return and, when the polls go up and it looks as if we are going to win, a lot of companies will give us money to get that influence. It will end up like Australia where Rupert Murdoch supports Bob Hawke. As far as corporate funds are concerned, we have always taken a principled position against companies that give money to the Tory Party without consulting anybody, compared to the trade unions that have to have a ballot.' I was against it.

Hattersley said, 'We need the cash. It won't be offensive to the Party. We are not a viable party. Cricketers and footballers give money.'

Dennis Skinner said, 'Yes, but they'll all expect peerages', which was a point I had whispered in his ear.

Tony Clarke said, 'Getting money from rich people deals with the charge that the LP is run by loonies.'

Dennis and I were the only ones to oppose it.

Picked up my Message Master, which is my latest toy and buzzes when there are messages. Trouble is I didn't have any messages, so I rang up and left myself a lot and they kept arriving.

Thursday 31 January

Arkady Maslennikov came over and I gave him a cup of tea and poured my heart out. I said, 'I feel so discouraged that all the people who defended the Soviet Union during the early years have been repudiated along with Stalin.'

He's a good socialist and said, 'This free-for-all has led to crime, and anybody can do anything. There are no values left. And, of course, the Baltic States have been encouraged by the Americans.'

I asked him about Gorbachev.

He said, 'Gorbachev is a very interesting man. He is very able, has a degree, but no depth of understanding. He is a brilliant tactician but no strategist.' He told a marvellous story about how Gorbachev said one day, 'I have been reading about Roman Property Law and it is very interesting.' Arkady told me, 'But the trouble is he had never read about any law since the Roman Property Law, so it wasn't frightfully helpful!'

I asked Arkady why he was sacked and he said, 'We went to the Urals together and I gave a press conference and said the visit had gone very well. And Gorbachev said it hadn't gone very well at all, it was an "overwhelming success". He just wanted me to present it his way.'

Arkady didn't like Yeltsin who, he said, was a complete opportunist and when he went to America and saw the great riches in New York, was like a country boy, excited without realising what lay behind it. Arkardy himself was shocked by the homelessness in London.

A very nice, decent guy. He said he was appalled by the British press and the way in which Britain kept jumping up and saying, 'Look how important we are in the Gulf.' He went on, 'You're going round with a begging bowl and you are only a minor part of the war', which is absolutely true.

He invited me to Moscow and he invited Ruth, and gave us his telephone numbers and said, 'Why don't you ring me up in Moscow.' I have got a few Russian friends, him and Boris Krylov.

The news today is that the American B52 bombers are going to be based at RAF Fairford for the bombing of Iraq, so we are now right in the heart of it at home, as well as having 45,000 troops in the Gulf.

Sunday 3 February

Went to the demonstration in Hyde Park, where the speakers were a German Rear Admiral, the Bishop of St Andrew's, Billy Bragg, somebody from the Green Party, Terry Marsland and me. Some Iraqis who had families in Baghdad were nearly in tears. CND said there were 30,000 people; the police said 15,000.

Came home and watched *Inspector Morse* and then worked till midnight.

Thursday 7 February

I turned on the television and it appears that a white van parked outside the MOD fired three missiles right over Downing Street, one of which landed in the garden of Number 10 and actually blew in the windows at the Cabinet Office and then blew up itself. I thought it was the Iraqis, but later the police said it was the IRA, though they might want to avoid a sense of panic about the Iraqi war. It was later confirmed that the IRA had done it.

Friday 8 February

Heavy snowfall, about 6-8 inches of snow, the garden like fairyland, London brought to a standstill, buses and trains cancelled and stopped.

I am wondering about my relationship with Labour MPs. I get on with Tory MPs because you don't expect to agree with them and so you just have a jocular chat with them. But with Labour MPs I still have this deep sense of betrayal, which influences me and draws me in on myself – I think rather like Enoch Powell must have been when he was in the House. If you talked to him he was friendly, but otherwise he was isolated. I dare say I should treat the Labour MPs as if they are just people you know, and not really worry about their opinions because you can't shift them. A strange conclusion to reach. I don't want to row with anybody, I'm perfectly happy to be friendly and yet there is no will to make change of any sort or kind to society – just a desperate desire by people at the top to get themselves into ministerial offices and an absolutely strident demand to everybody else to line up, or they will lose their seats and their chances of office, and, to the Party, just to get rid of the Tories.

Yesterday's bombing, which very nearly killed the entire War Cabinet, was the most sensational military assault on the centre of British power. The news has gone all around the world and established the vulnerability of Britain in two respects that interest me. First of all, that with all the high-tech equipment we have in the Gulf, we can't stop somebody in a transit van from firing a mortar bomb that nearly kills the Cabinet in the centre of London. Secondly, all the protests by Kinnock and Major and Ashdown saying that this bombing will only strengthen our resolve is never applied across the board to the other side – why don't they feel as we do about being bombed?

Mother said the other day that war seems to be necessary in some way and that is what I feel: it has got long-term consequences because it is a way of paying by a blood sacrifice for the selfishness of the last decade. People feel they have been selfish and jungle-like and they want to put it right by sacrifice – not of themselves, I might add, but by the sacrifice of young men who were sent out there. And in that whole process everyone starts thinking again about society.

Sunday 10 February

Had a phone call from Tunis asking if I would go to Amman on Sunday – Kenneth Kaunda, King Hussein, Daniel Ortega, Yasser Arafat. They are hoping they can make some progress on a peace initiative and I am sure it is a very useful idea, and it's just the question of summoning up £600 and the energy to get there. I am torn really. If I had a private secretary, I would send him out to do all these things. I gather that King Hussein will pay all my expenses while I am in Amman, but won't pay the fare.

Sunday 17 February

Collected Ruth, who drove me to Fairford for the demonstration outside the airbase there.

The cart, which was the platform, was covered in bales of hay, with blankets on them as seats. There were some lovely speeches. Bruce Kent spoke, a nun from Birmingham, a reservist and somebody from Iraq. Just before I spoke, a man jumped on the platform and unfurled a banner that said, 'No whinging Benns here.'

In the audience I recognised the Revd Andrew Hake, whom I had known in the Fifties when he was the industrial chaplain to the Bishop of Bristol. Then he went to Africa and wrote to me many times, but I haven't heard from him for more than twenty years. I went and spoke to him afterwards. Just as people began singing peace hymns, there was a roar and into the sky came three of these great B52 bombers loaded with bombs on their way to bomb Iraq. I stood there and cried. It was terribly sad.

Walked back to Fairford and the children from the married quarters threw eggs at us and waved the Stars and Stripes and the Union Jack.

Monday 18 February

An IRA bomb at Victoria killed one man and wounded thirty more and there was another bomb at Waterloo.

Tuesday 19 February

There was a fire today and the Central Line was not working, so with the bombing, the snow and the fire, the whole thing is just awful. London is almost paralysed at the moment.

Wednesday 20 February

To the Grand Committee Room, where John Smith and the Treasury team were addressing a lot of parliamentary candidates. I sat at the back. I hadn't been invited and John was explaining, in words of one syllable, what Labour economic policy was, which is in effect to cut the rate of interest by 1 per cent and stay in the ERM. There were all these candidates, all quite young, in their early thirties I would think, and I was looking at them from behind, not seeing their faces, with John Smith talking to them. It was like a regional manager talking to the sales reps, and when we get state aid for all parties and trade union money disappears, Parliament will cease to be anything other than a discussion group among alternative governments about how things should operate.

Sunday 24 February

The land war began last night, and land forces rolled into Kuwait and all the reports from the allies' coalition forces are wholly positive, and so on.

The Queen was wheeled out to do a broadcast, which I videoed.

Today the Archbishop of York, Habgood, came out in support of the war and Kaufman was on the radio: awful. I feel very depressed.

Monday 25 February
The world head of the Amadiyya Muslim Association in the UK arrived, accompanied by a former Pakistani Ambassador who had got in touch with me to say that Huzur (as he is called), the head of ten million Muslims with a presence in 120 countries, had been praying for peace in the Gulf and wanted to meet me.

I talked to them for over an hour. I asked about the sect and what it stood for, and Huzur said it believed in peace, social justice, the ethics of the Mohammedan religion, and that it wanted to spread the Muslim faith without violence and respected other religions. One of the things that interested me was that I heard it was the sect that believed that Jesus had been cut down from the cross, gone to Kashmir and died there. Of course, the whole idea that the myth of the risen Christ is false is a deadly blow to Christianity! Huzur said that the evidence was that Pontius Pilate had washed his hands of it, that Pilate's wife had said something indicating he was innocent, and that the crucifixion was fixed for a Friday when, of course, you didn't normally crucify; that it took three days for people to die on the cross, and Jesus was cut down within three hours; that the spears put into his side had gushed blood and water, whereas a dead man would only have oozed a little blood; that Jesus had been taken to a tomb, his wounds dressed and then he had gone to Kashmir, because he had rejected the idea of a Christ. Fascinating.

Thursday 28 February
Overnight, the ceasefire was announced by George Bush and that was the big news.

Went into the House and asked a question of the Prime Minister, and I am glad I did, because you can't run away at a moment like this, although Pat Duffy, the Labour Member, had congratulated Neil Kinnock, and said we had our faint hearts, pointing in my direction, and the House cheered him like anything.

Rushed to the station for the train to Canterbury. I was invited by the Religion and Society Group of the University of Kent. I had spoken to the Dean of Canterbury, who was very frosty and opposed to my visit. His press officer, an ex-military officer, was very angry. Today I had instructions that under no circumstances was I to give interviews while I was in the precincts of the cathedral.

Went into the precincts and it was a full moon. Canterbury is all pedestrianised and it was like going back to the Middle Ages. It was absolutely lovely. The air was warm, the sky was clear and the moon was over the cathedral, and I went in and looked around. Then I had to come outside the precincts to sit on the bench in the cobbled square to do this interview with a young reporter from BBC local radio.

Went back into the chapter house, where there were about 150 people.

It is a beautiful room with a marvellous decorated ceiling, probably from about 1200, and I gave my lecture on religion and the Gulf War. It went down very well and there were questions and answers and I thoroughly enjoyed it.

Sunday 3 March

The *Sunday Times* had an attack on people from the Peace Movement who, they said, were Jeremiahs who should now apologise, and there was a big picture of Ted Heath, Denis Healey and myself, quoting my figures about casualties when I talked about tens and hundreds of thousands. But on page 2 was a report from the Pentagon to the effect that 200,000 Iraqis, many of them conscript soldiers, had been killed. So I wrote a little letter to the *Sunday Times* pointing out the discrepancy between their request for an apology and their confirmation of the forecasts.

To the Young Vic Theatre for this performance of *The Peloponnesian War*, a play written by John Barton, a marvellous show. Michael Kustow, whom I had met somewhere, was director. There were Enoch Powell, Anthony Barnett from Charter 88 and *New Statesman*, and Brian Clark, a playwright. After the play we went on the stage, with Mike Kustow in the chair and John Barton sitting on the floor – he having written the play and also playing the part of Thucydides. It had been a marvellous production, every word of it was absolutely relevant 2500 years later, and we then discussed it. Enoch was very good, having done his Fellowship thesis on Thucydides. We had a good discussion. Brian Clark said language was corrupted, Anthony Barnett talked a bit about democracy, then there was a discussion from the floor. It did show how the theatre can become the media, and how important the theatre is as a medium because the theatre and the churches were both media before televisions and newspapers. Having been in Canterbury Cathedral and with the Royal Shakespeare Theatre, I felt I was moving into new ground and I enjoyed it greatly.

At the Campaign Strategy Committee there was a paper from John Underwood, the new Director of Campaigns and Communications, who took over from Peter Mandelson. Michael Meacher thinks Peter Mandelson wants to get rid of Kinnock and take over the Party, with Tony Blair as his Deputy, which I think is a ludicrous conspiracy. Such a Party would have no appeal to anybody. I said I thought John Smith and Gordon Brown would take over the Party if we lost the election, and Michael was full of realignments and this and that, but things don't happen like that.

Friday 8 March

Took Caroline to the airport.

Tonight there is the vote on the revived War Crimes Bill; I had voted for it last time because I thought anti-Semitism is on the increase, and why should these old Nazis get away with it, and so on. But a lot of Tories were against it and the House of Lords threw it out. To my amazement, the Government decided to resurrect the Bill under the Parliament Act and asked us to pass a resolution. It had to be drafted exactly as it was when it went through last year, because that is the provision of the Parliament Act. I thought very carefully and I cannot vote for it – the hypocrisy of it is too much. I know these old Nazis live here and should be brought to justice, but then I think of Suez and Vietnam, and of the massacre on the road between Kuwait City and Basra recently; and then I think of the judges who would be trying the case, who would be the same as those who tried the Birmingham Six and resisted justice for them. Then I think the argument that we shouldn't let the Lords veto Commons legislation is so hypocritical, when the Tory Party believe in the Lords and would be quite happy to encourage them to veto Labour legislation. I am just not going to vote. I am tempted to make a speech about it, but it would be a very unpopular speech. It would be very difficult to explain it because the papers would say, 'Benn backs Hitler just as he backed Saddam, he now comes out for the Nazi war criminals.' So I will just do nothing about it at all.

I have a feeling that as there is only a one-line whip, they may have a job getting it through. I record this because it is one of those occasions when your feet won't take you through the Lobby, even though you feel in your heart that war criminals shouldn't get away with it. But somebody has got to protest about hypocrisy.

Thursday 14 March

Big news today is that the Birmingham Six were released after sixteen years in prison.

Gail Rebuck and Kate Mosse from the publishers came to the house to reassure me, following the dismissal of my commissioning editor Richard Cohen, that my diaries were safe. Gail Rebuck is married to Philip Gould, who advises the Labour party on publicity for the election and employs Nita Clarke, so there are sort of Kinnockite and family connections. If it hadn't been for Richard I would never have published my diaries at all, but I haven't got a contract with them for the final volume and I can't pull back. Richard wants Caroline's book on Keir Hardie, but that's a matter for her to decide. Hutchinson are continuing with the book about Mother, but it is all terribly painful because Richard is such a kindly man and such a distinguished editor.

Friday 15 March

The release of the Birmingham Six is absolutely dominating the headlines and there is a demand for the resignation of Lord Lane and I signed the motion that had been put down.

Caroline got back late tonight.

I left early for Swansea and was taken to the university, which was run-down like most other universities. There is graffiti everywhere, and the windows are broken or painted over.

The Student Union has lost its control over the students and there are stories of the selling of degrees in the Philosophy and Medical Ethics Department to people who haven't really qualified; and one of the dissertations was pure plagiarism, and two people who had objected had been sacked and given redundancy pay, on the understanding they never said a word about the university. It was a very interesting reminder of the absolute corruption of everything in the public services – Health, Education – everything is corrupted and destroyed by Thatcher.

Monday 18 March

A young lad called Charles Crowe, a student, came to work for a few days.

Voted for the War Crimes Bill, despite the doubts I had had: 88 voted against, 254 for, but nothing whatsoever will happen, though I suppose if you come out against it, it looks as if you are retrospectively endorsing fascism in Europe and there is a growth of anti-Semitism again. Also, it was an opportunity when the Cabinet decided to override the House of Lords, so that is a useful precedent.

Wednesday 20 March, Chesterfield

On the train a distinguished gentleman came up to me, looked down and said, 'I want to speak to you about the Gulf War.' There were a lot of Tory businessmen sitting around me and I wondered what this was going to amount to. He said, 'I just wanted to tell you that I agreed with everything you said about the Gulf War.'

I said, 'That's very kind of you. What do you do?'

'I am retired but I was in the Colonial Office in Arabia in the old days, and what you said was absolutely right and has even made me think again about the Falklands War.'

I was quite staggered.

Thursday 21 March

Michael Heseltine made a statement in the afternoon in which the Poll Tax was abolished. An astonishing week. In future, we are going to have a property tax based on ability to pay.

Friday 27 March

To the Speaker's House for the ceremony where Eric Heffer was given the Freedom of the City of Liverpool, a lovely occasion. The Speaker's Dining Room is a beautiful room with huge oil paintings of the Speakers around it. All these Liverpool people came in – Jack Spriggs, Tony

Mulhearn; a mass of people and all the Militant Tendency councillors who had been expelled.

The spirit of Liverpool just took over that room. They were saying, 'Look at those carvings,' quite unimpressed by the important people who were there – the Speaker or anybody else – or by the paintings, but, 'Look at those carvings, only the working class could have done that.' They have a real pride. We had drinks and canapés and one of them came up afterwards and said, 'Do you know, they have charged us twenty-one pounds a head for this.' I spoke to the Speaker about it – I thought it was disgraceful.

At the ceremony itself, Neil Kinnock was sitting there looking absolutely frozen, because the room was full of the councillors he had expelled. So the thing had a poignancy about it.

Eric spoke, looking thin and weak, but he made a good speech.

Wednesday 3 April, Stansgate

Now I am sixty-six, I have to think about what I am going to do with the rest of my life.

I hereby resolve that I will not do more than vote against the things on the NEC that I think are wrong. I can give an opinion, but they don't listen, and there is no point fighting the Party at this stage, certainly not before the election. Secondly, I have got to give more attention to Chesterfield, because the books, the speeches and the Gulf War have been an excuse for not doing as much in Chesterfield as I should have done.

I am a conscientious constituency member as far as the casework is concerned but my diary should be full of things I am taking up for Chesterfield. Certainly in the early Eighties I wasn't doing that for Bristol, though I think I have been better since I have been in Chesterfield. I should take a bit more interest in Parliament and contribute my opinions more there on matters that are of concern to Chesterfield, and not always be floating off on great international activities or constitutional matters that don't make an awful lot of sense to the people I represent in Parliament.

Altogether I think I have just got to think a lot less about myself and a lot more about what I am elected to do, because I have had a bit of a shock reading the diary and this is a bit of a confession. Six years ago, on my sixtieth birthday, I resolved that I would publish the diaries and this volume will complete them.

Age catches up with you. I haven't the energy I had before and I wonder whether these years of defeat didn't, in the early days at any rate, sour me and prevent me from making constructive suggestions that would have been welcome to my colleagues in the House and to the Party generally, who desperately want to see a Labour Government. That's been a bit of an eye-opener to me, and I think that is one reason why I dreaded reading those volumes. All that time wasted on Militant when really they aren't a part of the normal mainstream of the LP, which is radical, socialist, at least in essence. On the one hand, you have got all these people who are simply concerned with power; and on the other hand, you've got sectarians who are simply concerned with ideological purity; and somewhere in the middle somebody has to try and use that skill to bring it all together for the good of the people we represent.

Thursday 11 April

In the evening I invited people working in the office, including Charles Crowe, Simon Fletcher and Jennie Walsh, to come to Television Centre for *Question Time* with David Mellor, Simon Hughes and Stephen Fry. Peter Sissons was in the chair. The audience has apparently risen to between five and six million since the Gulf War. The first question, obviously, was on the Kurds and I thought I got that case across quite well. Then there was a question on whether Major was a wimp, which allowed me to distance myself from the whole sort of personality cult in politics. Then there was a question on school testing and finally one on the zoo.

Friday 19 April

The really big news today was that Nita is expecting a baby in December, so that will be our seventh grandchild. She and Stephen are leaving tomorrow morning for the South of France.

Sunday 21 April

The day of the Census.

I fixed the window sash cords. Went to see Mother.

Caroline had a phone call from a Welsh academic who had met a woman who claimed to be Keir Hardie's daughter. She was the daughter of Rose Davies, whom Keir Hardie had known in the early years of the century.

Worked until 2 a.m.

Tuesday 23 April

There has been a lot of speculation about whether John Major would offer David Owen a place in the Cabinet, and there was a marvellous cartoon in the *Evening Standard*. There was the Cabinet Room, with Major sitting there with the usual figures round the table. Heseltine came in with his papers and Major was saying, 'I wonder why we should stop with David Owen?' And there was David Owen next to Major; next to him was Ted Heath; I was at the end of the table with my pipe; and round the corner were Michael Foot and Roy Hattersley.

Thursday 25 April, Birmingham

We were picked up by Peter, the Bishop's chauffeur, in a very fancy car and driven to Hartlebury Castle, the home of the Bishop of Worcester, Philip Goodrich. We drove through the country, through the great gates, along the widening path into a sort of walled garden. Through a gap in the brick wall there was the castle, where some of the vicars and curates were gathered for this general clergy conference. There were a few media people and the Bishop's wife, a very nice woman. I met the former Bishop of Rochester, Richard Say, and Bishop Hugh Montefiore was also there.

Talked to the Bishop, and then we went into this crowded meeting in the Great Hall where there where about 200 clergy including one West African minister, one Romanian Russian Orthodox and one American woman minister – the second ever to be ordained, a very jolly woman in her mid-sixties.

I made a speech, which Ruth said was too funny, but I thought I had better make them laugh. I went into the British Constitution and really made fun of it. Then there were some really good questions: Is God a democrat? Is democracy a good thing?

Then two Evangelicals got up and said, 'Do you accept that Jesus is our Lord?'

I said, 'I don't like the word Lord. I don't believe in Lords.' This brought us on to the whole question of the Kingdom of God, and I did describe my Constitutional Reform Bill. What you realise is that an authoritarian Church, where power comes from the Creator mediated through the bishops to the clergy to the laity, can't really take on board democracy at all because everything is done from the top.

Friday 26 April

Did a bit on LBC about disestablishment.

Had a lovely letter from the new Archbishop of Canterbury, George Carey.

I had written to him a year ago when I was asking all the bishops whether they were in favour of putting a single name forward to succeed Runcie and he had written in his own hand, 'Dear Tony (if I may), thank you for the strong stand you take on moral issues.' So I then congratulated him when he became Archbishop and he said, 'We hope to get to know you when I am in London.'

So I wrote another note when he was enthroned:

Dear Archbishop,

Good luck at Lambeth. Don't let the media get you down.

I thought you might be interested to see this bit I wrote about Elsie Chamberlain because it will remind you of what some of your predecessors thought about the ordination of women.

I hope we may meet soon.

Yours,

Tony

I got a letter back this morning, signed in his own hand:

Dear Tony,

Thank you so much for your kind letter of 19 April.

I am determined not to let the media get me down, because it seems to me that they are knocking every public figure at the moment. Obviously I have got to get used to this kind of thing, and it is especially helpful when you know they are completely wrong.

Thank you for the copy of your obituary of Elsie Chamberlain. Wasn't she a marvellous person?

With every good wish,

George.

Sunday 28 April

Neil Kinnock was interviewed by Brian Walden, who is a very clever man. The first thing he said: 'Well, what's the difference between you and Major?' Kinnock waffled for half an hour and then the more he went on, the more obvious it was that there wasn't much difference. When he got on to the Health Service he did much better, but then he got stumped at the end because he wouldn't agree to increase taxation to pay for public services, so Brian Walden said, 'It looks to me as if your methods, as well as your aims, are the same.' I don't think Kinnock, who was smiling and giggling and gesticulating, had any idea how bad it was.

Sunday 5 May

Hilary brought the boys over and we went up to Chesterfield. Michael is now nine and James is seven. They were watching something on the television where a couple were kissing passionately, and they rolled on the floor, turning away from the television, saying, 'How embarrassing, how embarrassing!' Then James said to me very earnestly, 'You know, Dan-Dan, they must be very good actors to agree to do that.'

Tuesday 7 May

Worked hard on my evidence for the Select Committee on Members' Interests, which is being televised. I rang the Clerk of the Committee, Jim Hastings, to discuss what I could and could not do. At 5.15 I went into Room 15. There were two cameramen standing high above, with their cameras looking down at me as the witness.

I heard John Biffen give his evidence. He put in a paper, which was waffle in my opinion, and answered questions in a very moderate and waffly way. When he had finished, Geoffrey Johnson Smith, the Chairman, said, 'The Committee is going to deliberate in private, and then for a moment with Mr Benn, before we take evidence in public.' I knew that was about the fact that one of my appendices was a photocopy of the relevant passages from the *Questions of Procedure for Ministers* issued to me by Jim Callaghan in 1976 under the classification of 'Confidential', which

I deliberately left in because I didn't want there to be any doubt about what I was doing. I was claiming parliamentary privilege for it. But predictably, in the private session they decided they couldn't agree, called me in to explain and I tried to argue with them, but they wouldn't change their view. Although they didn't take me through my evidence (though they will publish it) they did ask me a lot of questions and I brought out everything that I wanted to say.

Clearly there is a real political divide between the Tories, who are anxious about this whole business of declaring interests, and the Labour people, who in general want it. But the questions were good and interesting and I took various extracts of Erskine May and made reference to various bits of literature I had, and so on. It is a new dimension in parliamentary life.

Monday 13 May

Worked on my Commonwealth of Britain Bill, and faxed a letter with a summary of the Bill to the Queen's new Private Secretary.

Went into the Commons. We had the NEC International Committee: nobody there from the Shadow Cabinet and, when we were discussing the international situation, I said I wanted to warn on the Central Bank. 'This new proposal from Jacques Delors we heard about over the weekend, under which, if Britain signed, it wouldn't have to join until it was ready, is a trap. I don't want to find that the Party has been committed to this, on the grounds that the Government might be reluctant.' To my amazement, John Prescott supported me and so did Jo Richardson, saying, 'Don't commit us.' Geoff Bish said, 'We are cautious on this.' The matter came up again, and I just get the feeling this is the moment when we can turn the tide against this mad rush to European federalism.

Tuesday 14 May

Went to St Thomas' Hospital. This is a personal part of the diary and not for public record. I was told I had leukaemia two years ago and had probably had it for five years, so I have had it now for seven years. It gets very slightly worse every year and is something I shall die with, but not of.

To the Commons. Walked across the bridge, a lovely day.

I saw Norman Tebbit and asked him how his programme on disestablishment looked and he said, 'It's fine. Your bit was very good' (when I mentioned the monarchy). I said, 'I'm surprised you used it.'

'I just don't want to elect a President, that's all. I'd want to have a non-political monarch,' he said. I replied, 'Well, what about the Prince of Wales?' He seemed to think he was just feeble-minded.

I got the feeling that Tebbit's link with the monarchy was pretty tenuous.

Wandered round to look for a new room, because there will be people leaving with the end of Parliament and there is a new building over in Parliament Street so I think I will probably get a room over there.

Sunday 19 May
Went to see Mother, who is in good form.

In the evening I went to this dinner that Patricia and Richard Moberly and Ruth Winstone were giving for Chris and Ngoc Mullin, for Mike Mansfield, QC, and his partner Yvette, for Gareth Peirce and her husband Bill, to congratulate them on their great triumph over the Birmingham Six case. Three of the Moberly children were there.

Ruth played a leading part in organising it all, which was extremely good of her. Tony Banks and Sally were also there. It was a really lovely evening. Mike Mansfield is unorthodox and very radical and good, and his partner Yvette is a film-maker. Gareth Peirce is modest and quiet and her husband, Bill, is a photographer and is also very modest.

At seven, I heard the news that Rajiv Gandhi had been assassinated in India about an hour earlier. A terrible tragedy. I met him in Delhi eighteen months ago and he was very charming to me. I knew his mother, his grandfather and also Mahatma Gandhi.

Voted, and then I watched the Tebbit programme on disestablishment in which I appeared once or twice.

Friday 24 May, Chesterfield
At Abercrombie School the headmaster, a very nice man who is retiring this year, introduced me to all the children, who were as bright as anything. Having grandchildren of that age, I just went in and talked to them as if they were my own grandchildren. I went and looked at the bit of waste ground where I had arranged for them to have access in order to extend the playground. Then I gave a talk to the older children, who asked me a lot of questions about dogs because of the attacks on children by pit-bull terriers. They didn't like the fact that the Government is considering destroying all dangerous breeds. Very bright children. Had school lunch with them and then went on to do a long surgery.

Got back just after four and had a phone call that Eric Heffer had died at about 2.45. I was planning to go and see him this afternoon because I have almost finished reading his book on socialism, which is a very magnificent book, beautifully documented. So scholarly, so knowledgeable, so human, so clear. His brother-in-law asked what we should do about the press, so I said, 'Leave it to me.' I rang the Press Association and within minutes the phone began ringing. For most of the afternoon and evening I was doing interviews about Eric.

Eric was a very remarkable man with working-class origins. He was born in Hertfordshire, served in the RAF, joined the CP, was a Christian and a choir boy. He met Doris in the Young Communist League and was active in the trade union movement in Liverpool. He was a shop steward in ship repairing, became President of the trades council, got into Parliament in 1964 and fought a magnificent battle against the Heath Government's Industrial Relations Act. He wrote a book called *Class War in Parliament*, got on the NEC, became Chairman of the Party and was in the DTI with me, refusing office earlier from Wilson, saying that he would only agree if Jim Callaghan was sacked. Eric was sacked himself when he made a speech against the Common Market.

Tuesday 28 May

The papers were absolutely full of obituaries for Eric Heffer – *The Times*, *Telegraph*, my bit in the *Guardian,* and it obviously made a profound impression. Later today I was asked to write an obituary for the *House Magazine,* which I did, and another one for *Socialist Campaign News*. I heard that the funeral was to be arranged for Monday in Liverpool.

To lunch at *The Independent*. The purpose of the lunch was to discuss the Commonwealth of Britain Bill. I found it very awkward. First of all, I find myself a bit of a peasant because I don't normally go to lunches any more. Fortunately I had remembered to ring and say I was a vegetarian, and so is Andrew Hood and funnily enough so is Peter Jenkins. So there were three steaming steaks and three vegetarian dishes. They hadn't seen the Bill in full, so I gave them a copy and they were quite interested in it. To cut a long story short, they were quite sympathetic to it but didn't really know how to proceed.

Andreas Whittam Smith, the editor, said, 'How can we get a discussion going? It's all hopeless, it's impossible, nothing will ever happen.'

Peter Jenkins was keen that the lawyers should play a leading role in the future. He said 'the under-class', because that's what he was talking about, was quite incapable of organising anything itself and therefore would have to rely on the courts to help.

I pointed out that you didn't have to win an election, you could run a campaign, like the Poll Tax campaign. And Andreas Whittam Smith agreed that, without an election, mass action had actually brought down Thatcher and the Poll Tax. So that shook them slightly.

Monday 3 June, Liverpool

Caught the train for Eric Heffer's funeral. Went by taxi to Doris's home: full of family, all tremendously proud of Eric, and quite properly so. Doris was very brave. I was taken by car just behind the coffin to St Mary's Church in Walton for the funeral. As the car drew up outside the church, it was clear that not only were the streets crowded with people genuinely grieving, but the churchyard was also packed. There was a Campaign group banner, the Anfield Anti-Poll Tax Union banner, the Militant banner and other trade union banners. Unfortunately I didn't have the order of service because there weren't enough to go round. There was a choir and David Sheppard, the Bishop of Liverpool, was in the background.

I was asked to speak and it was quite a difficult thing to do really. The mourners were so mixed. There was Stan Orme, Peter Kilfoyle (the new candidate for Walton), Derek Hatton, with his hair all slicked down, in a bright suit. Also Tony Mulhearn, who was expelled from the Party, Dennis Skinner, Tam Dalyell and a lot more MPs. I tried to say what Eric would have wanted me to say, because there is a danger that when a socialist dies, the Church has them back and forgives them for what they have done and Eric wouldn't want that. So I made a radical restatement of Eric's position. Talked to a lot of people in the churchyard afterwards – I knew so many of them. Derek Hatton came up and shook my hand.

Tuesday 4 June

Went into the House and, as I was walking down the corridor, a man came round the corner and bumped into me and said, 'I'm awfully sorry.' I looked up and it was the Prime Minister hurrying to vote. He is a nice man, John Major, whatever you say. I wrote to him today because a woman who was born in the same ward of Queen Charlotte's in the same week as Stephen, and who has remained a friend of the family, told me that her mother had collapsed a few days ago and was rushed to Charing Cross Hospital, where they wouldn't admit her but kept her in a bed for five hours without food or water. Then she was taken by ambulance to a nursing home that charges £600 a week. I said in my letter, 'I am not going to make any reference to this publicly, but you ought to know what is going on.'

Saturday 8 June

Going on all week has been the forced resignation of John Underwood, the Director of Campaigns and Communications, who replaced Peter Mandelson last summer. I had done a programme called *After Dark* with him about two years ago, so when he was appointed I invited him to come and see me. He's a very decent chap and I have seen him at the NEC ever since. The trouble for him was that he was anxious to give a fair account of the work of the NEC and the Shadow Cabinet, whereas Kinnock wanted it to be only about himself and his favourites. As the journalist Steve Richards told me the other day, Mandelson kept getting the press to concentrate on Gordon Brown and Tony Blair, which has led to a conflict between Mandelson and John Underwood after his appointment.

So here is another example building up of the total dictatorship of Kinnock, where he not only treats the Militant councillors and the left of the NEC with contempt, but also even his immediate colleagues. But if you look at it, Mandelson concentrated exclusively on trying to promote Kinnock personally and Gordon Brown and Tony Blair, but he himself didn't do terribly well in respect of Kinnock's reputation, because Kinnock is still the least popular of the party leaders, falling behind both Major and Ashdown.

Thursday 13 June

William Whyte, this schoolboy who has been here for the last ten days,* and his father came to the office and I took them into the Commons. William had read a life of Anthony Eden by Robert Rhodes James and is extremely knowledgeable about Suez. He had read both the first paperback volumes of my diary and asked me to sign them – very, very intelligent, brilliant in fact.

The Institute of Contemporary British History had a seminar on the IMF crisis of 1975. It was given by Alec Cairncross and apparently it was as dry as dust and wholly economic in character. Ruth went and talked to Denis Healey, who said to her that my diaries were much too long and she replied, 'You should have seen the full version!' She also met somebody who is a bit of a know-all and said that Princess Diana was having an affair with one of the men on her staff. This is the sort of gossip that goes round and I put it down in case it comes up later.

Monday 17 June

Had terrible toothache and in the end I capitulated and rang my old dentist, although he is no longer on the NHS, but I just had to have something done until I can get an NHS dentist.

Kaufman was on the one o'clock news, coming out in favour of a federal Europe, an EMU and all the rest of it, quite without any authority from the Party at all and we are pre-empted again. I am going to speak in the debate on this matter on Monday and set out my views as clearly as I can. If we go on discussing it in terms of a Tory Party split and the Labour Party being united, it is completely misleading, because the LP is not united on the matter. There is no discussion on the NEC about economic and monetary union or political union. Kaufman just speaks for himself and pre-empts everything. In a way, nobody wants a row. I certainly don't. I'm not going to vote for it and I'm sure a lot of other people aren't, either. I think it will be a democratic versus a federalist argument, because nobody can argue that the EEC is in any way democratic.

*During the late 1980s and 1990s a number of young people came to help in my office to gain work/political experience. They became known as the Teabags, an acronym for The Eminent Association of Benn Archive Graduates. See Principal Persons, p. 681, for full list.

Wednesday 19 June

Arthur Scargill's court case came off in his favour; they dropped the prosecution against him or it was dismissed. So he and Peter Heathfield went to court, and the government, wanting to get them removed as unsuitable persons to run a trade union, lost. It was a brilliant success. God knows, Peter had been hounded and persecuted mercilessly by the Government.

Caught the train to Chesterfield, did a surgery and came home on the train. There were some fantastic cloud formations and, on one horizon, there was this mass of white billowing cloud making mountains, and the sun was coming through the cloud above it in bright shafts of light. Somehow, you could imagine people looking at that cloud and horizon and seeing in it what they would imagine heaven to be like greeting them, because it was so clearly defined and yet so ethereal. Then, as we got to London, there were the red sky and the smoking chimneys and somehow that was like hell.

Monday 24 June

The big world news at the moment is this enormous, flaming row about whether Europe should enter a federal Europe. And John Major, who is a European, is wet, and that's why the right and Mrs Thatcher are so angry. He is quite happy to go along with it, and the LP also are quite happy to go along with it because, as far as Kinnock and Smith are concerned, it lifts any responsibility off their shoulders. They are trying to dodge the responsibility.

At the NEC we discussed John Underwood, the Director of Campaigns and Communications, who has resigned, and there was a little note on that and then new terms of reference for the new one. It said, 'The Director of Campaigns and Communications will report to the General Secretary.' I intervened and said, 'I want to move an amendment: "The Director of Campaigns and Communications will work for the NEC as a whole and will report to the General Secretary"'. I say this because when I was asked to do *Question Time*, I discovered from the producer that Peter Mandelson had objected to my being invited. He did what Bernard Ingham did – bullied the press by hinting at a withdrawal of co-operation unless they did what he wanted.

Friday 28 June

Went into the Commons because my Commonwealth of Britain Bill was on the Order Paper. I saw Christopher Hawkins, a Tory MP, one of the Members for Derbyshire, who had been paralysed in a road accident and decided not to stand again, though he said he was better now. I asked if he was going to stand, but he said they had selected a successor. I think he was a lecturer at some college and he has always been very friendly to me. He said, 'What do you think of the debate on Europe on Wednesday? Didn't you think Kaufman was awful?' Well, he was. He went on, 'Did you notice that although Hurd made an elegant speech and Kaufman made an abusive speech, neither of them really addressed the question of what should be the proper relationship between Britain and the EEC?'

Today Mrs Thatcher announced that she was going to retire from parliament and this has led to another great surge of coverage – this great woman, the greatest Prime Minister, will she be an influence? She says she wants to go to the House of Lords, and will be the Countess of Finchley, and so on. The fact is, of course, that she quit. She quit the premiership because she wasn't prepared to run a risk of being defeated in a second ballot; she quit Parliament because there was no future for her. Ted Heath said at some stage that she was defeated because of her opposition to Europe and I think that is true.

Wednesday 3 July
The war in Yugoslavia is now getting out of control, because the army has thrown over the political control of the federation and is just busy suppressing Croatia and Slovenia, because it is mainly a Serbian army. The whole world is in a state of complete flux. It has got to decentralise and put certain powers at the top. Very interesting, but very worrying.

Thursday 4 July
Geoffrey Goodman arrived at 11 and I had brushed the garden and mowed the lawn. He was terribly friendly and we talked about the old days. I said I was anxious to mend my fences with old comrades with whom I had fallen out. Geoffrey said Michael Foot and Jill were at dinner last night, and he thought Michael was very blind now and probably couldn't read and that Mervyn Jones was writing his life.

He said, 'Although we had our differences in the Eighties, you mustn't think it was ever personal. I thought you would have made a marvellous Leader. I was sorry that that wasn't really what you wanted', which was the kindest way of saying, 'You threw it all away.'

I said, 'Looking back on it, I don't know whether it was right to have contested the leadership. It might have been better to have argued the case for what I wanted.'

He said, 'A bit of compromising, and you would have got there and it would have made a difference.'

Possibly that is so. Caroline and Ralph Miliband had agreed. I think I probably did the wrong thing in the Eighties to carry this campaign out from an ultra-left position, if that's the way it was seen. But I said I thought that if I had got there, I would have got there on what I called Kinnock's terms and I wasn't prepared to settle for that. Anyway, Geoffrey was very kind.

He then talked about his relations with Bob Maxwell. Geoffrey is married to a Czech Jew whose whole family were killed. And Bob Maxwell is Czech too and apparently his father and some other Jews were put in a boat in a lake and they pulled the plug. The only time Geoffrey had seen Bob Maxwell cry was when he asked about his father, and Bob told him that story.

Geoffrey thought that Bob's role in all this security business was very strange, because Bob had once told him that at the end of the war he and a Russian colonel had broken into General Zhukov's headquarters in Berlin and had opened the safe and copied all the documents about the Russian plans to dismantle East German industry and take it back to the Soviet Union. Geoffrey didn't believe it and later on, when somebody wrote a book about Maxwell, and Maxwell had it pulped, it contained a reference to the story and how Geoffrey didn't believe it. Maxwell called him in one day and said, 'You don't believe me.' Geoffrey said, 'No, I don't.' So Maxwell opened a drawer and brought out the documents that he claimed to have got out of the Berlin safe. It made Geoffrey wonder whom he was working for at the time.

About the future, Geoffrey thought socialism would reappear; technology would change everything; the Third World would have massive unemployment. He has got a very boyish quality about him, though he is seventy now, white hair and a friendly smile. It was very enjoyable.

Monday 8 July

Up at a quarter to four, just as the sun was beginning to rise, and got to London from Stansgate in about an hour and twenty minutes. Another lovely summer day. I take a thermos cup in a specially constructed tray, which I have on the passenger front seat so that I can drink tea while I'm driving; and I've got my tape recorder and I listen to my favourite records. Altogether it's just a very agreeable journey and I like getting home on a Monday morning when I've been to Stansgate.

I went to the Home Policy Committee where the big debate was on the question of the EMU because Kinnock, Smith and Kaufman are very keen to get the Party totally and completely committed to economic and monetary union and a Central Bank. A statement was put before us trying to make it look as if this new move is in line with our Party policy, which is not true. Bryan Gould said he would accept the statement, although by doing so he was turning on his head in his opposition to the Common Market – but then his position on the Shadow Cabinet and National Executive depends on not alienating Kinnock, that's the absolute truth of the matter.

Clare Short said that if there is convergence of our economies, she would accept it. When I was called I said, 'I can understand the reasons why the Party leadership wants this – membership of the EMU would supposedly safeguard us from short-term speculation, it would provide wage discipline and it would be like the gold standard. The one thing we should be absolutely clear about is that there is no difference of opinion between Labour and Tory front benches. The Tories are going to go in because the Establishment will not accept a political leader that isn't in favour.

'However, there are problems. Britain is itself a common market with a common currency and a nationalised bank, and it hasn't dealt with problems of unemployment or homelessness. America has a common market with a federal reserve bank and that hasn't solved their employment problems.'

When the electors discover that whoever they vote for they can't do anything about it, British policy will revert to the most awful nationalism. 'It's no good asking me to support it, because I can't, I haven't got the power to support it,' I concluded.

Neil then moved two amendments. On convergence, he said, 'All social democratic parties in the EEC agree about this and it is an inexorable move.' The Delors compromise suggested that Britain might accept a second-division status, so he was against the Delors compromise.

I was the only one who voted against it. And we are now committed to EMU and a Central Bank.

Wednesday 10 July

To the Commons for the Committee of Privileges. Just before it began I said to John Biffen, who is on the Committee, 'This can't go on long because I'm going to St Margaret's to Eric Heffer's memorial service and I'm speaking.' Biffen said, 'I know, I'm coming with my wife to hear you.' So I said, 'Mrs Thatcher's going.' 'I am still coming!' he replied.

Anyway, Caroline had come up from Stansgate today and we walked over to St Margaret's, Westminster and stood in the garden a bit as the church filled up. There must have been over 100 people there. The order of service had been beautifully prepared by the Rector of St Margaret's, Donald Gray, who is also the Speaker's chaplain.

There were quotations from Eric about socialism and Christianity, and there was a vicar from Liverpool who took some of the prayers. The Speaker, Bernard Weatherill, was in the front row with his predecessor, George Thomas; the Clerk of the House; John Smith; and Derek Foster, who is Chief Whip. Dennis Skinner couldn't make it. There was Mrs Thatcher coughing away with a bad cold. As I left the church afterwards, I just said to her, 'Thank you very much for coming', and she burst into tears. I think it was decent of her to come and I wrote her a note afterwards thanking her. Geoffrey Howe was there, Patrick Mayhew, John Biffen. Very impressive that Eric should have had such support from the Tories.

There were three addresses. The first by Ian Aitken, who was extremely amusing. He referred to 'Comrade Heffer, the class warrior' and went on to talk about how Eric used to come to Annie's Bar and have a couple of drinks. And how they came to expect his morning telephone calls when he thought that what had been said about him was unfair. There were warm tributes to Doris from everybody. A Conservative Member, Robert Rhodes James, gave the next address – a very warm and modest speech about how Eric was proud that he, like Jesus, was a socialist and carpenter. He said that the only time Eric ever let him down was by dying before the end of the Parliament, because they had agreed they'd have breakfast together and go out in style – a breakfast at which alcohol would 'not be expressly forbidden'.

I had worked terribly hard on my speech. I felt it was my job to project Eric's political faith and so I talked about his commitment to trade unionism and the working class and socialism, his belief in internationalism, his intolerance of people who tried to give orders at the top, his sense of dissent, his commitment to conscience being above the law. 'He was elected in the far-off and happy days before people had a political minder who told them what to wear and what to say, and I suspect that anyone whose job it was to mind Eric Heffer would have had a difficult time.' I talked about his books, and said that he was a teacher, and that teachers leave deeper footprints in the sands of time than those who pass by in their ministerial limousines.

It was really quite a gathering – and Doris and her mother and brothers and sisters-in-law were all there. Mrs Thatcher spoke to Doris.

In the evening I went to Lime Grove because the old BBC studios there are closing at the end of July, after over forty years, and they'd found everybody they possibly could to invite. I must say it was fun. Robin Day was there, Ludovic Kennedy, Andrew Miller-Jones, who is eighty-one and had been involved in the first television broadcast ever, in 1936. John Birt had left when I arrived; he is absolutely detested by the old creative people. He's been appointed to take over from Michael Checkland and his idea of current affairs is that you decide what you want to say and then you find people to enable you to say it which, of course, is my whole complaint about the BBC.

I saw Roy Jenkins who was frightfully friendly, Anthony Howard, David Jacobs, and Margaret Jay was there. There were one or two who had axes to grind, still fighting old battles. Andrew Miller-Jones was still going on about how disgraceful it was that so many tons of film were thrown away, literally lorryloads, because the BBC couldn't afford to keep them.

Thursday 11 July

In the evening I went to do *A Week in Politics*, with Vincent Hanna, Andrew Rawnsley, Enoch Powell, Professor David Starkey about the monarchy. I was a bit angry to find, when I got there, that there was a cheap introduction saying, 'Benn, having given up his own title, is trying to dethrone the Queen', and so on and so on (a reference to my Commonwealth of Britain Bill). At the very end when the question 'Will there be a monarchy in twenty years' time?' came, all that Enoch Powell could say was, 'God save the Queen'; all that Starkey could say was, 'Yes, and it'll silence you lot.' But it was quite jolly.

Sunday 14 July, Stansgate

The grandchildren all came into our bedroom early in the morning and played very happily. Michael went out bird-watching. There was football and cricket on the lawn.

Monday 15 July

Went into the Commons for the Organisation Committee of the NEC.

We came to the question of Terry Fields, the Member for Liverpool Broad Green; a motion was put saying that because he'd been sentenced to prison for refusing to pay the Poll Tax, he was guilty of conduct prejudicial to Party interests and damaging to the Party. Neil said, 'He could pay, and people who don't pay cause great resentment.' Hattersley thought it was not the prison question, but his disobedience of the law. Clare Short said, 'It is sometimes right to defy the law and we must modify the motion.' I defended Terry. I said that he was a fireman, who had been radicalised by the use of the army in the firemen's strike; his wife had been very ill; he was a good Member of Parliament and, I said, 'The Poll Tax campaign brought down Mrs Thatcher, while the Party did nothing about it.' They all shouted at me and I said, 'Well, we didn't. We didn't even have a demonstration, on the grounds that the Party couldn't afford it.

'Terry could pay, of course, but he decided to share the suffering of his own constituents. What we're doing is retrospectively expelling the likes of George Lansbury and Fenner Brockway, who went to jail for disobeying the law. It is disgraceful and conscience is above the law' – a point I made in the memorial service to Eric Heffer.

Dennis Skinner said, 'This is just going for the left. We tried all this in 1985 and just went down to a massive defeat in 1987, and millions haven't paid their Poll Tax. What the NEC want is a gang of clones.'

It gets worse and worse and it won't help the Party. Just keeps alive the idea that the Party is deeply penetrated.

Anyway, I hurried from that and met Peter Hennessy for this evening's meeting in the Grand Committee Room, organised by *The Independent*, on constitutional change. About 250 people, I should think, and everybody had a copy of the *Guardian*'s summary of my Commonwealth of Britain Bill. Andreas Whittam Smith began and I gave my lecture.

It was a strange audience. I think many of them had never been to a public meeting before. They were overawed by the House of Commons, and by the platform; they weren't familiar with the subject. But it was useful and I made a few little jokes and was cross-examined on the monarchy. It was a sort of SDP meeting.

Friday 19 July

I cancelled my Chesterfield surgery and, alas, a meeting for the old-age pensioners at Northern College and stayed in bed with a high fever and a bad cough. My doctor came to see me. A very nice woman. She wanted me to go into hospital – said she thought I had got bronchial pneumonia. Well, I didn't want to do that, so she put me on some antibiotics anyway.

Saturday 20 July

I stayed in bed all day with a high fever, taking these drugs and coughing and feeling awfully unwell. I just lay in bed. I couldn't move really.

Monday 22 July

Caroline took me to St Thomas' Hospital for various check-ups. We had a Coke and an ice cream and a bun together, and I went through various tests, I think about six blood tests and X-rays and I was given more antibiotics. So, unfortunately, today I had to cancel my visit to Sheffield for the local radio *Desert Island Books* item because I was so unwell.

Wednesday 24 July

I got up today. My temperature's pretty well normal.

Sheila Yeger came in. She's working on her play about Keir Hardie.

Caroline went to Hammersmith Hospital and, as she came back, a van behind her bumped into her and broke off her bumper, so a young man of about twenty-five to thirty got out and fixed her bumper on again. Caroline thanked him and he said, 'You're an American, aren't you?' And she said, 'Yes.' And he said, 'I'd like a mother with stockings and a suspender belt.' So Caroline said, 'Well there are lots of them about.' Then he asked her, earnestly, 'Will you give me a date?' And she said, 'No, I won't.' 'Well, why not?' So she replied, 'Well, I've got somebody.' He said, 'Is he young and virile?' So Caroline said, 'He's old, and he'll do.' He became quite persistent and aggressive, so Caroline got into the car, closed up the window and drove off.

Today the National Executive met and I missed it – probably for the first time since the IMF crisis. I deliberately stayed away, but I wasn't really well and I heard on the news that 170 were going to be expelled from the Party, and that Terry Fields and Dave Nellist were going to be investigated.

It makes you want to leave the Labour Party, because our civil liberties would not be safe in the hands of such people, and to hear the Labour Party officials talk about Militant is like hearing Ian Paisley talk about the Pope. Just deep, bitter, irrational hatred. I suppose if Terry and Dave are expelled, they'll stand as candidates in their own constituencies and they might do rather well.

Friday 26 July

Today I faxed an appeal to the Prime Minister of Grenada to plead for mercy for the people who are due to be hanged for the murder of Maurice Bishop in 1983. It is the most ghastly story. The Americans invaded the island, allegedly because of the murder of Bishop, and arrested Phyllis and Bernard Coard and accused them of the crime. They've been in prison now for nearly eight years, and the trial has dragged on.

There is no appeal to the Privy Council because Maurice Bishop's own administration terminated it, but in fact the new government has agreed that it will revert to the right of appeal to the Privy Council on 1st August. However, the executions are likely to take place before then and Phyllis and Bernard Coard are just waiting hour by hour for news of the executions.

Saturday 27 July

Had a late lie-in. Tony Gifford rang me this morning about the Grenada executions. I suggested he might get on to Nelson Mandela, who is now in Havana with Fidel Castro, and that Tony might even use his role as a QC to approach the Queen, who is Queen of Grenada and has no obligation to take any notice of what Downing Street says. Possibly he might mobilise Arthur Bottomley and Judith Hart to assist.

Sunday 28 July

A late lie-in and read the newspapers. The BCCI scandal is roaring ahead and there was a little bit of coverage of my letter to the Prime Minister asking for payment in full to the people who have suffered as a result of the bank collapsing after serious fraud.

Gorbachev now wants to move to a more pluralistic society generally, which is highly desirable, but if he's going to be bullied by the West into adopting a full free-market economy, the price of suffering in the Soviet Union will be enormous. The Russians have just lost confidence in themselves, and the media and the intellectuals have taken over and are just knocking everything Russian. It's actually very depressing.

On the home front, only just over 30 per cent of Labour supporters think Kinnock is any good, and Major streaks ahead in terms of popularity because of his charm. And, of course, he's got a popular sympathetic press, which helps; but the persecution of the left continues.

The Labour Party is politically bankrupt and, according to today's

Sunday papers, if it did go bankrupt, every single member of the National Executive would have a legal liability of £98,000, which would be a sort of surcharge on the Labour Party and that simply isn't acceptable. I shall raise this at the NEC in September because I'm not going to be bankrupted by policies I never supported and expenditure I never backed, particularly the wildly extravagant public-relations expenditure and the extravagant expenditure on witch-hunting and legal fees, and all the rest of it.

I think Kinnock will be remembered as the man who did destroy the Labour Party, and yet the individual rank-and-file members and the trade union leaders go along with it because they think he's the only man who can lead them. It is an extraordinary historical disaster of a kind that will be appreciated one day. But I don't know when. It may be that Kinnock himself has concluded that the Labour Party is a dead duck just as Gorbachev has concluded that the Communist party is a dead duck and that pulling out and dealing with it by individual political action may turn out to be the right course to adopt.

Tuesday 30 July, Chesterfield

Tom Vallins and I went down to the medieval market, which is an annual celebration in Chesterfield – people in medieval clothes playing medieval instruments and music, somebody juggling and lots of stands organised by charities. And I must say the sense of community and gaiety and joyfulness in Chesterfield is extraordinary. People were having a marvellous time. Then I did my surgery and went to sleep during it. I'm terribly tired at the moment.

When I get up here I'm very happy. I just wish I wasn't so tired. But there you are. Most of the family are in Corfu.

The Moscow summit is taking place today between Bush, Gorbachev and Yeltsin, the joker in the pack trying to humiliate Gorbachev and establish the right to an individual arrangement for Russia. Although I loathe Yeltsin – think he's a real right-wing demagogue opportunistic capitalist rogue – the idea that countries should be able to run themselves without too much central control is, of course, very much in line with the way in which I think Europe should go.

Wednesday 31 July, Chesterfield

I was at the Mines Service Centre at Duckmanton all day – the old Markham workshops. It used to be a huge centre employing over 1000 people, one of five workshops; now it only employs 453. As a visiting Labour MP, I was given a pair of leather-tipped shoes so that my feet wouldn't be injured going around where all the heavy equipment was. I spent an hour and a half with the manager, Mr Leatherbarrow, who is hanging on by his toenails because, under the new arrangements that the

Government have insisted upon, the workshops have to compete with private contractors. This is a real problem because it's quite obvious that British Coal would like not only to reduce the number of pits in the UK down to perhaps thirty or even fewer, but to sell off or privatise the workshops. So these guys are living in a state of high uncertainty.

We walked around, and every time I go to an industrial site, to a factory, I'm always overcome with depression at the way in which our skill and craft have been allowed to run down. Most of the workers are older workers (they're not taking on any apprentices this year), a workforce of enormous skill. I went into one of the electronic shops where they were repairing control gear and I asked about diversification, because they're in a similar position to those who might be working in defence. What about computers, I asked? One man, who must have been nearly sixty, said, 'I've got computers. I build them at home.' Another lad said, 'Oh, yes, I've got computers at home, I can cope with them.' Well, the manager had never heard that before. Two guys with great skills that had never been recognised.

Thursday 1 August, Chesterfield

The days, the weeks, the months race by and there is a part of me now that is just longing for retirement and another part that knows that, if I did retire, I'd sit about, do nothing, be depressed, be a hypochondriac. I am kept going by a combination of an interest in the job and the fear of what would happen if I stopped.

I had a surgery this morning. Not an awful lot, about four people. Then to a centre where they run a little discussion group for quite seriously mentally impaired people, and people with Down's syndrome. There were some people there who were getting one-to-one care. One tall lad who was wearing a leather helmet because he kept banging his head on the floor looked distressed, and he had somebody looking after him all the time. I was just very jolly with them. Then I sat in a discussion group and told them a little bit about the work that I did. I was frightfully tired and I dozed off at one stage and they said, 'You're tired! you're tired!' So they were watching me like anything.

Monday 5 August

The office was absolutely full. William Whyte, that nice lad, turned up for his last day. Very bright and helpful and knowledgeable; a really brilliant boy. Andrew Hood came in and humped a lot of stuff out of the attic down to the basement, ready to go to Stansgate at the weekend in the truck. Ruth was in, planning what should go.

Wednesday 7 August, Liverpool

To Walton jail where Terry Fields is. This huge building, with its enormous wall and smooth top, designed to make it allegedly impossible for people to climb over. Outside was what looked like an enormous bus queue under a semi-circular shelter – the families waiting to go in. Ken Stewart, the MEP, was there. The awful thing was that I know Ken as well as I know myself, and I asked him, 'Is Ken coming?' And he said, 'I am Ken!' So I said, 'I'm Tony Benn!' and laughed. He and Bob Parry and I went in; Eddie Loyden's secretary Fiona had to wait outside. The press were there, and Fiona handed out my press release.

We went into a brand-new cell, with a lavatory in the corner, because slopping out is obviously not something they want visitors to see. And there was Terry, in prison outfit, looking very well really. I gave him a big hug and we sat around this table, the four of us, and he was allowed to smoke while we were there, so I smoked my pipe.

The cell was completely ceramic with shiny tiling. I could have touched any of the four walls from where I was sitting, but I found it very hard to hear because of the echo. At any rate, Terry said that he was all right. Apparently he runs a surgery for other prisoners. He does his own parliamentary correspondence there. He said his job is cleaning which, as an old fireman, he was used to. He said there was a man in there, also for a Poll Tax offence, who was given thirty days – a man of sixty-three who had lost a leg through diabetes and who, when he came in, had had to strip and give up his possessions and have a shower; and he had to take off his artificial leg. It was utterly appalling. Terry said the food was bad, and sometimes had been cooked for two hours before they ate it, but you had to eat it because you were hungry. He was a bit worried about his wife, Maureen, because she's due for committal for Poll Tax non-payment in a couple of weeks, so that when he comes out, she'll be in. It was very sad. Terry was very affectionate and I told him he must speak to me before he comes to the National Executive on 24 September. He had had a letter that morning from Larry Whitty saying he was being charged, or was likely to be charged, with being a member of Militant. I thought, 'How bloody disgraceful: a Member of Parliament, a fireman, a decent working-class man, a good socialist, in prison, and all he gets is a letter from the Labour Party saying, "You're likely to be expelled."' It made my blood boil.

I only stayed for about twenty minutes because I had to catch a train back. Then the cell door was unlocked, so I went back to the office and picked up my bag. Just before we went into the cell, I'd said to the four prison officers there, 'You're under a lot of pressure at the moment, aren't you? It must be very difficult if you've got people in prison who you think are innocent, like the Birmingham Six or the Guildford Four.' And the senior officer, who had one silver pip on his sleeve said, 'Well, I was at the prison to which the Birmingham Six came and I can tell you it was a traumatic experience.' Quite what role he had played I will never know.

One of the other prison officers, a bearded man, took me out to the gate so that I could meet the press and catch the train. I asked him, 'How long have you been in the Prison Service?' He said, 'Eight years.' 'What did you do before?' He said, 'I was unemployed for two years, and before that I worked for Bowater, the paper company. I couldn't find work, so I joined the Prison Service because they'll take you up to the age of forty-nine. I've got another few years to run and then I can retire.' He went on, 'There's no chance of work in Liverpool.' 'Well, like Terry Fields you're a victim of the system.' 'You're quite right,' he said.

Granada Television were outside. I said that I'd been to see Terry, that I admire him, that he is a good Member of Parliament who was taking a principled position. I saw a couple of people selling *Militant* trying to get behind me, so that they would appear on camera. I said, 'Please go away, I'm talking about a friend.' They moved round, but truthfully I thought that was disgraceful. I might have been able to do Terry Fields a bit of good and they just wanted to make it into a Militant occasion. They are an impossible crowd of people, they really are, I must say. The whole city is in shock that one of its MPs is in jail.

Saturday 10 August, Stansgate

Up early, working in the garage on my Black & Decker work bench. At twelve o'clock Jeremy Corbyn and Claudia and little Ben and Sebastian arrived. It was again another perfect day at Stansgate, which makes a hell of a difference, and we had lunch. We went around the nature reserve and Jeremy enjoyed that very much. Took some photographs and then after tea everybody returned to London.

Saturday 17 August, Stansgate.

Caroline worked on Keir Hardie and let me read a couple more sections. It really is brilliant.

In the evening, watched an extraordinary programme on TV made up of home-movie shots, in colour, that the German soldiers took when they attacked Russia in 1941. I found it quite eerie. First of all because the soldiers looked very much like the young people I'd been with in the air force, and secondly because they did it with the swastika shown in a sympathetic way. It seemed almost to be rehabilitating the Nazi war machine and Germany in the eyes of people watching at home. The fact that they were our enemies does not seem to come across at all.

Monday 19 August

Woke up this morning to hear the news that Gorbachev has been displaced by a coup led by Vice-President Gennadi Yanaev, supported by the military and the KGB, and others widely described as the hard-liners. The news bulletins have reported nothing else all day, with comments from Bush and Kinnock, Major and Kohl and everybody else. Tonight the news bulletin showed tanks on the streets of Moscow, and Boris Yeltsin standing on a tank telling people to take to the streets. Mrs Thatcher said that there should be mass demonstrations and civil disobedience which, coming from her, I thought was a bit much. And Caroline said this is just an argument between two groups of Tories – Gorbachev and the hard-liners both being Conservative in their approach to economic and social questions.

Nobody's given a real explanation as to why it happened. I can't claim to be an expert, but it seems to me that Gorbachev's reforms, particularly his scaling down of the Cold War, made him immensely popular abroad and he was presented as a man with whom Mrs Thatcher could do business; as a man who wanted democracy; as a man who favoured a Western-style liberal capitalism, but actually as a result of his reforms the Soviet economy got into one hell of a mess. Production has fallen, living standards have fallen, food is short, the USSR is breaking up with the Baltic States and the Ukraine – and even Russia itself – wanting to establish their independence from the Soviet Union as a whole. And there must be a lot of people in the Soviet Union who say, 'Well, this hasn't worked.' Certainly, when I was there two years ago the popularity of Gorbachev was not very high, although maybe his arrest and imprisonment will make him a hero – you can't tell. But any military and security force is bound to want to protect the Soviet Union and its integrity, though as they've increased wages and cut essential food prices with subsidies, it may be that they will be quite popular. We must not allow ourselves to be driven back into a Cold War posture in Britain, with pressure for rearmament and the cancellation of Defence cuts.

Yesterday the *Observer*'s MORI Poll showed that the Tories were only one per cent behind Labour.

Tuesday 20 August

The media is full of news from Moscow and Boris Yeltsin is the hero. Andrew Hood rang me this afternoon on behalf of Charter 88 asking me to sign a letter but I want to think about it a little bit more. There's something funny about it and I'm not quite sure what it is. I think the problem is that the British people have not been told of the economic crisis in Russia or of the danger of disintegration. Gorbachev gave freedom to the intellectuals and the media and the managers. He invited foreign capital in and they all love him. On the other hand, with the disappearance of the tight grip from Moscow, he was faced with the disintegration of the Soviet Union. And because the reforms were talked about but not introduced, ordinary people in Russia suffered very substantially.

Wednesday 21 August

Yeltsin is the absolute hero of the media. It's Yeltsin this, Yeltsin that, Yeltsin the other all the time and Caspar Weinberger, one of the million commentators on television, called for the break-up of the Soviet Union. It's quite clear that although they didn't want the coup to succeed, the West does not want Gorbachev either and neither of them is very attractive.

Anyway, later in the day it was quite clear the coup was over. The coup leaders were leaving Moscow, some flying to Central Asia and some, apparently, going down to the Crimea to apologise; then there were resignations from the committee that was set up. I must admit I was tremendously relieved, because if the coup had succeeded, then we'd have gone back into the Cold War and the West, and rearmament, and all the rest.

Thursday 22 August, Stansgate

Gorbachev returned to Moscow looking very informal with Raisa and his little granddaughter.

This crisis is being used by the West as an opportunity to displace Gorbachev and replace him with Yeltsin, which would be an attempt to introduce capitalism and repression. The All Union Treaty, which was to be signed on Monday or Tuesday, will now be rewritten to incorporate far, far bigger disintegration, and Yeltsin, I think, says that the USSR officials should be elected by the republics, which would mean that they would have an opportunity of getting rid of Gorbachev that way. So I can't say my heart is singing, though I'm glad that the Old Guard failed, because I think it is a state of moving on.

Monday 26 August, Bank Holiday, Stansgate

Kids came into our bedroom as usual. PC, our old friend Peter Carter, arrived on his Moto Guzzi bike. Caroline worked flat-out on the meals. The little portable swimming pool was filled and it was a perfect day. We had the Stansgate Olympics, organised by young Michael, with the one-legged race, the relay, the egg-and-spoon, the four-times-round-the-house race, the three-legged race, the babies-round-the-pond race. Afterwards medals were awarded – little cockle shells attached by Sellotape to bits of string, Michael is so good, such tremendous fun.

Wednesday 28 August, Stansgate

Dave rang up and read me an extract from Churchill's book, *The World Crisis: The Aftermath*, published in 1929, quoting minutes Churchill had written to the Cabinet about the intervention in 1919, saying that the problem is that the anti-communists in Russia and in the Ukraine can't agree and that there is a terrible danger of Russia breaking up into warring factions. Denikin was to try and reach an agreement with the Ukrainian anti-communists. Dave made the point that the crucial question now is not whether Russia will be communist, but whether it will be democratic, because the new constitution that was declared last year guaranteed press freedom and Yeltsin immediately banned *Pravda*. Dave reminded me that Lenin, when he banned the papers, said it was only temporary because of the emergency – and they weren't freed until 1990. 'Now Yeltsin controls everything,' Dave said.

Tuesday 3 September

Jyoti Basu, the communist Chief Minister of West Bengal, came for a talk. I have known him now over two or three years. West Bengal has got a population of 90 million and he's won four elections in a row and, of course, to discuss with him what's happening in the Soviet Union was absolutely riveting.

He said the Chinese Communist Party had invited him to China to teach them about how to succeed in winning elections, which I thought was quite funny. He said he was afraid that the Soviet Union would no longer supply military equipment to India and he though the implications for the Third World of what had happened in the Soviet Union were absolutely appalling. Basu thought communism was actually dead, and although there's no question of him changing the name of his party, he felt that that whole period was over. I'm so torn because I loathe the dictatorship of the proletariat; on the other hand, the Soviet Union was a great buttress and safeguard against the United States and the Western imperial nations dominating the Third World, and that safeguard has been removed.

Sunday 8 September

Late lie-in. I bought the papers and there was a profile in the *Observer* of Tom Sawyer of NUPE, the Chairman of the Labour Party. One of the things that apparently converted him from being a left-winger to a right-winger was when Eric Heffer and I tried to get the NEC to back a general strike in support of the miners. There was quite a chunk about this. Well, Doris Heffer rang me up and said that can't be right. I had also thought it was strange, I'm not sure it's correct. Anyway, she rang me up and said Eric would never have advocated that, though I did remember having made a speech that at some point we might have to consider a general strike. So I wrote a rather pompous letter to the *Observer* and faxed it off to them. However, I then had second thoughts, a bit too late, and went back to look up the minutes for December 1984, when there'd been a motion from the Yorkshire Women's Council calling for national industrial action. Dennis Skinner had espoused it, and in the end Eric and I had called for support for this, which did amount, in effect, to a general strike. So I was quite wrong in the letter I had written.

Then I looked in my diary and found that when this matter had come up, I reported Tom Sawyer saying that he would like a general strike, but didn't see how we could get one, which was quite a different slant from the *Observer* story. So in the end, feeling very embarrassed, I faxed the *Observer* withdrawing my letter and saying that I was doing further research on the matter. I hope it doesn't become a news story, because if it does I shall be in difficulty. It worried me inordinately because I have prided myself on quite exceptional accuracy backed by archives; and to say firmly that such a matter was never raised at the Executive, when it was, could do enormous damage. But I dare say they won't really notice it at the *Observer*. I hope not anyway.

I am engaged at the moment in discussions about Vic Williams, the soldier who declined to go to the Gulf, spoke at many anti-Gulf War meetings and is now on a charge of desertion and of conduct prejudicial to good order and discipline. A court martial begins tomorrow. I spoke to Helena Kennedy, who is the barrister representing him, and she thought I didn't know him well enough to be put forward as a character witness, but asked, 'Can we call you an expert witness?' I said, 'Well, I've served in all three armed forces, I'm a former Secretary for State with responsibility for military matters and I'm also a Privy Councillor and a Member of the Committee of Privileges.' And so she's going to try and get me on.*

Monday 9 September

I rang the *Observer* this morning. Fortunately, the Letters Editor wasn't there, so I got onto his secretary who found the faxed letter and tore it up.

There was a burst pipe in my office – a lead pipe began leaking – and there was a big pool of water in the back corridor where some of the archives are. I must say I was absolutely terrified that there'd be a major flood, but I found a stopcock and switched it off. Fire and flood are the two hazards for papers, apart from the general problem of deterioration over the years.

Wednesday 11 September

Vic Williams was convicted of desertion and of conduct prejudicial to good order and discipline, for leaving the army just before his unit was sent to the Gulf. I heard later in the evening that he was sentenced to fourteen months imprisonment. I wrote a letter to the Prime Minister on the question of conscience and sent the *Guardian* and PA a copy, and I must say I think it's a good case on which to fight, because the man took

*In the event I wasn't called as a witness.

a moral stand, surrendered to the military authorities as soon as the war was over, and fourteen months in a civilian prison is probably quite a light sentence given the damage that he really did to the Government. But still I dare say they were influenced in that by the fact that an air-force officer left all the secret plans in his car and they were pinched, along with his car, during the Gulf War, which must have imposed a catastrophic risk on the allied military planning.

Saturday 14 September

Went and did a bit of shopping and bought something I'd been looking at most lovingly for a long time, called a Dymo Electronic Labeller, which has got a QWERTY keyboard and will produce beautiful labels. It was frightfully expensive, including all the gear I got with it – it was £263 – but it will enable the archives to be professionally labelled and I must say that really is attractive.

Then I went to see Mother, who I'm afraid is very confused.

I rang Ken Coates, who told me that, in fact, the whole Soviet economy is breaking up. He said the sarcophagus at Chernobyl, which had been built around the nuclear power station, was leaking and there was radioactivity in the air again. It was an absolutely major disaster, which has cost millions and millions and millions of dollars or pounds to put right. There was a real crisis there; the Russians were in a state of total confusion and he wondered what socialists should do. It was very interesting.

Sunday 15 September

Another lovely day. Caroline got the breakfast, we read the papers. The big political news, of course, is that the Tory lead is between 4 and 5 per cent and all the figures show that Neil Kinnock is just wildly unpopular; 15 per cent of the voters said they would vote Labour if there was a new leader and only 13 per cent think the Labour Party has a problem of extremism, whereas 28 per cent think the problem is Neil Kinnock. So that will be satisfying in the sense that it may somewhat limit his capacity to drive the Executive towards further purges.

In the evening the Independent Left Corresponding Society met at home, the first time we've been together since January, because Ralph Miliband was terribly ill after his heart bypass went wrong and somehow I haven't wanted to meet without him.

There was Ralph, Jim Mortimer, Jeremy Corbyn, Denise Searle, the editor of *Socialist*. Jim Mortimer said he was doubtful about a Labour victory. Kinnock was an embarrassment, he was inconsistent, he was also a gabbler.

Monday 16 September
Andrew Hood came in for a second hour-and-a-half session about the monarchy for our Commonwealth of Britain book. He's a very brilliant guy – he put questions and I tried to answer them and give anecdotes to explain.

Tom Vallins rang from Chesterfield to say that Terry Hawkins, who is a milkman and a councillor in Chesterfield, has a wife whose brother works for the Royal National Institute for the Blind. Last week Tory Central Office rang the RNIB up and said, 'How long would it take you to put our manifesto into Braille?' The RNIB said, 'About six weeks', and the Tories said, 'Well, you'll have to do better than that.' All of which suggests that the election may be closer than we think.

The newspapers today are full of the Neil Kinnock business. He said why should he resign? He was the successful captain of a successful team. But patronage is very powerful and, if people think that by staying with Neil they're going to lose the election, then they get a bit jumpy. I would be surprised if he had quite that triumphant success at Party Conference that he's had in the past. I do not think that we can possibly win, but I may be wrong because polls can go up and down.

Tuesday 17 September
Caroline spent all her free time finishing the Keir Hardie book and for about an hour, until one o'clock in the morning, I read the pages dealing with the years after the death of Keir Hardie. I do find it absolutely riveting. She's just totally changed my perception of Keir Hardie, from a sort of prophetic figure standing head and shoulders above everyone else to a man who was a bit of a loner, an agitator who liked doing meetings and making speeches, but at enormous cost to his wife Lily, who was actually a drug addict, and his daughter Nan, who looked after her. He broke, alas, with his son, Jamie, who went to America. Caroline follows these stories up.

The book is about Sylvia Pankhurst; it's about Aggie, Emrys Hughes's sister, and how Emrys married Keir Hardie's daughter. It's about Keir Hardie's relations with all the Labour leaders, Ramsay MacDonald, Hyndman, Robert Blatchford and Victor Grayson, Philip Snowden, George Lansbury and Fenner Brockway. It made me wish I'd spent much, much more time talking about the early days to Fenner and the people that I knew. I dare say young people are so busy with their lives that they can't take the time to talk to the old pioneers whom they know.

Friday 20 September
Paul Foot rang me. He said, 'Tony, I've got some marvellous news. We have got hold of the full list of 22,000 names on the Economic League's blacklist.' This is the list of 'troublemakers' that is circulated to those companies that subscribe. I think he said there were twenty MPs on it,

and I replied, 'I hope I'm one of them.' And he said, 'You are, but it says: Caroline Benn and then after that Tony Benn.'

So this confirms the idea that Caroline is, in some special way, seen as a suspect by the Establishment. He says the *Mirror*'s going to give it big coverage and that the Economic League had told a parliamentary committee they didn't have a blacklist.

Monday 23 September, Chesterfield

To G.B.Glass, a factory that makes the most beautiful glassware. What was interesting wandering around was to see the high quality of the glass manufacture that went on there. The equipment looked very old – I think like many British firms it has probably failed to re-equip. It's half-owned by Siemens and half-owned by Jules Thorne and employs about 800 people, a very big employer in Chesterfield.

It doesn't recognise trade unions properly. Tom and Margaret Vallins came with me and afterwards we had a buffet, but there was no attempt whatsoever to introduce me to the trade union representatives, so I'll have to meet them separately.

Later my surgery included one sad case, an argument about school boundaries. A constituent was absolutely determined that her son, who was eleven, should go to the old Chesterfield School, which is now called Brookfield Community School; but they live on the wrong side of the boundary and the school is oversubscribed. He has a brother there and so she'd made this little lad dress up in school uniform and stand outside the school every day, but they wouldn't take him. He was crying, there in my surgery, just so distressed.

I said to the boy, 'You go out of the room for a moment', and, then I said to his mother, 'Can I talk to you candidly – how old are you?' 'I'm thirty-seven.' I said, 'Well, I've got a daughter of thirty-seven and you shouldn't do that to that little fellow.' It was really sad.

Tuesday 24 September

A really awful day.

I had a note from Joshua about the installation of the new computer system; the office felt it wasn't going to help them with the diary and were cross they hadn't been consulted, and I was so depressed and angry.

I went off to Chesterfield again, but before I went Caroline said that she'd just heard from Anthony Whittome of Century Hutchinson that they really love her book on Keir Hardie. They think it's marvellous – they're going to produce a hardback. She's worked on it for five years, all by herself, without help of any sort or kind. An absolute triumph and I'm so delighted.

I came home on the train and there were two Russians. I thought they were businessmen who'd just arrived to do a deal with a company in Chesterfield, but actually they were both Ministry of Foreign Trade officials who had moved into a commercial status for the purpose of building up trade. We had a fascinating talk all the way back to London.

They thought the coup was a fake. They took the Kargalitsky view that the troops didn't have to be sent, that they could have got rid of people from outside the White House, which is where the Russian parliament is. There was no attempt to cut off communications, to arrest anybody. They said about 40 per cent of the people in Russia supported the coup; sixty million pensioners couldn't understand why, having worked so hard for the Soviet Union, they were poor now, and they would support the coup.

Not that the coup would have solved anything, but it was a reflection of people's disenchantment with Gorbachev's total failure to solve any problems. Five years of talk and nothing happening. I said I thought Yeltsin was a demagogue and they said, 'Oh, we absolutely agree. He's a complete demagogue. He can't solve any problems either: we must have efficiency; there's too much corruption; forty per cent of the food supplies are lost on the way, or looted or robbed.' Mind you, I must make it clear they were people from the old apparatus.

Wednesday 25 September

I record this as another horrible and disgraceful day in the history of the Labour Party.

Went off to the Executive early. There was a crowd outside because Dave Nellist's and Terry Fields' cases were coming up. I did a little interview saying what outstanding, loyal, committed members they were and went in. And the Executive lasted from then till about half-past five.

We discussed, first of all, the programme and the speakers at Conference. I haven't been put down to speak. At 11.29 Dave Nellist came in and asked to tape-record the proceedings. So they asked him to leave and there was a discussion. Then it was agreed that he could tape it.

At 11.46 he came in again.

Nellist repudiated every charge in a detailed way. It was a brilliant exchange. There's no doubt he's got sympathies with Militant, and nobody has ever denied that, but he repudiated the charges made. He said, 'I accept the NEC and the Conference decisions, though I didn't agree with them. I'm not a member of Militant, and you have no power to expel me for my ideas.' That was a sort of summary of his argument.

Blunkett asked, 'Will you dissociate yourself from Militant?' Nellist said, 'If you give me a form of words, I'll consider it.' Clare Short said, 'Militant is deceitful. You must promise to have nothing to do with it.' Nellist said, 'I want to stay in the Party and abide by its rules.'

Kinnock asked, 'Did you know it existed?' Blunkett said, 'The NEC and Militant both admit it.' 'Well,' said Nellist, 'I accept it exists. I'm not a member.'

Gould said, 'Well, there's a closer connection, a sympathy, an involvement. You know Militant; do you dispute or accept that it exists?' Nellist: 'The newspaper has to be organised.' Gould said, 'Is there an organisation?' At this stage I said, 'Look, this is pure McCarthyism.'

John Evans asked, 'What about the Young Trade Union Rights and the Poll Tax campaigns? Did you know that Militant were involved?' 'Yes,' said Nellist. Skinner added, 'So were a lot of other organisations.' I said, 'Are you aware finally that you will be denied the right to stand, and your constituency and all constituencies will be disenfranchised?' 'Yes,' said Nellist. When he left, Evans moved his motion that Nellist be suspended and prevented from coming to Conference. Joyce Gould said, 'There's a lot of press interest. Nobody should make a statement to the press.' I said, 'I don't accept that. I am on the Executive to represent the constituencies and my loyalty is to them.'

After a long discussion, by a recorded vote with myself, Bill Connor, Dennis Skinner and Barbara Switzer against, Nellist was suspended by 21 to 4 votes, and by 19 to 6 he was kept out of Conference.

I watched the Party Political Broadcast by Kinnock, about Kinnock and for Kinnock, and it was absolutely drained of any content whatsoever. Just a lot of people saying in Welsh, 'Oh, Neil is one of the most brilliant men I've ever met.' And Glenys saying, 'Oh, yes, great talent.' And I don't think it even mentioned the Labour Party once, actually.

Thursday 26 September

In the evening I watched this programme called *Timewatch*, I think, about the alternative view of the Gulf War, with Ramsey Clark, the former American Attorney General, Marguerita Papandreou, and a whole range of people, American and British – coverage of the situation in Iraq, which the British media never mention: starving babies, bombed buildings, the way the sanctions had been used to stop food and medical supplies. It was really riveting.

Friday 27 September

A smashing article in *The Times* called 'Kinnock's Betrayal Explained':

> Peter Mandelson, Labour's former Communications Chief, provided a revealing insight last night into the reasoning behind some of Neil Kinnock's policy U turns (Philip Webster reports). Referring to the age old accusation of the left that Labour Prime Ministers forsake policies and principle as soon as they get to Downing Street, Mr Mandelson said Mr Kinnock had told him, 'I would rather get my betrayal in before the election than after.'

There was a little bit after that saying that what Kinnock meant was facing the harsh realities. But it was actually an interesting comment.

Tuesday 1 October, Brighton

I watched Neil Kinnock's speech on television at our accommodation in Brighton. He gave a very polished performance. It was all stage-managed of course: the whole layout of the platform, with the people around at the side of the platform and a great stand and flowers behind, and it was a sort of Nuremberg Rally. It was awful. But Neil made a speech that was positive and full of perorations and alliterations, and so on.

He got a good response, but I got the feeling that a six-and-a-half-minute standing ovation was a bit stage-managed. Then he went back to the rostrum, having kissed and cuddled Glenys as if she was a rag doll. He went back to the rostrum and said, 'Let's sing a song.' So they all sang 'We Shall Overcome'. And I thought it was a bit strained, but any rate it was generally regarded as a great speech.

Central TV party. Sir Patrick Nairne was there. I think he'd been Jim Callaghan's private secretary and he was number two at the Foreign Office or something. He said to me, 'I've never forgotten when I was told to produce a bill for a referendum, you came out of the Cabinet and gave me a bill you'd already drafted and presented!' He's now working with the Freedom of Information Campaign. Like all these senior civil servants, terribly respectful when they meet a former Secretary of State.

Tony Bevins had done an interview with me in *The Independent*, on Monday, in which I said policy would change again after the election. In the afternoon the *Evening Standard* had a huge banner headline: 'Benn's Time Bomb for Kinnock', but it's a good argument to use because it gives the left hope, it indicates confidence and, of course, it's very difficult for the Labour Front Bench, having changed its mind once, to claim that under no circumstances – whatever happened – would they change it again. So I thought it was a very skilful move and I'm terribly pleased that I said it.

Wednesday 2 October, Brighton

I had asked Tom Sawyer yesterday whether I could speak in the debate on the Modern Constitution, which he said he would think about – he couldn't be sure.

I didn't want to be humiliated again by going to the floor, as I did last year on the Gulf, and then finding that I wasn't called.

I put my hand up to speak and people cried, 'Tony Benn, Tony Benn.' I thought. 'That will settle it, Tom Sawyer will never respond to such pressure.'

But I was called, and I felt the Conference was taking me to its heart again and although, according to people who watched from the floor, Neil's face fell when I was called, apparently he perked up and laughed and applauded, and so on. So that was all right.

I thought it was well worth using the Conference this year to get myself seen as a constructive and helpful member of the Party, despite everything that's happened.

I haven't got a lot more to do. I've just got a few more fringes and then I'm going home. I don't know that I'll go to Conference on the Friday morning. It's getting more and more like a Tory conference

Saturday 5 October

I finished reading the script of Keir Hardie which Caroline has completed, and what an extraordinary story it is – the story of how Keir Hardie neglected his family to pursue his interests, had a huge influence, but his children suffered terribly.

And about Sylvia Pankhurst, the impossible self-publicist and propagandist who thought she was right about everything, well in advance of everyone else. When you read it all you've got the history of the Labour Party, the ideological arguments between socialists and the Labour Party; you've got the family's story; you've got the personal relationship; you've got everything. Caroline lived through a similar experience, and the way in which political men dominate their families and ruin their families' lives is a theme in the book. Only she could write it.

Sunday 6 October

Well, today was a day at home in the morning, and we had a lovely family party in the afternoon and the six grandchildren came down to the basement. They've all got their own files. Michael said, 'I'm in charge of this office, you sit there and you sit there.' So one sat at the computer, one sat at the typewriter, two sat in the kitchen. They said, 'You can't come into the kitchen, Dan-Dan.' So I said, 'Why not?' They said, 'We're having a press conference.'

Well, they must be the only children of that age whose idea of a game is to come down, play with office equipment and have a press conference. It was lovely. And then they all went off and I worked for a bit.

Monday 7 October

Andrew Hood came in the morning and we went over the premiership. He warned me that my previous comments about the powers of a medieval monarch had been mocked by academics, so I modified them in terms of legal powers, executive powers, administrative powers, and political powers and political interests, and how it all worked.

Charlie Crowe, a student who's going up to New College shortly, volunteered to do a couple of days' work and undertook to index my speeches, which is the most burdensome job. He gets on very well with Ruth.

Wednesday 9 October

To my great delight, when I rang Chesterfield they said that the canvassing arranged for tonight had been called off – I had dreaded going up and canvassing, and coming back down, for two hours on the streets. I virtually commute to Chesterfield, so that was a great relief.

Mrs Thatcher got a six-minute standing ovation at the Tory Party Conference, with Tories crying – she thoroughly embarrassed the platform. As my brother Dave said afterwards, on the phone, it was the Twentieth Congress without the leader.

The truth is, John Major is a wet. The Nineties are going back to the old consensus, a sort of SDP-Tory Wet-right-wing Labour consensus, with no choice of any kind.

Anyway, in the evening at eight o'clock Corin Redgrave and his wife Kika Markham came to visit with Vladimir Guefenider, who is a young man in his late thirties, I would think, President of the Committee on Administration and Law in the Department of the Mayor of Moscow. And when he came in he kissed Caroline's hand and all of a sudden you felt you were back to Tsarist courtesies.

He had a bright young lad of about the same age translating, who did very well. I had a long talk with this guy Vladimir, asking about the Moscow Mayor. He appoints the prefects in all the districts, and the local council has really no control over the Executive. It's like an elected Tsar of Moscow, and I put that to him and he laughed.

Apparently, quite recently the Chamber of Commerce in Moscow met to say they would stop investing in Moscow unless the Mayor, Popov, withdrew the very rigid price-control measures that he'd introduced. Well, I thought that was very amusing, because actually it's an anti-communist dictatorship being built up and that became so clear from talking to Vladimir.

This young man is a lawyer, and was being asked really, in effect, to set up a new administrative structure for Moscow to get rid of the old Soviet apparatchiks, and it looked to me just as if it was a replacement of one dictatorship by another.

He said, 'We are not going for capitalism. We want natural relations between people, as they have in the rest of the world.' And I said, 'Well, capitalism is a political system. It doesn't like democracy any more than communism did, which is also a political system.' And I think I planted some thoughts in his mind, but I was very friendly and gave him a photocopy of *Comrades in Arms*, the booklet published by the British Government in 1941 in honour of our Soviet allies, which interested him very much.

Corin Redgrave said, 'Of course, there has to be some capitalism in Russia. But we must preserve the collective things that are good in Russia.' And I mentioned the Chinese economy and how successful it was, because nobody took any notice of what was dictated. They were much more decentralised. Corin also said there never was socialism in Russia (because he used to be an old Trotskyite and so he would be critical of it for that reason). But I was confirmed in my view that this is a middle – class counter-revolution against the old regime and no doubt necessary because of its corruption, and we'll see what happens as the situation develops.

Sunday 13 October
Caroline's sixty-fifth birthday. She looks about thirty-five. She's more active than she's ever been. She's very happy, and we had a late lie-in and I gave her my presents, including a bed warmer you put in the microwave to heat up. And some plants, scent and various other things.

Defence debate today, and there is a huge Tory row about cuts in the old regiments. Gosh, when there were redundancies in the mining industry, the Tories whooped with glee. When there are redundancies in the army, they start threatening all sorts of things. It's quite funny. Tomorrow I expect I shall vote against the Government because of nuclear weapons.

Tuesday 15 October
I left early to go to Charing Cross to have an X-ray, because I had bronchitis in the summer and they want to check it. Then went back to the Commons to see Henry Cobb, who is the Clerk of the Record in the House of Lords. He's retiring next month and is being replaced by somebody called David Johnson, who was on holiday. We also met, while we were there, Stephen Ellison, who's looking after the computerisation of the project, and also, up in the Victoria Tower, Katharine Bligh.

Cobb is a real archivist – modest, shy. He's actually a medieval economic historian. He's been there thirty-five years.

Two kind ladies brought tea and then we went up to Victoria Tower. You go through many security locks and up in the lift, then you change to another lift and there is this huge spiral staircase, which in the old days used to go right to the very top, but now has been replaced.

We went up to the twelfth floor, where there were models of the House of Commons stored on one side, and scrolls of the early Parliaments, parchments of the early parliamentary bills and writing on them of the clerk, saying *La reyne le veult* – the Queen wishes it, which was the royal assent.

Then we came up to Father's papers, which are beautifully kept. They're in blue boxes, every one of them numbered, and although it's not on a computer they have got an index and a printed hand-list. And they've also brought all Father's files back from Colindale – his *Times* cuttings files.

Ruth went to see Jim Callaghan for an interview for the *House Magazine* on his maiden speech. She said he was a bit grumpy to begin with. At the end he asked what she did and she told him, 'I'm an editor, I work on Tony

Benn's *Diaries*.' Then he told her he hadn't come to the launch of my books because he thought I'd done too much damage to the Party, and what a nice and attractive young man I had been, and how I went wrong.

He said, 'As I get older I don't want to have quarrels with anybody.' Which is exactly the way I feel. Altogether he was really quite friendly.

They had about forty-five minutes, and she picked up on a lot of things – the fact that his father was in the navy; he himself had been in the Inland Revenue and the navy; he hadn't been to university, which worried him. She reminded him that he had once said to me, 'I'm not as nice as I look', and I'd replied, 'Neither am I.'

I think that probably that interview will make it possible for relations to improve with Jim. Just as Geoffrey Goodman is trying to improve my relations with Michael, so Ruth has been helping with Jim. The trouble is the next volume of the *Diaries* will deal with Michael Foot so devastatingly that I'm not sure how possible it will be to improve relations.

At five o'clock I went to the Committee of Privileges. I happened to say to the Attorney General, after it was over, because he was sitting there talking to Merlyn Rees, 'I ought to tell you that the next volume of my diaries is coming out next Tuesday and it covers the 1980s and of course, during the 1980s, I was put on the Committee of Privileges, therefore my diary will include reports of what was said.'

'Oh,' he said. 'You can't do that.'

'Well, I reported in my diary what happened in Cabinet meetings and nobody ever raised objections.'

He said, 'Oh, but the Committee of Privileges is quite different. It's a question of confidentiality; members of all parties reach a consensus.'

'Well, it may be so, but my duty is to my electorate, not to the House of Commons.'

'It will be breach of privilege.'

I said, 'If you want me on that basis to leave the Committee of Privileges, I'm quite happy to do so, but I can't accept that the House of Commons is more secret than the Cabinet.'

'You'd better bring any extracts you want to use to the Committee of Privileges to get them authorised.'

'I'm not doing that,' I said. 'I'm awfully sorry. I was elected by people in my constituency and what I learn when I am here, I have an obligation to convey to the people who elected me. It's as straightforward as that.'

He looked very uncomfortable and said, 'You'd better write to the Chairman.'

So anyway, I went upstairs, back to my room, a bit discouraged, and I did write a letter to John MacGregor, which might be quite a useful cover if ever I am hauled up. I doubt if the House would take action, but the House is a pretty brutal place when its own privileges, in a general sense, are threatened, so I might be in serious trouble.

When I got back to my room there were messages that Mother was taken ill. So I dashed back in the car to the Goldsborough Homes where she is, and she had a pain in her stomach and they decided to put her in hospital, in St Thomas'.

So I waited till the ambulance arrived and then saw her into the ambulance, drove back to the Commons, voted in the Defence debate, which was dominated by a lot of grumpy old colonels who saw their regiments being merged and cut back, and so on. I found myself in a lobby with these old Tories. I nearly said to them, 'Well, the Chesterfield Fusiliers are being threatened and the last time they were in action was during the Orgreaves picket!'

I went back to St Thomas'. Mother was in a little room and the surgeon, came to see her after the registrar had examined her and thought she might have peritonitis, so she had to be X-rayed. At ninety-four she is terribly frail.

I went out for a smoke for a moment and a stocky young man of about thirty came up to me and said, 'Have you got a light?' So I said, 'Yes.' And asked, 'Do you work here?' He said, 'No, I'm just about to admit myself to hospital. I've taken a hundred paracetamol.' So I said, 'Why?' And he said, 'Well, my father died of cancer and I'm very depressed. It's the second time I've done it.' I said, 'Well, you'd better go in quickly.' 'Oh, no, it won't take effect for a number of hours.'

So anyway I popped in and I spoke to the staff nurse, who was a very busy young woman, very nice and active and friendly, and she went out and said, 'Well, when you've had your cigarette, you come in.' So he went in, and no doubt they pumped his stomach out.

Wednesday 16 October

I went over to see Mother in hospital and I talked to the surgeon. She was really quite beyond communication, looking awfully haggard and old. The surgeon said he might have to give her a stomach operation and a colostomy, but at ninety-four it's very risky.

I'm afraid that it looks pretty bad.

Saw George Thomas today in St Stephen's Hall with some guests. He's eighty-three. He's had cancer twice, and was amazingly fit. I dropped on one knee and he said, 'Oh, get up, you naughty boy.' Which is typical of George.

We were talking for a bit and I said to his guests, 'Of course those were in the days when George was radical.' 'Oh,' said George, 'I'm getting more radical now.'

I think what happened to him was that he started as a radical and then swung to the right. He was a very right-wing Secretary of State for Wales. Then, when his mum died, because he was very devoted to her, in a strange way he transferred his affection and allegiance to Mrs Thatcher.

Friday 18 October

I cancelled my Chesterfield surgery because I am so concerned about Mother, and I went to the hospital and she's in a coma now. She was breathing in a rather shallow way, and I thought to myself, 'This could be the last night.' So I found a camp bed in the corridor and I brought it in and simply lay down and went to sleep.

I think I was coughing so much that the nurses kept coming in to see if it was Mother, but it was me. She didn't speak all night.

Saturday 19 October

I woke at 5.15 and stood up and looked over the river and it was absolutely beautiful. There was hardly any traffic. It was dark, the stars were out, the sky was clear and I could see all the places where Mother's life had really been spent, since she came to London to see her father in Parliament in 1910.

Sunday 20 October

Labour has a seven-point lead, according to the *Observer*.

I rang the hospital and they said that last night a nurse had gone in, and three times the nurse had asked Mother on three separate occasions, how she was and she said, 'I'm all right, I'm comfortable.' So it looks as if she's coming back from it all. What a will to survive!

Went to the hospital and saw Didi and she was able to talk. So I said, 'It's Anthony.' She said 'Hello' in a very croaky voice and she understood. I talked to her a little bit and stroked her head. Dave was there and I felt she'd rallied a bit.

Monday 21 October

Steve phoned from the hospital and I heard him talking to Mother and I heard her saying, 'Hello, Anthony' in a croaky voice.

At ten past two the phone rang and they said, 'This is St Thomas' Hospital. I'm afraid your mother died about ten minutes ago.'

So I phoned Dave and I phoned Caroline, and Dave went straight to the hospital and I updated and issued by fax a little obituary statement. Didi was very peaceful. She was lying there, still warm, her skin still soft, and I stroked her hair and I must admit I just stood and sobbed and sobbed and sobbed.

By pulling the bed out with her lying on it, and raising it, I was able to get one or two lovely photographs of her profile against Big Ben in the background, which was so appropriate.

Dave was there and Frances arrived. She was very upset – of course the family are all very upset. And Steve was there and he was upset, but he had his camera and took lots of lovely pictures.

I phoned Nursey – Miss Winch – and she was terribly upset. She'd known mother for sixty-three years and said she was her closest friend and adviser, and that is true.

Mother's life was really a very remarkable one, and her book, *My Exit Visa,* is coming out next year so that will be something to look forward to. I think she will be recognised as having led a useful life. Certainly it was an active one, and a long and a very progressive one. Considering she was not allowed by her parents any sort of education, she became a great scholar and put an awful lot into life. And everyone who knew her liked her very much.

Tuesday 22 October

To the Moses Room at the Commons for the party that Cledwyn Hughes had invited me to, to celebrate his forty years in Parliament either as MP or peer. Neil Kinnock made a speech saying how he looked forward to seeing Cledwyn as Leader of the House of Lords after the next election, and all the rest of it.

While Neil was talking, Fred Mulley was standing next to me and said that we need to get a round robin, we'll never win under him. I said, 'Shhh'.

Then Cledwyn made a speech. Long and rather pompous, but very amusing. He made a reference to me, which I missed because I'm very deaf. He apparently said that he'd been to St Helena on a Labour Party visit, though actually the Party had originally wanted to send Tony Benn, 'for obvious reasons'. There was a lot of laughter.

Indeed, it was what Father said about there being too much goodwill in the House of Lords – unbearable goodwill.

I went up to Jim and I said, 'I hope Ruth Winstone did convey to you my affection for you, Jim.' He said, 'Well, I've noted that.' I said, 'We've had our differences, but I've a great affection for you.' He's sort of grumpy and friendly.

I went up to Hailsham and I said, 'Quintin, my mother died yesterday and it reminded me of the marvellous tribute to my father you made when he died in the House of Lords. I've got the Hansard, very carefully kept.'

He said, 'Fancy your remembering' and he added, 'Life is never the same when your parents have gone', which I thought was profound.

So that was the evening, and I stayed for about an hour and a half and enjoyed it, to be honest, even though I found the whole atmosphere of it absolutely cloying and inward-looking. It was the 'club' meeting privately, and nobody would want outsiders to know what was going on because these were people who normally abuse each other.

Wednesday 23 October

Three lovely obituaries today. *The Times* gave Mother pride of place, with the photograph I had sent.

Sunday 27 October

Caroline and I and Stephen and Josh went to see Mother's body at the funeral directors, Kenyons. It was in the chapel, and of course a body is never the same as a living person. Although if you watch it by candle-light, the flickering of the candle gives a little bit more movement. We stood around and I touched her head and kissed it, and there she was in her dress, beautifully laid out.

Stephen had his video and I had my camera. Then we came home in the evening. Caroline went on with her Keir Hardie book, which occupies all her time.

Monday 28 October

We all headed off for the Golders Green Crematorium.

I set up various tape recorders to record it, three of them in fact. I think at about 1.15 Didi's body was brought in, in the coffin, and placed on the table in front and the service began. Dr Janet Wootton, the Congregational minister, took the service.

There was no written service, but we sang the old 100th Psalm, 'All People That On Earth Do Dwell', and we sang 'How Bright These Glorious Spirits Shine'.

Piers read a bit from St Augustine which Mother liked, and I read extracts from her interviews with Rebecca Abrams last year about how she came to the Christian faith, stories about her difficulties with two Archbishops of Canterbury on the ordination of women.

Then Stephen played the air he composed on the organ – she loved it so much – and afterwards we went out. Everyone was in tears.

I'm afraid that when I read my passage I was blubbering and everyone else was crying. It was immensely sad.

Then the children cried and had to be comforted, and afterwards we all came back here for sandwiches, a drink and tea and coffee. And then they all went off and Caroline and I cleared up.

It was a very moving occasion. I think Mother would have liked it very much indeed.

I'm sure somewhere she noticed it and enjoyed it.

The recording fortunately came out very well.

Tuesday 29 October

I went in to the Jerusalem Chamber at Westminster Abbey for a reception for His Holiness Alexei II, Patriarch of Moscow and All Russia.

The new Archbishop of Canterbury, George Carey, made a speech and it certainly was very interesting. He welcomed the Patriarch, and said something about the Jerusalem Chamber, its history, that Henry IV had died here, that Henry V had taken the crown here and contemplated the awesome responsibilities of the transfer of power.

He said democracy is about a transfer of power as in South Africa, 'in the general election here, maybe, though I'm not predicting'. Everybody laughed. After the coup in Russia there were new moves to democracy and the market economy, he said.

Then he talked about the Russian Church and the close relationship with the Anglican Church, and the need for parish ministers. And he said, 'Higher up the Church, you have the bishops and the Patriarchs working with governments, all agreeing that all authority is with God.'

Now, of course, that's what his homily – or rather his homage to the Crown – requires him to say, but all of a sudden I felt that we were going back and back centuries, to the idea that the clergy and the Church and the State ran society, with democracy left out.

The Patriarch, Alexei II, was wearing a white helmet with a great bit of material hanging down, like somebody in the Foreign Legion, and robes and a lot of jewels; he thanked the Archbishop for his greeting and said the Archbishop of York had been to Russia, they had much to learn from the Anglican Church.

He said, 'The terrible events of 1917 are now over, and we are moving to a market economy and we shall need your help'.

Well, after that, I made a beeline for the Patriarch and, as I got there, the Archbishop said, 'I want you to meet Mr Benn, one of our most distinguished British Parliamentarians,' which was very nice of him.

I said to the Patriarch, 'I've been in Parliament for forty-one years. I've been in the Soviet Union many, many times, to Moscow, and I love it; but I hope you will not equate democracy with capitalism, because capitalism imposes great hardship on people.'

The Patriarch, looking a bit uneasy, said, 'Well, we are moving slowly towards a market economy.'

So I said, 'Well, what the West wants from you is low wages and high profits out of your skilled labour force.'

'Well, we know some people want that.'

So then I said, 'Capitalism and British imperialism have exploited the world; and what I fear is that the only form of capitalism you could have would be a military form of capitalism, like Pinochet's in Chile.'

He said, 'We must liberate our agriculture.'

'But under the Tsars, the landlords owned all the lands *and* the serfs before the serfs were liberated.'

By this time he was looking extremely uncomfortable. The interpreter, who spoke absolutely perfect English and apparently lived in Britain – a woman, I should think in her late fifties, possibly early sixties, with jet-black hair glued to the side of her head and a black dress, was sweating profusely. But I made my point and wished them goodbye and left.

Wednesday 6 November

Robert Maxwell is dead.

His body was found off his yacht near the Canary Islands, and now that he's dead and can't issue writs against people, everyone is free to say what they really think.

The man was financed by MI5 to get Russian trade secrets and publish them in the Pergamon Press. He worked with the Israeli Intelligence services. He is thought to have been the man who shopped Vanunu, who revealed the fact that Israel had nuclear weapons capability and who is now in jail in Israel.

Maxwell was a really nasty, crooked man. I find it very difficult to say anything good about him, but of course there are tributes from Kinnock and Ashdown and Major and everybody in the papers. It's not absolutely impossible that he may have been killed by Mossad; but the fact is that he is the second *Daily Mirror* person to be an Intelligence man – Cecil King was also MI5. Talk about a free press when the *Daily Mirror* is run by MI5 over a period of years – it does make you wonder.

Maxwell financed Neil Kinnock's private office. Why? Was he really trying to get a Labour Government elected, or to wreck the Labour Party so it wouldn't get elected?

Saturday 16 November, Chesterfield

Slept much of the way, but on the train I met a man who told a horrific story. In June, his wife, to whom he'd been married for two years, and their little girl of nine months had disappeared. He rang the police on the Friday, and they said, 'There's nothing we can do.' He rang on the Saturday and they said, 'There's nothing we can do.' He rang on the Sunday, and they said, 'Come in on Monday.'

They sent a police constable back to his house with him, who looked through the house and kept commenting on the expensive things he had there. 'Where did you get these from? Where did you get all this money from?'

His great pride and joy were some fish. He had some carp in a pool that he'd dug in the garden. After that six policemen arrived and began digging his garden. They said, 'We think you killed your wife.' They left a policeman with him all night, or a succession of policemen.

The following day, the Tuesday, he was called into the police station, and interrogated from nine till three by four plain-clothes detectives. They said to him, 'You're a fucking liar. We know you killed your wife Your neighbours have told us you killed your wife.' To cut a long story short, they bullied him and bullied him.

Then, on the Tuesday evening, they sent twenty policemen, who dug his whole garden up to six foot in depth. They punctured his pool, so the water ran out and all his carp died.

Now he suffered from blackouts and depression, and he collapsed several times while the police were at his house and in the police station. On one occasion in the police station they accused him of sexually assaulting his nine- month-old daughter, and he hit one of the policemen and they shouted at him, 'Ah, there you are, it shows you are a violent man.'

On the Wednesday evening his wife reappeared. She'd disappeared with her child. She'd had a breakdown of memory; she didn't know where she'd been; she'd been very depressed by the problems that they faced. The police never apologised. And that was the end of the matter.

That was the story he told me. I wrote a letter to the Home Secretary about it because I was so incensed, although looking back on it on the Sunday morning, the following day, I suppose I ought to have checked whether any of it was true or entirely fabricated. But it was a most extraordinary story.

I was taken to the Speedwell Rooms, where there was a North East Derbyshire Labour dance. There were about 200 people, mainly in their sixties and seventies. And I thought, 'If that's the local Labour Party, we are in a jam.' Harry Barnes, the local MP was there. We both spoke. I thought it went down pretty badly, truthfully. I looked around and there was no particular response, they all looked a bit impatient. Then as soon as I sat down the dancing began. I asked about it afterwards and they said, 'Oh, these people come dancing in the Speedwell Rooms every Saturday.' So in fact they weren't Labour people at all; they were just elderly people who liked dancing. They danced beautifully. The men were in patent-leather shoes and the women were all coiffeured up; maybe they were Labour voters anyway.

Sunday 17 November

The Tories are faced with a serious anti-European revolt in which Thatcher and Tebbit are playing a part. They don't like foreigners and they think that the Common Market is going to be the Ministry of Technology re-created on a European scale, interfering with the power of British employers to dominate their own workers.

On the other hand, Major knows that the City of London will never accept a Prime Minister or political leader who is anti-Europe. That's why they got rid of Thatcher, or one of the reasons.

The Labour Party have swung completely. Kinnock, who was very anti-Europe, is now very pro-Europe. Indeed, not only pro-Europe, but criticising the Government for going too slow. He's carried his view through the National Executive, through the Shadow Cabinet, he's publicised it, he's got it through the Conference with the trade union votes.

Meanwhile the opinion polls show a great hesitation by people in the country as a whole, because they don't want to see sovereignty handed over. They suspect that this is really a German-dominated Europe, a re-creation of the Europe Hitler wanted, only without the war, being done by diplomats and bureaucrats and businessmen and bankers.

So you have a funny situation, where that could be the factor which brought the Tories back to power, by being cautious on Europe. I've been as active as I could, but it's difficult because some people in the Labour Party have got no confidence in Parliament.

Ken Livingstone, in the Campaign Group, is just a federalist because he is not interested in the House of Commons and Parliament.

Wednesday 20 November

Debate on Maastricht.

Major opened terribly quietly, as you'd expect of a Prime Minister entering negotiations. Kinnock was awful, not least for calling Robert Adley a jerk when he intervened. Mrs Thatcher spoke for half an hour; it was amusing to see her again. She left before I was called.

During my speech, Tebbit and Biffen were nodding away. Even the people on our side, who didn't like what I said, did really enjoy it. I was terribly pleased with it. It was about democracy. None of the other MPs talked about democracy at all.

Thursday 21 November

I saw Mrs Thatcher leaving the House, and I walked over and had a word with her. She said she was very sorry that she hadn't heard my speech yesterday, but she'd just flown in from America, spoke and left because she was extremely tired. I'm a bit embarrassed actually by the support from the right-wing nationalists, Tebbit and Thatcher and others.

John Smith later cleverly made fun of the Tories and truthfully, if there was an election for the leadership on a secret ballot tomorrow, Smith would win, with only about five votes going to Kinnock, and our standing would rise in the polls instantly. But that's not on.

Friday 22 November

Rushed to the station to catch the last train to London from Chesterfield and it was forty minutes late. I went into the little waiting room and there was a young woman sitting there. I asked her where she was going and she said Derby. I said, 'What do you do?' And she said, 'I'm a signal-maintenance trainee at Derby.'

I said, 'It must be very difficult for you.' 'Yes,' she said, 'the men don't like it.' She was only seventeen.

Then another young woman came in, I think this time in her twenties. She was training to be a teacher in further education. Then a man came in and said he was an unemployed builder. Then another man came in who worked as a grinder at Rolls-Royce.

So the five of us got talking. The woman who was a trainee teacher said that she had to catch the connection at Derby to go to Matlock. So I said I would ring and ask them to hold the train. I pulled out my cellphone and got the number from Directory Enquiries. I got through to Derby and said, 'Can you hold the train to Matlock?'

I didn't say who I was or anything. A few minutes later, in puffed one of the staff at Chesterfield Station, saying, 'Oh, Mr Benn, are you going to Matlock? We heard a message that you were going to Matlock and had rung about holding the train.'

I said, 'No, it's that woman over there who's going to Matlock.'

'Well, they've arranged a taxi for you.' Then he disappeared, and a few minutes later he puffed in again and said, 'It'll be all right, the taxi's for her.' So she got a taxi. It was really rather amusing. They had recognised my voice at Matlock!

I finally got home frightfully late. I went to bed about half-past two. I was terribly, terribly tired.

Wednesday 27 November

National Executive this morning where we stood in silence for Robert Maxwell, which I found a bit much.

A paper on the political union of Europe was put up and my amendment on a referendum was accepted as being valid for consideration. I argued that we could not on the one hand say that the Labour Party insists on a ballot before even a one-day strike at a single factory is called, but not be prepared to have a ballot or a referendum when it comes to the question of the whole future of the government of our country.

I said there was a grave misunderstanding of what's happening, because public opposition is quite strong. The Liberals favour a referendum.

Kaufman said, 'There is now a four-to-one majority for the EEC, the referendum would confirm it, there is a split in the Tory Party, and do we want Thatcher to hijack the Labour Party?'

Robin Cook said that he felt comfortable with the document. He welcomed the widening of the Community. There were problems in Eastern Europe; they wanted a strong EEC. In 1975 he'd argued against, but we lost, we're in, and if we're left alone what would happen to us? He was doubtful about a referendum.

John Prescott said, 'Well, I'm for turning it down. The attitude to democracy is an issue, but there are political realities. The idea of a referendum in 1972 was to get Labour off the hook and it was a tactical question, so look at what would happen.' He said he was not in favour of control of our budget deficit by the Community, he didn't believe in a federal Europe, he favoured widening.

Anyway, by 22 votes to 2 we voted for the paper on the European Union; and on the proposal for a referendum, we lost by 24 to 2 (Dennis and me).

Went to Chesterfield for a ward meeting. Then I got back to the station, caught the train and saw a vaguely familiar figure with white hair at the other end of the carriage.

I stood up to see who it was and it was Lord Mackay, the Lord Chancellor, whom I'd always wanted to meet. I walked along and he was sitting in a non-smoker; I had my pipe.

I said, 'I do so admire you for having gone to that Catholic funeral and facing the anger of your own Church.'

'Well,' he said, 'the man was a Catholic and he was a friend, and they asked me to promise never to do it again and I couldn't.'

He's a charming man, he's two years younger than me. We sat and talked for two and a half hours. I asked him about ecclesiastical appointments. He said, 'I have five hundred livings that I appoint lower down and I'm advised by the Patronage Secretary to the Prime Minister.'

He said he was the son of a railwayman and so he, and the Archbishop of Canterbury whom he spoke very highly of, and John Major are all people who've got to the top by virtue of policies from a Labour administration. They may be Tories now but they are really a product of the opening up of society.

He told me about his own career and how he was really non-political. He said he liked Carey very much and had met him in Salisbury, when Heath had invited them both to a meal.

I asked him about the intimidating atmosphere that courts offer to people who go there and he said, 'Well, there has to be an element of awe.'

I said, 'I've written letters to you on a few cases, and I don't suppose you've seen them personally?'

'I read them very, very carefully,' he said.

I asked him about the Birmingham Six and the Guildford Four and the Tottenham Three and he said, 'Well, we're going to have to look at all that.'

He talked a bit about religion and he said the severe, austere Scottish Christianity was something that he couldn't quite go with, but he said, 'I don't work on the Sabbath, although I work very hard on other days', which I'm sure is true. But he did favour the Establishment of the Church, in order to maintain better moral standards.

We talked about people in the Lords. Harold Wilson came to the House of Lords but was so confused it wasn't possible to talk to him.

We had a very amusing discussion about the plaque to Emily Wilding Davison which I had screwed up on the door of the broom cupboard in the

Commons crypt. Lord Mackay was slightly upset that I'd said he was against it. 'You did put it up without permission,' he said.

Then I told him the story about how I'd seen the Speaker to ask permission to have it put up, and the Speaker suggested that I see the Lord Chancellor, but that he might not like to see me because I'd renounced a peerage; and how Mr Kitcatt, the Speaker's secretary, had written a letter saying that.

He was very tickled by that.

He offered me a lift when we got to London, but I had a car. It was amusing and he's got a great deal of charm, just like Major, just like Carey.

Thursday 28 November

In the evening I went to do this *Clive Anderson Talks Back* show. I've been very doubtful about it, because he's a clever right-wing lawyer who is a bit hard to cope with. He makes jokes at people and the audience laughs at people. It's not very comfortable.

I just argued with him and laughed at him.

I had one minor problem – there was somebody with a boa constrictor also on during the show, and I wasn't prepared to appear with or be near anyone with a boa constrictor. I'm terrified of snakes. So I insisted on being kept separate!

Sunday 1 December

I went off to St Martin-in-the-Fields from where about 100 people, or perhaps a few more, marched quietly with banners down Whitehall to the Ministry of Defence to present a petition of 5000 signatures for the release of Vic Williams.

Lots of police there. Police trucks, police cars, up at the top of Horse Guards Parade. I could see two policemen, one armed with a sniper gun with a telescopic lens and another one with a camera. I drew attention to that in my speech. I went to the door of the Ministry of Defence and there was a doorkeeper, so I asked if he was the Duty Officer, which he was. So I handed the petition over and that was that.

From there I went to the Turkish-Kurdish Centre, where there were 800 people or more, absolutely packed in.

The walls were covered in graffiti. On the platform were the former US Attorney General Ramsey Clark, a former Deputy Prime Minister of Pakistan, Harold Pinter, and a few others. I'd never actually met Clark before. He's an outstanding man. The best type of American radical. He was wearing an informal corduroy jacket and blue button-down shirt and a striped tie. He spoke without a note for about twenty-five minutes.

He's as straight as a die. You could tell that immediately. Had the genuine indignation of the radical at the injustice in Iraq.

He told personal stories about a little girl of ten who'd had her leg amputated without an anaesthetic, gave statistics about the number of babies that were born with malnutrition and then went back to the history of the Middle East.

After him came Harold Pinter, who read a short poem full of vulgar language: 'We've kicked the shit out of the Iraqis, the fucking asses,' etc. I thought it was quite unnecessary, but nobody was particularly shocked.

Monday 2 December

Caroline and I went to dinner with the Deputy High Commissioner for India, Krishna V. Rajan, and his wife and daughter, and also there was B. K. Nehru, whom I'd last met in 1971 and I'd dug out my diary entry for that day. He's eighty-two now; he was born in 1909 and he's in very good health.

He told us he'd just been in New York for an economics conference and he said, 'I was staggered to discover that in the world every year the south pays fifty billion dollars worth of aid to the north in terms of interest payments, which is far more than so-called Third World aid.'

And he said, 'You can't have an economic structure worldwide whereby capital can move but labour can't, and if you're going to follow this, then labour must be able to come to wherever it's more profitable. These are the people that are being kept out by the Asylum Bill, on the grounds that they are economic migrants and all of that, but of course all the money that's invested abroad is economic migrant money.'

I was sitting between the High Commissioner's daughter, who's an interpreter, a very brilliant girl, and an American woman who said that her grandfather was a millionaire. She had been in Italy, had set up a consultancy business in design, had worked for ICI for a time and then twenty-six years ago had married. They had a child when he was sixty.

I told her about my diaries. She said, 'I write a diary, but I try to write personal things and I'm thinking now about the problem of ageing.'

So I said, 'It applies to everybody and it's very interesting.'

'Well,' she said, 'Take sex. Nobody ever thinks about sex for older women, but I want sex just as much now as I did when I was young.'

Well, this began to get a bit near the bone and I said, 'You're trying to seduce me.' So she laughed.

Then she said, 'Now, you could have a young woman if you wanted one, but I would have to have a toy boy and I'm not prepared to do that.'

And it got uncomfortable, so we moved on to politics.

She said how everybody hated Kinnock. 'Well,' I said, 'That doesn't matter very much. You don't have to be popular to win an election.'

It was enjoyable. Caroline and I hadn't been out to that sort of a dinner for ages, for about ten or twelve years.

Tuesday 3 December, Cambridge
Drove through the East End and got to Cambridge just after four. Ruth went to see Dr John Adamson, who is the history tutor at Peterhouse College, and he took her around Cambridge.

Meanwhile I drove to High Point Prison about twenty miles away to see Vic Williams.

I went to the gate of the prison and I produced my House of Commons card, parked my car and they let me in. I was taken down and Vic Williams was let in from a door. We were put in an absolutely empty visiting room with bare walls and a table.

I said, 'Can I smoke?' Vic doesn't smoke. I gave him the tape recording of the demonstration in his support. I gave him a copy of the letter to the Prime Minister, and other letters of support.

He said they were pouring in at the moment, and I also gave him the *Diary of a Coward,* a photocopy of a manuscript diary written by Emrys Hughes in the First World War.

Vic said the prisoners were quite decent and were getting quite political. Some of the prison officers thought he shouldn't be in prison at all. Others were much more reserved and less friendly.

He said that when he was awaiting his court martial he was put on to clean the gold and silver plate in the Officers' Mess, which I think he said must be worth £100,000. And he said, 'I threw myself into it and did a brilliant job and officers were saying, "I say, This mess is very clean". I wanted them to realise that they were losing a good soldier.'

He then said that at the court martial Helena Kennedy had been very soft and skilful with them. And, of course, he was lucky to get fourteen months and not twenty years, which he could have done.

He said that in the army, in the guardroom, he'd had a rough time. At Colchester they were careful of him because they knew of the public interest there was.

I asked, 'Is prison like the army?'

He said, 'It's frighteningly so.'

He told me that when he left prison he'd arranged to go to South London Poly and do a course.

Here's a perfectly loyal young soldier, who had volunteered, but thought the Gulf War was wrong and had taken a stand, handed himself in at the end of the war and been punished, and was now content living at ease with himself. His political understanding has grown by leaps and bounds. He's doing study skills, he's learning the word processor. In a way, prison life must be very harsh and the regime very harsh and the loss of freedom tremendously severe; but he's using it well.

Drove back to Cambridge.

Outside Peterhouse I met Sir Henry Chadwick. He's a Very Reverend, so he must be a canon. He's Professor of Theology and Church History, educated at Eton. His *Who's Who* entry cross-references to Judge Chadwick and Sir Owen Chadwick. So he comes from an absolutely top-class academic family.

He's interested in inter-communion between the Catholics and the Protestants and the Church of England; he's very much opposed, I assume, to the ordination of women. He's about seventy-one. He had that air of superiority and a slightly watery but courteous way. Anyway, I sat next to him at dinner. I'll come to that.

Went out into the Fellows' Guest Room, where all these young Cambridge students were, in their best suits, really looking like a lot of tailor's dummies, drinking orange juice and champagne. I was taken back to before the last world war. This was the old Oxbridge re-created. Ruth said it was *Brideshead Revisited*. I found it very interesting, but also unattractive.

Then we went down and met the Master again and were taken into dinner; there was a long Latin grace and we were told that the hall was 700 years old.

I sat on the left of the Master, and on my left was Dr Adamson and next to the Master on the other side was Ruth and Norman Hammond, who is the *Times* archaeological correspondent and also an archaeologist at the college. What I picked up slowly in the course of the evening was that this was the most right-wing college in the whole of Cambridge. Very few women in it; indeed, it had the reputation for having a lot of homosexuals there, I don't know if that's true. We were told while we were there, 'This is the queers' college.' Very right-wing.

Anyway we had dinner and I talked to the Master about early Church history and about Cromwell, the Commonwealth, and so on.

He said to me, 'That battle over the peerage must have been quite a lark, a lot of fun.'

So I said, 'It wasn't very funny to be thrown out of Parliament.' I told him a few stories about Lord Salisbury.

Then we went to the Fellows' Parlour where the meeting was to be held. It was a darkened room, which I think had been decorated personally by William Morris.

There were two round tables in front of a burning coal fire and two candelabra, and a silver tea service had been put in front of me. The secretary of the History Society (it was student-run) introduced us. Ruth spoke for about a quarter of an hour about the diaries.

I think they were horrified that a woman was addressing them. Then I spoke and there were questions, and all the questions were so anti-democratic. 'You talk about open government,' one of them said. 'What about the national interest?'

Norman Hammond asked whether, by publishing my diaries, I was breaching the Privy Council's oath.

And somebody else said, 'Well, I'm an American and I think they'd prefer to do it in secret in America, if only they could.'

Then somebody else said something about, 'Isn't this all idealistic and, if you trust the people, you would end up with a referendum in favour of hanging.'

It was quite an unresponsive audience. One or two laughs, but they weren't political, they weren't sympathetic, they weren't in favour of democracy. Afterwards some of them came up and argued most passionately with me and one student said, 'Isn't it very unfair of you to write your diaries, because your account will get much more attention than the accounts by other people?'

It quite frightened me in a way, because a sort of monastic, elitist, privileged group of people was being trained. They had had their morale restored fifty years after the war and the growth of the Labour Government and the Welfare State, when the morale of all these sort of people had been greatly diminished.

Anyway, that was it and afterwards we packed up and left. Caroline said later it was the think-tank of Essex Man, and I thought it was the place where the *Sun* newspaper was translated into Latin.

Thursday 5 December

Did a little briefing with people from Walworth Road in preparation for *Question Time* tonight. *Question Time* has now been privatised and in the chair is Peter Sissons, who's taken over from Robin Day. It was quite unlike the old one, where you had a meal first and got to know each other.

There was Gillian Shephard the Tory Treasury Minister, whom I'd never met, a very nice woman; Howard Davies who apparently was in the Embassy in Paris when I went over there and is now Chairman of the Audit Commission and has been making life absolute hell for David Bookbinder in Derbyshire; and Christine Crawley, one of these bland Labour Euro MPs. Peter Sissons introduced us thus, 'Gillian Shephard, Treasury Minister, former inspector of schools. Howard Davies, so clever that he left the Foreign Office, went into the Treasury, took over the Audit Commission. Christine Crawley, one of the great Chairmen of some committee, Member of the European Parliament', and so on. 'And Tony Benn, whom John Mortimer once described as a mad, Marxist, werewolf and who is now totally isolated in the Parliamentary Labour Party.'

So before he got onto the first question, I interrupted him.

I said, 'Look, that introduction was most offensive. You could have said I was forty-one years in Parliament, eleven years in the Cabinet, Chairman of the Labour Party. You just dredged out all the old abuse. You should just introduce people factually.'

There was a tremendous round of applause.

Friday 6 December, Edinburgh

Caught the plane at Heathrow at eight and was met by two students in Edinburgh, and by Fergus, who is the chauffeur of Professor Hamlin, the Principal of Dundee University, and was driven to Dundee.

When I got there I had time just to look in at a class of students who were studying my Commonwealth of Britain Bill, as a standard text for discussing the British constitution. It was handed out to all of the students doing politics and social studies.

Did a series of interviews with the media about constitutional reform. Then to lunch with the Principal, Professor Hamlin, and various other people. John Berridge is the lecturer in politics who'd invited me up and organised the study of the Bill; he was formerly a Chairman of the Conservative Association, but moved out of active Conservative work into a more academic role. He was very friendly.

On the left was a Labour man – the leader, I think, of the Tayside Regional Council. We had a good old talk.

Hamlin was very funny. He told one marvellous story about Robert Maxwell, who'd seen somebody smoking in an office and so had gone up to him and said, 'How much do you earn a year?' The man said, 'Eighten thousand pounds.' So Maxwell had written a cheque for £1500 and said, 'Here's a month's salary, get out.' And the guy said, 'Okay. By the way I work for British Telecom.' And he pocketed the cheque and walked away.

Hamlin also said something else – that Maxwell had worked for the Ministry of Defence in Intelligence and had been sacked after the war for taking a bribe. Of course, everybody comes out with anti-Maxwell stories now he's dead. But it was a very interesting lunch.

After lunch I went to give the lecture on the Commonwealth of Britain Bill. The interesting thing about Dundee University is it's so different from Peterhouse. Peterhouse is just the intellectual elite. Dundee was very respectable, in the serious Scottish academic tradition. Half the students there come from Northern Ireland, Protestants of course.

I was absolutely exhausted by the end of the day, I must tell you.

Monday 9 December

Organisation Committee, where I asked whether it was true that Denis MacShane had been offered the constituency that belonged to Dave Nellist. Joyce Gould said, 'No.' Well, Joyce wouldn't know that. I said, 'Thank you very much. Because if he is then subsequently appointed, it will turn out to be a complete coincidence.'

Ruth arrived with the children of her friends, the Leighs. Toby, aged fourteen, and little Harriet, aged eleven, came around and I took them everywhere: down to the crypt and into the House of Lords, into the House of Commons, down to the engineers' control centre, where they looked through the periscope which peers into the Chamber, and they seemed to enjoy it very much. Harriet is as bright as a button, and questioned everything.

I sat in the Tea Room. There is general discontent with Kinnock, you just can't avoid it and there's nothing much can be done about it, although people are now asking will it be Brown or Blair, or John Smith or Margaret Beckett?

Well, actually, I couldn't give a damn. I don't think it's got any particular relevance because they're all the same, they're all right-wing.

Tuesday 10 December

Nita had her second little baby, a boy, Daniel John, born at the Mayday Hospital in Croydon this afternoon. Lovely, lovely news.

Wednesday 11 December

Caroline went off to the Mayday Hospital to see the little baby Daniel and I followed later. He's so perfect, he's just a tiny little person, he's not a baby at all. Absolutely perfect in every respect, but on a tiny scale. So content, opens his eyes and looks around. Mother died on 21 October; on 10 December a new baby is born. Life and death are cycles and you take them in your stride, but it was so thrilling. He is now second in line to the peerage. When I die, it will be Stephen; if Stephen dies, Daniel. So if Stephen and I were killed in a road crash, that little monkey would be Lord Stansgate and he's under a week old.

Thursday 12 December

I tried to spend the day, which was very, very difficult, typing up the memorial service for my mum on Tuesday. I made about 200 or 300 copies of the programme. All I've got to do now is buy the booze and the biscuits for the party in the Commons on Tuesday after the memorial service.

Tuesday 17 December

Left early this morning for the House of Commons with the orange juice and the wine, and the plastic cups and biscuits and everything.

I went over to Parliament's church, St Margaret's, and we had a simply lovely memorial service. There must have been over 300 people there.

Stephen played the organ so well, Janet Wootton gave a passionate address, Canon Gray was so graceful at the beginning and the end, Rabbi Jackie Tabick read a lesson and said the grace in Hebrew. It was just overwhelming.

Afterwards I stood and greeted everybody as they came out.Then we went over the road to the House and into the Jubilee Room. We had also booked the Grand Committee Room, but in fact the Social Security Select Committee was meeting there, waiting for Robert Maxwell's sons to arrive (which they never did), so we were crowded into one room; but it was awfully friendly and the wine and orange juice and biscuits were circulated. I felt we'd done Mother proud.

She'd have been absolutely overwhelmed if she'd seen it. It was a bigger turnout than for Father's memorial service, and it was an indication of the tremendous links she had with so many people. And she'd have been terribly pleased about a woman rabbi and a woman minister in the parliamentary church, absolutely delighted.

Thursday 19 December

In the evening to *A Week in Politics* with Denis Healey, Barbara Castle and Merlyn Rees.

It was absolutely riveting – forty minutes on what the next Labour Government would do. What was so interesting was that Denis Healey was the old tough iron Chancellor of 1975 saying we must now face the unions, and Barbara and Merlyn had swung back to a left position. So, far from being alone, as I would have expected with them all turning on me, it was 3 to 1 against Denis.

Friday 20 December, Chesterfield

I went to sleep on the train and woke to find a little note saying, 'Please appoint Lord Mackay of Clashfern as the next Labour Lord Chancellor' (he being the current Conservative Lord Chancellor). I don't know who sent it, but I posted it off later:

> Dear Lord Chancellor,
>
> This was left on the table in front of me when I was sleeping on the train. I don't know who sent it, but his admiration for your qualities exceeds his judgement about my powers. I enjoyed meeting you.
>
> Yours
>
> Tony Benn

When I got to Chesterfield I went to the Child Development Centre where they deal with disabled children. It was a very moving scene, these little kiddies with all the new equipment, computers and laser beams, which stimulated them.

Tuesday 31 December

On Christmas Day Gorbachev resigned and Russia is now a group of very uneasy partners: Russia, the Ukraine, Byelorussia, Kazakhstan, Georgia, and so on. It is the disintegration of a great superpower, with nuclear weapons left all over the place and the Americans anxious to see they're properly controlled.

Kinnock has succeeded, I think, in destroying the Labour Party financially as well as politically, morally and intellectually and organisationally, and that is the effect of his eight years as leader.

Friday 10 January, 1992

Caught the train home. The labels for the letters I wrote over Christmas still haven't been done. It is just impossible. I will have to have a typist come in and tackle the backlog of work. I settled down and began to write letters by hand.

Another IRA bomb today by the MOD. Nobody killed, because they gave warning, but a lot of damage. The one thing that nobody will recognise is that this is a civil war in the UK, triggered off by the partition of Ireland by British troops by force, against a ballot-box decision for Irish unity and independence seventy years ago. Until that is recognised, the problem will never be solved.

The other news is that Bush collapsed yesterday or the day before, apparently with gastric flu, but the truth is that you have to be fit in politics and if word gets round that you are ill, that's your problem. People don't want an unfit person to have responsibility, particularly if he has got his finger on the nuclear trigger.

Monday 13 January

Teresa Gorman told me she was going to introduce a Bill on Tuesday for each constituency to be represented by one man and one woman, which is based on my idea. She said Bernard Shaw had first thought of it.

I have a feeling I have got to start packing for my last journey, now that Mother's gone and I don't know how long I have. I am not very well. I have got a backache and this leukaemia problem, so there is a sense of urgency about my life now.

Wednesday 15 January

Caroline and I went to the Pipesmoker of the Year Award in the Savoy. We haven't been to a do like that for ages, and it reminded me of those business dinners which would be addressed by the Minister. There was an absolute battery of photographers. One of the presents given to me was a Big Ben pipe, which had been manufactured by Stephen Wilson, one of the designers for Dunhill: a wooden base and the bowl of the pipe was the clock face of Big Ben. I lit it at once because it was so attractive. Lots of photographs.

At the lunch there were about 350 people, only about four women. Laurence Marks, the TV writer, had talked me into it though I had some doubts on health grounds. His wife Brigitte is an actress and had played in *Auf Wiedersehen Pet*. There was a table with parliamentarians – Dick Caborn, Alan Meale, Ted Leadbetter, Robert Adley. It was full of ceremonial, with the toastmaster who said, 'Pray be upstanding for your distinguished guests,' the slow hand clapping etc. Absolutely revolting and I thought to myself, 'This is a *Daily Express*-reading audience.'

After a couple of ceremonies Laurence Marks presented my life story on a huge screen, using slides of me at every stage, Caroline having provided them.

Then I made my speech and I thought I had better make some jokes, then made a point about the 'pipe of peace' and pipe smoking stopped you going to war, and so on. It went down very well. I was given the gold award and the Dunhill pipe, which must be very expensive, and about 200 grams of tobacco. It was very jolly and friendly.

To the Campaign Group where, after I left, there was apparently a flaming row between those who support the Anti-Nazi League in its re-created form – including Peter Hain and Glenys Kinnock, and Paul Holborrow from the SWP, supported by Bernie Grant, the black Member for Tottenham – and the Anti-Racist Alliance, which is supported by Ken Livingstone and the Black Sections. Apparently Marc Wadsworth, who is a black journalist with Thames Television, attacked Bernie Grant for his record as an MP.

It is absolutely absurd that there should be these arguments between anti-racist organisations. It is left-wing politics at its most ludicrous.

Went to the *Week in Politics* party and, as I left there, William Cash – that tall, rather elegant Tory MP who is a constitutional lawyer and a committed Thatcherite – said to me, 'As you know, Tony, I am very close to Mrs Thatcher and she often speaks most warmly of you' (because I have opposed the road to a federal Europe). He said, 'You have only got to look at this place, look at this building. All this would be thrown away.' You realise their opposition to a federal Europe is not democratic at all. They just want to hang on to the privileges of a feudal Britain. I have got nothing in common with them.

Thursday 16 January, Chesterfield

I was met by Tom, Margaret and Ann Denman, who took me to the Royal Hospital to present a petition signed by 3500 people against the opting out of the hospital from the NHS. There was quite a crowd there and one of the managers said 'The protestors should come this way.' I said, 'We are not protestors, we are elected leaders of Chesterfield.'

We went to the first floor and the Unit General Manager greeted us and said, 'I am prepared to receive the petition from Margaret Vallins and Tony Benn. And will you come this way, I have got a small committee room.'

She said she wasn't prepared to see anyone else. I had my tape recorder running in my pocket, so some of it was picked up.

I said, 'What do you mean, picking and choosing who you will see. The leader of the Labour Council, Councillor Flanagan, is here and the leader of the trade-union representatives. Who are you to decide? Who appointed you, who are you accountable to?' It got very tense.

Somebody asked about the lecture theatre and she said it wasn't free. So I said, 'We'll do it here' and, in the darkness of this hallway with the *Derbyshire Times* present, the petition was presented.

What annoyed me was the arrogance of the Unit General Manager and the obsequious nature, frankly, of the citizens. In the end, Margaret presented the petition and we all left.

After that there was somebody from Yorkshire TV trying to organise us – 'You stand there. Do this, do that. Look this way, don't look at me.' Of course, if you are an ordinary citizen, you can't look at the camera; the only people who can are the journalists and the presenters. I didn't take any notice.

Back to London on the train.

Friday 17 January

Worked a bit this morning and left for Highgate Cemetery for Tony Gilbert's funeral. He was eighty-five, a lifelong communist who came from a Jewish immigrant family, fought fascism in the Thirties, joined the International Brigade, was captured by Franco's troops and tortured, got out, came to Britain, joined the army, went to Burma, was bayoneted by the Japanese, came back, joined the trade union movement, was sacked by the railways, was victimised, then became General Secretary of the Movement for Colonial Freedom (now Liberation). His wife Kay Beauchamp is in an old people's home.

It was a clear sunny day and the average age was over seventy, I think. We walked behind the hearse with two banners – the International Brigade and the Liberation banner – past Marx's monument, a huge head resting on a piece of granite. We sang one of the International Brigade songs and then we sang the Internationale. Very moving.

Monday 20 January

Tea in the afternoon with Clive Soley and Harry Cohen in the Tea Room. Clive Soley is a decent guy, whom I have always regarded as being an honest centrist member of the Party, and he said he didn't know what socialism was! He said it was all out of date, no relevance, we could be against capitalism, but what is socialism for?

Harry Cohen was fine. I got slightly angry and shirty about it, but I suppose you have to face that that's what people think.

Tuesday 21 January

Andrew looked in. He didn't get the job with Charter 88, which rather discouraged him, or with the Democratic Audit, which is run by Stuart Weir with a huge grant.

In the afternoon Ralph Miliband came and we had a marvellous talk. He said he thought there was a danger of my being presented as a sort of lovable, eccentric socialist, and I have sensed that myself. He is always very wise. I told him I thought he had been right about my not standing for the leadership and deputy leadership in 1981 and 1988. He said he didn't think it mattered very much. He said he had now come to the conclusion that the Labour Party was such a durable organisation that it couldn't be destroyed, but he thought there might be some room for a little socialist party, and if there was proportional representation then the prospects would change.

Friday 24 January, America

On the plane the industrial correspondent for the *Guardian* came up. He was on his way to the G7 meeting, where Yeltsin and others are discussing help for the Soviet Union.

I was told I couldn't smoke my pipe by the Chief Steward. I was asked to be photographed with two of the stewardesses.

Arrived and was met by John Catalinotto, who teaches mathematics at a community college, a man in his mid-forties, I should think. He looked a bit like a Russian dissident, a very nice man. A cab-driver friend of his had agreed to take me into town for nothing and we talked all the way there. John edited a paper called *Workers' World,* which is a break-off from the SWP.

To the Martin Luther King auditorium, spoke for about ten minutes and then an hour of excellent questions, as usual. It is a very radical place and people aren't allowed to know that there is a thriving socialist, trade-union tradition in the US, which is absolutely marginalised but which represents a lot of marvellous, dedicated people. WBAI is a sort of socialist broadcasting station with an audience of about 150,000 to 300,000 listeners; it links with five other Pacific stations.

The most important thing I discovered was that in the elections to the NY City Council recently, of the eight million people who live in NY, five million are eligible to be on the register, only three million registered and only 250,000 actually voted.

Saturday 25 January

Breakfast in the hotel. Worked on my speech and then took a taxi to the Peace with Cuba Office, and the cab driver was a Hispanic, I would think. He had served in the Vietnam War. He said there wasn't a single homeless person in NY who wasn't responsible for it, either through lack of education, because they were illiterate or had mental problems. A real potential Nazi supporter. He defended the Vietnam War, said the US was protecting the world and that benefits were poured out to those who won't work. He said, 'You don't seem to understand. There are twenty-three thousand violent deaths every year in America and there are tigers about, absolute animals, and even if you put them in a palace, they would still be animals.' I argued openly and frankly with him.

Got to the coalition office on the fifteenth floor of a rather crummy office block, about six people wandering round answering anti-Castro phone calls, drafting press releases. I was told I was going to do an interview with Radio Havana, but it never came off.

I drafted a message, then got a taxi back after buying some milk and biscuits. The driver was a young black guy, unmarried. He said things were hard, but, 'Many years ago Mr Roosevelt seemed to be able to find ways of dealing with this.' So there was the first time the slump was connected with the New Deal – interesting.

Back to the hotel, brought my diary up to date, and I'm just going off to the rally at about 11.50 a.m.

The speeches went on for about four hours and they were interrupted by people standing and shouting 'Cuba libre!' 'Viva Cuba!' and all that stuff. It had a very excitable flavour.

Afterwards I was invited to the house of the Cuban Ambassador to the UN for light refreshments. They have a full Ambassador to the UN and an Interests Section in Washington, and I met the Minister Counsellor there and his wife. I asked, 'What would happen if the Americans normalised? What effect would that have on Cuba? Would Cuba be taken over by American capital?'

He said, 'It is very difficult arithmetically to see how we can survive, and we think the danger of an American invasion of Cuba on some trumped-up pretext could well occur before the presidential elections, to give Bush strength.'

It was very interesting and I felt much committed to it all, when you think of the utter hypocrisy of the American Government supporting the sheikhs and Saudi Arabia, and Pinochet and all that.

Sunday 26 January

Last night, at the Cuban Ambassador's house, I had a talk to Frei Detto, the liberation theologist, who told me that he had worked with Lech Walesa in Poland, and Walesa had said to him, 'Socialism is the worst system of government in the world.' Frei said, 'You think that because you have never lived under capitalism.'

Had tea and watched TV, a discussion of the relationship between Church and State, and one thing I got from the discussion was that in polls 90 per cent of Americans said they believe in God and 38 per cent attend a Church every day. So one can honestly call America – although it separates Church from State – a Christian country, in the sense that it is fundamentalist in its belief in Christianity, though it is divided on how it should work.

Went downtown to have breakfast with Ramsey Clark and the taxi was driven by a Jamaican who had lived in Stoke Newington for eighteen years. He said he liked the American way and he was very much part of the American myth, although he struggled to survive.

Ramsey and I had a good old talk over breakfast. He said he had been sent by President Carter to Iran in *Airforce 2* to try and talk about the situation, but the Iranians wouldn't let him in so he had had to go in an unmarked plane. He had not been put on the National Security Council when he was Attorney General because of his known opposition to the Vietnam War.

He also described his relations with J. Edgar Hoover and the FBI, and said what they did was to hand him masses of minutes to read and he annotated them, then they had his comments and could use them against him, but if he didn't they implied he had agreed with them. So he said what he did was just to issue instructions to the FBI, numbered minutes, and he was very much in favour of that as a way of dealing with officials, which is exactly my view.

Caught a cab back to the hotel. The cab driver was a woman, probably in her late thirties, called Ilena who had come from Romania eight years ago. Her husband had been what you call a middle-man. She said the present Romanian regime is absolutely crooked. The leaders have got money salted away abroad and they had actually rehabilitated Antonescu of the Iron Guard movement, the fascist leader before the war.

She said the old Communist Party regime at least provided the essentials; now it was almost impossible to live with the new programme of austerity and privatisation and free markets.

Wednesday 29 January, London

Long discussion at the NEC on proportional representation for the Scottish Parliament. Professor Plant was there. He introduced a scheme which is in effect the Executive recommending that the Scottish Parliament or Assembly has the additional member system. Plant in fact said that the Labour Party had such a lead in Scotland that there had to be a closer correlation between seats and votes.

Dennis Skinner was in favour of the winners getting all the spoils – why destroy the Labour Party in Scotland?

I said the Scottish system will be applied elsewhere if we recommend it. I asked whether the proposals would be put to the people in Scotland. I then pointed out that you could have a system where there was no choice open, and I gave the voting figures for New York.

Robin Cook said, 'If we defeat this, the SNP will be delighted.'

Hattersley said he was passionately opposed to PR, but in Scotland it was different.

Kaufman said he wanted to know the answer to two questions: 'Does the Scottish LP want it, and do they need it?'

Plant said the decision would be thought to have an impact elsewhere, but the political context in Scotland is different and you can't recommend a system that keeps Labour in power permanently.

At 11.25 a.m. we had the policy document on London Government, calling for a Greater London Authority. I asked if it included the City of London, and they said yes. I queried the reference to directors from commerce and industry who would be responsible for the delivery of services and compulsory tendering. I said, 'Why do we always have to repudiate the GLC?'

Kinnock said, 'We never have repudiated the GLC.'

'Well, Bryan Gould has just said we have got to make it clear this isn't the GLC again.'

Dropped Dennis back at the Commons, and went to the Campaign Group's AGM. We re-elected Bernie Grant as chairman, Jeremy Corbyn as secretary.

There was rather a tense moment when Marc Wadsworth, who is active in the Black Sections movement, tried to distribute a paper on the Anti-Racist Alliance and Bernie Grant said, 'You can't distribute papers without my permission.' So Ken Livingstone went absolutely quivery and said, 'I am leaving, if this sort of behaviour continues . . . This is how Kinnock behaves. We have always been able to distribute literature', which is true, and he got up to go. It is this boiling hatred between the Anti-Nazi League, supported by Ernie Roberts and Bernie Grant, Paul Holborrow and Peter Hain, and the Anti-Racist Alliance, supported by the Black Sections, CLPD and Ken Livingstone. It is so crazy.

Voted, and then Caroline came and we went to a Random Century party, very upmarket, on the top floor of the Random House building in Vauxhall Bridge Road. There were four or five top authors there. I saw Kingsley Amis in the corner, whom I had met some years ago and who wrote some very rude and untrue things about me in his book, which I had quite forgotten, but Caroline reminded me. We wended our way through publishers and agents; the publishing world is precious and chic, a sort of upmarket version of the media – about the same level as the BBC, but more like the theatre. Had a brief word with Simon King, Kate Mosse, and Bridget Sleddon, said goodbye to Gail Rebuck and then we left. Caroline was very pleased to get away. I didn't like it, either. Still, Hutchinson have done me proud over the years.

I went to the Commons. I had a meal with Chris Mullin and we talked about the possibility of doing a sequel to *A Very British Coup*. We discussed the political situation and he said, 'After the election, you realise you will be asked to stand for leader.' I said, 'You must be joking.' He said, 'You will be. You won't be elected, but you will be asked.'

I said I have had enough of party in-fighting. I'm not doing any more of that. I'm going to try and persuade people, as best I can, of what course of action should be followed. He advised me not to stand.

Saturday 1 February
Went and bought a new Panasonic telephone/fax machine, which is marvellous and has an answering machine, and if you leave it on you can receive faxes without having to adjust it. It was quite expensive, but it does mean that I can send press releases.

I have got so much equipment at the moment and I can't use it all. The problem of training on new equipment is something I have under-estimated.

Big news today, which did make me laugh, is that the Tories, through the security services, have got access to the KGB files in Moscow reporting meetings between Neil Kinnock and the Soviet Ambassador over the years, which is a natural thing for the Leader of the Opposition to do, and they are running a sort of Zinoviev letter story. Of course, instead of dealing with it in the proper way, saying, 'Of course the Labour Party maintains contact with the Soviet Embassy and so indeed did the Tories', the Labour Party is claiming it's a smear and are running a mile. It's absolutely terrified when it's attacked; it runs and runs and gives the impression of being totally gutless. If I were asked, I would say of course I had had contact throughout the whole period – I visited the Soviet Union when I was a Minister. They have no self-confidence really.

Wednesday 5 February
Afif Safieh, the PLO representative in London, came to see me for about three-quarters of an hour. A very charming, intelligent man, a Roman Catholic.

It's a black time for the PLO and we exchanged our analysis and we both agreed that America needed Israel less, because the Americans have moved their allegiance to the Arabs; that the Russian disappearance had left Israel a bit less needed in the Middle East, and the Israelis are now whipping up anti-Islamic feeling to try and continue to get support.

At 12.30 Leo Panitch came to lunch. Charming guy. Speculating about the future of Britain, he wondered if there'd be a coalition government after the election when the crisis would be so bad, and I said it was a possibility either then or later. He said, 'Well, do you think there's a vacancy for a George Lansbury?' 'Who do you mean?' And he said, 'You.'

So what he was thinking was that if the three party leaders came together into coalition, the Labour Party would have to have an Opposition leader and perhaps I might do that job. I said, 'You must be joking', because quite honestly I have not a shred of ambition to lead the Labour Party and it would entirely ruin my life and the work I want to do; but at the same time somebody would have to do it. I suspect there'd be a lot of ambitious young men, like Livingstone and maybe even Bryan Gould or John Prescott.

Today and yesterday, the really big news was that Paddy Ashdown had gone to solicitors to try and get advice on the consequences of an extra-marital affair. And apparently – surprise, surprise – there was a burglary in that solicitor's office. The report by the solicitor on what had happened was stolen, and Ashdown tried to get an injunction out to try and prevent all this from being published.

Then it was clear he couldn't succeed, so he gave a press conference yesterday; it was all over the papers, pages and pages in the *Evening Standard* and a lot of sympathy in the papers today.

Obviously MI5 had done it. I think the Liberals are getting a bit too strong for the comfort of the Tories. Ashdown reacted by clutching his wife and saying he was very happy, and she said they'd been very happy. I found the whole thing totally revolting but my objection to him is his politics and not his private affairs.

Monday 10 February

Sheila Yeger came to talk about her play on Keir Hardie and she had a funny idea that part of the play should be set in my office, in order to draw the parallel between Keir Hardie and me, which would be absolutely laughable. I'm not Keir Hardie, we haven't the same origins, nor do I play the same role. Also it would butt in on Caroline's book. Caroline persuaded her anyway, and so did I, not to do it.

Home Policy Committee had a long paper on the NHS, which I'd only opened this morning and which was presented by Robin Cook. I tried to raise a couple of points at the beginning about democratic control and the absolutely arrogant style of the management.

We raced through it. No consultation now with anybody. These things just go through on the nod, written always by the parliamentary spokesman.

I heard a joke arising from Paddy Ashdown's affair being brought to light: someone raided a safe where Neil Kinnock's papers were kept and found he'd had an affair with socialism, and he issued a statement saying it was long before he was Leader of the Party. I told that to Roy Hattersley and he laughed outrageously.

Tuesday 11 February

Went to the Campaign Group. There was a terrible row because *The Socialist*, the Socialist Movement paper, had an article saying Ken Livingstone was planning to replace me as leader of the left and set up a new group after the election. Ken was very upset about it.

Well, he writes a column in the *Sun*, of all papers, though I understand the case for doing so. Of course in a way the article was quite right – that is what he's trying to do. Ken is in with John Ross, he's in with *Marxism Today*, he's in with the *Morning Star*, he talks to the Tribune Group, and I think Ken does have the funny idea that after the election, if we win, he'll move into the centre and hope to get a job; and if we lose, he'll lead the left in the party, a broader left.

Thursday 13 February

I wonder whether the balance of my work is right. I've no role whatever in the leadership of the party, I'm a good constituency member, I speak in the House when I want to on a matter that I think is important, and I work in my office providing material for people who are making programmes, and taking part myself.

I don't know whether that is the right thing to do. It certainly isn't a parliamentary-oriented job of work, but it is a continuing one of trying to get the case across.

Friday 14 February

To the Commons and spoke in the Wild Mammals (Protection) Bill debate to ban hunting. It was an interesting debate because the Tories came out in their true light.

Nicholas Ridley made an incredible speech accusing the proponents of the Bill of wanting to stop entertainment. And I was called and spoke for five minutes, which is an absolute model length. The Bill was defeated by twelve votes with a huge turnout.

Tuesday 18 February

Dave came to lunch to talk about my mother's will and all the complications arising from that.

To Church House, where the Synod is meeting for the BBC Debate on Disestablishment, with Brian Redhead in the chair.

I moved the motion that we disestablish the Church of England. It was opposed by the Bishop of Peterborough, and Michael Alison MP and various speakers; and then at the end Emma Nicholson, the Tory MP, supported me and Frank Field opposed. We lost by 77 votes to 73, which is very close, given the fact that it was full of Church people. I wasn't surprised.

Frank Field was talking about the need to see that the Church didn't fall into the hands of activists, but was controlled by the whole nation, in order to see that the memory of Christ was never removed from the memory of the nation, and so on.

There was a black Anglican from Uganda, no doubt a very courageous man, who, when you listened to him, sounded exactly like an Islamic fundamentalist saying we must take over the State.

It was another reminder of what's coming out of the woodwork with the collapse of socialism and equality and democracy.

The Church is incompatible with democracy. Christianity may demand democracy, but the Church is opposed to it, because it all depends on authority: authority from God through the bishops; authority of the State through the appointment of the bishops; the authority of Parliament through the Church; the control of Church measures. And you can see why secularism was such an important factor in earlier generations, and it will be again, because the Church is rapidly trying to occupy – in terms of power – the role it once performed.

Wednesday 19 February

There's a big press story at the moment that people are dissatisfied with John Smith because as Shadow Chancellor he's so conservative, so cautious; doesn't want to give any impression that the Labour Party will do anything; keeps reassuring the City.

In the evening I went to the Conway Hall for the Memorial Meeting for Kay Beauchamp, who died at the age of about ninety-two last month, following Tony Gilbert who died aged about eighty-five. The two of them, being lifelong communists, had given themselves entirely to Liberation. They were devoted to each other. The audience was absolutely typical. It was an ageing audience, men and women; you do get this feeling that the socialist/anti-socialist divide is partly the old versus the young.

Saturday 22 February, Chesterfield

I did a surgery all morning from 9.30 until two o'clock. Tremendously long.

Then I went shopping. Bought myself a little tape recorder, a very cheap inflatable mattress and sleeping bag, because Hilary and Sal and their children are coming to stay tonight and I thought I might just as well spend £40 on getting something I'll be able to use again and sleep on the floor, rather than book into a cheap hotel.

The grandchildren arrived and I blew up my mattress, unrolled my sleeping bag and I thought I'd just try and see what it's like. And I went sound asleep at about quarter past eight and when Hilary and Sally came in at a quarter past nine, far from my being babysitter, Michael and James said to them as they came in, 'We *think* Dan-Dan's all right.' So it was really very funny, but whether they'll ever trust me to babysit again, I don't know.

Tuesday 25 February

Josh came this morning, bless his heart, and gave us a computer lesson on the IBM-compatible machine.

Wednesday 26 February

The Executive was pretty grim really. Not very long – it only lasted about an hour and a half. Then we came to the European Parliamentary Labour

Party Report and we were told that the European Directive might make telephone canvassing illegal.

So I said, 'What the hell's it got to do with Brussels whether we do telephone canvassing? I'm not taking any notice of it.' We were told it was because it upset the consumer. So I said, 'Well, they're not consumers, they're electors. I get on a train and I'm called a customer; I go to a hospital and I'm called a customer. I'm a patient, a passenger and an elector. It's all this rotten market-forces argument.' There was some sort of sympathy for that.

At 5.30 I went to the Campaign Group and we had quite a discussion about what we'd do after the election, on the assumption that we would lose.

Ken Livingstone said we must put up a candidate, and so on, and I said, 'Well, look, half a minute. First of all we shouldn't be discussing it now. Secondly, if we do lose, the Party will be so shattered that the first concern will be saving the Party, it won't be what we can do in obstructing the Government or putting up a candidate; we've go to think about seeing the Party isn't killed by what's happened.'

I went back to my room. I listened to *Face the Facts* on Radio 4, about freedom of information, and what interested me about it was that for the first time ever, I think, they played a bit of my diary from 1979, from tape – actually dictated when I had a filthy cold.

Thursday 27 February

Went off by taxi to see Lord Goodman, Arnold Goodman, whom I don't suppose I've spoken to probably since the Labour Government left office in 1979.

I'd written to him for advice about how to get funding for the British Library to index my archives. He lived in a very luxurious flat in Portland Place, just above the BBC and below the park.

When I arrived I was shown into his living room. He came in, very frail, aged seventy-nine, sitting in one of those chairs that lifted you up and put you down.

We had a general talk about Wilson and about the Open University and Jennie Lee. He said one or two interesting things. First of all capitalism must redistribute wealth. Now, to hear an old Jewish solicitor still use the word capitalism was quite astonishing.

'Of course, the trouble with the judges is they all come from the upper middle classes, and have been to major or minor public schools and then to Oxbridge and have no contact whatever with reality,' he said.

Lord Goodman said he thought that Neil Kinnock was weak; he nevertheless thought Labour would win the election. He knew everybody. He told me how he'd refused to work for Robert Maxwell, but was quite a friend of Rupert Murdoch.

He said to me several times during the course of the discussion, 'Mind you, these foundations you might try for funding are very right-wing, you've got to get some people who are sympathetic to what you want to do. You see, you are a threat to their property.' He said that three or four times.

He made a number of suggestions as to whom I might approach, including Jennifer Jenkins and Peter Tapsell, whose partner was Japanese and might be able to get Japanese money involved.

I mean it was very much a general talk, nothing specific about it, but he said, 'How much do you want?' I said, 'I should think about a quarter of a million would do it.' And I think he thought that was just about a reasonable amount to ask. If I'd asked for £5000, he'd have written me a cheque and sent me off with a frown for troubling him!

But I couldn't get away. I was there for an hour and a half. And I know what it's like. People of that age just like talking.

Friday 28 February

I got up at six, left at seven, caught the eight o'clock from St Pancras, which was lucky, because at 8.30 there was a bomb at London Bridge and all railway stations were closed, so I wouldn't have got to Chesterfield at all.

Went to the Winding Wheel Centre. There were fifteen people at the Derbyshire Welfare Rights seminar and I got a marvellous brief, which I read all the way up on the train, so by the time I got there I really understood it.

Went over to the office, where we discussed the election campaign. Tom and Margaret have been working really hard. They've got the posters out, they've got the election address ready, they've got everything absolutely ready.

Then I went back to the flat and I did a bit of telephone canvassing. Phoned about twelve people. One man said, 'I disagreed with you about the Gulf.' Another man said, 'I don't like all this left stuff. All this marching and petitioning; and Dennis Skinner never asks a proper question.' He was obviously an old, right-wing Labour trade-unionist guy. The real Labour Party.

One number was a wrong number. When I rang through I said, 'Is that Mr Jennings?' and a woman said, 'No, this is the Pizza Parlour in Hasland. Is that Mr Benn?' 'Yes.' 'Oh, we're all for you.' It was really smashing.

Then I was picked up by Alan Self, an awfully nice guy, who's lost a leg; works in the Registrar's Office. He took me up to see an old people's home where they were having a pea-and-pie supper, and I chatted to a lot of people there. Very friendly, the old people. I have such an affection for them because of my mum. There were these old ladies, some of them were a bit gaga, and old gentlemen with straight backs sitting there, having their supper. And I bought one or two bits of old costume jewellery that was being sold – I should think probably things that had been left by people who'd died there.

Then I was driven back to the Executive, where we had an absolutely hilarious discussion about the election campaign. Of the forty-five minutes on the election, about half an hour was spent on this question: 'Shall we send the election address out in an unmarked envelope, or in an envelope that has Vote Labour printed on it, and shall we write the names and addresses on each envelope? Or shall we send the election address out without an envelope at all?'

There had to be two votes. There was a re-count and in the end, by 9 to 8 I think, we voted to send it out with a name and address on it. I said, 'Well, I think you've forgotten one option – the option of sending out the envelope without the election address.' It was very jolly and friendly and they're all geared up. I hope to God there is an election soon.

The train was late back to London because of the bombing and I got home after midnight, just absolutely exhausted.

Sunday 1 March

Family tea party at Melissa and Paul's, with everybody there: Stephen and Nita and Emily and Daniel, Hilary and Sally and their four children; Josh was there with William. We exchanged presents and had crowns – this time presidential crowns, instead of royal crowns, to celebrate republicanism. President Melissa, President Paul, President Jonathan.

Came home and worked in the basement, not doing what I really should have done but trying to assemble a portable box ready for the election, to hold my thermos and mug and pipes, and everything else.

Monday 2 March Chesterfield

To Brockwell Primary School. It was lovely.

The little ones of five, six and seven stood in the playground and they leapt up and down and they asked me to pick them up. Then I began jumping and they began following. I put my hands up, and they all put their hands up, they all touched their toes, clapped their hands.

'Pick me up, come on.' One boy came up to me and said, 'Are you coming to our class?'

I went round and looked at the school and there was a brilliant boy called Matthew in the assembly hall playing the piano. He was only eight and he was improvising and playing just like a professional. I asked him about his music and if his parents played the piano, and he said no, but he'd seen a piano at his uncle's. He was so self-confident, beautiful playing; he was so talented. I did enjoy it.

I thought, 'Well, if the future of the country rests with these people, we've nothing to worry about.'

Tuesday 3 March
To the Commons to meet a class from Abercrombie Primary School, who had come from Chesterfield on a visit.

There's something lovely about primary-school children. There were about thirty-five of them and we went up to the Committee Room and they asked lots of questions.

I said, 'If you were an MP, what laws would you vote for? Who's in favour of fox hunting?' Nobody. One little boy asked, 'What about hanging?' I said, 'Well, you've heard of the Birmingham Six, who were innocent, you can't hang innocent people.' I said, 'What do you think?' So they all voted against hanging, including the little boy who'd suggested it.

There was a vote on vegetarianism. I asked how many were vegetarians, how many wanted to get married, and they just were as bright as buttons – it was simply lovely.

Later Caroline arrived with a group from her further-education class. There was this guy with a beret and designer stubble and an earring, called Gary, whom she calls Bluto, and other students.

We went into the Lords, down to the crypt chapel, to the Emily Davison broom cupboard and down into the bowels of the earth, where the washing-up is done.

Wednesday 4 March, Zurich
Went over to the *Woz* office, a cooperative in Zurich absolutely crammed with people working at computers, where they produce 20,000 copies of this radical pluralistic left paper every week.

Zurich is a beautiful city and, as the plane came in, you could see the peaks of the Alps above the mist and then this lovely city with the lake; the Red Factory or Roten Fabrik is on the edge of the lake.

The Roten Fabrik has an interesting history. The municipality allowed what you might call the dissident community in Zurich to have this old factory, which has got a restaurant and an auditorium and is really run down and absolutely covered with graffiti and posters, but is used as a cultural centre.

In a way it looked like the remnants of the 1960s student rebellion in France and western Europe.

In the evening, I went to a seminar at the Roten Fabrik and talked to Professor Jean Ziegler, who is a socialist MP and a professor of sociology, and who has written a book exposing the Swiss banks and the corruption and the laundering of money. The result is that all the banks have sued him for libel and the man is facing the serious possibility of bankruptcy. He was very nervous.

Most of our discussion was about the new world order and the Common Market. Ziegler is in favour of the Common Market – he used all the arguments of what you might call the *Marxism Today* wing of the Labour movement; that's to say, there's no alternative, there are cultural links with Europe, the Common Market will clean up the Swiss banks, they can't do it themselves, etc., etc.

It was a very defeatist argument, but it was one with which I was familiar and on the whole I got a good reception.

Afterwards I heard that the Swiss banks really are corrupt. That drug dealers and criminals turn up at the airport with suitcases full of cash and just pay it into numbered accounts at the banks, and then go straight out again. Also I heard that the CIA had penetrated the Swiss banks, because of course the CIA also uses them for laundering money.

Also, a few years ago police files had come to light and apparently one million out of six million Swiss were on the computer files, and this had shaken them as they thought they were free from that sort of thing.

I got full marks for having looked up a little bit of Swiss history in the *Encyclopaedia Britannica*. Ziegler said to me afterwards it was amazing how much I knew about Switzerland!

Thursday 5 March

Up at 5.30 Zurich time, and I caught the flight to London, which was a bit delayed.

I later heard that apparently a Swiss fighter had a near-miss with that particular plane, only missed it by twenty feet, which is incredibly close, but I was asleep on the plane and I didn't hear anyone discussing it.

Friday 6 March

Got the train to Chesterfield and the League Against Cruel Sports had sent a man called Chris Williamson, their National Chair, to the Labour Club to present me with a little award for my speech in the debate against fox hunting. A beautiful little glass award saying that I 'stood up for wildlife on February 14'.

Saturday 7 March

At 10.30 I went over to the NUM building, where about twenty-five people turned up for the official adoption meeting for me as a Labour candidate.

The Tories have produced a 250-page book costing £30, I think, listing all the hard-left members of the Parliamentary Labour Party, which I think is smashing; it will do us a lot of good. It's been put together by Julian Lewis, who is a Deputy Director of Research at Tory Central Office. He was in the Newham Labour Party when the Right were supporting Reg Prentice.

Monday 9 March

At 1.30 Fiona Armstrong came along to do an interview about Civil Service briefs for Ministers. She was so overbearing, like all the *Newsnight* people, did a seven-minute interview and then said she'd use forty seconds. She wanted to do an 'establishing' shot in my office, which I wouldn't agree to, and she was cross about that.

I went off in the afternoon to Chesterfield. Looked in at the Trades Council Annual General Meeting for a few minutes. I had to leave before the meeting began, but it showed willing.

Then I went down to the Co-op Party Meeting where there were eight people. I should think the average age was probably about sixty and I talked to them for a bit.

For each person at the Chesterfield meetings I travelled fifty miles. For each person there the share of the first-class return train fare, which of course was paid for by the House of Commons, was £13.25, and for each person there I personally spent an hour from door to door going and coming back.

Wednesday 11 March

On the one o'clock news Major appeared outside Number 10 to announce the election for 9 April, so that's all done and settled and Parliament isn't meeting until 27 April, for the election of Speaker, and after that we shall meet on 6 May for the Queen's Speech, so we've got a little bit of a break.

At the Campaign Group we had some discussion about the election prospects. Nobody was very optimistic. There was a great sense of disappointment that Kinnock had fallen for the Tory trap, and we were committed to vote against the cut of income tax to 20 per cent on the first £2000 of taxable income. Dennis Skinner and others thought, and I agreed, that we should accept the cut but say, of course, that we'll put more tax on the higher range, which was actually what was in our Labour programme and apparently was quoted by Mellor in the House this afternoon. Our policy doesn't mean anything because we just vary it according to inclination.

Thursday 12 March

With the election announced, I got a little piece of Labour literature pushed through the door by the Kensington Labour Party. It had the candidate's picture on it saying, 'You're better off with Labour, a thriving economy is an essential foundation for a prosperous country where business makes profits and people know they have a job to go to.' The final endorsement of capitalism, then going on to say, 'That way we can earn the money to invest in things we all want like a better Health Service.'

Tom rang from Chesterfield saying that the labels (for my election address) from the Town Hall were not suitable for distribution by the Post Office, and he was up the wall.

I went into the Commons. At 11.30 we had the Parliamentary Labour Party Meeting.

Jack Cunningham told us that this morning we launched our campaign with a lot of media stars and celebrities. Neil will be in Scotland tomorrow, the alternative Budget will be out next Tuesday and the Manifesto as soon as possible. He said four million leaflets went out yesterday. 'We start in the strongest position we've ever been in. We have a small lead, a four per cent lead in the marginals.'

He said we had the best-prepared campaign ever. There were more party workers raring to go. 'We're on the way to victory, we must have confidence in each other, confidence created by Neil.'

Then Neil spoke. He said he wanted to look back at where we were in 1987, when the Tories were on 42 per cent, we were on 32, the Alliance on 24 and we'd just lost Greenwich. He was grinning and arrogant, and strident and raucous. I have to say that.

He said, 'Now the opinion polls show us at forty-one and the Tories at thirty-nine.' He went on, 'We've had a sustained success and we have confidence, the Tories are anxious, they will fight us along with Wapping and Fleet Street; they've abandoned prudence, the Budget does nothing for recovery or for industry, or for the services; they failed to impress the electorate, we are burdened with debt and unemployment, the British people's reaction to the Budget has been a credit to them; our alternative Budget will be out next week; Smith has done some excellent work on it; they will tell lies about us; the public want change; they want economic success, social justice and a sense of community.'

He said, 'We shall win with our values, pension, education, housing and so on, environment. We shall win, we must strengthen the means of enabling people to have care and to find personal freedom, and ways into employment and out of the recession.

'The combination, the mixture of strengths, shows we're fit to govern and to lead the world. We'll bring a new quality of government after years of stalemate and selfishness.'

He thanked the Shadow Cabinet, he thanked the House of Lords for all the work they'd done, at which there was applause. He said, 'No one is more loyal or has a greater sense of purpose than Labour peers.'

He thanked the retiring members and said that, 'We shall not forget them, but I don't want to mention any of them.' But he might have mentioned Michael Foot, his immediate predecessor, the only remaining previous Leader of the Party still in the Commons and the last survivor of 1945. But he didn't mention Michael.

He said, 'We've seen the arrogance and corruption of power and patronage.' And he quoted W. H. Auden.

He got a standing ovation.

Monday 16 March

Caroline went to see Jill Foot tonight to talk about the Pankhursts.

Jill kept her from five until nine, simply wouldn't let her leave. They went over all the ground and it confirmed Caroline's view, and it was useful and friendly.

I had a fax from King Hussein's office, saying that he appreciated my message about the possibility of a fresh military conflagration and thought this would inflict fresh wounds. He was particularly concerned about the redrawing of the Kuwaiti/Iraqi frontier.

To the Institute of Mechanical Engineers building in Parliament Square for the 'Manifesto meeting', which had been specially arranged there to avoid having to use Transport House, which would have shown too close a link with the trade unions. I had read the Manifesto, about 12,000 words long.

We started at 3.30 and went on till about 6.30 or nearly seven o'clock, I think. I might add that John Smith made a statement about the alternative Budget, which he published today. Very clever, attacking the rich and with plans to help the poor. Excellent, good socialist Budget.

We were told by John Evans that this was third time lucky; it reminded him of 1945; Neil was brilliant, and so on and so on.

Then we came to the actual Manifesto and I said to John, 'Well, as you mentioned 1945, I've brought along a couple of sentences which I think we might include in the Manifesto. "Labour is a socialist Party and proud of it. Members of the Labour Party, like the British people, are practically minded."' That was turned down with only three votes for it.

Then I moved another amendment, to leave out 'that fear was the greatest barrier to economic recovery', and that was carried. I also moved that in the phrase '. . . as with any proper-run business, our immediate programme' we delete 'business' and put in 'government' and add 'a strategy for a return to full employment'. That amendment was defeated, with only two votes for.

Then we came to the Exchange Rate Mechanism, and I moved the deletion of the Exchange Rate Mechanism in maintaining the value of the pound and said it was like the gold standard and it had brought down the '31 Government: three people voted for me on that, including Dennis.

Then I moved, on page 4, that we say, 'We shall not introduce a statutory pay policy.' Gerald Kaufman interrupted and said, 'Well, a minimum wage is a statutory pay policy.' So I said, 'In that case, we should say we shall not introduce a statutory pay *restraint*.' We were defeated, with Dennis and myself against.

Dennis moved that we delete the references to trade union legislation, the requirement for ballots before strikes and a ban on mass or flying pickets. There was a long discussion, which greatly embarrassed the trade unions, and in the end only two of us – Dennis and myself – voted for the removal of anti-trade union legislation.

There was a discussion about whether the minimum wage should move towards two-thirds of national income. Anyway, on the economic policy section Dennis and I voted against it altogether.

On the Health Service I moved that we say the Health Service would be democratically accountable to the communities it served; that was accepted. Dennis moved for the phasing-out of pay beds. That was defeated, with only two of us in favour. And I tried another one, to 'cease to subsidise private care,' but that was not really a major discussion.

On schools, I think the main discussion was on Muslim schools. I was opposed to Muslim schools, and I said we wished to see the key role of Church and other voluntary agencies secure, with admission policies on a non-selective basis, and leave out anything else. That was defeated. Then I moved that history be included in the National Curriculum. That was strongly objected to. Dennis moved for deletion of the whole passage on the National Curriculum and I voted for that, but we accepted the educational policy – the whole one – unanimously.

Then we came to democracy. Dennis moved that we delete 'that the Scottish Parliament would be elected on the additional member system.' That was defeated, with only Dennis and myself against it.

When we came to 'Britain in the world', Kershaw moved the deletion on page 1 of, 'Until the elimination of the stocks is achieved, Labour will retain Britain's nuclear capability with a number of warheads no greater than the present total.' I seconded it. In effect, it's a total change, and seven people voted for the deletion of that.

That was really quite a substantial vote. Dennis, myself, and five others. Then we came to the question of the EEC.

I said, we should say 'We shall defend the right of the British people to determine the laws under which they are governed by the Parliament they elect.' Only Dennis and myself voted for that. That would, of course, have given us a reserve position against Brussels; Gerald Kaufman said, 'Well, that was settled years ago.'

I shall argue for the Manifesto and put it forward with as much conviction as I can, but it can't be wrong to cast a vote in the argument. I don't want to be the guy who gets the blame for losing the election, and I'm sure they would try.

Then we were told that Neil was going to make a winding-up speech, but I was so late for a meeting that I slipped out and of course all the journalists thought I had walked out.

Tomorrow I'm off to Chesterfield to start the campaign.

Tuesday 17 March

Up at half-past six. Caroline got the breakfast, bless her heart.

I packed up my stuff, left at nine, drove to Chesterfield – took me about three hours in a very leisurely way.

Unpacked, which took me about two hours, setting my computer and fax and answering machine up, and sorting my letters and papers and everything.

Then I went over to see Tom Vallins, in the office – a very efficient agent, Tom Vallins is; Margaret was organising the canvassing and the distribution of leaflets and it really is a tremendously efficient set-up.

Labour's got a 5 per cent lead in the polls at the moment and it looks to me as if this is going to be a 1945-type breakthrough. That's my impression.

The Manifesto, if you leave out the bits I don't like, is really a very radical one and is much influenced by what was done in the Ministry of Technology in 1964–1970; very, very similar policy.

The only differences are: nuclear weapons, but they were maintained by the last Labour Government; commitment to Europe, but then that was maintained by the last Labour Government; the dropping of any reference to socialism, but that was not really ever explicit in the latter years of Wilson, and a distancing from the trade unions, but that began in 1969, so I can't say the Labour Party's changed. I think it is the old Labour Party coming back.

The literature produced by Walworth Road, the briefing material, is absolutely excellent, couldn't be better, but the idea that the Labour Party is an agency of social transformation is, of course, not the case. But whoever thought it was?

Wednesday 18 March, Chesterfield

I must say, the impact of the election on the electorate at the moment is absolutely zero. There are three men in their forties – a grey man, Major; a bald man, Kinnock; a macho man, Ashdown – going around using every sort of slogan about handing Britain back to the British, empowering people, and a better future and a new future and a better Britain.

It's just all sloganising without any content at all, and I'm sure this quiet door-to-door canvassing, or telephone canvassing, is infinitely more effective.

Went over to the Club, talked to a few mates. I must say, the whole election is fun to be involved in.

Caroline came up from London, which is marvellous.

Thursday 19 March, Nottingham

When I got to the Market Square there was a huge yellow campaign bus with Alan Simpson, the candidate for Nottingham South, there and this awful blaring Brahms music, which is the European theme song. I'm not quite sure which Brahms piece it is, but it's awful. Drives you bats.

As I got on the top of the bus I saw Edwina Currie, the Tory MP for Derbyshire South, on one side of the square, and Brandon-Bravo on the other and another candidate, and as I spoke they sort of converged and stood just below the bus. And there was one heckler shouting all the time, making it almost impossible to be heard.

Lots of people came up and it really was quite phenomenal. They were all encouraging, saying, 'You're going to win this time, you won't let us down, you will win', as if we decide the outcome of the election.

Had a cup of tea and did a little bit on Radio Trent, and then I went and talked to some of the canvassers. I was there on my feet for five hours, I should think, from one to six. I did a bit of folding of election addresses (for about five minutes).

The Duke and Duchess of York have separated. The only reason I mention it is because it's in all the newspapers, and it has slightly taken the shine off the three men who are running the campaign for the parties.

If I were asked to guess now, I would say that Labour will just pull it off. I think Kinnock will be Prime Minister.

Then the whole situation will be tested, because comment has been made of the fact that the word socialism wasn't used anywhere in the Manifesto, and of course I tried to move that it be included and it was voted down. The trade unions have been kept at a distance, but that won't last for five minutes if there's a Labour Government.

Kinnock is vaguely interventionist, like Wilson, and very right-wing, like Callaghan.

Friday 20 March

Came back to the flat and made a recording for the blind of my election address, which was rather enjoyable.

Was just about to get down to some work when I was called over to the Labour Club, because a former miner who'd been in the paratroopers had been got for his Poll Tax and had nearly hit a bailiff from Nottingham. The guy's unemployed, he's got diabetes and he was treated shabbily. And what came out of it was the feeling that we live in a police state, where the Welfare State is a form of probation – you put people on it when they're poor; they asked him, for example, 'Do you smoke? Do you run a car? You can afford your Poll Tax,' and so on.

I had a surgery. The one case that really interested me was a woman who had suffered a bad fracture to her arm last Sunday, went to the hospital and they said, 'We don't have anyone working in X-ray on Sunday. Come back tomorrow.' So she came back on the Monday. They X-rayed her, told her she had a compound fracture and told her to see her doctor.

She went to see her doctor yesterday, and the doctor said, 'The X-ray hasn't arrived.' Then she had a note from the hospital, giving an appointment on 31 March, so from 15 March to 31st she would not have any treatment. I was so angry that I rang the hospital through the switchboard, to the orthopaedic department. Then they rang back and in the end they said, 'Well, tell her to come back.' So she went tonight. But that's what it's really like in the NHS.

Saturday 21 March, Chesterfield

I sat for about an hour and a half and stuffed envelopes. In the afternoon I went out with Paul Vaughan and Alan Self, who's driving me about, and drove around with the loudspeaker and a tape playing the *Floral Dance* and my messages, which are very clear. Came across absolutely beautifully. The music is so much better than the Brahms, which is what we've been told to use.

Then I came back, did more stuffing of envelopes.

This evening I rang Steve and Nita. Stephen said the campaign was brilliantly organised, Nita said it was going terribly well. Major, forced out of his corner, was no longer a nice man. They said there were absolutely no Tory window bills up in Croydon, and Hilary said the same when I rang him in Ealing. He said there were no Tory window bills at all.

I think everyone has the same feeling I have, that it's going reasonably well.

Little Michael, my grandson, is the Labour candidate in the school election.

I would imagine that if there is a Labour Government, this whole clique of machine men who have taken over the Party at the top and locally will continue to dominate the Party. I should think probably Tony Blair will get on the National Executive this time because of the work that he's done.

Then I had a word with Josh, who works at the Party HQ at Walworth Road part-time, on the computer side. He said that the campaign at Walworth Road was quite mechanistic. There were people working away as if they were a business company, and there was no sort of motivation or anything. So Stephen picked up how terribly efficient Walworth Road was; Josh picked up how terribly mechanistic; I picked up how terribly remote; and Liss picked up how male-dominated. So we're getting, between us, a very clear perspective of it all.

Sunday 22 March

Had a couple of hours canvassing, knocking at people's doors.

I met a young man who was obviously a very thoughtful man, lived alone, a real male flat: it was clean, but absolutely without flowers or pictures, or any sign of feminine influence.

He was a great environmentalist. Very thoughtful and very influential, so I was told by Bob Burkitt. He was in favour of returning to the birch and capital punishment as a deterrent, and he had a deeply pessimistic view about human nature. He wanted to protect wildlife, thought the population would have to be cut back – people were pollution – but birds were part of the environment. He wondered whether the blacks had the capacity to run South Africa.

He was a deeply philosophical Conservative. So I said to him, 'That is your position'.

'Well', he said, 'I'm voting Labour this time.' He wasn't a brainwashed person, in the sense of the ordinary *Sun* reader and somebody glued to the television set; he was a thoughtful Conservative.

The *News of the World* had a little item, 'Benn's Law,' saying that I had threatened to return to flying pickets and everything. Ridiculous little piece, but they did quote me correctly from the *Campaign Group News* and they quoted me correctly after I spoke to them on the phone, so I couldn't grumble.

In the evening I heard Dennis Skinner was over in the Club, so I went to see him and he was very much himself, and I had a chat with him about the Liberals. He said, 'You should put out a last-minute leaflet saying the Liberals are in favour of the privatisation of coal and railways, and against the minimum wage.' It was quite good advice.

Monday 23 March

I rang Larry Whitty this morning to say I thought the tax thing was not registering – nobody mentioned it, we should get away from it.

Went out, in the pelting rain, to Holmbrook. It was so cold and the rain was pouring down, and it was absolutely impossible to write on the canvass cards, which were sodden.

One man said to me, 'What's the point of voting, Mr Benn? It doesn't make any difference.' I said, 'It's the one day in a year when you're as powerful as Mrs Thatcher.' So we went on like this, and I was just about to write him off when he said, 'Give me a poster.'

Then another man answered the door and I said, 'Will you be voting Labour?' 'Oh, yes, I will,' he said. 'This house was got for me by Tony Benn.' So I said, 'Well, I'm Tony Benn.' He said, 'What?' So I took off my hat and he still didn't recognise me. Anyway I went in and he said there were a lot of things wrong with the house!

I came back after about an hour and a half of this. Totally wet.

Tommy can't get any tickets for the Kinnock Rally in Sheffield on 1 April, and I have received absolutely no literature whatever from the Labour Party so I've no idea what's being pumped out to candidates. But the conclusion I'm coming to at this stage is that that whole campaign is really a takeover bid, like a City takeover bid, where the Labour Party's trying to take over the economy.

The widening gap between the leaders and the voters is really quite alarming; the only time you ever see the leaders is either on a podium, being interviewed by journalists, or among adoring crowds on a walkabout, but you never hear a single elector's voice ever in the news bulletins.

Tonight there is one poll that's put the Tories five points ahead. And of course Thatcher's come out and is warning everybody, and somehow the whole thing's very unreal. The whole election is between advertising agents, front benchers and lobby correspondents. They're the people who run it all. They run the election and they intend the electors to be spectators, and none of the leaders ever recognise that it might be different, there might be other ways of doing it; it's completely negative, completely mechanistic, completely managerial.

What Labour should be saying is; 'We've got to get back to full employment, it's a big job. It's going to be difficult, we've got to do it. We've probably got to do a lot of things that perhaps you might not like. We've got to do it.'

And if only Labour could resume its representational role and drop its management role, I think it would be better, because I don't think the City of London is all that impressed by John Smith and Mo Mowlam and Gordon Brown and all that crowd. I think they're going to vote Tory anyway, most of them, although they might be content to see a Labour Government if they could control it.

Tuesday 24 March, Chesterfield

At 9.30 I went down to the Market Square outside the post office and distributed leaflets on pensions and social security to anyone who went in and out of the post office.

We were told *Newsnight* was coming to film a meeting of the local party; when we got to the meeting, there was no *Newsnight*, but a journalist called Sebastian Faulks, basically a novelist, from the *Daily Telegraph*. He joined us for the day. Went to the Labour Club, where there were a lot of old boys all making political points in support of Labour, and Faulks was there with a photographer. Then we went to a school and stood at the gates with all the mums and the children, who were really friendly. I brought Sebastian Faulks back to the Club.

Saw on the ten o'clock news an ITN survey showing that of the C2s, the nurses, the council-house owners, policemen and so on, 10 per cent had shifted back to Labour from the Tories, and the survey gave us altogether a 5 per cent lead, so that looks good.

Thursday 26 March

Sebastian Faulks's really nasty article appeared in the *Daily Telegraph* today and I had a phone call from one woman who bitterly attacked me for being patronising. I said, 'Look, I didn't write the article.'

I calmed her down, but he succeeded in doing a lot of damage to me and Chesterfield by making out that I was a sort of patronising candidate, and made fun of my age and my clothes, and my tea drinking and my accent, and so on. It much annoyed the local party as well.

Anyway, I worked all morning dictating letters in my flat.

Friday 27 March, Chesterfield

All day again – as there has been for the last three or four days – enormous coverage of Jennifer, the little girl who features in Labour's NHS broadcast.

Journalists have been attacking each other. Julie Hall, one of the press officers for Kinnock, had to get up at a press conference and answer questions as to who was responsible for the story-line.*

The media has got complete control now of this campaign, and here was a very good broadcast which has been turned by the media into a row about Labour's blunders and all that, because they don't want the Party's real message to get across.

Went to Clayton Tannery, which was set up in 1830 and still uses the same technology. I don't think the technology of tanning leather from hide has altered much for hundreds of years. Indeed, there was a tannery that closed two years ago in Derby that had been opened in 1624.

The buildings were ancient. There was 'No Smoking,' because they would catch fire if anybody lit a match in there. There were deep pits of chemicals into which the hide was put, and then the flesh and the hair was rubbed off. The smell was pretty unpleasant.

There were only thirty-two people working there, and the man who was managing director was the son of someone who'd started as an office boy there in 1924 and had ultimately taken over the company in 1938, and he had a white coat and spectacles. His brother was in America, where they sell a lot of their leather.

We walked around and there were these absolutely ancient rooms, with the deep pits and the leather hanging on bits of string from bits of wood over the pits and old drums. It really was quite incredible.

They produced some very good leather, for polishing, for what are called military accoutrements, and so on. It's really a glance back to the last century.

Did a loudspeaker session in Tesco's and the manager came and turned me away.

Then in the evening Stephen and Emily and Daniel arrived from London by train, the train ahead of them having broken down.

From ten till twelve Caroline and Stephen, Emily and Daniel came with me on a motorcade to Poolsbrook and Duckmanton, two mining villages where all the houses were built by the Coal Board for people to work in the collieries.

*A Labour Party election broadcast about the treatment of common childhood illnesses by the NHS and the private sector, turned into 'the war of Jennifer's ear' over the authenticity of the case, and the political leanings of the family concerned.

Out of the whole community of two villages, only five people still work in the pits. Only five. It gives you an indication of the catastrophic effect of closing the pits – unemployment there must be about 25 per cent.

The atmosphere's very good. Labour appears to be leading some of the Sunday newspaper polls. The Tories are in disarray, and I came back to the flat and put all the clocks back, so it's now five minutes to midnight on Saturday 28 March.

Sunday 29 March

I drove to Halifax, it took me about an hour and a half.

When I got there I couldn't find the Labour headquarters and turned the wrong way into a one-way street, thinking I was in the right place. And a police car pulled up behind me, and I opened the window and an inspector with two pips on his shoulder said, 'Don't tell me. You didn't see the sign.' So I said, 'Well, it's worse than that. I'm lost.' So he said, 'Where are you going?' 'I'm going to the Labour headquarters at West Street.' 'Follow me,' he said.

So he guided me there and said, 'I have never in the whole of my life in the police ever met a famous person before. Could I have your autograph?' So I gave him my autograph and went into the headquarters.

Full of lots of lovely people, including one old man called Jack Gibson, who's ninety-one, born in 1901. Had a marvellous memory. And I chatted to people there and exchanged election addresses, and had a cheese roll and then went to a really old hall with bare benches. Then Alice Mahon spoke and I spoke, and I must say it was tremendously good fun. It was lovely, it was a revival meeting. I should think almost everybody there was Labour except for a few SWP people, and it was a great success.

When I drove back to Chesterfield again it took me about an hour and a half. When I got back had a bit of laundry to do.

To a candlelight vigil at the Royal Hospital. In the end about thirty people turned up, including Rogers, the Liberal candidate. He was the one who supported the Health Service reforms introduced by the Tories. Quite incredible really.

It was very wet and the candles kept blowing. All the people leaving after visiting hours, and staff who were going off duty, passed us in their cars and they didn't so much as look at us, except for one man who hooted. I thought, 'My God. They're fed up with the election maybe; maybe they feel it's got nothing to do with them. They have cars, they have jobs, they have patients who are being treated.' And it did really make me wonder whether this country hasn't been completely depoliticised by this type of election.

It reminded me a bit of people going by in their cars during the miners' strike when we were picketing outside Arkwright Colliery.

Tuesday 31 March, Chesterfield

I went to the Mary Swannick School and went round with the children, and in one class the teacher said, 'Who is this?' One little boy said, 'John Major' and another little boy said, 'My mum's got Tony Benn in her bedroom – only a picture of course!'

We were taken to the New Whittington Miners' Welfare Club and talked there for a bit to a few people, and then on to the Bull's Mouth. I was talking to a man who was a French polisher and up came a very smartly dressed gentleman.

I introduced myself to him. I said, 'I'm the candidate.' He said, 'Are you a councillor?' And I said, 'No, I'm the Labour candidate.' 'Who are you then?' I said, 'I'm Tony Benn.' 'Oh', he said, 'I'm a Conservative, I've always been a Conservative.'

So I asked him what he had done in his life. He said, 'I was a colonel in the Royal Engineers. I joined in 1947 when you were still at school.' So I said, 'Half a minute, I was commissioned as an RAF pilot in 1945 having joined the air force in 1942.' He said, 'I don't believe it, I didn't know that.'

And we talked and he said he'd learned to fly as well, and had won a Military Cross in Korea.Then he said, 'You're quite different from what I expected.' So I said, 'Nobody ever meets me after reading the press and says you're not as nice as I thought you were!'

So, to cut a long story short, we had a long talk and in the end he said, 'I've always been a Conservative, but I shall vote for you.'

This went all round the pub and everybody knew the colonel; it did a power of good.

Wednesday 1 April

Mark Lawson from *The Independent* appeared to do a profile of the constituency.

Very wet.

Tonight was the Kinnock rally in Sheffield: 10,000 people arrived from all over the country; there was a laser-beam show and big-screen television; and the screen showed Neil arriving by helicopter.

Apparently he mentioned socialism thirty-four times before John Burrows lost count, so obviously the impact of the socialist argument had got through, and I thought it was a great success from that point of view. The people who went enjoyed it.

Thursday 2 April

Mark Lawson's piece in *The Independent* appeared, and again it just made fun of the people of Chesterfield and me, although I don't care what they say about me. But it made me very angry.

When Alan Hamilton of *The Times* and later Andrew Rawnsley, this clever-clever *Guardian* journalist, arrived I really blew my top.

I said to Alan Hamilton, 'You come around here writing your funny pieces, making fun of the people of Chesterfield, sort of journalistic slumming.' And I said, 'This election is a matter of life and death for the people here.'

Anyway we took them around. We went to a couple of playgroups. I didn't enjoy it at all. After lunch I went around more schools and got back about four o'clock and Caroline arrived. It was so sweet of her, it's my birthday tomorrow and she said she'd brought herself as my birthday present.

Thank God polling day's one week from today. I wouldn't like to predict the outcome; the Liberals are coming up, Ashdown is being built up very, very hard now because he is thought to be the one chance of controlling the Labour Party. Of course, the effect of voting for the Liberals will be almost certainly to beat more Tories, but in Chesterfield where the Liberals come second, it could have an adverse effect on my majority. I'm not too worried about it, but in the back of my mind is the possibility that I might lose the seat.

Friday 3 April

Went over to the Club and when I got there, there was 'Happy Birthday Tony' hung up on the ceiling and a birthday cake, and I was presented with a mug, which I shall keep in the Club for my tea.

Saturday 4 April

To the market. I got on a bench and gave a speech up at one end of the market, and I used that speech to get across my opinions on matters that haven't featured in the election: the need for Home Rule for Northern Ireland, the need to cut our defence expenditure, the need to have a new arrangement with Europe.

There was a crowd of people who listened, and I deliberately did it because I wanted to be able to say later that I did tell the people of Chesterfield in the market place what my position was. I kept saying, 'I want you to know this before you vote. I'm bound to speak my mind,' and so on and so on.

It has been a rotten campaign, truthfully. David Owen is supporting Major but voting Liberal Democrat, which is an unbelievable thing to be doing, implying he wants a Major-Ashdown alliance. He's a busted flush, a curiosity factor.

I feel free now from the whole damn thing. I was alienated first from the Cabinet, then the Shadow Cabinet, then the Parliamentary Party, then the National Executive, then the Conference, then from Parliament, and I feel that I must be free now to represent people's interests and make speeches about them which illuminate the situation.

Monday 6 April
I think my *Diaries* coming out in October would be of far greater interest if Kinnock is Prime Minister, because people would want to know how he got where he did. And now we know that David Owen is a Tory, this idea that he was a Labour moderate was all rubbish. Looking back on it, I think the Labour left can be shown to be right on so many things. Right on the miners, right on the printers, right on the SDP, right on the Gulf War, right on the Falklands War. I just feel that we're in a very strong position at the moment. I hope we are anyway.

Tuesday 7 April
Went over to the party office at 9.15 and then out in the pelting rain and cold.

There was one man came up to me and said he'd been a Tory and that he was going to vote Liberal this time. He said we should bring back hanging. I said, 'What about the Birmingham Six and the Guildford four?' 'Hang them. They were all guilty anyway.'

There is a nasty element in the Liberal vote in Chesterfield, and today we heard that in Germany the Nazi Party had eroded Chancellor Kohl's vote in one of the *Land* elections, and in Italy the fascists appear to have been part of a coalition that defeated the Christian Democrats/Social Democrats/Socialist coalition; and of course in France Le Pen's doing very well. So the Liberals could represent the British version of that sort of a trend.

Watched *Newsnight*, which was questioning the link between the unions and the Party; Tony Blair was saying there'd be no inside track for the unions, and so on. It is no longer the Labour Party, but still it doesn't mean it won't win.

Part Two
April 1992–May 1994

The General Election of spring 1992 was fought by a Labour Party very much shaped by Neil Kinnock's personal control over the Party during the previous nine years. His strategy had included expulsion of the left and radical reform of the Party's image. John Major had been Prime Minister for less than two years, but the Conservative Party had been in power for thirteen.

The years that followed were marked by tensions in the Balkans and continuing action against Saddam Hussein in Iraq. European issues dominated much of the domestic debate in Britain, especially after the Government was forced to withdraw from the Exchange Rate Mechanism in circumstances that damaged its credibility and attempted to get the Maastricht Treaty ratified by the Commons.

The Government launched a second round of pit closures, tightened the legal restraints on trade unions and introduced further measures to privatise public services; these measures were severely criticised by the Labour Opposition in Parliament.

Attempts to secure a settlement in Northern Ireland failed to make progress, and those who were encouraging talks with Sinn Fein were accused of supporting terrorism. In South Africa the end of apartheid was manifested by Nelson Mandela's release from prison.

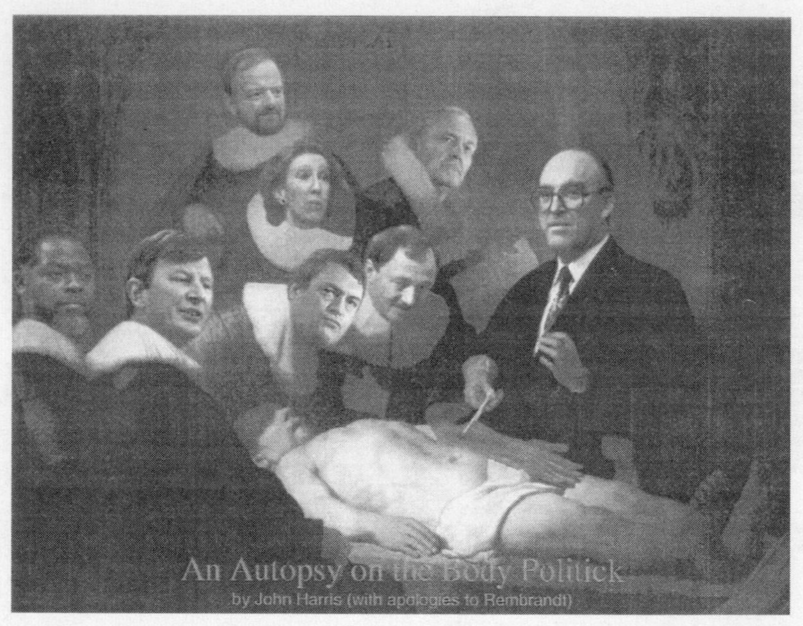

An Autopsy on the Body Politick
by John Harris (with apologies to Rembrandt)

Wednesday 8 April, 1992, Chesterfield

Eve of poll. I went over for the nine o'clock meeting in the Labour Club.

I put my fingers in my pocket, pulled out what I thought was a sweet, popped it in my mouth and it was a mothball. So I spat it out and drank a glass of milk, which I remembered was the best thing. At 11.45 I went off with Alan Self to Staveley Chemicals and we went into a little conference room with about ten people and I talked about the election. They weren't all Labour by any means; there were the shop stewards and a Tory councillor for Staveley Council, I think, who told me that Rogers had approached the Tories and asked them not to put up a candidate, so that they could combine to get rid of 'Wedgie Benn'. He said, 'If the Tories don't put up a candidate, we're bound to beat Benn.'

This Tory was absolutely incensed by it. He called Rogers all sorts of names. Then tonight Rogers put out a leaflet saying how the Liberals have had to fight off dirty tricks!

Absolute skulduggery the Liberals go in for – they're horrible.

The polls tonight suggest the Tories are strengthening their position and they say it's neck-and-neck, but I'm not really sure. I think Labour has a chance. Apparently Ladbrokes are taking bets at 7/2 on for a Labour overall majority, which means, I understand, that if you pay £7 and you win, you get your £7 back and £2 in addition. So that's something.

If I was asked to guess now, I think it will be a hung Parliament, with possibly the two parties absolutely in balance. I very much hope that in Chesterfield we get a bigger majority than last time, which we should do, given the East Midlands swing. It depends to what extent the Liberals have succeeded in immobilising the Tories to get rid of me, and whether the Tories vote.

Over a period this could be a town that went Liberal; it certainly won't go Tory.

That's the end of the 1992 election campaign and tomorrow morning polling begins. Indeed, in seven hours twelve minutes they'll be opening the polling stations.

Lissie rang to wish me luck.

Thursday 9 April

At half-past midnight we went to the declaration. It was clear from the television that the exit polls had been wrong and the public opinion polls had been wrong, and the Tories were moving towards a situation where they had an overall majority – a very substantial one. At about 1.40 we had the declaration and I won with 26,461 votes over the Liberal with 20,047 and Lewis, the Tory, with 9,473.

So I got 47.3 per cent of the vote, and my vote had gone up 1,929 and the combined Tory and Liberal vote had gone up by only ninety-one. But there'd been a massive shift, nearly 4000, of Tories who voted Liberal to get rid of me, so my majority actually fell from 8,577 to 6,414.

I made my speech and went back to the Club, and I spoke in the Club and they gave me a clap, but it was very depressing – they were red-eyed really at the thought of four or five more years of the Tories.

I thanked Tom and Margaret and we went back to the flat and went to bed about 4 a.m.

The nature of Chesterfield is changing very substantially, with mining in decline and new houses. It's becoming a more prosperous holiday centre and people are voting Liberal; Chesterfield is a declining constituency from a Labour point of view.

Friday 10 April

I drove to a hotel for dinner with the *Any Questions?* team – Sir Norman Fowler, who was obviously very cheerful as he'd worked with Major; Des Wilson, who I think is bouncy and whom I dislike, truthfully; Tessa Blackstone, who's a bit snooty, and Jonathan Dimbleby in the chair. I was quite amusing and cheerful and kept the thing going, but it was covering an aching heart.

Saturday 11 April

Today Steve rang to say that he and Nita had been invited to Neil's farewell party, which was being held in the Millbank Press Centre, so clearly Kinnock is going.

Sunday 12 April

Peter Shore rang. Very friendly. Thanked me for going to help in his campaign, said, 'You're the best leader we never had.' You could have knocked me down with a feather.

I rang John Smith and he rang me back, and I'm hoping to see him on Tuesday.

I spoke to Ken Livingstone. I think he's actually planning to stand for the leadership, but I don't think he can get the votes.

Rang Tony Banks and he said would I agree to stand for the Speakership, as Jack Weatherill is retiring?

Well, I don't want to be Speaker. I don't think I would be elected as Speaker, but I don't want people to think that I just want a job. So later in the day I rang Derek Foster, the Chief Whip, who told me that Betty Boothroyd had agreed to stand, even if Peter Brooke, the Northern Ireland Secretary, is put up by Major, that Heath would support Betty Boothroyd, and so there'll be a vote. So that settles that one.

Spoke to Steve on the phone, who said that Neil Kinnock had seen him last night and, before Stephen had had a chance of conveying my message, he said, 'Tony was bloody marvellous on *Any Questions?*' So I rang Neil's home and spoke to his daughter, Rachel. Neil was out to a meal. So I said, 'Will you tell your dad I'm thinking about him very much, thank him for all he did, and I know what this tabloid stuff can do.' And she said, 'Well, he'll appreciate that very much.'

Rang Dave Nellist to commiserate.

Rang Tam Dalyell about the Speakership and asked if he would hold himself in reserve, if we couldn't get a candidate, and he said he would.

Apparently, not only Neil is going, but Hattersley too. Potential candidates are Smith and Beckett, Bryan Gould, Gordon Brown possibly, Tony Blair. John Prescott for Deputy. Actually, I don't give a damn who gets it, because I don't think it terribly matters.

I think on the whole I'd prefer a right-winger who had to work with the left, than a so-called left-winger who had to prove his responsibility by swinging to the right. So that's my feeling about it at the moment.

Monday 13 April

I rang Neil. Got through to him in Ealing. I said, 'It's Tony Benn. I just want to thank you for the work you did in the campaign, wish you the best, and I have some sympathy with the tabloid attacks on the family.'

'Oh,' he said, 'you were bloody marvellous on *Any Questions?*'

Then Larry Whitty's office rang to say the NEC was meeting at two o'clock tomorrow.

I rang Bryan Gould; he rang me back. He said, 'I've got this difficulty about getting nominations.' 'Well,' I said, 'I'm going to leave the decision as to who I support to my General Management Committee.'

So he said, 'Well, Smith will declare, and if I don't declare, I might get left behind.' 'Well,' I said, 'just put your name in and see what happens.'

Absolutely endless media invitations: Yorkshire, Radio Sheffield, LBC, BBC Breakfast, Channel 4 News, BBC News, ITN asking if I would go on to talk about Kinnock's resignation. Well, I wouldn't.

At three o'clock he made his announcement in the Shadow Cabinet Room, using a little lectern at the end of the room; the camera panned around and there was Julie Hall and Colin Byrne, I think, a pathetic little bunch of people going out with him. He's getting his full euphoric funeral now and I'm keeping my mouth shut, but when it's all over it'll be as completely over as Thatcher was over.

Tomorrow I'll go to the House of Commons early and install my computer and everything. Then I've got the Executive at two, the Campaign Group at four. I might see John Smith, but I'm not sure I want to get mixed up in the leadership issue at all.

Tuesday 14 April
The Independent rang me up and asked if I would write an article on the realignment of British politics. So I said, 'No, I'll write an article on the future of the Labour Party.' 'Well, we want it on the realignment.' 'Well,' I said, 'I'm not going to let Peter Jenkins, who's been wrong on everything for years, tell me what I've got to write about.' So in the end the Features Editor got really angry, 'You're better off writing for the *Guardian*!' So that was another media contact broken.

To the NEC, and Tom Sawyer came up to me and said he was so glad I'd won at Chesterfield. So I said, 'I'm surprised you're so friendly, because I saw you on television last night saying the Party couldn't succeed until it had exorcised Bennism.' He said, 'Well, we all made mistakes.' Anyway I just made the point.

Then Neil came in and there was a standing ovation, and I was about to rise to my feet when I noticed everyone else starting to sit down; it didn't last very long.

John Evans was in the chair. He said this was the worst meeting he had ever had to attend in his life – we had a huge debt to Neil, who had made the Party electable.

It's a marvellous phrase when the Party has lost four elections in a row!

He wanted to commiserate with Neil, and Neil and Roy had said they wished to go and therefore we had to consider procedures.

Neil said there would be plenty of opportunities for analysis later, 'Don't mourn, organise. Mourn only on behalf of the people who'll suffer. The last week settled it against us . . . If I was responsible I regret it . . . We must have a determination . . . reassert our values . . . commitment to get into power, because without it our values would never be put into service . . .' And so on and so on.

Blunkett said, 'Can I say thank you, not only to Neil but to everybody else.' And that was agreed.

Neil then said, 'I propose that we have a Special Conference to elect the Leader on 27 June, because of the danger of delay.'

John Evans said, 'Many MPs want to delay it. There's very strong feeling about it. Why rush it? Twelve weeks is in the constitution, it's a requirement. There are rights of members, and nomination and balloting to consider and, when you hand over, the new Leader must have the maximum support and be seen to be legitimate.'

Neil said, 'Forget the pressures, I've had them for eight and a half years. It's not worth delaying it, and anyway we've got to elect the Shadow Cabinet and people will think we're run by the trade unions.'

John Prescott said, 'Will you stay if we decide to delay it?'

And I think somebody said, 'What a stupid question!' I can't remember if it was John or Neil.

I said I didn't accept the Shadow Cabinet argument, because we'd elect a Shadow Cabinet when Parliament met. 'We're electing a man whom we hope will be Leader for five years and Prime Minister perhaps for another ten, talking about somebody well into the next century, and for the sake of three weeks it isn't worth rushing it. The House might rise early in July anyway. We need time and that is very important, particularly time for reflection, and I therefore move that the election of the Leader and Deputy Leader be conducted at the 1992 Annual Conference, in accordance with the provisions of the Party Constitution.'

Sam McCluskie said, 'I don't agree with Neil. I think his judgement in this case is flawed. You're quite entitled to resign, but you should not have laid down the timetable. It is difficult for the trade unions. If we rush it, it'll be said that it's all been done in smoke-filled rooms and you're bumping the trade unions.'

Blunkett proposed that we delay it till 18 July.

Hattersley said, 'I've decided to stand down and to tell my AGM tonight. But Neil took the view that he did and I've accepted his judgement. I would stay till October, but I will go when Neil goes. We'll be accused of a trade union rap anyway. I shall go on debating the Party future long after October, and Neil was the best we could have had for the Party and we owe it to Neil to trust his judgement.'

Sam McCluskie said, 'Don't you give me any lessons in loyalty.' So that was another angry comment.

Joan Lestor said, 'Neil's dignity is not a factor, and it'd be nonsense to say we were undermining him. We can't break the rule book.' She said she would prefer to go to October but would accept the Blunkett amendment. 'The Party's shell-shocked – not ready for a choice.'

Well, that's a short summary of the debate, and my amendment was put and defeated by 18 to 7.

Blunkett's amendment for 18 July, which is purely nominal, was carried by 15 to 10, with Neil voting against, and the whole thing was made a substantive motion by 22 to 1. The one being Eddie Haigh.

The only choice now is between Gould, a barrister who got on to the media on Thames Television, and Smith, who is a right-wing Scottish conservative, a passionate European whom I know and like, but with whom I profoundly disagree.

There's no choice really. And I'm not even sure Prescott could get enough nominations; nor Margaret Beckett, nor anyone else.

It was really very friendly. I felt as though there was a warm reconciliation after bitter struggles in the past.

Thursday 16 April, Chesterfield

In the afternoon Caroline went to Stansgate for Easter and I went up to Chesterfield for the party officers' meeting.

Darryl Alvey was there. Paul Vaughan, Margaret Vallins, Tom Vallins, Johnny Burrows, Dave Walsh, Paul Barry and Leslie Shooter and myself.

John said, 'We don't really want a post-mortem.'

So they then did what the Labour Party always does when it's facing a difficult problem; they had a long technical discussion about whether we have 'thank you' leaflets. Will we put an ad in the *Gazette*? Can we afford it? We have a balance of £3,900 – should a letter be written to the *Derbyshire Times*? Should Tony write an article for the *Derbyshire Times*? And so on and so on.

Well, that took most of the time. Then I gave my report.

Easter Sunday 19 April, Stansgate

We had an Easter-egg hunt and I heard Caroline, who is four, saying to Daniel, who's only one, 'Don't be frightened, Daniel, we're not monsters, we're just children and persons.'

So then we had my belated birthday party, with a crown and presents and everything. It was lovely and in the evening we watched *Spitting Image,* which was absolutely hilarious – it's a marvellous programme.

In the course of the day I had some fierce political arguments with the family about the way the election had been run, and I'm afraid my criticisms are not very welcome.

Thursday 23 April

Vic Williams, Gunner Williams, telephoned. He came out of prison today. I had a marvellous talk to him. He really enjoyed the Emrys Hughes *Diary of a Coward* that I'd sent him.

He said that prison was like the army, and they'd treated him carefully because they thought he had influential friends. And he had £1,700 debt and might have to sell his car, and intends to study the law.

Monday 27 April

To the Party meeting. I saw Hattersley and he said that he hadn't really wanted to go out, but Neil had decided to leave. He said Neil was very dispirited.

I said we could have worked together, you and I, much more easily. He said that he was only shown the part of the Manifesto relating to constitutional questions, and the Manifesto had been written by Patricia Hewitt. An outrage.

I went and met a few new Members. Estelle Morris, Charles Morris's daughter, is a Member of the House. So pleased about that.

Saw Ted Heath doing his rehearsal for the election of Speaker. I said that I want to speak in the debate, and he'd had my letter.

To the Party meeting at twelve – Neil's first appearance at the PLP with all the new Members since the election. There was heavy clapping. Stan Orme was in the chair and said everyone admitted what a marvellous role Neil had performed. Neil said that a reception of that kind for a Leader could only mean he was leaving!

I went from there to the Campaign Group, which I must say was very, very painful. Skinner was in the chair.

I said I thought we should have a discussion on the Speakership but, truthfully, they didn't think the election for Speaker was important. I mean, there isn't really much democracy in the Labour Party. No feeling that decisions should be made by agreement at all. None at all. Then we discussed the PLP and the impending Leadership.

Audrey Wise said she was very unhappy, and she had been going to support Ken Livingstone, but she wasn't quite sure. She was going to support Ann Clwyd.

Dawn Primarolo said she would be supporting Gould and Ann Clwyd.

Alan Simpson said, 'We should not put up a candidate, unless we've nominated Skinner or Benn.'

Alice Mahon's General Committee thought we should do nothing.

Then Ken Livingstone spoke, and Bernie Grant absolutely blew his top, 'effing this' and 'effing that': 'I sacrificed myself for the Campaign Group, and I resigned the Chairmanship of the Campaign Group, and I've been attacked in my GC because the Labour Co-ordinating Committee controls it.' Dawn and Audrey just walked out.

It's the second time the candidature has split the Campaign Group. Anyway, after that I went into the House and we had the Speakership election and Betty Boothroyd was elected.

It was quite interesting. The House was packed. I've never seen it so crowded in my life – all the new Members and everybody else. And the Speaker's a very important appointment.

A couple of things I said annoyed people very much. One was that the Poll Tax had led to disfranchisement, and the other was that there would be social unrest; but otherwise my speech was very funny.

Tuesday 28 April

I went to swear in and had decided I would make a sort of protest, so I put a tape recorder (a little one) in my pocket, and when I got to the Clerk he said, 'Are you going to swear or affirm?'

And I said, 'As a loyal republican and follower of Charles Bradlaugh, I shall affirm.' I then affirmed and I ended up by saying, 'According to law', so at least I made a modest protest. You couldn't refuse to take the oath as such.

Shook hands with Betty Boothroyd, who's very happy as Speaker.

Wednesday 29 April

To the National Executive, where Neil spoke. He thanked the Chairman, said that this was *not* the time to speak – then did so for forty minutes. We've got to review the policy; the polls showed us ahead; the NHS was an appeal to self-interest; fear was dominant, 25 per cent of the unemployed voted Tory. The pollsters got it right. After Chernobyl we all went wrong on nuclear power. 'Tony said that one of the lessons was to stop talking about self-discipline, but it is essential – debates are rubbish. They drop a curtain of fear between the Party and the public, and it makes the Party be seen as a babbling rabble, which bewilders and demoralises our supporters and our people hate it. We can't be preoccupied with ourselves; we should deny the enemy a free ride – it's a long way to come back. We're not the puppy dogs of the unions. We have to be responsible and respectable and a leadership election now is a small price for me to pay. And every statement has got to be about fighting the next election. And going after power is the key. Get rid of recrimination and we'll win.

It was an awful pep talk. He's quite unchanged by his defeat.

Friday 1 May, May Day.

Caroline went to the dentist in the morning and later spoke to Richard Pankhurst, the son of Sylvia Pankhurst, but didn't have the courage to ask him whether Sylvia had been Keir Hardie's lover, because he's such an old gentleman.

That's the end of May Day 1992, with America still riddled with riots and looting and God knows what. I wasn't wrong when I said in my speech on the Speakership that we were in for troubled times and there could well be social unrest.

Saturday 9 May, Glasgow

Came up to Scotland for May Day celebrations in Irvine.

Up at seven. Fortunately, I had a thermos that holds a litre of tea, so I polished that off and an Easter egg and a Mars Bar by the time Alex Smith (MEP for Scotland South) appeared at 8.30.

I had an interesting talk to him.

We discussed the money made available to the political parties for Common Market information programmes, channelled from Brussels, and got the distinct impression that the way this was interpreted in London was that it could cover general publicity expenses.

We went over the Maastricht Treaty, which is coming up for ratification quite soon. He had looked at some of the information given to one of the committees by the Bundesbank, saying that in the event of a nation not fulfilling the requirements laid down by the European Bank, member states would be able to be fined, their Common Market money would not be paid to them and the Ministers might lose their votes in the Council of Ministers, until they complied. So that would confirm that Britain would be reduced to a municipal corporation rate-capped by Brussels, with the possibility of disqualification and so on. It is absolutely hair-raising, so I am going to make that my first big intervention in the new Parliament.

Then we went to the May Day march. There were about 200 – 250 on the march, with about four banners – the Spartacists, SWP, Militant, Tommy Sheridan's mother. There were two women who were non-aligned socialists, both teachers in their late forties or fifties, and an old pensioner who knew Harry MacShane. And a marvellous five-man pipe-and-drum band called the Marauders – just buskers really – marching and dancing on the road and playing their pipes. They just entertained people all the way to Irvine. As we went through the housing estates, people were laughing and cheering and the kids came out to look. When we got to the high street in Irvine, a lot of heads were shaken at the Scots presenting themselves in such a disreputable way.

Tuesday 19 May

I went to see my consultant at the Haematology Department at St Thomas' Hospital, and the result of the tests he did showed that my leukaemia is stable and in some ways receding.

Wednesday 20 May

Went into the House and the Maastricht debate was opened by Major, who made a very good speech. He is quiet and serious and presented his case.

I had a note after my speech from Nicholas Fairbairn, an absolutely maverick Scot, saying how much he had enjoyed my speech – most exhilarating. 'Château Benn is improving,' a typical comment from Fairbairn. When nuts like him compliment you, it makes you wonder.

But the European thing is really settled now. This is the last fight. There may be one on the common currency later, and maybe on the Social Chapter later, but there is nothing to stop this country being completely absorbed. And what is so extraordinary about it is how people have been misled from the beginning to the end about what is happening. I am not in favour of nationalists and nationalism, and I find some pretty funny people taking the same view as I take, but there are good and bad reasons for taking it.

Sunday 24 May

A story in the *Independent on Sunday*, which I added to my Gulf file, indicated that President Bush did finance Saddam right up to the invasion of Kuwait, and $2 billion of food aid had actually been diverted by Saddam to build his military arsenal and even his nuclear arsenal. Some of the food aid had been diverted to Russia to buy weapons. And now this guy Ross Perot – the billionaire, maverick, right-wing Independent candidate for the presidency, whose popularity is above Bush's – has highlighted this and Governor Clinton is doing nothing about it.

If America were to go really hard-right, the whole world would be in a very serious situation because it would clamp on us as well.

Got back and prepared for tomorrow's trip.

Monday 25 May

Whit Monday. Up at about four, collected Ruth and we drove via Bristol to the Hay-on-Wye Literary Festival.

At eleven, we went to have tea with Sheila Yeger and Roger Stennett and a friend. Sheila has completed the play on Keir Hardie, and Roger is engaged in the most fascinating project of animating the Bayeux tapestries for television, with French money. I saw a few seconds of it on video. We drove on into Wales for the Festival.

By the time we set off back to London it was getting dark and, as we got to Oxford, we heard banging and the silencer had fallen off, so we had to stop. Fortunately I had some food and a thermos, so we had a bite to eat; and I had my cell-phone, so I rang the AA; and I had a flashing light and all this gear that I had prepared for years for emergencies, which came into play. About an hour later a very nice AA man called Stewart, from the Chilterns AA, turned up. He said, 'I wouldn't have come out for John Major!' He said there was nothing he could do and he would have to tow us to Oxford. I haven't been towed for years and it was night-time. He put a rope on and towed us at about 40 mph to a garage near Oxford. It was quite frightening.

From there a relay truck driven by a guy called Dennis turned up, engaged by the AA to run a relay service to take you home. He put the Mini on the back of his truck and we drove through the night to London. There was a two-way radio going on between him and his base, and I heard someone say to him, 'We have just picked up an RAF officer. Which unit do you think he was in?' Dennis said, 'Bomber Command?' 'No,' said the voice, 'he is in RAF Intelligence, and guess what was wrong with him? He had run out of petrol!'

Dropped Ruth off and finally got to bed about three but it had been a marvellous day. Those festivals are a new life for me. I went last year to Hay-on-Wye, when I gave my Tom Paine lecture, and I hope I am invited back next year.

Thursday 28 May

It is very hard to see my way through this current depression. The world is in a ghastly state, with enormous poverty, preventable deaths and disease, and the arms trade here. Really a quite disreputable response by a frightened nation that isn't very democratic and is brainwashed by the media into believing that things are going well, when actually they aren't. The Canary Wharf development in Docklands has collapsed and gone bankrupt, but nobody speaks about it except in a sort of clinical way. The media don't say, 'This is the terrible failure of Thatcherism'; they simply say, 'This is the situation. What will the banks do? We'll have to go on with it; public money must go on going into it.'

Sunday 31 May

I had a very moving phone call from Felicity Arbuthnot. She has just come back from Iraq and said the conditions there are quite horrific, with no proper medicines or treatment, and people are dying.

She told me one story, which she had heard from a Norwegian doctor there, about a little boy of thirteen living in a house, and the house next door had been destroyed by a bomb. And the little boy had clambered into the wreckage, where his neighbour was dead. 'A dead mummy,' he said. And then he found a dead baby and said, 'I picked up the baby and put it on the mummy and put her arm around it.'

I tidied my drawers, which I don't think I had done for about twenty or thirty years.

Monday 1 June

There was a letter today from the RAF Museum at Hendon asking people who served in the RAF to write something for its seventy-fifth anniversary, and would I like to write a piece of 2000 – 4000 words? I decided I couldn't really say anything about the war itself, so I would try and write something about the air force that was not aggressive in any way.

I found my logbook for 14 June 1944 and then looked up my diary, and there were about ten manuscript pages about my first flight and one or two other things, and I thought I might send it off. Here was a nineteen-year-old schoolboy so excited at being able to fly. My brother Michael was killed nine days later, which added a special poignancy to it all.

Caroline went to the Quaker Museum and came back with a couple of diaries written by conscientious objectors in the First and Second World Wars. Quakers are remarkable people.

Tuesday 2 June

Spent a lot of time putting together material for the RAF archives. I found a photo of the plane I flew in, a picture of my dad, my brother and me, my airman's book, my ID card. I sent them all off to Hendon.

I heard the result of the Danish referendum, where by a majority of 1.5 per cent (55,000), people had voted No to the Maastricht Treaty. I had heard rumours that it might be close, but not that close and not that way.

Got to bed at about two.

Wednesday 3 June

PLP meeting. At 12.15 John Smith came in. He could really be a nice Tory in the Tory Cabinet – there was no difference. He called us colleagues. He said the issues of policy and organisation were important. Campaigning publicly for the Party is how he would use the campaign for the leadership, and he welcomed the spirit of the election. He said we needed a strong economy and a fair society, and they go together. He said education and training were important; the balance of payments was bad, although we were in recession; there were structural faults in the economy; we need to emphasise science and technology, education and training; we must have a just society. He talked about the problems of the consciences of the rich, implying that the rich had to lift the poor up, instead of the working class lifting themselves.

He said he had supported an alternative Budget because we had an unfair tax system. Labour must be the party of redistribution, must deal with environmental issues, constitutional issues, decentralisation issues and new issues after the Cold War.

He said internal Party democracy was important and that battles were won and lost on the floor of the House of Commons. Well that, of course, was totally parliamentary-oriented.

There was no mention whatever of the trade unions in John Smith's speech.

Friday 5 June

The *Daily Mail* had a huge six-page extract from some book about Princess Diana's attempted suicide. It really is a sensational story in its impact on the monarchy.

Sunday 7 June

Again the royal family stories are crowding out everything else from the papers.

I'm working solidly every day and it is terribly damaging to home life. I don't know when I am going to recover from all this. I don't know what it is: whether I just can't stop working, or I need continually to keep myself up to date with what is going on, or what, because I have no sort of ambition in terms of a career any more. It's a habit now, a sort of obsessive habit.

Monday 8 June

The big news in the papers is the scandal about the Prince and Princess of Wales and their marriage, and the Archbishop of Canterbury has made a speech.

Tuesday 9 June

Went to the Dentist.

Voted at seven and then drove Tony Banks to the Theatre Royal, Stratford to see Sheila Yeger's play, *A Better Day*, which is the story of Keir Hardie. It was great fun, though it had no politics in it. The cast were fine, the director was very nice and the whole atmosphere was very radical. It was really a feminist critique of male politicians, and it was also a sort of worship of the man. Keir Hardie himself never matured or developed in the play. He just spoke about socialism and the workers, and all the rest of it. I enjoyed it. It got panned in the *Evening Standard* the next day (I am dictating this two days later). But I hope it is a success.

Wednesday 10 June

Overslept a bit, frightfully tired after last night, but when I got in I found a message from Dennis Skinner saying everybody thought I should drop my motion at the PLP meeting for a referendum on Maastricht, because the Shadow Cabinet is completely committed to Maastricht.

He said Jeremy Corbyn, Bernie Grant, Alice Mahon and Dawn Primarolo all agreed with his view. It disoriented me a bit, because you don't like to go against your own people.

Anyway, I spoke to Dennis and said, 'I feel I must go ahead.' And he said, 'I knew you would, but just keep that point in mind.' I said I would. Then I sat down to think what I would say at the Party meeting but the phone rang incessantly.

Went to the meeting and I was enormously nervous. First of all, there were lots of new Members who didn't know me, and I hadn't played an active part before and to come up in opposition again on this question was a difficult one.

I said my motion didn't touch on the merits of the Maastricht Treaty, it dealt solely with who should decide – the Commons or the electorate. We had been told for years that there was only one option, whereas there were many: the full Maastricht minus the Social Chapter; a two-tier community, a Europe based on the Treaty of Rome without the union; a democratic united states of Europe; a Commonwealth of Europe; and so on. And this wasn't the moment to commit the party to Maastricht.

I said, 'The case for a referendum is that, whatever the outcome, it is of major constitutional importance.' You couldn't decide the future government of Britain by a single vote on a single day in the House of Commons. The Danes and the Irish were allowed to vote, and we had gone for referenda in 1975 and 1979. And we favoured one member one vote for the Deputy Leadership, strike ballots, the entrenchment of individual rights, but not a vote on this.

'Whatever you feel, I hope the Parliamentary Party doesn't vote for the Shadow Cabinet amendment because it would commit us to Maastricht, it is premature and it is against a referendum. We would be saying to the Liberals, "We agree with you on Maastricht, but we disagree with your demand that people be consulted." It is not a sustainable position. I urge you to vote against the amendment tabled in the name of the Parliamentary Committee. Peter Hain has ruled out a referendum as well. Even the Liberals agree with that.' There was a bit of laughter then because, of course, he had been a Liberal.

After I had spoken, Kaufman spoke. 'The Government is in difficulty. Don't let the Labour Party be dragged into the maelstrom, let us be agile. The Government has got problems; see the Labour Party doesn't get caught in them.' It was purely tactical and had no merit in it at all.

Peter Hain said it was too early to decide about a referendum, and therefore he had left the referendum option open and wouldn't withdraw his amendment. He said the Treaty was fatally flawed, clear conditions were required and a new and radical vision of Europe, and we should renegotiate the Treaty or oppose it.

John Reid said there were two debates going on – the referendum and the issue – and 'Tony Benn always splits the party whatever he does', which I thought was a bit rough. 'Tactically, the case against a referendum is very strong. The Treaty has got no basis in law, we will be helping the Tories and splitting Labour, and both amendments allow a referendum and it will split the Party.'

Neil said, 'We want the UK in Europe. Labour can't go back to the Seventies . . . I have devoted my entire life over the past eight years to getting party unity and I hope you will support the Shadow Cabinet.'

To cut a long story short, Max Madden then moved next business, seconded by Bob Cryer. And then David Blunkett said, 'I move that we remit everything.'

I said, 'Well, I won't remit. I think we should have a right to a vote, you know. It is an important issue.'

Then they overwhelmingly voted to remit my motion and the two amendments to the Shadow Cabinet.

I went out to face the press and I was terribly cheerful and said, 'It was an excellent discussion, very good debate.'

Ken Livingstone made a good speech; quite a lot of people did. There is a lot of discontent with this ranting by men on the Front Bench and the Party doesn't like it.

Margaret Vallins phoned and put me on to John Burrows, who is the President of the Chesterfield Party and a senior officer of Derbyshire

NUM. They heard yesterday that British Coal are preparing to close half the Markham colliery and sack 500 people, half the workforce, and concentrate all the work in one particular seam. On that basis, that particular seam would be competitive, allegedly, with Colombian coal. Very difficult, and John didn't want to say anything publicly until the people at Markham decided what they wanted to do.

Friday 12 June

Filthy toothache all night. Bed late, up at six.

Went to St Pancras, where I had agreed to meet Danish television at eight, before I caught the 8.30 to Nottingham. Left my bags on the train and went and did the interview on Maastricht and the referendum.

As I went back into the station I heard over the loudspeaker: 'Leave the station immediately. Everyone is to evacuate the station.'

I got to the platform and the security officers said I couldn't go on. There were two security women and a huge gathering of people. They said 'There is an unidentified bag on the train.' And I said, 'It's mine.' So I took them and opened my bag and showed my thermos and sandwiches. They were a bit cross.

Went to Parkside School, the old Boythorpe School, to participate in the business studies course: five students between fourteen and fifteen. The task they had been given was: 'You have been told to close the school and move people elsewhere, due to economy cuts. How would you do it?' One boy had been given the role of an estate agent and he had had the school valued, and it and the grounds were worth £2 million. Somebody else was a developer; another was from the construction industry; another was an unemployed construction worker; another was the head teacher, who had been fired. I was asked to help them sort out the problem. Well, this was absolute capitalist indoctrination and I said so – not quite as crudely, but I said, 'Why close the school? If you want to make money, there are lots of ways of making money. You could use the school as a centre for drugs or prostitution or sell flick-knives.'

They said, 'We couldn't do that.'

I said, 'Well, that's the point, profit is not the test. Just forget for a moment who you are all are, according to this exercise. As students, do you want the school to close, and if not, campaign to keep the school open.'

There was a poor young Welsh teacher who was trying to teach the course and she was all flustered, because I wrecked the assumption on which the whole thing was resting. And they were a bit confused themselves, but I hope I made them think.

Came home and slept all the way on the train. Exhausted, and my tooth is killing me.

Saturday 13 June

By car to King Edward Memorial Park off the highway at Wapping, for a lovely little ceremony organised by the Unemployed Workers' Movement there, Ernie Roberts's movement. The dockers from Tilbury were there and other friends of Catherine, Jack Dash's daughter, to throw a wreath into the Thames. It was a beautiful day and, looking at the river from that particular point, I had never seen it before: you could see first of all that it was a dead river, no traffic going up and down; even though it was a Saturday, there probably wouldn't have been much on other days. And there were the old buildings that have been reconditioned, and stark as anything was Canary Wharf, that great white elephant of the greedy Eighties, staring at us. Then a bit further on was David Owen's house, where the Limehouse Declaration was issued, then behind this Wapping, the fortress that Murdoch had occupied. It was all very weird.

I met lots of people, old dockers from Tilbury, lovely people. Catherine threw this lovely wreath on to the Thames and the flowers came off as it hit the water and the wreath floated towards Westminster.

Bed at ten with aspirins and tooth tincture and I was able to sleep.

Wednesday 17 June

Our forty-third wedding anniversary. Took breakfast, flowers, chocolates and a cheque for £5000 for a new car for Caroline.

Campaign Group meeting, where we had a long discussion on the situation in Scotland where the Labour vote really failed catastrophically. Labour didn't appeal to young people, didn't appeal to women, got less than half the trade unionist vote. Dennis Canavan, who introduced it, was extremely anxious.

Malcolm Chisholm, the new MP for Edinburgh Leith, said he was not a separatist but he did think things had gone badly wrong.

Voted, collected Caroline and went to a little restaurant in Kensington Park Road. We thought we would like to sit in the garden so that people wouldn't overhear us so we asked the proprietor, a short man with white hair who had been there for twenty-five years, and he said, 'Oh yes, the head waiter would stand on his head for you.' So we sat in the garden. It was a lovely warm evening and, with all the foliage and two great parrots in a cage squawking and the sun coming in, illuminating the lovely painted buildings, we might have been in the South of France. People walked past and smiled, and who should walk past but Julie Christie, the actress (who had been a pupil of Caroline's and was now at University studying comparative religions, going on to sociology and history), and her husband, Duncan Campbell, the journalist.

Thursday 18 June

Saw Robin Day today when at Channel 4. I said, 'I thought you would be a peer in the Honours List and instead it was Archer!' He said, 'Archer is a crook and a liar, worse than Maxwell.'

Went to Walworth Road and gave a few interviews outside, and at ten the NEC began.

John Edmonds said the purpose of the meeting was to debrief, to analyse, to correct errors following the General Election. We would begin with a presentation by the Shadow Communications Agency, followed by a report from Larry Whitty. Then Philip Gould said his presentation would take forty minutes: he would talk about election polling. Daily polling had been of a sample of 1500 people, the same at the end as at the start. He said the alternative Budget had helped us, the Tory attack had helped them, the health campaign had helped us, the row about Jennifer's ear had harmed us. At the time of the Sheffield Rally, Labour seemed to be ahead. On the eve of poll there was a 1 per cent Tory lead and the strength of support was okay.

It was really mumbo-jumbo. Anyone could have said it, but these are people who are very expert.

On personal finances, 75 per cent thought prices would rise if we were elected, 75 per cent thought taxes would rise and 61 per cent thought mortgages would rise.

On the broadcasts, Labour were thought to have better advertising, better party political broadcasts and to have been most competent.

After the election 300 people had been interviewed and 20 per cent of those asked had explained our defeat with reference to Neil Kinnock himself, the last Labour Government, the winter of discontent, and the fact that people didn't believe us.

Skinner said, 'I notice there was no attack on the left.'

Philip Gould said, 'No, there was criticism of the left.' But Neil had been a 20 per cent factor against us, and the trade-union link had been 7 per cent against us. In 1987 Neil had been more popular than today – that is to say, only 13 per cent had voted against Labour because of him, but this time it was 20 per cent.

There was surprise that Labour had been defeated, but it might be a case of 'better the devil you know than the devil you don't'; the City would be safe, interest rates would drop, tax policies would be lenient, but of course unemployment would rise.

Tom Sawyer said, 'The advisers had been diligent. People ask: wouldn't it have been better to have had greater political control of the experts? Well, remember the times when Tony Benn and Eric Heffer and Dennis Skinner were in charge of the campaigns. That didn't help. I shall read Tony's diaries and Jad Adams's biography of Tony, and Caroline's book on Keir Hardie, but read Herbert Morrison if you want to know how the new working class has changed, and Martin Jacques has been saying the same. We need a wide range of opinion in the Party, we need people like

Skinner and Prescott as well as people like Blair and Cunningham. There is a limit to management solutions. We must stand up for the working class and inspire trust, and identify with them and represent them.'

Well, this coming from the man who led revisionism was something!

Skinner made a fine speech. We should scrap the National Membership Scheme and deal with the huge struggle ahead on the privatisation of coal and rail, because these are our issues. We should build socialism, starting at home. Don't rely on Chancellor Kohl or Jacques Delors. The EEC is a failure because of the slump. Britain must kick-start the economy itself. The halcyon days of the EEC are over. We must vote against Maastricht.

At 1.50 Neil Kinnock began his speech. 'I am the only Leader who has led the Party to two consecutive defeats . . . If it hadn't been for 1983 – 87, we would have won. We didn't lose in the election campaign, but years before.

'We wasted time in changing our rules, which preoccupied us. We should leave future Leaders to concentrate on the future – leadership and management.

'On the Monday before election day, Glenys asked me if I thought we could win. I replied that I hadn't thought so since last Saturday. The Tories thought they had lost and it was a battle between hope and fear. Our Manifesto had nothing to do with our defeat. An alternative Manifesto, nationalisation and stopping council-house sales would not have won it for us.' And he blamed the media, which he said was the worst media in the world. 'They destroyed the trust in the Labour Party.'

He finished after thirty-five minutes and there was a bit of mild clapping.

Tuesday 23 June

Up at 5.30 to go to Blackpool and, when I went to pick up my Mini, I found it had been stolen. I had left it round the corner, where I always do, at about eleven and it had disappeared. I knew exactly where I had left it, because I had had some heavy things to carry.

It's an awful nuisance because I've got to get a new pass, new permit, etc. insurance claim, tell the police and so on.

NEC tomorrow and we have papers relating to the expulsions – 688 pages to expel twenty-six people from the Brighton Labour Party. Absolute rubbish! I have never seen such rubbish in all my life, and if we are remembered for anything in the Kinnock era it will be that he hounded a lot of decent people and then gave the impression week after week and month after month: 'Kinnock beats the left'. Then he wonders why everyone says we are a divided party.

Thursday 25 June
As we were going off to a meeting in the Conway Hall, I saw John Smith. I said, 'I wrote to you, John. My local party have voted and they decided to go for Smith and Prescott.'

He said, 'Well, that's a good excuse for voting for me.'

'Yes. As far as my own position is concerned, I am not inclined to use my OMOV [One Member One Vote]. But can we have a word before you take over, because I do think there are things you could do that would help with the left.'

He said, 'Well, I've got a very open mind. They say I'm too old! I'm fifty-three, five years older than John Major.'

I said, 'Rabin has just been elected Prime Minister in Israel and he is seventy-six.' I went on, 'So, when you do retire, I'll be ready and available.'

Monday 29 June
With Caroline to the House of Commons because Jean Hardie Scott, Keir Hardie's granddaughter, and her own daughter, Dolores, arrived for this tea party Caroline had arranged.

We met them at 3.30 and we looked round the place. I showed them Keir Hardie's room, took them down to the Crypt, and so on. Then we had the tea and it was a very agreeable little party in Room B. The Keir Hardie picture had been moved from the Tea Room so that they could be photographed in front of it. Betty Boothroyd, the Speaker, came and there were quite a number of people; some of our children turned up, and two teachers with their children from the Keir Hardie School.

After they'd gone I was going to have a meal with Caroline, but the Coal & Rail Transfer Bill was coming up. I had dug out, for a TV programme called *Snapshots*, a leaflet issued by the Mining Federation of Great Britain about casualties in the pits between 1927 and 1934. In seven years 7,800 miners had been killed (this was in the privately owned pits) and over 1,200,000 injured, according to miners unions' figures.

I rushed into the House and made a speech based on those figures.

Tuesday 30 June
To the London School of Economics to join a panel made up of about eight people – much too large – chaired by Peter Hennessy; one of these middle-class 'let's get together and have a national government' sort of groups.

There was Vernon Bogdanor, who wants proportional representation; Matthew Taylor, a Liberal MP who wants links with Labour; Will Hutton, who's quite a decent Keynesian economist; and Patricia Hewitt. Well, it was really detestable. In the audience were Martin Jacques, Stuart Weir, Adam Raphael, Mary Ann Sieghart, David Butler – academics, spin doctors, media people, image makers, pollsters, Parliamentarians, and so on, who have made elections their study. I thought I may have been just a bit rude. I don't know why I was so fed up with it.

Thursday 2 July

Mrs Thatcher has made her maiden speech in the House of Lords attacking Maastricht. A packed House of Lords listened to her in absolute silence – nobody agrees with her in the House of Lords, and anyway by accepting a peerage she's de-gutted herself.

Addressing a message about democracy from there is totally incredible, as is talking about the danger of bureaucracy and centralisation, having abolished the Greater London Council, undermined civil liberties and punished councillors and trade unionists, and so on.

She's really killed herself off. Having quit the House of Commons, she now thinks that she is a great figure and, of course, the Tory Party will turn on her with absolute viciousness, because they are determined to get the Maastricht Treaty through.

Friday 3 July

I heard a couple of days ago that Martin Jacques and Gordon Brown were working on trying to relaunch *Marxism Today* as a new socialist paper called *Demos,* which would be soft left, and there is this Fabian Society relaunch, which is really very much the intellectual left, the pessimistic left, the ex-Marxist left, the chattering classes as they're sometimes called.

In the evening I was invited to a party thrown by ITN on the twenty-fifth anniversary of the starting of *News at Ten*. Robin Day was there; his escort was Shirley Anne Field. I had met Shirley Anne in 1961 at the time of the peerage case, and so I had a little chat to her. I asked Robin, 'How long have you known her?'

'Oh,' he said, 'three days, but at my age you have to hurry.'

I had a talk to Selina Scott, whom I hadn't seen since the Chesterfield by-election of 1984. On that occasion she'd written in the *Sunday Express* about people she admired and so on. And she said, 'I might even agree to have a date with the Right Honourable Member for Chesterfield, if only he'd give up his pipe.' So I reminded her of that. Then I said, 'I thought you were very friendly with the Prince of Wales.' 'Oh, you are an imp,' she said. 'What will happen to the royal marriage?' I asked. 'It will end up in a divorce,' she said.

Emma Nicholson was there and she and I are going to work together to oppose the 'Cost of Conscience' measure, which would provide for compensation for male vicars who leave the Church because women are ordained. She's quite a progressive woman in a way – sort of Save the Children Fund-Lady Bountiful.

I had a long talk to the ITN newscaster Trevor McDonald, whom I'd never met before. He's from Trinidad, and he reads the news and is mocked in a very friendly way on *Spitting Image*. Turned out he was quite progressive too.

I quite enjoyed it, but you could see how, in the end, the final corruption of radical politics was that you'd become a sort of well-loved old eccentric, seen at parties.

Caroline has been at the London Library and in the basement she found a book published in 1874 called *Christian Sects, Heresies and Theological Errors,* or something. And in it she found a great deal about Pelagius, who apparently was a Scot, not a Welshman, was a monk in Bangor who took the name of Morgan, then went and got to know St Jerome and St Augustine. His great heresy was that he opposed original sin and supported justification by works. He was expelled, chased and pursued, and 450 bishops met to excommunicate and outlaw him.

I would love it if Caroline wrote a book on Pelagius because I think it would be so important.

Saturday 4 July

I went and bought a second-hand car for £7000. Enormous expenditure! I got £1800 below the going rate, under warranty, and so on, but the Mini had got so small and you couldn't put anything in it – it was such a struggle. This is really a lovely car: four-door, sunroof, big boot.

Saturday 11 July, Durham

The weather was a bit shaky, but I got a taxi to the Royal County Hotel; there was Peter Heathfield with his new partner Sue, and Arthur (whom I warmly embraced) and Ann Scargill, and we sat and had a talk over breakfast.

Arthur said that Seumas Milne and Gareth Peirce, the radical solicitor, and Mike Mansfield and possibly John Hendy had been investigating an account that had been opened in Dublin in the name of the NUM, which was not an NUM account. It came to light because somebody tried to withdraw money from it, and the bank clerk at that stage had no details of the account. When she said, 'Will you tell me your name and address', the man ran out.

Tam Dalyell had raised in the House of Commons the role of Roger Windsor, asking whether he was an MI5 man, so it all began to come together.

Went onto the balcony of the Royal County Hotel to watch the march.

The first time I came in 1961 or 1962 there were over 115 pits in the Durham area and therefore 115 banners; now there are only five pits left. But some time ago they very wisely decided to make it into a Labour Movement festival, so they'd invited the Lodges to bring old banners from pits that had closed, which was very nice.

It's impossible, standing on the balcony of the Royal County Hotel, where I've stood fifteen times, not to be impressed by the sea of faces. There are old miners, people in wheelchairs, indeed, later I met two young miners who were paralysed from the waist down in an accident only three months ago.

There were babies, and in front of one banner was a man with a bowler hat, looking very formal – had probably served in the Brigade of Guards, like many Durham miners. Then in front of another band was a man with Down's syndrome, sucking a lollipop and smiling indiscriminately.

I saw Chris Mullin marching with his wife Ngoc and little Sarah in front of their banner.

Tuesday 14 July

I had a long talk to John Ross, who'd been in the Soviet Union recently. The situation there is absolutely tragic: hundreds of people in the streets selling unwrapped food, and food poisoning is rife.

Factories that produce perfectly good products but aren't as good as, say, Japanese televisions, are closing. There is 40 per cent unemployment, terrible poverty. Some people driving around in Porsches and BMWs, making millions selling art treasures, and the Communist Party on trial for its life.

Academic institutes have been closed. The one that's doing long-term forecasting of the Soviet Union – the most sophisticated model of the economy – hadn't got a ribbon for its printer.

Ross is going to advise the trade unions in Moscow.

Wednesday 15 July

I went to the Vote Office to pick up the statement to be made by Heseltine on coal, but it was not there. So I went up to the Press Gallery and there was a copy of it. I was going to pick it up, but the official there said, 'You can't have that. It's only for the press, you've no right to be here at all.' So I said, 'Please give it to me.' He said, 'I won't.' He was very excited and just so miserable. I asked one of the journalists for a copy and he gave it to me.

So I rang up the Serjeant at Arms' Office, but they said, 'Oh, it's a clear understanding that Members don't go into the Press Gallery.'

Then I went to the Speaker's Office and had a word there.

The media just think they run the place, and if I had time I would make an issue of it in the House, because I really do not see why journalists should get a statement to be made to the House before Members do.

Saturday 18 July

To the Royal Horticultural Hall for the Labour Party Conference to elect the Leader. Apart from John Evans's chairman's address, there were no speeches – nothing allowed. We just sat about waiting for the ballots, so I had a cup of tea and talked to Peter Shore.

Anyway I stayed for the result and then slipped out.

We have a new Leader, John Smith, and Margaret Beckett as Deputy. They've both won overwhelmingly and everybody wants them to succeed: I've got to remember that the desire to win is back again now, and therefore I don't want to get locked into a lot of combat with a new leadership. I'm just so pleased Kinnock's gone. He's such a shallow man, and although at the moment they're paying tribute to him because the media and the Establishment thought he was trying to destroy socialism and the left, I hope John Smith has the good sense to disregard such advice.

Monday 20 July, Chesterfield

The news today is full of David Mellor and this actress. The Prime Minister has said he'll stick by him through thick and thin. I've no doubt Mellor will weather this particular storm.

I'm certainly not prepared to support restrictions on the press, but I think you just have to counter-attack in some way and deal with the behaviour of the press – it's a far greater crime not to report things or to distort things than it is to harass people.

I went to Newbold Community School for another of these business studies courses. The students were working on an Eco Dome idea – a huge 300-acre domed leisure park where they reproduce a rainforest and Arctic conditions, have a lagoon and a hotel, and so on. It's a sort of ecological Disneyland really.

Two people – one a furniture maker and the other a very well-to-do public-school boy – had wanted to be socially responsible and set up this company to try to raise £300 million for this project, on the site of an old open-cast mine. They reckon they can have it open by 1996. I personally don't think it has a cat in hell's chance of succeeding, but anyway this project, which had been outlined in glossy brochures, had been handed out to groups of students at the school, sixteen and seventeen-year-olds, to work out a business plan.

The first group presented an assessment of the Eco Dome and said how marvellous the facilities would be. The students representing the planning committee said how desirable it was; the environmental group said how desirable it was; then people representing the unemployed (not trade unionists, I might add, but people representing the unemployed) said it would create 3000 jobs; then the group representing local residents said how marvellous it would be for Chesterfield.

I listened to all this politely, applauded, and then was asked to comment.

I said, 'Supposing you had three hundred million pounds to spend, would this be your top priority? We need the River Rother to be cleaned up, we need hospital treatment, lifelong education, and so on.'

So one of the Thatcherite students said, 'Yes, but that wouldn't be profitable.'

I said, 'Is profit the only test?'

Then one of them said, 'Well, maybe the jobs there would be low-grade jobs, but we haven't got the qualifications for good jobs.'

I said, 'That's the point, that you should spend the money on helping students get the qualifications.'

It was a bit embarrassing, because the teacher felt I was criticising him; the people from the company were worried because here I was criticising their scheme. In the end I said to them, 'Well, the point is you've got to question all these things and think it out for yourself. Don't believe me or anybody else.'

After I'd gone they'll have some discussion, but I hate these business studies courses.

Thursday 23 July
At the NEC we discussed who should speak from the platform at Conference. It was agreed that members of the National Executive would wind up the debates.

Dennis Skinner asked very sarcastically, 'What about the beautiful people? Aren't they going to be allowed on the platform? Tony Blair, surely, because he's after John Smith's job.'

Clare Short said, 'We know he's after John's job, we all know that.'

Then I moved that Cuba be invited to send an observer to the Annual Conference. I said, 'Cuba is being squeezed by the Americans. The US have applied sanctions to all shipping companies that trade with Cuba; they've got a huge military base there. We've always said the Russians should withdraw from Afghanistan, but we've never said the Americans should withdraw from Cuba. There are double standards. The Supreme Court recently ruled that it was legal to kidnap people from foreign countries and bring them to America.'

Kaufman said, 'You couldn't admit Cuba, because of human rights.'

So Clare said, 'Well, why are you admitting China?'

Anyway, the motion to include Cuba was defeated by 13 votes to 11.

It was all very friendly, in the sense that it was a little bit more than the usual 22 votes to 2 – although on all the key questions it was. And I got the feeling that John Smith was listening.

It was just so nice not to have Kinnock there.

Saturday 25 July
Tomorrow I'm going off to Stansgate to prepare the way for this great visit of ten people there for four days – the Teabags' visit – which is taking

place from 4 to 8 August. I designed a 'Teabag T-shirt' and I'm going to give one to each of the Teabags as a memento. My body is yearning for a holiday.

I'm thinking at the moment very deeply about old age.

Wednesday 29 July

I went to visit Donkins in the morning. This company, which is one of the world's major engineering companies, making equipment, gas valves and so on for the British gas industry, is now placed in a real crisis.

The reason is partly the recession, partly the fact that British Gas is now in effect being broken up into artificial markets, where gas traders buy gas individually and then pay British Gas to pump their gas through the pipelines and charge the customers for the gas used.

So these gas traders neither do the exploration nor transport the gas, nor do they actually deliver the gas, but they get a rake-off.

They're not investing in any way in gas equipment, and British Gas are pushed by competition from the gas traders into greater difficulties, so they are not investing, so the result is there's absolutely no certainty about the future.

Tuesday 4 August

Up very early and the Teabags began gathering at home: Simon Fletcher, Charlie Crowe, Andrew Hood and his sister Catherine, Laura Rohde. We packed up two transit trucks with boxes of archives and drove to Stansgate in about two and a half hours, where we met up with other Teabags.

There were notes from Caroline on domestic arrangements, and from Ruth on the archival tasks, and I gave everyone a Teabag T-shirt from me. We had a lovely meal and it was just like having all the children there.

There was a conducted tour, and late into the evening we talked about the book. This is the book on the constitution that we are supposed to be writing, and so we worked out whether we could write something that was really different, to break out of the total stagnation of British politics.

Wednesday 5 August

A very early start. The work began in earnest on the archives.

It's the first proper holiday I've had for ages. I'm finding it exhausting – all the physical work of lifting and humping – but tremendously useful.

Thursday 6 August

I was out in the garden in one of the buildings, sorting my papers and archives and somebody called out to say that I had a phone call from King Hussein of Jordan, who wanted to have a word with me. So I ran in and picked up the phone and he said, 'Sir, this is King Hussein speaking.' I can never recover from the fact that he always calls everyone sir.

I said, 'I am awfully sorry, I was in the garden.'

'What a good place to be,' he said. 'I wanted to thank you very much for your message' – because I had sent him my letter to the Secretary General of the UN about a visit to Baghdad. 'I agree strongly with the line you take. It's difficult, people don't take much notice of us.'

'Would I be right in saying that the Gulf War had really played some part in stimulating fundamentalism in Egypt and Algeria?'

'Oh, yes, certainly,' he said. 'I much appreciate what you're doing. I'm just off to Bandung for the Non-Aligned Conference.'

I told him I wished I could be there, because the Non-Aligned Movement needs to find its own world now that the Cold War's over. I asked him about the Secretary General of the UN, and he said that he was taking a more independent line and was balancing the various crises: Somalia, Iraq and the situation in the Balkans, Yugoslavia.

I wouldn't be human if I didn't admit that I was much flattered that the King rang me personally.

Sean Arnold, who is an absolute tower of strength, cleared the 'Temple' of books so that we can have the room made watertight and the books properly housed, and some of them were in very bad shape.

The Teabags went out to the Cap & Feathers pub in Tillingham and came back late. Caroline is an absolutely marvellous host.

Saturday 8 August

The Teabags left for London.

Tuesday 11 August

I haven't commented a great deal on the situation in Bosnia. There are the most horrific atrocity stories, almost all concentrating on what the Serbs are doing.

Mrs Thatcher has said the Serbs should be bombed. Bush says he wants some form of military intervention, allegedly to protect humanitarian supplies. The French and the British are a bit more doubtful. The Germans have been very active, but can't possibly send troops to Yugoslavia because of the memories of the appalling slaughter by the Nazi troops of Yugoslavs in the last World War.

The Muslim world is beginning to take an interest in the fate of the Bosnian Muslims.

The new Secretary General of the UN, Boutros Boutros-Ghali, is a very impressive man, seems to be trying to get the UN a bit free of American influence, which I think is a good thing, and to operate more on its own.

One fundamentalist Muslim sect is bombing and shelling Kabul, so that the fall of the Afghan Government hasn't produced the peace it was supposed to, despite the enormous amount of military material that the

Americans poured in through Pakistan to try and topple the Afghan regime.

Really the world without communism looks much worse, even from the point of view of the West, in a way.

Gorbachev recently warned that what was happening in Russia could lead to fascism. It's very hard to make sense of it all. The old socialist arguments, class war, and so on, don't really fit the facts. With the collapse of the socialist analysis and its disappearance as a force, nationalism, fundamentalism, xenophobia, racism, fascism are all beginning to appear again.

It's going to look more and more like the pre-war world and unless some action can be taken to make the Non-Aligned Countries assume a greater role in the UN, and American power can be broken, and Europe can be reformulated on a basis that doesn't commit us to capitalism run from Brussels, and unless the Russians can find some way round the absolute crudity of the market-force Mafia that run everything, we're in for a very, very troubled time.

Monday 17 August

Sean Arnold came in to work on listing and assessing the condition and extent of all the archive papers, using a modest grant from the Wolfson Foundation, which has reached us through the British Library.

I said to him, 'You do exactly what you want to do. Treat yourself as an independent consultant.'

Tuesday 18 August

Today Major arrived back in London. There was a five-and-a-half-hour Cabinet meeting and at the end a statement was issued that Britain had decided to send fifteen Tornado aircraft and two Hercules air tankers to the Gulf to join with French forces of a comparable size and American aircraft. There will be an exclusion zone below the Twenty-second Parallel, which will allegedly protect the Shi'ites from being bombed by Saddam. There is an exclusion zone in the north anyway to protect the Kurds.

After the announcement from Number 10, I wrote to the Prime Minister saying:

> Following the announcement tonight that the RAF is to be committed to possible military action against Iraq, I'm writing to demand that Parliament be recalled at once to allow the decision to be debated and voted upon. Millions of people here and worldwide will see this as a crude attempt to secure the re-election of President Bush, launched at the Republican Convention. 200,000 Iraqis were reported as having been killed by US, British and other forces in the

> Gulf War last year, and the Harvard Medical Team said that up to 150,000 babies under five would die of disease, caused by the destruction of Iraqi water supplies. No one will take British demands for peace talks in Bosnia seriously if we are simultaneously preparing for further bloodshed in Iraq. I'm copying this letter to Madam Speaker, who has certain powers in the matter of the recall of the House during a recess.

I faxed the letter to Number 10. I faxed it to the Speaker. I sent a copy to John Smith via the Labour Party Headquarters, as a courtesy. And I sent it out to a mass of newspapers and press agencies so that at least somebody will be reporting it. When there's going to be military action, the media rally around and pump out the propaganda; they don't ask any questions or have to be given any instructions.

I also sent off my letter to King Hussein, who was attacked on the radio tonight for breaching the sanctions against Iraq; altogether I find the whole thing very frightening.

The Labour Party, I should add, in the form of George Robertson, is on the television. The only time the Labour Party is ever used at all is to confirm the necessity for military action; indeed, to support everything the Government is doing and to comment as if they were media people.

Wednesday 19 August

I heard this morning that at 3.30 during the night Olive Winch died. We always called Miss Winch 'Buddy' or 'Nursey'.

I first met her on 28 September 1928 when she came up to Greenock to be the children's nurse for my older brother and myself, and was there when the new baby, who was David, turned up in December.

She'd been a close friend of the family ever since. A lovely, kindly woman. Always gave her full attention to the people she was with. The only thing that makes her death less sad is that she'd had a whole series of strokes over the last year or two and life had been an absolute misery.

When I saw her last week she was unconscious, but I think she probably knew I was there and heard what I said. But she's the person I've known longer than anybody else apart from my parents. A lovely person, so interested in everybody: all the children, all the grandchildren she knew and took an interest in.

Of course the real heroine is Myrtle Maltravers, her niece, whom she took on when her husband left her and who then took Bud on, and looked after her to the very end.

I ought to record that the entire summer has been carried by Caroline, who did the shopping, made the breakfast, entertained the children, did the laundry, found time for everybody, played with the children. She is the absolute centre of the family and everybody relates directly to her.

What an extraordinary woman she is. I've never in the whole of my life met anyone like her.

Friday 28 August
Ibrahim came to see me at nine, stayed till ten. He brought an invitation from the Baghdad Government for me to go to Iraq.

I said, 'To do what?'

'To look around and see that there's really no trouble with the Shi'ites.'

I said, 'It wouldn't be credible if I came as your guest, and said that and came back again. Nobody would believe me. Perhaps I could say to you what I think ought to be done. I think, first of all, that Saddam ought to recognise that he is in acute danger until the American elections are over; second, that he should do nothing provocative; third, that if he really wanted to take an initiative that might register, he should invite the UN Secretary General there.'

'Ah,' said Ibrahim, 'your suggestion about Bhoutros-Ghali, the Secretary General, to visit Baghdad was very welcome, but it was decided it wasn't the appropriate time.'

I said, 'He should go, or somebody from the Non-Aligned Movement, and you could have a peace process in Iraq where you negotiate arrangements for devolution, without partitioning Iraq, with the Kurds and Shi'ites.'

But he said, 'I will put forward your suggestion to Baghdad.'

'Well, I hope it doesn't cause ill will, but that's what I feel.'

Monday 31 August, Stansgate
We had the Stansgate Olympics, organised by Michael.

There were the usual tears because not everybody won something, but I had made some little medals and drilled holes through coins and put string round them.

One of the curious things this summer is that little Emily cries her eyes out at the sight of my brother Dave, of whom she's frightened. She's only two and a half. She's very advanced, but is just frightened of him.

Dave asked why and Jonathan said, 'Well, you're so ugly, but I'm not frightened of you.'

Children are very candid.

In the afternoon I phoned Sir Alfred Sherman, who had rung me earlier. He's this old Marxist who became Thatcher's adviser. He wanted to emphasise the tragedy of getting involved in the Bosnia situation and what could happen.

Wednesday 2 September
In the evening I drove up to a reception given by Jonathan Cape at Random House to launch Peter Hennessy's book *Never Again,* the history of the 1945/51 Labour Government.

I had great hesitation about whether I'd go, because I'd heard Neil Kinnock was going to make a speech, but then my curiosity overwhelmed me.

Neil spoke from a rostrum below which was draped the Union Jack. I couldn't understand why it was there, though Peter Hennessy later told me it was to remind us of 1945 and the troops coming home. Still, it was singularly inappropriate.

Neil was very fat and sleek and well dressed, and he was back to laughing boy Kinnock. People giggled courteously at some of his gags, but he spoke from a text, which I thought was quite incredible. You'd think that a Labour Leader could talk about a previous Labour Government without a text.

What he said about the 1945 Government was so incredibly banal. He said it had no ideology; it was very British, it didn't try and force its view on anybody; it was all done by Parliament and through Parliament, as if there'd been no social forces that had led to the Labour victory.

Then he ended up quoting Nye, who, of course, resigned from the Government; and then he quoted Eric Hobsbawm, who was a communist anyway and one of the *Marxism Today* people whose position has changed over the years.

I found it very embarrassing.

The insight into Kinnock's thinking now that he's left office was so clear. There was nothing malicious about it – just that the Labour Party is finished, I think; at least the Parliamentary Labour Party.

Yesterday I had a letter from the Prime Minister saying he did not think it necessary to recall Parliament and that he had briefed John Smith fully. This morning I had a letter from Betty Boothroyd, the Speaker, saying that she had no power to recall Parliament unless Ministers requested it.

Sunday 6 September

I noticed in a magazine called *The Oldie* an article by Roy Greenslade on Bernard Donoughue and Joe Haines, describing in detail – and obviously carefully checked for libel – why it was that they did so well from Robert Maxwell, while the Maxwell pensioners are left absolutely without any money at all. It was a really devastating piece of serious journalism and I put it in my press-cutting file for today.

Tuesday 8 September

Worked on my letters this morning. My car radio is out of action because it's got one of these anti-theft devices, which means that if it's switched off you can only switch it on if you put a code in. And I was given a code, put the code in, and it didn't work; the machine said that if you tried to put it in more than ten times, the whole radio became totally inoperative.

So having had the car stolen once and having bought a new car, the new car radio's out of action because the battery's flat. That really is modern technology.

Sunday 13 September

In the evening, about 7.30, I went out to get some tobacco and there were four beggars between our house and the Notting Hill underground station.

There was one man who had stopped me last night and had said 'Mr Benn' in rather an aggressive way, and I gave him a quid. Today he was following people again; he looked drunk.

There was an old black woman sitting absolutely upright and silent in a shop doorway; there was a young woman, may have been only eighteen or nineteen, screaming in another doorway; and there was somebody else wandering about unsteadily.

It really is a reflection of the world we live in. The slump is really hitting people: at the top end the money isn't pouring in as they expected, and at the bottom end people are absolutely on the breadline.

Tuesday 15 September

The news today is that, despite the quarter per cent fall in the base-rate by the German Bundesbank yesterday, which was supposed to be a life-saver for the European economy (all rubbish) combined with the devaluation of the Italian lira, despite that the pound has now dropped to within one-tenth of a pfennig of the German Deutschmark within the framework of the ERM. And if I were a betting man, I would bet that within a matter of weeks the pound would be devalued, although they'd push up interest rates to try and stop it, but it won't help because the speculators who gamble with currencies conclude that the pound is overvalued, which it is, and they'll go on campaigning against it until they get its value down.

So I don't think even the £7 billion that the Chancellor borrowed in foreign currency from the banks to prop it up, and the continuing statements of no devaluation and the quarter per cent fall in the German interest rate – none of these things are going to save it.

When I look back on yesterday's Executive in the light of all this, it is quite incredible that at this very moment, when there is an absolutely massive crisis, the Labour Party should be frozen into the most bland and absurd anti-socialist statements in the hope that it'll occupy the middle ground. I don't think it's going to be like that, but you never know. Things operate in a funny way, and it may be that because the Government has made an obvious hash of the economy, and because capitalism is no good the credit will come to John Smith, the moderate man. But my feeling is that what the Labour Party needs now is some more charismatic and visionary person to lead it and frankly, I don't see any of them there at the moment. I don't think Smith the lawyer, the conservative Scottish lawyer, utterly committed to Europe, is going to be able to achieve very much.

Wednesday 16 September

The world currency market is in a state of absolute chaos.

The Italian lira has been devalued, the Germans have lowered their interest rates; later today the pound was devalued, we withdrew from the Exchange Rate Mechanism, the pound fell, interest rates were raised first of all by 2 per cent then by another 3 per cent and they took the 3 per cent off and the speculators have made about £10 billion at the expense of the British tax payers.

Monday 21 September

Had a word with John Grist, the Supervisor of Broadcasting at the House, who said the Clerk of the House was creating real difficulties about the grade of the Supervisor's post. He said that the Clerk was absolutely determined that when John left, the power of the Clerk's Department would be undiminished. John complained at how terribly conservative everybody was in the House of Commons.

I said the one case for Maastricht and the European Union is that it would wind up the House of Commons, where MPs have traded power for status. He said, 'I'm inclined to agree about that.'

The House has been recalled for 24 September, and Ruth suggested that I should call a special meeting of Labour MPs for that morning because there is not going to be a PLP meeting.

So I rang up to confirm that with John Smith's office. Then I rang up the Leader of the House, who said there would be a substantive motion on the Thursday, then a motion on the adjournment on the Friday.

Tuesday 22 September

I spoke to Nita this evening. She said, 'This is the moment to launch the idea of a referendum, appealing to everybody: Labour, Liberal, Greens, people of no party. Make that the keynote of your speech in the House on Thursday.' I think that she's absolutely right.

Wednesday 23 September

I went over to the National Executive and there were quite a lot of press people outside, and I decided that I would launch the idea of a national petition informally on the steps of Walworth Road. I said that that was what was necessary, quite briefly, straight to camera.

When we came to the statement on the economic situation and Maastricht, which John Smith briefly introduced, Dennis moved his amendment, which was that we withdrew from the ERM permanently and had a referendum on Maastricht.

Gould said that the ERM was flawed and the real crisis had been the recession, and he thought that the paper that John Smith had produced would not carry any conviction. Cook said you can't leave the currency to market forces. Prescott spoke, very inconclusively, I thought.

Coming out, I reiterated the referendum point, because I want to plant it in the minds of the press.

I went over to the Commons and took my Treaty of Maastricht Referendum Bill to William McKay in the Public Bill Office and he said I could present it on Friday. I went to the Journal Office and cleared the wording of the petition, then went to see the Clerk of the House and got a manuscript amendment and he showed me the Government amendment. The thing is catching alight a bit now.

Thursday 24 September

John Major opened the debate. He was slightly less sure of himself, and John Smith made his first speech as Leader of the Opposition.

Neil Kinnock was sitting on the backbenches, his face frozen in an artificial smile. For the first time I felt somewhat sorry him, totally destroyed, having tried to use his influence to destroy the Labour Party as a political force. One or two people spoke to him, but when you lose the power of patronage you lose everything, and everyone was of course gathered around John Smith.

Wrote letters to every single editor of every single newspaper and posted them off, asking them to report the fact that a national petition had been launched and a Bill introduced, asking people to write to me at the House of Commons. I should think I will get thousands and thousands of letters. I have totally lost confidence in the House of Commons, but here's a piece of extra-parliamentary activity taking the argument to the people, not to the hard left but to the people. I think Maastricht is cracking up and Major's speech was much more nationalistic, and Ted Heath made an arrogant speech today about the peasants. And I just had a sort of feeling that I'd broken through and found a new way of presenting the argument. When I'm on a democratic theme I always get public support – that's what's so thrilling about it.

Friday 25 September

I went into the Commons early, picked up my Treaty of Maastricht (Referendum) Bill and presented it at 9.30.

Saturday 26 September

Left for Blackpool. At Euston there was no trolley, no porters, the escalator was broken and I had a bad blow-up with a man in a plum-coloured suit, who was the 'customer officer' or something.

He was very apologetic, and I said I knew it wasn't his fault. So anyway he whistled everything up and I got more than I'd expected; a little truck drove us straight to the train, bypassing the ticket collector.

When we arrived in Blackpool we went to our old friend, Mrs Shaw of Florida Apartments, where we must have been for about the last five or six times in Blackpool: it was the same old flat, same uncomfortable bed with a rubber sheet, same electric light bulb, which is broken; but still we're very fond of it.

Monday 28 September, Conference, Blackpool

The press was full of Bryan Gould's resignation.

I did the *Jimmy Young Show* from my mobile phone, and I simply argued for the referendum and described the petition. If the whole cost of the mobile phone had been to justify that particular broadcast, it was worthwhile.

I spoke at Conference solely and simply on the referendum for four minutes, and at the end there was a crushing defeat for the opposition to Maastricht and a crushing defeat for the referendum.

We had the NEC election results, and it was awful. Dennis Skinner was defeated. He's such a fine man, absolutely incorruptible, you can't even buy him a cup of tea. He's in the House from 2.30 to ten o'clock every night; he spends all his free weekends stomping around the country addressing Labour rallies and talking to strikers.

The yuppie Labour Party is prepared to live with me, but not Dennis, and it's an indication of the disappearance of the working class from the Labour Party; that's a real tragedy because many of them may be attracted to the fascists, where there's a high class consciousness and a low ideological consciousness, and racism. There's not a single working-class man or woman left on the Constituency Section, except possibly John Prescott.

Anyway, Neil Kinnock topped the NEC result, as you'd expect; Gordon Brown and Tony Blair, who've had mass coverage got on; Bryan Gould was heavily defeated, and I survived, with an increase of 1120 votes.

We all went over to the Ruskin Hotel, and Caroline gave an absolutely brilliant speech on Keir Hardie. It was clear, it was modest, it was knowledgeable; there was a lightness of touch, and the parallels with today were drawn.

A momentous day. The Labour Party leadership and the TUC leadership made disreputable speeches, saying that if you want a referendum you're supporting Le Pen, you're a Little Englander, and all that. With a right-wing Labour Party and the growth of a sort of fascist movement, which I think will happen, and a sectarian left, we're in deep trouble.

Wednesday 30 September
John Smith passed my seat on the edge of the second row at Conference, and I said, 'I enjoyed your speech very much. You had a word with Caroline yesterday, and she much appreciated it.' I said what a pleasure it was that he didn't hector.

Thursday 1 October
There was a review of the *Diaries* in the *Guardian* by Michael White and of Caroline's book on Keir Hardie by Kenneth Morgan.

Michael White just gave me a rap over the knuckles from a suburban commuter! Kenneth Morgan used Caroline's book in order to trot out his great expertise on Keir Hardie, and said Caroline was married to Labour's leading troublemaker, which was both sexist (because it referred to her husband and not to her) and offensive. I don't know that I should bloody well agree to see Morgan for his book on Callaghan.

To the Conference and there was a debate on the constitution. Tony Blair said 'colleagues and friends' instead of comrades, which is the normal language of the Conference, which amused me. He was slick and it was a series of soundbites, but he included some liberal ideas.

It amused me that he picked up the policy for which I had been denounced in 1978 on the control of the security services. It had led to someone coming straight over from the CIA to see me as a Minister.

Dennis Skinner was hilarious and got a standing ovation from everybody.

Friday 2 October
Looking back on the Conference, Smith was uncharismatic, but so much better and more honest than Kinnock, who looked like a man in a mask with a fixed smile and no expression. Callaghan, Jack Jones, Ray Buckton, Clive Jenkins, Michael Foot, quite a number of the old boys were there. It was nice to see them. I have a sort of warm feeling about Callaghan, but not about Kinnock.

Talked to Ian Aitken, who seemed very bitter that on his retirement after twenty-seven years on the *Guardian*, he had had a letter simply saying, 'Thank you for your service, I hope you've enjoyed working with us as much as we've enjoyed having you.'

Saturday 3 October
Unpacked, went to the House of Commons to photocopy blank petition pages, copies of the Maastricht (Referendum) Bill, an article in *The Times* calling for a referendum and a speech I made in the House, in order to send them out to anyone who writes about Maastricht.

Bob Burkitt, up in Chesterfield, has offered to send out letters to all the local constituency party secretaries. I'll have to pay for the stamps myself because I can't use House of Commons facilities, but it was a really useful exercise. I got back about eight o'clock, had a meal and worked down in the basement office.

Monday 5 October
The stock market is in a state of total turmoil. The pound has dropped, shares have dropped worldwide and there's a developing row between Britain and the EEC partners about subsidiarity.

Thursday 8 October
Lamont spoke at the Tory Conference today. Very unconvincing speech, with those autocues that you have on glass panels, which are very obvious to anyone watching on television but are not noticed by the audience. The thing is so mechanical and it's destroyed the vitality of public speaking.

Sunday 11 October
Caroline did a quiz in the Sunday papers; 'Is Your Marriage on the Rocks?,' and answered all the questions very candidly, including, 'Have you ever considered a separation?,' to which she wrote 'Yes.' It ended up by saying, 'Your marriage is made in heaven!'

We watched *Spitting Image*. It showed Kinnock and Smith meeting in the street, Smith looking very respectable and Kinnock distributing newspapers as a paper boy in Ealing, rather pathetic. Also Maggie and Tebbit mugged Major at the Conference. It is a marvellous programme.

Monday 12 October
Andrew Hood came, and brought an extremely interesting article he'd written, based on our discussions, for the *New Statesman,* on constitutional reform, which I hope they publish.

To Cheltenham for the Cheltenham Literary Festival.

Barbara Castle was there looking absolutely dolled up to the nines. She's a remarkable women. She's eighty-three and although she's obviously very frail, she's still got this terrific vitality. I went up to my room at the Queen's Hotel, made a cup of tea, then walked to the station to meet the train that Caroline was coming on from London. I could see Roy Jenkins getting out of the train from the first-class compartment and Caroline was behind.

There were 900 people there for this discussion about political memoirs and diaries, chaired by Hugo Young, with Roy, Barbara and myself. It was really quite well structured. Hugo read little extracts about what each of us had said about each other, which I thought was going to be just a personality exchange but then he asked us why we wrote diaries and then a lot of other questions, such as: why don't Tories write diaries? Are diaries true? Did you make mistakes? What about memoirs?

Roy was very generous, as he always is to me. He's finding my *Diaries* absolutely riveting, reads them all.

I said, 'I don't read diaries, I just write them.' Which was honest.

When I accused Roy of having launched monetarism, he said, 'Well, if we're going to have an argument, I must say that Tony is very honest, he wrote in the seventies, "I can't wait for Arthur Scargill to be president of the NUM", which shows how honest he was, but threw doubt on his judgement.'

I said, 'Arthur was right – he said the Government was going to butcher the industry, he told the truth. And whereas Mrs Thatcher was thrown out by her people, Arthur was re-elected by his, and anyway he didn't want a peerage.'

That got a huge applause. I think it must have slightly surprised some of the Cheltenham Tories who'd turned up.

Barbara was quite blunt and amusing, and Roy was very huffy and puffy and pompous but it was a good evening.

Afterwards I signed tons of books, and I noticed Roy got about three people to sign his and Barbara signed a few, so it was a success.

Then we came back to the Queen's Hotel. It's just getting on for midnight and it's Caroline's sixty-sixth birthday in about two minutes. She's sitting in the bed in this luxurious room with a bedspread, couch and flock wallpaper; probably costs about £150 a night. She's preparing for her Keir Hardie lecture tomorrow and I'm bringing my diary up to date, as I've talked about the contemporaneous nature of diary writing.

Tuesday 13 October

Caroline and I went down to Cheltenham Town Hall and she gave this brilliant lecture on Keir Hardie, absolutely packed to the doors and they all sang 'Happy birthday to you' at the end, because Richard Cohen announced it was her birthday, and somebody brought her some flowers.

Bought a new telephone. I have so many gadgets that don't work and this one doesn't seem to work very well, either.

The Government has announced a programme of further mine closures. The closure of all those pits is just vicious, absolutely vicious class war by the Government against the mining industry, due to the privatisation of electricity. They're not going to buy British Coal, they're moving to gas and subsidised nuclear power, it is an absolute outrage. I think the House of Commons should be disruptive, but it depends whether there is action outside. You can't do anything inside if there isn't anything outside.

Wednesday 14 October

The newspapers today absolutely full of the closure of two-thirds of the nation's coal mines and overwhelming support for the miners, for a whole range of reasons.

Gordon McLennan, the former General Secretary of the Communist Party, came to see me, stayed about an hour and a half. We sat in the kitchen together, he in a garden chair, and had a cup of tea and talked.

He said that his wife was involved in the Scottish Communist Party, but he hadn't actually joined it. He felt that the democratic left had lost all contact with the working class and in effect what he came to tell me was: you've got to work with the Tribune Group.

I said, 'I've no hostility to the leadership or to anybody else, but I sit in the National Executive, and Blunkett and Clare Short and Robin Cook and so on are all engaged in hammering the left and it's very painful, so I've worked on a parallel development.'

He said, 'You should ring Robin Cook and try to get something done about the mines closures. What is needed now is leadership, and you have a new function to perform.'

He was very friendly and flattering. After he left I thought I would get down to it, so I rang Larry Whitty and asked for a special meeting of the National Executive.

I rang John Smith and told him I'd done that. I rang Norman Willis's office and said there should be a big demonstration. I rang the Archbishop of Canterbury's office and spoke to his chaplain, who said the Archbishop was in Turkey, but he'd have a word with the Archbishop of York.

Rang Tom Vallins, and we're going to have a big demonstration in the Market Square in Chesterfield.

I tried to get hold of another bishop, who was being very helpful; and indeed he's called a special meeting of the Church Commissioners to try and get them to withdraw their investment from PowerGen, which is responsible for refusing the contract.

Andrew Hood said, 'Why don't you write an article for the *Daily Mirror*?' So I rang Richard Stott, the editor, and said, 'I'm ringing you wearing my hat as a former Secretary of State for Energy and a Chesterfield representative. Can I write a piece?'

'Yes,' he said, 'five hundred words'.

So then I did a draft and Andrew and Simon Fletcher worked on it, and mid-afternoon I faxed it across. And Stott rang back and said he'd print it on Friday.

By early evening I was utterly exhausted, but the whole thing looked as though it was moving into place and I think, in fairness, the Labour leadership is probably going to come out.

Thursday 15 October

The national response to the decision to close two-thirds of the pits in Britain has been astonishing. Right across the political spectrum. We learned later in the day that the decision wasn't even taken by the full Cabinet, and the Welsh Secretary was heard on the radio saying he didn't know, and Teddy Taylor and Edward Heath joined in the attack. An amazing story.

Rehabilitated Arthur Scargill in twenty-four hours as the man who was right. Tremendous sympathy.

Had a word with Arthur. He said that Norman Willis had been very helpful. They've now worked out that sixteen coal-fired power stations and six railway depots would close, and this could cost 100,000 jobs.

The Bishop of Sheffield said he couldn't come to the demonstration in Chesterfield, but Tony Atwood, the Rural Dean of Doncaster, rang me up and said he'd be happy to speak.

Friday 16 October

Up at six and the *Daily Mirror* front page said 'March With Us'; they gave me page 6, they gave Paul Foot page 9, and it really was smashing coverage. I think it's guilt on the part of the *Mirror* and a lot of other people at not having supported the miners before, but anyway, for whatever reason, this is very broad.

In the course of the day all sorts of Tories came out in support, like Winston Churchill, who visited a colliery where the UDM are strong, Elizabeth Peacock, William Cash, Marcus Fox. Quite astonishing really.

I think tomorrow will be the biggest demonstration there has ever been in the history of Chesterfield.

We're alerted to the possibility that there might be agents provocateurs, and Johnny Burrows rang up the police and warned them off. There's going to be a notional presence, but not a big build-up; but we've got to be sure that people don't throw bricks and stones and then get the miners a bad name. Also we're going to remove all the SWP posters. The excitement in the Club is so evident. So the old spirit is there, and it is not an accident really that Chesterfield is the focus once again of a huge new campaign. We've got Tories and Liberals on the platform on the Market Square tomorrow night and Arthur Scargill and Dennis Skinner as well as the Rural Dean of Doncaster. I feel immensely cheerful.

I'm sure the Government will try and get out of it. I think what they'll try and do is use the courts as an excuse, because today the courts gave a stay of execution for redundancy notices to four pits. That is a sort of partial victory, and I think Ministers will go to the courts and say, 'Get us off the hook,' because otherwise on the Wednesday night there is a serious possibility that the Government will be defeated in the House.

Meanwhile the European Summit in Birmingham, which was supposed to be the great event of the British Presidency of the Council, a special summit, has been totally overshadowed. Nobody's remotely interested in it any more.

There is a link between Maastricht and the miners of course, because the cuts in public expenditure are dictated by the need to maintain credibility with the Bundesbank.

Saturday 17 October, Chesterfield

The miners' campaign continues to dominate the headlines.

The Summit in Birmingham was a total failure, Major called it after the collapse of the Exchange Rate Mechanism, but nobody's taking any interest in it because the news today, hour after hour, is that more Tory MPs are saying they'll vote against the Government.

Major issued a statement saying there'd be more redundancy money, to be announced by Heseltine on Monday.

Everyone marched behind the banners to the Market Square, while Caroline and I walked down to the station and chatted to a few people and met Arthur off the train. He'd just come back from London, where the TUC General Council had met him. He said the atmosphere was quite different. Somebody at the General Council said, 'Look, we've never listened to this man for ten years. I think we ought to listen to him now.'

There were 10,000-12,000 people in the square and the Socialist Choir from Sheffield was singing. It was lovely.

The rally was organised in forty-eight hours by Tom and Margaret, who leafleted it; the local radio advertised it all day; and people went around with loudspeakers, telling everyone to turn up at the Market Square.

It was a crisp evening – coldish, but no rain, thank God – and in the bright lights of the television cameras it was unbelievable.

About 9.15 we went over to the Labour Club There were a couple of miners, who were in tears at the loss of their jobs and the destruction of their lives. It was really awful and I tried to cheer them up but it was very difficult.

A day to remember. And the theme of my speech today was that it was people like us who broke the Poll Tax, brought down Charles I, liberated trade unions, gave working-class men the vote, gave women the vote, introduced the Health Service, brought down the Berlin Wall, liberated Mandela. It's us – that's what it's about: us – and now we've got to raise our demands.

Sunday 18 October

Got to St Pancras and I'd left the car lights on so the batteries were flat – again. Second time I've done this in about a month or so. Got a taxi home.

I've got the most terrible pain in my ear, as if I've got a boil, and I'm also very deaf. I feel a bit low at the moment and I just haven't had enough rest. That's what I need, rest.

Monday 19 October
Went back home, but my battery was flat again so I had to get a taxi to the Commons.

Into the House. Heseltine made his statement, very much on the defensive because he said that ten pits would close at once, but twenty-one would be re-examined.

Just as I was leaving to come home in a taxi, Richard Shepherd, a Tory MP, a very nice guy, offered me a lift. He said, 'I live near you.' So he dropped me off and I said, 'Come and have a drink.' He came down to the basement, where Andrew Hood was working, and talked for about an hour and half. Richard's contempt for John Major is unlimited, and for Heseltine and for Lamont. I'm sure he'll vote against them in the House on Wednesday, and again on Maastricht on Monday.

He said that Mrs Thatcher had consulted him about his Referendum Bill* and she'd looked at it and had pages of amendments. And she said, 'You've got to spell it out, otherwise they'll wriggle out of it.' 'They' being the Civil Service and her own colleagues.

He talked about Major's speech at Conference, when Britain was mentioned forty-six times and how cheap it was.

Later a student appeared out of the blue at the front door and said, 'My name's Paul Fisher, can I come and help you? I've read the *Diaries* and I've read that you do take students on.' He looked a decent guy; he was from Queen Mary College, a pupil of Peter Hennessy. So he came in and opened letters – of which there were 400 – 500

Today it was reported that Petra Kelly, the German Green leader, and her partner, General Gert Bastian, were found dead. It was said that Bastian had shot her while she was asleep and then shot himself, and nobody knows the reason. It occurred about three weeks ago, on 1 October or thereabouts, and the bodies had decomposed. It's just such a terribly sad end.

The German Greens distrusted Petra Kelly because she was a bit of a self-publicist, but she reflected a very decent element in German life. Last time I saw her in Berlin was when I was doing my *Burning Embers* programme about two and a half years ago. She was depressed about the rise of the right, the reunification of Germany and everything. Extremely depressed.

Bastian was an interesting man. It was just a fated relationship. I think the Greens looked on her a little bit as the British Greens look on Sara Parkin, I'm not sure, but they hadn't nominated her for the Parliament. And this old general had retired – I think he was married, but separated from his wife. It's another sort of end-of-an-era story, because the Greens

*In late 1991 Richard Shepherd introduced a Private Member's Bill to make provision for a national referendum before the Maastricht Treaty could be ratified by the British Government.

were the articulate opposition to the right in the 1980s, both in Britain and notably in Germany, and now the two people most connected with the peace movement and the Green movement have been found dead. I hope there's a suicide note of some kind. I couldn't bear to think that we never really knew the explanation. Very, very sad.

Tuesday 20 October

Taxi to Hyde Park. When I got up there, there was this massive demonstration on behalf of the miners, the whole of Hyde Park was closed off. We set off at twelve and we got back at about two. My legs were so weak, I thought at one stage I was going to have to leave the march. I wondered if it was the return of my Guillain-Barré disease or just general degeneration, but it was a tremendously tiring march. People cheered and there was a band that played the Internationale. People waving from windows. A quarter of a million people were in the park.

After that we went to Central Hall, Westminster, which hadn't really filled up because most of the people were still waiting to leave Hyde Park. Afterwards I went over to the Commons. I just had time to eat a sandwich and a Danish pastry and made a quick cup of tea.

Then I went into the Chamber. I was so tired I was afraid I was going to go to sleep.

Robin Cook began with a pernickety, pompous speech. Very irritating is Robin Cook, I don't know why; but it wasn't about the central question. He was followed by Heseltine. I wasn't called until about ten past eight, and I was told to keep it very short and I took eight minutes despite an intervention. Very brief speech, but much more political and more confident, because when you come from a march you walk ten feet tall.

It was not like these awful managerial speeches that all MPs make about dollars per gigajoule of electricity and the marginal efficiency of coal against gas. No human concern there at all. That's what the argument's really about: human dignity versus profit, and I said that.

At the end of the debate at 10.30, after the vote, I presented the petition – about 30,000 signatures – so I did my duty.

The Government won by a handful of votes because the Ulster Unionists had been promised that it would review their need for electricity cable, and David Hunt, who wound up for the Government, just gave assurances all over the shop.

Thursday 22 October

The UDM were demonstrating outside the House of Commons yesterday and they all cheered me. I felt so embarrassed. They were wearing UDM stickers and they were allowed to have their banners outside. I've never known that outside the House of Commons before. The British Establishment loves the UDM and Roy Link, and I might add that Frank

Field, of all people, and Nicholas Winterton had jointly invited Roy Link in to talk about the pit closures. Just disgraceful when you think of what the UDM has done to the Labour Party.

Friday 23 October

In the evening I went to St James's, Piccadilly, for a concert given by Musicians Against Nuclear Arms, and I was introduced in a very elaborate way. I gave a little speech and I must say it is much better if you don't write anything down, if you just let it come out. I wish I could acquire that skill in the House of Commons, but I've never quite succeeded in doing it. I find Commons speeches still very difficult. I work and work at them – not as hard as I used to, when I stayed up overnight to write what were really extended Oxford Union speeches.

The world news today is that the GATT talks have broken down. The French are not prepared to concede anything on agricultural support, because Mitterrand presumably wants to be re-elected, and the Americans are stepping up the pressure, because Bush wants to be re-elected. The possibility of trade wars certainly does exist.

Sunday 25 October

Two marvellous reviews of Caroline's book on Keir Hardie, one by Tony Blair of all people and the other by David Marquand; really good reviews. Later in the day the *New Statesman* did an even better review, more sensitive from a woman's point of view.

Monday 26 October

I got up very early and went and did the *Big Breakfast Show* on television with Paula Yates, who's married to Bob Geldof. It was in her 'boudoir', sitting on her bed.

It was all right really. I behaved with reasonable dignity. Talked to the young people who ran the show, but it reduces politics to the level of *Blue Peter*. Silly really and made discussion almost impossible.

Paula Yates was a harmless woman and I got across a few political points – and 700,000 people watch it.

Wednesday 28 October

I went to the NEC and it was the first time I'd been there for many, many years without Dennis Skinner. Pretty miserable.

I got there early and found my usual place, and Robin Cook said, 'Do you mind moving along,' (because I was smoking). I thought, 'Damn that. 'No,' I said, 'you go and sit beyond me.' He then complained about smoking in the meeting.

They're merging the Home, International and Local Government Committees and making it the Policy Committee, which will meet four times in a year. They're just downgrading the whole role of the Executive. Kinnock behaved as if he was a new young member trying to make his number. It was embarrassing really – nothing offensive about any of it, but somehow in his circumstances he should only intervene on major questions.

I might add that Tony Blair, who had written this review of Caroline's book, said to me how much he'd enjoyed it and that the original review had been much longer, but they'd cut it.

Thursday 29 October

The *New Statesman* printed the article that Andrew Hood had written; it included a lot of thoughts I'd had in discussion with him and I think it could properly be said that much of it came from me, but I had said it must go into the *Statesman* under Tony Benn and Andrew Hood. They said it must have my name on it, and I thought they meant that it couldn't be Andrew Hood alone. Anyway, when it was printed, it was just in my name. So he's really been cheated of any recognition. Most unfair.

Sunday 1 November, Stansgate

Jonathan was having a punch-up with me and I held his hands and he butted me with his head. It really hurt. I thought he'd loosened a tooth. And he said, 'Don't worry, Dan-Dan. If the tooth falls out, put it under your pillow tonight and the tooth fairy will bring you sixpence and you'll grow a new tooth.' I thought that was very sweet of him, though at five he might have realised that old men don't have new teeth and that the tooth fairy doesn't exist!

Monday 2 November

Gordon Butler, the General Secretary of North Derbyshire Miners, rang to say that a fax had come to him from British Coal, and every single miner in all of the thirty-one pits had been given a redundancy notice that expired on 29 January. I tried to get a Private Notice Question asked in the House as an emergency, but I failed.

First meeting of the renamed, restructured Policy Committee. When we came to the new policies, it was said these wouldn't be expensive to develop, because the research was being paid for.

I asked, 'Who pays?'

Geoff Bish said, 'The Friedrich Ebert Stiftung, a German trade union and labour movement, paid some of the costs; the Institute for Public Policy Research, (IPPR) paid others; and the parliamentary spokesmen paid some of it out of their allocation of Opposition funding.'

Then we came on to international affairs and the Westminster Foundation for Democracy, which is funded by the Government and is used to promote democratic developments in former communist countries.

Michael Meacher gave a report on Yugoslavia, where he'd been. He said, 'We are involved in this country more than the Government admits. We recognised Bosnia and Croatia, so did the United Nations; the UN imposed an arms embargo; the Bosnian Serbs picked up Yugoslav weapons; there are two million refugees.' He went on to say that this would be a focus of unrest for decades to come – it was like the Palestinians, only in Europe; he was not in favour of deploying a large army, but an air-exclusion zone should be enforced; in Kosovo where nine out of ten are Albanians, there is a terribly serious situation. He added that one-third of Croatia had been overrun by Serbs; there was murder, rape, pillage, destruction, what he called 'recreational killing' and we should support the Prime Minister against Milošević because the situation there was impossible. Inflation is 7000 per cent and the Yugoslavs themselves, the Serbs in Serbia, would like to get out of it all. He said ethnic cleansing was an appalling thing and the massacres were on a huge scale.

I said, 'Could you tell me, Michael: was the German recognition of Croatia and Bosnia wise, given the history of the last war?'

Michael said, 'No it was a disaster; 700,000 to a million Serbs were murdered by the Croatians. The Germans pressed recognition on the EEC and they agreed, and the Serbs will win, and then where will the refugees go?'

It was quite an interesting little exchange.

Tuesday 3 November

I went to St Thomas' this morning for my leukaemia check-up. My professor didn't think it was too serious. He's absolutely obsessed with what the Government are doing to the Health Service, and I spent about half an hour talking to him before he did my blood test.

Wednesday 4 November

One item I forget to mention yesterday. A guy who had been at the Chesterfield rally wrote to me to say how moved he had been by the miners' rally. He also wrote, 'Did you know that Guy Fawkes lived in Maastricht before he came to London and tried to blow up the House of Commons?' So I rang him up, and it turned out he was the cousin of Peter Tempest, whom I knew at Oxford and was the *Daily Worker* or *Morning Star* correspondent in Moscow for many years. I mentioned the Guy Fawkes story to William Cash, who is a young constitutional lawyer, and he said, 'I knew that,' but I don't suppose he did. I found no proof of it, but it is an amusing little story.

The Maastricht discussion – who would win, would Major be humiliated, would the rebels be brought down, what would Smith do – was typical media coverage of a huge debate and the speculation went on all day. I asked a question to Heseltine about the redundancy notices issued by British Coal to all the miners at the thirty-one pits.

Then the Prime Minister opened the debate; he looked quite calm and cool considering the pressure he has been under. He argued the case, dealt with the concerns, claimed that British pressure had led to a much less federal Europe, and so on. I saw Heath looking a bit sick, but I think Heath is a sufficient tactician to know that was the only way Major could get it through the House. He said how the Danish question would be taken on board, and so on.

I did interrupt him at one stage and said, 'I understand your enthusiasm for taking Britain into the heart of Europe, but how could you do it without the consent of the people and merely by using the Whips'.

He said, 'I respect the Right Honourable Gentleman . . .' and all that sort of stuff, but still, I got the point in.

The Liberals are supporting the Government, which is disgraceful, particularly when you think that Paddy Ashdown was invited by the TUC to speak at Hyde Park on the miners, and then he goes and supports the Government. Had he voted the other way, as the vote showed, it was quite clear that the government would have been in real difficulty. But that's politics – very unattractive. John Smith made an amusing speech, a bit of knock-about, better than Kinnock would have been. Heath made a scornful speech about the rebels.

Came back to my room, very tired, but didn't have a sleep in case I missed the Division bell.

The Government won the first vote by 6 and the second by 3. The House was absolutely packed. I don't think I have ever seen it so full and, when the result was announced, there were Members standing in the central part of the House between the table and the bar of the House, which was quite out of order. There was tremendous cheering by the Tories who favour Maastricht, and our people looking a bit shifty and shouting at Ashdown. These great parliamentary occasions rarely rise to the level they are supposed to, and I didn't think the debate was that good. Major has saved his bacon for the moment at any rate, but he will be in trouble with various other things that are coming up.

I am disenchanted with Parliament, as anyone who reads this diary will discover.

I was absolutely knocked out and could hardly stand up when I got home.

Thursday 5 November

Went into the BBC. The messengers there have all been fired and the jobs put out to private contractors. The messengers had mentioned this to me last time I was there, and this time I saw all the new American-type uniforms and on their caps it said 'Securiplan', so I asked how much an hour they were paid. They get £2.40 an hour. I asked how long they had worked with the company, and the lad I spoke to said two months and another one had been there four months. I said, 'Are you unionised?' and they are not.

Went to the Commons, where I had an appointment with an Iraqi whom I had met on the plane when I was on my way to Jordan in 1990 on my visit to see Saddam. He was in trade and had given me a camel-haired cloak as a gift, which I appreciated. That may have been just a down payment! What he wanted to see me about was a $70 million deal to sell Malaysian cooking oil to Iraq, which had received an export licence from the DTI, but could only be paid for if they allowed Lloyds Bank (who held the frozen assets of the Iraqi Government) to release the funds for this consignment.

He then hinted to me that if this could go through, two prisoners held by Saddam could be released. He said the company he was dealing with in Baghdad was actually run by Saddam's son-in-law. All of a sudden, I could see myself getting up to my eyes in hostages-for-trade deals, money being offered to me for a charity, and I looked back at the cloak he had given me two years ago, which I took to be just a goodwill gesture, and got increasingly uneasy.

I said I would write to the DTI and see what they make of it, but I didn't care for him much, particularly the bit about hostages. At the end he said, 'I invite you to come to my house in Jordan,' but I suppose this is the way Middle Eastern people do it – there's nothing for nothing, you have got to exchange favours. It's not my way of doing business and it did make me uneasy.

Tuesday 10 November

Came back to the Commons, very, very tired. I looked up my biorhythms, which I don't usually do, but it is strange because my physical and emotional cycles are both at the bottom and my intellectual cycle is at the top. I just thought I would see if there is anything in it and sure enough, that's my position.

Wednesday 11 November

The Church of England Synod voted to ordain women priests. It was carried with a majority in the House of Bishops and the House of the Clergy, and only two votes determined it in the House of the Laity. It requires a two-thirds majority in every case. I must admit, I burst into tears, and Caroline was crying in front of the television and we hugged each other.

Later in the day I saw pictures of the women who had been in a vigil outside Church House hugging each other, and old ladies hugging each other, and young girls in dog collars who were only allowed to be curates and deaconesses and so on hugging each other. It was really exciting and I thought, 'Wouldn't it have been lovely if my mum had lived to see it.' Anyway, it came about and she always knew it would come – and it did. It was the backlash against the backlash against women, because the women's movement had been growing since the war and then you had this backlash against it in the Eighties, and at last women are on the march again. It will encourage women no end throughout the whole country, in every respect.

Friday 13 November
Heard the *News at Ten,* with an interview with Robin Cook about documents that had been released suggesting that John Major did know about the arms sales to Iraq. As I had a lot of experience of this as a Minister, I rang the BBC and got onto the *Today Progamme*. I described how Whitehall dealt will all these matters; how all decisions were taken at the highest level; how incoming Ministers got a brief; how red boxes at night contained all the letters; and how it was inconceivable that this would not have been decided at the highest level. And inconceivable that Ministers would not have known.

Saturday 14 November
I suppose, in a way, John Smith is a Clem Attlee, a quiet little man; and a Clem Attlee with a radical programme presented in a common-sense way has got a certain appeal. But Nick Raynsford, a Kinnockite MP, who was elected for Fulham, was then defeated and got back in Greenwich in April, has written an article in the *Fabian Review* criticising the soporific leadership and saying we need a more radical approach. As far as I could make out, he said Neil Kinnock had been prevented by the disciplines of the Party from being as radical as he would have liked to have been.

The newspapers are taking that as a demand that Gordon Brown and Tony Blair take over the leadership and deputy leadership. Smith and Beckett are being presented as dull and inadequate. I have reached an age now where I don't want to have any more rows in the Labour Party, so I am just going to concentrate on positive things and if I am asked for a view on the Labour Party, I will give it. But what is needed at the moment is a positive contribution and deadly analytical attack on the whole philosophy of the Government, to which I am afraid the Labour Party very largely adheres.

Friday 20 November
Spent the whole day in the office and wrote a couple of hundred letters, I should think, by hand. Sean was in and he's making progress at Stansgate. He is such a serious, scholarly man. He thinks there are about 30,000-50,000 items in my archives and about half a million sheets of

paper. That's quite a lot. I don't know what the equivalent would be in books.

There is a great deal of anger among people about who is going to pay for the fire at Windsor Castle, because the Queen hadn't insured it. People have asked, 'Was it Fergie's revenge?' If the taxpayers pick up the Bill, the Queen won't pay a penny because she doesn't pay tax, so that is quite an interesting issue. The whole monarchy thing is beginning to crumble. Caroline always said Charles III would never ascend the throne.

Monday 23 November

A man called and said, 'You have written to my mother and father on several occasions and I just wanted to let you know that they are both in prison for non-payment of the Poll Tax. My dad's in Bedford jail and my mother is in Holloway. They are both nearly seventy and I thought you would like to know.'

I said I would write to them. But what a bloody awful country this is.

At home, I found *Der Spiegel* had come out with their issue on the royal family, with puppets on the front page and inside a picture of me, with a long interview under the heading 'We are a banana monarchy' as a sort of joke on a banana republic. It was quite fun to read it.

Wednesday 25 November

We have a huge Thanksgiving party tomorrow and Caroline has spent the day preparing for it. She is an amazing woman. I don't seem ever to get anything done – piles of letters, tons of stuff.

If I am honest with myself, I am worried at the moment about how I am going to move into real old age. I am only sixty-seven which is no age at all, but in just over twelve years, I will be eighty, which is quite an age. I don't know whether I will be re-elected, but I hope I will. I don't know whether the constituency boundaries will be changed, and I hope they are not.

But at no stage in life is the way ahead absolutely easy, because you've never had any experience of it. I could go to the House of Commons every day and listen to the debates and be a sort of popular old uncle. I can't go on for ever pounding the country doing masses of meetings, which is too tiring. I am not really sure that I have got a book in me, because I am not an intellectual and what gives me huge pleasure is that Caroline's book has been a great success. Today a Labour peer came up and said he was reading it. It has had marvellous reviews and it is the authoritative book on Keir Hardie, and I am so pleased about that.

Thursday 26 November

Hilary was thirty-nine today, a lovely lad.

Caroline spent the whole day preparing for the Thanksgiving Dinner.

I missed the announcement by the Prime Minister that the Queen is going to pay income tax, and also about the state of grants to local authorities, which will take £37 million from Chesterfield next year – massive cuts.

In the evening we had our Thanksgiving party with eighteen of us – the kids, Ralph and Ann Gibson and their children, Mary and David and Rick and Liz, Peter Carter and the Reteys.

Ralph came down and had a talk in the basement, and he told me that although the judges have said there has to be a Public Immunity Certificate, signed by Ministers, when information relates either to security matters or to international negotiations, in fact, if a Minister didn't sign the certificate, there is nothing they could do to you. So Heseltine's defence that he had no option is perhaps questionable.

I also tried to get Ralph to see that the Scott Inquiry was a political and not a legal matter.

Caroline and I stayed up until one doing the washing-up, but it was a lovely evening.

Monday 30 November

Went to see the Chief Whip, Derek Foster, and said, 'I don't know what the Shadow Cabinet is planning to do on the Maastricht Treaty. I don't want to cause any trouble, but to me it is a very fundamental question and I am afraid I shall have to follow my convictions on this matter. I think it would be a great mistake if the Labour Party did actually do anything that let Major get away with Maastricht, because if we defeat him on Maastricht, there will be an election and we will win. Then John Smith, as Prime Minister, can get Maastricht with the Social Chapter.'

I didn't threaten him in any way, but I told him quite plainly and I think he understood. I said I thought many Labour MPs took the same view.

Foster said, 'I think it is unlikely that the Shadow Cabinet will vote for Maastricht on the Third Reading.' But that is not good enough. You can't abstain on it, because that gives the Government a majority.

At 6.30 I went to Room H, where Peter Shore, Austin Mitchell, Nigel Spearing and Gwyneth Dunwoody were planning the strategy.

Tuesday 1 December

Took my framed picture of Countess Markiewicz to the broom cupboard in the Crypt of the House of Commons and hammered it up on the back of the door. I am going to get a brass plaque for her put there – I have decided to put all my mementoes there because it is sort of 'outside' Parliament. This is where I am building up my little shrine to people who gave us Parliamentary democracy.

Wednesday 2 December

Sad news today from Irving Rogers that his father Herbert had died. He was ninety-six. I met him forty-two years ago, when he was very largely responsible for my being considered for the shortlist when Stafford Cripps resigned in Bristol.

Herbert was a very interesting old man. He was, I think, active as a young man in the ILP before the First World War. He worked with Walter Baker, MP, and was the agent to Stafford Cripps and probably the most efficient agent in the Party. He had a card index of every Labour voter. And he was thrown out of the Party when Cripps was thrown out, and kept the party together with Cripps, and came back with him and became his agent, and was my agent on a number of occasions.

He was an old Marxist and when I went to China in 1971, Herbert said to me, 'If you meet Chou En-lai' – which wasn't very likely, I might add – 'remind him that we met at the Bournemouth Conference in 1926.' So that, as far as Herbert was concerned, they were both working for socialism, Chou En-lai in China and he in Bristol East. And he kept a friendly eye on it.

He was a difficult man. He hung onto the Secretaryship of the Party into his eighties and, when Dawn Primarolo replaced him, he was very angry. But he was a character and one of the last of the pioneers really, because there aren't any of that generation left.

The Government is in the most frightful mess because of news stories about Lamont. I think Major, who is loyal to his Ministers, will probably have to get rid of him in the end. It is all just seedy; the Government is giving the impression of being very seedy.

I went to the School of Oriental and African Studies for the Alternatives to Maastricht Conference, which had been organised by Tony Chater and Ken Livingstone.

I must say, Ken is very active. He has a column in the *Sun,* which he uses to finance his *Economic Bulletin* and his trips to America for the presidential election, and he has been to Russia twice this year. He is involved in the Anti-Racist Alliance and he is building up a movement on Europe, on socialism and on race. Tony Chater tries to keep the *Morning Star* alive, which is pleasing.

Saturday 5 December

I watched David Dimbleby interview Neil Kinnock in a forty-minute discussion about his leadership. He said that when he was elected he didn't believe in the policies of the Party (i.e. nuclear disarmament, hostility to the EEC) but that he couldn't go too quickly. I really thank God that man was never Prime Minister. He lost us the election by the way he ran the Party, but if anyone ever wanted proof of the failure of Neil Kinnock and the failure of the Labour Party under his leadership, they have only to get hold of that programme, and it's all there from his own mouth.

Sunday 6 December

The news today is that the Home Office apparently went through their files to find out whether Bill Clinton, as a student at Oxford, had ever applied for British nationality to avoid the draft in America. I have never heard of the Home Office agreeing to answer such questions, so they are obviously working hand-in-glove with Bush. Clinton won the election and this has absolutely ruined relations between Britain and America, though in order to calm it down, Clinton said he looked forward to close relations with Britain.

Tuesday 8 December

There were two bomb threats, at Victoria and Waterloo, so I went by taxi to Broadcasting House for the Acting Director General, John Birt's, Christmas party in the Council Chamber. Trollope would have had a marvellous opportunity to develop his thinking about the modern Church of England, which is the BBC. I only stayed about twenty minutes.

I saw Anna Ford; Brian Redhead of the BBC *Today* programme, who wants to come and see me after, for a programme on the history of the twentieth century; Roger Mosey of *The World This Weekend;* and Esther Rantzen, the Lord Chancellor, Paul Fox, Robin Day.

Thursday 10 December

Little Daniel, our youngest grandson, is a year old and we rang him up and sang, 'Happy birthday', though what he made of it, I will never know.

Caroline went to do some shopping and to James's nativity play in Southfields School where he was a shepherd and was very shy and waved at her.

The Edinburgh Summit tomorrow, under the British Presidency, is the big news. Also a lot of Tory MPs are objecting strongly to the arrangements for Princess Diana to become queen, even if she is separated from Prince Charles. The Establishment is split on this.

Sunday 13 December

Dashed to the BBC to do *Breakfast News*. There was an interviewer, a freelance who had been on TV AM, and the sound man and the cameraman were freelance. When we had finished, we had a talk about the way people were being reduced to total insecurity. The great gains of trade unionism – decent contracts of employment and so on – have all gone by the board. The wages are down, uncertainty is great and, of course, the profit is accruing to somebody else. In the case of the BBC, it just means the BBC doesn't have to increase the licence fee.

Monday 14 December
It was a pretty exciting day. The Prime Minister made his statement on Maastricht and I got in on the Referendum, but the Tories were all waving their Order Papers on the triumph of the British presidency. What actually happened was that Major agreed to more expenditure than he wanted and gave the Danes the opt-out they wanted in order to win their next referendum. My question was about the denial of the rights of the British people to a referendum, and the fact that Europe was going to be governed by a succession of edicts from a junta of European leaders.

Tuesday 15 December
I saw Michael Spicer, the Tory MP, in the House of Commons and he said he had just come back from Copenhagen, where tonight an opinion poll had said that 63 per cent were still against the Maastricht Treaty. Of course, if they force through the ratification in Britain before Denmark, then Denmark will vote yes. If Denmark has a say and Douglas Hurd announces that we will not go ahead without Denmark, then they might say no. Apparently, Major is very angry with Hurd for saying that he wouldn't go ahead without Denmark.

Wednesday 16 December
National Executive. Larry Whitty produced a great flip-chart and slides about the Party finances, saying we had to make repayments of £1.2 million this year, I think. There were only 200,000 members, of whom 43 per cent were low-subscription i.e. unemployed or pensioners.

To cut a long story short, they wanted to make a drastic reorganisation in headquarters and cut the regions from nine to six.

I can't go through the whole debate, except that there was a lot of anxiety expressed about the number of regions and about the way head office was being organised. Kinnock spoke quite a bit, and others who had vested interests – Tony Blair, representing the Northern Region. I said that everybody knew there was an acute financial crisis but it was also a political crisis for the Party. Membership income depended on political commitment and political commitment to the Party had declined steadily over the years. And, I said, the restoration of that commitment is our major task.

I said I thought the working party had come out with the wrong solutions – it was commercial. For example, Larry Whitty, in presenting his finance report, had identified which conferences were profitable instead of which conferences would increase political commitment to the Party.

They are like a herd of sheep really; they go whichever way they are told to go. And although there was some detailed anxiety expressed, there was no will to do anything about it. And as I was the only one who opposed the whole thing, I put a little note to the chair, saying, 'Please excuse me, I am speaking at a miners' rally away from London. If it is permitted, I should like to register my vote against the report.'

Thursday 17 December
To Reading to do another miners' meeting. There was a group there called Velvet Fist, who had come together about eleven years ago. They were all in their late thirties/early to mid-forties, a very radical group who had, I think, originally worked together with the Communist Party. They sang and then there were speeches. Hurried back to the station, and the Velvet Fist were coming back to London and they sang on the platform and people gathered round. Then we got in the compartment and they sang all the way to London, beautiful part-singing – it was absolutely exquisite.

It was so interesting. It was typically British – people listened but nobody said anything.

Saturday 19 December
Went to St Martin-in-the-Fields for the PLO Solidarity Committee demonstration against the expulsion of 400 members of the Hamas group in Israel, following the murder of one Israeli sergeant. To my surprise, there has been a huge outcry against Israel, and since this is the Rabin Government, of course the Labour Party is being very sympathetic, as it always has been to Israel and the Israeli Labour Party.

Sunday 20 December
I decorated the Christmas tree, tidied the office as best I could, and we took the grandchildren to a pizza parlour in Chiswick. The three boys were most entertaining.

Monday 21 December
The Danes phoned to say they want to use my Commonwealth of Europe Bill for the campaign against Maastricht, which was really pleasing, so I sent them some copies.

Tuesday 5 January 1993
The *Guardian* this morning had a poll that had been commissioned by the Labour Party on public attitudes to the Party, revealing that people felt it had no real identity and was untrustworthy and incoherent, and so on. So I rang up the *Guardian* and asked to write an article about it. They said, 'Yes, send it in tomorrow.'

A big oil tanker off the Shetlands is on the rocks and could lead to a major disaster.

Bernie Grant rang me up this afternoon and said that he was thinking of issuing a statement in support of Jesse Jackson in America, saying that the Americans should stay in Somalia.

I said, 'Bernie, be careful.'

'Well,' said Bernie, 'they're such corrupt regimes in Africa, it will have to have some law and order introduced. That's the obligation that blacks in America and Britain feel towards Africa.'

I said, 'Bernie, this is the beginning of imperialism.' I was really quite surprised.

And he said, 'Well, we'll have a further talk about it.'

Friday 8 January

Got up at six for an interview with Radio Sheffield on the Iraqi crisis. The Americans, British and French have given an ultimatum to Iraq that unless it remove its missiles from the no-fly zone, they will take military action.

Saddam is very boastful. Bush is aggressive, because he's just about to leave office. And the whole thing is a nightmare; as soon as something like that comes, the BBC switches on the war machine.

There's no recognition that there's a denial of civil rights in Kuwait; that the Palestinians have been thrown out; that the Saudi Government has been engaged in ethnic cleansing – they sent one million Yemenis back to the Yemen. Quite terrifying.

I left home and went to Chesterfield. Spent an hour and a half with the owner of a little firm called Derbyshire Textiles. He kept talking about 'his ladies' who worked in the textile factory, and what a priceless asset the ladies were. I talked to him for a bit and he had a sort of aide-memoire for the visit. He talked about imports, job losses, the North Derbyshire economy, the Training Enterprise Councils, inward investment, and so on.

Then I went across to Scarsdale Hospital for a sandwich lunch with the Chairman of the North Derbyshire Health Authority and the Chief Executive, and Harry Barnes, the Member for Derbyshire North East, and we talked about the future of the Health Service, about the trusts, about fund-holding, about patient complaints and waiting lists.

What I felt increasingly was that this was a return to a form of colonial administration where everything came down from the top; the Minister appointed the Health Authority, elected people have been removed from the Health Authority, and if you want to make a complaint there's nothing really you can do about it. So I was totally out of sympathy. Of course what they need is more funding.

I had my surgery; a lot of people came. What really annoyed me most of all were two people representing B & Q and Comet stores about Sunday shopping. They produced a great petition in favour. I said to them, 'What about the law that says you can't open?' They said that the law was out of date and they took no notice of the law. I said, 'What does your union think?'

'Oh, we don't recognise trade unions. You can be a member of a union, but you can't negotiate.'

'Well, what about pay?'

'Two pounds fifty an hour, but double time on Sunday, and everybody wants to work Sunday.'

I listened very carefully, but I was fairly sharp with them, I must confess.

At the end of my surgery I did an interview with the BBC about Iraq, and later that night they showed it on television. I had fourteen seconds. They'd sent five people from Leeds to do fourteen seconds with me, and I realised when I saw it what the plan was. They showed a picture of me with Saddam Hussein in 1990, then a huge mass of support for what the Americans wanted to do and said, 'But there are, of course, the usual voices of protest.' Then they showed me, extremely poorly lit and grim, simply saying that the Americans want to run the world and that it is a question of double standards, and bloodshed is not the answer.

I'm glad I said it, because at least people will know that not everybody agrees. But my God, the propaganda weapon is something when it is used.

Saturday 9 January
I'm very depressed at the moment. I think the swing to the right is so strong. There's all this revisionist talk at the moment based on John Charmley's book on Churchill, in which he says that Churchill should have signed a deal with Hitler and made peace in '41. Then two things would have happened: Hitler would have destroyed Russia and therefore communism would never have come to Western Europe or Eastern Europe, and, secondly, Britain would have been able to hold onto the Empire.

The argument now is whether it would have been advantageous to Britain's imperial interests and capitalist structures to have done a deal with Hitler and prevented any social progress at all after the war.

Wednesday 13 January
When I got to the House I found that the whole place was in uproar because of the news about the bombing of Iraq.

At ten o'clock a statement was made by Malcolm Rifkind in the House, and David Clark, our Front Bench spokesman on Defence, made such an odious speech associating the Opposition completely and entirely with what had been done. It was awful. But the backbenchers who spoke on our side were very good: Bernie Grant and Bob Cryer, who was called 'a friend and ally of Saddam', Jeremy Corbyn, Tam Dalyell, George Galloway,

Harry Cohen. When Rifkind called Bob Cryer a friend of Saddam, there was uproar and, truthfully, although it began as a total coalition approach, by the end there was just a great sense of uneasiness. I must say our Front Bench is absolutely hopeless.

Friday 15 January

I dashed into the Commons this morning and presented the petition for a referendum on Maastricht. Thousands and thousands of people have signed.

Sunday 17 January

I'm very tired, and I've got an ache in my back and I've got a cough, and altogether I'm finding things a bit difficult at the moment.

The *Sunday Mirror* and the *Sunday People* have printed the 'Camillagate' tapes which prove that the Prince of Wales and Camilla Parker-Bowles had a passionate affair and used to discuss it on their mobile phones, through which it was picked up. It arouses curiosity; you're bound to be curious about all these things. It's got absolutely nothing whatever to do with anything serious, but it keeps people's minds off the slump and unemployment.

Got to Trafalgar Square for the anti-Maastricht rally.There were about 1000 – perhaps 2000 – people there. Very small; nobody, fortunately, from the National Front. I must say it was a really weird experience. The organisers were standing there with sashes, like the Masons, and there was a merchant banker there who was wearing a city suit, a trilby hat and this thing round his neck. The whole thing reminded me completely of a Northern Ireland march by Protestant loyalists. I felt very embarrassed. There was William Cash; Teddy Taylor, who's a real populist; Richard Shepherd, whom I like. None of the Tory MPs had ever been on a march before. I'd been on a million such marches, but never with such an audience.

Peter Lewis, whom I fought in Chesterfield, is organising the thing. He gave me a funny handshake, which made me wonder whether he was a Mason. And on the platform was one Liberal Democrat who's against Maastricht, somebody from the Green Party, Tory MPs, Labour people like David Stoddart (Lord Stoddart of Swindon), Peter Shore, Austin Mitchell, Douglas Jay, who must be about eighty-seven – he was standing in the crowd, he didn't want to speak.

There were Union Jacks waving, and when Mrs Thatcher's statement was read out, they went almost hysterical. Teresa Gorman said, 'Welcome, fellow Britons.'

One BBC guy caught me and said, 'Isn't it funny to be campaigning with Teddy Taylor?'

And I said, 'I have campaigned for the referendum since 1968 and a lot of people have caught up with me.' But I felt uneasy.

Tuesday 19 January

One thing I forgot to mention yesterday is that the Home Affairs Select Committee, or some of the members, led by Sir Ivan Lawrence and including Chris Mullin, had asked to see Stella Rimington, the Head of MI5. She'd refused to give evidence to the Committee, but suggested they have lunch with her.

So, believe it or not, six MPs got into two cars and were driven to some building – probably the MI5 building in Mayfair – for lunch.

I thought that was the ultimate: the subservience of MPs, distinguished members of a committee that had the power to send for persons, papers and records, to an official who, at best, is only a Permanent Secretary. I thought it was outrageous.

The House of Commons isn't worth protecting, it isn't worth defending; it's just a fraud. I shall make some reference to that in some debate or another.

Wednesday 20 January

Today President Clinton, the forty-second President of the United States, was inaugurated and sworn in.

I must say, to see Bush go was one of the great pleasures of this year. Whether Clinton is going to be better, I don't know, but he gives the impression of youth and idealism and he's given American people hope.

Friday 22 January

I had a quick word with Chris about the Home Affairs report on the security services. I said to Chris, 'Well, what happened when you saw Stella Rimington?'

'Oh,' he said, 'we swore that we wouldn't say anything about it to anybody.'

So I said, 'So you've joined the Establishment now.' He looked a bit discomfited, but the point is that once you agree to receive information in secret, you are tied. That is the difficulty.

Anyway, the great news this afternoon was that Ray Powell's Bill, which restricts the opening of shops on a Sunday, was passed. It was an amazing vote: 240 to 40. It's a second great victory on the Sunday shopping laws.

Saturday 23 January

I went to Worcester today to speak for the Worcester Miners' Support Group. It was a long, boring journey via Oxford. On the train I had a friendly argument with the people on board, because the train from London to Oxford had no compartments for smokers. I think that's intolerable. So I said to the guard, 'I'm going to light my pipe.'

'Oh, no you're not,' he said with a friendly smile. 'Come in and we'll smoke in my compartment.'

So he took me into the driver's compartment and we had a chat. I really do feel somebody's got to take a stand on behalf of smokers. You should take no notice whatever of No Smoking notices unless somebody asks you not to smoke; and, if they do, then you put out your pipe or cigarette immediately. I think that's the principle that should be established.

On the train there was a man who looked rather German, and had a German accent and said he was a chemist. He was a smoker too, and said there was no proof that smoking had anything to do with lung cancer. He said that if you ask people what causes liver cancer, bladder cancer, stomach cancer, nobody knows, but with cancer of the lung then they just tell you it's smoking. I shouldn't really make a fight about this, but a certain libertarian instinct builds up in my mind.

Anyway, in Worcester I went to the hotel and they'd laid on a meal for me. Had a little press conference.

Came back on the last train; was a bit more courageous. With my fingernails I removed the No Smoking notice from the window and just sat there and smoked my pipe. The guard came by and didn't say a word.

Wednesday 27 January

At the National Executive John Smith said that the pit-closures campaign had been very successful, that unemployment had become a big issue, but, 'I must warn about the leakage of information, which is quite intolerable, and all the sniping that's going on. There are some parliamentary prima donnas, and higher standards are required.'

Well, it wasn't entirely clear to me at that stage who he was talking about.

Gordon Colling said trade union colleagues were angry; there had always been arguments about what sort of a party we had, but Clause 4 of the Labour Party Constitution, 'to secure for the workers by hand and by brain the full fruits of their industry' was there for a reason. The new technology was causing suffering; there was homelessness; sick pay was cut and manufacturing was one-fifth down. Modernisation would have to be debated, but he would not accept that we were going to be a different party and he wanted a more collective leadership.

By this time it was clear he was talking about Tony Blair and Gordon Brown, with all their modernisation stuff. Then Diana Jeuda echoed all this.

I said these were all very elliptical references but as a member of the NEC I was just a spectator of them, I didn't know what was going on at all. I read the poll results in January, which suggested that we weren't very popular, and I said that I wrote an article about it and hoped that wasn't what John Smith was referring to.

He began shaking his head vigorously.

I went on, 'What I'm afraid of is, whereas different leaders over the years have tried to move the Party in different directions, there's now an attempt to dismantle the Party, to weaken the links with the unions, to go for proportional representation, to have a Lib/Lab pact and be like American Democrats.'

Replying, John Smith said, 'This idea about "Clintonisation" is absurd. We've got to study experience from elsewhere. I hope this meeting will be kept secret, because we've got oppositionitis and there's a terrible danger.'

Then Robin Cook reported. 'We've got to make a cut of one-third in our expenditure and one-third in our workload; our forecast for this year is going to be £100,000 less income than we thought because the trade unions can't afford it. We'll have to consult about what contributions we get from MPs.'

I raised the question of the closure of the Party's library and said that we must be the only Socialist Party in the world that won't have a library. We were told that the costs and space didn't permit it and that we'd only be keeping three years of archives, and no books.

Saturday 30 January, Chesterfield

Had a long talk to Margaret Vallins. She thought the local party was moving to the right. One or two things were being said on my reselection. She also told me that last Monday she had been called out very early by a woman who was absolutely demented because the bailiffs were coming to evict her family from their house.

The background was that Mr X had been a piano tuner and had been very popular, but hadn't kept proper accounts and didn't charge very much. The VAT Office had in effect bankrupted him for non-payment of the tax they said he owed. His wife was doing all the accounts and she never told him of the trouble he was in.

His house is worth about £70,000 and his wife never even told him the bailiffs were coming. Margaret arrived with Father Flynn, the local Catholic priest, to see what was happening, and they found the locksmith already there to break in and change the lock, the bailiff standing by, and in the house Mr and Mrs X and her mother, who's ninety, just about to be thrown into the street.

So Margaret, who's a tough cookie, rang up the Housing Department and got another house allocated to them, which has three bedrooms. And she got the bailiffs to defer action, on the grounds that it would be a scandal if they evicted a ninety-year old woman.

Sunday 31 January

I went to Donald Soper's ninetieth birthday service at the West London Methodist Church.The church was packed to the doors. I found myself sitting next to Michael Foot, who said what a marvellous book Caroline had written about Keir Hardie – by far the best that had been written – how it gave such a perfect insight into the early days of the Labour movement.

I was really pleased about that. Apparently Ken Livingstone said that it was the book that had changed his life in 1992. Peter Brooke, the Heritage Secretary, was in the front row. Donald clambered slowly and painfully up the steps and then gave the most marvellous address about faith, hope and love; how faith had to be approached through the stepping stone of doubt and how hope was the most important thing in the generation of a desire for improvement; and how love spread and produced miracles.

It was marvellous. It was wise and his voice was clear and strong. He spoke without a note. He really is one of the great public speakers of our time.

Afterwards I had a word with Donald and met his wife Marie and his daughters. That man has kept alive a tradition of the improvement of mankind over so many years. It's really an inspiration; he offers much more to the public than any archbishop or cardinal in Britain, or any political leader.

In the evening Arthur Scargill rang me, boiling with anger that Dick Caborn and Michael Clapham had gone along with the Trade and Industry Select Committee Report on the coal industry, suggesting in effect that only sixteen pits should be saved. He told me that there would be a ballot for action on 5 March, involving the railway and mining unions, and that a day of action would take place. What I fear is that the Front Bench will support the Select Committee and therefore leave Arthur isolated, and then if Arthur has a ballot for industrial action they'll blame him, this time for *having* a ballot. In 1984–5 the Front Bench blamed him for not having a ballot. It's just an outrage and it looks as if the Tory MPs, like Elizabeth Peacock, are doing more than the Labour MPs.

Monday 8 February

I went into the Commons and looked up the second reading debate on the British Petroleum and Submarine Pipe-lines Bill of 1975, in which John Smith spoke. I found the most marvellous quotation from him which I photocopied and sent to him with a little note: 'Dear John, In memory of our happy time together.' I think that may just slightly alert him to the danger of this silly attack he has made on nationalisation. It's not going to get him a single vote.

At five o'clock I went to the Select Committee on Broadcasting, which was meeting to consider my request that I could use some of my parliamentary speeches in a video of speeches that I wanted to produce. This has never been done since Parliament was televised.

Tony Newton was in the chair, the MPs were Mark Lennox-Boyd, Sir Anthony Grant, Bruce Grocott, Matthew Taylor – it wasn't a very fully attended Committee.

I put my case, and Tony Grant, who's a nice old man, said, 'I've no objection at all. I think we can agree that that can be done.'

Tony Newton said, 'Oh, yes, there's general agreement.'

Then Bruce Grocott asked, 'What if you make a lot of money out of it – if there is a profit?'

'Well,' I said, 'You can make an arrangement, if you wanted to, for a share of the royalties, if there are any.'

Anyway I got clearance to go ahead and make the video and they will tell me exactly what the conditions are when it's done. Bruce Grocott told me that the Canadian Parliament actually has a little studio where Members can make videos and circulate them to their constituencies.

Later the BBC asked me to do a discussion with Peter Mandelson tonight on John Smith's speech. I said, 'I'm not going to have a cockfight to entertain your listeners. If you want to know what I think come and record one of my speeches.'

Thursday 11 February

A man from Videotron, the cable TV company, arrived to remove my cable system, which I have not paid for because it simply isn't worth it. He left the TV in a quite unusable state.

Friday 12 February

Ralph Miliband came for about an hour and a half today and we had a lovely talk.

He was saying how his sons, David and Edward, say to him, 'Oh, Dad, how would you do that? Would it work?What are your positive proposals?'

I said, 'Well, it's the same with my sons.'

He was very relieved to hear that. I think he thought he was very out of date.

Saturday 13 February, Chesterfield

A really big row is blowing up now about whether the Government might possibly ratify the Maastricht Treaty excluding the Social Chapter, even if Parliament voted for its inclusion.

This has caused a storm of protest for obvious reasons, because it would mean the Government using the Royal Prerogative to deny to Parliament its rights of legislation.

The idea put forward first was that the Government would ratify the Treaty in the form in which it was signed, which would mean bypassing Parliament. Then this caused such a sense of outrage that now Number 10 is backtracking.

The longer this Maastricht business goes on and the deeper the economic crisis becomes, and the greater the risk of a trade war with America and the growth of hostility to the whole business, the more it looks as if the Treaty might actually be defeated. Of course, far from solving our problems, it would put the responsibility for solving them back on this country, with a Government party and an Opposition party who haven't got two ideas to rub together as to how.

Monday 15 February
Incredibly, the *Guardian* had a leading article endorsing my view that the Royal Prerogative should not be used to ratify the Maastricht Treaty if Parliament votes an amendment to it to include the Social Chapter.

I went to the House of Commons, having discovered that there was to be a statement on the Maastricht Treaty and the Royal Prerogative as a means of ratifying it; Douglas Hurd did a complete U-turn and said that the vote on the Social Chapter amendment would not affect ratification.

Thursday 18 February
A most terrible day because of Caroline's accident, but I'll go through it consecutively.

I left at ten o'clock to go to Bristol for Celia Roach's funeral at the Lord Mayor's Chapel. When I got back to London I went straight to the Commons and had a meeting with the National Union of Students Gay Lobby. I came home, having looked in on the TUC Lobby on unemployment at the Commons, where there were about twenty people At 5.35, not that I knew it at the time, Caroline was driving her car to Stansgate for the weekend, came out of a road between Latchingdon and Cold Norton and was struck at about 50 mph on the driver's-seat side and the car was driven right across the road, knocking down the sign-post the other side. It was an absolute miracle she wasn't killed.

I went off to Charing Cross Hospital to talk at a demonstration, came back and at ten past eight the phone rang and somebody asked if my secretary was there. I said, 'No, why?' She said, 'It doesn't matter.' I asked, 'What's it about?' She said, 'Well, it's about a Caroline Benn.' I said, 'What is it?' The voice said, 'She's in Broomfield Accident Hospital in Chelmsford.' So I said, 'What's wrong.' She said, 'We don't know, she's been injured.'

I jumped in my car, left at 8.25, got to Chelmsford in an hour and twenty minutes, which must have been at an enormous speed, went to the Accident & Emergency Department and went to the little cubicle, but Caroline wasn't there. Her clothes were on the floor.

I waited, then in came the doctor, with Caroline lying flat on her back on a trolley with a collar, white as a sheet, complaining of acute pain and cold. I thought she was nearly dead. I felt her toes and hands, which she could feel.

Then the Senior Houseman for Orthopaedics and a man who was only about three years younger than Joshua, who was the Senior Registrar in Orthopaedics, came down. He examined her very carefully: she's badly bruised in the ribs, she's broken the pubic bone, but she hasn't broken the pelvic girdle, her hips aren't broken. Her hand is bruised.

Anyway they gave her a pain-killing injection and she sat up a bit, and I stayed till about midnight. Then they put her in a ward and about midnight I left for Stansgate, got there in about an hour, bitterly cold. It's amazing that woman is alive. I can tell you I had deferred shock.

Friday 19 February

I drove to Maldon to the car repair place and looked at Caroline's car, a little Rover Metro she'd bought just before Christmas.

The damage was unbelievable: the windscreen had popped out; the whole roof was cracked, as if it had sort of been bent like a banana; the full impact of the car had been on the driver's seat; a plastic bottle of milk had broken all over her head; a marmalade jar was broken in the back. The impact must have been horrific.

I drove into Chelmsford again, picked up Stephen and Lissie and took them to see Caroline. By this time she was sitting up, saying, 'I want this done, I want stamped envelopes, will you cancel my class', and so on!

I cancelled all my engagements over the weekend.

Sunday 21 February

Had a talk to Caroline, who's still in a bit of discomfort and she's got a bit of a fever, which implies there may be some internal bleeding. And she's full of aches and pains, but she's alive. The police have interviewed her and I think possibly she'll be charged with driving without due care and attention, but she's alive.

Wednesday 24 February

First engagement today was the National Executive Committee at ten o'clock.

In the Leader's report, item six on the Executive, Smith said the political situation was interesting because unemployment and crime are now being linked and we must exploit this as hard as we can.

Tony Blair's contributions were very good; he has come out with the line that Labour would be tough on crime and tough on the causes of crime.

I made a few points. I said, 'Every time you open the paper there's some new statement made by somebody. One Shadow Cabinet Member says we should drop Clause 4; there's a paper called *Renewal* with three members of the National Executive on the Advisory Board, with an article in it called the "Union Link, the Case for Friendly Divorce". You yourself, John, made a statement on public ownership and there have been other statements that can only be interpreted as meaning Labour supports US type Workfare policy. A political party is a cultural entity, and you can't win by repudiation of everything you believe in. I make the point and leave it.'

Somebody else asked about the Wages Council, and someone asked about Harry Barnes's Bill. And Smith replied to those two points, but he didn't comment on mine.

Sunday 28 February, Stansgate

Snow in the garden, and we heard the little children playing in the snow making a snowman. As usual on a Sunday, I took James and William and Jonathan to buy newspapers and some sweets.

Monday 1 March

Caroline has given up half her painkillers and is doing exercises and is much, much better, but her bruises are still bad.

Had an invitation from Copenhagen to go there this weekend to try and influence the People's Socialist Party to oppose Maastricht, but I can't do it.

I did some laundry today, took Caroline her meals – it's nice to see her in bed at home. Within a week she'll probably be walking a bit. The only problem is there are some days I'm going to have to be away, so I've got to arrange meals so that she can eat them whenever she feels like it.

It's a period of refreshment and rest really, and apart from three three-line whips this week, which I shall treat very loosely, and a visit to Chesterfield at the weekend, life is not pressing me too hard, apart from the book on the Constitution to do by the end of the month, the film to make for Yorkshire Television, the BBC Diary Programmes to do.

Tuesday 2 March

In the afternoon I went to meet Jeremy Corbyn about this World Appeal to leaders all over the world, to interest them in an appeal relating to peace and war, development, human rights and poverty, and I was charged with writing the letters.

Thursday 4 March

To the Commons for a meal, and sat in the Tea Room talking to Jimmy Hood and Jimmy Wray and Malcolm Chisholm. They say Smith is cutting up very rough with any Scottish front bencher who disagrees with him about public ownership.

We all agreed really that the sell-out had been on a massive scale. The question is: what do we do about it?

I'd been called back in for a ten o'clock vote, but there wasn't one and what a fraud this whole Maastricht debate is, because the Opposition want the Bill to go through. They say they'd like the Social Chapter in, but they don't really care. The Government's in increasing difficulty with its own back benchers, Major is attacking Thatcher retrospectively; and we could get the Tories out if we wanted to, but we don't want to.

Anyway, got home about 10.30 and massaged Caroline's back as usual.

Sunday 7 March

It's lovely to be able to do a proper job for Caroline, but housework is so boring. I've let her carry the burden for years. Doing the laundry and the washing, and the cooking and such cleaning as there is, is a huge burden.

I dare say incapacity will happen to me one day, and then we shall simply have to slow down and gradually live our lives out, enjoying our grandchildren. There are moments in life when you see a turning point and this is one of them.

Monday 8 March

I spoke to Bill Cash this evening and he said the referendum campaign was going well. Last Saturday the *Sun* printed my petition, so four million people will see that, and they'll be pouring in. It all begins to look a bit less happy for the Government and, with extreme right gains on the Frankfurt city council, the rise of fascism in Europe is becoming a bit more evident. It is all a very worrying time.

Tuesday 9 March

In the evening I redrafted and typed out twenty-five letters to world leaders, people like Mandela, Jimmy Carter, Trudeau, Nyerere, and so on. It might come to something.

Friday 12 March, Scottish Labour Conference, Inverness

It was a beautiful spring day, couldn't have been lovelier. In London the daffodils and crocuses were out, the blossom was out, and the weather was the same in Inverness. It was lovely. The atmosphere in Scotland is completely different from that in England. The Timex workers are on strike in Dundee; there's to be a day of action at the Albion shipyard on the Clyde; there's just a flavour of the old radicalism.

Alex Falconer walked with me over to the Station Hotel to the meeting of the Council of Non-Nuclear Authorities, then to the Campaign Group meeting – I was in Inverness for only four hours and fifty minutes, but I think it was worth doing.

On the train home I was sitting having a cup of tea when a young woman came up to me and said she'd like a word. She was a project manager with the Post Office, had been at Nottingham University and was reorganising their redirection service. She was twenty-five and I asked her how much she was paid. 'Twenty-five thousand pounds'. That's astonishing! As we sat there, a man came up and said 'You won't remember me' (I knew his face). 'I'm the father of William Whyte' – who was a very bright young lad who came for work experience in the office when he was fourteen.

I had ten hours sleep, in my bunk, it was absolutely marvellous.

Saturday 13 March

Luciana Castellana, who is a Member of the European Parliament, came to see me. She is a very interesting woman. She must be older than me, but her hair is dyed red and she was in the Communist Party, then in the Gingerbread group of the CP; now she is in the Reformed Communist Party. She told me in great detail what is happening in Italy where there is of course total chaos. She said the corruption between political leaders and industrialists had gone on for years, because the same Government had been in power for so long that the party and State were identical. She agreed that it was a bit like the situation under Brezhnev in Russia.

Luciana described what the capitalist establishment had done as 'subversion from above', a phrase of Gramsci's. Anyway, the judges had got to work and there were now hundreds of industrialists in prison, including the number three at Fiat.

But because Members of Parliament were covered by immunity, they couldn't be arrested. The anger and cynicism had grown. So then they said: we need a new, more stable system of voting, the British first-past-the-post system, instead of PR.

She said Maastricht is an attempt to impose on the whole of Europe what the German Bundesbank has imposed on the DDR, the former East Germany. The gap between East and West was wider now than when the Wall was up. She was also very worried about the nationalism of Europe, the terrible Euro-centrism.

She'd been here about forty-five minutes when the front doorbell rang and a policeman asked, 'May I have a word with you. We have found fifty bullets on the wall by your front gate.' I went out there, and there were fifty or more: a great pile of loose .22-millimetre ammunition shells! He said, 'The nuns in the convent next door saw them and called us.'

I said 'Can I have one as a memento?' I picked it up and I've glued it to my Notes for the day. It was mysterious and very disturbing. Later the police came back and asked for permission to search my garden, which I readily gave them, but they didn't find anything. I said, 'I hope I don't read in the paper that a cache of arms has been found at my house!'

Tuesday 16 March

Budget today. I haven't attended a Budget for years. They are the most boring parliamentary occasions and so predictable. John Smith said it was a cynical betrayal that the Tories had raised taxes when they said they wouldn't; but we said we would raise them and now we say they shouldn't. The whole thing is just a vacuum filled with scandal and abuse.

Thursday 18 March

Alice Prochaska, who is in charge of Special Collections at the British Library, came along to talk about Sean Arnold's report on the archives.

What she had to offer was accommodation for some of my papers, either at the Woolwich Arsenal or up in Boston in Yorkshire. I said that what I really would like to do is raise some cash from foundations to get the papers indexed. She said, 'You couldn't do that unless you virtually promised to give them to us.' Well, I'd be happy to do that.

John Birt, the Director General of the BBC, has apparently been found to have a private tax arrangement under which he set up a company and was on contract to the BBC, employing his wife and claiming 'wardrobe' expenses. He was forced to abandon the arrangement and then that focused attention on the Board of Governors. Today they unanimously supported him although they said it was a mistake. It has done tremendous damage to the BBC and to the Board of Governors as a whole.

Sunday 21 March

BBC *Breakfast* rang me and asked if I would like to be interviewed tomorrow morning because Jack Straw is publishing a pamphlet calling for the abandonment of Clause 4, and would I comment? It is typical that at this particular moment he should choose to court popularity from the right-wing press and the Liberals, but nobody actually takes Jack Straw seriously. He is just a little sort of weathercock blowing with every wind.

Wednesday 24 March

Had a letter from Alice Prochaska at the British Library saying that the archives were the best collection ever made by any British politician and offering to take them, so I have decided to do that.

Thursday 25 March

The statement on coal was made in the afternoon by Heseltine, who, having been backed into a corner, decided to devote a great deal of his speech to attacking me for pit closures when I was Energy Minister and for having authorised the Interconnector with France, through which a lot of French nuclear electricity is imported. I got in and said he was trying to mislead the House by suggesting that the Interconnector had been set up for diversity of supply, whereas it was for the export of British coal to France, by wire.

Wednesday 31 March

National Executive Committee was the first meeting today. We came to two emergency resolutions, one on the miners which deplored the pit closures, and I moved that we add 'and supports the action to be taken on 2 April following a ballot of NUM members'. Joan Lestor seconded. Robin Cook said, 'We understand their frustration, but it won't help to put that in the resolution.' Kinnock asked, 'Would it advance our ability to help the miners? It would paint us into a corner.' This is the man who ten years ago said he couldn't support the miners because they *hadn't* had a ballot. Anyway, to avoid the miners being defeated by the Executive, I withdrew the motion. When we came to railways, there was a resolution denouncing privatisation but simply saying, 'We reaffirm our commitment to a modern, safe and reliable system', so I added 'in public ownership'.

Prescott said, 'It is a complex matter, you can't support every strike.' Well, this wasn't about a strike.

Thursday 1 April

One thing I must report, that over the last few days the phone has been very funny. If I dial a number, I'm immediately cut off and a voice says 'Don't redial' and I get reconnected instantly. I get a lot of dead calls, where the phone rings and nobody is there. It does occur to me that as I'm going to Ireland over the weekend the security services might be beginning to take an interest in me and have started bugging me.

Friday 2 April

Went to the dentist at ten o'clock, and she glued a crown that had fallen out and said she was still on the NHS; that's something.

Caroline had made a lovely birthday crown out of a Hansard, and gave me a power pack that will allow me to restart my car if I leave the lights on, and some clothes.

At about ten past two I went to Heathrow for the flight to Dublin. Quite a comfortable flight. Taken to the RTE studios, for Kenny Live. In the car was Pattie Hearst, the granddaughter of William Randolph Hearst, who was jailed for seven years for a bank robbery, which she claimed she was forced to do because she was kidnapped; and her husband, a man called Bernard Shaw, a former inspector of police who is her bodyguard.

Helen Shapiro was on the programme first, then there was a priest with the mother of his child, who said they were reconciled; and at the end Pattie Hearst.

The interview with Kenny was very good – it covered a whole range of areas and the audience was very sympathetic. I didn't stay afterwards, I was so tired, but I did have a word with Helen Shapiro; she's a Messianic Jew who believes that Jesus was the Messiah, and they're not very popular either with the Jews or with the Council of Christians and Jews, or with the Christians. It is a very interesting position.

Thursday 8 April, Stansgate
Melissa arrived by train from London and we heard the fantastic news that she is expecting a baby in November.

Funnily enough, I'd said to Caroline only last night, 'I doubt if she'll ever have a child.' She said, 'Oh, I don't know.'

Stephen, Nita, Emily and Daniel arrived overnight. We're all so excited about the news.

Wednesday 14 April
Simon Fletcher had asked me to go and do a meeting for him up in North London where he is standing for the council, but he rang today to say that Frank Dobson, the local MP, had vetoed my visit.

Sunday 18 April
The *Independent on Sunday* quoted a lot of people on whether we should support intervention in Bosnia, including my comment that 'The UN can't make war, sell arms and make peace at the same time;' it read reasonably well.

If there is conflict there and the West is involved, it would be the first war hysteria created by the media without actually the full support of the government of the day. John Smith made a speech yesterday in which he came out strongly for military force. Of course, that is because Clinton has indicated it and the Labour leadership does whatever America wants.

Thursday 22 April
The former Italian Prime Minister, Andreotti, has been accused of Mafia links.* Italy has had a big referendum in favour of first-past-the-post. Caroline told me today that a poll of Liberals about electoral pacts showed 35 per cent wanting to join with Labour, 47 per cent with the Tories, so the whole basis of politics is dying.

Democracy is dying. I don't think young people look at Parliament as offering a choice. Older people know what is happening, but I think younger people just regard us all as part of the Government which, in a way, we are. The Shadow Cabinet have got the jobs, they get on the telly every now and again, they are well paid, they don't want to be disturbed. We are a defeatist nation, with a careerist political class ready to integrate itself with a Europe that will be run by bankers and Commissioners, and of course it will be a disaster.

Hilary had an interview today for Head of the Research Department at the Labour Party. His CV is fabulous and his presentation brilliant. He

*He was acquitted of association with the Mafia in 1999.

was treated with great respect by Joan Lestor, Tom Sawyer, Tony Clark and Larry Whitty. If it weren't for me, I think he'd get the job, but I don't think they want a Benn at Walworth Road. That is the real obstacle, so to that extent I am a barrier to the advancement of my own children.

Friday 23 April, Denmark

Up at four and off to Heathrow, where I caught SK500 to Copenhagen for this Red-Green International Conference against the Maastricht Treaty.

Who should be on the plane but Tristan Garel-Jones, who is the Minister responsible for pushing the Maastricht Treaty through the House of Commons. I had a jolly exchange with him and he offered me a lift into Copenhagen.

He said he was going to give up and be one of those very rare animals – a backbencher utterly loyal to the Government – and he would expose those Ministers who were less than loyal. I presume this was an attack on the remaining Thatcherites in the Cabinet. Garel-Jones is a very tough cookie, has been in the Tory Whips' Office and so on, but is jolly and agreeable to talk to and passionately committed to Europe. Apparently he lived for a time in France and Spain and said his grandmother, I think, was French. These things, rather than the more mundane political agreements, often explain people's attitudes.

There were four or five people on the platform, most of whose names I never got. When you are a Minister, somebody gets names and addresses for you, but there is nobody to do that now. One of the Greens had known Petra Kelly and Gert Bastian well, and I asked what happened. She said that Petra had been seriously ill and Gert wasn't very well, and they had indicated some time before that they thought their political work had ended; and that, presumably by agreement, Gert had shot her and then shot himself.

Saturday 24 April

It was a beautiful day and I went up and down a shopping area. Saw the changing of the guard. These Danish soldiers look exactly like the soldiers at Buckingham Palace, only they are in blue and look more like toy soldiers. There was one standing outside the palace, and three little children aged about three, four and five were talking to him.

Denmark was an empire, but now Queen Margrethe is a purely nominal queen and typical of what is called the 'cycling monarchs'.

You always see things in a different perspective abroad and everybody now is talking about networking. It is also clear that the leaders of the Labour and Social Democratic movements have joined the Establishment. They have policy committees, royal commissions, Shadow Ministers. They have abandoned representation; they are just part of the government – only not officially. There is a Shadow government and there will be Shadow Commissioners next.

Monday 26 April

Ibrahim, the Iraqi Minister who has been forced to work out of the Jordanian Embassy, came to see me with a letter from the Iraqi Minister of Health. He had brought the wrong letter and he was very embarrassed, so we had a chat and he went off. Later the proper letter arrived, with some horrific figures on mortality in Iraq since the bombing.

Tuesday 27 April

There was a huge IRA bomb in Bishopsgate over the weekend, which killed one *News of the World* reporter who had been tipped off and was going there to see the bomb go off. The estimate is that £1 billion worth of damage has been done.

The other big news is the Russian referendum result, held a couple of days ago, and it looks as if Yeltsin has won. The press coverage is totally biased and unfair. Yeltsin is presented as a great democrat and reformer; everyone who is opposed to him, because they are suffering brutally under his regime with the Mafia in charge, is denounced as a hard-line communist.

On Bosnia, there is a big build-up for military action after Mrs Thatcher's speech, which was widely denounced. Smith has come out for bombing. The Americans are thinking about it and will be announcing something soon. It looks as if the Muslims will be armed and Serbia will be bombed. Russia's view on this is uncertain, but the referendum is out of the way. Now UN action is pushed into the background and it is NATO action; and, of course, it is really the Germans.

Wednesday 28 April

I faxed an emergency resolution about Bosnia to Larry Whitty for today's Executive.

We discussed Standing Orders for the European Parliamentary Labour Party, the future of the BBC, and then I moved my motion on the war in Bosnia. The drift of it was that we should concentrate on humanitarian aid and not agree to air strikes. I pointed out the history of the matter and the danger.

It was seconded by Joan Lestor, and then Kinnock opposed it because he said it excluded the use of force. The German recognition of Croatia was wrong. What should we do? Could we stand back and let hundreds of thousands of people die? We should get UN support for air strikes, enforce the arms embargo, which would require military action on the frontiers, enforce sanctions, not arm the Bosnians. He recognised that there were no clear surgical air strikes; civilians would die.

I was defeated, with only me, Joan Lestor and Dan Duffy voting for my motion.

Monday 3 May, Chesterfield

We had breakfast and the grandchildren played football in the car park of the Labour Club.

Went to the Town Hall. It was a huge May Day march, Caroline couldn't walk on the march, so she went in the pensioners' bus. People had come from all over – the West Country, Scotland, Manchester; the Chesterfield Labour movement is a great movement. Rodney Bickerstaffe and his wife were there; Anne Scargill and Betty Heathfield, and lots of mates. All together, it was a really good day.

We came home on the train and fortunately there were only two people in the whole compartment, because the kids were just like a lot of monkeys, jumping about, firing their pistols, climbing in the luggage racks. At my age, it is just a bit much. I never understood as a child why people used to tell us to be quiet, but I am now in that position. Of course, the experience of life is to discover that, at every age, you go through every experience that everyone of the same age goes through and come to the same conclusions.

Tuesday 4 May

In the Tea Room, John Hume, the SDLP MP, sat down next to me and I said, 'I am so glad you are talking to Gerry Adams, because I have always felt that he had no more control over the IRA than the Sarejevo Serbs had on the situation in Bosnia.'

He said, 'I am not so sure about that.' Then he turned against David Owen. 'Once Owen said to me about Northern Ireland, "We should close off the frontier and send in the army and clear them up." He doesn't understand anything.' John said that the war costs about one billion pounds a year.

I asked, 'Do you think there is any chance of the British Government abandoning its claim to Northern Ireland, and the Republic abandoning their claim to Northern Ireland, and getting somewhere together?'

He said, 'Well, maybe. Anyway we all live within the Common Market now. There is no national sovereignty. The nation state is out of date,' and so on. John is a great European.

It's the first time he's spoken to me for ages because he was so angry when I voted against the Anglo-Irish Agreement.

I saw John Reid later, who used to be in Kinnock's Private Office, a very right-wing Scottish Member. He had just come back from Yugoslavia. He said, 'It is incredible. The Americans have got a strategy of their own. They think Russia is going to break up and they want to destroy Serbia, because they couldn't rely on Serbia in the event of the break-up of Russia.'

I think that is actually the truth. Cuba, Libya, North Korea, Iraq and Serbia are the new enemies, and Iran is quickly joining it, and America intends to use its power as best it can. And, of course, Germany wants to extend its role down the Danube and over the whole of Europe. Incredible.

Wednesday 5 May

Went to hear Nelson Mandela's questions and answers in the Grand Committee Room. Lady Olga Maitland asked about his relations with Chief Buthelezi of Inkatha.

I introduced myself and asked a question. 'We saw, and see, the ending of apartheid as the final victory of the liberation movement. I want to ask you about your view of the United Nations, because it seems to me that the gap between the rich and poor countries is widening, the arms trade is flourishing, human rights everywhere are denied, and I would like know how you see the UN developing, as the industrialised countries in the North appear to be dominating the world again.'

Mandela said he thought the UN was very important; it needed more resources, it could help in Africa and Africa would try to help the UN. It was a perfectly fair answer.

Afterwards, I went up and shook him by the hand. He was very strong and slim and looked fit. He must be seventy-five now. He had a strong voice, a clear head, a good use of language. Very impressive, and the place was absolutely packed out.

I waited in the Division Lobby, hoping I might hear from Joan Lestor or John Smith what had happened about Hilary's application. Smith came out and scuttled past me with Jack Straw, so I knew Hilary hadn't got it. At the next vote, Joan Lestor came out and I clutched her and said, 'Tell me what happened.'

She took me round the corner and said, 'Hilary did very well. Tom Sawyer voted for him, Tom Burlison was very impressed, but Smith had his own candidate, Roland Wales, from the Bank of England. And once Smith had indicated quite clearly that he wanted this man, everyone went along with it.'

I said, 'I never thought Hilary would get it anyway.'

She said, 'He was very good indeed.'

Joan said she thought Smith was angry with her for voting for Hilary, and for voting against him on Bosnia. It is the second time I have heard this from what you might call the genuine soft left.

Friday 7 May

Did my surgery, starting at 9.15, and then just after ten Margaret Vallins came in and said there was a fire in Littlewoods store in the Market Square, so I went straight down there.

There was smoke billowing out of Littlewoods. They had just removed some people who had climbed out of a window onto a ledge, and there were about ten ambulances, fire appliances, the police, a couple of soldiers. Of course, my first thought – and that of others – was: is this a terrorist attack?

I talked to a Chief Inspector, and the Chief Fire Officer allowed me through and I heard that two old-age pensioners had died, overcome with smoke, and their bodies were brought out.

I went to the United Reformed Church, where the staff from the store had gone, and there were people from the social services there and from the store, the WRVS providing tea, five vicars comforting the staff – every one of the staff had got out safely. The people from the NatWest bank were standing in the car park and I talked to them. But what was really impressive was the way in which the public services responded to an emergency.

At two, Tom drove me to a police press conference. I went into the Chief Superintendent's office and saw the Deputy Chief Constable, who was pretty aggressive. I said, 'Did you get any advance warning?'

He said, 'What are you suggesting? Are you suggesting it was a terrorist attack?'

'No, but people wonder.'

He said, 'There is nothing in it at all.'

I said, 'Well, thank you very much.'

Heard later that it was a fire caused by an electrical fault and the shop had no sprinkler.

At the end he snapped, 'It's a great thing to have *you* in the police headquarters.'

I said, 'Well, I had some differences with you at the time of the miners' strike because I didn't think you should have acted as agents for the Government, though I suppose, in a year or two, Group 4 will be doing all this anyway.' He didn't like that.

I went into the press conference in a tiny room with about three television cameras and about fifty journalists; all the hacks had turned up thinking it was a terrorist attack.

The Chief Superintendent gave a very good account of what had happened.

Monday 10 May

Went to the new Policy Committee, where we had a constitutional reform paper produced by Tony Blair. It was very weak. It talked about the Royal Prerogative, treaty-making and war, but not about patronage; said we should only get rid of the hereditary peers in the Lords, but not the life peers. It said nothing about a lot of things.

I had a word with Ian Paisley and said, 'Why don't you do a deal with Dublin?'

He said, 'Never! Never!'

'Well, what I am suggesting is, if they give up their claim to the North, Britain would give up its claim to the North; then you would be independent. You should think about it, because a lot of people in Northern Ireland would like to be independent.'

'Not many,' he said.

I replied, 'Well when I look at you, I can see Ian Smith trying to get out. UDI.' He laughed, but I think I might have registered.

Tuesday 11 May

I went to see my professor at Charing Cross Hospital and my leukaemia is stable. He said, 'You won't need treatment for six or eight years by which time things may be better.'

It is a funny thing going to see your doctor because it is a warning of your death. You wonder when the parallel lines will meet at infinity. He was very cheerful and said that the chief consultant at St Thomas' had been onto him (indeed, he rang while I was there), saying there was a bit too much potassium in my blood. Were my kidneys working properly? He asked about my prostate. I think these are all associated complaints. But if I live until seventy-five which is another seven years, I can't complain.

Wednesday 12 May

Big story in the *Sun* today that the security services had bugged Prince Charles and Princess Diana at Highgrove. The Home Secretary said there wasn't a word of truth in it. But then he doesn't know what's going on; the Prime Minister doesn't know what's going on. Stella Rimington, the head of MI5, would be unlikely to know what's going on. If the question of lifelong confidentiality to the Crown means anything, you would think it would apply to the Crown personally or to the heir to the throne.

Friday 14 May

Up early and caught the eight o'clock to Chesterfield and was driven to Barnsley for the mayoral dinner. God knows why I agreed to go, because I won't go to the mayoral dinner in Chesterfield, but Mick Clapham asked me and Barnsley is friendly. In the Mayor's parlour were nothing but pictures of every royal visit to Barnsley over the last forty years – George VI, Queen Elizabeth, Prince Charles, and so on – and lots of plaques about the Yorkshire Regiment and the Parachute Regiment.

The new Mayor had asked me to come. He and his wife are hairdressers from Worsbrough, which is where Arthur lives.

There were 220 people and it was a five-course meal, which went on from 7.30 to eleven with soup, fish, sorbet, main course, and I can't remember the other courses. There were toasts to the Queen, to the Mayor, reply by the Mayor, then I moved the toast to the Barnsley Borough. I decided that I would try and make a serious speech, but also with a bit of humour in it. I got a standing ovation, which I must say did surprise me at a dinner. I am glad I went because it persuaded me that you cannot make social progress while Labour people are content just to be elevated.

Sunday 16 May
Late lie-in. Read the papers. The *Sunday Mirror* had the first extract of a book by somebody called Lady Colin Campbell, saying the Queen's marriage to Prince Philip had been completely loveless for the last forty years.

Came home and *Spitting Image* is back on television. It doesn't mention the Labour Party now. There is nothing to say about the Labour Party – the whole of British politics is completely stagnant. It is all about scandal, the Government, the royal family, but there is no opposition at all. There is hardly anything about the Labour Party now. The media is all about getting rid of the block vote, proportional representation and doing a pact with the Liberals. It is SDP talk twelve years late.

Wednesday 19 May
John Smith gave the Leader's report to the NEC. He said, 'I want to talk about the relationship between the trade unions and the Party. I am in favour of One Member One Vote.' A campaign was needed; the £18 membership fee was too high; we should reduce it and review the twelve-month rule (people have to be members for twelve months before voting in Labour Party ballots); trade union members should have full membership at a reduced rate.

Blunkett said something, and I said that I was grateful to John for making a statement on which we can actually have a discussion. Membership is not about money, it is about commitment, and many old members in the Party, not particularly on the left, don't know what the Party stands for any more. The Party has existed for ninety-six years; I have been a member of it for fifty, half its life, and on the Executive for thirty-two years, which is one-third of its life. I think, candidly, what is happening is that the Party is being dismantled. The trade union link is to be broken; the economic policy statement we are considering today makes no reference to the trade unions. Clause 4 is being attacked; PR is being advocated with a view to a pact with the Liberals of a kind that Peter Mandelson worked for in Newbury, where he in fact encouraged the Liberal vote. The policy work has been subcontracted. These so-called modernisers are really Victorian Liberals, who believe in market forces, don't like the trade unions and are anti-socialist. The Party needs to be rebuilt by putting it back to local control, as it was before 1918.

I was listened to in silence. Whether anyone took my comments on board, I don't know.

Gordon Brown said, 'The principle is right. Trade union members should join the Labour Party. A lower fee would be right. We should ask the trade unions and the Labour Party to attract members and the whole NEC should support this.'

Blair said he agreed with Smith. This would strengthen our links with the trade unions.

Gordon Colling said, 'Trade union consent is necessary to secure this change and I am not sure you can get it.'

Clare Short welcomed the discussion. She said, 'The next election is a watershed. If we don't win next time, we will never win again.' There was no respect, however, by John Smith for the work that had been done by the working party; the membership was shrinking and was unrepresentative. She was fed up with all the insults to the trade unions. Older members were disillusioned. Then she said, 'In Max Madden's constituency in Bradford, when it was announced that he was going, the membership leapt from two hundred to one thousand, as people in ethnic communities just bought members in order to influence the selection. You could get serious corruption via OMOV.'

We came to the second major debate, which was on electoral reform. Whitty said, 'We have agreed to send out the Plant Report* and ask for comments by July.'

At 11.58 Lord Plant spoke. He thanked the working party. He said this had all been triggered by a Party Conference decision; we have got to look at electoral systems and he had made three reports. But of course the decisions were matters of political judgement and not technical decisions. He said, 'We need political pluralism in our electoral system and in the House of Commons, and PR in the second chamber would challenge the Commons, if the Commons didn't have it. I was sceptical when I started.' But he had come to the conclusion that socialism and electoral reform were interconnected.

I asked whether Lord Plant would comment on the 103 seats that were won by Labour with less than 50 per cent and what would happen if we had had his scheme.

He said, 'Well, you can't assume anything.'

Then Smith made another statement, which, again, was all written out. He said, 'The House of Commons should be left as it is.' He was not in favour of the additional member system, didn't want coalitions and was unconvinced by the supplementary vote.

At 12.50 we adjourned for lunch and I had a talk to Smith, who was very friendly and said he thought we'd win the next election. I get on well with John Smith, but he is a very right-wing figure.

*Professor Raymond Plant, professor of Politics at Southampton University 1979-94.

Thursday 20 May

Went to the Commons and met about sixty women from the pit camps at Houghton Main, Grimethorpe and Armthorpe. Dennis brought them in out of the rain and I took them to the policemen's cafeteria in Westminster Hall – quite against the rules. They had been at the court this morning for the hearing about the legality of pit closures.

Afterwards they went out and put up their banner outside St Stephen's entrance and sang 'Women of the Working Class'. The police were nodding and winking and something is happening. I don't know quite how to describe it. The women were so sweet and so courageous.

Went to the House for the third reading of the Maastricht (European Communities) Amendment Bill, opened by Douglas Hurd in his smooth, diplomatic way saying that federalism was dead.

He was followed by Jack Cunningham, who made an awful speech entirely without content, just point-scoring when the Opposition want the Bill to go through, and he announced that we would abstain.

Heath made a very trenchant speech. I was called quite early in the 10-minute limit section and spoke for nine-and-a-half minutes, and I felt it was the moment to let myself go. For the first time ever I hadn't prepared a note. I simply stood up and spoke my mind and my heart – very strong stuff – and the Tories liked it very much because I attacked the Labour Party and said they had given up everything they had ever believed in. Our Front Bench looked uncomfortable, but there was quite a bit of support on our side.

At the end Gordon Brown, our Front Bench spokesman, got up and it was a vacuous speech. The notes looked like ones he had used on many occasions before, because he turned over the pages so quickly and I could see over his shoulder that they were rather shabby and tattered. Absolutely no content. I wouldn't appoint that man as a research assistant. Funnily enough, I have not only never spoken to him, although he has been in the House since '83 or '87, but I have never heard him speak before and I was glad I hadn't.

Lamont tried to rally the forces at the end by talking about how Britain will be first, and so on, and Heath looked very sick. A very poor speech, I thought.

Only 290 voted for the third reading (it would require 324, I think, to be more than half the House) and 112 against – about sixty Labour and forty Tories, and a few others. So it was a tremendous success really. I think this story has ended on a sour note for the Government. They must wish to God it had never come about, and any serious federalist looking at the House of Commons or Maastricht will realise that there is not much enthusiasm for it.

Thursday 27 May

Kenneth Kaunda came to tea. I first met him in 1957, when he and Harry Nkumbula came to the House of Commons. He was born a year before me. He was President of Zambia for twenty-seven years. I met him again in 1960 or 1961 in India. He has got no official home, no income and no pension – he has got nothing. Unlike many political leaders in the world, he hasn't amassed money and put it in a Swiss bank; that's not Kenneth Kaunda at all. He is trying to set up a foundation that will allow him to work on peace and democracy around the world, and he went to South Africa with Jim Callaghan and with him to China. All these presidents like Gorbachev and Carter and Kaunda want their own foundations, but I don't know that he has raised any money. The woman who was his secretary in Zambia for all those years is now working as a temp in Reading – incredible really. When you're out, you're out in politics, it's a really hard business. I never got to those heights, but I had my period in the wilderness and I've been through it. And I am lucky now not to have been in the position that these people have been in.

He was very kind and gentle and said, 'We socialists must keep together.' And he agreed to have photographs taken because his old friends the Moberlys, together with Andrew Hood and Ruth, appeared. It was altogether very charming and friendly. We talked about old times a bit, but looking forward to what was happening in Africa. He had been to South Africa to try and bring about an understanding between the Inkatha movement and the ANC. He looked forward. He said he had written to Clinton recently that, 'You must take a different view. You are the only superpower left,' and so on. I really admire the man.

Wednesday 2 June

I did a CNN discussion with Peregrine Worsthorne, who arrived in a red bow-tie and green suit, looking so overripe it wasn't true. He hates the Prime Minister and his contempt for anyone who isn't in the upper classes is very evident. He said, 'Prince Charles will be crowned by the Archbishop of Canterbury who is the son of a butcher, under a Prime Minister who is the son of a trapeze artist.'

I said, 'You just don't believe in democracy.'

He said, 'If you got rid of the monarchy, the generals would string you up.'

'I dare say they would. They might want to do it anyway.'

He said, 'No, you're a national institution.' He was quite jolly in the end, but he must hate my guts. He did make a nice reference about the meeting I did in Trafalgar Square on the referendum.

I went to Leeds by train, with Andrew. Walked to Waterstone's book shop in Albion Street in the evening to talk about the book Andrew and I have published, *Common Sense*. About 250 people crowded into the bookshop and the manager introduced us and I spoke, then Andrew. Those bookshop seminars are quite something and they do it five times a week.

Saturday 5 June

I went down to Peterborough and was picked up by the Reverend Robert Van der Weyer, who is an Anglican priest and was mainly responsible for resuscitating the community established by Nicholas Ferrar and George Herbert in the early part of the seventeenth century. There is a church and some houses and they have a farm. He is High Anglican, a very clever man; has written twenty books, lectures in economics, is about forty-two and has had a strange life.

I talked to a few people, including an old Anglican minister, then we had the gathering outside the chapel. Nicholas Ferrar was a remarkable, wealthy young man who got to Cambridge at the age of thirteen, was elected a Fellow at fourteen, was a Member of Parliament and then gave up everything to set up the Little Gidding community which, because it supported King Charles, was destroyed by parliamentary forces during the Commonwealth and rotted away, until it was resuscitated in 1977.

The average age today was about sixty, and I put my papers on the Ferrar tomb, which acted as a table. I talked about the relationship between religion and politics, and faith and doctrine, and belief and action and the flame of hope. The vicar objected to the idea of collectivism. An old lady said she hated the word *Labour* Party and it should be changed.

Wednesday 9 June

Heard Norman Lamont's devastating resignation speech in which he said that the Tories were in 'office without power', which is the title of one of my volumes of *Diaries*. He also talked about soundbites and public relations, which is also one of my themes. I must say, it was a very effective speech and did an awful lot of damage to Major, who spoke later and didn't do very well.

Caroline came to the Commons and we sat on the Terrace until about 1 a.m. It was a beautiful hot evening. It is so rare in Britain to be able to sit out into the night.

Thursday 10 June

Went and signed twenty-five *Common Sense* at Waterstone's and I did hear today that the book is being reprinted. They originally printed 4000 and apparently Waterstone's have ordered 1000. To get a reprint in a week is something.

Sunday 13 June

Got home, had a kip in the office and then Caroline and I went to James's first communion at St Mary and All Saints in Chiswick. There were all these little girls dressed up like brides at the age of eight and little boys in shirts and ties, and all the male priests standing there, not a woman in sight except for purely subsidiary purposes. A great lecture was given to us about the Last Supper, and transubstantiation and the body and blood of Christ. When you hear it cold, it really is an extraordinary thing that we eat our god as part of our faith. A shaft of light came through the stained-glass window on to James while all this was being explained and you could see him yawning. Afterwards, he said, 'Thank goodness. I won't have to go to Communion again!'

Tuesday 15 June

I rang Mark Leonard this morning, this young researcher who works for Calum Macdonald, a very right-wing Labour MP in favour of a Lib-Lab pact, and who talks about the post-socialist consensus. He had asked me to do a meeting for students tonight and, when I got the publicity material on it, it said there was to be a debate between Tony Benn, Tony Blair and Frank Dobson. I rang Mark and said, 'You never mentioned a debate. I would never have accepted if I had known I was agreeing to that.' He was very upset and rang back and said Frank Dobson couldn't do it and Tony Blair would speak first, but I won't be engaged in a debate with Tony Blair.

Went into a studio to discuss *Common Sense* with Austin Mitchell and Norman Tebbit for Sky TV. Austin talks all the time, and Norman hardly got a word, in but Norman is terribly soft and good-natured and the book was given a huge boost. They said 3.5 million can watch Sky TV, but I suspect it is more like 200,000.

I met Teresa Gorman there and she has asked me to do something on the Women's Day celebration. She said, 'You're my hero!'

So I said, 'It's always nice to have young women Members in the House.'

To the Commons to a party of the Performers' Alliance – that is to say, Equity, the Writers' Guild and the Musicians' Union – and it was packed with MPs. Across the room from the far side came Joanna Lumley, who introduced herself, very warm and friendly. She is a marvellous actress. She is now in this show called *Absolutely Fabulous*. I had quite a talk to her and later I said, 'I enjoyed our talk and maybe we could have a chat about some ideas,' because I have got two ideas, one of which is the possibility of a socialist festival in Chesterfield, like the Hay-on-Wye festival.

Then a short man with long hair came up, and I asked what he did and he said, 'I'm only a composer.'

I said, 'Don't say that. What have you done?'

He said, 'I do the theme music for *Inspector Morse*,' which is one of my favourite programmes.

Alan Plater made a little speech and Bryan Davies replied on behalf of the Labour Party Heritage Committee – most inadequate, saying, 'Thank you for the lovely party and the good wine' – no politics in it at all. I think they just thought a visit to the House would be useful.

After a bite to eat, I went to the London Labour Students' meeting called 'Towards the Millennium–Labour's Agenda for Britain' and Blair was just winding up his speech when I arrived. I gave a most impassioned speech, but they were a bunch of Kinnockites and, I shouldn't say this, you just got the feeling that they saw the Labour Party as a quick ladder to the top.

Wednesday 16 June

I had tea with John Prescott in the Tea Room. He told me that Kinnock always had a caucus meeting with the trade union people before the Executive to square them, but Smith won't do that. Prescott didn't think Smith was interested in Party management at all and that's one of the reasons why the unions are upset. It's not just about the block vote, but the way he treats them individually. He also said Kinnock had told him not to stand for the deputy leadership in 1988, and Barbara had offered to sponsor Prescott but had, in effect, been told by Kinnock that if she did she wouldn't get a peerage. Kinnock had been delighted that I was standing for the leadership because, he said, 'That will smash the man.'

It is our forty-fourth anniversary, and I took Caroline roses and a box of chocolates and a cheque to help her buy her new car, and we had a hug before we went to sleep.

Tuesday 22 June

Up at 5.15, drove to the airport and flew to Glasgow, to the BBC to do *Good Morning Scotland*, then dropped off at a super, luxury hotel where Hutchinson put me up. By taxi to a book shop where I sold about forty copies of *Common Sense*.

There was a very disturbed lady who greeted me outside and said, 'I am the most important woman in Scotland.' She followed me in and, while I was signing books, said things like, 'And how are the greyhounds getting on, Mr Benn?'

I said, 'I don't have any greyhounds.'

'Yes, you do, I've seen you with them outside your caravan.' So in the end, I had to brush her away a bit.

Wednesday 23 June

I feel I have got an elephant sitting on top of me, partly the elephant of my own self-discipline in keeping the diaries and archives, and whether they are worth a row of beans, I don't know. I don't just want to be a historian; I want to be free, without retiring from Parliament, to start on fresh things.

My life has got into a sort of rut. I don't go to the Commons because I don't enjoy it. I think the Labour Party is busy committing suicide. The Government is in a frightful mess over all these foreign contributions, from Azil Nadir of Polly Peck, and possibly from Saudi Arabia.

I heard today that Markham pit has been closed. So in effect they have killed the last pit in North Derbyshire. It means that Gordon Butler and Johnny Burrows will be redundant, Tom Vallins is going to lose his job, Margaret's son-in-law Trevor has lost his job. It is a catastrophe really.

Thursday 24 June
This whole business of Michael Mates and Azil Nadir, who jumped bail of £3.5 million and lives in northern Cyprus, has been a major theme over the last few weeks. I can't say it interests me at all in respect of Michael Mates. In the end, Mates did resign because the *Daily Mail* had a report this morning containing the text of his letter to the Attorney General in support of Nadir.

Sunday 27 June
Went to the airport to meet Caroline who has been in Glasgow, and while I was waiting a very formidable man of about my age, with a very red face and a bristly white moustache, who looked as if he was the archetypal retired sergeant major, was sitting there waiting for his grandchildren. I said, 'Do you mind if I sit here?'

He said, 'Not at all, Mr Benn. I must tell you that, although our politics are very different, I enjoy your performances on television.'

That was a friendly thing. It turned out he had spent his life in the police as a fingerprint expert. He had been in the Hatfield police force for thirty years, and the last twenty years he had been an expert witness. He said, 'I have dealt with eight hundred cases and I have been in court one hundred times, and I have been meticulously careful in the evidence I have given. It has never been questioned by the defence.'

He was interesting. He was editor of a magazine, called *The Whirlpool* I think, and he said that he once saw identical twins in the street and asked if he could fingerprint them, just to be sure they didn't have the same fingerprints. It was interesting and I liked the old boy.

His grandchildren appeared, and then Caroline appeared and we went to Stephen and Nita's for a lovely tea party. Andy McSmith, who has just written the life of John Smith, was there and he kindly signed it 'To Tony Benn, my friend and mentor'. It was very nice of him. He is an absolute hack Kinnockite, but a great friend of Nita's.

Read today in the paper that the Americans have bombed Baghdad, allegedly in retaliation for the attempted assassination of President Bush in Kuwait two months ago.

Monday 28 June
A man from Swindon telephoned and told me a tragic story. He is Lebanese, of Lebanese and Syrian parents who lived in Iraq, had Iraqi citizenship, came to Britain, has been here twenty-five years and is now a British citizen, an exporter of medical equipment. His brother lived in Iraq and was killed, with his eighteen-month-old baby, on Saturday night by the American bombing. The mother of the baby was seriously injured.

I asked, 'Can I make use of this?' and he agreed, so I sat down and wrote a long article for the *Guardian,* which I hope they will print.

To the American Embassy for a demonstration by the Committee for a Just Peace in the Middle East. I was told that when you take a letter to the embassy, they will only allow you to hand it to the janitor. Six of us went over and the guard from Pinkerton's, a private security company, said that the others had to stay outside the building, so I stood there and said I was an MP. Up above I could see an American marine, no doubt heavily armed. I said I wanted to see the Ambassador's private secretary. After about ten minutes of waiting in the security area, a plump, jolly woman of about fifty-five came down, and said she was the secretary to the American Minister. I think she was probably the woman who typed his letters. She didn't seem to know much, but she took me up to the Ambassador's suite, and I handed over the letter and told her about the man whose brother and baby had been killed. She was genuinely concerned and I gave her the letter and the article that I hope is appearing in the *Guardian* tomorrow.

Thursday 1 July
A beautiful hot day.

Went to University College Hospital, which is in imminent danger of closure. There were about fifty people there – porters, nurses, maybe some doctors. Apparently it has a reputation for having a Trotskyite trade union branch. But then, of course, nowadays anyone who is a socialist is a Trotskyite; there's no such thing as being a socialist other than being a Trotskyite or a Kinnockite, which is not being a socialist at all. I spoke and then there were questions. They did take strike action last November to prevent the closure of a ward, but they were considering what the right action is. I asked them if they thought there was the possibility of simply ignoring the management's instructions, and somebody took up that theme. I said, 'Maybe you should think not of a strike but of a mutiny, where you simply isolate the management and get on with the job of running the hospital.' I think the idea of a mutinous response is quite an interesting one.

To the House of Commons for the launch of my mum's book *My Exit Visa*.

I thought nobody would come, but Archbishop Lord Coggan appeared first, then Lord Jakobovits. Coggan was Archbishop of Canterbury and retired, I suppose, in 1980 when he was seventy, and was replaced by Runcie. Jakobovits was Chief Rabbi and has recently been replaced. Paul Mendel of the Council of Christians and Jews was there, and Gerry Noel. It was the old crowd of the Council of Christians and Jews – one or two rabbis, Christian ministers, and so on. Coggan took the chair, and Jacobovits gave a very carefully worked out lecture attacking the excesses of the media. He talked about hope, attacked communism, homosexuality and children without marriage, partnerships, and so on. But as he was there in honour of my mum, I just had to take it.

I spoke a vote of thanks and the Archbishop wound it up. A few of us had tea on the Terrace afterwards. Coggan was absolutely charming – couldn't have been nicer.

It is quite an honour that a former Archbishop and Chief Rabbi should join together in memory of my mum. I don't think I really appreciated the old lady while she was alive, although I did enjoy going to see her. But perhaps that's the way it is. You do learn more about people later. I think I was slightly overwhelmed by the support. Coggan was terribly pleased when I said in my speech how delighted Mother had been that we had an Archbishop of Canterbury who knew something about the Bible (he was, I think, a professor of Old Testament history).

Friday 2 July
Crown Prince Hassan of Jordan telephoned me from London to thank me for the line I had taken on the bombing of Iraq.

Monday 5 July
Today was the coal debate, and about thirty or forty women from Women Against Pit Closures began applauding me in the Central Lobby. I said, 'Be quiet or you'll all be thrown out!' They wanted tickets for the Gallery and I said there was no hope, but I went to the Admission Order Office and the man there gave me six tickets. I couldn't believe my luck. One of the women said that I had saved her husband's job twenty years ago when he worked at Meriden, and that was really pleasing.

Anyway, there was a statement then on the coal debate and I have never in my life heard such a disgraceful speech as was made by David Hunt, the Employment Secretary. Cheap – I put him in the John Patten/Selwyn Gummer category – and abusive without any content. Robin Cook was very pompous, but his speech will read well. I was called immediately after Hunt and I spoke for about fourteen minutes. I got very angry, but when I read it afterwards, it was all right.

Martin O'Neill made a fumbling speech for the Labour Front Bench and Tim Eggar, the Under Secretary who has got a broken nose and looks slightly strange, like a sort of damaged boxer, made a most offensive speech with no substance in it at all.

In the Members' Lobby, John Smith, who had actually listened to my speech, congratulated me on it; not that these things matter in career terms, but it was a generous thing for him to do. I had referred to the work that he and I had done together in the Department of Energy and gave a trenchant defence of Labour Government policy.

Tuesday 6 July

I went to meet fifty-seven primary-school children from a private Catholic school, St Peter and St Paul, in my constituency, and the little girls were all in dresses and the boys in grey flannels and shirts, and their parents were doctors and lawyers and accountants who owned companies, etc. I said, 'Will you ask me questions, or shall I ask you?' 'You ask us,' they said. So I asked them questions. What laws would they pass to ban smoking, to clear up pollution? What work would they like to do? They were lovely kids, very polite. I moved them towards political questions without pushing my views down their throats and I think they enjoyed it.

Came home. Terrible traffic jam in London. Fourteen women had broken into Buckingham Palace and there were armed police everywhere. There was a huge bomb explosion in Ireland yesterday, and security has just built up to the point where our civil liberties are being affected. They have closed roads in the City of London, so you can only get in at certain police checkpoints. It is absolutely crazy.

Saturday 10 July, Miners' Gala, Durham

We got the minibus up to the cathedral. I have never been to the Durham Miners' Cathedral Service before, but I felt this time I ought to: this huge cathedral built in 1093, almost half as old as Christianity itself. In the cathedral, the bands were playing and a brass band in a cathedral is just overwhelming. The place was packed to the doors. We were put up in the choir stalls, so I didn't actually see the canon who gave the address, but it was a marvellous address.

But the language of the prayers – 'We are unworthy and only God can help us' – is of course the very opposite of the message of the Gala, which is that only we can help ourselves. I do think the Church has got to look awfully carefully at the whole question of its language, because it is one of subservience in the hymns and prayers, while the sermon itself was about self-confidence.

Afterwards the Bishop, David Jenkins, gave his blessing and as he came by the choir-stall I bowed to him and he inclined his head, and I shook hands with him as he went out. He is retiring this year so you have what is, in effect, the end of the Durham coalfield; the end of the Bishop of Durham in this cathedral in its 900th year, and coal has been mined, I think, in Durham for almost as long as the church has existed.

I couldn't fight the tears. They just rolled down my cheeks and I couldn't look to left or right as I left the cathedral, because I thought of all these lovely, decent people who had worked so hard and made such enormous sacrifices, and been utterly betrayed by a government that tried to destroy them and treat them as if they were the enemy. It was so unfair.

As we went out, the band started again and we marched all the way down to the Royal County Hotel. Spoke to lots of people who had met me before. I got a lift back to the station with a man who said he was so glad to do it, as his father had driven me to the station after an earlier gala. I have been elected to go to more galas than anyone has in the whole of its history – sixteen times.

I was emotionally disturbed all the way back on the train. I couldn't work, couldn't sleep – still fighting back the tears at the injustice done to these people.

That was the end of the 109th Durham Miners' Gala.

Sunday 11 July

I overslept and didn't get up until about 10.30.

The newspapers are awful at the moment, full of crime and violence and war, and the Labour Party simply arguing about the block vote. Frank Field has come out with a proposal for private pensions, and Blunkett on the radio called him a maverick. Here is the collapse of a whole economic system, and all we are doing is discussing our internal affairs and demanding inquiries into this and that, and clear answers to this and that.

Tuesday 13 July

I found myself at short notice put on the Statutory Instruments Select Committee, which didn't please me, and I have in the past just avoided committees. But I looked at the Order the Committee was considering and it was to exempt Common Market countries from the present Post Office Act of 1953, which had made it illegal to import fictitious postage stamps and dies. This was a nonsense. The Minister read a short brief, which he expected would go through on the nod.

I got up and drew attention to the absurdity of this provision – if it was wrong to import this material, it should be wrong wherever it came from; anyway, why should we agree to it? I went on and on and intervened many times and even though I say so myself, I ran rings round the Minister and made it amusing by talking about fictitious bank notes that might be printed by the Bank of France, and why should we discriminate against Nigeria and Third World countries? The Tories cheered like anything. Nicholas Winterton, passionately anti-EEC, was in the chair and Tam Dalyell and Geoff Hoon spoke, both of whom are passionate pro-EEC people. I tried to get the whole debate adjourned, but it went through.

Wednesday 14 July

Today there is a motion in the Lords for a referendum on Europe. I have got mixed feelings about it, because the House of Lords is totally undemocratic and have got no right to counteract the House of Commons. On the other hand, the Lords can be overridden, whereas the power transferred to Brussels can't. To cut a long story short, despite speeches by Lady Thatcher and Tebbit and old George Thomas, the Lords defeated the referendum by about 3 to 1, and I wasn't surprised because a House that depends upon inheritance and patronage is not likely to come out for democracy.

I forgot to mention that yesterday Mark Tully, the distinguished BBC correspondent in India, launched a blistering attack on John Birt about the rule of fear and threat in the BBC. Everyone in the BBC is absolutely delighted.

This afternoon, a man came and said I hadn't paid my TV licence. I had paid £80 a month late, and a couple of weeks before my cheque went in the licence fee went up to £83, so I gave him an amended cheque.

Sunday 18 July

In the evening we watched the first of four programmes on London Weekend Television about Kinnock. It was odious.

He pretended to be surprised when someone first mentioned him as a parliamentary candidate; he pretended to be surprised that anyone had thought of him as a Leader; he absolutely left out of his account his own radicalism and the left; he had people like Healey comparing him to Gorbachev; he had Dennis Skinner saying he had a left image to begin with; he had comments by Livingstone, comments by Smith, and so on.

It was terribly dishonest. I am so glad I refused to be interviewed for it.

My main feeling was just absolute delight that the man no longer has any responsibility for the Party and is pretty well a busted flush. The programme may have got him back on the National Executive Committee and that would be, from his point of view, worth doing. He never talked about what was happening at the time, just about what was happening to *him* at the time.

Monday 19 July

National Executive meeting in the House of Commons, and when we came to the item on OMOV, I pointed out that OMOV wasn't in fact One Member One Vote, because MPs wanted to retain half of the whole vote in the election of the leadership and 100 per cent when electing the Shadow Cabinet. Tony Clarke said, 'Oh, that's just a comment. Next point.'

So I said, 'Don't be so bloody insulting.' I don't usually lose my temper, but I went on, 'I've been on this National Executive in the 1950s, 60s, 70s,

80s and 90s, and I'm entitled to have my view taken seriously.'

Clarke was a bit taken aback. He said, 'I recognise your contribution to the movement' and so on.

Tuesday 20 July

I worked at home this morning and turned my mind to the coverage in *The Independent* of the court case where Lord Justice Watkins and Mr Justice Auld agreed to accept an application by Lord Rees-Mogg, backed by Sir James Goldsmith, to declare the Maastricht Treaty illegal.

I spoke to the Clerk of the House about this, because it seemed to me to be a breach of the Bill of Rights, and he said, 'Yes, I agree.' And he was furious at the courts. He referred to the Pepper v. Hart case of 1982 when the courts decided that it was open to them to examine speeches in the House of Commons to interpret legislation.

So I wrote a letter to the Speaker and faxed it across, and asked her to declare this as a breach of privilege and to refer it to the Privileges Committee. I even drafted an Early Day Motion which, in the event, I didn't table.

Went to the House, saw Jean MacLean, a member of the Australian State Legislature, and had a chat to her.

I said, 'Have you been to England before?'

And she replied, 'You gave me lunch when I was last here.'

So I said, 'That must be the first signs of Alzheimer's disease.' I felt a bit embarrassed!

At 3.30 I got up in the Chamber and asked the Speaker if she was in a position to reply to my letter. She said, 'No, I'm giving consideration to it.' So I didn't press it. Later she said, 'Please come and see me tomorrow at eleven o'clock.'

Of course I'm against Maastricht, and Rees-Mogg's trying to kill Maastricht, but that's not the way to do it.

Wednesday 21 July

Went to see the Speaker at eleven and she was tremendously supportive. Had about a quarter of an hour/twenty minutes with her. She said, 'I'm going to make a statement. I don't want to respond simply to a complaint of privilege. I want to speak myself about it and make it clear. I'm drafting and redrafting the statement.'

I said, 'That's fine, I'd much rather you did it that way.'

So I dropped the Committee of Privileges idea and she said, 'I'll be very firm.'

I had a phone call later from the Speaker saying, 'I'm going to make a statement and you can reply.'

So I drafted a speech, took it to the Speaker's Office and the Clerk's Office. Told Michael White of the *Guardian* how important this was and he just seemed to brush it aside. You just can't persuade journalists to believe you at all; they know best.

At 3.30 the Speaker made her statement, which was very good. I then made a statement almost as long, which was very well received, and the House really responded because I was defending Parliament against the courts.

I put out my response in the lobby for the journalists, who can't write anything about anything unless they get advance notice.

Then *The Times* rang up for an article, and while I was doing that, Rees-Mogg rang up and said, 'I'm just trying to use the courts to protect Parliament.' Well, it's not for a Tory peer to use an appointed judge to defeat the House of Commons.

Thursday 22 July

Absolutely mass coverage of the Speaker's ruling. Couldn't have been bigger. *The Times* and *Telegraph* had it on their front page.

Drafted a letter to Stella Rimington to find out whether Roger Windsor of the NUM had been employed by MI5. Tam Dalyell and George Galloway tabled a motion yesterday noting the use of Windsor as an agent of the Security Service during the coal strike.

Ruth was doubtful about the letter. She said 'You weren't the one who took the issue up in the first place.' I mentioned it later to Tam, but he didn't want to pursue it. I didn't send it.

Gradually, a few people who are anti-Maastricht are beginning to realise that the whole purpose of my campaign is to make the case for Parliament against the right of the European Court to interfere, a point Peter Shore made in the House this afternoon during the debate on the inclusion of the Social Chapter in the Maastricht Treaty.

But the media have hyped it up all day. The two speeches to begin with – Major and Smith – were both perfectly serious speeches arguing their case.

I'm not optimistic, but I say this two and a half hours before the vote.

David Hunt, the Employment Secretary, was absolutely appalling, as he was in the debate on Tuesday shouting, seeming to tempt interruption, and so on. Rumours went around as to what would happen.

I personally thought that the Ulster Unionists would be bought, which they could be, and that party loyalty was very strong. Therefore I didn't expect for one moment that we would win either vote.

I spoke to George Gardiner, the absolute right-wing MP who used to be political correspondent for the *Western Daily Press* about thirty years ago. 'Haven't given up hope,' he said.

Went into the House at the very end and, of course, it was absolutely packed. The Speaker's Gallery was full, the Serjeant at Arms' Gallery was full, the Public Gallery was full.

The first vote – on the amendment to include the Social Chapter – took place; the lobby was crowded and the Speaker was there. The place was tremendously tense with excitement, the Press Gallery was absolutely jammed with people standing.

As the rumours spread, Richard Ryder, the Tory Chief Whip, came in and nodded at the Prime Minister, and the Prime Minister smiled so we thought we'd lost; then Derek Foster came and had a word with our people – it's like seconds in a ring in a boxing match.

Finally, at about quarter past ten the tellers lined up and the word went round: 'It's a tie.' And so, indeed, it was: 317 for the Labour amendment calling for the Social Chapter to be included, and 317 against.

So the Speaker got up and read a statement saying, 'I have a duty to cast my vote. It's not a political vote, in accordance with precedent. I declare that the Noes have it.' She said, in effect (which was fair enough), that the amendment had not really got a majority.

So then there was a second division on the Government motion. People were watching again, and the Ulster Unionists went in with the Government. This is what proportional representation would mean if you had a little National Front Group; they would be selling their support for all sorts of things.

People didn't know what the Tories would do and, to cut a long story short, I went through the lobby, and everybody was jostling and talking; it's funny when you have Tories in your lobby. Then we waited again, with great tension and excitement.

One of our whips came out and put his fists in the air, so obviously he knew what had happened and a Tory whip is supposed to have said, 'Well, you win some and you lose some.'

So it was. Ray Powell (first time I have seen him win, except on private business) was the Chief Teller and he said, 'Madam Speaker, the Ayes to the right were 316, the Noes to the left were 324.'

So both motions were defeated and we're back where we were. Well, of course, the House was in state of tremendous excitement, I must admit I waved my Order Paper, a thing I've never done before in my life, but I was so excited.

Major got up. He had a prepared statement. He said, 'I'm going to put down a motion of confidence tomorrow, incorporating confidence in our handling of the Social Chapter, and if that is defeated there will be a General Election.'

John Smith got up and said something.

Then I popped up with Article 1 of the Bill of Rights, but constitutional questions in high political moments don't arouse much interest. I fired a shot across their bows; they couldn't just ignore Parliament and ratify.

I had, I might add, intervened during the Prime Minister's statement about the voice of the people, and so on. And then, of course, everybody exploded.

What a day! There has been a tie before – on the Aircraft and Shipbuilding Bill in 1975, I think there was a tie, but it's a very unusual thing and on a vote of confidence is unprecedented in my recollection.

Friday 23 July

Got everything ready for Chesterfield. Whether I'll get there tonight I do not know, but I ought to be there if I possibly can, if there is to be a General Election shortly.

I think the Government will win today. I have little doubt the Ulster Unionists will vote for them again, because they've got some sort of a deal: the Tory rebels will come to heel, I should think. Major's threatened an election, and an election would involve a threat of suicide from his point of view.

Got there a bit early. The place was buzzing, but, of course, when the Government announces it's a vote of confidence, everybody falls into line at once.

The Ulster Unionists have obviously had some sort of an understanding given, and funnily I heard George Galloway asking in his speech, 'I want to know exactly what offer has been made to the Ulster Unionists.'

At that point I slipped out and I saw the Prime Minister also leaving, and I heard him talking to himself, saying, 'Nothing, the answer is absolutely nothing.'

When Major made his speech, it was quite all right in terms of his presentation; he sounded quite confident, coming back to the fact that the Social Chapter would cost jobs and how he was gradually persuading other Common Market Community countries to drop it; how competitiveness in Europe was less than it was in America, and so on.

Smith was very good – he made fun of Major quite successfully. And I got called fairly early on, and spoke for much too long: twenty-three minutes. It was a bit rambling.

At the end, at four o'clock, it was quite clear that the Government had a majority on the first vote and that all the Tory rebels had come back into line. I didn't stay for the result of the second vote, but jumped in the car and drove to St Pancras to go to Chesterfield.

Sunday 25 July

The big news in the papers is that, owing to the fact that a mike was left on after an interview by Michael Brunson of John Major, everyone heard him saying that Cabinet Ministers who disagreed with him, and who were against the Maastricht Treaty, were bastards. That will do an enormous amount of damage; it really will do a tremendous amount of damage.

Four or five nights ago I dreamed that I was doing a meeting in Manchester in November, when it was pelting with rain and terribly dark. And there wasn't a train that would get me back, so somebody said, 'Why don't you fly a Tiger Moth back? You know how to fly.' On the face of it, it seemed a good idea. Then I thought, 'My God. First of all, can I remember how to fly a Tiger Moth? Secondly, it will be pelting with rain and pitch-dark. How do I get from Manchester to London?' And I got really quite worried.

I think what the dream was probably telling me was that I am no longer a young man, I've got to recognise my limitations. But it was very vivid.

Monday 26 July

Talked a bit to Nick Jones of the BBC at the House of Commons, who agreed that Kinnock was basically a student politician. He, Peter Mandelson, Charles Clarke and Jack Straw were sectarian student in-fighters, and Smith is so much better.

Wednesday 28 July

Before the NEC began, John Evans leaned across to me and said that he'd heard what the nature of the deal between the Government and the Ulster Unionists was, and it was that Ulster would get £200,000 – or perhaps it was £200 million, I can't remember; must have been £200,000 – that otherwise would have gone for development in Merseyside and Scotland.

When we came to the Education Green Paper, the really big debate turned out to be on higher education. Claire Ward, the Young Socialist, said that students were very worried because there was a phrase in it which suggested we might move towards student loans, rather than student grants. And Gordon Brown said this would be open to misinterpretation, and would give the impression that Labour was shifting its opinion.

John Smith said he was also anxious; he said there might be another scare about a graduate tax.

Then Neil Kinnock said that, despite thirty years of opposition to the idea of student loans, 'I have now come to realise that loans must be a part of the debate.' There was Kinnock, preparing for another U-turn; he does a U-turn on everything.

Then Ann Taylor said that grants to all students couldn't be sustained. Clare Short remarked that student loans were not very good, and Diana Jeuda said, 'Just leave it.' Kinnock said we must face the facts.

I said, 'I do think our purpose in publishing this is to restate our commitment to education, to attract the right support. Some people seem to be suffering from ministerialitis, even though they've never been Ministers.'

This one was absolutely as a body blow to Kinnock and he looked most miserable. Anyway, I said I agreed with John Smith and we ought to be cautious about it.

Smith said we should shorten and clarify this passage, and Prescott said, 'Neil Kinnock says we can't raise tax, but why not? What's wrong with that? If it's necessary to do it, we'll do it.' Kinnock looked as sick as a dog.

Got to Chesterfield and went to the Club; they were talking about the mining industry a lot of the time, and Johnny Burrows said there's no doubt they will privatise a lot of the pits; Markham and Shirebrook might be reopened. He didn't think it was a good idea to say that Labour would renationalise, because he thought that would frighten off the private companies who might keep the pits open, and that would at least provide an opportunity for development. We could nationalise it when we got there.

Monday 2 August, Chesterfield

There's a lot going on now about the purchase of the Labour Club from the NUM who owns it. Then they're going to convert the shed at the back as a cottage for me, and I will then be able to put the money for the rent into the Labour Club.

In the afternoon I went to 'Our Vision, Our Time' in Schoolboard Lane. It is a day-centre for mentally handicapped people. The social worker asked them all to explain who they were, and they were all very hesitant and shy at first and then, as the discussion began, it bubbled and bubbled and became extremely amusing and entertaining.

They were being trained really to resist the way in which disabled people were talked to like children, and jargon was used. And they'd got hold of these ideas: we want to be treated as adults and we don't want any jargon, and we want our rights.

Today the ERM collapsed.

Tuesday 3 August

What I'm beginning to learn from this week in Chesterfield is the absolute jungle they've created among voluntary organisations.

They've taken statutory functions and farmed them out to voluntary organisations. The funding is very largely (but not exclusively) through non-elected bodies, so these voluntary organisations become very suspicious of each other because they don't want to find their funding's been interfered with. It would be terribly easy just to cut off the money and close them all down.

I think that is a real danger; this is what the Government has in mind. But lots of people working in this sector have to work within this framework. I've got to think a lot about that.

Thursday 5 August

The civil war in the former Yugoslavia dominates the papers, has done for days. It's a terrible, bloody war, and all wars are terrible and bloody, but they don't usually get the news coverage this one gets. If we became combatants, then the humanitarian aid would end, the role of the UN as a peace-making agency would end, and NATO would take it over; it would be an extension of Western European military power in Eastern Europe and I think it's wrong, but it's hard to say that when you see this terrible suffering every day. I suspect that the suffering would be just as bad if we were there.

Friday 6 August

The news from the Balkans continues to be absolutely tragic. You've got Paddy Ashdown and Clinton and other people demanding the bombing of Serb forces or Serbia, and the United Nations commander there warning against it, because he says if you bomb Serbia, they will attack our forces and, of course, we'll be involved in the combat.

The awful thing to recognise is that all wars are settled by the strongest side. You have to be prepared to put a huge army in and occupy the whole of the former Yugoslavia and impose a settlement. This is one of the difficulties.

It doesn't really meet the bill, although Chris Mullin and my brother David compare this to the Spanish Civil War. 'Why don't we do something about it as we should have done in Spain in the 1930s?' It's hard to argue with that.

On the other hand, all wars are tragic and horrible. It's only the media coverage that differentiates between that and what's happening in Iraq, where we're killing children by the thousands because of the sanctions and the shortage of food and medicine.

Sunday 8 August

I watched Kinnock on television – the last episode of *Kinnock: The Leadership Years* – and it was awful. He shouted, 'We are all right, we are all right!' at Sheffield, as if it was a sort of pop festival. He felt that was a mistake, and then he said he was a personal and political failure, but that he would be ready to stand again if we lost at some stage in the future.

Tuesday 17 August, Stansgate

It was a beautiful day. Caroline worked all day in the garden watering the grass.

Gordon Brown, the Labour Shadow Chancellor, was on television saying that Labour is not a high-tax, high-spend party and certainly does not intend to penalise the rich. The most ridiculous statement ever. He's so unconvincing; he just looks as if you could not trust him with a corner shop.

Wednesday 18 August

Keith Jones, the BBC producer of the *Benn Tapes*, and his wife Julia and their little three-and-half-week-old baby Jonathan arrived, and Caroline gave them a lovely lunch.

Friday 27 August

I went to meet Arthur Scargill at St Pancras. He was due to arrive at 2.50, so I got there ready to meet him. He wanted to talk to me about Roger Windsor, who apparently said to Johnny Burrows that MI5 would deny his involvement, and that would clear him.

So obviously Roger Windsor's got a big campaign going on, now that Tam Dalyell and George Galloway have tabled a motion in the House of Commons on the MI5 connection, which they're both quite sure about.

Anyway, that's what Arthur wanted to tell me. I can't say it was extremely important. We went on to talk about Charles Clarke and Mandelson in Cuba.

Sunday 5 September

There was an article in the Sunday papers on Roger and Angie Windsor and MI5. I've put it in my miners' file for 1992/3.

Tuesday 7 September

Sarah Clancy was in for a week's work experience, a very nice young woman of nineteen, and Charlie Crowe.

I should report that John Smith made his speech to the TUC today. He made no reference in it to One Member One Vote, but came out with a passionate commitment in favour of trade unionism and its importance, and it knocked everybody sideways.

It is an interesting confirmation that only the right-wing leaders can do that. I mean, Kinnock would have had to follow the line of the so-called new realists, and Smith decided to take that line, which will enormously help him with One Member One Vote, so that was interesting.

Thursday 9 September

In the evening, to the twentieth birthday party of BBC Radio 1's *Newsbeat* in St George's Hotel, just opposite All Saints, Langham Place, in the rooftop restaurant.

When I got there they were all very young, I didn't recognise any of them.

Lots of people came up to say how much they enjoyed the *Benn Tapes* series on radio, and one said, 'How long did it take you to script your diary before you dictated it?' He had no idea it was dictated straight off the top of my head every night, so I said, 'I shall go home tonight and record what you have said to me.' He was the Head of Sports and Outside Broadcasts.

There was no ill will, as there is among superior Radio 4 people who are all fighting a battle to reform the Labour Party and make it Liberal; none of that. I think the generation of young people there were sort of Thatcherites, but there you are – it was Radio 1, they were younger and the only problem is there was music being played the whole time and I heard nothing of the conversation because I'm as deaf as a post. I was overwhelmingly the oldest person there and the only politician who'd bothered to turn up.

The PLO have renounced terrorism and the Israelis have recognised Arafat as representing the Palestinian people, so a peace deal of some kind will go ahead. It is a betrayal of the Palestinian cause, but it's the best they can get. It will establish a Palestine; the Arab states will put money into Gaza and Jericho and make them very prosperous; Palestine will be recognised by the UN; and bit by bit Israel will have to come to terms with its new position. Despite the weakness of the PLO during the Gulf War, the Americans don't need Israel any more now that the Cold War's over, and they've got to get on with the Arab states.

Monday 13 September

Hilary was appointed Head of Research at the trade union MSF. He's worked there for eighteen years and finally he's got it and an increase in salary. What a hard worker that lad is. He plods away, he's reliable, he's lovely to work with and finally he's been recognised, and to be the Head of Research in one of the three biggest unions is a huge job in the Labour movement.

The other big world news today is that on the White House lawn, in the presence of thousands of people, Rabin and Arafat made statements and then shook hands in a formal way, and so there may be some new way forward.

The Palestinians have not got what they want or are entitled to, but the Israelis have conceded more than they wanted to, and it is a first step.

I had a word with Peter Hain on the phone; his pamphlet, 'The Future of the Left', was published today. He sent it to me and asked me if I'd go to Neath to his party's Annual Dinner, but I can't do it.

He said, 'I must tell you something in great confidence. We've had a survey in *Tribune*, among 5,000 people (I already knew, but didn't say I knew it); 2000 replied and, when asked who *Tribune* readers identified with most, it was overwhelmingly yourself.'

Mark Seddon, the editor, had told me. I was apparently 2 to 1 votes over and above the next runner-up, Robin Cook.

Thursday 16 September

To University College Hospital which has been partly occupied in protest against its closure. There was a nervous-looking man, who was obviously one of the managers, and a nervous-looking woman, who said she was the Personnel Manager. So I shook her warmly by the hand and said, 'Well, we pay your salary, so I hope all goes well,' and then brushed them aside.

When we got to the occupied ward it was blocked with a bed and a gas cylinder, but we banged and they opened it up and inside there was this meeting going on. The patients had been moved, and there was this deserted ward with masses of people smoking, drinking tea and standing on beds and arguing. Someone said they should occupy another ward; somebody else said they should occupy the whole hospital; another person said that the union branch meeting had decided it would be better to march on Downing Street.

It was thrilling really. It was a bit like St Petersburg in 1917, and reminded me of the movie *Reds*.

I came home, and I've got to go off to Chesterfield at six o'clock in the morning. I'm stuck up at Chesterfield for so much of the time. Still, with reselection coming up, I don't think I have a choice.

Saturday 18 September

In every newspaper is the huge challenge to John Major's leadership. No question that a lot of people are trying to get rid of him. The Establishment no longer thinks that Major can win the election, so they want the Tories to have a new Leader.

They're not prepared to accept any anti-Market leaders, because in Britain you're not allowed to be against the Maastricht Treaty and be treated as a respectable or serious political person, so they'll look for a Euro-enthusiast like Kenneth Clarke. They're foolish to do it at this stage, because they need the new guy to get into the saddle in time for the honeymoon to be over before the election comes.

Paddy Ashdown, with the Liberal Conference coming up, is saying he wants to be Prime Minister – and can be.

I think the British Establishment is looking for a Lib-Lab arrangement, and of course that's what the Labour Party's all about, breaking the links with the unions, getting rid of the left, going for proportional representation, paving the way for a Lib-Lab Government, which the Establishment would then support to the hilt in getting the cuts that they want to the Welfare State.

Monday 20 September

Anna Ford phoned this morning to ask me to supper with her on Saturday fortnight. I've only met her twice, but I've always admired her. She's a Liberal really, a decent straightforward Liberal, but I wasn't entirely clear whether it would be just the two of us or what. Anyway, I thought it out and rang her back later, and it was a little dinner party she was giving at home. I said I couldn't do it that day.

Friday 24 September
BBC Television came along to record from 'Paradise Regained' by Milton which I chose for their one-and-a-half-minute poem 'fillers' – it's a very good idea, opens up all sorts of possibilities. I really enjoyed it.

I rang the BBC to complain about coverage of the situation in Russia, where they simply treat the Parliament as rebel and hard-line and communist and give 100 per cent support to Yeltsin. They said, 'Oh, well, we do have people representing the Parliament.'

I said, 'That's not the point. You haven't had a single voice in this country expressing a view.' I didn't make much impact really.

I went to the Ritz for the attempt by the unemployed of Lambeth, Chesterfield and Liverpool to have tea at the Ritz: an idea based on Wally Hannington's scheme in the 1930s when they did the same at the Savoy. The police were there, although actually they were quite friendly.

Tea in the Ritz costs £13.50; an unemployed person might get four times that in a week.

Saturday 25 September, Brighton
I went to the flat that had been lent to us for the Conference – Brunswick Place, a beautiful luxury – by Helen Leigh. I dumped my stuff.

Sunday 26 September
Taxi to the NEC in the Grand Hotel, Empress Room.

I won't go through what happened at too great a length, except to say that I forced about twelve votes.

We voted to treat all sexual partnerships on the same basis.

Then, on Trident, I moved the resolution to phase out Trident; I got three votes.

On the motion to bring our defence spending into line with other European countries, I moved we accept. That was defeated by 11 votes to 9. So I got nine votes: a partial victory.

On the Middle East, there was a perfectly respectable resolution supporting the Palestinian state and condemning the imprisonment of Vanunu. I only got four votes for that.

Then we came to Clause 4, being debated on Friday, and it was recommended that we remit the resolution supporting it. I said we should accept it: Clause 4 is on all our membership cards. Kinnock said we should remit it: we're not hog-tied to the words of Clause 4. At any rate only four people voted to retain Clause 4, so with that the Executive adjourned and if (as I hope and believe) I am not on the Executive again, that was the end of my last meeting – to see them do what Gaitskell had never succeeded in doing, namely defeat Clause 4.

Afterwards we went off to the Christian Socialists' meeting, 'Is God a Socialist?' where Chris Bryant and Chris Smith, who's a gay Christian

Socialist, were taking part. It was really good. I thoroughly enjoyed it.

Monday 27 September

All the rumours are that I'm off the Executive.

Lots of mates came and sat next to me. Stephen and Nita and Caroline and Hilary sat next to me, and Tony Banks and Valerie Wise came and sat next to me – all my old mates; it was what they call doughnutting: you gather around somebody who is in the news in order either to appear in the picture, or in this case, to give support.

Then the results were announced and my vote dropped dramatically. I got 299,000 votes, which was about 60,000 less than last time, and Harriet Harman leaped up to half a million, so I was genuinely defeated.

When that was over and all the cameras were there and so on, I looked very cheerful. Diana Jeuda, who was in the chair, said, 'I think the Conference would want me to make a comment on the fact that Tony Benn has been on the Executive for thirty-four years, has been defeated and we all want to thank him.' Or something – I couldn't hear what she actually said.

Anyway, to my amazement the whole Conference rose to its feet, turned round and gave me a huge standing ovation.

I mean, I was really pleased to be off actually, but at the same time to be defeated is to be defeated, and then to have this great wave of Conference sympathy was a bit overwhelming. I stood and clapped the Conference in the best European style.

So they were all crowded around and Jon Snow of Channel 4 News grabbed me and took me away, but all I said was, 'I'd like to express my thanks to the people in the constituencies who put me on the Executive for a third of the life of the Party – deeply appreciative of that. I'm glad a woman's got on, because we need more women on the Executive and I shall be free to do my own work.' It was a sort of funeral; to live to see your own obituary's a bit surprising.

So that was disposed of fairly quickly. Then we got back to the flat and had baked beans.

Then I went to the *World Tonight* temporary studio and found Harriet Harman sitting in the studio. I also saw Edward Miliband, who'd started today as Harriet Harman's research assistant, all very smartly dressed, just like Hilary Benn, a lovely guy; I think he was a bit embarrassed because he'd been a 'Teabag' working in my basement office. But he couldn't have jumped on the right surfboard at a better time and I was very friendly. I congratulated Harriet.

It was a traumatic day. I suppose in a way to be defeated is not a nice thing to happen; on the other hand, to be quite clinical about it, to be on that Executive is impossible. The constituencies didn't want me, a lot of people have left the Party and I think a lot more will leave the Party now.

I think it was the sympathy I found a bit overwhelming. On the other hand, truthfully I'm relieved and I'm going to get on with my job.

Dennis Skinner did very badly on the Executive, and so did Ken Livingstone. And now there are half a million people voting for Kinnock, Prescott, Gordon Brown, Blair, Robin Cook, Harriet Harman.

Tuesday 28 September

Earlier today John Prescott got a standing ovation for talking about the nationalisation of the railways. So the idea that the Labour Party has changed is ludicrous; it's coming to life again at this Conference, and that is what I rather hoped would happen.

I didn't want to hear John Smith's speech at the Conference because I know what happens; the television crews are given the speech in advance, then whenever he makes an appropriate reference, they mark who they will show on the camera. So Kinnock used to say, 'We're fed up with hard-line extremists', and the camera would flash to me. Or he'd say, 'What we want is to modernise the party', and they'd flash to Tony Blair.

I went and sat on the stairs, where there was a television set that I could watch and I could smoke without being spotted. Mick McGahey came and sat next to me and his stream of comment was very shrewd.

He said, 'What are you going to do, then? Aye, what are you going to do? Look at Robin Cook, he's a crafty bugger, and look at Tony Blair, he's no use at all.'

Smith's was a good Presbyterian Labourite speech, the kind Attlee might have made, ruined by the autocues, because the autocues make the whole thing look so totally insincere – there's no vitality, there's no sparkle about it. But it was a good speech, well presented and well read, and well received, so that was that.

Friday 1 October

When I look back on the week, the modernisers launched the biggest campaign against trade unionism I've ever seen in my life. They only got 47 per cent of the Conference, so it wasn't exactly an overwhelming triumph and Smith went down well.

The delegates voted to keep Clause 4, and we had the defence result today, it wasn't too bad; I think we could be heading for another 1945-type Attlee campaign, although I don't say as big a majority as that.

Saturday 2 October

A drunken signalman came up and talked to me for a bit. At one stage he said, 'I'm afraid I've had a bit of beer', which he certainly had. He asked, 'Is there a god?'

I said, 'I'm afraid everyone has to work that out for themselves.' It turned out that his fourteen-year-old son had got out of the bath and electrocuted himself on his record player, and he said he couldn't bear to go to the churchyard. It was all rather sad.

Sunday 3 October

At midnight I heard the news and there's fighting in Moscow.

All of a sudden people have rallied round the Parliament and they stormed the television station, which is guarded by Yeltsin's troops, and they stormed the Mayor of Moscow's house.

It looks as if Yeltsin has got a choice: either to go for a complete military coup, if he can rely on the army, or, in effect, to enter into negotiations with the Parliament, which Gorbachev says he should.

The Western statements are scandalous. The BBC was scandalous, 'hard-line rebels, violence, anarchy'. Nobody's saying, not even hinting, that it was due to the fact that Yeltsin unilaterally suspended the constitution.

The BBC is just not worth listening to but, of course, the comments have come from NATO, Brussels – they support Yeltsin because he's holding elections, even if they didn't they say they'd support him. I do just wonder if the thing becomes a civil war whether there won't be another war of intervention, as there was in 1920.

Sunday 10 October

The papers are full of the Thatcher memoirs: her attack on Howe, her attack on Lawson and her attack on everybody else. The Tory Conference has ended in chaos, truthfully. Thatcher spends her whole life now defending her record and I think, if I am learning anything from it (not that I needed to be taught after my own experience), it is that you cannot live in the past. I do diaries and describe what happened, and so on, but you've always got to keep your mind on the future, always keep it on contemporary affairs. She really hasn't made a contribution to that for ages.

So it's a warning – the public at large don't like old politicians quarrelling with each other about what they did years ago.

Saturday 16 October, Cyprus

Up at six and drove to the airport and went out on the 9.30 to Larnaca, arriving four and a half hours later. We drove on to Nicosia, straight to the house – palace – of the Archbishop Chrysos Tomas. He succeeded Makarios. His palace was absolutely beautiful – a real Middle Eastern palace with perfectly cultivated gardens and huge gates. The stone was all illuminated. Inside was a model of Kotziamanis's statue of a Cypriot freedom fighter, which stands about ninety feet high, and all these icons – the old Greek Orthodox icons. The Archbishop looked a bit like Santa Claus and greeted us very courteously – Tom Cox and me. Then about twenty-five MPs and MEPs came in, and there was a huge circle and we all sat round, and he delivered a political lecture in English on the problems facing the people of Cyprus. The Greek Orthodox Church is actually very political and the Archbishop – like Makarios – is the head of the whole society.

He went on at great length – rather soporific – on a very warm evening. Two boys of about eleven or twelve, very neatly dressed, brought in orange juice for all of us. And outside, coming through the open window, were the Muslim chants from the mosque just across the green line, which was how they describe the frontier with Turkish-occupied Cyprus. Pauline Green, the MEP was there, and Barbara Roche, who asked about the theft of works of art from northern Cyprus, which were being sold on the international art market. The Turkish came in 1974 and they just looted the place – a classic Occupation. Cyprus has a civilisation going back 8000 years. It has been occupied at various stages by the Egyptians and the Assyrians, the Venetians and the Greeks, the Romans, and the British at the time of Richard, Coeur de Lion (the Crusades) and by the French. It has had an extraordinary life really, because it is so strategically placed. It is a very attractive island as well.

Anyway, we listened to all this for about three-quarters of an hour and I was getting very dozy because of the heat, and I was very tired. The Archbishop came round and gave each of us – like Santa Claus – a little reproduction silver plate showing a ship that had been built in Cyprus 2000 years BC. When you think that the Christian era only began three-quarters of the way through the civilisation of Cyprus, it did give you a completely different historical perspective.

Sunday 17 October

Up at half-past six Cyprus time. We were picked up and taken by coach to a place called Astromeritis, which is on the Greek Cypriot side of the green line. As we arrived the service was beginning and there was the President of Cyprus, President Clerides. It was a beautiful whitewashed church – must be quite old, I should think – with lots of icons and lights burning and children there. I could see behind the altar there were some kids of about eleven or twelve all dressed up in bright yellow choristers' outfits, and they were fooling about having a marvellous time. The Bishop with his Greek Orthodox hat or mitre, was droning on and there were young priests who were singing and holding up the order of service for him to read, and he was sweating. The President looked very bored.

We walked from there to a restaurant that had a canopy stretching over quite a space, and at the very beginning everybody rushed in, presumably from the frontier, and lit a torch in a helmet – a soldier's helmet upside down, held in three rifles which had been bound together into a makeshift tripod. When the helmet began burning it made such a smell they tried to put it out, and it began smoking and they threw water on it, which made it worse, so finally it was removed. The whole thing was very Middle Eastern and informal and friendly.

A whole succession of speeches. The Mayor of Morphou made a speech; the Mayor of Sparta; Tom Cox made a passionate speech; and Alan Meale, Pauline Green and Eddie O'Hara, who is a Labour MP and was in Cyprus doing his national service. Then Clerides, the President, made a speech that aroused great cheers. I think, in effect, he said to the British: if you'll demand of your Government what you say you'll demand, I'll demand it too.

The Commonwealth Prime Ministers' Conference is meeting in Cyprus later this week. The Queen is going to be there. But here is the real rub – the Queen is staying in one of the sovereign bases, not actually staying in Nicosia, and there is a hell of a row. She is being given the gold key of the City of Nicosia and of course a lot of Greeks remember that EOKA fighters who wanted union with Greece were executed by the British. The Labour Government, of which I was a member, did nothing in 1974.

However, they were very well disposed towards us.

Then we began a long, slow walk, led by Greek flags and Cypriot flags and the boys who were all dressed up in yellow, towards the green line – the frontier. I don't know that it was so long, but it was certainly very hot and when we got there you could see the barbed wire, and in the distance was the town of Morphou under Turkish occupation. Lots of people came up to me and said they'd seen or heard me, and I did feel slightly strange to be known so far away. When we got to the frontier there were three lines dividing the Greek Cyprus from the Turkish-occupied part. There were the Cypriot soldiers first to let us through. Then we came to some UN forces – unarmed, and they'd been there for twenty years, I think. I talked to quite a senior officer in the Australian Police Force, who was wearing his Australian uniform with a little blue beret. Then there was an Irish captain from the Irish army, and an Argentinian officer there, wearing the blue beret of course. I must admit I do feel very emotional about that – it is the beginning of a world police force, and these people patrol this no-man's-land right along between the Turkish armed forces (of which there are 40,000 in Cyprus) and the Greek Cypriot Republic, which is the only republic recognised in international law.

It was a very interesting visit – terribly tiring and I'm beginning to feel my age now. One silly thing we had to do at the frontier: I had to jump over this ditch; quite a deep ditch and fairly narrow. A few years ago I'd have thought nothing of it, but as I pushed my leg to jump, it didn't push me as far as it should have done, and my other leg didn't grip and pull me up, so somebody caught my hand and rescued me. But I just feel my health is declining – not an illness exactly, probably just old age. After all I'm getting on for seventy.

Monday 18 October

I'd been summoned to see the Speaker, so I went to the Commons at eleven, feeling a little bit as if I'd been asked to see the headmistress on the first day of school. I couldn't think what it was about. When I went to her room she was very friendly. She said, 'Tony, I've asked you to come and see me because I see you've invited Gerry Adams to visit the House of Commons. I'm afraid this will cause some problems for the Irish Members.'

Well, I said I understood that, but let me give you the background. My grandfather was elected in 1892 on a Home Rule for Ireland ticket, and defeated a Conservative Minister, Ritchie, who said that if you give Ireland Home Rule, there will be anarchy and terrorism. I said in the twenties my father opposed the Black and Tans. I gave all the figures since the Emergency – 3000 killed and injured, 19,000 troops deployed, 18,000 explosions, – and I said we had to find a way of getting peace. Gerry Adams has talked to John Hume and it has been welcomed by Dublin, and I think that people in Britain ought to hear Gerry Adams's case.

Anyway, she thanked me and did not intend to prevent him from coming. I said that Adams had rights as a former MP to come to the Central Lobby. She was not going to prevent him coming, but there was a security aspect to it. Well, I know that very well, because I might get a bomb through my window from the Ulster Freedom Fighters. I said, 'Thank you very much – I appreciate that.'

She said, 'You know there's a debate on Northern Ireland on Friday. If you do want to speak, I'll call you early.'

Then I said I'd been in Cyprus. She said she had been twice this year and loved Cyprus. I said there was a lot of anxiety about why the Labour Government did nothing about it in 1974 – well, she said, it was Jim Callaghan who was responsible for that. And that was very interesting confirmation. I don't know what her interest in Cyprus is.

Tuesday 19 October

This morning I worked on letters, and at twelve ITN had the first programme called *House to House* with Maya Even, sitting in the restaurant at Millbank. It was just a sort of café-society atmosphere and I had been sent a flyer (as every MP had) saying, 'If you've got any news or gossip you'd like to mention', etc. Elinor Goodman began by describing what had happened at Cabinet, and then Maya Even was sort of flirting with David Hunt, the Employment Minister. So Ministers are now asked to comment on the authoritative statements made by journalists. Then they came to the Thatcher memoirs and they had various comments, including her editor talking, and then Robin Day dealing with today's press – all totally inconsequential. And I must say it just turned me off. I was very angry and I'm a bit depressed at the moment. I was rather difficult in the office this morning.

Went into the House after lunch and heard the end of Prime Minister's Questions, and then Andrew Mackinlay moved his Posthumous Pardons for Soldiers Bill. He made a powerful speech about how in the Great War 307 soldiers (many of whom were shell-shocked and ill or frightened) were shot within twenty-four hours of being sentenced, without any appeal or legal representation, on charges of cowardice, desertion in the face of duty or striking an officer, or something of that kind. And some awful Tory MP got up and made an awful little speech, but it went through on the nod – nobody voted against it.

Wandered about. Had tea with Michael Meacher, who travels about doing his World Aid job for the Front Bench – gets about one speech a year, and nobody takes any notice or reports anything he says.

Sunday 24 October

Robin Day's seventieth birthday at the Garrick Club. I've known Robin since 1946. He is about eighteen months older than me, and I knew him when he was a young barrister. He first came to prominence in 1955 when ITV went on the air and he was one of the newsreaders. From that he moved to interviewing, and he undoubtedly changed the whole nature of interviewing, from being so obsequious as to be revolting to being so aggressive as to be equally revolting. But he is a good friend and I have an affection for him. Robin made an amusing speech about how he wanted to thank his accountant and the cardiac surgeon, who both made the party possible. I didn't catch the name of the cardiac surgeon but he came up later and said, 'Show me your hands.' I didn't know what he was thinking about. Then he told me that in 1963, when I cut my hand with a circular saw and Caroline drove me to Hammersmith Hospital, he sewed it up – it was one of his first bits of surgery. It was highly amusing. His wife claimed to be very left and said how she'd always supported me but in the last election in Hampstead she had voted Tory because she didn't want any more changes in the Health Service, which I didn't think was very credible. I said, 'Well, don't bother to confess it to me!'

When we got there, Robin came up and greeted us, and we congratulated him and so on. Then he introduced me (not that I wanted to be introduced) to Maya Even, who is doing this new *House to House* programme. I tried to avoid her eyes because I had rung her up to complain about it and thought she would be wanting to raise my telephone call.

Norman Tebbit was there and his wife, who is still in a wheelchair after the Grand Hotel bombing in Brighton at the Tory Conference some years ago. I've never seen her before. I could see in the corner of my eye Paul Johnson, Woodrow Wyatt, Alan Watkins, Jim Naughtie, Dick Taverne.

John Biffen was there, and I asked if he had a mention in the Thatcher book, and he said 'I haven't read it.' Saw Geoffrey Howe there, and I said, 'You must be having a marvellous time' and he gave me an inscrutable smile as he passed off with his wife Elspeth. Norman Lamont was there and very friendly to Caroline. All these giants who preside in great departments of state do shrink in no time at all when they lose office. Sir Nicholas Henderson was there – that right-wing guy who was the Ambassador in Paris and whose last telegram to the Government was leaked after Labour was defeated in 1979. Every reactionary you could imagine was there.

I didn't see John Birt.

I have two serious social disadvantages at the moment. One is that I can't remember anybody's name any more – I put my mind on search and it usually comes up too late to be of any help. Secondly I'm very deaf, and cocktail conversation is difficult, so I lean forward and try to look interested even if I don't actually hear what's being said. I must give the impression of being quite senile. Caroline looked marvellous and was the belle of the ball. But when you looked at all those people – they were so old and decayed and decrepit.

At the end of the evening, Maya Even finally buttonholed me, so I sat down with her in the corner just as Andrew Neil, the Editor of the *Sunday Times* appeared with his latest partner. She said, 'I heard you'd phoned about the programme. I'm terribly sorry you don't like it. We've been trying to get it going and wanted every MP to know it was there and we'll have more serious discussions', and so on.

Monday 25 October

I forgot to mention that the new consensus – that's Harry Barnes, Peter Bottomley, David Knox, Simon Hughes and Calum Macdonald – had written to me asking me to withdraw my invitation to Gerry Adams.

I heard that the Home Secretary last Tuesday (that's to say, after the Speaker had cleared Gerry Adams's visit and before the debate in the Commons on Friday) had issued an exclusion order to prevent Gerry Adams coming to London. This of course is an absolute denial of civil liberties, so I talked to the BBC and then I came home with Caroline. It really does confirm what I knew all along, that the Government does not want the peace talks.

Tuesday 26 October

The phone rang continuously and I totted it up: fourteen radio and TV broadcasts today about the exclusion order against Gerry Adams.

To the House of Commons. I decided I would raise it as a Point of Order and at the end of PM's Questions fortunately there was no other business, so I got up and put it to the Speaker as a Point of Order in relation to the rights of former members to come to the House. As soon as I got up the Tories began jeering and about three times the Speaker had to protect me, so I just stood in absolute silence while order was restored. I put my point, the Speaker made a ruling and it was worth doing.

Later, when I was voting, Ian Paisley sidled up to me and said he'd like to have a talk. I said, 'I'd be happy to have a talk. I'm not hostile to your community,' and he said, 'Well, the Catholics vote for me and in the south the Catholics are different.'

I said, 'I know that, Ian, but in the end there is a school of thought among your community that knows the British Government will let them down.'

Oh I know that,' he said.

I said, 'Perhaps independence for Northern Ireland is the right thing, because you can't force Irish unity on anybody. Everybody knows that: Sinn Fein knows that, you know that, everybody does. If the British withdrew, I think it would help solve the problem.' He was blustery and friendly – I can't say more than that.

One of the things I think I must record is that the Speakership is run entirely by the Clerk of the House. The Clerk preserves the precedents, won't allow change, and Speakers aren't interested in procedure or history; and the security side is run by the Serjeant at Arms. The Speaker's private secretary is a sort of go-between. So although I go and see Betty Boothroyd and try to persuade her (as I tried to persuade Jack Weatherill or the previous Speakers), it is part of an absolute ritual of democratic representation, where the front person gets all the credit and some of the blame, but the real power is carefully guarded underneath. If ever I were Speaker, I would argue with the Clerk and reach my own judgement.

Wednesday 27 October

Talked to Chris Mullin about the interview tomorrow with the police from the West Midlands, about why he won't give the names of the people he claims he knows committed the Birmingham murders. Chris thought they were trying to get the Birmingham Six back into court and I said, 'No, I think they are trying to get you, Chris.' I don't think he quite understood it.

Thursday 28 October

Chris Mullin was interviewed this morning by the police, and Ruth Winstone sat there and made notes and she said he did very well. They were saying to him, 'Look, you are an essential witness. We must know – your evidence is really important.' And Chris wouldn't budge, on the grounds that he was not prepared to disclose his sources. But Chris is in a real difficulty because I think they're trying to get him. He thinks the police know who the real culprits are, anyway, but if they do arrest the people and ask him, 'Was this the man who confessed?' then Chris will be in a dangerous position personally. If he doesn't tell the court, they might put him in jail for contempt. So I have to try and help him.

Friday 29 October

Went to the House fairly early for the debate on the financial compensation to be paid to Church of England ministers who leave the Church because they object to the ordination of women. It was an interesting debate and Michael Alison, the Church Estates Commissioner, introduced it very delicately. Frank Field made a typical speech in which he said he was in favour of accepting the ordination of women but would vote against the specific measure on financial compensation. I got up and said: would he confirm that the effect of defeating the financial compensation would be that the whole thing would be set back? And Frank said, 'I hope the Rt Hon. gentleman for . . . [he pretended he didn't remember the constituency] is not trying to look into my soul.' But I think he was trying to defeat it.

Then we had an impassioned and stupid speech by Gummer, and I spoke and various other people. It was carried by 215 to 21 for the main motion, and the other was only 19 against, so it was overwhelmingly in favour of compensation. The House was packed for the vote. Excellent debate.

Came home briefly. The office is in a state of total confusion because my Psion computer has quite broken down so I lost my engagements.

Monday 1 November

I had a talk in the House with Chris Mullin, who is under terribly heavy pressure from the police and doesn't know what to do. I told him not to destroy the notebook and to stand firm and see what they do – we might be able to raise it as a privilege matter.

Wednesday 3 November

In the evening there was absolute chaos in the House. Points of Order and shouting – you just got the feeling the Government was on its last legs. We delayed the vote and made it last about forty minutes, and the Serjeant at Arms with his sword was sent in to tell us to go through the Division lobby or else he would take names. So I turned to the Members who were sitting and said, 'What he has done is absolutely contrary to the Speaker's Ruling of 1622.' They all roared with laughter and when the Serjeant had left, I said I'd made it up.

Thursday 4 November

Spent the whole afternoon working on *Question Time* identifying twenty-eight likely questions, and made notes on all of them. Then I went off to do the programme. The only questions that came up were Ireland, the Lords, Europe and the Commonwealth, and unemployment. The audience was very unideological – no structure to their thinking at all.

Panellists were Edwina Currie, Niall Ferguson (young don from Jesus College, Oxford) and Chief Emeka Anyaoku, who is the Secretary General of the Commonwealth – a nice guy. Afterwards I went into the green room and there were Sir Nicholas Henderson and his wife. He had been our Ambassador in France, and of course Ferguson was immediately attracted to him. We talked about diaries and memoirs. Henderson said he hadn't been able to get through Thatcher's book, which is very boring. I said, 'Do you keep a diary?' and he said, 'No.' I asked, 'Have you ever known anything secret?'

He thought of two things. Firstly he said, 'If I reported to you what Mrs Thatcher really thought about President Reagan, it would damage Anglo-American relations.' Secondly, during the Falklands War the Argentinian air force was using American bombs, where the fuse was set for 900 feet, and they dropped the bombs on the decks of British warships and would have sunk far more of them, except that the fuses didn't go off. The Americans knew this, and if they had rung up Buenos Aires and said, 'Reset the fuses for 200 feet,' then a lot of the fleet would have been sunk. Henderson said, 'You mustn't put that in your diary,' and I replied, 'Why the hell I shouldn't, I don't know.'

Monday 8 November

The Labour Party is in a terrible mess. Gordon Borrie, the independent chairman of the Commission on Social Justice set up by John Smith, has come out with a report, including a broad hint that the Welfare State is out of date. The Labour Party is left with absolutely nothing. There has been this perennial row about women-only shortlists for years.

It may be that, as has happened in New Zealand, a Green/Socialist Party will have to be set up. And if for any reason I was thrown out of the Labour Party, I think I probably would stand for that. It would be difficult to throw me out of the Labour Party but if there is a Lib-Lab coalition and proportional representation is introduced, and if that Lib-Lab Government really betrays the people who put their faith in it, then I think the Labour movement might recover in some shape or form.

Friday 19 November

Bitterly cold today and I walked down from the Labour Club to Chesterfield station and got the train to Bristol. On the train there was a No Smoking compartment in first-class, so I asked the man sitting opposite me, 'Do you mind if I smoke? and he said, 'Not at all. Actually I'm a pipe-smoker myself'. So he smoked too. I put up my little Smoking Notice, which I had peeled off a train some time ago, and stuck it over the No Smoking notice and we had a lovely talk. He was a chartered accountant working for the Royal Ordnance factory, which had been taken over by British Aerospace. He had been a Conservative, but he wasn't any more.

Monday 22 November

Caroline and I went to this musical evening at the Speaker's State Rooms at the House of Commons. Betty was all glamorous, and Ted Heath, Father of the House, was there. Lovely supper and lots of people. I must say, when I looked at it I realised what a total fraud Parliament was – a place where capital and labour were supposedly in conflict – because there were Tories and Labour people chatting; and Peter Mandelson in a black tie (without his moustache) kissing the Speaker; and a Tory MP who said, 'I do so agree with you about abolishing the Lords.' The whole thing was cosy, and I think if pensioners and trade unionists and unemployed miners could have seen it, they would have been utterly turned off. But still, that's what happens. It was like the period just before the French Revolution.

We had a lovely meal and David Steel and his wife came and sat with us and had a jolly talk, exactly along the lines that I mentioned. And then, when the music began, I slipped off. Caroline said she wouldn't allow me to stay (in case I went to sleep), so I went off and signed 100 letters.

Got back just as the music ended and the Speaker said, 'You ducked it, I'll never forgive you!

Tuesday 23 November

I went to the Groucho Club, which I had never been to, in Dean Street. Anna Ford invited me to go and I thought, as a courtesy, I'd go. I couldn't find anybody I recognised. Then moving towards me was a figure whose face I knew very well, but I had never spoken to him in my life – Stephen Spender the poet. I looked him up later and found he was born in 1909, and he is eighty-four and in very good shape with a shock of white hair and clear as a bell. I said, 'I'm so pleased to meet you. I was just thinking about you the other day and your book *Forward from Liberalism* which was published by the Left Book Club in the Thirties. He said, 'Oh, I'm ashamed of it', and I said it was a marvellous book. He got embarrassed and said it wasn't very well written. But it was an amazing book. Then Spender was sucked away by Mark Bonham Carter, but throughout the evening he kept sort of hovering round like a vulture and coming back to talk to me. In a funny way I think I made him uneasy. He said what we needed was a new Marx, and I said we've got the old Marx; he wrote some very interesting stuff about the conflict between capital and labour, and the widening gap between rich and poor, and the role of working people to improve themselves. Nobody says we need a new Freud or a new Darwin or a new Galileo. He'd disappear again and then he'd come back. Really interesting – of course he's one of the old left-wingers of the Thirties who have given up, like so many of them did.

Saw Clive Jenkins looking more and more like an old Roman emperor. I asked him what he made of the situation and he said, 'What a fundamental question to ask!' and floated off.

Friday 26 November

Hilary's birthday. I drove him back last night and was actually in the car with him when midnight struck for his fortieth birthday.

I forgot to say that I bought some Ryvita and cheese on the train and breathed in at the wrong moment, and got a bit of the biscuit stuck in my throat and began to choke. There was one woman in the compartment and I stood up and began coughing, but I couldn't breathe in and I felt myself going blue. I bent over double and finally I did succeed in dislodging, it but I really did think I was going to die. That explains my current gloom.

Sunday 28 November

I was dropped down at the station, and I brought a lot of the Sundays and read them very carefully. The big news today is that the Government has been in touch with the IRA and Sinn Fein, probably for twenty years, but certainly since February when the IRA apparently wrote to the Government. There is a real prospect of peace, but of course the Government can be presented as having lied and prevented Gerry Adams from coming to London, and so on.

Got home and wrote a letter to the PM asking him to lift the exclusion order on Gerry Adams's visit to London and the Sinn Fein ban on broadcasting, so that we could all hear what was being said. I faxed that out to the Press Association and to the BBC, who didn't use it on the midnight news. And I sent it to the Speaker.

Monday 29 November

I did five radio interviews about the Northern Ireland situation. Everybody rang me up, because I had invited Gerry Adams over, and what did I think? Radio Sheffield, Radio Derby, Radio Belfast, Radio Birmingham FM and one other. I think when you do six broadcasts in a day you realise there is a sort of role after top office in the Labour Party. Apparently, on Saturday night *Spitting Image* did an absolutely hilarious programme on the Shadow Cabinet just sitting there trying to think of something useful to say, and nobody could think of anything. The Labour

Party is dead; it just criticises the Tories and has no policy. If I am asked what Labour policy is, I say I don't know what it is on anything, which is true.

Wednesday 1 December

Tomorrow we launch the video of my Commons speeches; and I spent some time today trying to market it. Went to speak to the woman at the end of St Stephen's Hall who runs the bookstall, and she said I'd have to get onto the Fees Office for permission to sell it, and then they said I'd have to get onto the Speaker. So then I went to the Parliamentary Bookshop and the manager said he'd have to get on to the Select Committee for Broadcasting via the Deliverer of the Vote, who had do it through the Clerk. Then I went down to the souvenir kiosk by the Strangers' Bar and and they said they'd love to sell it – very friendly – but it had to be agreed by Sue Harrison, Director of Catering and she said she'd have to go to Colin Shepherd, Chairman of the Catering Committee. In effect it has come to a dead-stop because they say it's 'political'! I think the Speaker is the only person who could clear it. I don't know whether she will or not.

Back in my depressed mood tonight – don't know why. It's all a bit much – all this video stuff and diary and TV stuff – it's not really my political work. On the other hand, what else are you to do at the moment? You have no choice but to stick it out during this stagnant period of politics. The Budget was a vicious one, and Peter Lilley was talking tonight about the cuts in benefits and the new job-seeking allowance replacing unemployment pay. The invalidity benefit is going to be turned into an incapacity allowance and they are cutting and cutting, and the age of retirement for women will go up to sixty-five at a time when there is mass unemployment. Another five years of women going back into the labour market is outrageous. The Labour Party is absolutely frozen and the BBC doesn't mention the LP. Peter Lilley was followed by Emma Nicholson talking to Gordon Borrie, a former civil servant and Chairman of the Commission on Social Justice. I heard Gordon Brown doing his summary of the Budget and it was just negative, negative stuff. Nobody is talking about what needs to be spoken about. It's a very stagnant period, which could easily swing British opinion sharply to the right. I think that is the way in which it could well go.

Sunday 5 December

Reading the Sunday papers, a lot about Ireland. Terrible thing to say, but it has to be said because it is true that if it weren't for all the killing, there would be no coverage. It is the killing that has got the coverage, and the coverage forces the solution. And the Government have got into a position now where they have to deal with Dublin, so in a way it is a condominium and shared responsibility for the North, which is stage one. Stage two is when both Dublin and London renounce their claims on the North, and the North has to work out its own relationship with its own community and the relations between North and South. The Labour Party isn't mentioned at all in the newspapers because it says nothing of interest.

Came back and read all the papers – all gossip. All afternoon and evening I wrote out 105 names and addresses for the Chesterfield Christmas cards. I've always meant to do that, but I have a bit more time now. Various phone calls from the family and we watched *Spitting Image,* which is very funny. I watched a cynical play called *To Play the King,* about a right-wing Tory minister who clashes with Prince Charles when he's become King – he is all very liberal, and so on. An indication really of modern politics. It is difficult for anyone born in a particular period – the rise of the Nazis, the war, the Cold War, the challenge of the times, and all that; now there is no challenge – the thing has just sunk back into a decadent *ancien régime* like France before the French Revolution or England under Charles I. Something will blow – which way and when and how remains to be seen.

Monday 13 December
Enormously busy day. Reem Abdelhadi came to see me, a very charming Palestinian woman from Nablus whom I had worked closely with during the Gulf War. She came with two Palestinians from the Arab Association for Human Rights in Nazareth. They had asked to come, because I saw Reem briefly at the Marxist University and in effect she wanted to say that Arafat was negotiating without proper consultation. The PLO had always stood for the rights of the Palestinian people to the land that belonged to them. Arafat had abandoned that, without proper consultation, and he had now agreed to something that gives far less of the occupied territories, the return of which the UN had called for. The Americans were working hand-in-glove, of course, with the Israeli Government. The Palestinians would not enjoy the same guaranteed rights as Israeli citizens living in the new territories, which would be administered by the Palestinians – Jericho and Gaza. Some Palestinians were in Lebanon without proper rights and others were going to be sent to Iraq, where they would cease to have any rights; those Palestinians who were in refugee camps were treated as refugees; those who were not, were treated as citizens of the country where they had found asylum. They said the whole PLO would break. They wanted my advice, so I went over it all carefully. I said I thought that Arafat had engaged in both a betrayal and a beginning. I had hoped it might develop. They should get their case across, and it was a very useful meeting. They were friendly but keen to appear responsible, because if you are once classified as an enemy of the

settlement reached between Israel and the PLO, then you are treated like a criminal.

Thursday 16 December
To the BBC first thing for the *Moral Maze* with Michael Buerk, Hugo Gryn, Professor David Starkey, and Janet Daley and Edward Pearce. We were supposed to be discussing what had happened in Russia and democracy generally. It was just a madhouse. Janet Daley shouted and interrupted all the time; David Starkey was insulting; Edward Pearce said we had to have democracy slowly, we didn't want it yet; and Hugo Gryn was sensitive, but oh, what rubbish! I don't think I'll do it again because there's nobody even vaguely involved on the left in the programme at all.

Worked at home: the video is booming – another 500 orders today. Rushed into the Commons for an interview with Ulster TV about the Sinn Fein ban. The Prime Minister had written to me about the ban and indicated they might shift on it, and I put that out to the press. I did an interview with the BBC's *Financial World Tonight*.

I'm exhausted – I just don't feel like doing anything. I don't even get up to make a cup of tea because it would mean finding a mug and putting it in front of a kettle – I'm just longing for Christmas.

Saturday 25 December
Christmas Day. We opened our stockings in the bedroom and I got some lovely clothes from Caroline, and I gave her a garden vacuum cleaner and a new video. We phoned Dave, and I phoned Tom Vallins and Doris Heffer, and we had a huge family lunch. Then presents, and the kids ran around and decorated various things with their drawings and talked lavatory language. There were tears and lots of fun, and I took Paul and Lissie and Paul's brother Alastair back home, and then PC back to the Barbican and he showed me his model for the Bankside opera site. Absolutely beautiful: circular stage and then a slice of an orange for the auditorium, and behind it a curved circular building for rent, which will pay for the opera. He is just so keen; he's been hammered into the ground by the Prince of Wales and all that reactionary talk about architecture, but he keeps at it.

Tuesday 11 January, 1994
I had terrible toothache, an absolutely shattering pain in my tooth.

In the evening, five o'clock, Gerry McLoughlin, the representative of Sinn Fein in London, and Gerry Fitzpatrick who works for the Irish Centre came to work out an Irish agenda for us. We agreed that we would have a press conference on Monday to launch the Sinn Fein version of the talks with the British Government.

Wednesday 12 January

John Smith came up to me in the lobby: terribly friendly, almost put his arm round my shoulder, and said he'd just been to dinner with the American correspondents and one of them said to him, 'You are the luckiest man in world politics because the Government are in such a mess.'

I thought I detected just a sniff of alcohol on his breath. I wouldn't like to say as they say in Scotland, 'He was stinking wi' drink', but there was a slight alcoholic enthusiasm about him. We talked about the scandals, involving public and political figures, that continually appear in the press. I said, 'Scandal could work both ways.'

'Oh, no,' said John, 'the Labour Party is made up of people with happy marriages', and so on.

Well, I think scandal could be turned in our direction.

Thursday 13 January

I went to the dentist, who gave me some antibiotics.

Dame Shirley Porter and a lot of leading Conservatives have been accused by the District Auditor of having gerrymandered the sale of council houses in Westminster at the expense of the homeless, in order to sell them to people who would then vote Tory; indeed, they won three key wards on that basis.

Later I saw Ted Heath, who'd written me a nice little note the other day – the envelope written in his own hand – thanking me very much for having supported his trip to Iraq.

I went over to him on the Front Bench and said, 'Thanks for your note, Ted. I not only agree with you about Iraq, but I agree with you that we shouldn't bomb Serbia', which is a point he'd also made.

He laughed in a sort of friendly way and I said, 'You know, the old men have got it right; these young people are making a mess of everything.' And he laughed quite hard.

Friday 14 January

The bungalow next to the Labour Club is almost finished. I'm going to move in next month.

Saturday 15 January

I went out shopping, but spent most of the afternoon preparing for the Irish press conference on Monday, and I bound together the documents that Sinn Fein had produced and put out press releases.

In the evening Caroline and I went to Ralph Miliband's seventieth birthday party at his house off Regent's Park. He's really a distinguished old socialist. He's written a book called *Socialism in a Sceptical Age* and it's going to be a very important book, I think. Marion was there, and Ralph's sister, who had been left in Belgium during the war; also David Miliband, their elder son, who works for the Institute of Public Policy Research, and Edward, the younger one, who was a Teabag and who now works for Harriet Harman.

I did have a bit of a go at Edward about the sort of total failure of the Labour Party to say anything useful.

Sunday 16 January

Scandal still continues in the newspapers; a new Tory MP has been revealed as having a love-child. The press are just sniffing around for anybody they can find.

On Saturday twelve pounds of mail by weight arrived, and I just read it all and scribbled notes, but it's a huge burden, the mail.

In the evening I worked late on my letters, but I did take time out to see *Oklahama!*, the first of the great post-war or wartime American musicals, with the song 'Oh what a beautiful morning'. I'd never seen the film or the show but, of course, the music conveyed that huge confidence and happiness that really spread through America, and to some extent Britain, after the war.

Monday 17 January

I went into the House for the Sinn Fein press conference.

Tom Hartley, the National Chairperson of Sinn Fein, was there, a councillor in Belfast. A hard, decent, unemotional man. And he brought with him Joan O'Connell and Gerry McLoughlin and Gerry Fitzpatrick. Jeremy Corbyn and I talked with them in the cafeteria downstairs.

Then we went into the Jubilee Room, had got there about half an hour early and it was packed with television people. I think most of the top lobby hacks were at the Scott Inquiry listening to the Prime Minister. We had American television CNN, Australian Broadcasting, Swedish Broadcasting.

Lady Olga Maitland, MP, turned up and said, 'When will the violence stop?'

And Hartley treated her with great respect and said, 'Well, we're putting our case, and thank you for coming and listening.'

Apart from that one critical question, all the other media treated Tom Hartley as he is: as a statesman for the Irish people, really.

I talked to Richard Shepherd, who said that his local party was absolutely shocked that Major should refer to his colleagues as 'bastards'. And they were shocked by what was going on. He thought Major was just not up to the job, and that Douglas Hurd had a chance of surviving.

There was quite a bit of decent coverage on the television about the Irish thing, and when I came home I found a message on my answerphone saying, 'Good evening, Stewart Wheeler here. Mr Benn, I would advise you that under the Treason Act of 1351 anyone harbouring the King's enemies and levying troops against the King can be committed for treason. So that is one law, sir, amongst many other laws, that I think you may have forgotten. Anyone like Gerry Adams and all these other scallywags, I think, ought to be put up for treason. Now I may take summonses out for treason against them and I may take them out against you, sir, for aiding and abetting, also an Act of Parliament – I think it's 1851, something like that, I've got it in my books here. Anyway I bid you good evening sir, bye-bye.'

Very respectful, but feeling he had to make his point. Anyway it just makes a nice ending for the day and I might add that he gave his address and his name, so if anything happened I would know who had done it.

Saturday 22 January

Just as I was going to bed, I had a phone call from a woman who rang me up from Cheltenham in great distress to say that her brother-in-law had been on death row in Missouri for ten years. His death sentence is coming up, and could I do anything about it?

Well, I'm passionately opposed to the death sentence and I constructed what I thought was an extremely skilful letter to the Governor of Missouri, making clear what I was asking; saying something about my own position as a former Cabinet Minister and long-term Member of Parliament; calling his attention to the fact that the Judicial Committee of the Privy Council had said that more than five years on death row was really not right; hoping that he would show mercy and telling the human story.

I faxed it off to Missouri, which you can do now – amazingly. She gave me the fax number, I typed out the letter, popped it in the machine, pressed the button and within two seconds – it was by then about quarter-past 11 so it would be about a quarter past six on a Saturday evening in the Governor's mansion – it was gone, and if he doesn't get it today he'll get it on Monday. I also sent the letter by post to the Governor and sent some copies to her.

That is an aspect of political work that is very satisfying. I did take up the cases of some of the people on death row in Jamaica. Wrote to the Lord Chancellor, and the Privy Council considered it.

I had a letter from one of the guys who was reprieved, just overwhelmed with gratitude and so on. I don't say that my intervention makes a lot of difference, but the knowledge that somebody is intervening does raise morale for people in those tragic circumstances.

Monday 24 January

Went to the House of Commons. I'm very lonely at the House at the moment and, not being on the National Executive, of course you can't convey any information to anybody, so they tend not to come up to you.

It's partly my fault because I don't sit in the Chamber very much, I don't go to Parliamentary Labour Party meetings which I should or to other meetings, so I sort of cut myself off and I remind myself of Enoch Powell in his latter days. He'd walk along the corridor with his eyes straight ahead; if you acknowledged him, he smiled back courteously, and he was very jolly if you spoke to him. I'm disenchanted with the Labour Party and what it's doing at the moment, but I think I must be careful that I don't neglect the constituency because of all the broadcasting that I do, and that I don't absolutely abandon Parliament.

I had a very silly row with Hattersley tonight in the Division Lobby.

When the video of my speeches came out, *The Independent* asked him to review it and he absolutely rubbished it, so I couldn't resist – as I was standing next to him by the table where the clerks take your name in the Division Lobby – saying to him, 'Roy, a word of thanks. I only ordered three hundred copies of the video to be made, but after your review it jumped up to eighteen hundred, and now we've ordered another thousand. It was broadcast in full in New York and Norman Lamont's bought a copy.'

So he turned round and in an icy way said, 'Well, I still think it's rubbish.'

'Well, you can make a living publishing rubbish and nobody knows it better than you.'

It was a rather nasty exchange really, and Joe Ashton said, 'I ought to keep you two giants apart.'

I shouldn't have said it. He'll be angry with me and I feel guilty about it. And the old principle – 'Do not wrestle with a chimney sweep' – which is what my father taught me as a child, applied. So I shall make a point of being more jolly when I see Hattersley, but it did give me a certain pleasure that the video's gone like a bomb.

Tuesday 25 January

In the lobby this evening Ian Paisley came up with Peter Robinson – the two Democratic Unionists MPs – to have a chat.

Paisley's such an attractive old rogue really. He said he wanted to get a copy of the Sinn Fein account of the Government negotiations with Sinn Fein. We had a sort of jolly friendly talk. I must say he's totally different personally from his public persona, but that's very often the case.

Friday 28 January, Chesterfield

Bob Chesshyre was on the train, following me for this profile he's doing for the *Sunday Telegraph* magazine. He's a quiet, decent guy, but of course he's a professional journalist and it doesn't follow at all that he's going to treat me with respect. He asked me if I was a Marxist.

The train was a bit late and I dropped my bag, and he dropped his bag too, in my flat and we went down to the opening of the South Yorkshire Housing Association. The Housing Manager was there, although he's not allowed to build houses any more, but he administers a fairly big housing stock. There were also three Christian ministers; they were really liberation theologians.

Surgery lasted from 1.30 to six o'clock; about thirty-four or thirty-five people came. Robert Chesshyre sat in and nobody bothered at all – I asked all of them if they minded, said he's studying the work of an MP.

It was an absolutely typical surgery: housing cases, personal tragedies, two people who were mentally disturbed. I sat and chatted to them and dictated the letters to Margaret.

I took Bob back for a chat and a bite to eat in my flat and we went to the Executive meeting, and again they allowed him to sit in.

Later I walked him all the way back to the Chesterfield Hotel, through the market, which was nice: there was almost a full moon, a clear evening. Very tired actually; it had been an enormously long day from a quarter to six to pretty well quarter to one.

Monday 31 January

My new tea alarm woke me up with a shattering noise and a light this morning.

The Iranian Chargé d'Affaires, Mr Ansari, arrived this morning with the Embassy Counsellor. Two absolutely typical Iranians, neatly dressed with their white shirts and no collars, looking severe and puritanical, which is what they are. I welcomed them and said how much I appreciated their coming.

They said, 'We feel we'd like to talk to people, because there's a misunderstanding.'

I said, 'Let me tell you my view very simply. I supported Mussadegh, I thought he was an honest patriot. I thought the Shah was a CIA plant. I was opposed to the exploitation of Iran, I was opposed to the war against Iran, but I don't support the mujahidin who are the Iranian rebels in Iraq. I think the next U.S. target is going to be Iran because you're very powerful; they destroyed Iraq and now they'd like to destroy Iran.

'I understand deep religious feeling, but I think there are serious problems of human rights, and I think you've made a great mistake to issue a fatwa against Salman Rushdie.'

They said 'Thank you for being so open.'

I went and brought them coffee. Ruth wouldn't make them coffee because they wouldn't shake hands with her, for religious reasons, I presume.

We continued to talk. I think they appreciated the fact that I had been so frank, and they invited me to go to Iran, which I said I'd like to do in due course. Then they said that the fatwa was very difficult, because it was proclaimed by an expert who is now dead.

I said that Allah is merciful and the best thing for the Iranian Government to do would be to say, 'Recognise that Allah is merciful, and Allah will judge Salman Rushdie when he dies.'

They laughed, because in a way I had got at them through the theological argument. They said 'We've given an assurance that we're not sending people to kill Rushdie.'

I said, 'I'm glad to hear that, but it is quite unacceptable for a government to pronounce a sentence of death, even if they don't carry it out. Anyway, there may be Muslims here who feel it's their duty to Khomeni to kill.'

Went to the House this afternoon and the announcement was made that the Rover car company, the old British Leyland, had been sold by British Aerospace to the German motor manufacturer BMW.

I tried to get in a word because I really had a claim since I was the man who acquired British Leyland for the Labour Government, but the Speaker didn't call me. I thought that a bit rough, but still I can't complain.

Looking back on the day, the Government would sell anything – they've no interest in British industry at all; there isn't a British industry; there's a German industry, a Japanese industry in Britain, but there's no British industry left.

Tuesday 1 February

Talked to Joan Lestor a bit about Kenneth Kaunda and she implied very delicately that she and Kenneth had been very close when they were much younger; she sort of gave a funny smile and said, 'We were very dear friends. And anyway we were very young at the time.'

I said, 'You should write your memoirs.'

She replied, 'Oh, I can't while all my exes are still alive.'

She's sort of a nice old lady, is Joan Lestor. I say that but she's ten years younger than me.

This afternoon Jo Richardson died aged seventy. She'd been terribly ill.

There were four votes at ten o'clock and John Smith walked by me, turned around and came and sat next to me, then in a very jolly way said, 'How are you?'

'I'm fine. You're doing very well. What is our lead in the polls now?'

And he said, "Twenty per cent.'

I asked, 'What do you make of Major? He seemed to be such a nice guy; he doesn't seem to know what's going on.'

John said, 'I don't think he wanted the job.'

'Well, John, I came to see you two or three years ago, you probably remember, and I said you should be Leader and you said *you* didn't want the job.' So he gave me a funny sort of smile. Then I said, 'By the way, one thing about taxation: I was the Peter Mandelson of the '59 election and I remember that when Hugh Gaitskell gave a pledge in Newcastle in September 1959, after we had a huge lead in the polls, that there'd be no increase in taxation under Labour, morale just collapsed. And Wilson issued a statement saying there'd be no increase in purchase tax. There are two sides to all of this.'

'I know,' he said.

Wednesday 2 February

The new arrangement in the office is looking much better. The photocopier's in the kitchen now, and Sheila's got a desk of her own where she can open letters. There's more space to walk around and it's much improved.

Sunday 6 February

Today I drafted a New Labour Clause 4 called Clause 4a: 'To secure for the Shadow Cabinet the full fruits of ministerial office on the basis of the existing distribution of wealth and the present administration and control of each industry and service.'

This evening I watched *The Pope Must Die* with Robbie Coltrane, which was absolutely hilarious.

Monday 7 February

There was a bit of a row in the office because there are all these damned videos everywhere and I don't know what to do with them all.

Went into the House and the Under-Secretary of State for the Foreign Office made a statement about possible air strikes against Serbia, following the massacres in the market place in Sarajevo over the weekend, allegedly by Serbian artillery, though that isn't absolutely established.

As always happens, we got John Cunningham saying the Government was indecisive, the Liberal Democrats calling for stronger action, David Winnick calling for action, Andrew Faulds talking about a Christian Foreign Secretary and a Jewish Defence Minister failing to support the Muslims. It was an outrageous statement to make. There were one or two cautious voices from the Tory side.

I got up and said I thought the caution expressed by the Government had much wider support than it might appear from the House, and if you had air strikes, more lives might be lost. If the humanitarian aid ended, our people might be killed, and aid workers killed; the peacekeeping would end and you would get into a long-term war in the Balkans, the outcome of which you couldn't anticipate. I was the only voice from our side expressing caution, except for Dennis Skinner who said that the break-up of Yugoslavia was a deal between Britain and the Germans over opting-out from the Social Chapter which I think is probably true.

I am glad I made the point, and a lot of Tories came up afterwards and congratulated me on what I said. I know it is not very popular because the media are whipping it all up. But the horrors are being carried out by all sides, and just bombing the Serbs and 'surgical air strikes' are largely illusory.

At 5.45 Gerry Fitzpatrick, Gerry McLoughlin and Mitchel McLaughlin came for a further talk. We only had about forty minutes, but really what they wanted was my opinion about the Downing Street Declaration.

I was flattered to be asked and it was a useful thing to do. I wasn't trying to tell them what to do, but trying to suggest a framework. For them to simply lay down their arms now, hand them over and let their prisoners be treated as common criminals is an awful lot to ask, and I don't think all the IRA people would agree to do it. But it is quite clear to me that they want to make progress on the peace process and I think they are serious about that.

Tuesday 8 February

A Conservative MP called Stephen Milligan was found dead last night, apparently dressed in silk stockings with a plastic bag over his head, quite naked. Of course, this absolutely filled the tabloids, and the BBC refers to the tabloids disapprovingly but guarantees you know everything they say.

Went into the Commons at about 7.30 and on the Channel 4 News Perez de Cuellar, the former Secretary General of the UN, was interviewed by Jon Snow. He called for immediate air strikes and ground troops to end the war. I always thought he was pretty weak. At least it wasn't Boutros Boutros-Ghali, the present Secretary General, saying it. It is quite clear that this war is being whipped up by the media and of course, while you threaten air strikes, the Bosnian Muslims are not going to agree to any sort of settlement; they are just waiting for the strikes. This terrible massacre over the weekend could well have been triggered off by some operation by the Muslims to get Western air support against Serbia.

Wednesday 9 February

To Caxton House to join a delegation of Central Region Labour MPs to go and see Michael Forsyth, the Minister at the Department of Employment, about the Bilsthorpe Colliery disaster, which the NUM believe was caused by the use of roof bolts, which have never been supported by the NUM.

There were the MPs on one side – Paddy Tipping, Harry Barnes, Alan Meale, Joe Ashton, Dennis Skinner – and on the other side of the table were Forsyth, a dedicated Thatcherite; John Rimington, the Director General of the HSE; Frank Davies, Chairman of the Health and Safety Commission; and the Chief Inspector of Mines, Mr Kenneth Twist.

The chief mining engineer showed lots of pictures of rock, stresses and roadways – which meant nothing to me or anybody. Alan Meale started discussing the technical side. Joe Ashton asked for an independent inquiry.

I had read all the papers very carefully and Ken Coates had given me an excellent brief on it and, when I was called, I said 'What we want is an independent inquiry because there is a ministerial responsibility. I am not qualified to comment on the technical side. When I was at Energy in 1975, we agreed to transfer responsibility for mining safety from the department responsible for the production of coal to the Department of Employment, so that it would be independent. NACODS had a legal responsibility and it was done to make safety independent. The responsibility on you, Minister, is for safety and not production. You should call for total disclosure. In this case, it was the HSE that authorised the derogation of the Mines and Quarries Act to permit roof bolts to be used. There was pressure brought to bear on the Health and Safety Executive by the employment of American consultants who reported in January 1993, based on American experience. It was not even clear whether the derogation that had been given by the HSE had been fully carried out by British Coal. A former mining engineer for North Derbyshire, who had been employed by NACODS, has not been allowed to inspect the site. Certain figures are not being disclosed. We were given figures of accidents where roof bolts were used, but we were not given the figures (which I know are available to British Coal) of roof movements when roof bolts are used. Under the Citizens' Charter and so on we are entitled to know all that information. In addition to that, deregulation changes the regime and privatisation makes a difference. In effect, Minister, you – the Government – is a party to this inquiry and shouldn't therefore be conducting it itself.'

This had an absolutely electric effect. I was terribly pleased. I had put on a white shirt and a respectable tie – actually the centenary tie of the Durham Miners' Gala.

Forsyth said, 'Who would you appoint to be independent?'

I said, 'A judge. When I was responsible for nuclear power in 1966, when there was a corrosion of the soft steel bolts at the Bradwell power station, I wasn't satisfied with the way the Nuclear Inspectorate was handling it, so I myself appointed Sir Alec Merrison, the Vice-Chancellor of Bristol University, who was a nuclear physicist, to do an independent report.'

This was beginning to cause great anxiety. First of all, the Chief Inspector of Mines, Mr Twist, looked uncomfortable, but Rimington, of the HSE, looked even more uncomfortable, and Mr Davies, the Chairman of the Commission itself, looked very uncomfortable.

Then Dennis Skinner got in and said, 'Look. Let's be blunt about it. This is just another bloody quango and you are all in it together. It is all due to the '84/85 strike. After the strike, management was in the saddle. You didn't take a blind bit of notice of the union in this. As for you, Forsyth, you'd sell your grandmother if you could make money out of it.' And he picked up his papers and stormed out.

To begin with, I thought that was a bit harsh; on the other hand, it performed a useful function because it scared the Health and Safety Commission, who were terrified that their independence of government would be compromised.

I said, 'I think what Dennis Skinner said reflects the opinion of a lot of miners. You have got to take account of it, and you want to safeguard the independence of the Health and Safety Commission.'

Forsyth said, 'Well, it is open to the H&S Commission to recommend an independent inquiry.'

I replied, 'I know that, but I don't know if they will do it or not' – because we had been told they would report tomorrow – 'but, you, Minister have the right to appoint somebody over and above that. You can think of special reasons – new technology, new regimes of deregulation, privatisation – new factors that you can take into account that the H&S Commission might not take into account.'

We went downstairs and did a lot of television interviews. It really was very successful. I got the feeling they were a bit worried.

Came back to the House and drafted a resolution on opposing intervention in Bosnia which I took to the Campaign Group and Alice Mahon signed it immediately. Dennis said, 'Wait a minute. You have done very well' (this concerned my intervention last Monday), 'but don't put it in writing and divide the Campaign Group.' Of course, Ken Livingstone, Bernie Grant and Lynne Jones were for intervention, with Alan Simpson a bit wobbly.

I said, 'Well, I am a democrat and I put it before you for discussion.'

Today, Bryan Gould resigned from Parliament, having taken up the job as Vice-Chancellor of a New Zealand University, and said he couldn't honestly have supported a Labour Government. The soft left think this is a terrible tragedy. He is a sort of media man, and politics was all a career business for him. So I had no sympathy and anyway, if you are elected to fight for your people in a Parliament, you do not quit for a better job, and it will do us a lot of damage.

Saturday 12 February

Michael Foot was quoted on the radio strongly supporting the bombing of the Serbs in Bosnia, so the old peacemonger has now come round to the

Outside our London home of fifty years

LONDON REGION
C.N.D.
EX-SERVICES
CEASEFIRE
NOW
COMMITTEE TO STOP WAR IN THE GULF
STOP THIS BLOODY WAR NOW!
CEASEFIRE SANCTIONS NEGOTIATE
IRAQ OUT OF KUWAIT BRING THE TROOPS HOME ALIVE
NO TO WAR
STOP THE WAR! NEGOTIATE NOW!
CEASEFIRE NOW!
No blood for oil
OIL KILLS

The beginning of the end for the Conservatives under John Major.

Demonstrations against (*left*) the war on Iraq in 1991 and (*below*) pit closures in 1992.
Tony Benn, Arthur Scargill and Dennis Skinner campaigning.

Right: New Labour, Old Leader: Peter Mandelson with Neil Kinnock

Bottom: New Labour, New Men: Tony Blair and Gordon Brown plan their election victory

New Labour, New Era: The victorious Blairs in May, 1997

THE MESSAGE

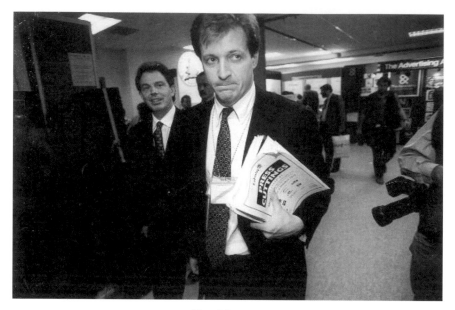

Top: Alastair Campbell, Tony Blair's Press Secretary

Bottom left: On message: David Blunkett

Bottom right: Occasionally on message: Mo Mowlam

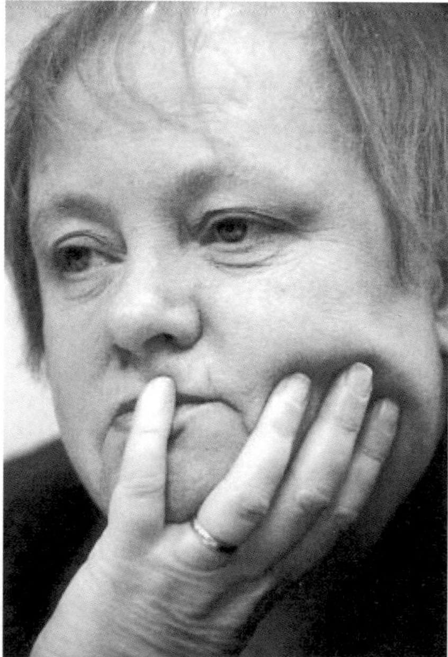

Off Message

Top left: Tam Dalyell, Father of the House, Mr Valiant-for-Truth

Top right: Chris Mullin, Chairman of the Home Affairs Select Committee, who pointedly refused to carry a pager

Bottom left: Jeremy Corbyn, human rights campaigner

Bottom right: Ken Livingstone, Mayor of London against all the odds

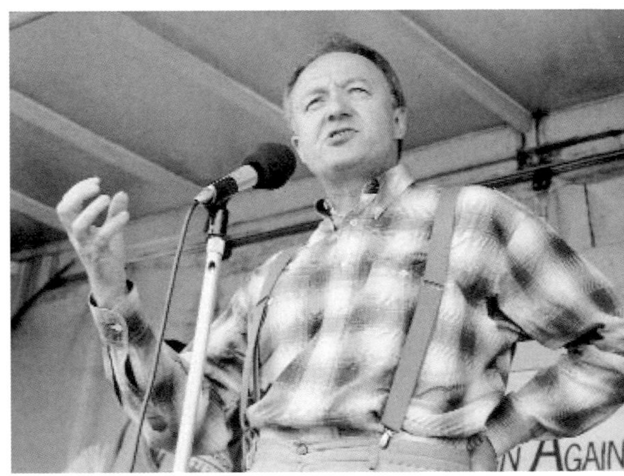

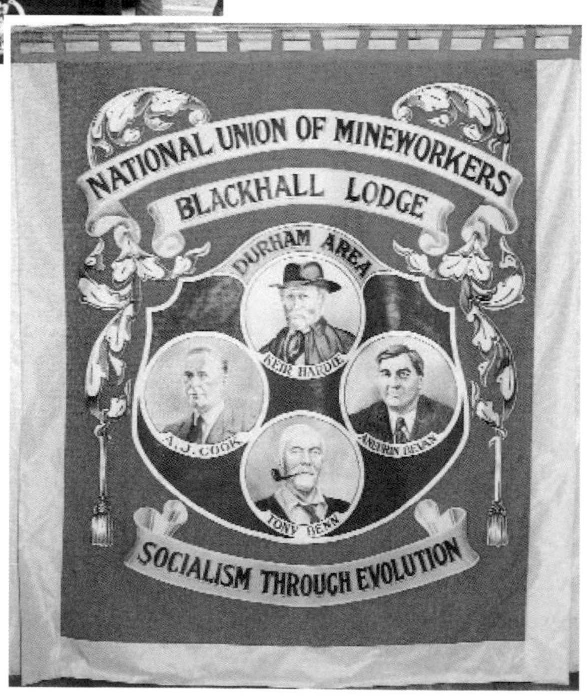

A tale of two banners:

Top: Chesterfield celebrates May Day with members of the Benn family, including grandsons William, Michael and Jonathan

Bottom: Keir Hardie, A. J. Cook, Nye Bevan and Tony Benn: the ultimate honour from the miners

militant stand shown during the Falklands War and the Gulf War.

Today I realised the great importance of not retiring. Gordon Schaffer is eighty-eight, Picasso painted until he was eighty-two, Frank Allaun is eighty-two. All these old boys kept going right to the very end, and I do think that is important, otherwise it is tempting to quit, like Bryan Gould. You can't split and you can't quit. You have got to fight and argue. That, I think, is what keeps you going. I certainly cannot imagine retiring. I would die of boredom and shame if I just gave up.

On the other hand, I have to recognise that it is an exceptionally depressing time because the ideas of the right have got such a grip.

Monday 14 February

Snow this morning.

Went into the Commons for the parliamentary photography exhibition: photographs by MPs. I had been asked because I had found in my mother's Kodak camera a film which, miraculously, was developed thirty years later, showing pictures of my children at the same age as my grandchildren are now. I had sent them in.

There was Peter Brooke, the Heritage Secretary. He told me an interesting story about the row the Government is having about the Churchill family, who want to sell Churchill's papers to America for an enormous sum of money. Peter Brooke said, 'We are challenging it because some of the papers are Government papers.'

Saw Denis Healey, who had submitted a photo of Edna surrounded by flowers in the garden, and then a picture of a wizened old Croatian lady with no teeth. Denis was very funny. He said, 'Of course, that's what Edna looks like now.'

Wednesday 16 February

I saw Alice Mahon this evening, who said she had seen the American Ambassador who was very doubtful about the bombing of the Serbs and said there were a hundred reasons not to bomb, which is why it hasn't been done before.

Thursday 17 February

In the papers this morning there was a report of the death of James Rusbridger, a former MI6 officer, whom I had met some years ago when I did a programme on the Intelligence services. He was found hanged, with his legs bound and a rope around a pulley, and I must say, it does raise the question of whether he committed suicide or was murdered. I don't know anything about it beyond the fact that his death was reported.

Sunday 20 February

Gordon Brown, Robin Cook and somebody else have come out with the idea of bringing private capital into the public service – Health and Education. If I am asked, it's nothing to do with Labour Party policy; we are not committed to it, and it's an interesting idea and I have got some interesting ideas too, but it does show how far we are drifting down the pan. If you want to bring private capital in, say that a percentage of the pension funds have got to be invested in the public services, gilt-edged or something, what's wrong with that?

Tuesday 22 February
I am listening to Denis Healey's *The Time of My Life* on tape and he is tremendously egocentric: 'I did this, I did that. I was the first to realise . . . I appreciated . . .' and so on. No affectionate reference to individual members of the Labour Party, to the trade unions, to Conference – they were all the enemy. You could see that Denis was clever – whether he is as clever as he makes out, I don't know – but he saw himself as an intellectual politician for whom office was everything and Opposition was hardly worth it. Whenever anything had gone wrong, he had been 'misinformed'. Fair enough, he made his case and it was interesting enough.

Wednesday 23 February
We had an interesting meeting of the Campaign Group on Bosnia. Malcolm Chisholm was in the chair. There were three people putting different points of view: somebody from International Workers' Aid, which has had a convoy going to Bosnia – very pro-Bosnian and anti-Serb; Ron Huzzard from LAP putting the view that I hold, that you shouldn't bomb or arm, but work on peacekeeping and humanitarian aid; then Malcolm Harper of the UN Association, taking a similar view but saying the UN would probably have to establish some form of a protectorate to guarantee food and aid and provide some sort of constitution, and drawing a parallel with what had been done in Cambodia.

Jeremy Corbyn's position I didn't quite gather. Bernie Grant is strongly in favour of arming the Bosnians and bombing the Serbs, and so is Lynne Jones, and the debate went backwards and forwards. The Campaign Group is always good when an issue like that crops up. We didn't reach a conclusion, but at least we had it all out and without disrupting our personal relations.

Saturday 26 February
Today an American Israeli doctor, one of the settlers in the area which it has been agreed should be handed over to the Palestinians, got a submachine gun and killed about thirty to sixty Arabs and the whole peace talks have been put at risk. I must admit I wonder whether all the effort I put in during my life to helping the developing countries to rid themselves of imperialism hasn't led to a new tyranny of some kind or

another. It is not that I am intending to give up in any way, but the one thing that does happen when you get older is that you see it all in a historical perspective.

Monday 28 February

I heard this morning of the shooting down of two allegedly Serb aircraft by two American F16 fighters in the former Yugoslavia.

Went to the Commons to hear the statement on Bosnia, having notified the Speaker that I would raise the matter on a Point of Order. Jack Cunningham, our Shadow Foreign Secretary, had asked for a PNQ and the Speaker had turned it down. Well, I couldn't remember ever in my life hearing of the Opposition asking for a PNQ and being turned down, so there must have been a lot of pressure put on the Speaker.

I did get in and the Speaker said she would consider an emergency debate under Standing Order No. 20 later. I got up at the very end and asked if she would accept it then and there. It was an effective parliamentary point and well worthwhile making.

Wednesday 2 March

Arthur Scargill came to tea with me at the House of Commons; we talked for about an hour down in the Strangers' cafeteria.

He said that the security services had opened a bank account in Dublin in his name and had sent a lookalike of Arthur Scargill to draw the money out, ready to be photographed; but the bank had not received the money that the security services had intended to pay in, owing to a muddle at BCCI which was the bank they were using for the purpose and so this scheme went wrong.

Arthur said that Leon Brittan, as Home Secretary, had used the police as a military force with helicopters, and so on; that 13,000 miners had been arrested, 7000 injured and eleven died and not a single police officer had ever been charged, and the riot charge was a fraudulent charge. He said that defeatism leads to an inward-looking, inward-fighting movement and it was like the '30s.

Thursday 3 March

The Scott Inquiry into Matrix Churchill* has exploded in such a way that it looks to me as if the Attorney General, Sir Nicholas Lyell, is in trouble, because he apparently told Ministers they had to sign a public-interest immunity order to keep certain key documents out of the trial of those charged.

*Customs and Excise prosecuted directors of Matrix Churchill for the alleged illegal export of machine tools, used in munitions manufacture, to Iraq. The trial judge directed the men to be acquitted in November 1992.

The Pergau Dam scandal, where the British Government appeared to be providing development aid from the Overseas Development Agency for the dam in exchange for British military equipment bought by the Malaysian government, is exploding. You've got Lynda Chalker and Douglas Hurd being cross-examined by the Foreign Affairs Committee on that, and these Select Committees are very powerful and influential. It's a much better standard of cross-examination than you get in the House.

Sunday 6 March

Read the papers.

Heseltine's name is back in the news. Will he challenge John Major because Major ditched Lyell, the Attorney General, and is now moving towards the right?

I do think Heseltine would probably make mincemeat of John Smith. The thought idly crossed my mind as to whether another attempt at the leadership would be appropriate. But I think Smith's failure has got to become apparent and then somebody would have to be found, and I don't know who it could be. I don't see anybody on the Front Bench who would be capable of doing it. Prescott's got a certain flair, but otherwise there's nobody there at all and if Labour loses next time, we have a whole new ball game.

Thursday 10 March

There was a statement made this afternoon about the decision to send more troops to Yugoslavia, and I said it would be an outrage if the Turks were invited to take part, partly for historical reasons and partly because they still had troops in northern Cyprus, contrary to UN resolutions. But that was brushed aside and I think the Turks will go in, and I think the Serbs will fight the Turks like tigers.

Caroline had a marvellous letter from Michael Barratt Brown about Keir Hardie, saying it was by far the best book ever written about Hardie. So she's having a big success. But alas, they are 'remaindering' the book. It's only eighteen months old and they've got 398 copies left; they won't do it in paperback, which would make it really successful.

Wednesday 16 March

Had a card from Ruth reminding me that it was the year of driving safely.

Walked to the Treasury to speak at the Annual General Meeting of the Civil and Public Servants. The Treasury made a room available and it was an interesting event. I hadn't been in the Treasury since Denis Healey was Chancellor. Huge building, so old-fashioned it's hardly true really; just like going to a Third World country.

Quite a number of people turned up – there must have been sixty or seventy – and some of them looked to me as if they were from the First

Division Association, that's to say senior civil servants.

I made a speech setting out my view of economic policy and privatisation, and democracy and market forces, and so on. Walked from there down to the House, where I met some trainee teachers of English from East Germany.There were these kids between eighteen and twenty-three and I've never met a more defeatist group in my life. They were pessimistic, beaten, confused; some of them looked back to socialism under the old system and said it was better than the present; others said it wasn't socialism. One girl said, 'How can we have democracy we're so poor?' I said, 'Democracy gives you the power of the vote to influence your future.' The same young woman said, 'Well, money is all that matters.' Then the others said, 'We never had socialism under the old Eastern German system; what we want is real socialism.' Then another girl said, 'What we need is absolute equality of income.'

They were stumbling towards something. I had actually wondered whether all those years of some form of socialism in East Germany would have built support for it, but they looked back on it as bureaucratic, oppressive. They don't like the West German takeover, they don't like anything. I argued with them and said, 'I haven't convinced you, but you haven't convinced me.' But they were all very friendly.

Friday 18 March, Chesterfield

I was tidying the flat without dressing when the phone rang and Tom Vallins told me the firefighters at Chesterfield Fire Station wanted to see me about the refusal of the County Council to allow them to have a fully manned heavy cutting vehicle at the station. So I went over and met the Fire Brigades' Union and one of the officers looked in.

Chesterfield covers a big chunk of the M1, and it's got railways, and the heavy cutting equipment and decontamination unit are regularly needed.

I listened carefully and then dictated a letter and wrote it off to everyone I could think of: Home Secretary, Chairman of the Public Protection Committee and the Chief Fire Officer in Derbyshire.

They said they weren't a fire station any more – they were a 'service delivery outlet'; all this 'managers' and 'customers' jargon, and so on, has crept into the Fire Service. It was awful!

Sunday 20 March

Got up at five o'clock, after three hours' sleep and drove to LWT. When I got there, I discovered that Lady Thatcher's daughter, Carol Thatcher, was also doing the papers. It put me out a bit, so I said, 'I didn't know there were two of us.' 'Oh, we always do it like that.' As a matter of fact, she was very polite and courteous and said, 'I'll leave the heavy stuff to Mr Benn.'

She dealt with six pages of Lady Buck's revelations of her sexual relations with Buck and with the Marshal of the Royal Air Force, Sir Peter

Harding, who had to resign last week. Honestly, the level of reporting of scandal is appalling, and she dealt with some of that.

I had a word with Carol Thatcher afterwards and told her about the video of her mum's speeches on Europe, called *No! No! No!* which Parliamentary Films – who made my *Speeches* video – are putting out with a commentary by Norman Tebbit. She said, 'I'll get my mum to ring you.' I don't suppose she will, but I'm trying to help to get that launched.

Monday 21 March

Assad Khan, a young man of sixteen or seventeen has come from Christ's Hospital School to do a couple of weeks' work experience. He's deaf, and he's shy and he's brilliant; Ruth had this great idea of putting him onto writing a brief on John Wesley for a television programme that I've been asked to do, and as he's absolutely university-standard, we gave him all the background papers.

He'd never heard of Methodism before, and he said he didn't think he liked Wesley very much. So I had a discussion with him and he worked away this afternoon.

When I got home I decided that I would ring Patricia Hollis, Lady Hollis of Heigham, who's a lecturer at the University of East Anglia, a friend of Tony Crosland. A very beautiful redhead, and I think Tony Crosland must have taken a bit of a shine to her. She's now a peer. She was always very friendly and charming. Anyway, she's writing this life of Jennie Lee and she wanted me to comment on Jennie's role in the setting up of the Open University.

I had dug out all the papers from my archives to send to her, and I spoke to her on the phone. She was very interesting. She said that men didn't like Jennie Lee, and Nye's family loathed her. She married Nye on the rebound from Frank Wise, with whom she'd had a long affair; her first lover was a Chinese lecturer, in the 1920s, I think, when she was at college. She was absolutely shattered by Nye's death. They spoke of her in her constituency of Cannock as the dowager; she was very sort of arrogant to them, didn't treat them at all respectfully.

The *People* newspaper had a poll as to who was the most 'normal' MP – squeaky clean – and David Alton came top and I came second. I thought what an old fraud I am. Everybody's closets are full of skeletons, things they've done and are a bit ashamed or shy of. And democracy keeps a spotlight on you, but at the same time it also makes you vulnerable to the most terrible, scurrilous smearing and scandalising, of the kind that is pouring out at the moment on Sir Peter Harding and the former wife of Sir Anthony Buck. The whole thing is utterly revolting and the *News of the World* paid this woman £125,000 to write a lot of the stories.

Rushed home, where I heard that Donald Swann, whom I'd known for fifty-six years, had died.

Sunday 27 March

The clocks went forward and at 3.08 a.m. British Summer Time, the phone rang (we were both asleep) and it was Paul saying that little Hannah Benn Gordon, eight pounds in weight, had been born at two o'clock this morning and they were all fine. So we went back to sleep. Couldn't have been more exciting.

I went over there at about three o'clock and was the first member of the family, other than Paul and Lissie, to see little Hannah, and she was adorable. She was like all newborn babies: looked very old, and her fingers were all crinkly and her face all crinkly, and a head of dark hair. She was just sweet: she had hiccups and she cried and I put my tape recorder on. I had taken my Polaroid camera and I took about ten pictures and I gave them about six and kept four myself.

Later in the day Caroline went, then Hilary and Sally and their four children, so it was a perfect day. Lissie is such a lovely mother, and all the anxieties I'd had that she would resist childbirth and that she was a career woman evaporated. But getting her novel accepted last Friday and having a baby on the Monday is just wonderful.

Wednesday 30 March

Assad Khan brought flowers for Sheila and Ruth and a book for me, and I gave him a copy of my tapes. He's a very strange boy; he queried the comments that Ruth had made about his work experience, and wanted them changed, so Ruth negotiated with him. She likes him enormously. He's a brilliant young man.

Sunday 10 April, Stansgate

Tonight we heard about the bombing by the Americans of Serb forces in Bosnia, apparently asked for by General Sir Michael Rose, the UN Commander. This is the first bombing of Serbs on the ground, and I am not sure what effect it will have. The UN is gradually being sucked into the civil war, and they have got over-confident because they managed to lift the siege of Sarajevo.

Continued violence in Southern Africa. Rwanda is in a state of civil war. It is a terribly troubled world. Clinton is involved in further sex scandals.

Tuesday 12 April

Sitting in the Tea Room when Alice Mahon came in in floods of tears and said Bob Cryer had been killed. Nobody believed it and thought it couldn't be true. So I went to see the Chief Whip, Derek Foster, and Derek said, 'I am afraid it is true. He was killed at one-forty on the motorway. Ann was with him. She was injured, but not seriously, and is in hospital.' Alice was just so distressed and it came as a tremendous shock to everyone. He was a very popular guy.

Wednesday 13 April

I had been asked to do an obituary for the *Daily Mail* on Bob Cryer. In the House at 3.30 I asked the Speaker, having given her a bit of notice, if some provision could be made for tributes to be made, because Bob was a good friend. Dennis and Nicholas Winterton supported me. I think the Speaker will make a move.

Thursday 14 April

I have been asked by Ann Cryer if I would speak at the graveside, in lieu of a vicar, which is a terrible responsibility.

This morning I was so tired that I left the bath running while I got breakfast, and I should think a whole tankful of water came down and poured into the living room, soaked everything, fused some of the wiring, came right down to the office and it is a miracle there wasn't a disaster. Caroline was so sweet about it. You would have thought she'd have done her top.

She had a nice letter from a man who had written another life of Keir Hardie. He is now at Nuffield College and said that her book was far and away the best book he had ever read on Hardie; it got closer to Keir Hardie than either he or Kenneth Morgan or the other biographer.

Sunday 17 April

I went to Broadcasting House to do a Radio 5 programme on the role of the United Nations as a peacekeeping force. Alastair Stewart was in the chair, and there was a former Syrian diplomat who is now at the Department of War Studies at King's College London working primarily for the Americans now, Joe Adamov from Radio Moscow, and Sir Anthony Parsons, former Ambassador to Iran and to the UN.

What really came out was the determination of the Russians just to re-create big power politics, rather like the Tsar, the King and the Kaiser. Adamov said he thought NATO should take over the role of the UN, thus excluding the rest of the world, and pointed out how strong Russia was militarily with nuclear weapons, vaguely threatening without having any ideological content. Parsons said we were in a muddle.

It was quite useful, except that they had a bloody great news bulletin in the middle of it all about the London Marathon, which totally destroyed the continuity of the discussion.

Friday 22 April

Caroline and I got up at about five and drove to St Pancras and caught the train to Bradford for Bob Cryer's memorial service and interment. On the train were Jeremy Corbyn and Claudia and one of their little boys, Bernie Grant and Sharon, Jimmy Hood and Edward Barber. We went to St George's Hall in Bradford. Dennis Skinner was there, Derek Foster,

Stan Orme, Malcolm Chisholm, Chris Mullin. It was a huge turnout.

There were 2500 – 3000 people in the hall, and on the platform was a long table with a red tablecloth and flowers. It was tremendously impressive, and somebody was playing the organ. At eleven, Bob's coffin was brought in and Ann and their children, Jane and John, were there; the coffin with flowers on it was laid just below the platform in front of the audience. Dennis Skinner, obviously very moved, took the chair. There were about thirteen speeches, reasonably short – local councillors; people who knew about his work with the Railway Society, his interest in films; Jeremy Corbyn, Bernie, Alice Mahon, Arthur Scargill and I spoke. Then we sang 'Jerusalem' and the coffin was taken out.

There was a coach to take us to the funeral but as I was to speak at the graveside I was put in the Rolls-Royce with Ann, John and his partner, and Jane and her husband. Not much was said up to the cemetery. It was a beautiful day and the cemetery overlooks the city.

I had a word with the man responsible for the undertakers and asked what to do, because I had no idea about a graveside address. He said, 'The coffin is lowered in and then you normally say something.' So I stood there, frozen, in front of the grave and right opposite me were Ann and the family. The coffin was lowered uneasily on ropes down to the bottom and, when it was safely there, I spoke. I found it very, very difficult. I quoted from Tom Paine: 'My mind is my church, my religion is to do good.' Then I quoted Johnny-Head-in-Air from the film 'The Way to the Stars', which the family had asked me to read. Then we stood in silence for a moment and came back to the coach.

To the Victoria Hotel, where there was a reception, and we talked to Ann who had stood up to it remarkably well, and to John and Jane, who certainly had stood up to it well themselves.

Tuesday 3 May

Went to the Commons and met about fifty student nurses from the Royal College of Nurses, and the people from the health unions in Chesterfield. I gave a talk on the Health Service, how it had begun, and we discussed finance, taxation, democracy, relations with parents, community care. It was quite thoughtful and there were some mature students there – one former miner who had moved into mental nursing. But my general impression of them was – as I feel about so many young people – that they seemed totally beaten, totally defeated, totally confused, totally cynical, with a sense of powerlessness. That is the biggest change, and how you get people to come back with some vitality is the biggest problem. I think morale-boosting is the key job.

Friday 6 May, Chesterfield

Just had time for a quick meal in my flat and then we had the Chesterfield

General Committee, which was inquorate, with only twenty-one people there. There was some argument about what we should do, because the last one was inquorate too and if you can't get a quorum, you can't get a legal majority to reduce the quorum and can't transact any business or reach any decisions. You could see the Labour Party dying at the roots. I have said this a million times, but when it happens in Chesterfield as well, it gets a bit alarming.

Sunday 8 May

Came home and at midnight on the news the BBC said the Hungarian elections had led to a 'lurch to the left' and that the Leader of the Hungarians had himself been a long-time serving member of the Communist Party.

So I rang up the BBC and spoke to somebody from the News Service. I said, "Can you tell me why, when the left wins, it's a "lurch," but when the right wins, it's a "victory"? And could you tell me when you last mentioned the fact that Yeltsin had been a card-carrying member of the Communist Party?' He was very shirty, but he took it down.

Part Three
May 1994–May 1997

This chapter records the inevitable decline of the Conservative Party – which, after so many years in power, had come to be associated with sleaze and complacency – and the birth of New Labour following John Smith's unexpected and tragic death in 1994.

Describing New Labour as a new political party Tony Blair began by challenging Clause 4 of Labour's constitution, the cornerstone of its socialist principles. He expressly distanced himself from the trade unions in pursuit of what became known as 'the Project', a strategy embodied in a Manifesto that was carried by a referendum of Party members rather than by the Party Conference.

The Project aimed to build a new centre party around Blair's own vision of a caring capitalism, free of sleaze, and committed to market forces, globalisation and a strong federal Europe; he believed that in this way, he could attract Liberals and Europhile Conservatives to the Project, and appeal to Middle England, the middle classes, the business community and media proprietors.

The election of Bill Clinton as President of the United States seemed to provide some hope that New Labour would find a natural partner across the Atlantic within the framework of a shared political analysis.

These events were set against a background of spreading conflict in the Balkans and the Middle East. In Northern Ireland, Unionist pressure was strong enough to frustrate real talks with the Nationalists, and the Unionist presence in the finely balanced House of Commons ensured limited progress. John Major's Government had, however, made a significant breakthrough with the Mitchell recommendations on decommissioning in 1996.

THE ADVOCATE
OF CAPITALISM!
John Kent

Thursday 12 May 1994
John Smith died today. I first heard he had been taken ill and then the *Evening Standard* rang and finally it was confirmed.

It is terribly sad. I have known him for twenty-five years, worked closely with him in the Department of Energy and have been with him in the Cabinet. I liked him very much. He performed a completely different function from Neil Kinnock – he healed the wounds of the Party.

The House met at 2.30 and was suspended until 3.30, and the tributes were paid. Major was good, Margaret Beckett was good and Ashdown. I spoke for about forty-five seconds. Dennis Skinner ended up.

Everybody is so sad about what has happened. I saw a young girl of about sixteen with blonde hair, who came up the steps at St Stephen's Entrance and said, 'Where can I leave these flowers for Mr Smith?' So I told her to take them to the Central Lobby. That is something really – an indication of the character and strength of the man.

Sunday 15 May, New York
Phoned home. Looked out of the window and saw homeless people sleeping in the doorways below. The new right-wing Mayor of New York has now arranged that they will be cleared off the residential areas and put in hostels in the industrial areas in New York, in a piece of right-wing social engineering.

Got a cab to the Washington Irvine High School, where this big meeting on fascism and democracy was being held, organised by WBAI. There were about 500 people there. In the chair was Gerald Horne. Michael Parenti, a socialist professor from California, spoke first. It was a simple socialist analysis. He said one thing, for example, 'The ruling class only want one thing – everything,' then he analysed it, very much in the way I do. He talked about GATT and the effect of having a World Trade Organisation with powers overriding democratic decisions on environmental protection, and so on, and how they were all advised by experts who were not accountable.

It was a useful day. Noam Chomsky didn't come, which was a great disappointment, but you realise that the radicalism in America is just as great as you find on the left in Britain.

Tuesday 17 May

The Labour leadership contest has begun in earnest, with Blair in the lead, Brown not knowing what to do, Prescott pushing, Beckett pushed aside, Cunningham ignored, Cook hopeful.

I saw Alan Simpson in the House of Commons, and he says we should repudiate all candidates. Would Ken Livingstone stand? Dawn Primarolo says we couldn't have a contest in July. The papers today are saying the Party couldn't afford to have a special conference; it would all have to be done by postal ballot; the National Membership Scheme isn't very accurate. It's a bit of a shambles.

Wednesday 18 May

Went in to the Campaign Group meeting, which was extremely interesting. It was very crowded, and after getting through our business quickly, we discussed the leadership. Harry Barnes introduced a paper. He said, 'We should seek to influence the outcome. The Campaign Group shouldn't run a candidate, because we couldn't get enough nominations, and we shouldn't look for an alternative left candidate. We should nudge and push candidates in our direction and get commitment from others. Individuals can support who they like. We should ask for a democratic and socialist outcome.'

Ken Livingstone said, 'The election should be postponed until October. The Deputy Leader, Margaret Beckett, is in charge and she was in the Campaign Group, and if she doesn't stand, we should put up a candidate. We have enough Members to nominate; we would have the only candidate with a policy. The Campaign Group is 3 per cent of the electoral college, and if we don't run, the Campaign Group would in effect give up.'

Thursday 19 May

Edna O'Brien came to have tea with me. She had written to me and sent her book and I had sent her a video. She must be getting on for sixty-two, a very handsome woman, bright red hair, slim and glamorous. She wanted to talk about Ireland and is very committed to the Irish cause. This idea that she is 'just a writer,' which they tend to say about authors who have a political view, is quite wrong. 'Oh, no,' she said, 'I have been kept off television. I've not been allowed to do this and that. My books have been hammered. One man said, "I hope this book dies and I hope Edna O'Brien dies."'

On the other hand, she has quite a lot of influence. She said she had published an open letter to President Clinton and he had invited her to have dinner with him in the White House, and someone had turned it down in advance without telling her, so she was furious. Now she is going to have dinner with Clinton in June when she goes back to America. You do realise that great writers, great politicians, great media people, great actors do move in a sort of top echelon of some kind. She said how she liked Kinnock. I tried not to look too concerned about that.

She has been asked to write an article for the back page of *Newsweek* in America, which is very influential. She asked, 'Well what does this devolution mean?' She wasn't well informed on the details, but why should she be?

Friday 20 May

I got up early and went to Heathrow to catch the nine o'clock shuttle to Edinburgh for John Smith's funeral. It was cutting it a bit fine and to my horror, the plane was itself twenty minutes late. Malcolm Wicks, the Member for Croydon, came up to me and we were both worried about not getting there on time, but we finally arrived at Edinburgh at about 10.40. We got in the last car with Stan Orme, who had come from Manchester, and one or two others. We were driven to the parish church and were in the last row but one in the church.

It was a beautiful Presbyterian church, almost the size of a cathedral, with up to 1000 people crowded in. Callaghan came in in a tail-coat representing the Queen. Kinnock and Glenys were there, Michael Foot, the Shadow Cabinet in full, half the parliamentary party, the Prime Minister and Norma Major, Norman Fowler, Ian Lang, the Lord Chancellor, Jon Snow, Elinor Goodman, Melvyn Bragg. Robin Butler, the Cabinet Secretary, was also there.

The service was dignified, very much the Scottish Presbyterian Establishment really. It was Scottish even to start with – very Presbyterian, very severe and at the same time very gentle about John.

There were three tributes: by somebody called James Gordon, I think; somebody called Derry Irvine; and Donald Dewar, MP, who had all been contemporaries of his. John Smith was a student politician who went to the Bar, just as Kinnock was a student politician who went to Parliament. There is a sort of student element in all this. What came out was the character of the man. I think John's death will have an impact on the future of British politics – that's my impression.

There were people in the street standing quietly and crying. It was very moving.

We had a slow ride into Edinburgh. Got to the Parliament House where the reception was. Only the bigwigs had been invited. The first person I saw was Lord Mackay, the Lord Chancellor, and he came towards me with his wife. He introduced me to her and said, 'I knew John Smith very well as a colleague, as an adversary and as a judge. I heard cases where he put evidence forward.' I told him that Tam Dalyell had thought he should be the Lord Chancellor if *Labour* won the election – that was an amazing story. He is sixty-seven.

Then I moved away and there were Jim Callaghan and Ted Heath standing side by side, Jim looking very distinguished and Ted with his bulging belly looking as curmudgeonly as ever. So I asked, 'Do you ever remember anything like this?' Somebody said, 'Gaitskell.' Jim said, 'I don't remember Gaitskell's funeral at all. Perhaps Dora wanted it to be quiet. What about Iain Macleod?'

I thought I would take the opportunity of asking Jim and Ted what they were doing with their papers. Jim said, 'I have got fifty-three boxes and they are now in the Victoria Tower, but they will have to go to the LSE.'

Ted said, 'I have got a hundred and fifteen tons of papers and they are going to Balliol.'

I said I had a lot of papers and I thought it was shocking that the Churchill papers were being sold by the family.

Ted said, 'I hope you haven't got any Government papers.'

I realised what an old civil servant he was. 'No, just a few photocopies.'

Then I went to the PM and said, 'I just want to thank you for the tribute you paid to John.' He then caught Norma by the arm and said, 'Now, here's a man who never introduces personalities into his speeches.'

I said, 'I'm not a goody-goody. If I had a meeting in Chesterfield saying why I hate John Major, no one would listen. But if I said what prospects are there for work and jobs in Chesterfield, they would pour in.'

He said, 'I thought thousands would turn up if it was a meeting about me!'

Then we got onto the weakness of Prime Minister's Questions. I said, 'You know, the way to deal with this problem is to answer real questions, instead of "What is the Prime Minister doing today?" and "Will the PM visit Chesterfield."'

So then he pulled someone over and said, 'Listen to Tony. This is exactly what I have been saying.'

So that was useful.

Had a brief word with Michael Foot and then a Church of Scotland minister came up and said, 'My wife has Alzheimer's and, before she became unable to cope, she wrote to people asking for childhood stories, and you sent a Tubby story about a little man who lived in the plughole in the bottom of the bath.'

I said, 'I remember the letter very well, because she is the only person who has ever written to me for a children's story.'

He replied, 'I am afraid she has got Alzheimer's, and I haven't been able to communicate with her for four or five years now.'

It was rather touching.

I realised at this stage that I was going to miss my flight, so I turned to the PM and said, 'Would you give me a lift in your jet?'

He said, 'Of course I will. I am going in a few minutes, so you had better be ready.'

I was really grateful. I rode to RAF Turnhouse in a car with John Wakeham, Richard Ryder, the Chief Whip, Norman Fowler and the driver.

I said to Wakeham, 'What job did you enjoy doing most?'

He said, 'Chief Whip, without any doubt.'

It was an absolutely grand thing to do, and I realised I was going to have a good time.

We got to RAF Turnhouse and there was the Group Captain saluting and I said, 'I was an "Aircraftsman Second Class" and a Group Captain still frightens me!'

We got into an HS146 of the Queen's Flight. Now, the HS146 was the plane they tried to cancel and I saved it, so I was really pleased about that. Ted Heath and Wakeham were on board, and the Prime Minister's Principal Private Secretary. I asked, 'Where shall I sit?'

Norman Fowler said, 'Well, the Prime Minister is writing a speech, but do sit next to him, I'm sure he would be glad to have your advice!'

I said, 'No, I'll sit in another compartment.'

Opposite me was Ted Heath's Special Branch man and we discussed the security arrangements for former prime ministers and Northern Ireland Secretaries. He said it took six people to guard Ted.

Norman Fowler was wandering about like a sort of impresario and said, 'By the way, I did enjoy your letter in *The Times* about the media coverage of politics.'

I said, 'Well, I have a lot of letters about it,' which is true.

So we sat down with Richard Ryder and the Prime Minister's Private Secretary on the left and two policemen on the other side of the aisle.

The Private Secretary said he was reading Crossman's diaries on the Cabinet, and was surprised at how much time the Cabinet as a whole spent on public expenditure. So I said, 'Well, we did spend a lot of time. By the way, when did you join the Civil Service?'

'It's funny you should ask that. I joined the Treasury the very day that the Treasury was considering a response to your paper on an alternative economic strategy in 1976. Of course, we had our own contingency plans. We had to have contingency plans.'

I was interested in that, and he might perhaps be a man to talk to later.

Richard Ryder asked, 'Did you read Alan Clark's diaries?' I said I hadn't, but I had listened to them on tape, and he went on, 'Well, he was a Thatcherite, not a Tory.' He also said to me at some stage that Walter Harrison (our former Deputy Chief Whip) was a real thug. I told him I thought that was a bit unkind and he said, 'Well, I meant it as a compliment really!'

I said to Ryder, 'Well, the Chief Whip knows everything that goes on and how it can be used.'

He said, 'We'd never do that.'

But it's true. Walter Harrison used to go through all the papers of dead MPs so that their wives wouldn't be upset by personal revelations.

Tea and sandwiches were served and the Prime Minister came and sat down opposite me.

I said, 'We were just talking about public expenditure cuts.'

He said, 'I wouldn't know anything about that.'

I went on, 'The Cabinet minutes are very dull.'

'Yes, they simply say, "The Chancellor said this. One the one hand, it was argued; on the other hand it was argued. The Prime Minister summed up."'

I said, 'But the two Deputy Secretaries write the discussions down, and that's the real record.'

'Oh,' said the Private Secretary, 'They are all destroyed.'

I replied, 'I am not saying you are wrong about that, but I find it hard to believe.'

Then we got onto the question of leaks, and the Prime Minister said, 'It happens all the time now. People just think it's the right thing to do.' I said, 'Well, Wilson once tried to stop them. We spent so much time discussing one leak that we never got onto the business, and then when we returned to Cabinet in the afternoon there was a big headline in the *Evening Standard*: "Wilson raises leaks in Cabinet."'

The PM, I think, said that Douglas Hurd kept a diary.

Then we got on to scandal and the Prime Minister said to his Private Secretary, 'Do you remember the time of all that stuff about me in the papers?'

I said, 'I wouldn't support a *New Statesman* appeal for money when they ran that scurrilous story. I had a lot of this. I got blackened.'

John Major said, 'Well, when I was appointed Prime Minister, the media interviewed everybody I have ever known to try and find some scandal.'

I said, 'It's very difficult. Look at poor old Clinton.'

It was a useful, friendly talk and I promised I would send him – and I did so that night – the Cabinet minutes for 1931 to which I had referred, which I thought would interest him.

We landed at Northolt and of course my car was at Heathrow but they had kindly arranged for a government contract car to take me to Heathrow.

It was a momentous day really and I did feel – having had the opportunity of travelling with the Prime Minister and a former Prime Minister, and so many other Ministers – that I had been moved up in to the top scale.

Saturday 21 May

Edward Miliband phoned to say his father, Ralph, had died this afternoon. It was terribly sad. He had a bad bypass operation two years ago and hadn't been well. He had been in America, water had built up, and he had had kidney failure and died. Frightfully sad.

Sunday 22 May
Came home and decided I would send an open letter to David Blunkett calling for the leadership elections to be postponed until October, for which I think there is a strong case. I rang Colin Brown and spoke to Chris Moncrieff and put it out, because I think planting that idea is seriously useful and, as I am not a candidate, I can do all these things, which I probably couldn't do otherwise.

Monday 23 May
Up at five and to Chesterfield for my surgery. On the train the ticket inspector, who is an old friend of mine and was on – may still be – on the Executive of the RMT, said life was absolutely impossible on the railways now: 'All this rubbish about calling people customers.' He said there was a rule that railway officials were not to wear their trade union badges. That's absolute dictatorship.

Caught the train and David Blunkett was on it, so I sat next to him for a while. He said he had heard – indeed he heard while we were on the train – that I had written a letter to him about deferring the election until the Conference. He said he inclined towards going ahead with it early. He is obviously very critical of Gordon Brown. I don't know who he will support, but he did promise that he would circulate my letter to the Executive, which I think he probably will do.

Bill Michie was on the train, and at the end of the journey I saw Arthur Scargill.

Tuesday 24 May
At ten, I caught a cab to Russell Square, and from 10.50 to 11.30, I had a talk to Noam Chomsky, the American philosopher, in the Russell Hotel. I had never met him before, although I had seen his face many times; a modest, shy man of sixty-five years old, a few years younger than me. He asked me a lot about the Labour Party, but my response on that was not as interesting as his comments.

When I said that America seemed to be declining, he said, 'No. American state power, put behind American corporations, makes America the world's masters, and does it matter whether the workers in America sink to a Third World status? It doesn't matter so long as the corporations and the government are all-powerful.'

He drew a parallel historically between 1800 and 1830 and Ricardo and the communists at the time.

I said I thought there was a danger that a left analysis, however accurate indeed, even if very accurate, perhaps even *because* it was very accurate, might be effectively depressing and reinforcing the view of the right, who said there was nothing you could do about it.

He asked about the Labour Party and socialism and had it been totally abandoned? About class analysis, about the possibility of a new party, about the growing radicalism of the unions in the United States. He was a modest and charming man, and when I asked about the film of his speeches and lectures, he said he hadn't seen it himself, which is quite incredible really. We had a meeting of minds.

Then at 11.30 John Pilger, the Australian journalist, and Hilary Wainwright arrived. Pilger said he thought Smith had had such a tremendous obituary because the British Establishment had seen in John Smith their best hope for killing socialism. He said, 'Did you notice that there were no political tributes paid, they were all personal?'

Then Pilger and Chomsky talked to each other, both saying how difficult it was to get through media censorship. Chomsky gave me his home number and address, so that I can be in touch with him. He is here to publicise his new book.

As I was waiting with him for a cab, a taxi driver rushed over and said, 'You're Mr Chomsky, nice to meet you. Oh! Tony, how are you?' It was a man called Tony Cavoni, an old socialist cab driver.

Thursday 26 May

On the leadership election, the press have got it absolutely clear in their minds that they are determined to have Blair; and by telling everyone that Blair is the only one who can win, of course, the Party, which wants to win, wants Blair. So that is the game. I have never seen a critical word about Blair anywhere.

Brown must be disappointed but, of course, he has been disappointing. Cook is an angry little man. Beckett might be the best bet. I would vote for whoever stood against Blair in the last ballot and if one had a choice between Beckett and Prescott, I don't know what to do. There is great hostility in the left towards Prescott because he sold OMOV to the Conference.

Seumas Milne said one interesting thing: 'You know Chris Mullin is very conservative.'

In a way he is reverting to his normal self. People do move, you have to accept that. I try to keep abreast but not to give up, which is what I think most of the moves are really all about.

Friday 27 May

At 11.20 I was up at Golders Green Crematorium for Ralph Miliband's funeral. It was an interesting occasion – a huge crowd on the left: John Saville who, I think, had been his teacher or colleague at an early stage;

Leo Panitch all the way from Canada, Tariq Ali, who knew Ralph very well; Robin Blackburn, Professor John Griffiths Bernard Crick, Ian Aitken, Dick Clements, Sheila Rowbotham, Hilary Wainwright, Richard Kuyper. Anyone on the real left of any significance was there. Jeremy Corbyn couldn't make it.

We went into the chapel, probably the same one where Mother's cremation took place. The service was interesting. Ralph was a secular Jew. They started with music. The first speaker was John Saville, then I read 'Questions from a worker who reads', with a word or two afterwards, then Leo Panitch, who was very moving; then Vanya del Borgo read from 'The Sociological Imagination' by C. Wright Mills, then Ralph's son, Edward; then Tariq Ali reading 'And Death Shall Have No Dominion' by Dylan Thomas; and finally David Miliband. The two boys were absolutely marvellous, very controlled, sensitive, talked about their father in an objective and tender way. Then to music we walked out. Richard Gott was there.

Ralph was only seventy. What was nice about him was how encouraging he was. He was very clear, very analytical, never got angry or personal. He encouraged me in an extraordinary way from the time the Independent Left Corresponding Society was established. Then he brought Tariq, Robin Blackburn, Perry Anderson, Hilary Wainwright, Jeremy Corbyn and me together occasionally for the Independent Left Corresponding Society, which went on until about 1992.

Sunday 29 May

Believe it or not, the BBC has hired a train with two carriages with all-over carpeting, and a chef and staff, to take Solzhenitsyn all round Russia to comment. There was a picture of the old man ranting away at Vladivostok harbour saying that the new Russia was completely immoral. I wondered what it cost the BBC to do this. Then I contrasted it in my own mind with what happened to Ralph Miliband, who was a distinguished socialist dissident here, whose life passed without any comment. And the BBC gave all this attention to Solzhenitsyn who, when he came out of Russia, went to Madrid and praised Franco to the skies. But that is the state of politics – it is awful.

Monday 30 May

The big news at the moment is the leadership of the Labour Party; a bit of scandal about Alan Clark; a killer bug; and the Prime Minister's attack on beggars.

Tuesday 31 May

The Alan Clark story has got bigger and bigger. He had an affair with a woman who is married to a judge in South Africa, and with both of their daughters. They decided to come to London, and there is a rumour that they asked for £100,000 not to reveal it. Alan Clark is angry, and his wife has said, 'If you bed somebody below stairs, you expect them to go to the newspapers.' An incredible story.

Thursday 2 June

To BBC Television Centre, where Ted Heath and I and Margaret Ewing, a Scottish Nationalist, and Claude Cheysson, the former French Foreign Minister, were discussing the future of Europe. Cheysson is a socialist, I suppose, because he worked with Mitterand. He is now a Member of the European Parliament and the French Assembly and he said, 'The European Parliament is nothing; nobody takes any notice of it at all. The French Assembly can't intervene on European Union matters because that is an executive power. We must mobilise the media to try and get people interested in Europe by opening up the Council of Ministers.'

I said, 'Well, I proposed that in 1977 and they just laughed at me.'

Ted Heath emerged as his real corporate self. 'The Commission is most important. It was that that rebuilt Europe after the war. You can't have the Council of Ministers meeting in public. It's like having the television cameras in Cabinet. Their job is to reach agreement.'

He was actually terribly friendly to me, and I like him, but he is a corporatist and wants capitalism imposed in Europe by Commissioners and bankers.

Cheysson was talking about Franco-German cooperation, on which Ted Heath places a lot of importance. Ted said, 'To try and separate France and Germany would be to live in cloud-cuckoo land.'

But Cheysson, interestingly, said he thought the Germans were now turning eastwards more, were more interested in Eastern Germany and in relations with former communist countries than they were in France.

He said, 'Don't forget, we killed each other, murdered each other, raped each other for centuries and we resolved we would never do it again.' I understand that, and indeed I mentioned something to that effect when I was on the programme. It wasn't a bad programme, but it was much too short and my point about fascism and nationalism and the need for a Commonwealth of Europe was something they didn't really want to discuss. They wanted to discuss minor reforms. But I do think that this whole European enterprise, as far as Britain is concerned, is grinding to a halt.

Cheysson revealed that Chancellor Kohl said to Mitterand, 'Don't have a referendum in France, because if we had a referendum in Germany, the Germans would vote it down.' Now, from a former French Foreign Minister, that was very significant: the Germans would have voted against the Maastricht Treaty. All this stuff about the British holding back, and so on, is rubbish.

Before we went on the air, Ted Heath joked with me. 'When are you going to announce your candidature against Blair?'

I said, 'Well, shall I do it during the programme?'

'Well, that would certainly take attention off us, but you would be much the safest candidate to put up against him.'

I said, 'I suppose Blair is one hundred per cent with you on the European question.'

'Absolutely,' said Ted, as if Blair was one of his children, and I think that is the position. But Ted is curmudgeonly – just an awkward old so-and-so – but I am rather fond of him.

Friday 3 June

Sharon Wentworth rang me. She had written to me in 1975 at the time of the referendum, and is now thirty-eight, was a sister at St Thomas', had five children. I had a talk to her and she told me that, during the last election, the TGWU for whom she now works hired forty cars and provided drivers for the Shadow Cabinet. Her job was to drive Tony Blair, so she was with him throughout most of the campaign. She said, as so often, that drivers are just invisible – people in the back don't take any notice of the driver. She said that whenever Tony Blair got a bad press which he did occasionally, he became very upset and would phone Gordon Brown, who would say, 'Don't worry Tony, it will be all right tomorrow.' She got the impression – and I found this a real insight into Blair's character – that he was a weak man and wouldn't stand up to criticism. She said he was very charming and pleasant, and couldn't have been nicer.

Monday 6 June, Chesterfield

I went to Chesterfield for the Co-op Service. It was a nice evening and I walked up from the station to the Spire Church and heard the bells ringing out across the streets of the town. I went in for the service and all of a sudden a very traditional feeling came over me. Here was a church, which over years had maintained the idea that we were all brothers and sisters, and here was the co-operative movement, which had put it into practice as best it could. I thought, perhaps in that conservative atmosphere – because the Church is conservative and the co-operative movement is conservative – that some little flicker of hope was kept alive.

Tuesday 14 June, Chesterfield

I went to the special meeting of the Chesterfield General Committee to discuss the leadership. For Leader, Prescott got 23 votes, Blair got 2, Beckett none. For Deputy Leader, Prescott got 2, Beckett 20 and Jeremy Corbyn 3.

Wednesday 15 June
To the Campaign Group, where Ken Livingstone explained why he had withdrawn from the leadership contest.

He announced that he was going to be a candidate before the Campaign Group met, then later he said he was going to vote for Beckett; then he announced that he was a candidate and Jeremy Corbyn was his running mate without telling Jeremy Corbyn, then today he withdrew on the grounds that he couldn't get any nominations.

It caused an awful lot of ill will. Jimmy Hood said, 'Who would have supported Ken if he'd stood?'

Billy Etherington said, 'We should learn the lesson, there's no support for Blair.'

Diane Abbott said she would have nominated any Campaign Group Member, but was sticking with Beckett.

Bernie Grant said he wasn't in favour of nominating anyone, but Beckett might be a Deputy Leader.

Banks said, 'Only Tony Benn and Skinner could get the thirty-four nominations. Ken has completely blown it and it's pointless now. I shall nominate Margaret Beckett.'

Alice Mahon said, 'I'm going to nominate Margaret Beckett.'

Not very good really – they were all over the shop, and Ken's behaviour was that of a total maverick, with no sort of collective responsibility to the group. Of course there is disagreement: the women want Beckett; most people there want Beckett, and not Prescott, but they all agree they don't want Blair.

Friday 17 June, Manchester
To the Town Hall, where Ann Taylor was speaking. She looks like a Permanent Secretary or a Tory Minister, though that's being a bit unfair to her.

She was trying to tell the SEA how important education was; how we've got to move it forward; how Labour would deal with the problems of lunchtime supervision, and so on – absolutely superficial stuff. No commitment of any kind to funding or, indeed, legislation, and making a great thing about consultation – they were consulting *everybody*.

If you have a policy, you put it out; you don't consult people to find out what your policy should be, as if you were starting from scratch. That Green Paper that had come to the Executive last year, when I was still a member, doesn't mention comprehensive schools.

There were some good points made from the audience. One man said, 'What's in effect happening is that selection is returning at the age of about fourteen – people are either being prepared for university or they're being prepared for a non-academic career, which is right back to the 1944 White Paper.'

Another man who's passionately against church schools asked, 'What are you going to do about church schools?' Somebody pointed out, I think, that Tony Blair had said that he had an open mind on public schools.

Ann Taylor was put under heavy pressure, but she just calmed it all down as if saying, 'Now, just relax' – and she was dealing with some of the greatest educational experts in the country. They were very patient about it and it was quite an interesting thing to watch. I had no role. I was just sitting there as a visitor and I kept my mouth shut.

It was our forty-fifth wedding anniversary, and afterwards Caroline and I walked back to the hotel and moved into this very nice suite that I'd booked.

She'd already had a meal, so I had my sandwich and made some tea, then we watched Goldie Hawn and Dudley Moore in some film or another, a sort of comedy thriller. It was quite funny, and we went to bed at getting on for midnight.

So that was our wedding anniversary – it was very nice to be together.

Saturday 18 June

I got on the stationary train at Manchester. There was hardly anybody on it, so I lit my pipe. No smoking on the train anywhere.

The train driver who passed through my carriage saw me and said, 'This is a no-smoking train.' So I asked, 'Who said so?'

'The management.'

I said, 'We used to own these railways, until they sold them off, and who gave them the authority?'

'Well, it's the rules.'

'Now that I'm not a passenger any more, but a customer, the customer is always right. But, I won't smoke if anyone objects.'

So he said, 'I object. I'm very anti-smoking.'

I said, 'Well, you're up in the front.'

'Some of the smoke gets through the doors.'

Well, there were three sets of doors, – it couldn't possibly get through the doors, particularly as the train would be going forward and all the wind would be blowing back. So I continued to smoke and I took my little Smoking notice, which I'd peeled off the window of a train some time ago, and stuck it on the window and sat there. But a lot of other people got on, so I took it off and stopped smoking. But it is a tyranny really. It says 'penalty £50' and I'm tempted one day, so long as I don't offend other people in the compartment, I'm tempted just to smoke and see what happens. That's all by the by. It's just a minor irritation at the moment.

Sunday 19 June

Caroline was at the SEA Conference in Manchester in the morning and she came back in the afternoon.

Ruth turned up, having worked right through the weekend on the manuscript for *Years of Hope*, the new diary volume. She really has worked incredibly hard and it's terribly difficult working from corrected typescript that's been photocopied, but at any rate progress is being made.

Tuesday 21 June
I had to vote a couple of times on the Sunday Trading Bill Lords' amendments, then I went to a meeting in Committee Room 14 organised by the Committee to Defend Mordecai Vanunu. To prevent him talking to anyone during the trial, he was put in a helmet so that he couldn't speak, and it was a secret trial. He's been in solitary confinement in a cell nine foot by six foot since 1986.

Wednesday 22 June
Kenny Seth looked in. A very bright black work experience student. He began reading the published diaries with a view to selecting extracts for an abridged edition.

Thursday 23 June
Fifty years ago today my brother Michael was killed, aged twenty-two; he'd have been seventy-two now. He died of wounds on operations, and I still think of him with tremendous affection. Dave put a little notice in *The Times* today commemorating his life.

Kenny Seth came in again. He's reading the 1940–62 diary years, making proposals for abridgement. He's only eighteen, he's a bright lad who's going to Cambridge this autumn. He's the first youngster who's read the book, and I wanted to know what he thought about it. He said it was very good, and to appeal to a lad of eighteen like that is extraordinary.

Went to give the prizes at CAVE, the Community and Voluntary Education centre in Clapham, south London.

Douggie Moncrieff, an old communist of seventy-six was there. His wife, Queenie, had founded CAVE twenty years ago, and the head teacher, Anne Bromwich, had previously taught Stephen, Hilary and Melissa at Holland Park School.

These national awards were presented to those who had stuck it out – they're youngsters who've played truant at mainstream school, been in difficulties, got thrown out, wouldn't go back and have been really encouraged. They obviously have a marvellous time and a teacher said something about each of the pupils, and I presented the prizes. It was really impressive.

I heard today that if Blair is elected Leader of the Labour Party there'll be a vacancy on the constituency section of the NEC, and as I was the runner-up at the Conference, I'll go back on the Executive from July to October. It amuses me no end that I shall have served on the Executive not only with Gaitskell, Wilson, Callaghan, Foot, Kinnock, Smith and Blair, but I'll have sat on the National Executive Committee with seven Leaders of the Party, and so I'm just tickled pink.

Sunday 26 June

A lovely sunny, warm Sunday. We got up fairly early and read all the papers, which are full of the leadership election and of the European Union Summit at Corfu, where Major is absolutely refusing to accept Dehaene, the Belgian Prime Minister, to succeed Jacques Delors as President of the EU.

Monday 27 June

I am definitely back on the NEC if Tony Blair or Prescott wins the leadership. Indeed, I'm back anyway, because if Beckett wins I replace Blair and if Prescott wins then Dennis Skinner comes on, so it could be that Dennis and I are both back on the Executive.

Sheila came in today, having typed up the first half of the abridged *Years of Hope,* which I've got to record onto an audio book next week.

I went to the House of Commons and the Prime Minister made a report on the Corfu summit and got massive support from the Tories for standing up to the French and the Germans. And Margaret Beckett, acting Leader, was totally destroyed when she tried to say he would be marginalised; Major just quoted something she'd said in the past about if the Common Market stands in the way of the policy we want, we'll have nothing to do with it.

Peter Shore and I were the only anti-Maastricht people who were called on our side.

Tuesday 28 June

Keith Jones, who produced the *Benn Tapes* for Radio 4, rang me up last night saying would I like to phone in when Nick Ross was doing his Radio 4 call-in programme on disestablishment, because the Prince of Wales is supposed to be dealing with it this week in a documentary.

He said Norman St John-Stevas, Lord Fawsley, or whatever his name is now, is going to be the one answering questions.

I didn't think I would but then I switched on the radio at nine and decided at about half-past nine that I would ring. So I rang the special number.

I explained that there were certain serious defects in the system; that the only oath the Queen took was to uphold the Church; the Prime Minister appoints the bishops and the House of Commons rules over the Church. And it was time to liberate the Church, to liberate the people to elect the Head of State, and to liberate the royal family so that they could do what they like.

I then pointed out that as a Privy Councillor I could veto the proclamation of Charles as King by objecting to the proclamation – there's a special phrase, which I had remembered: 'with one voice and consent of tongue and heart' – but if I do so object, it won't be unanimous. I compared it to the veto of the President of the European Commission.

So this discussion went on for about ten minutes and then I rang off. After that all hell broke loose. The *Financial Times* rang and said would I write an article; everybody rang for interviews. I did *The World at One*, though they didn't use it.

I was bloody angry, I must admit. I then decided that I would hold a press conference, so I typed a letter to the Lord President of the Council and sent it to Buckingham Palace and Prince Charles, saying that I intended to object, and sending the wording of the proclamation. Put a note out for the Lobby that there was a meeting in Room W1. I've never known such a crowded press conference. It was as crowded as when I stood for the deputy leadership six years ago. Absolutely packed, with three television cameras and all the journalists.

I did a very amusing press conference. Described it all and somebody said, 'Well, they will never let you do it.'

I said, 'I dare say there'll be some trouble with my taxi getting to St James's Palace.' At that moment one of the bulbs in one of the television lights burst, with a noise like a shot, so I said, 'There you are, they've started already.' That's all on the tape – it was frightfully funny.

Wednesday 29 June

I went and had a quick bite to eat, then went up to watch the two-and-a-half-hour Prince of Wales documentary with Jonathan Dimbleby, broadcast by Central Television.

All the press interest in it has been because it was widely assumed that the Prince would talk about his adultery, and so on – and he did say he had been unfaithful, 'but only when the marriage had broken down'. He also said we might consider national service; and he wanted to disestablish the Church of England and be the Head of all Faiths.

What came out really was not a very clever man: a puzzled man, an unhappy man, an insecure man who's trying to do what he thought was a good job on environmental questions, hammering modern architecture. But he came over terribly badly, bored to hell with all the foreign trips in part, but also with the round of domestic duties at home, which can't have done him a lot of good because he always pretends to be so cheerful.

Somehow it was very unsatisfying. My objection has never been to him personally, although I do think he isn't a very modern or sensible person. Of course it was all Lord Bountiful stuff; it wasn't anything to do with helping people to win their own battles. You saw the Prime Minister having an audience with him, you saw John Smith at the launch of the Prince of Wales's Trust, and I just feel that if the Head of State is Prince Charles and the Labour leader and Prime Minister is Tony Blair then you might as well throw in the sponge because nothing will happen.

Thursday 30 June

The papers full of comments on the Prince of Wales's programme.

The tabloids anti, the heavies divided, but really it hasn't done him a lot of good.

Friday 1 July

Went into the Commons for our annual family tea party. There were seventy or eighty people there, mainly friends of the family.

Andrew Hood and his mother and sister were there. Michael and Betsy Zander arrived and I made the most frightful goof. I've known Betsy since before she married Michael but somehow I fixed in my mind when she approached me that it was Marilyn Butler (not that they look at all alike), so I kissed her on both cheeks and said, 'This is the first time I've ever had the opportunity of kissing the head of an Oxford college.' (Marilyn Butler had just been made Rector of Exeter College.)

Betsy said, 'I am not the head of an Oxford college.' So I apologised to her and said that I didn't have my spectacles on or my hearing aid in.

Tuesday 5 July

I haven't spoken in the House for nine months now, but I don't think the House is really worth doing; nobody reports it, the place is empty, nobody's interested. Blair is drifting through. The Tories have come out with full employment as their theme. David Hunt, the Employment Minister, and Howard Davies of the CBI addressed a conference on full employment organised by the TUC. I can't think of anything more revolting than that.

Thursday 7 July

I feel at the moment that I'm in a dungeon with nothing but damp walls and water running down them – no hope, no light. I'm terribly tired. I need ten years to clear up before I die.

Saturday 9 July, Durham Miners' Gala

Got up at seven or eight, went and had breakfast with Arthur Scargill in the dining room of the Royal County Hotel. It was a lovely day, a bit overcast to begin with, but warm and windless.

I stood on the balcony, and from ten in the morning right through until about 12.30 the banners went by. It was the usual moving event. When you're on the balcony at the Royal County, the whole of human life goes before you.

There were babies being carried by their parents; there were triplets being pushed; one little child on top of her father's shoulders was given drumsticks and beat to the music on his head.

There was a man of about thirty-five, wearing a policeman's helmet, marching and smiling in front of one of the bands. All the bands played 'Gresford', which is that hymn written in memory of those who died in the Gresford Colliery disaster. I wept, and I wept even more when at one stage the Durham Miners' Home for Disabled People brought through four or five people in wheelchairs, very old ladies, some of whom were waving and holding up their fists. It was lovely; it brings out the good in you.

The gala's been kept alive in part by a rich New Zealand-born man, who's provided £60,000 to fund it for three years.

There were two police sergeants when I walked back to the hotel. One of them said, 'You know sir, ten years ago we didn't agree with a word you said but now we know you're right.'

I said, 'Well, you've been used by the Government to clear up the mess of their policies.'

'Yes,' he said, 'We're piggies in the middle.'

'You're in the middle but I'm not sure you're the piggies,' I said.

Sunday 10 July

Up early again because I was asked to go on the *David Frost Show*. There were various people interviewed. David Frost is an old hand. Jim Thompson, the Bishop of Bath and Wells, was there. Bishop Jim from Stepney was the great radical, but my God, to listen to him talking about disestablishment – saying how it was spiritual guidance for the nation, how he was in favour of the monarchy because it meant that politicians had to be humble before somebody – it was revolting. Apparently he'd been a chartered accountant, but I never knew that

David told me privately, 'We're considering what would happen if the Queen Mother died, and we had to announce it in the middle of a programme.'

I said, 'That's easy: send somebody to North Korea and find out how they've dealt with the death of Kim Il Sung.' So they all laughed uproariously.

BBC Television News rang about two Tory MPs who had apparently accepted £1000 to put down a parliamentary question, although the offer was made by a journalist, planted by the *Sunday Times*. There's such an uproar about it that the Prime Minister has suspended them and there'll be an inquiry. It may come to the Committee of Privileges, of which I am a member. Of course the BBC have no record of the Register of Members'

Interests, so they rang me up. I had it, so they sent someone round for it, photocopied it and took it away. I really am a public resource now.

Tuesday 12 July
I went to the *Newsnight* party. I'm treated with courtesy and all that, but the people who go to these dos are all centre-party people really.

Chris Mullin was there. It's worth mentioning his name because he wrote an article in *Tribune* coming out for Tony Blair.

Monday 18 July
I went into the House and there was a debate on the economy, which occupied most of the day. It was a terrible debate as far as the opening speeches were concerned. The Chancellor of the Exchequer, Kenneth Clarke, was just contemptuous and arrogant, and Gordon Brown was absolutely pathetic, every time anyone interrupted him he just read what had been in their election address.

It was knockabout of the lowest level. Gordon Brown is right, the Government has mishandled the economy; but Kenneth Clarke was right when he said the Labour Party had nothing whatever to offer.

Heard the winding-up speeches and to my amazement Harriet Harman, who wound up and made quite a good speech, drew special attention to the point I'd made about taxation, because I intervened on the Chancellor, saying that the test of taxation was what it was for and who paid for it.

Tuesday 19 July
I went into the House in the afternoon and had tea with Alan Simpson. It was really sad because his sister, Carole, who is only in her early forties, is dying of a brain tumour. She was in a wheelchair looking very, very weak. It was painful, but he had asked me to come and meet her. I tried to be cheerful and talk to her and she was very brave and joined in the conversation and joked and laughed, but knowing all the time that she was under possible sentence of death. Alan had said to her, 'What would you like to do now?' and she had said, 'I'd like to go to the House of Commons and meet Tony Benn.'

Thursday 21 July
A young lad called Sam came in for a few days on work experience. He's seventeen, his mother's a homeopath, his father's a graphic designer; both his parents are Buddhists; he's at Pimlico School, is as bright as a button and anything you ask him to do he does beautifully. He's fifty-two years younger than me.

At eleven o'clock the Electoral College met and, predictably, Tony Blair and John Prescott became Leader and Deputy Leader.

It was on television live. There was David Blunkett saying the obvious things, as you'd expect from the Chairman of the Party – you know, 'we've had a marvellous election, everybody has behaved very well, we're proud of the way the Party has responded.' But while the cameras remained on his face, a commentator said, 'The Labour Party is very proud of the way it's going, the way it's been conducted; all the candidates are marvellous', and so on so.The media apply a sort of Sinn Fein ban, under which they have to tell you what's being said; they can't let you be told by the people concerned.

I watched Blair carefully, because I've never heard him make a general speech, and it was really quite radical. He talked about ending quangos and ending hereditary peers, about right and wrong, and I think he drew in part on Caroline's *Keir Hardie,* which he had reviewed very sympathetically.

I don't know how he's going to do any of these things; he may just be a Felipe González or a Bill Clinton. But he did give people hope and vision. I think he's frightened the life out of the Liberals. The Tories must be frightened in the South. He got a huge ovation. It was a good and radical speech and I have no complaint about it at all.

I voted of course for Prescott and Beckett, but I'm inclined to send Blair a note congratulating him and offering to help, because I don't want to end up as a bitter old man, which is not my inclination.

Went into the House. Sam came with me and I got him a seat in the Gallery. I've never seen the House, on adjournment of course before the summer recess, so absolutely empty. There was one Labour MP, Paul Flynn, on the Back Benches: our Front Bench was empty; there was one Minister on the Government Front Bench and two Tories on the Back, four people in the whole House.

At two o'clock the Committee of Privileges met, and exactly as Big Ben struck I said, 'I was advised by the clerk that, as the senior member of the Committee, I could fix the time of our first meeting.'

I also said that I called the meeting at this time because we couldn't meet in the recess, and we wanted to discuss the *Sunday Times* story. There was some question about whether we could even go on after the time the House adjourns, at three o'clock.

The Lord President of the Council then took the chair and said, 'The first thing we have to consider is the recommendation of the Select Committee on Members' Interests that when a Select Committee meets for the first time, it must begin with a declaration of interest of all those who are on it.'

This caused some anguish among Tory members. Sir Peter Hordern, a tall, elegant, pompous old Tory said, 'No, we can't decide this matter now.'

Alan Williams said, 'What about the declaration of interest by the

Chairman? Surely we must know that?'

Tony Newton said, 'There's no problem as far as I'm concerned, because as a Minister I can't have any interests!'

Doug Hoyle asked, 'Couldn't we defer the interests issue until we've had a chance of studying the papers that have only just been handed around?'

So it was agreed that the question of interests would be deferred.

Then the Chairman said, 'We must move on to business and the two things we've got to do in the Sunday Times affair is decide what papers we want to commission and which witnesses we want to call.'

We agreed that we'd ask the *Sunday Times* for all the tapes and transcripts; we'd do our own transcripts; and we'd invite other MPs who refused to go along with the *Sunday Times* to give evidence, if they liked.

I said, 'We should force the *Sunday Times* to submit all the evidence.'

Then Hoyle said, 'I think we should consider having the witnesses in public.'

Peter Hordern said, 'No', and Tony Newton said, 'Well, the Committee has no power to deliberate in public.' Several of us argued for witnesses to appear in public.

Peter Shore was against. Jill Knight said, 'We'd be packed with press and television. It would make us into a media circus.'

I said, 'I would like to test opinion on this. I move that witnesses be heard in public, because of the public interest.'

Hoyle said, 'We can't sweep all this under the table.'

David Mitchell said, 'We can't have the witnesses playing to the gallery. The pressure on us would be tremendous.'

James Spicer said, 'It can't be swept under the table anyway, because we're going to publish our findings.'

We were just about to have a vote on whether witnesses were to be heard in public or not when Peter Shore said, 'I don't think we should vote. We should have papers setting out the arguments, for and against.'

By this time it was a quarter-past three and the television camera on the wall showed that the House had adjourned. And so, like Cinderella at midnight, our mandate to meet had gone. But the Lord President was quite sensible and said, 'I think if people do want to vote, we should settle that.'

David Alton, whom I knew supported hearing witnesses in public, said, 'I think we should defer it.'

I realised that if I didn't get Alton and Shore's votes, I was lost, so I said, 'All right, in those circumstances I won't press it, and we'll have the papers and decide at the next meeting.'

At that moment the Committee of Privileges vanished until 15 October, because we have no power to meet during the recess. Extraordinary really.

One or two Tories, including Cranley Onslow, said to me, 'I suppose all this will be in your diary?' I replied, 'Yes, of course it will.' That is the one advantage of being there.

Looking back on the Committee, the Labour members are not too bad. We've got Doug Hoyle, Alan Williams, and Alf Morris, and Peter Shore. I think that the interest of the Tory members is to protect the two people who took the thousand pounds, keep it as secret as you can, dispose of it quickly and attack the media (but not too strongly, in case they respond). It is a cover-up, actually; that's what it is about.

Got in the car, came home. Long traffic jams because of the royal garden party, as usual.

Went off to Stansgate.

The first thing I did was to take off my suit, put on an open-necked shirt, sandals, dirty old trousers and really begin to enjoy the pleasures of the holiday.

Friday 22 July
Another lovely day.

I'm sitting unshaven, without having had a bath, having done an LBC interview over the phone with Donald Trelford about Tony Blair.

He described the leadership process as 'the coronation of Tony Blair'. I said, 'Can I stop you a minute. It wasn't a coronation, it was an election.' I am developing a new idea that Blair is the spokesperson for a new generation, and I specially said that Blair's speech had a touch of Keir Hardie about it. I must not get into the business of being seen as critical of the new Leader.

Livingstone said Blair was the most right-wing Leader we'd ever had – I'm not going to get into that scenario.

Monday 25 July
Yesterday Sinn Fein had their conference and issued a statement that fell short of accepting the Downing Street Declaration demand that they would abandon their military action.

Although the media have churned out a lot about them, the reality is that Sinn Fein have to be taken into account if we're going to have peace. The British Government won't give up the Unionist veto, the Irish Government won't yet give up their claim to the North, and the IRA won't give up their weapons. This has got to come together at some stage.

Tuesday 26 July
Another absolutely perfect day, warm, close, humid and beautiful.

There was a vast bomb outside the Israeli Embassy – twenty people injured – in Kensington Palace Gardens. I heard this huge bang (apparently it was heard eight miles away) coming on the day after King

Hussein and the Israeli Prime Minister Rabin had been shaking hands on the White House lawn with President Clinton, who is a sort of impresario of these strange marriages.

The media immediately said that it was due to the extremist Hamas, and probably supported by Iran, without having evidence of any sort or kind.

Spoke to Bill Cash. I said, 'If Blair offers a referendum on Europe, which he's talking about, then we can have a couple of years of campaigning and we can probably get the single currency and all that defeated. I'm quite optimistic about it.'

Cash is a strange guy; he's a lawyer himself and always speaks to me as if I were a young pupil in his chambers. But still, he did say at the end that people of different opinions are coming together on this. I said, 'Of course they are, because the fault line in British politics now lies between the political class and the public at large. That's where you've got to do the work, down the line.' Tories are not well equipped to do grass-roots work.

Then I went to Chris Moncrieff's retirement party and had a friendly talk to Jim Callaghan. I told him there was a picture in the new volume of the *Diaries* of Sailor Jim, later Lieutenant Callaghan, later Prime Minister. He said, 'Where on earth did you get that from?' I told him that Ruth had found it. Then he said, 'I've just listened to another of your diary *Tapes* programmes and you're so generous to me.'

I said, 'There you are! Do you remember the time I sewed a button onto your suit at the Socialist International in Vienna?'

So we had a friendly old talk. I'm fond of Jim. He looked over to Blair. 'He's much taller than I thought.'

I said, 'Well, look at his heels!'

Blair was holding forth with everybody. Masses of people there, Tories and Labour.

Chris Moncrieff is very popular.

Wednesday 27 July

I heard that a Conservative peer had been to Highgrove for a dinner arranged by the Prince of Wales for people in the environmental lobby, Greens of one kind or another. What had become absolutely clear from the dinner was Charles's great fear of the animal rights movement, and the possibility of his reputation for hunting going against him. He said the trouble is that they don't understand anything about country life, and all that.

But it was interesting because it shows how vulnerable he is. And I think that argument is one that needs to be kept very much on the boil.

Sunday 31 July, Chesterfield

I went out with some councillors, walking up and down the streets; it was just marvellous. Friendly people standing at their doors, lovely gardens; some had bought their own council houses.

There was one man of seventy-eight who said, 'Tony, I heard your father in the Azores at the end of the war. He was a very senior air-force officer and I was a warrant officer' (I think he said warrant officer). 'Your father was talking about the post-war world. He was so amusing.' That was the first time I'd ever met anyone who'd heard Father – you'd have to be nearly eighty to remember him from the war. That gave me huge pleasure.

Came back to London, worked in the office, and then I went to the movies to see *The Remains of the Day*, a marvellous film about the upper classes and the lower classes and fascism in Britain, and a butler who was totally repressed, and the housekeeper who loved him and married somebody else.

Tuesday 2 August

I had a nice personal handwritten letter from Tony Blair, saying how much he enjoyed Caroline's book and referring to the fact that I spoke for Cherie, his wife, when she was a Labour candidate. I must find that recording of the meeting in my archives.

Wednesday 3 August, Chesterfield

Up early and caught the train to Chesterfield. The rail strike didn't begin until noon, but the train terminated at Derby so I had to get a taxi to Chesterfield.

I went from there to Chesterfield Transport. It was a municipal bus company that was bought up by its employees, and this was an opportunity to go over some of the problems that faced them.

The truth is this. The really big operators, Stagecoach and Main Line, have been gradually building up a monopoly position, and Chesterfield Transport is a minnow in a very big pond. Stagecoach might try to take it over and their offer might be tempting.

Chesterfield Transport have a very tight profit level; they've had to limit their pay, make five compulsory redundancies and forty voluntary redundancies, and they've only got 280 people in all. They can't afford to buy new buses. They said that every year the number of cars on the road means a 7 per cent drop in passengers.

They said that the really big operators, having concentrated on the profitable lines and neglected the rural lines, will want subsidies to keep uneconomic services open. So having made a huge profit by their policy of concentrating on profitable lines, they'll then get more money from the Government. They said, for example, that Peak Transport are now running minibus services on profitable routes in Chesterfield. They said that the British bus industry has really been killed. The drivers are expected to do five and a half hours non-stop driving, fuel costs are high and the rebate is being steadily reduced. They needed an integrated transport system because otherwise you'd get higher fares, poorer services, and so on.

It was really useful discussion and you realise that privatisation – even on a cooperative basis – just squeezes and squeezes the little people.

Thursday 4 August

To the Newbold ward meeting; there were only about six people there.

It was an absolutely classic example of why ward meetings don't attract people. From 7.30 until about 8.55, when I was asked to do a brief parliamentary report, there was an item about whether the accounts had been done properly, about membership, about issues of a purely administrative character. I chipped in and said, 'I hope that the Labour Party will begin reducing the Liberal vote.' They were all very pessimistic about that.

I did think to myself that really they should leave all the business to the officers, or the chair, and report quickly and get on with the political discussion. An absolutely classic old Labour Party meeting.

I forgot to mention yesterday that I thought it would be sensible to make known to Tony Blair that I was ready to help him in an area where I might have some expertise. So I rang up David Miliband, who's only thirty and has been made Head of Policy in Tony Blair's office. I said I'd had a nice letter from Tony and if I could help in any way I'd be glad to. I said, 'There's one area where I might have a bit of expertise and that is in the question of helping with the abolition of hereditary peers in the House of Lords.'

David was quite excited about that. He said he'd like to come and have a talk about the business of going into Government and what would happen. I've established a link, and through David I can get through to Tony Blair whenever I want to.

It might be that something would come of it.

Wednesday 10 August

I went to a meeting on a housing association estate in Hasland called Heather Vale. Beautiful houses, lovely little squares, and so on, but the meeting was angry because a footpath leads to a council estate called Gorse Valley. They were livid that the footpath was open because they said there was vandalism, crime, drug addicts; needles were found on the footpath, and bikes came through. They wanted the footpath closed. There was a lot of shouting and anger.

Thursday 11 August

Tony Blair is now accepted by everybody. Roy Jenkins says he's good;

Shirley Williams says he's good; Bill Rodgers says he'll make a fine Prime Minister; Paddy Ashdown is on the defensive; Major doesn't know what to do. There's a hint that Blair may aim to reduce income tax to 15per cent.

Friday 12 August
I went in the afternoon to Lambeth Palace to do this *Everyman* programme on relations between Church and State.

I had never been in there in my life. I was born across the river, I've worked for forty-four years in the House of Commons, and I'd never been into Lambeth Palace.

It's beautiful, with its courtyards and grand libraries; the librarian, a very modest man, showed me around respectfully, then said, 'I don't know which unit you're with. Are you with the Japanese television unit?' There were some Japanese there with a camera.

Monday 15 August
At four o'clock this morning Caroline woke up and heard somebody shouting at the front door. She went downstairs and there was a drunken Scotsman outside the door, hammering and saying, 'Is Tony Benn in there? If Tony Benn's not there I'll fucking well vote for Tony Blair.' Caroline said through the door, 'Please go away.' And he said, 'Are you a servant girl.' Caroline continued, 'Would you mind going away.' Then he lifted up the letter box and said, 'I don't think much of your legs.'

Tuesday 16 August, Stansgate
Caroline was working in the garden, watering the flowers, and I must say it looks absolutely beautiful; she's planted trees and flowers – it couldn't have been more attractive.

Friday 19 August
The little lap-top computer on which I've been working began smoking, and I thought it was going to set on fire so I switched it off. Switched it on again and it stopped.

Monday 22 August
Got up at six and took Hilary to catch the train with James, who found a £20 note at the station. After a long discussion – obviously he'd like to have kept it – he agreed to write a letter and send it to the police.

Thursday 25 August
Caroline, her friend Phyllis, Jonathan, James, Carrie and I went to Bradwell, to St Cedd's Church, built in AD 654. It must be one of the oldest buildings in England.

We were curious about the Othona Community, which is a Christian community in which people gather for communal living every summer. We had been there about ten years ago, and the people recognised us and said, 'Come in for a cup of tea.'

There was a nice guy with a beard and a T-shirt who welcomed us in. He was a vicar. 'I first came here many years ago. I was struck by it and now I'm in the Church.' He was very progressive: in favour of the ordination of women; against the dismissal of a vicar for his unorthodox theological views; against the idea that you couldn't put 'Dad' or 'Mum' on a gravestone.

There was a notice outside saying, 'We are primarily a Christian community, but we don't exclude others.'

Wednesday 31 August, London

I went to 4 Millbank to do a programme for Radio Scotland on the question 'Do all political careers end in failure?' But just before I left, I heard that Sinn Fein had announced a ceasefire and the whole of the rest of the day was occupied with that.

Roger Stott, who's the number two Northern Ireland Shadow spokesman for the Front Bench, was apparently told by Blair that he couldn't broadcast. Kevin McNamara was also told he couldn't broadcast. When the BBC rang and asked Blair if *he* would do an interview there was a hesitation, so they said, 'Actually we don't need to bother you, we've got a Labour spokesman already.' He asked, 'Who's that?' 'Tony Benn.' There was a sort of explosion, audible in the office, which was quite funny. And Blair did finally come on, but simply repeated what Major had said: 'It's got to be permanent.'

To cut a long story short I did eleven television and radio broadcasts.

Thursday 1 September

Mitchel McLaughlin and Gerry McLoughlin and another guy from Sinn Fein came to review the situation following the ceasefire. They were extremely cheerful. We reviewed everything that might happen: the possibility of Loyalist violence; that Gerry Adams might be assassinated; the way in which the British Government would respond. I said the jobs I would do were to write to John Major to ask for the exclusion order to be lifted, to try and arrange for Gerry Adams to come to the Labour Conference where we could have a discussion, and look at the Sinn Fein broadcasting ban again. They asked me if I would join an international commission, which they're hoping to set up with Nyerere, Kenneth Kaunda, Jimmy Carter, and so on. I'm quite happy to do that if ever it is organised.

I had a phone call in the evening from Edna O'Brien. She said, 'I just wanted to tell you, Tony, that your book (she'd obviously read the extracts in *The Times*) is absolutely brilliant, so deep, so personal.' She went on, and on so I said, 'Would you like to review it?' 'Oh, no, I don't want to review it, but I might mention it as the best book of the year.' On the basis of that I'm going to ask her to our launch party.

I asked her about her book. She said it had been rubbished by the British journalists but it's doing all right. I think this was an important element of the phone call. She said how disrespectfully David Dimbleby treated Gerry Adams – 'That poor man, he lives on forty-five pounds a week unemployment pay in a cage in Belfast, with guards and Rottweiler dogs to protect him; he's such a sweet and intelligent person.' And she continued, 'After the ceasefire I rang up Gordon Brown and asked him to ring me back, but he wouldn't reply. When I ring President Clinton, he replies. I spoke to Neil Kinnock, who denied absolutely that Nelson Mandela had ever been a terrorist.'

Then she went on to say that she had had dinner at the White House with Clinton, and Jack Nicholson was there. She said the trouble with Clinton is, 'He doesn't know who he is, he simply doesn't know who he is and he's so frightened.' She said he said to her, 'Have you written anything in which Jack Nicholson plays a part?' She said, 'No, I haven't, but he'd make a perfect Irish terrorist.' And Clinton absolutely froze. It was an interesting comment.

Saturday 3 September

I wrote to the Prime Minister asking him to lift the exclusion order on Gerry Adams for the Labour Conference.

Today, when it was known that I had issued the invitation to Gerry, Tony Blair's office put out a statement saying that it was ill-judged and ill-timed.

I can't say I care very much, because I've no particular time for Tony Blair, but it was the first example of what has become standard practice by Labour Leaders that, when asked by a Tory paper, they will always, always, always repudiate one of their Parliamentary colleagues, or anybody else.

Sunday 4 September

I went to join Keni St George, who was doing a meditation in Trafalgar Square. He's a most imaginative man, a Nigerian Buddhist. Joshua knew him because he played an instrument in one of Josh's pop groups – Oz, I think it was called. Keni is very keen on animal welfare. He had a lot of farm animals being carefully looked after in pens outside St-Martin-in-the-Fields; he had a refreshment tent; then on display he had dead meat, half a pig's head, fish, chicken, and so on – really disgusting; and a coffin that said, 'Meat is murder.'

I'm rather of that inclination. I like him. I went and he hugged me, he was so pleased, introduced me to quite a few people he knew. There was no press interest, as far as I could make out, although there may be – I'll find out tomorrow.

I idly wonder whether my Gerry Adams initiative (which Major made clear in a television interview will not lead to the exclusion order being lifted) will have alienated Tony Blair at the very beginning of my attempt to be helpful on the Lords reform. I think, in the back of my mind I had wondered whether I might be asked by the Labour Government to undertake such a job, but I'm certainly not going to make sacrifices of principle at this stage in order to have the entertaining experience of sitting in all the Labour Cabinets there have been from 1952 to 1995 or, 96. It would be fun, but I'm not going to think about it.

Tuesday 6 September

Gerry Adams has seen Bertie Reynolds and John Hume in Dublin. And Ian Paisley went to see Major and Major asked, 'Will you accept my word as a Prime Minister' that he had not done a secret deal. Paisley refused to reply, so Major threw him out.

It's all very exciting.

Thursday 8 September

I leaped out of bed at twenty-past four this morning with the most shattering cramp in my right thigh. It really was so painful that I cried out. Finally it subsided, but cramp is a big problem, and if I were totally disabled, I wouldn't know what to do.

Monday 12 September

The National Executive Committee was held at five o'clock at Walworth Road, and I must say I've never approached a meeting with such gloom and doom. I felt miserable, I didn't want to go – it was a strange experience actually.

I parked my car where I always did until a year ago, because I haven't been to an Executive Meeting at Walworth for almost exactly a year.

As I entered the building, I found there'd been a lot of repairs and there was a new carpet and names on the doors, like a business company, confirming what I had discovered from reading the NEC papers, which were mainly about cash forecasts and business plans and all the things you would associate with a business.

I went into the room and sat in a place that I didn't realise until too late was absolutely within an inch of John Prescott and Tony Blair. Dennis Skinner came and sat next to me.

David Blunkett was in the chair, and welcomed Tony Blair and Wayne David, the new leader of the European Parliamentary Labour Party.

At 5.08 Tony Blair began making a statement about the future of the General Secretary Larry Whitty. He said he'd asked Larry to take on the job of European Co-ordinator; Labour policy towards Europe was the key in the General Election and beyond, it was of central importance, we wanted somebody of weight and authority, and he'd offered Larry the job. Larry had agreed and there would be a vacancy for the General Secretary's job.

Larry Whitty responded. He explained the position, said it was not easy for him but that circumstances change, and that undoubtedly our interests in Europe were the key. He said the Party was solvent, well organised and electable, and it was an appropriate moment to go after ten useful years.

Kinnock then said that this was the happiest of relationships: Larry Whitty had been an agent of change, and he thanked Whitty.

Dennis Skinner said, 'Well, the party's shocked. Larry was threatened, the NEC had not been consulted and it was a shabby deal.'

Then Vernon Hince of the railwaymen said he was concerned about it, he was sorry it had been announced just before Conference and he also regretted the fact the NEC hadn't been consulted. That's quite strong stuff for a member of the RMT.

Clare Short said, 'It's a fait accompli, but it was a disgraceful way to do it – an unforgivable way to do it.'

I said that I'd probably known Larry longer than anyone else because he was my private secretary thirty years ago in the Ministry of Technology, and I was very glad when he joined the Labour movement. The position of General Secretary is an important one. We had a situation now where the NEC didn't have any opportunity to discuss the new job of European Co-ordinator, and the NEC would not have an opportunity of filling the post because the offer had already been made and accepted. We would be in great difficulty because Larry, presumably, would not attend Conference.

'Oh,' said Larry, 'I'm not resigning today.'

Then Tony Blair spoke again. 'This is a new job. It will not be an NEC appointment; it will be under myself and John Prescott, and it will therefore not be responsible to the NEC.' He said he understood the anxieties, was sorry it leaked out, but it was the right time to do it – all change is difficult. Today's NEC was called to involve the NEC, and it was the only way it could be done.

Dennis Skinner said, 'I don't want to accept this. I want a vote.'

David Blunkett remarked, 'Well, we could note that.'

I said, 'Well, there's another point, if I may, and that is that we've learned that the new European Co-ordinator will not be answerable to the NEC, so you'll have European policy made directly to the Leader of the Party. That's a very serious thing.'

There was further argument about Larry's terms, and Blair ended it by saying, 'There will be some overlap of responsibilities, but the Socialist

Group and the European Parliamentary Labour Party are big issues. Anyway, we've got the chairmanship of the Socialist Group ourselves, the Labour Party has. We don't want lobbying at Conference; we must act quickly.'

So the nominations will close during the Conference, and Conference will be all about lobbying for the General Secretaryship.

That was the meeting. It lasted until almost quarter to seven and I drove Dennis back. It was like the old days.

Looking back on it, Blair was quite tough. He got what he wanted; he said he had to do it, there was no alternative. People didn't want to go against him in terms of voting but it's quite clear that his stand – and the peremptory way in which he virtually sacked the General Secretary of the Labour Party – has caused considerable anxiety among the trade union people.

I find it interesting. I was happy to get out of the building really.

I'm glad to get a glimpse of the new Labour Party, the business-management party with a Leader who treats the General Secretary as if he was his agent or candidate. Blair was very charming, and smiled at me; I gave him two Polo mints, as I did John Prescott – I was sitting absolutely between them. I thought I would make the point, and I think it is an important point, of the transfer of power from the delegates and members and the Executive to the Party Leader.

I went to do a Radio 5 Live interview. I must comment on the BBC, because the receptionist at the front hall was overwhelmed with work, and there was a huge queue of people trying to find out which studio they should go to. Somebody asked where a studio was, and the commissionaire didn't know because the commissionaires are these Securiplan guys who've replaced the old BBC commissionaires, who knew the BBC inside out.

In the studio there was a line failure and I had to wait for a long time. One of the engineers I spoke to said that the whole costing of every item was absolutely mad, and they hated John Birt and his regime. And one woman who's a researcher there said, 'It's just one long anxiety.'

Saturday 17 September

It's a strange world at the moment. The Labour Party is utterly frozen: it comes out for nuclear weapons just before the Cold War ends; comes out for the broadcasting ban ('not an appropriate time to lift it'); opposes me for saying anything about inviting Gerry Adams. The Party is just wrong about everything. It's a bureaucratic machine, although it isn't the bureaucracy, now I come to think of it – it's just the leadership.

My brother David whom I spoke to tonight said that John Birt was a great friend of Peter Mandelson – they were both at LWT – so I'm sure that Birt will use Mandelson to get through to Blair.

Thursday 22 September

Going up to Edinburgh and waiting at Heathrow I met two Chief Constables; one the Chief Constable of Fife and the other the Chief Constable of the Central Region. They'd been down to some conference in London.

We had a very friendly talk. I asked about cannabis, which they do not wish to be decriminalised.

They told me one funny story about three candidates who went to canvass at a house. The first one knocked on the door and the man said, 'And what'll ye do fer us?'

'Aye, well, we'll look after you from the cradle to the grave.'

The second one came along and knocked on the door. And the man said, 'And what'll ye do fer us, because the last candidate will look after us from the cradle to the grave.'

'Aye, 'said the second candidate,' we'll look after you from the womb to the tomb.'

Then Ian Paisley came along and they said to him, 'Now what'll ye do for us, because the other candidates have said they'll look after us from the cradle to the grave or from the womb to the tomb, but what'll ye do?'

And Paisley said, 'Oh, don't bother with the cradle to the grave or the womb to the tomb. I'll look after you from the erection to the resurrection.' Quite a clever joke.

Saturday 24 September

Absolutely exhausted: Muswell Hill, Manchester, Bath, Bristol, Edinburgh, Preston, Rochdale, London, in a week.

I'll be glad when it's all over. I'm going to have a much quieter life this year, I really am.

Monday 26 September

Today the Labour Party launched a huge campaign against high taxation, thus repudiating Keynes, and there are articles now appearing in the Tory papers saying: can anyone think of anything that Tony Blair believes in?

Modernisation has just emptied the cupboard completely – there's nothing.

Tuesday 27 September

I completed my last four 'letters to historical figures' for BBC Scotland. I must say the Grace Darling one is excellent. I used the shipping forecast, 'South east Iceland, Faeroes, Fair Isle, Viking, Forties, Cromarty, Forth, Dogger, Tyne, Humber' to lead into Grace's lighthouse.*

*Grace Darling, the daughter of the light house keeper at Longstone, was famed in 1838 for rescuing passengers from a wrecked steamship. She died of TB, aged 26, in 1842.

Wednesday 28 September
Gordon Brown has said the old Labour Party was a high-tax, high-spend, high-borrowing party that believed in nationalisation and corporatism and that it was no longer relevant; and that we used to believe in full employment for men, but women should be kept at home – it was an absolute lie, and he just repudiated the whole past of the Labour movement.

Saturday 1 October, Blackpool
Packed up for Conference in an awful hurry. Queued for about twenty-five minutes for a taxi at Blackpool station. I was dropped off at the Florida Apartments – we must have been here probably every other year since 1982. I gave Mrs Shaw a hug, and came up and noticed immediately that the bathroom had been refurbished, there was new linoleum in the kitchen and a new chair in the living room.

I think nature prepares you for the next stage. And the next stage, as far as I'm concerned, is the gradual phasing-out of the organisational aspects of the Labour Party.

Sunday 2 October
To the National Executive at the Imperial Hotel.

I raised the fact that GEC Marconi Avionics had sponsored the international reception being given on Monday for international delegates. It was a big arms manufacture, and I made quite a meal of it.

I said, 'Here is this absolutely ghastly arms trade, and we've asked them to pay for us to meet international delegates.' This did create a great deal of shock, I must tell you. I was very pleased about that. Then we came to the agenda and resolutions.

At the end I said, 'As this is the last time I shall attend the NEC after thirty-five years, I would like to thank everyone for listening, and I hope to see many more Labour Governments come into power.' They all clapped.

Then Clare Short said, 'I think we all appreciate Tony's inimitable style.'

So I said, 'You should try imitating it.' So they laughed and that was the end.

I went up to Blair and said, 'I haven't spoken to you personally to congratulate you on being elected, and I'm sure you'll do very well.' I asked, 'Did Cherie get the tape of the speech I delivered when I came to speak for her?'

He said, 'Yes.' (She hasn't responded.)

Then I said, 'I must give you a copy of my *Diaries* because you'll be interested in the Bevan-Gaitskell business.'

That was my last meeting in the Executive. I'm really glad to be off it, to be honest, genuinely and honestly glad. There's a lot of work to no purpose. I did quote in the Executive this morning Ian Mikardo, who said he'd never known a bird that could fly only on its right wing. People laughed.

Monday 3 October
Behind the Conference platform was a huge green sign with New Britain, New Labour and a very faint red rose. The Executive members were told to sit on the platform only on Monday morning during the Leader's speech and on the final day.

The platform was terribly crowded. I was sitting in the back row, which didn't worry me much.

Jimmy Knapp was specially put on to speak before television coverage began. The televising of Conference has become a complete fraud, because instead of showing the speeches, the interviewers go up into the gallery and interview people. So you can't hear the speeches; you just hear people being interviewed and journalists commenting. They've stolen the conference from us really. Full coverage is what we used to have – and should have – but don't have.

The economic debate was begun by Gordon Brown, who made a sort of exciting speech. There were one or two good phrases, like 'The teachers should teach and the nurses should nurse, instead of being managed,' and so on. He gave a lot of hostages to fortune, none of which could be realised with the Central Bank and Brussels, but still it went down quite well.

Then we had Robin Cook and all the motions being moved and seconded.

I was called first from the floor. I spoke for exactly three minutes: a very short speech saying that the Labour Party represented the use of the ballot box to redress imbalance, and we should liberate Labour and make capital democratically accountable, have more democracy and raise hope. It wasn't marvellous, but it was useful.

Tony Booth, Cherie Booth's father came up. He really is an extraordinary larger-than-life character. He used to be in that programme *'Til Death Us Do Part*. Anyway, I talked to him and then we wandered around a bit and the Conference went on in the afternoon.

Caroline went off to the MSF Party and met Cherie Booth and had a chat to her, liked her very much.

Tuesday 4 October
Blair made his first Conference speech as Leader. He said Marx was dead; he talked about Europe, he talked about partnership with the private sector, full employment, health care, technology, opportunity, responsibility, civilian task forces (which are really a sort of workfare arrangement). He said we've got to reform the Welfare State, we must tell the truth, and 'I'm not prepared to say we would repeal trade union ballots.'

He said he was tired of dogma and promises, and he wanted a Bill of Rights. There'd be a Scottish Parliament, a Welsh Assembly; we would end quangos; and he made a reference to Ireland, said he agreed with the line taken by the Government.

He then said something about the House of Commons need for more women, about ending hereditary peers. He said we have changed and that there would be a new statement of objectives to replace Clause 4.

The speech was made with the help of teleprompters, and the camera moved over to Mandelson, who clapped desperately hard.

It was a clever speech. Of course, by attacking Marx and saying he would end Clause 4, Blair opened up a huge and unnecessary debate within the Party, in the hope of isolating the left and making them look like troublemakers.

Wednesday 5 October

The newspapers today inevitably are absolutely packed with 'Labour Party to drop Clause 4' stories.

In the course of the afternoon I did a live BBC television interview, surrounded by Labour people who clapped like anything, so you realised you weren't alone – really interesting.

Thursday 6 October

Got up very early, packed up at the Florida Apartments, said goodbye to Mrs Shaw and carried my heavy bags to the station.

The debate on the Clause 4 vote was to be held this morning and I felt terribly depressed.

At Manchester got on the train for Chesterfield.

I went with a few people in the bus to the funeral of Brendan Pashley, the partner of Jackie, who is Margaret Vallins's daughter. Brendan died while swimming in the sea; he got into trouble and Jackie, Tom and Margaret witnessed it, helplessly.

The church at the crematorium was absolutely packed with people. A young lad of thirty-two dying so tragically and unnecessarily made it especially sad. Jackie was very distressed.

The vicar gave a very good address about the nature of the tragedy, and then some popular music was played on a tape recorder. I noticed during the service that there were a lot of young men of about the same age, who obviously had been miners with Brendan when he was at Arkwright Colliery. When we sang 'The Lord is My Shepherd', they knew the words of the hymn without using the hymn book. It reminded me of the deep roots that Christianity has in our society.

In the car I heard that Tony Blair had been defeated, on defence and on Clause 4, and he said it didn't matter. So democracy means that you just carry on, whether you're defeated or not. So much for democracy.

Came back to London.

I rang the BBC to say, 'I notice on your news bulletins that you say that the Conference defied Tony Blair. Now, what is the meaning of defiance? I mean, in 1979 did the British electors defy Jim Callaghan or did they defeat Jim Callaghan?' The woman news organiser laughed and said, 'I think you've got a point.' But they went on saying 'defied', of course.

Saturday 8 October

At the end of Conference they played 'The Red Flag' in jazztime and people waved Union Jacks, just like demonstrators for the Queen. Another Mandelson gimmick. Just turns your stomach.

There's a semi-fascist element in the Labour Party at the moment, a 'hand over to international capitalism, wave your little Union Jack' tendency.

Sunday 9 October

I went off to the demonstration against the Criminal Justice Bill in Hyde Park. It was very orderly. Anthony Barnett from Charter 88 and Arthur Scargill were there; Jeremy Corbyn chaired it.

On the ten o'clock radio news and the 10.30 ITN news there were descriptions of pitched battles. I gathered that what happened was that the police, after the demonstration (which was quite peaceful) was over, blocked off any exit to Park Lane where people were going to pick up their buses. And maybe a few anarchists did engage in a battle or maybe they were agents provocateurs, or maybe it was all caused by the police. Anyway, there was a bust-up and eleven police were injured by CS gas, of all things, thrown by the demonstrators; and seventeen demonstrators were injured, and so on.

As a member of an elected body I shouldn't say it, but historically riot has played a role. And something has got to be done to get this representation back again, because all the vote is, is just a chance to vote between Blair and Major, and there's nothing in it. And it only happens every five years so whoever you vote for you're going to end up with the same policies. A real problem this.

Monday 10 October

To Doncaster, where there was a great big Toyota minibus and I was driven to Cleethorpes, with Claire Rayner and Bill Owen, for a literary lunch.

Bill I'd known of old; he's eighty, he's a good socialist, comes from a communist background, a really solid, serious man. He's just written a book that is his life story.

Claire Rayner is a plump woman of sixty-three, an agony aunt with a medical bias.

We talked all the way in – it was very friendly.

Afterwards we came back together in the car to Doncaster. We began talking about working-class roots and working-class songs and working-class habits.

Claire Rayner is a great one for singing these old songs about the workhouse and so on. Bill Owen then chipped in with songs he knew. He'd spoken in his speech about death and how he remembered exactly the moment when his mother and father died because of the tunes that were played and how music was for him a sort of marker.

Anyway, we had a jolly time, though it got a bit bawdy at one stage when we were talking about combination underwear and I said I still had my wartime combination underwear and they've got some other name for them now: aerobic underwear or something. Bill Owen said, 'I've never forgotten those liberty bodices. You'd spend ages fumbling about to undo her liberty bodice, and then you missed the last bus home when you were a kid and you had to walk home – it was awful, and anyway I'm so short that my nose used to rest between their bosoms.' We were all just giggling and laughing and having a marvellous time, like a lot of kids on a family outing.

Tuesday 11 October

I had Mr Ibrahim, the Iraqi Minister in the Iraqi Interests Section – now officially run by the Jordanian Embassy because we've broken off diplomatic relations with Iraq – come and see me because there is a huge crisis building up.

Saddam has moved soldiers down to the Kuwaiti border, and the Americans have sent thousands of troops. Ibrahim thought America would actually now bomb Iraq, as a warning. He said the suffering in Iraq is absolutely terrible, with starvation and death and so on. And people were paralysed and numb, and a lot of the Iraqi intellectuals were leaving Iraq. American policy here's a disgrace, and Britain goes along with it, as they always do.

Ibrahim told me some interesting things. He said the Pope had sent a delegate to Baghdad, who had suggested that Saddam should recognise Israel. Saddam had denounced this.

I said I hadn't heard that, but it was an interesting idea, because you'd bypass the Americans if you recognised Israel. I think it's quite a clever idea and it certainly would have an effect, but if the Americans kill more Iraqis to no good purpose, just to frighten Saddam, it'll be a terrible thing to do.

A useful, friendly talk. I like Ibrahim very much although he knows my attitude to the Saddam Hussein regime. Ibrahim is totally loyal to the government he represents.

Friday 14 October
Today's the day that Shimon Peres, Rabin and Arafat are all given the Nobel Peace Prize. There are bumpy roads ahead, and there will be for Northern Ireland as well.

Sunday 16 October
The Prince of Wales's biography by Jonathan Dimbleby is published, and it's all come out and it's just a tragedy really. He and Diana are totally unsuitable. I had lots of invitations to do broadcasts, which I've refused.

Monday 17 October
I drafted an Early Day Motion in support of Clause 4 and took it into the House. Blow me down, I was told by the clerks in the Table Office that the Speaker had ruled that you couldn't put a quotation on the Order Paper. Well, I said, 'It's not a quotation it's a statement of policy.'

Anyway the clerk wouldn't table it, so then the Clerk of the House was brought in and I really lost my temper.

I said, 'Look, Parliament is a bicycle with four-wheel brakes. If we can't discuss politics in the House of Commons, what can we discuss?'

Obviously I made an impact because later, when I went back, I heard that it had been agreed.

There was a statement on Iraq and what came over quite clearly from Douglas Hogg, the Foreign Minister, was that the Government retained the right to take military action against Iraq without further United Nations authority. They blamed Saddam for not selling oil in order to relieve the tragedy of the sanctions, and they required all sorts of periods of testing.

I should say that Jack Cunningham, our Foreign Affairs spokesman, strongly supported the Government but criticised them for letting arms go through to Saddam, which is a minor point really compared to the enormity of the suffering.

I drew attention to the number of people killed in the Gulf War and the number of babies who had died, and said that the humanitarian consideration should predominate. Anyway, there wasn't agreement between Russia and France and China about this, and it was more to do with Clinton's attempt to get re-elected.

It didn't go down very well, but Tam Dalyell gave support on the humanitarian side and so did Llew Smith. The points were made, but the Labour Party's utterly useless.

I was taken in a taxi to the *James Whale Show*. James Whale is very respectful to me, I must admit, but the programme's an absolute nightmare. When I went to have my make-up done, I entered this tiny make-up room and, as I opened the door, there was a black dancer, almost completely naked. She had a G-string on and a few things covering her enormous breasts. I thought, 'Well, I will just have to sit there', and she was bending down and doing herself up, and so on. She said, 'I hope I'm not embarrassing you.' I said, 'Oh, no, not at all.'

So I just sat there. Then I had a few minutes' discussion with James Whale and rushed back to the Commons. They kept me an hour and a half, but still it's an audience reaching 3.5 million people.

Later Tam Dalyell came up to me and said he had absolute concrete proof that Mark Thatcher had been involved in some sleazy deal – the one that's been in all the papers on selling arms – where it is alleged that he made a lot of money on a contract Mrs Thatcher had signed.

He said, 'I know you don't agree with fighting these things personally, but I have enough information from American Intelligence sources to persuade me that this is correct, and I intend to name him in the House tomorrow.'

I said, 'I don't disagree with that. I'm not in favour of turning political issues into personal issues, but you go ahead.'

Tuesday 18 October

The Committee of Privileges met at six o'clock. We got on to the agenda that had been submitted by Tony Newton, who was in the chair, and it was agreed without any discussion that we would divide the inquiry into two halves: First of all, the conduct of the Members and the press in respect of the incident that led to the issue being referred to the Committee of Privileges; and, secondly, the wider question of the alleged corruption.

I spoke next, and I said I did move in the summer that we should meet in public. And as the Attorney General has said that the law here is not clear, my approach was that we recommend what the law should be. 'For that reason, I am less interested in pursuing MPs or journalists than in clarifying the law for the future. The issue really is the credibility of Parliament, and that requires publicity. The hearings, in my opinion, and the deliberations, should be in public.'

The Attorney General said, 'I'm in favour of evidence in public for the second part of the inquiry.'

On my motion that we hear all the evidence in public, there was a vote of 4 to 8; the four included David Alton, and against were all the Tories. As I left, the press were outside and they asked me to make a statement so I said, 'I'm not going to make a statement. The chair will make a statement.'

But Bill Michie and Doug Hoyle had been going round telling everybody they intended to resign, and I heard later they had decided to resign.

Caroline had said to me, 'Don't resign, this is the one committee on which you sit where you have some influence.'

So, what I may do is simply not turn up for any of the meetings that are held in private, just simply not turn up, and then resume my attendance at meetings when we get on to the general question. In this way, of course, we would totally undermine the credibility of the inquiry into the Members, because the Tories would have an overwhelming majority.

What I'll do is draft a letter and send it round to the other Labour members of the committee, saying that in the circumstances I don't feel able to attend for the hearing, in private, of the evidence relating to the press and to the Members who allegedly accepted the £1000, because it's not very appropriate or in line with what the House of Commons is supposed to do, which is to protect the electors against the possibility that Members might be influenced by money. But I won't resign from the committee. They may throw me off, but I won't resign.

The rumours of a royal divorce are denied by the solicitors for the two sides.

Wednesday 19 October

John Reid, who used to be Kinnock's assistant and then became an MP, came up to me and said, 'Tony, I've had too much to drink.'

I said, 'Well, I hope the beer in your belly hasn't put out the fire.'

He replied, 'I want to have a serious talk with you.' So we walked along and stood just outside the library. He went on, 'Tony, you don't seem to realise, because you come from a privileged home, what the working class really feel. They want victory; they don't want everything, they just want improvement. And there are you – all you learn about socialism you learn from your books; you and your Holland Park home with your big log fire. Why don't you come and have a meal with me and my wife and meet some real working-class people?'

Anyway, he was trying to be friendly so I said, 'Thank you very much for saying what a lot of people think.' But, I continued, 'What moves me? It isn't bloody books, I hardly ever read them. It isn't that I was a revolutionary student when I was young. It's the fact that the working people I represent are bloody badly treated. I see all these people who came up from the working class and ended up in the House of Lords, and I'm bloody well not going to accept it. I'm not going to accept it.'

I was very harsh with him. I said, 'I appreciate what you're saying and why you're saying it, but that's my philosophy. And the other thing I'm worried about is that a new political party has been formed in the heart of the Labour Party, a new SDP.'

'Aye, well,' said John Reid, 'I never had any time for Kinnock.'

I said, 'He bloody well lost! I've sat on the Executive with seven leaders and not a single moderniser has ever won an election. I'm bloody well not going to accept that I've got it all out of a book.'

I think I was so strong and powerful and foul mouthed that he said, 'Aye, well, that's the best case I've ever heard you make.'

I replied, 'That's what I believe.'

It was interesting. Then he said, 'I hope you're not going to retire.'

I said, 'Of course I'm not going to retire.'

He said, 'I think you've a bigger role to play now than you've ever had to play. Well, Tony, don't give up, don't give up. There are more people in the parliamentary party agree with you than you may realise.'

Stephen looked into my office. We went out together.

There were 2500 riot police, including mounted police with helmets and horses with visors, who had driven some of the demonstrators against the Criminal Justice Bill into Whitehall and along the Embankment.

Sunday 23 October

Fresh revelations in the *Sunday Times* about the Prince of Wales; another book or programme coming out about the Princess of Wales. That couple are fighting themselves to the death. The public on the whole are more sympathetic with Princess Diana, but the effect of it all is that the monarchy itself has become a really big issue now.

Also the 'cash for questions' thing is building up. Neil Hamilton, who is a Minister at the DTI, is refusing to resign, because he denies the claim that he was ever paid anything as a backbencher for putting down questions for Harrods.

John Major's been in Northern Ireland building up the peace process. If he pulls that one off, he might do better than we think.

Monday 24 October

The Home Secretary is being accused of having intervened in the application for naturalisation by the Al Fayeds who own Harrods. Obviously the Fayeds who gave, I think, a quarter of a million pounds to the Tories are now furious with them and determined to destroy them.

Neil Hamilton hasn't resigned. The Prime Minister says he'll publish Robin Butler's report on Neil Hamilton and Tim Smith, the other Minister, who has resigned. It's getting more and more complicated.

The other thing is that today Peter Lilley announced that they're going to abolish unemployment benefit and substitute a job-seeking allowance, which is an incredible thing to do. Just throw away the whole unemployment entitlement under the Welfare State! Patricia Hewitt is saying there's going to be no link between pensions and average earnings.

Friday 28 October, Chesterfield

Tom and Margaret had said to me that Dave Walsh, who's a young active member of the local party, had been putting it about that when reselection comes they need a younger candidate, and so I said, 'People are entitled to have whoever they like. I'd like to go on – I'm doing the job, I'm working very hard.'

Margaret said, 'I think if they did get rid of you and put somebody else in, Chesterfield would go Liberal.' I think that is a possibility, because it is totally changing its character and, though I'm reasonably well respected in the town, I have to think a lot about age. Ageism is not just a prejudice; it is that young people have got to get rid of older people in order to make room for themselves. It's a necessary process, it's like the queue – you've got to get to the front of the queue.

I remember my dad saying in 1945 how he objected to the fact that whenever his name was mentioned, it said, 'Sixty-seven-year-old Lord Stansgate.' Well, I'm sixty-nine now and they always call me a veteran. They never call people they approve of, like Roy Jenkins or Mrs Thatcher, a veteran. 'Veteran left-winger, veteran fighter for socialism' and so on.

Monday 31 October

I decided this morning that I would announce in the House in the debate this afternoon that I intended to issue a statement on the proceedings of the Committee of Privileges. I'd already faxed the Speaker asking to be called. I then faxed another request to the Speaker to consider a manuscript amendment from me, which would instruct the Committee to meet in public.

I rang Sir Clifford Boulton, the Clerk of the House, who was extremely helpful. He told me today is his last day at the Clerk's Table. He was very helpful indeed and his secretary said they'd miss him very much because he had such a good sense of humour.

I gave a copy to Sir Clifford, to Ann Taylor and John Prescott, because they were speaking in the debate. Prescott opened the speaking as Deputy Leader, and made a good speech.

Tony Newton was very hard-line on opposing open meetings, and what's really frightened the Tories, I think, is the possibility that Al Fayed will turn up and publicly smear all sorts of people.

Before the debate began, the Speaker announced that she took a very serious view of Peter Preston of the *Guardian* using House of Commons notepaper to forge a letter to get the account of Jonathan Aitken's hotel bill from the Ritz in Paris.

Really, they talk about high standards in Parliament but what about the *Sunday Times* trying to bribe people? And the *Guardian* forging documents? On the other hand, it was quite clear from the debate that the Tories were determined to protect their own Members.

I made a speech in which I argued the case for looking after the interests of the electors, and then read, very carefully, to the House my statement about issuing reports of the Privileges Committee proceedings. This led to a great gasp from the House itself.

Ted Heath said there should be more openness but it was quite impossible to go as far as I had suggested.

Tuesday 1 November

Banner headlines in *The Times* and *The Independent* about the statement that I made that I intended to publish my own report on the Committee of Privileges.

I went off to the House of Commons, having been alerted to the fact that complaints would be made about my statement yesterday. I was there when Peter Emery and Sir James Spicer I think, raised what I'd said.

The Speaker said, in the House, 'It's nothing to do with me, it's for the Committee to decide.'

At four o'clock Labour Members of the Committee gathered with the Chief Whip (Derek Foster), the Deputy Chief Whip (Don Dixon), the Shadow Leader of the House (Ann Taylor), and we had a discussion as to what to do.

What's quite clear is that Doug Hoyle and Bill Michie are still contemplating leaving the Committee. On the other hand, they think they've done a deal with the Tories that will get something, although the Tories have actually made no concessions whatever.

Peter Shore, who's now on the Nolan Committee on Standards in Public Life, was keen to continue.

The line that I'm taking is quite different. They were polite and they didn't criticise me, but obviously they're hopping mad that I said what I said, because they think it will interfere with their status on the Committee. And somebody asked, 'Why don't we talk to the Tories on Privy Councillor terms?'

Well, that's the very thing I object to, this whole 'coalition' spirit. Anyway, I said I'd do whatever they did. We went into the Committee at five o'clock. I made manuscript notes. We had this long discussion and then adjourned after nearly two hours.

A great crowd of journalists was outside Committee Room 16 and I said, 'I shall issue a written account of the proceedings later.'

Back to see the Chief Whip, with the same little group in the same little room and it came out a bit more strongly there. Bill Michie was livid with me for not consulting him – though he'd decided to resign from the Committee of Privileges without consulting me.

Peter Shore said I'd destroyed the Committee of Privileges and made it quite impossible to reach an accommodation. He was white with anger.

I said, 'Peter, we've disagreed about open Government for twenty-five years. My interest is in getting rid of the cosy club; your interest is in exposing the Tories. And they're quite different interests.'

So it was all very sensitive and touchy, and Doug Hoyle still thought a compromise might be reached.

I went up to my room, turned on my BBC computer, and I typed from eight until ten, nearly 2000 words. When I'd done it, I photocopied it, took the first copy to the Lord President's Office, handed a copy in to the Speaker's Office, then gave a copy to the Clerk at the Table to give to the Clerk of the Committee of Privileges. Then, having done that, I stood in the Lobby during a vote and gave copies to everyone I could see who was on the Committee of Privileges, including, I might add, the Chief Whip, the Deputy Chief Whip, Ann Taylor and David Alton. I gave a copy to David Mitchell, a Tory Member of the Committee. I was being quite fair.

Then I left it in the Press Gallery; even dropped a copy in Hansard.

Then, while the machine was rolling off copies, I did an interview on *The World Tonight.*

It was about eleven o'clock by now and my little pager had received so many messages that it said 'Memory Full'.

I also heard tonight that it is possible that tomorrow a motion might be moved and carried in the House that I should be removed from the Committee of Privileges. I thought it couldn't be done until the Committee itself met again and moved such a motion, but apparently it might be done by the House.

It's so obvious that this is a cosy club protecting its own against the press, against the public, and I just don't want to be part of it.

I hope I've done the right thing. Caroline was a bit doubtful about whether it was sensible to get slung off the Committee. If it comes up tomorrow and there is a vote and a debate, I shall have to say something about it. I did what I thought was right, and the House must do what it thinks is right. And if it thinks it necessary to remove me from the Committee, it's a matter for Members. But we are responsible to our electors and not to each other.

I'm quite clear about that.

Wednesday 2 November

Got up at six this morning.

The Times had an extraordinary article by Simon Jenkins called 'The Case for Secrecy', describing me as an anarchist, and saying that no institution could last if information about how it worked were to come out. It really was the clearest statement I've ever read. I've been called a communist, a Trotskyite, an anarchist and a Maverick, but that was a really interesting insight into the attitude of the British Establishment.

I went into the House. The Speaker began by saying, 'I want to make a statement about the Right Honourable gentleman the Member for Chesterfield's issuing of the proceedings of the Committee of Privileges.' She said what a serious view she took of it – it was for the Committee to take action and report back to the House. Very, very stern and conservative.

Anyway, I didn't try and get in on that.

Then we came to a debate on Peter Preston, the editor of the *Guardian* who had forged a letter and sent it by fax to try and find out what Jonathan Aitken's hotel bill had been in the Ritz in Paris. Really just trifling stuff.

Peter Preston was up in the Gallery chewing and chewing. I could see him, sitting next to Hugo Young and Andrew Rawnsley.

I had originally decided to vote to refer it to the Committee of Privileges because I thought a forgery was serious. Then I thought, 'Well, I'll abstain, because this is a bit phoney. It's just the Tories have found some way of hitting back at the Labour Party.'

Then I thought about it further. 'Why should I refer him to the Committee of Privileges, which will hear his case in secret. Particularly since it became clear that he wanted to have it in public and they wouldn't let him.

In the end I was one of 38 who voted against it, with 331 voting to refer Preston to the Committee of Privileges.

They will be very angry with him and, of course, I'm now a block because they can't hear any evidence until they've dealt with me. I shall write a report of the next Committee of Privileges meeting, where they will be discussing whether or not they're prepared to recommend my removal from the Committee. I shall then put in an amendment to their report and in my amendment I shall argue my case. I'll do it properly.

They didn't move a motion to expel me tonight but when they do, no doubt the Labour Opposition will support that motion.

Thursday 3 November

I went over to the House. Parliament had risen and I was hungry, so I said, 'Is there anywhere I can get a meal?' I was told, 'There's the Sports & Social Club.' I never knew there was a club. I asked, 'Where is it?' It turned out to be in the basement of the Palace and it was absolutely packed with people. It was just like a pub; was even called the HoP Inn!

They were so friendly and I got a couple of cheese rolls and a cup of tea, went to my room for a bit, and then on to the National Union of Unemployed Workers meeting in the Grand Committee Room. But there were only eight people there. I feel so sorry for them.

Monday 7 November

Today I stumbled in the office. I had felt faint a few days ago, and today I stumbled quite stupidly and fell, not on the floor, but on my hand, and bruised it and hurt my chest and felt a bit shaken.

I noticed yesterday that President Reagan said he had Alzheimer's disease and everyone said how courageous to admit it. But you do get to the point when you get a few little warning signs.

Tuesday 8 November
We heard that Andrew Hood had got the appointment that he had applied for with Robin Cook. There were 500 applicants and Andrew got it, so it's a great coup for the 'basement university' and the Teabags.

Friday 11 November
Caught the 9.43 and got to Chesterfield just after eleven. Tommy Vallins took me to Springwell Community School where, three of the students – three girls actually – are working on Radio Emerald, which is a green station and they are going to get a licence next spring for a couple of months. They were serious, rather like Michael, my grandson; shy, but asked questions; unhappily, the first time round the microphone hadn't been switched on, so I agreed to do it again.

Tuesday 15 November
William was rushed to hospital today. He fell in the playground and hit the back of his head with a terrible crack. The head teacher went with him in the ambulance to the hospital and Josh was notified. The awful thing was that when Josh rang he said, 'Dad, it's Josh. William ...' and we were cut off and I thought 'Oh God!' Then he rang back and said William had had an accident. They let him out again, but this evening he was sick and Josh took him back to the hospital, just in case. The hospital was marvellous. Thank God for the Health Service. The school was marvellous. Thank God for public education.

Came home and hadn't paid my phone bill so it had been cut off.

Melissa brought Hannah for tea. That little creature! She's seven months old and is so observant. She just sits and watches everything and sometimes gives a little kick when she gets suspicious, but she's awfully sweet. She's exactly like the little doll 'Suzy Walker' that Melissa had when she was a little girl. Suzy Walker is the same size as Hannah and has the same-shaped face and same-coloured hair, and wears a woolly jacket just like Hannah's. It was really quite extraordinary.

Wednesday 16 November
I watched the opening of Parliament on television, and this year I felt more of a rejection of the whole thing than I have ever felt before. I used to think it was ridiculous, embarrassing and silly, but now – with the corruption in Parliament, and with the absolute absurdity of the royal family, and the sickening sight of Major and Blair walking side-by-side, and Prescott with David Hunt, and so on – I just felt for the first time that parliamentary democracy would offer this country no prospect of any change whatever. It is there to keep us in order.

Rifkind made a speech this week about the need for new institutions to supplement NATO (an Atlantic Union of some kind), institutions that would in effect protect the white races against the challenge from Africa and Asia. Considerable overtones of colour and class, because he said that democracy and the market economy were integral parts of the Atlantic community.

It is difficult for me to do more in Chesterfield than say to people, 'Well, look, if you vote for me, I'll fight for you. But don't vote for me thinking I can change very much', because Blair agrees with the Government on almost everything.

I listened to the Queen's Speech, which wasn't very exciting. They have dropped Post Office privatisation.

I was summoned to the Whip's Office for a meeting of the Labour members of the Privileges Committee – Doug Hoyle, Peter Shore, Alan Williams, Bill Michie and Ann Taylor.

There were two issues. One is whether a compromise can be arrived at under which witnesses would be able to decide whether they wanted to give evidence in public or private; and if they decided to go private, then we would have to accept it. The Tory problem is that not only do they want to protect their own members, but they also want to prevent other witnesses, such as the *Sunday Times,* or Al Fayed of Harrods or Peter Preston, from coming and spilling the beans. So I don't think they will accept it.

Then we moved on to the question of my written report of the proceedings. I said, 'My position is very simple. The press want to increase circulation and make money out of sleaze. We, as a party, may think we can get an advantage out of exposing the Tories but the real thing is that this has spread over into us and we have got to come out for openness. I object to the commercialisation of the Commons. For example, I had a letter this morning from two MPs – one of whom is Janet Anderson, a Labour MP, and Sir Graham Bright – inviting me to a champagne reception in the House to launch Safeway's new version of cola. Well, I think it's absolutely disgraceful.' I also mentioned David Mitchell's invitation to an El Vino's wine reception. I also had a letter about how to get a cheap car if you are an MP by consulting a colleague. It's disgraceful.

Peter Shore said, 'If you do this, you will be seen to be delaying reaching a proper solution to the problem.'

I said, 'Well, I'm sorry, but I think the real question is not whether it is quick or not, but whether it is open or not.'

Bill Michie was very angry with me and said, 'You didn't consult with us. We were negotiating and you went out on your own.'

'Well, Bill, truthfully, you said you had resigned from the Committee, without consulting me. Anyway, there are not negotiations going on with the other side.'

So it will be interesting to see what happens. I think what will happen is that my recommendations will be turned down, and then they will decide whether to report me to the House. I am going to go on writing reports about what happens in the Committee, so I suppose I will be thrown off.

Saturday 19 November, Chesterfield

I didn't get up all day. It's 4.40 p.m. and I haven't shaved and am still in my pyjamas. I have this awful cold and Caroline is at Stansgate. I have got to be in Derbyshire this evening, so I just lay in bed because I felt I needed a rest and nobody bothers me in Chesterfield; the phone doesn't ring. Lying in my little bedroom, looking up at the ceiling, I did sort of wonder what the hell I was doing with my life. I have been so busy for the last ten weeks that I have had no time for family, for friends, and I have almost forgotten how to enjoy myself. I have just been on a treadmill that I have manufactured myself.

Monday 21 November

I went to the Committee of Privileges and I won't go into what happened, except to say that, when the vote came, twelve people voted to remove me from the Committee, including four Labour Members – all Privy Councillors, I might add. And on the second vote, which was about whether my report of the last meeting should be published, nine voted against and three for, with some abstentions. That will have to go to the House for approval.

It was quite a remarkable meeting really, and although I am sorry to be thrown off the Committee, I do think a principled stand is right and I am glad I have taken it.

In the House this afternoon I got in a question about the thirty-nine NATO aircraft that bombed the Serbs in the former Yugoslavia, apparently the biggest air-raid in Europe since the Second World War. Of course, what it will do is make the humanitarian position in Yugoslavia impossible. This is American pressure.

Saturday 26 November

Up at 5.15 and caught the 6.35 to London.

Caroline went to the socialist Labour school governors meeting with Stephen Byers, whom she likes very much.

Leo Panitch and I had lunch together at a very expensive restaurant. I didn't care for it much. We talked about Ralph Miliband's boys, David and Edward. Edward is now working for Harriet Harman and the Treasury team, and David is Chief Policy Adviser to Blair.

Leo had asked David if he had seen the programme about MI5 and the miners which had been shown this week, and David said he had. So Leo asked, 'What's your policy?' David said, 'Well, they are very, very strong and we haven't really got a policy.' And David didn't think that Blair had yet been briefed by the Intelligence services.

So I developed the argument that, in order to get anywhere, to be a legitimate Leader of the Labour Party, you had to come to terms with MI5, the City of London, the monarchy, Brussels, the press lords and the senior civil servants, and so on.

I am interested in David. I am meant to be meeting him for tea this week.

Leo commented that David had said to him of me, 'What a giant of a man.' That may be his personal view, but in his little gang at the top of the Labour Party they will dismiss the left. He is, of course, of that generation. He was about twelve when Thatcher came to power and he has never seen or heard anything else. Leo said that David was seen as being a figure of the left in the little team at the top, which was interesting.

According to Leo, David and Edward would like to be in Parliament.

I am very, very tired and I have got this annoying cough – I was sick with the cough on the train this morning. I wonder if my lungs are in bad shape. Still, threescore years and ten I have nearly had, and I can't complain. But I must say I would like to die in harness. I couldn't bear the thought of retiring or rotting away, because I would bore myself to death and I would be an awful old hypochondriac, I know that.

Monday 28 November

Talked to a few people in the Tea Room, and at the moment there really is a feeling of utter cynicism and despair about Parliament – right, left and centre. It is not just the left that is fed up with what Blair is doing in Parliament, but the right of the Party feel that this little gang has taken over and has no connection with the Party. I felt more sick tonight than I have done for ages, because here was a vote of confidence in the Government and we were told not to vote.

Tuesday 29 November

Came home and found a message from the Leader of the House's office on my answer phone saying that the debate to remove me from the Committee of Privileges would be tomorrow night at ten; it wouldn't be 'exempted business,' so in order to prevent it being got through on the nod, someone has to shout 'Object'. So I'll get a few people to come in tomorrow night to do that. But the business managers will carry it forward every day. It is really a dirty device.

Wednesday 30 November

Went to the Bob Cryer memorial meeting in the Grand Committee Room at the House. Two former Speakers were there – George Thomas and Jack Weatherill; the Serjeant at Arms; William McKay, the Clerk;

Jim Mortimer, the former General Secretary of the Labour Party; Gordon McLennan, the former General Secretary of the Communist Party; Peter Bottomley, Ted Knight, Alan Clark, Alan Simpson. Gina, the cafeteria manageress, spoke and made a lovely speech, which moved Ann Cryer to tears. John and Jane were sitting in the front row. I spoke and Dennis wound up – a marvellous meeting.

Thursday 1 December

Went up to my room and David Miliband, who is about twenty-nine and is Chief Policy Adviser to Tony Blair came for a talk. I asked how he was getting on and he said he had only been there for ten weeks and it was difficult to settle down. I asked who the key people were and he said, 'Tony Blair works very closely with Prescott and Gordon Brown and Robin Cook.' I didn't ask about Mandelson, but obviously he's a big force. And Derry Irvine, who was Blair's pupil master when he was a barrister and is an old friend of John Smith's as well.

I asked about the staff and he said, 'I am in charge of policy,' and somebody called Alastair Campbell is the Press Officer; and he mentioned a couple of other people. I said, 'Do you have regular meetings?'

He said, 'No, we meet once a week.'

'You ought to meet more frequently, because it is very valuable.'

David said, 'It is a point. We have been under such pressure. We want to act more vigorously.'

I said, 'Also, you want to get out more.'

He asked what I thought and I said, 'Well, for a start, I think the attack on Clause 4 was a great mistake.'

'Oh, is it? I thought you would agree that we need wider objectives.'

'Well, it is the de-gutting of the Labour Party. It means a lot to me.'

'Surely you want broader objectives.'

'Yes. The Chesterfield Labour Party has got much broader objectives, but in *addition* to Clause 4. Nothing in the world will ever persuade me to accept a dynamic market economy. I just won't accept it.' I think that slightly shook him and surprised him.

'You'll probably get away with it,' I continued, 'because nobody wants to embarrass the Leader, but it will be at a fairly considerable price. It's like taking crucifixes out of a church. It just separates you from your traditional background.' I told him about the trade union ticket collector on the train who said, 'Mr Benn, I am a right-wing Callaghanite Labour man and I don't identify with the new leadership of the Labour Party.' I said to David, 'The answer is that you have to keep Clause 4 and add others, as Gaitskell did.'

David said, 'No, we won't do that.'

'Well, anyway, I think you are trying to dismantle the Labour Party.

You sack the General Secretary, distance yourselves from the unions; we're told not to vote on a motion of censure on the second reading of the European Fianance Bill.' I think he was genuinely surprised. I went on, 'Don't underestimate Major. He might settle the Irish problem. His gimmick was very effective. Don't Clintonise the Labour Party.'

He asked, 'What would you do?'

'I think you really have to recognise that fear is the factor. We have got to give people confidence in themselves. You'd have to have a big housing programme, the public services strengthened and a fair tax system. You have got to take back some of the tax that was given away to the wealthy. Anyway, to get investment, you'll have to solve the problem of Brussels.'

'We're powerless in respect of Brussels.'

'You are never powerless.'

David had got my letter about reform of the Lords, and I said, 'I'd like to help, but I don't quite know what the objective is.'

He said, 'We have got to be very careful about the House of Lords and the Church, because they go right up to the very top' – meaning the Crown.

I said, 'The Queen will agree to anything.'

'It's very difficult, and anyway, there are more Tory life peers.'

'Well, you could cram more life peers in, you could do what you like, but you would get reform through under the Parliament Act.' I think what I might do is to draft a Bill and send it to him, but I got the feeling that all Blair really wants is to stop hereditary peers from voting.

Then David said, 'What will the left do when there is a Labour Government?'

'What I think will happen is that expectations will go through the roof and then they will squeeze the Labour Government.' And in a funny way, I had a sort of feeling that the Establishment half-wants Tony Blair, because they think he will make the cuts in the welfare services that Major isn't strong enough to make.

I added, 'I hope you don't mind my speaking plainly.' And David said, 'No,no, we must keep in touch.' We talked a bit about his father Ralph.

Tuesday 6 December

Looked in at a meeting George Galloway had organised for the leader of the Saudi Opposition who, because of British arms contracts with Saudi Arabia, is being deported back by Britain to Saudi Arabia, where he will certainly be executed. A most awful thing. I met him briefly – he's a distinguished atomic physicist.

At ten o'clock there were about six votes in the House. The first was on the proposal by the Government to raise VAT on fuel from 7 to 15 per cent and we won. A number of Tories abstained and others voted with us, and the Government was beaten by eight votes, a clear defeat.

Just before midnight the Chancellor got up and said he would drop it, and there was uproar in the House. I didn't hear the result of the actual VAT vote because I was working, but I went up to the Gallery and watched the scene when the Chancellor made a statement saying he wouldn't proceed with the VAT; somehow the total failure of the Labour Party to have an alternative took away all the excitement, other than the excitement of seeing the Government defeated.

That's the first substantial victory in the House of Commons against the Tories since 1979, and the Government is in great disarray, and quite rightly so.

Wednesday 7 December

Went into the House later and saw the Tory Deputy Chief Whip, Greg Knight, who said they're going to put down the motion to remove me from the Privileges Committee on Monday night.

Believe it or not, I heard on the midnight news that the Labour Party was suggesting that the gap in revenue (as a result of the defeat over VAT) be filled by selling the Grid, so the Labour Party comes out for privatisation in order to avoid tax increases. It's just unbelievable – you just can't believe such things are being said.

Saturday 10 December, Chesterfield

To Phyllis Silver's 100th birthday party. She looked at me searchingly when I first won the seat in 1984 and said, 'Mr Benn, I'm ninety and I've never been to Derby.' So I said, 'I don't advise you to go now, at your age.' So she said she'd vote for me; actually she was a very solid Labour person. Tomorrow is her actual birthday, so I had got a copy of *The Times* for 11 December, 1894, the date of her birth, and I put on the front, 'Happy Birthday, Phyllis.' She's in an old people's home part of the time, and she'd come home and her daughter Betty was there.

I asked her what she first remembered. 'I remember the First World War.' Well, the First World War started when she was twenty. I said, 'Do you remember Queen Victoria?' 'Oh, yes, I remember Queen Victoria.' Well, that was when she was about six.

She shed a few tears and I gave her a hug. She said to me, 'Are you the Labour man?' So I said, 'Yes.' She said, 'Oh, I'll vote for you.'

Ten years ago, when she was ninety, we'd arranged for a car to take her to the polling station, and she actually walked to it, so I said 'Well next time I shall expect you to walk, Phyllis, and I hope you'll come to my one hundredth birthday in thirty years' time.' So she laughed; it was really rather touching.

Today Keith Joseph died. He was elected to Parliament in 1956. He was a very clever man indeed. Very nervous; he used to be sick sometimes before doing *Any Questions*? He was tense and drawn and white. Although he'd been a perfectly ordinary, middle-of-the-road Conservative in the 50s as a Minister, he then began in Opposition (after the Tories were beaten in 1964) moving rapidly to the right. He was supposed to be one of the great architects of the 'Selsdon Park' policy, which was the beginning of Thatcherism in 1970, and then Thatcher made him Secretary of State for Industry.

Sunday 11 December

I worked all the time I was at home on my speech on the debate tomorrow to remove me from the Privileges Committee. I don't often type out a speech, but I did type this out because I wanted to get it absolutely right.

Then we went over to this lovely family party at Hilary's. The whole family was there. There were eight grandchildren; they bounced, jumped and everything.

It was a birthday for Hilary, who was forty-one, for William, who was ten, for Daniel, who was three, and there were presents and crowns and cakes, and it was lovely.

Monday 12 December

One thing I've learned: in the old days there was a press lobby upstairs in the House and if you put out a press release they all got it. Now, of course, there is this huge television and radio headquarters at 4 Millbank, about six minutes' walk from the House of Commons. Hundreds of people work there: Sky, ITV, ITN, radio, foreign television companies, and so on. They never come into the House – why bother? You can watch it on a screen over at 4 Millbank and write your stuff just as well as if you were in the lobby, and you can smoke and have a cup of tea while you're doing it.

Journalists used to come to hear what politicians said; now politicians traipse over there, three, four, five times a day, to have a little interview, and the commentators talk to each other.

My speech on the motion to remove me from the Committee of Privileges lasted about half an hour. I had continual interruptions and it was like opening a furnace and being blasted by everybody, including Peter Shore, who spoke against me. Not a single one of the Committee voted for me.

What's happened (and I suspected this for a long time) is that Members of Parliament have found a way of escaping from public scrutiny into the secrecy of the Select Committees, which are really little coalitions where you're expected to fall in line on the grounds that a unanimous report is more effective than a report based upon Party lines.

That came out very, very strongly, and so you can see that at the heart of Westminster, despite all the shouting and abuse, which is completely synthetic, all the parties are really living in a coalition atmosphere. Coalition with civil servants in coalition with the Minister, in coalition with each other, and one day that really needs to be brought out.

It's one reason why I didn't like the Privileges Committee because when I asked them to vote on it, they were all so embarrassed; it wasn't the thing you did on a Privileges Committee.

Another thing they didn't like was that I was appearing to be high and mighty about selling influence for money, which only a handful of MPs (mainly Tories, but not probably exclusively Tories) do. One of them talked about my making money by publishing my diaries, as if there was a parallel between being a writer and a politician and being an MP who would pick up cash from wherever they could get it – Al Fayed in Harrods, or Glaxo, or whoever.

What was interesting was that the Cabinet were got out of bed at twelve to come back and vote! The Labour Front Bench abstained, Peter Shore voted with the Tories, and I was duly removed.

I saw Kenneth Baker, who is in favour of a referendum on Europe. I said to him, 'Maybe you and I should get together and get an all-party referendum motion tabled, or a Bill to bring about a referendum.'

Well, he said, 'I've got to persuade a few more people in my camp.'

Tuesday 13 December

Went into the Tea Room and Michael Martin was there, the Chairman of the Administration Committee, the rather tough Member for Glasgow, Springburn.

I'd been told by the Serjeant at Arms that I'd have to ask Martin about making a video about the workings of Parliament behind the scenes. I had a word with him about it and he said, 'My advice is just do it. Do it unobtrusively and it'll be all right.' So that was a huge advantage and it helps me when I go back to the Serjeant at Arms.

Wednesday 14 December

To the Campaign Group meeting, where most of the attention was on Clause 4 and here a real problem has arisen.

Dennis said there was real hostility on the Executive to the ending of Clause 4, but they all said that we can't let Tony Blair down. So they agreed, with only Diane and Dennis and one other (I forget who it was) opposed. But it is very foolish . . .

Thursday 15 December

Went to Wallace Heaton, where I bought this most expensive 'View Cam' camera, which you can rotate without necessarily having to move the camera; instead of having a little viewfinder, you watch it on a screen about three inches in diameter. It's very, very good.

Now that I've got clearance for the video in the House of Commons, I've got the camera and I can make a bit of a go of it.

Sunday 18 December
Went back to the House and went into the Tea Room and had a talk to Joan Lestor. We were talking about Dr David Pitt, Lord Pitt of Hampstead, who'd recently died, and who had been one of her intimate friends.

Then we talked about Clause 4 and she said, 'Tony Blair has absolutely no awareness at all of the Party.' She had tried to speak to him, but he simply wouldn't listen. 'He's empty, there's nothing in him at all.' And she's very suspicious of Peter Mandelson, like everybody else.

I put to her that the way to deal with Clause 4 was the way Gaitskell dealt with it: keep Clause 4, but add aims and objectives and publish them separately. So she's going to do something about it. She said, 'Of course, the Executive goes along with it because they don't want to embarrass the new Leader.'

I said, 'You may just have to embarrass the Leader to stop him doing worse things. Why don't you make a speech?' So she said she would make a speech about it.

At the very end, I was talking to Bryan Davies, the MP. He's a nice guy; he used to be Secretary of the Parliamentary Labour Party and he was there in 1983 when Bristol South East disappeared.

I mentioned to him that there'd been a court case which delayed the Boundary Commission in respect of the redistribution of the Bristol seats, and that it had been paid for privately and I wondered where the money came from. And he told me something absolutely fascinating. He said that it was all stitched up by Mike Cocks, a Bristol MP, and that the court case cost £75,000. So I'm going to do a little bit more enquiring about this, because I always knew that the whole thing was an attempt to delay my adoption as candidate to prevent me from campaigning in my new constituency.

One or two other things happened today.

I sat in the Tea Room and had a long talk to Derek Foster, the Chief Whip. He said that he tried to persuade Tony Blair to march at the Durham Miners' Gala with his own local pit banner, but he wouldn't because it would damage his image.

He also said he'd talked to Blair about his kids' school, without any success, and that he'd talked to him about Clause 4, without any success. While we were sitting there, who should come in but the Chaplain of the House of Commons, Canon Donald Gray, who's a really lovely guy, and he sat in the Tea Room and we had a smashing talk.

Apparently, according to him, when Mrs Thatcher was asked about Willie Whitelaw she said, 'Well, every Prime Minister needs a Willie.'

And later she was asked whether she ever had a holiday and she said, 'No, no, I'm always on the job.' And we were just giggling about it.

So this great Prime Minister, who'll be remembered for all time as the first woman Prime Minister and a most powerful one, is really now a bit of a figure of fun.

Friday 23 December

When I was out shopping I met Richard Gott, who used to be the Features Editor of the *Guardian* but has recently been 'exposed' by Gordievsky, a former KGB man in London who defected to MI6, as having received money from the KGB. Gott resigned immediately. When I saw him, I just gave him a hug. I said, 'The Cold War's not over; it was a war against socialism and it's still going on. I wish you hadn't resigned.'

He said, 'It was difficult, because it was a bit embarrassing keeping me. On the other hand, resigning appeared to be admitting my guilt.'

But he didn't look too upset actually.

Monday 26 December

Drove to the Gibsons – that's Ralph Gibson, my best man, and his wife Ann – and we had a marvellous time. Ralph has retired, and his photographic albums were full of trips to America and art galleries he'd visited. And, although he still sits as a supernumerary Lord Justice of Appeal, he can pick and choose what he'll do and he was tempting me into retirement. I can see the appeal of it. It's a funny thing but when you get to threescore years and ten, which I will be in April, the call of leisure is a very strong one.

Maybe in the next Parliament, if there's a Labour Government, they will remove hereditary peers. And if they rename the House of Lords the Senate, it might – after fifty years in Parliament in the year 2000 – be too much to resist. But I think I'd make myself ridiculous if I had to call myself 'Lord'.

You can see, as you get older, the appeal of a home for retired politicians, so long as you weren't propping up the hereditary system in any way, although there still remains this terrible problem of patronage. Maybe Major won't be Prime Minister by the time I've done fifty years in Parliament, and I might be asking Portillo for that privilege!

I shouldn't really set all these things down, but there you are – the diary's meant to be honest.

Sunday 1 January 1995, Stansgate

New Year's Honours List and Elizabeth Smith and Sarah Hogg have got peerages: Elizabeth Smith in the tradition of Dora Gaitskell, who got a peerage when Hugh died, and Sarah Hogg because she'd worked with John Major. Nothing really changes.

The 1964 Government papers have been published and, apparently, when Hartley Shawcross was a Labour front bencher, he received £40,000 from MI5 on the instructions of Harold Macmillan, the Tory Prime Minister, to help finance the Industrial Research and Information Service. It was an anti-communist organisation designed mainly to expose and remove communists from the trade unions and Labour movement.

As I get older, I wonder if I've been naively pursuing one course while all sorts of other skulduggery was going on. But there you are.

We had a flood warning in the evening and were told there might be a flood at high tide at midnight, so we stayed dressed, got torches and so on, but it was all right. There were the first flurries of snow – not very much tonight. The house is icy cold in the winter.

Monday 2 January

A couple of political points that I should make.

First of all, Labour's U-turn on nuclear power. Apparently Martin O'Neill – who is, I think, our spokesman (I don't know on what) – has said that now Labour is a pro-nuclear party.

I think the reason for this is that, first of all, there're a lot of trade unions within the nuclear industry; secondly, almost certainly the Americans, having cancelled their last three nuclear power stations, desperately need plutonium. Very recently a renewal was made of the agreement with America that plutonium from our nuclear power stations would be transferred to the United States, in return for which they'd let us have Trident warheads, and so on.

The second U-turn is on VAT on school fees. This was an idea that Caroline had suggested ages ago, and it would only affect a tiny percentage of the population who could afford to pay private school fees. Once the *Mail on Sunday* had reported this, Blunkett was forced to say that it wasn't being considered. The BBC said that Tony Blair didn't want to upset middle England or middle-income groups. He is a Conservative in every sense. Policy is being made on the hoof by Blair, and certainly he'll do nothing whatsoever to alienate Tory voters.

Wednesday 4 January

I had a very funny letter from a man in Canada who was writing a book about the pilot who flew with my dad in the First World War and who dropped the Italian spy, Tandura, behind Austrian lines. He enclosed the extract about my dad and it said: 'Lord Stansgate's son, Anthony, is now in Sir John Major's Cabinet.'

So I photocopied those two pages and sent a note to the Prime Minister, marked 'personal':

Dear Prime Minister,

You'll see from the enclosed that you have been knighted and I am a member of your Cabinet. Why didn't you tell me? I've corrected it and thought you might like to know – there's no need to reply.

Wednesday 11 January

An advertisement has appeared signed by thirty-two out of the sixty-two MEPs supporting Clause 4, and Blair has let it be known how angry he is that it ruined his visit to the industrialists in Brussels last night.

This morning I had a letter from the Prime Minister in his own handwriting:

Personal & Private 7 January

Dear Tony

Many thanks for your note. I too was surprised to hear of my secret knighthood and your membership of the present Cabinet.

At first I thought this might be an example of over-secretive government, but, as you surmise, Mr R had got his facts wrong. Thank you for correcting them. Which, of us, I wonder, would have been most embarrassed if Mr R had been right?

With my warmest wishes for the new year,
Yours sincerely
John

It was extremely funny. Later in the day I saw John Major in the Lobby as we were going in to vote. I hadn't seen him for ages.

I said, 'John, thank you for your amusing letter.'

He said, 'Thank you for *your* amusing letter. I don't want a knighthood.'

'No, you're entitled to an earldom!'

So, with lots of smiles all round, this little story ends.

I went to the House and ordered a copy of the Act of Settlement from the Library, because now that Camilla Parker-Bowles is getting divorced, the royal story is taking a new form.

Heard that Blair had addressed the MEPs this morning and had told them that they were infantile incompetents, and that it was insulting to him and had blunted the edge of his Brussels initiative.

Friday 13 January, Chesterfield

The man next to me on the train asked what socks I was wearing because he could see a logo of a candle surrounded by barbed wire. I told him they were Amnesty socks. Turned out he was a former Tory councillor in Derbyshire, a man called Vernon Colquhoun, a country lawyer.

We had a nice time. He said how much he'd enjoyed *Desert Island Discs*, then he dropped me off at the Labour Club.

Saturday 14 January
Ruth and I went to the House of Commons to film in the evening, the second proper day of filming we'd done. We were stopped by an Inspector in Westminster Hall, and I gave him my little card saying what we were doing; he seemed satisfied.

We got some marvellous shots of Westminster Hall at night; talked to somebody who was on security, used to be head of the dustmen in Kensington, a very thoughtful guy, who said, 'Democracy here stops outside the gate.'

We went to the 'bandstand', which I'd never heard of before. It is right under the Central Lobby – fantastic; and then from there to see the Victorian sewage pump, which has been operating since 1867 and still pumps sewage up from the basement.

Tuesday 17 January
The world news today is this absolutely massive earthquake that has affected Osaka and Kyoto and Kobe. About 1800 people have died – possibly 2800 – and fires are raging. It is just like an atomic bomb attack really. Terrible, terrible tragedy and the worst earthquake for fifty years in Japan. Really ghastly.

Wednesday 18 January
I lost all my evidence to the Nolan Committee (3,000 words or more) on the computer. I'd worked on it morning and evening.

I went to the Commons this afternoon and found a letter waiting for me from the Deputy Serjeant at Arms, saying I'd been seen 'photographing with an unknown person in the telephone exchange' and that I would have to get permission before I continue. It's a bit of a setback really.

Thursday 19 January
I went and had a meal in the Members' Tea Room with Derek Foster and Clive Betts. Derek told me that he'd warned Blair before Christmas that this decision on schools would be very damaging and would affect the Clause 4 campaign.

Clive Betts was very determined. 'We've got to get rid of all grant-maintained schools and have comprehensive schools.' He said that the different social classes live in different parts of the town, so neighbourhood schools tend on the one hand to be middle-class and on the other working-class, and we had to move money to where it's needed most.

To the Campaign Group, where Dennis reported that John Prescott had had an accident and fallen off his chair; that Blunkett had lost all his chairmanships and was almost in tears and had to be persuaded not to walk out of a meeting; and that it was established that Mandelson had attacked Bill Morris, after Morris had made his speech about the Clause 4 debate.

Saturday 28 January

Blair is going round the country arguing for his new Clause 4, and he came out with a new draft about fairness and opportunity and binding people together, and so on. It was quite incredible. Absolute Liberal, SDP, Tory-wet stuff.

When the left advocates constitutional change, it is divisive and an arid constitutional struggle. When Blair does it, it's marvellous, it's essential; anyone who disagrees with it follows the old hard-left shibboleths.

Thursday 2 February

Surgery and then straight into the Chesterfield General Committee.

It began with the announcement that there'd been twenty nominations for me, and that I'd been reselected without the need to go to a ballot. People clapped and I thanked them briefly.

Then Bob Pont said, 'I hope we're going to begin to train up a successor to Tony Benn', which was a way of saying, 'I hope this is the last time he's the candidate.' So Johnny Burrows chipped in and said, 'We never trained anyone up when Eric Varley was here, and we got a much better candidate.'

We went on to the Clause 4 issue. There were one or two wobblers, but the overwhelming majority were furious with what Blair had done and felt we should confirm Clause 4. We have been told we've got to have a ballot, and Walworth Road is apparently going to send a pack and a ballot form; we're not going to be guided by that, we'll put out our own question and that question is: 'Do you want to keep Clause 4 and possibly add other things, as may be decided at Conference?'

Sunday 5 February

I have suggested that we have Clause 4 inserted into the Campaign Group Aims and Objectives or standing orders, and that the Socialist Campaign Group of Labour MPs rename themselves the Socialist Group of MPs. I think you've just got to be ready for something big that's going to happen.

Meanwhile, having safely been reselected, I'm going to settle down and do what I've intended to do for a long time: write a few serious letters to the electors of Chesterfield.

Monday 6 February

Major, having made a speech at the Monday Club or the No Turning Back group (one of these right-wing groups) has made it clear that he would not be ready to contemplate a single currency after the Governmental Conference in 1996.

No British Prime Minister would be allowed to come out against Brussels, and although they pretend they'll do this, that and the other to protect our interests, when it comes to it, the power of international business and the media will drive Britain into a federal Europe and a Central Bank because they hate the power of democracy; and capitalism requires a one party state, just as communism did; a coalition run by bankers and bureaucrats, just as communism did.

That is the long-term consequence of accepting the view, so called, that 'there's no alternative'.

Tuesday 7 February

At seven o'clock I said to Alan Simpson, 'Have you got two minutes?' I took him down to the Crypt, to the broom cupboard where I had put up the plaque to Emily Wilding Davison, and he helped me put up my new plaque, which is 'To all those people who dedicated themselves to democracy, civil liberties, freedom and representation in Parliament', and then I listed them all – at least as many as I could think of.

Then we screwed it up with a battery-operated drill. I think, having got away with one plaque without permission, I'll probably get away with the other.

Thursday 9 February

Got in my car and went to a meeting of two wards of the Hampstead Party for a debate with Paul Boateng.

Boateng was so aggressive and personal, and waved his fist, that at one stage I did have to say, 'You're not prosecuting O. J. Simpson, you know, Paul.'

So he retorted, 'What has Tony Benn ever done? When he was in the Cabinet, he sold uranium to South Africa! What did he do about public ownership?'

'Well,' I said, 'At my age I'm not concerned to defend my record, but I put down the first motion in 1960 for sanctions against South Africa; I spoke in 1964 in Trafalgar Square when Mandela was arrested; I introduced the Giro, the National Enterprise Board, brought oil into public ownership, shipbuilding and the motor industry.'

He was so nasty. He kept saying that the working class depends on us, we're powerless, we've got to win; it was really demagoguery.

Friday 10 February

I went to see the BBC people at 4 Millbank about the *Under Big Ben* project – going behind the scenes in the House with my camera. Charles Frater, whom I know well, has agreed to be director.

Monday 13 February

Got up extremely early, and Ruth and I went to the House of Commons for filming – we got there at about quarter past six. We talked to some of the cleaners, went on the terrace, up above the dome over the Central Lobby, where all the apparatus for lowering the chandelier is – it is a most extraordinary building. I can't believe how much there is that I've never seen before.

At eleven o'clock an oil engineer from Iraq came, with a plea to see if I can do anything about the Iraqi sanctions being lifted; they're causing horrific consequences in Iraq. It's the Americans who won't budge. Tam Dalyell, Ted Heath, Denis Healey and others are involved in trying to get them lifted.

To the House, and just before the debate I went up to the Speaker's Chair and had a word with Betty Boothroyd.

I said, 'Can I have a quickie?'

So she covered her mouth with her hand and said, 'I've just had onions for lunch.'

I replied, 'Well, I'd rather have the Speaker with onions than not have the Speaker at all', at which she giggled. Anyway, I said, 'Just to let you know – I thought you'd be interested – I've had permission to go round and make a video for schools, a tour of the House of Commons, and I've got some marvellous shots. I've been up Big Ben, down to the Victorian sewage plant under your house, above the Central Lobby – you've probably been everywhere yourself.'

She said, 'Oh, no, I certainly haven't.'

I went on, 'It's a video for schools, but the BBC now wants to broadcast it. Would you like to come round with the camera?'

'Oh, no, I'd much rather see the video.'

I can now say that I've spoken to the Speaker about it, I was pleased about that. I'm not going to ask for permission in writing.

In the course of the evening Andrew Mackinlay, the Member for Thurrock, who's a very keen and active lad, came up during the Liberal debate on Europe and told me of an interesting exchange with the Chief Whip, Derek Foster.

He said that Derek called Andrew to his office earlier today and asked: 'Are you going to vote for this nonsense tonight?' (It was a Liberal debate so it hardly mattered to the Whips.) Andrew said, 'I am voting because I feel strongly about it.' Derek Foster said, 'I've got to tell you that you won't get any promotion. Tony' (that's Tony Blair), 'has made it clear he feels very strongly about this.'

Andrew said to the Chief Whip, 'I assumed that I had burned my boats already.'

Derek Foster: 'No, you haven't. I spoke to Tony about you last week, you have a future.'

'Well, I'm sorry,' replied Andrew. 'I've said I'm going to vote. I feel strongly in favour of referenda generally.'

That's the first time I've ever had a documented account of the way Chief Whips frighten young members.

Caroline went in to Holland Park School, where she is a governor. She told me that the problem at the moment in the school is marauding gangs of youths, young Moroccans whose parents were brought over to work in the hotel industry. When the recession came, they were made redundant and their kids had nothing to do, and attacked and intimidated children as they left school. They beat up one little Bosnian refugee.

Sunday 19 February

I don't want to retire from politics, but I don't just want to be the same old Tony Benn. I don't want, either, to make the same mistake of the so-called democratic left who began coming to terms with Thatcherism and the new times. That would be a corruption, and I'm simply not going to do that.

I'd like to throw a light on the future, the next century: what can we reasonably expect; how will it all develop; what about the environment, about animal welfare, about housing, about local government, about democracy, about Europe? I'm a bit nervous that if I tried to do it I wouldn't have the intellectual capacity to produce anything any good. That's why I tend to stay in the old grooves.

I was thinking the other day that if Clem Attlee and Ernie Bevin were still in Parliament at the age of 110, and were still asking questions of the Prime Minister and writing Early Day Motions and trying to chip into debates, people would say, 'For God's sake Clem and Ernie, you've had your time – move over.' And if Gladstone died now, they wouldn't know what to write in the obituary except, 'It's believed that he was the Prime Minister 120 years ago'.

I've got to learn to cope with old age.

Caroline is doing it already: she's going to give up teaching when she's seventy, which she will be at the end of next year. She's working on this huge survey of comprehensive schools, just nose to the grindstone from six in the morning till two the following morning. She has a capacity for work which is phenomenal.

After that she wants to write a book on socialism in America, then an account of her own life.

Monday 20 February
Caroline's computer went on the blink today, which is an absolute disaster; all her work on the book on comprehensive education is on it.

Tuesday 21 February
In the House at 3.30. Anthony Steen, the MP for Totnes, complained to the Speaker that I'd been to his constituency on 4 February and that I hadn't told him I was going. He said there were 700 or 800 people at the meeting. Of course the Labour MPs cheered like anything and the Speaker said that he had possibly raised a Point of Order that had given further publicity to my meeting. It was extremely funny.

There is a big statement between London and Dublin coming out tomorrow, the framework for discussion on the future of Northern Ireland. Major is appealing to the Irish Protestant community over the head of Paisley and it's a significant step forward.

Wednesday 22 February
In the afternoon the Prime Minister made his statement about Northern Ireland, which was long awaited. He and John Bruton, the Irish Prime Minister, had issued the framework document at Hillsborough Castle; Blair gave full support, and so on.

It is quite a clever document because it has devolved power for Northern Ireland on everything but law and order and the power to tax. It then established joint structures, north and south, which the new Northern Ireland Assembly would negotiate with the Irish Government; then there would be a continuation of the inter-governmental conference between London and Dublin, and European support would come in via the north-south arrangement. So it was very clever, and Sinn Fein seem quite happy with it.

Ian Paisley and Trimble and the others describe it as an absolutely major betrayal, so at least the Unionists are now emerging in their true light as the enemies of any sort of settlement in the north other than full integration with Britain, which is an impossible idea.

I then went to the Campaign Group, where I put forward my proposal – which I must admit I did think would be widely supported – that we should decide to take action ourselves in advance of the April Special Party Conference. We should change our name to the Campaign Group of Socialist MPs and we should absorb Clause 4 into our constitution or standing orders.

The Group met at 6.30 and I moved my proposal in very simple terms.

In a nutshell, I was soundly defeated. Thinking of the mistakes I made, first of all I hadn't consulted properly, which is a terrible problem and a real fault of mine. I assumed there would be general support.

Secondly, it was absolutely clear that Blair's arguments had penetrated the Campaign Group – this is the only way to win the election, and we weren't going to nationalise everything.

Thirdly, with the onset of a Blair Government and the patronage that he would have, some people there (I would imagine) wouldn't want to get into Tony Blair's bad books or even be expelled.

Fourthly, I just don't think they wanted a lead from me. And this is one of the lessons of age, really. I mustn't assume that anything I say wins the support of the Campaign Group; the Group's all over the shop on Europe, all over the shop on Bosnia, all over the shop on all sorts of issues.

So I came home really licking my wounds, and of course tomorrow it will be 'Benn rejected by Campaign Group'. And I'll just have to learn to live with that.

Friday 24 February

Blair made a statement, reported this morning, saying that he represented middle England. And in no time at all he'll represent the Tory voters, whom he's courting as hard as he can, and the press is giving him a huge build-up.

Major went to Glasgow and said he was totally opposed to devolution for Scotland, while Ireland is of course to get an Assembly under the framework document.

Tuesday 28 February

Lissie and Hannah came to the office. Hannah is now eleven months old and is so enchanting. She's such an interesting little girl, she observes everything – she was given a hairbrush to play with, and she pulled out an individual hair and examined it carefully. When she meets people she's cautious. She went to Sheila quite happily and was very friendly, but Paul Fisher was there and she'd never seen him before, so she gave him a sort of look as if to say, 'I'm glad to have met you, look forward to getting to know you better, but meanwhile forgive me if I'm a little bit shy.' With me she's just smiling, putting her head on one side and crawling a bit.

Caught a taxi to see Ted Heath at Wilton Street. I had been about four and a half years ago to ask his advice as to whether I should go and see Saddam Hussein, and this time it was about the sanctions against Iraq.

I got there, and there was a policeman with a pistol in his holster and two police on motorbikes. So I asked, 'Do ex-Prime Ministers normally have three policemen?' He said, 'No, one, but because you were coming we brought the other two!' He was very jolly. I rang the doorbell and the door was opened by his housekeeper, whom I had met before, and there in the front room at a round table with his old Prime Minister's box open was Ted.

He said, 'I'm sorry to have brought you over to my house.'

I replied, 'I won't take five minutes, but before I start I'm so pleased you're not standing down and that you're staying in the House of Commons, because you and I were elected in the same year and both of us should see the year 2000 and fifty years in Parliament.' So he smiled – he's very noncommittal is Ted – he smiled a bit, and I said, 'Well, I imagine you didn't want to go into the other house and find yourself sitting next to your successor, Mrs Thatcher.' He gave another smile.

Then I said, 'Really I came for your advice about sanctions against Iraq, because this awful American woman Madeleine Albright is coming to try to whip up support for the continuation of sanctions. Do you think the British Government will take a different view?'

'No, no,' he said, 'the best hope is that the French will break the sanctions and, if they do, the thing might crack.'

'Anyway, that's all I wanted to say.'

'Well,' he said, 'It's worth a try.'

But Ted's very mellow, and of course he's passionately pro a federal Europe and we disagree. I reminded him that the first time we'd met was in about January 1951 or '52. We had a debate about appeasement, I think; I can't remember exactly what it was about.

When I left, Ted stood up and brought me to the door and stayed there until the taxi drove off, and I was rather touched. He and I are the last survivors of 1950.

There was an animal lobby back at the House, so I filmed them with my video camera. They had big banners: 'Stop the Live Export of Animals'. I took out my camera and walked along the line, talked to a few people there, got their comments; they were all very friendly. Most of them were older women – there were more women than men.

Then I went into the Central Lobby and took a few pictures surreptitiously. Nobody stops me now, I just do what I bloody well like.

Went and had a bite to eat, and by then it was almost time to drive to Wimbledon, to the old Labour Hall. Paul Boateng had turned up for the meeting in place of Kevin Barron, whom I'd expected, and he was just as unpleasant and aggresive as he had been in Hampstead.

He said, 'We're not a class party. We don't believe in a class party, we represent the middle classes as well.'

Wednesday 1 March

The debate began at 3.30. This was supposed to be the great critical debate on Europe. Blair opened by trying to make fun of Major, saying he hadn't made up his mind on the single currency; he couldn't face the actual difficulties of going in. What would be sacrificed if you went in?

Major gave a measured reply in which he said that if you do go in, there could be very considerable consequences. And although he didn't say it explicitly, if Britain stayed out, then of course there would be pressures on the pound.

I put in one question to the Prime Minister about the effect on domestic democracy, but nobody in Britain cares about domestic democracy; you can wind up local government, wind up trade unions, introduce the Criminal Justice Bill and nobody gives a damn – Parliament is just happy to be there. They've got everything they want in the House of Commons: a marvellous job, secretaries, allowances, travel warrants, a rifle range, a gymnasium – a lovely life.

The Government won by 5, with Norman Lamont (of all people) actually voting with Labour which has destroyed his credibility with the Tories, and even with us, I think. Then there was a second vote, which they won more respectably.

Thursday 2 March

To Number 10 Downing Street with the million-signature petition against hunting. There was a huge crowd outside Downing Street. Somebody had a fox, which I filmed. The police were very difficult; they said you can't use a wheelbarrow to take the petition to Number 10, you can only have six people. Six people couldn't carry the petition, and they wouldn't let us go backwards and forwards carrying the petition until we'd carried it all, they wouldn't allow any interviews with the media outside Number 10; so they really made it as difficult as possible. I did feel that we were back to petitioning the king, not that the king (or the Prime Minister) would take the slightest bit of notice of the petition.

At any rate, I went into Downing Street with my video camera.There was another petition against landmines, with a Cambodian lad whose legs had been blown off by landmines and who was now working on designing better types of wheelchairs.

Friday 3 March

Into the House for the Wild Mammals Bill. Took my camera in and photographed the Speaker's procession.

The British Field Sports Society had decided that discretion was the better part of valour and therefore they wouldn't oppose the Bill. Of course people like Tom King, Sir John Cope and Sir Cranley Onslow and all the pro-hunters spoke.

But it was an interesting debate because you felt the tide had turned as a result of all the activity outside. And I did something that I'd never done before and would probably never dare to do again: I took my video camera into the Division Lobby and filmed MPs filing past the clerks where they take the names.

In effect, in this film I'm going to make animal rights and fox hunting the issue that brings together all the various elements of extra-parliamentary and parliamentary activity on animal rights, which is a good one to do, because it's not party political.

Saturday 4 March

I got to Skegness from Chesterfield in time to hear most, if not all, of Tony Blair's speech as Party Leader. He was standing at the rostrum smiling, talking about the need to project our values in a new way, and so on. It was a speech of the kind you might have heard at an American Democratic convention.

Paddy Ashdown would have agreed with all of it; the delegates clapped and applauded, and gave Blair a little standing ovation, and it was an example of his skill. He's a smiling person with a clear political agenda, but not much knowledge of – or sympathy with – the Labour Party, in my opinion.

I walked to the station, icy cold. Skegness station is just like a cattle shed. I had to get a train from there to Grantham; then I had to wait for an hour in Grantham, pretty well, to get a train to Peterborough; and then I had to wait for fifty minutes in Peterborough to get a train to King's Cross. All in all it took me about five hours to get home, and if you include the time going from Chesterfield to Skegness, it was seven or eight hours of travelling today.

I thought it was a complete waste of time in a way, except for its value as an observation of the Labour Party at this particular period. The Labour Party is unquestionably at a time of transition. The Leaders never believed in Clause 4, but there was a sort of place for socialists. There isn't any more – young people come in who don't know anything about socialism; we don't talk about socialism, we just prattle on about values and fairness and equality, without any substance at all.

I suppose, in a sense, I am a bit of a dinosaur in that I really do believe that the purpose of the Labour Party was to make changes in the structure of society and the economic system, whereas Blair and his cronies just want to get there. And they will get there because the tide of opinion against the Government is so strong.

Dennis Skinner said the other day, 'When the Tories came in in 1951 they did practically nothing to change what the Attlee Government had done for quite a number of years, and this will be the same. We'll have a Labour Government administering Tory policies, and that is God's truth.'

Sunday 5 March

We had a leak today, water dripping. I'm probably going to have to get up three times in the night to empty the bucket so that it doesn't come through into the kitchen. Incredible old house this; it needs a major refit, like its owners.

Tuesday 7 March
Andrew Hood looked in this morning. He's working with Robin Cook now, as his research assistant. He was very excited at the thought he'd be in the Foreign Office in a couple of years.

He said that the Party was run by Blair, Prescott, Brown and Cook, and that Mandelson was enormously influential.

I talked a little bit about the single currency and Andrew said, 'I think what the Labour Government will do to preserve international confidence is to say that for every one per cent that inflation goes up, we'll raise interest rates one per cent.'

Of course that would be the end of the prospect for ending unemployment and Andrew said, 'Well, the alternative is to bang on capital controls.' Well, that is true actually. Still, I didn't want a row, so having just made the point I left it.

Wednesday 8 March
I went off to the House of Commons with my camera to meet up with Abercrombie Primary School from Chesterfield. It is a simply lovely school. The kids are as bright as anything.

We went round with two guides. One of them, with a beard, was rather boring, explaining that this was done in leather, and that was bas-relief, and this was something else; the other guide was absolutely brilliant and he got them all so interested. It allowed me to go round as a tourist really and to listen to it all.

There was a little boy called Michael who was the cleverest of all. When the guide asked them about the English Civil War, Michael said, 'It was a war between the Roundheads and the Vauxhalls.' He'd muddled up, of course, the Vauxhall Cavalier with the Cavaliers. It was so sweet.

We went into a committee room and I asked them about hunting and the majority of them were against it. I think nobody was in favour of hunting.

Then they said, 'Can we have a debate?'

I asked, 'What do you want to debate?'

Well, they said, 'Are you in favour of violent sport, like boxing?' One boy got up and said, 'I think boxing's a good idea.' Then a girl got up and said, 'You could get damaged.' Somebody else said, 'You should have more padding.' And another girl said, 'Yes, but that doesn't always help.' It was a marvellous debate and in the end we had a vote on that. It was 19 to 7 for the abolition of boxing.

Friday 10 March, Inverness
Had breakfast downstairs with Alan Simpson and others, and then went over to the Scottish Conference.

There were the usual stands all over the place for British Nuclear Fuels and banks and the Law Society and the Police Federation.The Labour Party Conferences are now just a market place for other people to show their exhibits.

Alan Simpson told me of a plan he had. He said, 'The Government are taxing holiday flights to raise money. Supposing we taxed the flight of capital? One-eighth of one per cent tax on the movement of capital across the frontiers would bring in fifty billion pounds, so you could wipe out the public-sector borrowing requirement in a year.'

He's very bright, Alan. I like him, and if there is any person who looks to me as if he might get really far with the socialist case, it is Alan Simpson.

Tony Blair gave his speech. Very clever because he pulled out all the right points, struck the right chords about public ownership and freedom and fairness, and mentioned democratic socialism en passant. Never mentioned capitalism at all.

Saturday 11 March

Steve sent me an article written by Auberon Waugh and focusing on my opposition to hunting:

> It will come as no surprise to see Benn has now jumped on the animal rights bandwagon; never mind what rubbish is being stuffed into our poor children's heads, this revolting old ham has so far managed to achieve very little mischief in a lifetime devoted to it. May I suggest that on April 3rd this year, and every year until he's dead, Tony Benn should be burned in effigy in every village on every hill in the country. We've reached the moment when Tony Benn night on April 3rd should replace Guy Fawkes' night on November 5th . . .

Though I didn't like reading it, because nobody likes reading that they should be burned in effigy, it certainly is an antidote to the fear I have that at the end of my life I shall be subjected to the final corruption of being a kindly, harmless old gentleman.

Tuesday 14 March

I saw Chris Mullin today, and I did express my great sadness at his letter to *Tribune* about Clause 4 saying that the chaos in Vietnam was caused by common ownership. I made it up today by saying that he'd made a brilliant speech on the Criminal Appeals Bill, which he had done. I think I've mended my fences there.

Wednesday 15 March

I was picked up by a black guy of thirty-six in his Mercedes and taken to do a broadcast with London News Talk Radio.

He told me he had been a building engineer for Wimpey in Docklands, earning £30,000 a year, was made redundant and had now decided to use his car for chauffeur work. His wife was a social worker. It was a perfect example of the way we are progressively de-skilling ourselves. Just as we got to the studios in Hammersmith he said, 'Of course I need the money because I'm putting my two children into private schools.' I thought that really said it all.

Friday 17 March, Chesterfield

When I got to my bungalow Tom Vallins and Ann Denman arrived, then who should appear but David Blunkett for a cup of tea and a sandwich and talk in my bungalow before our joint meeting tonight.

Then I walked over to the Winding Wheel centre and there were maybe 300 people for this meeting on the cuts in education. David Blunkett made a very woolly speech, I thought, but still he was trying to give all sorts of pledges – I've heard worse.

I'm going to be up in about six hours because I've got to attend a big demonstration in Trafalgar Square against the export of live animals.

Monday 20 March

Caroline went to Mothercare this morning looking for a bunny to replace one that Hannah has lost; the woman said, 'I think there is one in the stockroom' and brought it out. Caroline brought it home and we looked at a photograph of Hannah with the original bunny, which fortunately Caroline had taken, and it was the very same bunny. To cap it all, we were rung up by the Dumfries branch of Mothercare which had another one in stock, so we're going to buy a 'reserve bunny'. Apparently, when she was given it, Hannah was terribly happy.

I did a bit on Radio Sheffield disagreeing with Peter Tatchell's outing of homosexuals, his Outrage project.

Friday 23 March, Chesterfield

I heard that I have had a letter from the Serjeant at Arms saying that the Speaker had ordered the removal of my two new plaques and it was waiting to be collected at the Serjeant at Arms' Office. That depressed me no end and made me extremely angry. I felt utterly depressed at the hostility of the Commons to anything progressive, and I felt I had been overconfident – I just felt over the last few months that I could do what I liked. It worried me a bit because I wanted to interview the Speaker about her work, and she may say no and may try to get my film stopped. At my age you should be treated with respect – I suppose at my age you should also obey the law.

I went back to the Club and Tom had received from Walworth Road 800 sealed envelopes inviting every member of the Chesterfield Labour Party state if they want the new Clause 4 or not. He opened one of them and it was also a letter from Tom Sawyer (a standard letter of course) with a little request for money. The cost of this exercise must be phenomenal – a quarter of a million envelopes, ballot forms. The purpose is to try and undermine the general committees of local parties. I've no doubt they'll do it.

Saturday 25 March

I packed up my stuff, drove to Heathrow and flew to Belfast for the Campaign for Democracy seminar on the peace process. On the train this morning I wrote notes of what I wanted to say, because when you go to Ireland – north or south – you have to be *very* sensitive to the language you use. You can't talk about Ulster of course in the north, if you're talking to Sinn Feiners, because they talk about the Six Counties (though of course Ulster is actually eight counties), and so on.

I am so deaf and the Irish accent is so difficult to understand that I really didn't pick up anything at all, except one guy who was a Loyalist and who bitterly criticised me for inviting Gerry Adams to London.

I flew home, terribly tired. Home about half-nine I suppose and had to put all the clocks forward – so many clocks in the house, computer clocks and so on; frightfully difficult to do, but still I did it and went to bed at about quarter to twelve.

The thing about Belfast was of course the total difference as a result of the ceasefire. The first time ever in the last twenty-five years that I have been to Belfast and the streets were not absolutely full of soldiers in tin hats with rifles, machine guns and military vehicles. Only one policeman at Aldergrove airport and no soldiers in the streets at all. Peace has come as a huge relief to everybody and there is no going back. Sinn Fein are patient; they wanted to know what I thought about the Establishment position, and I said I thought the Government was trying to extricate itself from Northern Ireland. That is what worries the Protestants and Loyalists. Four Church of Ireland bishops and archbishops went to see Major this week to convey the anxiety their flock felt. I am not needed now that this whole thing has moved further forward. But when I look back – I think it was January 1992 or '93 that I decided to give a fresh lease of life to the Irish thing by writing to the Secretary General of the UN – clearly, along with an awful lot of others including John Hume, we were sensing that this was the time to move forward.

Sunday 26 March

Went to the House of Commons for another morning of filming. If the Speaker does clamp down, we want to get as much 'in the can' as possible. When we got there we went to the Engineers' Control Room where the periscope is, and obviously that is the great centre of activity. They have the keys to everywhere. They took us to the top of Victoria Tower. When

I got to the top – there is a lift, thank God, because it is taller than Big Ben – the view was unbelievable, just beautiful.

The people in the House are so friendly to me and their comments on 'upstairs and downstairs' and on the Serjeant at Arms are extremely revealing. What they didn't believe was that MPs are treated like dirt as well, and accept rules that have been cooked up by officials and put to committees. The Civil Service runs the whole place. The senior people, the Speaker's secretary, the Serjeant at Arms, the Clerk of the House, just float about like permanent secretaries. They don't know anything about the *real* running of the place. The filming 'downstairs' is absolutely fascinating.

Tuesday 28 March

I might add that yesterday I saw the film-maker Richard Attenborough (Lord Attenborough now) in the House. I had a word with him – I don't think I've spoken to him in about thirty years, maybe even longer.

Friday 31 March

Tom Vallins took me to the Royal Hospital at twelve for a visit. My relations with the Royal Hospital are very poor. I was taken round by a bevy of business managers, corporate planners, corporate forward-planning officers, and so on – mainly women – and they showed the facilities, which are very good, though I think the medical staff are pretty short. Taken to the renal unit, the AIDS unit, and then I was asked to unveil a plaque.

We had a buffet lunch and I talked to some of the business managers and said, 'Do tell me what is the point of having this internal market of providers and purchasers and services – what does it achieve?' And they said it allows you to plan. I said you could argue that about the fire service, or the police force, or Members of Parliament. I think I made them uneasy. Caroline told me when I got back that Tony Blair has said today that he wasn't in favour of the internal market.

I talked to Donald Trelford, who was the Editor of the *Observer* and is now acting Head of Journalism at the University of Sheffield. He told me that he was called to the Board (of Lonrho, I suppose) and somebody said, 'I want to get rid of Tony Howard' (Deputy Editor of the *Observer*). Trelford said, 'There is only one way of doing that – you'll have to get rid of me.' Later Tiny Rowland rang him and said, 'Take no notice of those people, you keep power.' Trelford said Tiny Rowland just liked running a paper and didn't particularly care what was said. He told Rowland that he was going to support Labour in the 1992 election and Rowland asked why. Trelford said, 'I think it's time for a change,' and Rowland said, 'That's all right by me.'

Trelford was very candid.

Monday 3 April
My seventieth birthday and there were masses of cards and telephone calls. I really think I'm going on to the Internet – move into the high-tech area – because when I was fifty-eight in 1983 I was ready to move onto BBC computers and they really have been such a success.

Dave sent a beautiful colour TV set, which is awfully generous of him.

I went into the House of Commons by taxi for the birthday party that Ruth, Sheila, Tony Banks and Chris Mullin had organised. I don't know how to begin to describe it – it was beautiful and lovely. There must have been sixty or seventy people there. Sheila did the food. Parliamentary colleagues included John Biffen, Ivan Lawrence and Richard Shepherd. The Teabags were there – all the young people who have helped in the office over the years. Tony Whittome, Keith Jones, Patricia Moberly, Maxine Baker, Charles Frater, Jack Jones, Marion Miliband, David and Edward Miliband, Caroline and the family – lovely.

We talked for a bit and all of a sudden there was a bit of a scuffle, and who should come in but Velvet Fist – a group I met on Reading station about two and a half years ago, a radical group – and they sang unaccompanied songs: 'We're Alive', 'The World Turned Upside Down' and a song on the South African revolution. I was quite overwhelmed. The cake was a large model of the Houses of Parliament, which Ruth had had commissioned, with Big Ben at five to three: the moment that I was born.

We all went down to the Crypt, where Tony Banks made a speech by the broom cupboard and presented me with a beautiful plaque. It says, 'This historic broom cupboard is dedicated to Tony Benn, MP, on the occasion of his 70th birthday in recognition of his lifelong work for Parliament and the people, Monday 3rd April 1995.' Well, as the Speaker has removed the other plaques, I don't really know what to make of this, but I made a little speech and we went upstairs again. There were more speeches and a cutting of the cake – just lovely. I'm overwhelmed by it.

Friday 7 April
Caught the 8.30 train to Chesterfield for a surgery and canvassing. Caroline's car had been towed away because they had suspended the parking bay where she had parked. It is all highway robbery now really – these private companies are given the right to put tickets on, and tow you away and there is nothing whatever you can do. I had an angry exchange with the council about it yesterday.

Monday 10 April
The newspapers this morning are full of a *Guardian* report about Jonathan Aitken, who gave a press conference at the Tory Party HQ saying that he would sue the paper for libel. In the evening Granada did a programme about him, which I thought was a bit of a smear, truthfully. They had

actors reading and it wasn't absolutely clear, except that he has obviously been up to his eyes in links with the Saudi royal family.

I watched *Homecoming* about the return of Alexander Solzhenitsyn to Russia, which I must say is very disappointing. I didn't feel it got to the nub of the problem at all – just anti-communist propaganda as usual, with a little bit of doubt expressed about the new Russia.

Tuesday 11 April

Tonight it was announced that Labour would get tough with failing schools and wouldn't hesitate to close them, sack teachers and appoint new governors. It is just outflanking the Tories to the right – everything coming from the Front Bench is totally and completely right-wing. Very difficult to know how to cope, but I think the answer is that you get into power and then you just treat a Labour Government the same way as you would a Tory Government – you campaign, you vote, you argue and see what happens. There will have to be some countervailing pressure brought; Caroline is utterly discouraged by it.

Wednesday 12 April

Up at six and caught the train to Bradford. With this new franchising of different lines, it is almost impossible to get a through ticket. I had a chat with the conductor. He said there was absolute chaos now, and the new people being employed were on six-month contracts; and his company had to pay money to use the stations, they had to lease out the restaurant car and then lease out the buffet attendants – absolute chaos.

Got on the train and slept. Woke up and found that the guy from the buffet had brought me a cup of tea and a Danish pastry, because he said he knew that was what I liked. I paid him, thanked him and went back to sleep.

The courts have ruled that local authorities have no power to ban the export of live animals, on the grounds that it is a legal trade and they don't want mob rule. Really the language of judges and the protection of profit are disgraceful. Old ladies in woolly hats, who go out there because they believe that cruelty to animals is wrong, are described as a mob, and all the courts are doing is protecting profit. Utterly revolting, but there was a marvellous interview with Nancy Phipps, whose daughter, Jill, had been killed at Coventry Airport by a truck, saying that nothing would stop them.

Thursday 13 April

I picked up Ruth, and Charles Frater who is directing the film, and got to the Commons by eight to do a day's filming. This time we had the support of Michael Cummins, the Deputy Serjeant at Arms, and there was always someone from his staff in attendance. Charles had two cameras, lenses, lights, mikes, stands, umbrellas to reflect the light, and so on – enormously time-consuming. We worked from eight until six. It was so slow and you can't get people to talk when they're all wired up and there is a light shining on them. But he is producing some fine photography of the palace.

Wednesday 19 April
I woke up at 5.30 very breathless, with a pain in my chest, and thought I was going to have a heart attack. I felt very down – I don't want to do anything.

I went down to the office at nine I guess, and sat about. Sent a telegram to somebody for their diamond jubilee wedding anniversary tomorrow. Had a fax from the Land Reform Group, who are going to occupy some land on 23 April in memory of the Diggers. Drafted a couple of Early Day Motions, one on teachers' action and the other on the export of live animals.

Friday 21 April
The rumour is that the Oklahoma bombing was not Muslim extremists at all, but possibly a right-wing group of Militia, who are armed soldiers who hate the Federal Government – real brownshirts/fascists. At least it's a relief that they're not going to start a new war in the Middle East to punish the suspects, but it is also an indication of what's happening in America. Maybe that will scare people away from that right-wing view of life.

Saturday 22 April
To Trafalgar Square for the commemoration of the Armenian massacre by the Turks in 1915, when a million and a half Armenians were slaughtered. The Turkish Government still to this day won't recognise it.

On the way there I saw a demonstration against abortion, which was quite effective. Every twenty yards there was a person – man, woman, child, priest – with a red balloon standing absolutely stationary, and in their hand was a placard saying 'Abortion Kills Children'. Considering how many people were involved – thirty perhaps – it was an immensely effective way of getting a simple message across, and I must remember that for campaigning in the next election in Chesterfield.

Monday 24 April
One of the slightly bright sparks is that, contrary to all the media said, Lionel Jospin, the French socialist leader, came out top in the first ballot. It looks to me as if Jospin might do rather well, and that would be very good news. Unemployment in France is terribly high – 10 per cent – and that is because they have followed all these wretched Common Market policies.

In general though, it is all awfully depressing. Ron Huzzard, who is an old Quaker who ran Labour Action for Peace, rang me up; his local general committee had had serious discussions and they voted against the new Clause 4, but a ballot of all local members (none of whom has lifted a finger for the Party or played any part in it, and who may have only joined in the last few weeks) overturned it by voting for the new Clause 4. We have got the same problem in Chesterfield. I think the Blair Terror may really be beginning. Looks as if there may be the possibility of a legal challenge to the 29 April Conference and, were that to be the case, then of course it would get everybody off the hook.

Saturday 29 April
I got a taxi to the Central Hall, Westminster, where the Special Conference was called to consider the new Clause 4 that Tony Blair has put forward. It was, of course, in the very Central Hall where I sat on the evening of 26 July 1945 when Clem Attlee came back from the Palace and said he was forming a Government. I found that MPs were up in the Gallery, so I went up to the balcony where I had sat before (not exactly the same seat) and put in an application to speak. The place was fairly crowded – about 1000 delegates they said. The Conference Arrangements Committee Chairman described the procedure and Arthur Scargill claimed that only Annual Conference could change the Party constitution. What was so horrible about it was that when Arthur made that point, a slow hand-clapping began, and that began making me feel as if I was at a Nuremberg Rally. Legal arguments never carry a lot of weight at Labour conferences.

Blair made a twenty-minute speech, with a smile from ear to ear, full of the language of marketing; really very clever and well presented: we've got to do this, we've got to be up to date, I really believe in the new Clause 4 and no Leader has ever believed in the old one. Of course that isn't true, because the wording is full of incredibly bold pledges that Blair hasn't the slightest intention of carrying out.

Then we had a debate – I can't recall everything that was said. John Edmonds spoke in favour of the change; Bill Morris against; Rodney Bickerstaffe against; the AEU in favour; Roger Lyons in favour; Ken Cameron against. I just wasn't called; I really did think I had a pretty good claim, as the most senior member of the Party and a former Chairman, but there you are. I sensed the atmosphere – I thought at one stage I heard vague hissing at Rodney Bickerstaffe who came out against the change. I can't say that I terribly wanted to dig into a lost cause when the battles have got to be fought on the policies. I slipped out as soon as Prescott finished his speech and everyone was waiting for the result, so I wasn't caught by the media, and I had refused a couple of media invitations.

It is true that no Labour Leader has ever believed in Clause 4. Blair says he believes in the new one. But does he? He has had to pay some price in wording to get it through. The Party desperately wants to win and thinks Blair is an electoral asset, which maybe he is – though not as much of a one, I think, as John Smith would have been. There is no need whatever to abandon our faith in order to win now, because we have such a lead. Lots of people have joined the Party and joined in the ballot who actually know nothing about the Labour Party, but then that is true of elections as well, so you can't grumble about that.

It is and it isn't a turning point. When I think of my last year or two as a member of the Labour Cabinet, Callaghan was passionately anti-union, passionately pro-nuclear, and Denis Healey was a monetarist so that, in that sense, just as the last Labour Government paved the way for Thatcherism, so Tony Blair is carrying on Thatcherism, and I mustn't allow myself to get depressed. As I dictate this I am desperately depressed, in part because I didn't get called. Fifty years ago I was too young to play a part, and now I'm too old to be thought necessary. The media tonight are dancing on the grave of socialism and I think Blair's honeymoon will probably have part-run its course – though not completely until he gets rid of the trade-union link, which is what he wants more than anything.

Sunday 30 April

The newspaper headlines this morning were full of the end of the workers, by hand and by brain; socialism is buried; trade unions are a thing of the past. Blair followed it up with an article in the *Sunday Mirror* saying that the trade-union role had got to be reduced following their vote in the Conference on Saturday. So this is only the beginning of the process to clear the Labour Party of any sense of its past. I really felt so offended.

Thursday 4 May

Polling day in the local elections. Back at the club there was absolute hostility to Tony Blair, whom they simply cannot stand. Ian and Fran Street, a lovely couple, decided to leave the Party over Clause 4, so we are going to find a way of keeping them by making them honorary life members, or something of that kind

Friday 5 May

Fiftieth anniversary of VE Day with a celebration in Westminster Hall at the Commons. I went in early at ten and found my seat in the front row on the right hand side as you go in from the north door; in the front row were the Prime Minister and Mrs Major, Tony Newton and his wife, Ted Heath bang in front of me (with such a big head it was difficult to film), then Tony and Cherie Blair, then Blair's father, Ashdown and his wife. Took a lot of film and chatted with the Royal Scots band that was playing, and got pictures of the women hoovering the red carpet for the Queen. The splendour of it in terms of Hollywood drama is unbelievable – you had the thrones, the Lord Chancellor, the Speaker, and the maces, which had to be covered when the Queen arrived because the Queen's authority supersedes that of the Lord Chancellor and the Speaker. Stephen had earlier got a picture of the Beefeaters getting out of their bus.

Then it all began and it was a typical British Establishment event. The Lord Chancellor presented an address and then gave it to the Queen, and then made a speech which passed over the war quite quickly and concentrated on the Cold War and how totalitarianism was defeated. So it was clear that the British Establishment regarded the accidental conflict with Germany as quite irrelevant, compared to the importance of defeating Soviet Russia. Betty Boothroyd talked more about the popular struggle, and after that the Books of Remembrance were brought in. The Chaplain of the House of Commons gave a prayer, and then the Archbishop of Canterbury, and the whole thing began to break up.

I got round with the camera as easily as anything, although Michael Cummins, the Deputy Serjeant at Arms, saw me and said, 'No more filming after the fanfare.'

Stephen spoke to the No. 3 Serjeant at Arms, who had confessed to him that he was the man who had actually removed the plaque that I'd put up in the broom cupboard. The No. 3 said, 'I think the way round this is to put them up between the dissolution and the summoning of the new Parliament, because then the Speaker has no authority.' Then there was a youngish guy (about 35) dressed up in braid and I asked, 'Who are you?' And he said, 'I'm the Lord Great Chamberlain!'

I filmed the band packing up in their bus and the trumpeters doing the fanfare – all the young household Cavalry, I suppose. They gave refreshments to the veterans, and outside Westminster Hall cafeteria there were three waitresses having a smoke and joking.

Roy Jenkins told Caroline that he would buy Melissa's book, and she told Melissa, who was very chuffed.

Thursday 18 May

Sheila was at home and she gave me a homeopathic remedy for my hand, and it is improving.

To the House of Commons and we had a debate on the Nolan Report. The Tories were very angry and there were a lot of interruptions, and then Ann Taylor said we must implement Nolan immediately. But the right-wing Tories, understandably, think that their whole capacity to make money out of Parliament will be taken away. Labour MPs think it's a Party matter; but it isn't really – nobody sees it as a democratic question. Tony Newton said there would be another committee of senior MPs set up, and I asked if they would meet in public and he said, 'We haven't considered that.'

Monday 22 May

A man from Plymouth, for a fee of £98, came to advise me on how to use my Psion organiser. I wanted to know how to transfer material from the Psion organiser to my PC and back, and how to send a fax. He didn't know, and he rang his partner about five times from the office, because he said he was used to Windows and this was a DOS system. It was terribly frustrating. The whole thing has cost about £145 and I got practically nothing out of it. In the end I did manage to work out how to send a fax, but I was very cross.

Went to see Major Mike Charlesworth, Superintendent of Works in the House of Lords. The Lords want to charge £250 an hour to film there, which is a bit much. We filmed Nora Wooll, the parliamentary florist, whose mother had also been florist there; and we went up to the Post Office and had a lovely talk with the old postmen. They talked about the effect of animal rights, abortion and the Gulf War on the volume of mail they had.

Tuesday 23 May

Went up the Victoria Tower and into the bindery, where people bind books for Parliament and other organisations. So we filmed the book-binders. There were four women in one room doing the sewing, and two men doing the beautiful leather toolwork.

Got a cab to the Lexington restaurant for lunch with Rory Bremner, an absolutely brilliant mimic. Also there was his partner in the enterprise, Elissa; his research assistant; a man I didn't know, late forties, and John Fortune. He and John Bird do these marvellous discussions. We all sat down and talked about politics. Bremner wanted to find out my thoughts, and I said all these things I'm saying at public meetings at the moment. He even suggested I might come on his programme, and he said he'd had Norman Lamont and Robin Cook to lunch, and so on. He said the Labour Party hated the attacks he made on the Party, and he asked me about the new Labour Party. He asked if I'd like to have lunch with him and Anthony Sampson and Will Hutton, this Keynesian economist who writes for the *Guardian* – I rarely read his stuff, but his book *The State We're In* is very popular.

Wednesday 24 May

Harold Wilson died at St Thomas' Hospital at midnight, and the whole day was occupied with interviews. The phone rang continually.

Went into the House and the House paid tribute. John Major made a very sensitive speech and Blair made a rather empty one; Heath made a fine one; Paddy Ashdown said something. I made a speech about Harold the socialist, his links with the unions, and the vilification of him for resigning in protest against the defence budget in 1951. Full of humour. I went upstairs to the Strangers' Gallery afterwards, and Marcia and Mary were there, and her son Giles. I gave Mary a kiss. Marcia gave me a huge hug when I met her – and a huge hug at the end. She said, 'I'd love to come and have a talk.' I said, 'I wish you would.'

On *Newsnight* later were Ben Pimlott, Anthony Howard, Barbara Castle, and Peter Mandelson – God knows why he was there. They showed the most unfair film about 'the pound in your pocket', and the pipe-smoking and the trips to the Scilly Isles, and trade union demonstrations. I really got angry – I said it was most unfair and insubstantial. Barbara came in gallantly. I think Paxman was a bit surprised – he hardly got a word in edgeways. They just picked out bits about this kindly old man with his pipe and his Labrador. The Establishment will use anything (a funeral or anything else) to hammer home their point that Wilson was the old Labour Party. At the same time they try to make a link with Blair – is there a parallel between Wilson and Blair? Wilson came in after the death of Gaitskell, Blair's come in after the death of Smith, and the public mood is changing. Barbara at eighty-five was just so glamorous, all dolled up.

Thursday 25 May

Martin Kettle rang from the *Guardian* and said would I like to write a piece to compare Wilson with Blair? And I said, 'No, I certainly wouldn't do that.' I let fly at him and I think he was a bit shaken. I said, 'The *Guardian* is totally uncritical of Blair – he has no experience, no policy, just soundbites.'

Friday 26 May

Very nice letter from Tony Blair, of all people, congratulating me on my speech on Wilson, which caught the mood of the House, so I wrote and thanked him very much.

> Dear Tony,
>
> I was touched to get your letter. Harold was a very remarkable man, and when you are at Number 10, I think his experiences in office will be helpful to you.
>
> All the best. Yours,
>
> Tony

Obviously a peace offering of some kind, and should be taken as such.

Saturday 27 May

I picked up Josh and we went off to Wembley for the play-off between Chesterfield and Bury for elevation to the Second Division of the Football League. I had never been to Wembley before and Josh was marvellous. He found the way to the VIP car park, and we went up to the banqueting suite and there was a huge room with lots of little tables. I had been invited to go by the Chairman of Chesterfield Football Club. I was taken to a table by somebody from Endsleigh Insurance, who sponsors the Football League, and we sat at a table with food on it. I couldn't make out who they all were – someone was from the National Union of Women Teachers, who somehow were sponsored by Endsleigh, or helped Endsleigh. I was totally puzzled!

Then the President of the Football League came up and the MD of Endsleigh Insurance. Then, blow me down, I met a few people from the North Derbyshire Health Authority and they sponsored the Football League. And I asked how on earth they could justify the NHS putting money into sport, rather than into health. 'Oh, it helps to publicise good health,' and so on. I must say I've known about it theoretically, but the whole commercial sponsorship thing exploded in my mind. Huge money involved. Then I did meet somebody who is the secretary of the Players' Union, and the Players' Union defends the football players, because thirty years ago the maximum pay for a player was £20.

I knew nothing about football but fortunately Josh did, and he said to me that this was as important a game as when Chesterfield beat Stockport by 8–1 in 1902. I kept that in the back of my mind.

Chesterfield beat Bury 2-1, and I was so pleased that Chesterfield won because it will boost morale in the town.

Came back. I found the whole thing very exhausting.

Wednesday 31 May

Recall of Parliament.

Major opened the debate – the emergency debate on Bosnia – and said we weren't planning to withdraw, we didn't want to become combatants and we had to protect the hostages. Bosnian Serbs were barbarous terrorists. Blair supported him. Ashdown is a sort of gung-ho former major in the Marines, and he talked in effect about the need to go to war. Ted Heath made a cautious speech in which he revealed the weaknesses of the position taken by Ashdown and in effect said the air strikes were the cause of the trouble. I said at the end of my speech that I intended to divide the House. Tam Dalyell sent a message to me saying he would support me; but Jean Corston didn't think it was right; and Alice Mahon didn't think it was right because of the fact of the hostages; and Bob Wareing was nervous, and so on. Dennis wouldn't be a teller when I asked him later, so it was to be Tam and myself but there was no vote.

Thursday 1 June

I had a letter from the Postmaster of the House of Commons saying that he was shocked that I had been filming in the Post Office, because security considerations made it absolutely vital that nobody should know that there is a sorting office in the House of Commons. Well, how any ordinary person seeing Royal Mail vans arriving, and knowing that 40,000 letters come, could believe there was no sorting office there is ridiculous. He wanted all the film handed over! I'll have to lie low on that.

Wednesday 7 June

I went to the National Portrait Gallery to have lunch with Dr Charles Saumarez Smith, the Director. They wrote to me in February and said they wanted to commission a portrait of me – I suppose that's what happens when you're seventy and getting respectable – and they suggested a painter called Humphrey Ocean, who has painted Willie Whitelaw and Freddie Ayer, Paul McCartney, Philip Larkin and others. He was there and he'd written me a very nice letter. The Director of the Twentieth Century Collection of Portraits was there, and the exhibition director. Trouble is there would be ten sessions of two hours each, which is a hell of a lot.

Thursday 8 June

I had a long talk in the Tea Room with Derek Foster and Andrew Mackinlay, Ann Taylor, Chris Mullin and others. We discussed Murdoch. Chris thought Blair should humour Murdoch before the Election and then strike straight away afterwards, once in power. Of course he won't do anything of the kind. Derek Foster has no time for Blair at all. When I put to him that Blair wasn't a socialist and wasn't even Labour, he agreed. He was Neil Kinnock's PPS, so he's rather more affectionate about Kinnock. Andrew Mackinlay, the young member for Thurrock, asked my advice as to whether he should stand for the Shadow Cabinet and I said I thought he should. Gerry Bermingham, somebody who sits for St Helen's, South, said that the working-class vote wasn't growing; it was the discontented middle class or lower middle class – C1s and C2s – who supported Blair. And of course that is true.

It was a political discussion in what Brian Sedgemore calls the 'thought-free zone' that is the PLP.

Saturday 10 June

The British and French are getting together on a rapid reaction force and this is obviously the build-up of a military capacity for the European Union. The Germans can't come into it because of the fact that they had troops in Yugoslavia during the Second World War. Meanwhile an American captain, flying an F16 fighter, was shot down by the Serbs, hid for a few days and was rescued, and has not just been given a hero's welcome, but treated as a media star. He burst into tears and said that God and the Marines had saved him. Very sinister.

Sunday 11 June
The *Sun* rang and all of a sudden my heart froze and it reminded me of the awful period when the press were after me all the time. I said no, I didn't want to speak to them. Then I wondered what the story was, and later the *Mail* and *Independent* also rang – it was about the Boy Scouts declining to swear an oath of allegiance to the Prince of Wales because he had committed adultery. I just never want to go back to that degree of hostility from the media. Just the words 'the *Sun*' struck terror in my heart.

Tuesday 20 June
Shell have announced that they are not going to ditch the Brent Spa oil rig in the Atlantic, so all the campaigning by Greenpeace and the boycott of Shell in Germany have been successful, and it just shows that if you keep at it you win.

Thursday 22 June
My pager buzzed and I pulled it out as I left and there was a message from Stephen to say that Major has resigned. Well, I didn't believe it – I rushed home and saw the news, and he has given up the leadership of the Tory Party because of all the press speculation. It is a gimmick, but it is a very clever one because he will look much stronger. I might add that this morning the new educational policy, which actually sells out on comprehensive education, was announced.

I went over to the House as quickly as I could and we went to College Green, where the media always gather for a crisis. It was an absolute circus. Everyone was saying that Major has done the right thing. This is the first time in my life that this has ever happened.

Sunday 25 June
Media absolutely full of stories about the Tory leadership: will Redwood stand? Will Lamont stand? What about Heseltine, Portillo, Shephard . . . ? Absolute gossip politics.

Monday 26 June
I went to a meeting on Bosnia organised by the Peace in the Balkans Committee, with Alice Mahon in the chair. There was heckling and shouting when I was speaking, led by Quentin Hoare who used to be a member (and perhaps still is) of the New Left Review Board. He shrieked at me. It was quite clear that the Bosnians and the Croats and those who

take the Michael Foot view – that this was an act of aggression and these people are war criminals – were there.

There were really violent views expressed: that we on the platform were paid for by the Serbs; we supported fascism and war criminals; we were responsible for the killing. Alice Mahon was very fair. There were about fifty pro-Bosnian Croats; the rest were probably just the usual Peace Movement people, with a few pro-Serbs. Sir Alfred Sherman spoke. I have never met him before, but he rang me up and he supports the Serbs completely.

Tuesday 27 June

My back is hurting like hell and my leg is swollen. I'm very, very tired, I've got eczema on my hand and I'm a bit under the weather.

I nearly went to St Thomas' Hospital and checked in with my swollen leg but, I thought if I do, they'll take me in overnight and it will be 'Benn in Hospital' in the papers.

Wednesday 28 June

Sheila gave me a remedy for my back (she's a homeopath) and said it would be all right in an hour – well, it was a little bit longer than that, but truthfully my back has completely cleared up and I am so relieved.

Thursday 29 June

Major's reputation is rising and the Tory Party's reputation is rising, while Blair's is falling and the Labour Party's is falling, because the LP has absolutely failed to get hold of the right point, which is quite simply that everybody should have a chance to vote for the new Prime Minister in an election. That can only be done by a humble address to the Queen, which I have suggested, but they won't touch it.

Tuesday 4 July

Ben Bella, former President of Algeria, came to see me. He and Hugh Stephens, who is very active in the Afro-Asian solidarity movement, want to set up an international commission on economic sanctions. They want a conference in London with myself, Daniel Ortega and Ramsey Clark, former Attorney General of the United States, to form this commission to examine sanctions against Cuba, Libya, North Korea and Iraq. I asked Hugh Stephens later where the money would come from; he didn't know.

But as I shan't be receiving any of it I can't say that's a great problem.

To the Commons and went up to the committee corridor where in Room 12, the Tory ballot was going on for the leadership. The corridor was packed – senior police officers, security people, Serjeant at Arms and his Deputy, Michael Cummins. No filming allowed at all. I positioned myself at the end of the corridor –I got some pictures of the scene and they are absolutely unique – and nobody stopped me.

I went on to the terrace and there was Larry Whitty with his new wife; he must be getting on for fifty-five and he's married this girl who looks about thirty-two. We talked and he unburdened himself, now that he's been sacked as General Secretary. He said Blair had tried to stop the singing of the 'Red Flag' at the last Labour Conference, and had tried to stop 'Auld Lang Syne' because the new Labour Party didn't sing that either.

Sunday 9 July

At twelve I went to see Reem Abdelhadi and her husband at St Petersburg Place. I had visited the flat earlier in the year, just after the police had raided it and, they told me, had done £22,000 worth of damage. She is very unwell and described what happened to her in prison, with strip-searching and the terrible food. She was strip-searched before and after visitors – even though when she had visitors there was a glass panel between them. I didn't ask about the evidence but, looking into their eyes, it was absolutely clear to me that they were innocent. People in their position would have said something to indicate anxiety about the trial – they were anxious that they might be punished – but had no anxiety as to their guilt. So I came away totally convinced that they were innocent.*

Came home and watched *Undercurrents*, a video of two hours that had been sent to me about direct action, covering everything from stag hunting, the export of live animals and anti-motorway demos, to invading the annual meeting of banks that invest in repressive regimes. Marvellously produced.

Monday 10 July

Very depressed at the moment. Blair is going to Australia as Rupert Murdoch's guest to talk to the Murdoch press editors. He tells the TGWU Conference that the unions will have no armlock on a Labour Government. He is a Tory – it's like having John Redwood as leader (well, not Redwood exactly) but Blair is the most popular Tory leader in Britain at the moment.

Thursday 13 July

Sitting on the terrace at the Commons was so luxurious, and so all-party, that I felt Parliament is not about improving the lot of people; it is a very easy life. I was tired – my leg and hand are still hurting, and truthfully I'm feeling a bit under the weather.

*Reem Abdelhadi was a Palestinian student who approached me for advice and help after she was charged with engaging in terrorist activities; I gave evidence for her at her trial, where she was acquitted.

Friday 14 July

The ASLEF train drivers' strike has really stopped the entire transport system. Marvellous. I did a 'telephone surgery' from the Commons, which was interesting. I talked to the constituents on the phone, then dictated letters straight onto a cassette and put that, with notes, in an envelope and sent them straight to Margaret – marvellous, compared to six hours there and back by train for just four cases.

Saturday 15 July

We had something for our meal tonight called 'Rasher', which looked like bacon, tasted like bacon, smelt like bacon and was absolutely delicious – and it's vegetarian. I don't normally think about food, but I do like the vegetarian foods we have.

Sunday 16 July

The papers are full of the horrors of the war in Yugoslavia, with the Serbs revealed as having been guilty of terrible atrocities and public anxiety growing rapidly.

Caroline and I went to Hyde Park for the Indian vegetarian picnic – about 200-300 people sitting round a little platform, and some Hare Krishna people with drums singing, and little Indian girls dancing.

Monday 17 July

A very hot day again.

The reverberations of Tony Blair's speech to Rupert Murdoch's worldwide managers and editors in Australia have been phenomenal. It has really really shaken the right of the Labour Party. The language, the repudiation of the past, the denial of a vision, saying there is no ideological difference between left and right – terrifying really, but you have to keep your mouth shut until after the election.

I heard from Andrew Mackinlay that the trade union group of MPs had met Blair last week; Gwyneth Dunwoody, Derek Fatchett, Kevin McNamara and others had put to Blair that the unions had saved the Labour Party many times in the past, but Blair didn't seem to understand. He said he didn't mind the unions supporting individual candidates, but that – after Nolan – sponsorship was very dangerous. (He himself being the guest of Murdoch in Australia.)

Friday 21 July

Caught the 7.30 to Chesterfield and slept all the way. I have a marvellous system – I have two balloon cushions: one fits up my back and the other stops my head from wobbling. I've got an airline eye mask, and I have made two little foam-rubber arm rests (because the arm rests on first-class trains are very hard), with an ashtray in each one. I put a newspaper under my feet (though I have airline socks as well) and I leave my ticket on the table, and I'm usually sound asleep for an hour. Sometimes I set the alarm clock so that I don't go on to Sheffield, which has happened.

I saw about twenty army trucks today, painted white with 'UN' on them. I had such mixed feelings, because when I see army trucks I always think that means we are going to war, but when they are painted in white with 'UN' I think that's good. But then I thought, 'Oh, God, they are going to be used for going to war against Serbia.'

Saturday 22 July
Went to Hilary and Sally's. We sat late, talking to them by their little pond with candles floating on it and little frogs developing from the tadpoles. They are so happy and lovely.

Wednesday 26 July
Caroline cancelled her trip to Greece because of the pressure of her book on comprehensive schools.

Sunday 30 July
In Bosnia the Croatians have launched an attack on the Croatian Serbs in the Krajina area. Bob Wareing has been much criticised for going to talk to the Bosnian Serb leader and the military commander, both of whom have been named as war criminals. The *Mail on Sunday* had a whole page about it but hardly mentioned the fact that Wareing is the Chairman of an all-party group – the All-Party Yugoslav Group – and that going with him was Lord Harlech, who was our ambassador in Washington; they didn't mention that.

I did one interview strongly defending Bob Wareing, but this war hysteria is building up. Caroline said she saw something on TV where the Krajinian Serbs, who were refugees like the Muslims, were seen crying after being driven out by the Croatian Army, and the BBC said they can't expect much sympathy in view of what is happening elsewhere.

Tuesday 1 August
My little Psion hand-held computer is an absolute dream. I just type out the letter I want, press the button and it comes off the printer – it is absolute bliss.

The situation in Bosnia is that the Croats, who I think must be being supported by the Germans, are now launching an attack to drive the Serbs out of their part of Croatia. Willy Claes, the NATO Secretary General, has made a dangerous speech about air strikes and so on. The House of Representatives followed the Senate in voting to lift the arms embargo. Clinton says he'll veto it. Portillo's in Washington. It's hard to follow, but I must say my instinct that this conflict is not all it appears gets stronger and stronger every day.

We had the hottest July on record, I think, or something like it.

Wednesday 2 August

A very, very hot day again.

Went to a little Greek taverna round the corner, had a lovely meal sitting out and it was just such fun. It is forty-seven years since Caroline and I met. Caroline was wearing the same dress that she wore when I met her at Oxford, she can get into it quite easily – she didn't look more than about thirty-odd and she's touching seventy, unbelievable.

Friday 4 August

The big news today is that the Croatians have launched a major attack on the Serbs of Croatia from the Krajina region. This means that war has broken out on a large scale. The risk is that the Serbians under Milosevic will go to the support of the Serbs in Croatia. I'm dictating this a couple of days later; the Germans and the Americans were very soft in their criticism of Croatia, and I think what happened was that the Germans persuaded the Americans that, if the Croatians were armed and helped, they would attack the Serbs and that would take the pressure off the Bosnian Government.

Saturday 5 August

The Croatian attack is mounting and the media in Britain make nothing of the Serbs, who are being made refugees as a result of the Croatian attack; indeed, there's some pleasure really that the Croatians have done to the Serbs what the United Nations are not able to do.

Sunday 6 August

At twelve o'clock I did an interview for Radio Wales with Ken Livingstone, who said it was just fascism in Serbia.

Now the Croatian occupation of the Krajina region of the country, where the Serbs lived, has been completed, and 150,000 Serbs have moved into Bosnia; there is frightful bloodshed, with Croatian soldiers setting fire to buildings and the media using the words 'ethnic cleansing'. It is incredible.

Tuesday 8 August

Caroline worked from midnight until three because she couldn't sleep.

Wednesday 9 August

Another very hot day.

The situation in Bosnia is developing in a terrible way. I'm getting letters today from people who do understand that the Croatian attack on Krajina was triggered off by German and American pressure, America wanting to beat the Serbs without involving themselves, and the Germans wanting to use Croatia to destroy Serbia, their old enemy. A most tragic situation and the media coverage has been disgraceful.

Sunday 13 August

The papers today are still full of the Blair business. Blair's issued a statement saying that power without principles is barren, but principles without power are futile. A soundbite that was no doubt cooked up by Mandelson.

Wednesday 16 August

The latest rumour is that Blair is going to drop the Labour Party pledge to have a referendum on proportional representation; Professor Raymond Plant, who I think is a most boring old academic but is very keen on PR, wrote an article about it in *The Independent*.

Thursday 17 August, Stansgate

This evening James, who is nearly twelve, came and sat down and asked me about what a Prime Minister did. I did just idly wonder whether a second son of a second son of a second son of a second son* might be getting interested in politics too. He's a bright lad and has very good school reports; he's rather sort of silly, like boys of that age are, but I was pleased he was interested.

Saturday 19 August

To a meeting of the Commission of Inquiry on Economic Sanctions. Hugh Stephens had done all the organisation and Ibrahim, who is the head of the Iraqi Interests Section in the Jordanian Embassy, came up to me and handed me a personal letter from Saddam Hussein, thanking me very much indeed for my work. Well, I didn't think it would be helpful if I announced that at the conference! I thought if the press picked that up it would destroy the conference, so I explained this to Ibrahim and he fully understood.

George Galloway was there. Had a bit of a talk about Blair. Now that Bryan Gould's article has been published in the *Guardian*, it's quite clear that his attack is not on Blair but on Mandelson, who, he said, had been working to undermine Kinnock even while Kinnock was Leader, with a

* James Benn, second son of Hilary Benn (who became an MP in 1999), second son of Tony Benn, MP, second son of William Wedgwood Benn, MP, second son of John Williams Benn, MP.

view to getting Gordon Brown as Leader or, failing that, Tony Blair.

Mandelson becomes more and more clearly a sort of Rasputin figure.

Masses of people gave evidence; it's all in my diary notes. Some of it very powerful. Ramsey Clark said that both nuclear weapons at Hiroshima and Nagasaki killed a quarter of a million people; the sanctions in Iraq had killed half a million – twice as many.

It became clear that this is really a question of war crimes.

Sunday 20 August

Sent a fax to King Hussein:

> Your Majesty,
>
> Yesterday and today in London an International Conference, which I chaired, met to discuss the grave effect of sanctions on Cuba, Iraq and Libya. I was asked to write to you personally to appeal to you not to close the Jordanian-Iraqi border.
>
> I enclose some details of the conference.
>
> With my best wishes to you personally.
>
> Yours sincerely
>
> Tony Benn

Tuesday 22 August

Caroline had a pain in her chest this morning. She'd had a bit of a cough. She said it was very painful and thought it might be pleurisy.

At 5.30 I had to see our doctor because I'm going to India shortly, and Caroline came with me, which is surprising because she doesn't actually like to go to the doctor. At any rate, I got some hepatitis and cholera injections. Then the doctor had a look at Caroline.

Then very much to my surprise, having asked a lot of questions, the doctor decided to send her into hospital at once. So we drove, got there about half-past six, went up to Accident & Emergency, and there was the usual crowd of people in the early evening at St Mary's, Paddington.

Caroline saw the 'triage' nurse (I'd never heard the term before), a male nurse doing a preliminary assessment.

I went to get a cup of tea and a Coca-Cola and some sandwiches. When I came back Caroline was seeing the doctor, so I sat outside the hospital smoking my pipe. It was a typical Accident & Emergency department: ambulances arrived every ten minutes or so – one man brought out with blood right down his face and body, so much so that they had to slop out the ambulance afterwards.

To cut a long story short, I went into the cubicle and sat with Caroline. There was a very plump male nurse with a crew cut and a little beard who, after he had trained as a nurse, did a degree in music and was the choirmaster and organist in a church in Willesden.

A young doctor came to see Caroline and what they suspect it might be is a pulmonary embolism; this was why they had taken her in. They gave her an X-ray, which was normal; they then tested the aeration of her blood, which wasn't perfect. It didn't exclude the possibility of an embolism, even if it didn't establish it, so they decided to keep her in overnight.

By then I realised it was serious. I found it hard to believe because there she was, sitting smiling, happy, laughing, and having a marvellous time. At about a quarter-past midnight she was finally found a bed in the Intensive Care Unit on the eighth floor. I went up with her there and she gave me a list of things she wanted: mainly chapters 1, 4 and 8 of her book, her Filofax, her creams, some blank paper and a toothbrush, knickers and a nightie.

I walked out of the hospital really not quite knowing what was going on. Came home, found everything she wanted, packed it up and went to bed at about half-past one.

Wednesday 23 August

Got to the hospital at half-past seven. I gave Caroline all the things.

I still find it very hard to believe that she's got an embolism, but Caroline thinks she has – she has a cautious disposition.

Thursday 24 August

At 6.30 a doctor from Bihar in India came and said the tests were completely clear – absolutely nothing on the lungs. So Caroline nearly gave him a hug. I knew all along that it must be all right.

So that's the end of a very, very happy day.

The last two days I've been really in a daze and I think Caroline has, too. She's still got this pain in her chest. I think it must be muscular, or a bruise or something.

We're going to have a lovely weekend.

Friday 25 August

Caroline had a very bad night; she's in great pain, but it must be muscular because it isn't her lungs or her heart. For the first time in ages I got her to take a Nurofen, a painkiller.

Tuesday 29 August

NATO has declared that the market massacre in Sarejevo was an atrocity, so obviously air strikes will take place.

Wednesday 30 August

Massive NATO attacks on Serb positions around Sarajevo.

I think what's happened is that this is not a civil war really; it's the

Germans, Americans, European Union and NATO supporting the Croats – back to where we were in the war when there was a right-wing German-dominated Croatia attacking the Serbs.

NATO has entered the civil war as a belligerent; the United Nations has been totally edged aside by NATO (Yeltsin wasn't even told by Clinton that the bombing was going to take place); British troops are at risk; and it won't work.

Saturday 2 September

I went off to the Spinney, a Derbyshire County Council old people's home, for a fête; its so different from the private nursing homes where they charge £400 a week. The atmosphere's so different – it was a genuine community business, which was so different from these private homes, which I loathe. But the decoration's beginning to decline because they haven't got any money to make it really nice, and there was just that feeling that everything in the public sector is running down. But the care and the love are so much better.

David Howell, the Tory chairman of the Foreign Affairs Select Committee, has criticised British policy for being craven and simply following the Americans by agreeing to the bombing. *The Times* had a leader saying that you had to take all this seriously. So I feel, bit by bit, that attitudes are shifting.

Monday 4 September

Rory Bremner came to see me. He'd really come for ideas for the autumn. He's a serious student of current affairs and, like all satirists, really wants to get the guts of an issue.

I said to him at one stage, 'I know you're a friend of Mandelson's . . . '

He said, 'No, not at all, I have no present intention of making a friend of Mandelson.'

Wednesday 6 September

The Times had a very interesting cartoon this morning based on a woman who has been sleeping in a glass case in the Serpentine Gallery. People come and look at her inside the glass, so *The Times* cartoon showed Blair in a glass box dreaming of Number 10 – very entertaining.

Thursday 7 September, India

Got to bed at about half-past five, Delhi time, and was woken three hours and twenty minutes later by the Prime Minister's office, saying the Prime Minister would see me at eleven o'clock, at his residence.

I made some more tea and had breakfast; accidentally brushed my teeth with the cortisone cream for my ulcerated leg, instead of toothpaste.

Rao had been Chief Minister of Andha Pradesh, had held various ministerial posts and is by far and away the most senior Indian statesman – born in 1921, the same year as my older brother Mike.

Was taken by car to the Prime Minister's residence, which was where, of course, I'd met Rajiv Gandhi six years ago. I went in to see the Prime Minister at about five past eleven and, instead of getting ten minutes as expected, I got forty minutes, which was a great honour. Rao reminded me a bit of Jim Callaghan. To begin with he looked a little sleepy, but he perked up almost immediately.

He said, 'The pendulum swings one way and the other, you know; you have to keep movement and change, and moderation is a very powerful force,' which is pure Jim Callaghan.

Then, on the IMF, I said, 'I'm a little concerned about the power of the world bankers. For example, in 1976 the Labour Cabinet of which I was a member capitulated to the bankers and cut public expenditure, and we paved the way for Mrs Thatcher.'

Rao said, 'India didn't capitulate. We told the IMF that we were not prepared to accept their conditions and that they'd have to go away. But the thinking of the IMF is changing. The rigid mechanical criteria are beginning to go, and everybody's adjusting to the new situation.'

I asked about the multinationals and Rao said, 'Well, we have to work with them, but they're not going to dominate us.'

Then I asked about the market more generally and about the ethics of profits. Rao said, 'Yes, but we don't talk about markets, we talk about market planning – i.e. the element of planning coming into it. We never talk about privatisation as such. We try and look at it from a common-sense point of view.'

Then I raised with him the question of the media: 'Rupert Murdoch has ninety million viewers of his satellite channels in India. That makes him more powerful than Ayatollah Khomeini.' Rao gave a wry smile.

He indicated, as you do – saying something like, 'Thank you very much for coming' – that we had come to the end. He also said, 'The Labour Party has always been good friends with India.'

At three o'clock, Mr Singh from the Protocol Department of the Institute for Cultural Relations took me to see one of the Mogul palaces outside Delhi. He wasn't very knowledgeable or interested in politics. When I put questions to him, he really couldn't answer them; also, I'm very deaf and I didn't hear what he did say, and I find Indian accents very difficult to pick up.

When we stopped at the traffic lights, mothers with young babies tapped at the window and looked very sad, and the babies held out their hands. There was a little boy of about seven holding a baby of about eighteen months doing the same. Mr Singh said, 'They're just professional beggars.' But it distressed me very much.

There was a snake charmer, whose eyes were darting everywhere, and as soon as he saw me look at him, he lifted the lid and out came the cobra.

Later I met a tall, elegant Englishman who turned out to be the British High Commissioner, who said he hadn't seen me for a long time. I told him about the time I'd met Gandhi. He said, 'When I was a student, I wrote to Gandhi to ask if I could do an interview. I didn't say I was a journalist, because Gandhi didn't like journalists; I was told that Mr Gandhi was fasting one day, but I could go along. I went along and he was praying and I handed him written questions. On old envelopes that he'd cut up, so as not to waste paper, Gandhi wrote his replies to those questions and I still have all those papers.' Well, they must be enormously valuable. I asked him if he kept a diary and he said, 'No but I've kept some notes.'

No dinners have been arranged in Delhi; I would quite have liked to have had dinner with somebody, but I'm tired and I'm quite happy to be back in my room.

I'm a rather fussy old gentleman now and I haven't got the strength that I had, bouncing up and down the great big stone stairways of the temples. Also my deafness is a real barrier, because when two Indians are talking to each other I can't even tell whether it's English or not.

Friday 8 September

Looking back on India. Just a quick reflection on it – they certainly went to an enormous amount of trouble and I was treated like a Head of State on an official visit so from that point of view it couldn't have been more flattering.

On the other hand, it was a depoliticised India, and I suppose that in the back of my mind I'd thought that when Russia collapsed and India played a more important role in the development of the world, they would have something to say, but not at all. I suppose Indian politics is corrupt but then British politics is full of careerists – it attracts people who just want a job.

Saturday 9 September

Somebody from the High Commission in London met me with a car and I got home at about six o'clock.

Jack Straw has come out with a statement about clearing the beggars off the streets, which would earn him a standing ovation at the Tory Conference. The Labour Party has said nothing denouncing the French nuclear tests. The minimum wage commitment to £4.50 has been dropped in favour – if we're lucky – of £4.

Monday 11 September

I rang the BBC to complain about the censorship of all opposition in Britain to the bombing of the Bosnian Serbs.

Monday 18 September
In the afternoon I drafted my speech on Yugoslavia and at 7.30 went to the Committee for Peace in the Balkans at the Friends' Meeting House.

About 100 people there, with Alice Mahon in the chair. Somebody from Workers' Liberty, which supports lifting the arms embargo (the Michael Foot, Ken Livingstone, Chris Mullin view) spoke and was shouted down. Anyway I did the best I could.

Thursday 21 September
I must note that the three minicab drivers I've had in the last couple of days have all been men who were in business and were bankrupted. One was a Cypriot who had had a little restaurant, and the bank had foreclosed because he owed them £12,000, even though his restaurant was taking £4,000 a week. Broken by the bank.

This morning the driver who drove me had been a small businessman importing spectacles from China and the money had been put in by two Israelis, who then had a row with each other and withdrew the money. Coming back there was a man who had been a managing director in the rag trade and his company had gone bankrupt. They'd all gone into minicab driving.

Tuesday 26 September
Went over my programme for the Labour Party Conference.

Liz Davies is due to have her endorsement as a parliamentary candidate for Leeds North East refused by the NEC tomorrow morning. My reflections on that are very simple. Frank Field, MP, has encouraged Labour voters in the past to 'Vote Liberal' and that's all right. Roger Liddle, who was an SDP councillor until May and voted against Labour, is taken into Blair's private office. But Liz Davies, who voted twice against her Labour council – once to save a nursery school – is not allowed to be a candidate. Blair can go to Australia as a guest of Rupert Murdoch, who owns the *Sun*, the *News of the World* and *The Times*, which have knifed the Labour Party for years, and that's okay. But Liz Davies supports *Labour Briefing* and that's not okay. The way to deal with it is to say that this is what New Labour is: a party open to Liberals and Tories but not to socialists.

Wednesday 27 September
In the afternoon I went to see Silverglade, who are editing my film, loosely called *Under Big Ben*. It is very good, I must say.

Tuesday 3 October, Brighton
Conference. The first debate was on Liz Davies. Clare Short spoke for about twenty-five minutes – the most scurrilous, scandalous, disgraceful

speech that I think I have ever heard a member of the Party make. She called Liz a Trotskyite and spoke all the time about Militant. Well, Liz isn't a Trotskyite and has nothing to do with Militant. Anyway, Liz was defeated on a show of hands.

A police inspector, a very tall man of about 6′ 3″, the Chairman of the Police Federation, came up to me and said, 'Sir, I was a young constable outside Number 10 in the Sixties when you used to attend as a Cabinet Minister. I have listened to your *Diaries* on tape in my car and, now that I know what went on inside, I found it really riveting.'

I said, 'Well, I have introduced a Bill that said the Police Federation should join the TUC, and I met a couple of your lads who came to see me.'

He said, 'Yes, I heard.'

I said, 'Well, they weren't very interested in that.'

At the Tribune rally later I made the case that we in the Labour Party had inherited the greatest instrument for social change there ever was and that we should use it. It didn't go down that well really, particularly my reference to Clare Short's speech being utterly disgraceful. The jokes didn't go down very well, either. They are a tough bunch, the Labour Party, and this was a sort of praetorian guard around the Leader.

The Liz Davies story has been totally overshadowed by the Blair speech, and the Blair speech has been totally overshadowed by the acquittal of O.J. Simpson for the murder of his wife.

Wednesday 4 October

The left has been obliterated with the abandonment of Clause 4. It is the biggest victory for the right that there has ever been at a Labour Conference, I would think. It will pave the way for a Labour victory – a very right-wing government may be the way in which we are going.

I do, for the first time, think I might be expelled from the Labour Party under the new constitutional rules, whereby the General Secretary can decide whether you are fit to be a member. It has never been like that before.

Thursday 5 October

Caroline went to see the doctor, who has referred her to hospital.

Friday 6 October

Caroline and I went to St Mary's, Paddington to see the registrars, who said she must go in next Friday (her birthday) and have a biopsy.

Saturday 7 October

Caroline is not at all well and it suddenly hit me what a terrible danger she was in. I burst into tears and sobbed. I have told the children it is serious.

We watched *Casualty* which she loves, and then *Kind Hearts and Coronets*.

Tonight Alan Howarth, the Tory MP for Stratford-on-Avon, joined the Labour Party and he will be welcomed, though Liz Davies is unacceptable – he having been a Tory MP for twelve years, she having worked for *Labour Briefing*. The Labour Party will accept him and not even insist that he resigns to fight as a Labour candidate.

It is quite clear to me that my political and personal lives have come to an absolute turning point. I have got to devote myself single-mindedly to helping Caroline now.

Sunday 8 October

Caroline woke at 4.43 and started on her book.

I dozed, bought the papers and came down to the office to do a bit of work.

But it is a day for reassessing everything. Caroline is obviously potentially very ill, and my job now is to support and sustain her in every way I can. What she must be feeling, I can't imagine, but I mustn't divert her positive thoughts for her own recovery to sympathising with me. I may be being unduly gloomy, but whatever it is, she is the main priority now. What I must do now is repay Caroline with all the love and attention she has given to me over forty-six years of knowing her. What an amazing creature, a courageous, bold, intelligent, loving person. I hadn't meant to put all this in a political diary, but I can't not put it in because it is the central feature of my life at the moment.

Sunday 22 October

Michael Meacher telephoned. He said he was 'very, very worried'. Michael Meacher is always worried! He said, 'It's worse than it has been for the last twenty-five years. Blair called me in and said he wanted to take away Transport and give me Shadow Chancellor of the Duchy of Lancaster.'

Well, that's an absolute non-job, working with Prescott to have a go at Heseltine. So he asked Blair, 'What have I done wrong?' And Blair said 'Nothing.'

Then Michael said that his speech at Conference had been checked with the Leader's office, but the following day Mandelson had put out a story saying he had 'gone further' than he should have done, which was quite outrageous.

Tuesday 24 October

At ten, Mr Ansari, the Iranian Chargé d'Affaires, came to see me. He wanted specially to talk about the Labour Conference and what the British attitude to Iran was. I told him that there was hostility to Islamic fundamentalism and to Islam generally; that on the whole the British

Government took the view that the Americans took, and always had done on these matters.

He said he would like me to visit Iran at any time I liked. There is a delegation going next week, but the two MPs who had been invited – Lynne Jones and Elizabeth Peacock – had both pulled out. It was, I think, because women see Islamic politics as very unattractive. He said that forty-eight per cent, I think, of students at school are women and 38 per cent of university students are women. 'You must remember that women accept the culture of the Islamic state.'

I said, 'Well, I know, but then *you* are told that *we* accept the culture of the monarchy. We don't really, but there is not much we can do about it.'

Wednesday 25 October

Went to Silverglade, the video-editors, on the South Bank and from nine until nearly six, I worked on the editing. Ann Tyerman, the BBC commissioning editor, came. She likes it. By Monday night the whole thing should be finished.

Sunday 29 October

There was a tremendous row because on the David Frost programme Clare Short said she was in favour of legalising soft drugs. She has just been boosted to the skies because of her attack on Liz Davies, and now she has put up a big black – as we used to say in the air force – and infuriated Blair and Straw. I did laugh, I must admit.

Monday 30 October, Stansgate

Every time I go to Stansgate I really wish to retire, because the thought of having lots of spare time and a late lie-in, then wander round, do a bit of shopping, meet people in the neighbourhood, is terribly attractive.

Michael Meacher rang. I have given some thought to Michael's position. I said, 'Look, Michael, you are the Employment spokesman, an absolutely crucial job. You should spend the next twelve months making really strong speeches about the importance of the trade union movement. Go and see all the General Secretaries, make some speeches; don't clear them with Blair.'

He said, 'I hear what you say.'

'Well, it's no good telling me you hear what I say – that's management-speak. Are you going to do anything about it?'

'Yes, I will.'

'You've lost your old constituency by going along with the Party and now Blair has no time for you. You must be nearly fifty.'

'I am fifty-five.'

'Well, there you are, you see.'

Tuesday 31 October

We went to the hospital to see Caroline's doctor. We came home and gradually unwound. All of a sudden the future opened up again; having thought that her sixty-ninth birthday might be her last and that she might not live to see the book published and the bulbs she was planting grow, life opens up again.

I am emotionally drained, physically exhausted and I have got toothache. I get shaky on my pins, dizzy when I stand up.

Thursday 2 November

Up very early. I went to see my consultant at St Thomas' and my leukaemia is marginally worse. He is such a nice guy. We had a talk and he has a total contempt for the way the Health Service is run, chasing the cost of every ball of cotton wool, right down to the last one. He also told me how he had got a taxi from St Thomas' to Guy's Hospital and the taxi driver said, 'We do very well out of St Thomas'.' The consultant asked what he meant and the driver said, 'The other day, I had to drive to Newcastle to pick up a patient and it cost £240.'

Friday 3 November, Chesterfield

Had a talk to Tom and Margaret because I am very gloomy about the Labour Party and about the Chesterfield Labour Party.

Went and did some shopping, and then I went to the Party Executive meeting at six. The only business that came up was whether we could afford to send people to conferences. Dave Walsh said we shouldn't send delegates if we didn't have any money. That went on and on and on. There were fourteen present, but I just felt that I had no role there. I caught the last train home, and I was really depressed.

Saturday 4 November

Ann Denman, Chair of the Chesterfield Labour Party, rang me because she had heard from Tom that I was very depressed. She said, 'I hear you feel you are not wanted in Chesterfield. You're the only reason I am in the Party. If you are not there, I shall pack it in,' and so on.

I said, 'It's not that I take it personally. I just feel that the Chesterfield Labour Party is moving in a non-political direction.'

You have to face the fact that the Labour Party has been killed at the top, because Blair spends all his time attacking the Tories for what they do and attacking the Labour Party for what it believes, which is a much more serious line of criticism.

Watched Rory Bremner and went to bed.

Sunday 5 November

Turned on the radio and heard that Rabin, the Israeli Prime Minister, had been assassinated – by Jewish extremists, they say. Clinton is going to the funeral and there were all the usual expressions of regret and everything. It is a serious setback, but this whole situation is very dangerous and Arafat might well be assassinated by Hamas.

Wednesday 8 November

On my way back from Central Hall, I walked over to the Field of Remembrance by Westminster Abbey and placed a a little wooden cross with a poppy on it for 'Flight Lt Michael Benn DFC 1944' in the little area for the RAF. I thought it was a nice thing to do. He did die in 1944 as part of that great effort to prevent fascism defeating us. But it is a long time ago now and, when you look at the world we live in, you wonder how many of those sacrifices were wasted by the politicians who supported Hitler before the war and went back to Hitler's ideas after the war.

Thursday 9 November

The Labour Party came out with Workfare today: cutting benefits for young people if they didn't take low-paid jobs that are subsidising the employer.

I don't want to be thrown out of the Party. I will be quite candid in my diary. I do want to be in the next Parliament and that is a factor to be taken into account, but after the next election I shall vote according to my conscience, and between now and then I shall speak my mind. But I also have in mind that I don't want to embarrass Hilary.

Sunday 12 November, Chesterfield

Went to the Remembrance Day service. I walked over with some of the old right-wing members of the council and their husbands and wives. They all loathe Blair. The more I think about this, the more it takes a while to get it straight. Blair doesn't inspire anyone. Nobody loves him, because he doesn't want them to do anything except admire him, obey him and give money. Rather like what the Postmaster in Bristol said to me on my first visit after I had been appointed Postmaster General. 'What shall I do as Postmaster General?' I asked, and he said, 'Do nothing.' That was in 1964.

Walked back to the Cenotaph and all the cadets were there, and upstairs the Duke of Devonshire in his bowler hat and the Mayor in his three-cornered hat, and so on. Talked to a few of the old veterans who really had seen some service.

Monday 13 November

Ruth looked in in the morning with her twin sister Diana, and we had terrible trouble thinking of a title for the film, and Diana said, 'What about *Westminster Behind Closed Doors?*' And blow me down, later in the day

Ann Tyerman rang to say that it had been agreed. I am just so relieved. We spent more time arguing about the title than anything else.

World news: there was a bomb in Saudi Arabia at an American training base and five Americans were killed and sixty injured.

The other news today was Tony Blair's long-awaited speech at the CBI in which he said, 'We will not tax wealth. We want wealth. We want people to be successful. The CBI and the Labour Party have got to leave their baggage behind.' He got sort of warm applause. But he said, 'We have dropped Clause 4', so that's what it was about, satisfying the CBI; he had to drop Clause 4 before he went there. Every night I go to bed and say to myself, 'I won't think about Blair any more. It will be all right when we win.' But it is so obvious that when we win it will be a Tory victory – just a reshuffle.

Today Blair said that the minimum wage and the Social Chapter were simply a set of ideas, playing them down, when of course they are absolutely fundamental to the Labour Party. So it has almost got to the point where the CBI would sponsor Labour candidates. I should think the sense of unease now in the Party must be rising to fever pitch.

Wednesday 15 November

Parliament opens in about two minutes, and I am going in to the Speaker's party and shall be in the House in the afternoon, and Caroline is going to Stafford today.

Went to the Speaker's party and when I saw Betty Boothroyd I dropped on one knee, a rather exaggerated sign of politeness. I shall need all the support I can get when the film comes out.

Went to the Tea Room and there was Joan Lestor. She told me she had seen Mary Wilson, who had had a terrible time over Harold. Apparently his pension was only £28,000 a year and he had to have round-the-clock nursing; in the end friends had gone to Westminster City Council to try and get some home help for him, which it did provide.

I asked about his illness, and apparently Mary had told Joan Lestor that when Harold came round from his first operation for stomach cancer, he said that he thought he had heard three surgeons saying to each other, 'I am afraid we gave him too much anaesthetic.' So he became convinced that he had been accidentally or deliberately injured, and many people thought that might explain why his memory had gone.

Thursday 16 November

Rushed to the station and, as I ran down the steps, the doors were shutting on the train for Chesterfield. I saw the driver and put my head in the window and asked, 'Are you going to Chesterfield.'

'Yes, and I wouldn't have waited for anyone other than you.'

So I got on the train and the ticket collector said, 'The driver said he wouldn't have waited for John Major!'

Got to Chesterfield for my surgery. There was a man who had been involved in an accident with a dog and wanted something done about dogs running on the road; two people worried about their Poll Tax; somebody living next to a bungalow that was being converted into five bedsits and said it would reduce the value of his property; and an unbelievable story of a Labour member who had been assaulted by a Liberal Democrat when he distributed literature to his house.

Went to an adult-education centre to present certificates to 120 people who had been attending the centre. It was marvellous.

Sunday 19 November

There has been an explosion in Islamabad launched by Islamic extremists, killing people in the Egyptian Embassy. You can see Islam being built up as the great enemy of the West, but it's more complicated than that, because of the damage the West has done to Islam. A holy war would not be good for any of us.

At about eleven, I rang Michael Meacher and spoke to him for half an hour. There have been reports about rows in the Shadow Cabinet over this idea of cutting benefits. Apparently Blunkett, Straw, Harriet Harman and Meacher himself came out very strongly against cuts, were strongly supported by Robin Cook, who was apparently absolutely furious. The back-stabbing going on is on a very big scale without us even being in Government.

Monday 20 November

Went to my room at the Commons and watched the Princess Diana interview. She is a very disturbed person. She absolutely destroyed the Prince of Wales by what she said. She also admitted that she had had an affair with James Hewitt. The interview was full of self-pity and harassment. She did great damage to the monarchy. She said she wasn't sure Charles would ever be King, but William was a bit too young, and so on. I think she will just soar to the top of the popularity poll; but I also think it is the end of politics. We have seen socialism killed; we have seen Parliament diminished in public esteem; we have seen democracy undermined. And now we have seen the end of all politics, I think. Just back to a gossiping nation wondering what will happen to the royal princes and princesses.

Tuesday 21 November

Every front page of every paper is about Princess Diana. Even the *Guardian* had about five pages on it. I refused all invitations to comment.

I went to the Commons. Caroline went to teach. All the pupils have to sign learning agreements, and this is just a mass of paperwork that diverts from the teaching. Might just as well have lavatory agreements, where you agree to use the lavatories and the college agrees to provide the lavatories. It is complete madness.

Monday 27 November

Coming back from a television interview, I was driven by a Nigerian engineer and he described the enormous poverty and inflation there, and the money from 2.5 million barrels of oil a day that is all going into Swiss banks to protect the Government and buy off – indeed shoot – the opposition. It was quite horrific.

At five, Dr Romesh Chandra, the President of the World Peace Council, came to see me. He is seventy-six, an Indian and a very interesting man, an old communist of course. He told me that Cuba was going to survive because the Cuban Government lived at the same standard of living as the Cuban people – there was no elite there.

He was interested in the idea of a Fifth International, a popular layer below the NGOs and the General Assembly and Security Council of the UN. I really liked him and will keep in touch with him.

Had a real old gossip with Joan Lestor and Andrew Faulds. Joan said when that man had broken into the Queen's bedroom and was put away in a mental establishment, the following day the Queen had gone into hospital, allegedly to have a tooth removed; Joan thought she might have been attacked. This was absolutely tabloid gossip, but I put it down because it was interesting.

Came home and Rory Bremner had sent me the tape of the 'Benn and Skinner' sketch he had done. And I must say it was brilliant.

Wednesday 29 November

Late last night, John Bruton arrived in London and made a joint statement with John Major about Ireland. There are going to be preliminary talks now; then an international commission under Senator Mitchell, an American, on the arms question; then all-party talks no later than February. It was all pressurised by the fact that President Clinton arrived today, put a wreath on the Tomb of the Unknown Warrior, went to see the Prime Minister and the Queen and spoke to MPs. The fact that the Ulster Unionists are very angry indicates that, although it may be a fudge, it might be a helpful one.

I forgot to report what the Cuban Ambassador said to me this morning when he came; I may have forgotten to mention his visit. He told me about the changes in Cuba, where they are allowing cooperative farms to be set up instead of state farms, and how there are some private workers – plumbers and carpenters, and so on.

He said that when Fidel Castro went to New York for the fiftieth anniversary of the UN, he had been invited to lunch by David Rockefeller;

American industrialists are beginning to see the merits of investing in Cuba. The Ambassador said they were prospecting for oil there.

He was pretty sure that Cuba would pull through. He said there was some support in America, and Latin America, and that South Africa was supportive. So I got a rather encouraging account.

Friday 1 December
I got the train to Liverpool from where the Chairman of Warrington Constituency Labour Party drove me to their Annual Dinner. Doug Hoyle is one of the Members for Warrington, and the other is Mike Nichols. He must have come in in 1992. I spoke after the dinner and then they suggested questions and answers, and I must say it went down well. It was very friendly, and people came up and I signed menus and had photographs taken, and I did feel a bit of a celebrity; it is nice to feel the warmth. There is no doubt that that constituency is Old Labour.

Saturday 2 December
I forgot to mention that at the dinner last night there was a little girl of eleven called Erica who had helped in the election, and so they had recruited her as a member of the Labour Party. Walworth Road had said, 'Don't tell us how old she is' as she is an honorary member. She was a sweet, shy girl, passionately keen on politics. There were lots of pictures taken with her and other people there.

I have got to look ahead. My job is to be an MP and provide some support for the Labour movement and make some intellectual contribution. In January we will only be fifteen months away from the General Election.

There is quite a lot of interest in Arthur Scargill's new party. I have said nothing about it publicly. I am hoping, truthfully, that the failure of the next Labour Government will revitalise the Labour Party. Anyway, I don't want a row with Arthur, whom I greatly admire.

Monday 4 December
Melissa came to see me at the House. We had a lovely talk in my room. She had an excellent article in the *Guardian* this morning attacking the Government and the Archbishop of Canterbury for saying that the state of marriage was better in a long-term partnership, which really upset her.

There are huge strikes in France against the cuts in welfare, which are necessary to bring the franc into line with the Deutschmark in order to have a single currency. The French situation is fascinating because it is all sort of self-generating. When they show on the television that pensions and unemployment benefits in France are better than those in Britain, people will ask, 'Why the hell are they?'

Wednesday 6 December
Sheila and Ruth bought mince pies, quiches and bottles of wine and we went to the Jubilee Room in the Commons to set up for the launch party of *Westminster Behind Closed Doors*. Charles and Julia Frater, who directed and edited it, were there. The Chaplain, Canon Donald Gray, was there and Sir Patrick Cormack, the chairman of the Works of Art Committee; we had invited the staff who had taken part, and some of them were also there; Chris Mullin turned up. It was a lovely occasion. Ann Tyerman, the commissioning editor from the BBC, was there, very worried because we hadn't had permission to film everywhere.

I had received a really lovely letter from the Prime Minister saying:

> Dear Tony,
>
> Thank you for inviting me to attend the preview and for your kind references to the shot of me and Norma on VE Day. Sadly, I fear I will be unable to join you due to my absence in Florence. I shall certainly hope to see a copy of the broadcast next Monday.
>
> With all good wishes.
>
> Yours ever,
>
> John

Then underneath, in his own handwriting:

'Many congratulations on 45 years. An astonishing achievement that few will match, and what's more you enjoyed it. I am sorry I missed the programme, I will try and tape the broadcast. John.' I must say, I do rather value my relations with the Prime Minister; first of all, because he is very powerful, and secondly because I am keen to make it clear that politics is not about personalities. But also, as a mark of this friendly relationship, I am hoping that he will let me bring my cameras into Whitehall to film *Whitehall Behind Closed Doors*.

Monday 10 December
I had another letter from the Prime Minister in manuscript:

> Dear Tony,
>
> Many thanks for the video. <u>I thought</u> I knew the House well, but I learned a lot and it is, as one of the ladies said, a village. And <u>you</u> were dead right about the media.
>
> Yours,
>
> John

Well, the funny thing was that the letter had been sent to Tony Blair's office in error. They had opened it and read it and forwarded it on. So I thought I had better tell the Prime Minister. So when John Major came through the Lobby I said,

'Thank you very much for your note.'

He said, 'Norma and I watched the video on Saturday.'

I said, 'I must tell you this John. your letter was opened by Tony Blair's office and returned to me.'

'Will he think there has been a plot?'

Thursday 14 December

There were very serious riots in Brixton last night. A twenty-five-year-old black man was arrested in a burglary raid and then died in custody. The police said he died of a heart attack, and a lot of blacks gathered outside the police station and, from what I can understand, the police brought out the full riot squad. There was burning and looting. And of course the police said it was criminal elements.

When I got to the House, I found a very shirty letter from the Speaker saying:

> Thank you for sending me a copy, and I know you will not object if I describe it as an affectionate if idiosyncratic portrayal of Parliament . . . Our rules and procedures are set in place to protect the privileges that underpin our democratic freedoms and I am sad that so senior a Member as you should have thought fit to disregard them.

Then she wrote in her own hand, 'All good wishes for the festive season, Yours, Betty.' So I suppose the letter was written by the Speaker's secretary and then she probably tried to soften it a bit. I thought it was better not to reply, but I'll have a word with her and be really cheerful.

Sunday 17 December

Read the papers in bed. Maggie O'Kane had an extremely interesting article on the Gulf War. She described how the American troops who advanced on the Basra road pursuing the retreating armies had simply used bulldozers to bury them alive. It was a war crime on a massive scale.

I decorated the Christmas tree.

The euro is the name of the new single currency that is going to be imposed on us and the Tories are beginning to revolt. I think it is time the left took some initiative in the House of Commons.

There was a lot about this head teacher Philip Lawrence who was knifed to death outside his school in London – obviously a very good man.

Monday 18 December

Sheila said something to me today, 'You know, people think of you as a leader of the left and if you appear in a new role as a sort of interpreter of Parliament they may like you very much, but they won't look to you to provide a lead.' I have a lot of time for Sheila.

So I think it may be that I shouldn't pursue this idea of becoming a television star. I mustn't opt out of Labour politics. So that is my thought at the moment: go back into politics in 1996.

Tuesday 19 December

I went to Bush House to do *Outlook* for the World Service. The first item was on genetic engineering and they quoted the Prince of Wales saying that it was absolutely disgraceful to play the part of God. I was asked to comment, so I said, 'It is strange, coming from the Prince of Wales, because the monarchy in Britain is a piece of genetic engineering, depending on who your parents were, what bed you were born in and at what time.' The whole crew in the control room just killed themselves laughing.

Came back to the House and plucked up my courage to go up to Betty in the Speaker's Chair. I said, 'Thanks for your note, and best wishes for Christmas.' She gave me an absolutely charming smile which confirmed what I had suspected: namely that the letter she had written was a formal letter that she had to write; but it hadn't really altered her perception of the programme.

Thursday 21 December

Rodney Bickerstaffe told me a lovely story by Tommy Douglas, the Canadian socialist: the story of Mouseland. In Mouseland, the mice were always ruled by black cats. So one day they got together and said, 'It's not very good. Let's elect white cats.' So they elected white cats, who immediately set up a speed limit for mice so that it was easier for cats to catch them, and introduced bigger mouseholes so that they could get their paws in and pull the mice out. So then the mice said, 'Let's elect black cats with white spots.' But that didn't work. Then they elected white cats with black spots, and that was no better. So one of the mice said, 'Why don't *we* put up a candidate?' and he was immediately locked up as a revolutionary.

It is a very nice story.

Saturday 23 December

A woman rang me from Chesterfield; she had been to one of my surgeries. She said she was in a council house that didn't have a cooker or a bed, and she had a boy of seven. Her husband had left, but they wouldn't give her any money from the social fund. So I rang around, and finally Social Services did send somebody to go and look at her circumstances. I had done what I could, but she said she was going to go to the press; however, the report I had from Social Services was that nobody believed what she said and that she was very violent when she went to their offices.

Tuesday 26 December
The *Daily Mail* gave a lot of coverage to the book that Peter Mandelson and Roger Liddle have written, a sort of manifesto for the Labour Party calling for a Lib-Lab coalition, the abolition of child benefit, keeping the unions under legislative control, breaking the power of local education authorities – absolute Tory ideas. *The Independent* rang and asked me for a comment, so I said they ought to get Michael Portillo to write an article denouncing it as having gone too far to the right. The fact is that the Labour Party has got within it a nest of right-wingers who would be on the right wing of the Tory Party. But, just as the left were defeated in the mid-Eighties, so they will be defeated in the late Nineties, because you can't have a situation so totally remote from reality.

Friday 29 December
Emma Nicholson, the MP for Devon West and Torridge, has defected from the Tories to the Liberals.

Saturday 30 December
Dick Taverne has been made a Peer. My God, those who defect get rewarded.

Wednesday 3 January 1996
This evening there was a marvellous programme on Channel 4 called *How to Tell Lies and Win Wars*. Maggie O'Kane revealed the lies told about Iraqi brutalities in Kuwait, lies organised by a PR company, and how Bush took them up. Depleted uranium has caused quite serious radiation problems and there were very evasive answers from Tom King. The programme dealt with the burying alive of Iraqi soldiers by American bulldozers; the oil slick caused by the West bombing tankers in the Gulf; the so-called 'smart bombs' that could hit a man in the corner of a room, which comprised only 6 per cent of the total, the rest being free-fall bombs. It also dealt with the media and how it had been taken in.

Thursday 4 January
At ten, Mr Ibrahim, the Iraqi Chargé d'Affaires, came to see me. He said the suffering as a result of sanctions is quite appalling, and was there any chance of changing it? He keeps in touch with Ted Heath and Tam Dalyell. The Labour Party is quite hopeless and won't see him.

Ibrahim thought the American strategy was to divide Iraq, an idea that King Hussein had come up with, which would mean that the south was under the Shi'ites, the centre part would be under Baghdad and the north would be under the Kurds; Iraq, which has plenty of land and natural resources, could rehouse all the Palestinians who couldn't be taken back to what is now Israel.

I asked about Ibrahim's family. His daughter is at Brunel doing a degree in interior design and architecture. His son is dyslexic, but after some years of hard work has just got near his Bachelor degree.

To Chesterfield, where Ruth set up the camera and filmed the whole surgery. Only one of the thirteen people didn't want to be filmed. There were three single-parent mothers; two women, one of whom had a son imprisoned for rape; a man who had been in prison for trying to abduct his wife and child; an old couple with problems with noisy children; a woman who had been denied the gravestone she wanted for her father. It really was an interesting surgery.

Monday 7 January

I rang Alan Clark this evening about the history of the Tory Party that he is writing and thanked him for his invitation to go to lunch at Saltwood Castle, but said I couldn't manage it. He is going to come here instead.

He is very interested in oil policy under the Tories. He thinks the Tories made a muck of it. They had really just given the oil away from 1970 to 1974 and we tried to grab it back; I got about 25 per cent before we were defeated in 1979. He said, 'That was probably Britain's last chance and we wasted it.'

He went on, 'It's funny, Macmillan's name is never mentioned. He used to be known as Grandfather Harold. He was a very shrewd man really, but he was just obliterated by the memory of Maggie.' Alan Clark, needless to say, was a great supporter of Thatcher. 'Ted Heath is going a bit gaga, but I occasionally talk to him.'

Of course, the man is a serious historian. He is very right-wing, absolutely unashamed of his sexual adventures. He is very nationalistic. He said, 'If this Europe business goes too far, the Tory Party will be in trouble after the election.'

I said I supposed the party would go mainly Euro-sceptic.

Then Clark said, 'Redwood is a fool.'

'I thought he was more of an intellectual than Portillo.'

'Maybe, but Portillo has got a much higher standing in the Party.'

Monday 8 January

Lot of coverage of Tony Blair's speech to Singapore businessmen about 'the stakeholder economy'.

This had been taken up as the big idea, comparing it to 'never had it so good' and the 'classless society'. Of course, there is absolutely no substance of any sort or kind in it. If you are unemployed or homeless, what does the stakeholder economy mean? It must mean the dismantling of the Welfare State in favour of the tiger economies of Asia.

It is meaningless. But they got Austin Mitchell on tonight to say he thought it would have great potential, and Blunkett said the same.

I went to Humphrey Ocean's studio in Lambeth. He is very charming, a youngish man born in 1950.

Tuesday 9 January

Heard – very sad – that Bruce Kent had left the Labour Party because he could no longer defend it. It reminded me of an occasion not so long ago when, in a discussion with Bruce Kent, he was defending Kinnock and accusing me of splitting the Party.

First day of Parliament after the recess, and I do feel a bit lonely there. There is a part of me that says, 'Look, face the facts, Tony, you are an old man, you are out of date, things have moved on. There is a whole new generation that believes in market forces, capitalism, the lottery, doesn't like the unions, likes globalisation. You don't, but how many people do you represent?' So there is a part of me that thinks it is time to move on.

Wednesday 10 January

Went to the Commons and was stopped in Hyde Park for speeding by two policemen with a new electronic device. They said, 'We are not going to report you, though you were doing forty-one mph.' I said, 'Thank you.' and he said, 'And do up your seat belt.' So I thought I escaped quite lightly.

Thursday 11 January

I went over to see Margaret Beckett. I have somewhat fallen out with her over the years, particularly when she was Deputy Leader. She is now the Shadow Secretary of State for Trade and Industry.

I asked her about Millbank Tower and she said the Party had taken part of the ground floor and first floor. She described how it was wired into all of the media outlets, and so on; and the new Head of Policy who has just been appointed was previously in charge of the Rebuttal unit which responds to Conservative attacks. So all policy has really been subordinated to fighting the campain.

I asked about policy and the Manifesto and she said, 'I think Tony has got that in hand.' They are not going to issue policy statements, but make speeches on certain subjects and then it will all be drawn together in some way.

She asked about the DTI. I told her it was a big department (not as big as it had been in 1969); I mentioned to her the oil round the Falkland Islands, which is greater than the oil round the UK. I said, 'I don't know how you would get hold of any of the revenues, because they will be leased to private companies and some will go to the Falkland Islands'.

I continued, 'After the election, there is obviously going to be a lot of pressure for high interest rates.' She did admit that in 1992 John Smith had asked the Treasury if it had a contingency plan for raising interest rates.

I asked her how we would cope if we found the Treasury empty when we got there. Beckett said she thought that John Smith's Shadow Budget was a mistake, which I did too – it came too late. She was very vague about the stakeholder economy, but said, 'I think, if we are a stakeholder economy, that means nobody is excluded, which must mean full employment.' She went on, 'I know that when John Smith mentioned full employment at the TUC in 1993, Tony Blair was horrified and thought it was a totally irresponsible thing to say.'

Then I said something about the proposal for the Welfare State and the tiger economies. She said, 'I think a lot of that is just for show. There won't be any basic change in the Welfare State.'

'Well, what about Europe? It would seem to me that a referendum would be sensible.'

'John Smith was never against it in principle, but he wanted to get a bit nearer before he agreed.'

'I think John Major will do it.'

'He won't, because of the Euro-enthusiasts. They would never agree to it.'

At the end I said, 'We have had a few differences, but if there is any way I can help, I would be happy to do so.'

I don't know what she expected. I was interested in what she had to say, particularly on proportional representation – that Peter Mandelson and Blair were both bitterly opposed to it, which I didn't know. I said, 'Well, I think it would be crazy, if we got a clear majority, to cut it immediately by introducing PR.'

Her difficulty is very straightforward. She and Michael Meacher and Gavin Strang, figures of the old left, will be ditched in the first reshuffle, just go without trace, and I think she knows that and may be looking for friends.

Friday 12 January

Mrs Thatcher in a speech yesterday praised John Redwood and rubbished the One Nation policy idea; and there was an interesting article in the *Telegraph* reporting Sir Keith Joseph's last speech, in which he said that he wanted a stakeholder economy. So we are in a situation where there is a total meltdown in British politics.

To Chesterfield later, and I went to the Labour Club to talk about what a Labour Government would do when it was elected. It got very tense. I realise that the working class and socialist element in the Chesterfield party is diminishing, as Chesterfield moves from being a mining and manufacturing town to being a leisure town. One young lad asked,

'What's wrong with the House of Lords? They are independent. We must have independent people.'

It has been eleven years since the miners' strike ended and there has been a big change in the political climate; Blair represents that sort of group.

Saturday 13 January

It was announced that Arthur Scargill had decided to launch the Socialist Labour Party on 1 May. Mike Mansfield is involved, Caroline Sikorski, and others.

Tuesday 16 January

At three, Alan Clark and his research assistant, who has got a PhD from Cambridge, came to the office. He was very friendly.

He wanted to talk in more detail about oil: BP should have been the instrument, they should have taken the whole of the North Sea over and developed it entirely; we should have sold the oil at the cost of production – about $7 or $8 a barrel – instead of at the world price, which was $30 a barrel. He really made the point that the Conservative Party had abandoned the national interest, and he looked to me as somebody who had defended the national interest, which I had. He is a funny, maverick character really – the son of Sir Kenneth Clark, whom I met when he was Chairman of the Stamp Advisory Committee. I reminded Alan of that and showed him some of the stamps I had commissioned without the Queen's head on them.

We gossiped a bit. He had no time for Blair, and thought Major was much underestimated. He is going to try and get into the next Parliament as an MP. He gave up in 1992 because it was all so boring, but he thought next time round – when the bloodshed began in the Tory Party – he would like to be there. He is anti-European and a Thatcherite in a way, but a humanitarian Thatcherite; a strange and complex person.

He said Heseltine would never get the job, although, after another series of catastrophic local-election defeats that he anticipates in May, he thought Heseltine might try to take over the leadership.

Clark commented, 'It is quite untrue that Edward VIII was got rid of because he was pro-fascist, because the Government was pro-fascist.' And he continued, 'National Socialism is very appealing, it has populist appeal.'

I said, 'Well, if you separate fascism from the gas chambers, it is in a way what we have been having.'

He didn't disagree with that. He said he thought that when Rudolf Hess came to England in 1941, he had so many contacts that the whole file had to be suppressed and hasn't been released. When it is released, it will be an amazing story.

He was very candid and courteous, and said he thought I was 'the greatest Labour figure since Ernie Bevin', which I thought was an interesting and unexpected parallel.

Clark also said, 'I want to get back into Parliament because, if you are not in, whatever you say, nobody takes any notice unless you have submitted yourself to the electorate.'

That is the case against retirement.

In the House tonight, sitting in the Lobby, nobody came up to speak to me. It is very lonely really.

Wednesday 17 January

I went to Number 10 with a whole group of Iraqi primary-school children and two or three secondary-school children, who had all written letters to the Prime Minister about the sanctions. Five of them and I marched up to Number10; the policeman was very friendly and the children handed in their letters. They were told that the Prime Minister would reply. It was very moving and the kids were so excited.

Monday 22 January

Harriet Harman has decided to send her son to St Olaf's grant-maintained school in Orpington, and the row is boiling and the media is enjoying every moment of it. The Tories are laughing themselves silly. According to the evening papers, Tony Blair has ordered the Shadow Cabinet to keep quiet about it. Joy Johnson, the Party's press officer, has resigned, no doubt under pressure.

It is the first serious setback Blair has had and I think it will have considerable repercussions. Blunkett had to cancel the launch of his new education statement and the debate went wrong in the afternoon.

I now have to make a major speech shortly saying that New Labour is a new political party and has very little to do with the Labour Party.

Tuesday 23 January

The Harriet Harman story is dominating everything.

Prime Minister's Questions was absolutely hilarious on television. Kenneth Baker began by asking John Major whether he didn't agree that the decision by Harriet Harman to send her child to a grammar school showed that she must be a stakeholder at heart. Major agreed. Then Blair got up and said, 'You can't use an eleven-year-old child to undo the damage done by the Government.'

So Major said, 'Well, all I am doing is being tough on hypocrisy and tough on the causes of hypocrisy,' which was a mockery of Blair's famous phrase that Labour was tough on crime and tough on the causes of crime.

Then another Tory got up and said, 'Shouldn't the Prime Minister congratulate the head of St Olaf's school on attracting children from fifteen miles and two boroughs away.'

The Tories just collapsed in laughter and the Labour Party was incensed with anger – left, right and centre. Allan Rogers, who was a great Kinnock loyalist, was furious and said, 'After the election is over, I am going to speak my mind.'

I don't think Harriet Harman has any idea what has happened. Jack Dromey, her husband, who tried to get elected as General Secretary of the TGWU, was interviewed saying, 'She'll tough it out.' Blair is supposed to have said that his job was on the line, and Prescott is supposed to have gone into the Tea Room and exploded, and said 'Harriet Harman should resign.'

Hattersley was on television saying it was the worst week for Blair since he became Leader.

Wednesday 24 January

The Party meeting at which Harriet Harman's statement was discussed, was at 11.30. It was one of the most crowded meetings I have attended. Doug Hoyle, the Chairman, said he had had a lot of requests from people to speak.

The first was Michael Martin. He said, 'We are a deeply wounded party. I chose a comprehensive for my children. I had exactly the same choice to make as Harriet and, although the kids had a difficult time, it made us a better family. People will say: if you can do it in Education, why not in Health? Harriet is our spokesman on Health. My constituency Labour Party won three council by-elections recently and I can tell you that there are old stalwarts, who fought in the 1945 election, who are deeply worried by what has happened. Harriet should reconsider her decision.'

Then we had Judith Church. She said, 'London schools are no good and I want to make an appeal for unity. I had to pay £150,000 to get a house in an area with a good comprehensive school. Now you have to pay £450,000 for a house, to get into that same school. ILEA messed up education in London and nowadays, for a child to survive in a London comprehensive, you need knife skills; and there is terrible bullying. You can't sacrifice your children for your principles.'

Alice Mahon said, 'Harriet got us into it, and now she has got to get us out of it by resigning. I am not saying you are not a good parent, but you can't do both jobs.'

Gerald Kaufman, who sits for a Manchester seat, said, 'I represent a prime inner-city area. There are three independent schools there that get two million pounds for "assisted places". We need a Labour Government in order to get that money from the assisted places scheme into the deprived areas. There will be tremendous pressure on a Labour Government and, regardless of the decision, we must be united. I have been twenty-six years in the Commons, twenty-one in Opposition – we can do nothing in Opposition.'

'My fear,' said Roy Hattersley, 'is that the Party is retreating from comprehensives and saying we dare not alienate parents who want to send their children to selective schools. Well, we dare not alienate the parents who want a decent comprehensive system. We lost the 1992 election because of all this gossip about Lib-Lab arrangements just before polling day. We should reaffirm our position. We need money for schools in London. The best answer to criticism would be a strong reaffirmation of our comprehensives.'

Bernie Grant supported Harriet Harman. 'The schools in London are rotten. I kept quiet in the PLP when our principles were being trampled on but I am not keeping quiet now. A friend is someone who lends you money. A comrade is someone who helps you when you are in the shit.' Everybody laughed, but it was amazing that Bernie came out like that.

Paul Flynn said, 'In 1945, Labour was seen as representing ordinary people, and the Tories the fat cats. You can't preach equality and practise privilege. What I am afraid of is that there are a lot of beautiful people around the Leader, admiring each other all the time, and they are more and more remote from the PLP. You get all these tortured editorials, and so on, but the image we are getting is that the Labour Party is like the Tory Party and this approach is stealing our idealism and the core of our conviction. All parents don't have the chance to make a choice. Harriet Harman has given the Tories ammunition and she should resign.'

'I don't like what Harriet Harman has done, but Labour v. Tories is the issue; we are uniting behind the Tory Party in making an issue of this. The greatest damage that could be done is if we lost the election. We must be united.' That was Glenda Jackson.

When Harriet Harman got up, she said she understood the distress of her colleagues. 'Education matters to all of us. I am opposed to selection. I support the policy. Our decision was for our son. I know how tough it is. I was dismayed that the Tories attacked me, and I am sorry for any embarrassment.'

Tony Blair got up, smirking all the time. He said he always knew a story like this was going to be an issue. He understood the hurt felt by the Party – decisions cause anguish. He would say two things: firstly, there was no change in our policy on selection and in favour of comprehensive education; secondly, the issue was not about Harriet, but about how we handled ourselves. 'The Tories want a scalp. I won't give them a scalp, or be like the Tories. Every morning I wake up and realise that my responsibility is to see Labour get into government. These are very tough judgements that have to be made; they test you to the limit and beyond. I see what the Government has done to my country. I won't allow anything to prevent me getting there. The public will look at our character, and I won't let them take away a member of my Shadow Cabinet.'

It was the most insubstantial speech really. He isn't all that tough.

I am glad I went to the Party meeting because otherwise I wouldn't have picked up the flavour of the passion against Harriet Harman. Mandelson was sitting there, no doubt having drafted every word of Blair's speech – and Harriet's as well.

After that I went into the House, and the Prime Minister made a statement on the Mitchell Report. Everybody welcomed it – Blair, Ashdown, Tom King; David Trimble, the Ulster Unionist Leader, was overjoyed by it.

The media are now trying to get on to Stephen and Hilary about their time at Holland Park School.

Tonight the press reported 'Blair crushes the revolt'; the BBC reported on the defeat of Old Labour. The media just take the spin from Mandelson and the others who explain what has happened, without any regard for the truth. So the press are still prepared to keep Blair going, and yet the reports they give are wholly false. But that's the BBC; you can't rely on them for anything.

Thursday 25 January

I am a bit depressed really because it is not just the policies that have moved on, but this repudiation and rejection of anyone who did anything before Blair came to be Leader is very wounding.

Saturday 27 January

Today the Tories launched a big poster campaign with a picture of Blair and Harriet Harman saying, 'Do as we say and not as we do.'

Monday 29 January

I went and had a third two-hour session with the artist Humphrey Ocean and all he has got is a rough outline. He worked on my eyes and eyebrows. I asked how many more sessions and he said three or four. Well, that would be another eight hours and it is a bit much really, but he is a charming man. It is a bit boring, really, except that I can smoke my pipe.

Tuesday 30 January

At Prime Minister's Questions, once again, Major did very, very well against Blair. Major is relaxed and amusing, and he is very good; Tory morale has gone through the roof.

I had a word with Joan Lestor about him and she said, 'Well, there you are, that's the working-class boy dealing with the public-school boy.' I thought there was something in that.

I was depressed last night, but I am a bit more cheerful today.

Wednesday 31 January
Very busy day. I should record, to give some indication of the change in the balance of work of a Member of Parliament, that I had three cases – telephone calls and faxes – about international issues. I had a message from Turkey that some Iranian refugees had been arrested and were likely to be sent back to Iran, where they might be tortured or killed. I had a fax from a group of Pakistani workers saying that the General Secretary of their union was having trouble getting a visa to visit Britain. And I had a fax from Alex Falconer, the Member of the European Parliament for Fife, saying that the European Union was trying to lower the level of human rights and other requirements to justify Turkey entering the EU.

Saturday 3 February
I was thinking of my life today, how well organised it is. I have got Sheila working in London and Margaret in Chesterfield. I can take my car and park at the House of Commons. I have got a room at the Commons. If I go to St Pancras, they let me park in the station, so I just drive there and get straight onto the train to Chesterfield. I have got my bungalow in Chesterfield. I have got my Psion organiser with all my contacts on it. I am quite happy to spend most of my day, as I did today, on organisation rather than actually doing anything! But when I do get round to doing it, it is all very efficient.

Monday 5 February
I took a taxi to Kettners restaurant for a meeting of the Conservative Graduates Association. I suppose the average age was thirty-five or forty. They had written a nice letter saying that they respected me for sticking to my principles, and I thought it would be rather fun to put an argument and see if I could answer their questions.

It was a very interesting evening. First of all, on Europe, they were sympathetic. They were obviously – by an overwhelming majority, I should think – anti the single currency.

They were worried by what I said about profits, and tried to make out that customers and profit were the way to spread prosperity. But what I felt was that their ideas on this line had been so unchallenged for so long that, when you challenged them, they couldn't think of the answers. But they laughed at all my jokes and, at the end, warm compliments were paid.

On the way back I asked my taxi driver what he did before he became a driver. He said, 'I was a molecular biologist.' So that was another to add to the list of people who have been driven by market forces from a high degree of skill to driving a cab.

Tuesday 6 February
To a lobby at the House of people protesting against the supply of Hawk aircraft to Indonesia; the Indonesian Government has used them to crush East Timor. I think 200,000 people have been killed. There was a very tough crowd of people there from Greenham Common, I think. Paul Flynn and I were the only two MPs.

The women had apparently got into a BAC plant and hammered a Hawk aircraft and done £1 million worth of damage. I was interviewed about it.

Wednesday 7 February
I had instructions, as did every MP, from Labour Party headquarters as to how pictures of Blair, and his autograph, were to be used in any Party publicity. A form of words was given, and no other form of words was to be used unless they had been cleared with the Leader's Office. And clipped to this were about thirty photographs of Blair. It is absolutely the cult of personality. Incredible.

This evening Tony Blair made a speech on constitutional reform, saying that hereditary peers would lose the right to sit and vote, but of course many of those who are active would be made life peers. In future, he said, the Lords would be an appointed second chamber. Also, there would be an Assembly in Wales, a Parliament in Scotland. We would adhere to the European Convention on Human Rights. Local authorities will be able to elect mayors instead of having councils with a leader. Tony Banks was quite enthusiastic about it. He said, 'Well, whatever you may think, it is a cautious economic policy, but it is radical in this direction.' He himself had advocated an elected Mayor of London, like the Mayor of New York or Paris or Berlin. Tony also thought that getting rid of hereditary peers removed a brick in the edifice of the hereditary system, and that may be so.

Friday 9 February
The seven o'clock news announced that there was a bomb at Canary Wharf; clearly the ceasefire in Ireland has been suspended. The IRA admitted planting it. Gerry Adams said he was very saddened by it, but that peace was his main objective. Obviously he is embarrassed by it.

Monday 12 February
There was a storm in the night and when I went into the bathroom there was water coming through the ceiling. Caroline got out onto the flat roof and, though it was pelting with rain and icy cold, she scooped the leaves away with her fingers. I should have done it, but with the effects of my Guillain-Barré disease, I was afraid I would fall over the wall into the garden.

Steve Richards came to my room. He is a great friend of Joy Johnson, who was appointed by Blair a year ago to be Head of Campaigns in the Labour Party. Apparently she got the job because Gordon Brown, the Shadow Chancellor, had said he was entitled to have somebody he liked and trusted. She was apparently to the left of Brown, which is not difficult. Blair asked her if she could get on with Peter Mandelson. She said she was sure she could, but she had only been there a week or two when he began undermining her. Richards said he had interviewed Blair about the bombing in Docklands before Blair had had a chance of getting on to either Alastair Campbell or Peter Mandelson, and he didn't know what to say.

Wednesday 14 February

I went into the Commons in the afternoon for a meeting in the Moses Room which is in the House of Lords, to discuss Ireland. But because there was going to be a Sinn Fein speaker present, Black Rod got on to Lord Boston, the Chairman of Committees, who said he felt he was interpreting the will of the House of Lords in denying access to Sinn Fein. So we moved rooms. Utterly disgraceful.

We all crowded into a little room off Westminster Hall, packed to the doors. Brian Fitzgerald, the Chief Whip of the Irish Labour Party and active in the Forum for Peace and Reconciliation, and Francis Molloy for Sinn Fein both spoke. Fitzgerald said the bomb had changed the agenda. He condemned the outrage and regretted it. He said the IRA had reopened the war and he expressed his condolences. It was now the IRA versus the people. He said Sinn Fein had been shocked. He welcomed Francis Molloy coming and called on the IRA to stop the violence. It was a very good speech.

Then Francis Molloy said he welcomed the initiative, and he was equally impatient. You mustn't isolate the leadership of Sinn Fein. He said Adams spoke for everyone when he remarked that a great opportunity had been missed because of the bombing.

Fitzgerald also said that the IRA could not accept the fact that 98 per cent of the Irish found the bombs unacceptable.

Sunday 18 February

There was a a bomb in Wellington Street tonight, just off the Aldwych, which blew up a double-decker bus. Obviously the ceasefire is completely over.

Monday 19 February

I went to the House to hear the Attorney General, Nicholas Lyell, defending himself against the charge that he had wrongly handled the public-interest immunity certificates in the Iraqi arms situation. He is a bland guy and smiles, but he didn't go down very well with the House. The hunting of William Waldegrave and Lyell is not what it's really about.*

I had a bite to eat with Joan Lestor who is frightfully depressed. She said she knew perfectly well that she was going to be sacked in the first reshuffle after the election. I can understand how she feels and I said, 'Look, hang on, because just to be there and to see the Blair Government and how it works will be of great value, and if you don't want to stay you don't have to.' She said Clare Short has gone completely; she is not standing for the Executive this year. The NEC is simply not worth being on.

There is snow in London. They appear to have caught one of the guys who blew up the bus – one man was dead and they've picked another up. There was a gun on the bus, but probably the bus was not the intended target.

Wednesday 21 February

Worked in my office telephone-canvassing my constituents. So far I've only spoken to ten people, of whom two said, 'You're joking' when I said it was the MP speaking. I said, 'In a few minutes you'll hear Big Ben striking,' which they did in one case. People were cautious – a bit suspicious, I think. I asked them if they were in work and if they had any problems. If I phone five people a night, that's 500 people in a year.

Sunday 24 February

Lissie told me that she was expecting a second baby on 29 August. Caroline hadn't told, me but she never does!

Monday 26 February

An article by Julie Kirkbride in the *Sunday Telegraph* claimed that the Labour leadership was very worried about all the old MPs there might be in the next Parliament; photos of me, Dennis Skinner, Geoffrey Lofthouse and Bob Sheldon and saying they were afraid we might not live through the next Parliament and there might be by-elections at awkward times. It is the second or third time this story has appeared. It just creates a flavour of anxiety and it is ageist, because there are nine million pensioners who need to be represented.

Went to the Commons and we had the debate on the Scott Report after lunch. The House was packed because of all the rumours that the Government might be defeated – how would David Trimble vote? What would Paisley do? Robin Cook delivered a devastating attack on Waldegrave, who had been at the FO at the time, and on Nicholas Lyell,

* Sir Richard Scott's report into the export of arms to Iraq in breach of Government guidelines had investigated the basis for strategic export controls and the procedures and practices followed by departments.

but the thing was totally unsatisfactory, as if the whole question of our relations with Iraq and the Gulf War and the arms trade could be summarised in this issue.

I didn't think my speech – which was about our relations with Iraq, the sanctions and the arms trade – went down very well with our side because we were just hoping to get a Tory defeat and the heads of two Ministers, whereas I broadened it out.

But Patrick Cormack, the Tory MP, congratulated me on my speech and William Waldegrave said, as he passed me, 'Yours was the best speech.' I thought that was a bit odd.

The Government won by one vote; every Labour MP, including people brought in in ambulances, was there: Roland Boyes, who's got Alzheimer's; John Fraser, who has a neck brace; and others. We lost by one vote. Ian Paisley abstained, and David Trimble and the Ulster Unionists voted with us because they were angry that they didn't get a deal on elections in Northern Ireland.

Friday 1 March, Chesterfield

A surgery from twelve to five with a succession of Child Support Agency cases. It is simply unspeakable. All these cases are dealt with in Northern Ireland by the agency, with circumstances changing all the time. As an MP you get both sides of a case and it is a disastrous Act.

Ron Davies, the Shadow Welsh Secretary, said on a TV programme tonight that the Prince of Wales, who talked to trees and flowers and then let his sons hunt, was quite unsuitable to be King. Blair and the Prince of Wales were both in Wales today, and Blair forced Davies to recant.

Tuesday 5 March

I had a leaflet sent to me, published by the British National Party, denouncing the fact that Merton Council has approved planning permission for a mosque in Morden. On the back of it was written, 'Rat Benn – Here it is spelled out – you are part of a treason on your own race and people for the Jew Communists – one world mongrels.' Well, the idea that Jewish communists would be demanding mosques is a bit absurd; but the way in which the fascist movement does appear from time to time is interesting.

Wednesday 6 March

Caroline and I got up early and we walked to the Tate Gallery for the Cézanne exhibition, to which I'd been invited by Humphrey Ocean, who is painting my portrait for the National Portrait Gallery. Probably the finest Cézanne collection ever brought together in one place. What I noted was that the whole Establishment was there. Really quite amusing. Lord Palumbo, Sir Crispin Tickell, Margaret Jay, Peter Parker, former

Chairman of British Rail. He said that railway privatisation was an absolute tragedy, and corrupt: 'The whole thing will collapse and really good people are being sacked.' He was really quite moved and I agreed with him entirely.

I saw Peter Mandelson slithering in. Had breakfast with some of Humphrey's friends.

Friday 8 March

Had a phone call from the *Independent on Sunday* saying that, following their announcement two weeks ago that they were a republican newspaper, they had asked for nominations for an elected president and the result was that I came well to the top, with Betty Boothroyd next, Jarvis Cocker third and Helena Kennedy fourth. That did make me laugh.

Saturday 9 March

Up at five and had breakfast and a bath, then caught the train to Doncaster. On the train was Simon Pirana from the Workers' Revolutionary Party, who edits the *Yorkshire Miner*. We talked about Gerry Healy and Vanessa Redgrave and the split in the WRP eleven years ago, precipitated because Gerry Healy's sexual behaviour was so outrageous. It wasn't just that he was a womaniser, but that he used sexual harassment and terror on young women. They came to the movement with a desire for socialism and then found they were in his bed.

Caroline once heard Healy – an old seaman – speak and she said he made a most passionate speech, had an electric personality; he certainly captured the imagination of Vanessa Redgrave and Corin, and so on. But these little groups are really out of touch with reality. If you take the left now, there is the Socialist Organiser, Socialist Workers' Party, Socialist Movement, Socialist Labour Party, and the Socialist Alliance formed by Ron Brown, the former MP for Leith, which Arthur refers to contemptuously as the Libyan Connection. Then there is Militant. There are lots of socialist parties, but not enough socialists. So I think I'm happier in the Labour Party.

Wednesday 13 March

Was picked up by car on the way to do a CBS broadcast; on the one o'clock news there was an absolute tragedy. Sixteen people aged five and six have been victims of a shooting incident at a primary school in Dunblane in Scotland. The whole nation is in shock and I heard later that it was a Scout master who had been involved in some trouble in the past.

Came back to the House and to the Campaign Group, where we had a discussion on the Child Support Act, led by Mildred Gordon and Jean Corston. Mildred said that Labour had supported it because they thought absent fathers should pay their whack towards children. The Tory aim was to cut benefits and discourage divorce. More than 40 per cent of absent fathers were unemployed, and the CSA could now deduct £4.80 a week from their income support. Most mothers getting CSA help were worse off, and the old court settlements that dealt with maintenance had now been pushed aside. By the time Labour comes to power they would be millions of pounds in arrears, and imprisonment of absent fathers might occur.

The Act led to tension between the two wives, when there was a second marriage. Jean Corston talked about pregnant girls from Bristol East who had been on the radio and said they simply wouldn't put the names of the fathers on the birth certificates. The Tories were quite ignorant of the workings of the Act.

Sunday 17 March
I feel I'm on a chicken run at the moment – just going round and round. I don't want anyone listening to this to think I'm finished, but you go up and down, and tonight I am a bit down.

It's an awful thing to admit, but you can see how attractive the House of Lords is: to be there without a constituency, without elections, just making the occasional speech in the place. I couldn't ever take one of Mr Blair's peerages, but I can see the appeal.

Wednesday 20 March
The Government has had to admit that mad-cow disease may affect human beings, which will have a huge effect on the sale of beef, which has already fallen by a quarter since rumours of this.

Saturday 23 March, Chesterfield
Had breakfast and walked down to the Winding Wheel centre for the Women's Institute Science Exhibition. It was tremendous. The Police Scientific Department took my fingerprints and gave me a bookmark with them on. But the WI is shrinking. Nobody is joining it. It is mainly composed of old people, and I had a certain feeling for them because the Labour Party has a lot of old members too. The Methodists are also shrinking at a rate of 2.5 per cent a year because nobody joins. Maybe it is the function of organisations to die – it makes you very affectionate towards them. It makes you wonder whether the Labour Party is dying.

The banning of British beef abroad is big news, and what has come out is the Government deregulation of the industries producing bonemeal using offal for cow-feed. A farmer on *Any Answers?* on Radio 4 said that he had cattle and he could not get the suppliers to tell him what was in the bonemeal that he bought. An organic farmer said he only feeds cattle in his own fields on grass and natural products so there that was no possible risk of BSE.

Trimble spoke at the Unionist Conference in Belfast, and Gerry Adams spoke at the Sinn Fein conference in Dublin, and the Irish situation is going wrong in a really big way. The Unionists will never sit down with Sinn Fein, and Sinn Fein will not easily be able to get the IRA to have a ceasefire; it is a problem for Major – if only the Labour Party would take a bit of a stand it would be so much better.

Monday 25 March

Sir Alfred Sherman, the old ex-communist who worked for Thatcher and is now violently anti-EU and pro-Serb, rang me up. He said, 'I want to tell you two things. First, about this mad-cow disease: it is due to the fact that the Common Agricultural Policy excluded American soya bean, which was used for feed, and drove farmers to go for bonemeal. Second, AIDS was brought to this country by sodomites from abroad.' Well, any remaining shadow of doubt that I'd had about Sherman ended at that moment.

Wednesday 27 March

To the Campaign Group at the Commons. This new Manifesto plan of Blair's was discussed – that he will draft the Manifesto and send it out for consultation, then to Conference, and then it will be put to a ballot of the whole membership on a one-member one-vote basis. The idea emerged that everyone, particularly candidates, would be asked to give a pledge of support. I'm not giving a pledge.

Spoke to Peter Kilfoyle, MP for Walton, who had written a devastating review of Mandelson's book. Later I had a cup of tea with Kevin McNamara, who said he wasn't going to sign anything. But this authoritarianism governed by plebiscite to overturn the democratic institutions of the Party is absolutely wrong. The truth is there is no affection for Blair – we want him to win, and we're frightened of him because of his patronage, but it may be that he will want some exemplary expulsions, particularly of MPs and parliamentary candidates, before polling day.

Thursday 28 March

Got a taxi to Paddington for the train to Truro. It was a lovely spring day and we went through Reading and right down through Exeter and Plymouth; the West Country looked absolutely lovely. The daffodils and crocuses were out and the weather was warm and the sun was shining. It was really quite a nostalgic journey – I don't get to the West Country much now, being stuck up in Chesterfield. It took me back to the many times that I had been there when I was Member for Bristol. Arrived in Truro and was met by a monk who I quickly realised was the Bishop of

Truro himself, Bishop Ball, a man of sixty-five with this grey habit and pectoral cross.

He said the cathedral was full tonight for my lecture and he drove me to his house, where I met his chaplain and his secretary, who is a devoted lady – all bishops have devoted ladies.

While I was there I saw another man who looked exactly like the Bishop – also in grey habit and pectoral cross – and it was his twin brother. I walked round the garden with the twin brother, and there was this marvellous view. He said he was very dissatisfied with Blair and talked about the prejudice against gays.

We had dinner with the Bishop Suffragan of St Germans and his wife and then drove to the cathedral.

Many people had written to me and said they hoped to see me – the Penzance Labour Party, and the parliamentary candidate for Falmouth, Candy Atherton, whom I had known when she was with CND. Thankfully I was not put in the pulpit, but provided with a little podium.

It was a lovely, lovely evening. The response was a bit like a Labour Party Conference in the 1980s. The bishops laughed and the very last question was, 'Which party do you think Jesus would belong to, if he was alive?' A warning bell sounded in my mind, so I said, 'In the presence of bishops and clergy, I don't think I can give any credence to the idea that he isn't alive.' The clergy laughed at that very much.

I was driven back to the Bishop's house where we talked and had tea; there was a lot of gossip about bishops – they loved Runcie. The Bishop had told me he had been against the ordination of women, but had ordained them and it had worked very well.

I left at 10.30 and caught the sleeper back to London – I didn't have any tea from my thermos, I just got into bed and went straight to sleep.

Saturday 30 March, Labour Party Regional Conference, Skegness

Skegness is a tolerable place and the hotel was only £17, which was very cheap. When I went to the Conference Hall I was absolutely shocked. In the old days they used to have a red tablecloth and trade union banners, lovely agricultural workers' banners. This time there was a blue tablecloth and blue chairs and a white backcloth, and all it said on it was 'Regional Conference 1996' – nothing about the Labour Party or anything.

I had got there early so that everybody saw I was there. At about eleven Harry Barnes and Dennis Skinner and I met with the firefighters, who are having a ballot on industrial action because huge cuts are being made in the fire services in Derbyshire. It was agreed that I should ask the Home Secretary to come and see us.

At 11.20 I saw no reason to stay, so I walked to the station and caught the 11.50. Skegness station is the most godforsaken station I have ever been in. The buffet was boarded up; it was not properly covered; the wind blows; there's only one person in the ticket office – ugh, terrible place.

Got the train to Grantham, thinking I'd have an hour to wait, but I didn't and about ten minutes after I'd arrived there was a fast train to London.

Monday 1 April

I rang my grandson James, because it was April Fool's Day, to say that the Prime Minister had resigned and there was an election, and he said, 'April fool!' So he's pretty smart.

Thursday 4 April

Ruth and Sheila gave me a new Ericsson mobile phone for my birthday. A beautiful thing with a mass of features – it will take me ages to understand, but it's unrecognisably better than my old Motorola. Lighter, and a longer lasting battery.

Monday 8 April

Tony Blair has written an article about why Christians would find it hard to be Conservatives. Of course Blair's idea of Christianity is that you all do what the Archbishop of Canterbury tells you to do, so it wasn't a radical article. Meanwhile the Tories have provided a dossier for the right-wing press in America, reminding them of all the left-wing things Blair said in the past – how he was against the bombing of Libya, against the aggression by America in Nicaragua, a member of CND; these have been described by the Labour Party as dirty tricks.

Tuesday 9 April

Every day there is some new horror. The Labour Party has now dropped its idea of absorbing the City of London into the new London body that is going to be set up to replace the GLC. Then I read that the Party was going to drop its intention to control cross-media ownership, in order to satisfy the demands of Rupert Murdoch. Blair is going off to America and says he doesn't intend to alter the Thatcher reforms, and he's getting a glowing press in the US. Jack Straw has decided that an incoming Labour government will change the rules about internal exile under the Prevention of Terrorism Act, which the Ulster Unionists have demanded.

But an old friend of mine in Bristol called Reg Gregory, whom I've known for forty-five years, sent me a copy of the *Observer* for 20 April 1969, which he found under his carpet covering the floorboards, on the front page of which was the headline 'Benn Warns Last Labour Government in Our Life Time'. The report said that Tony Benn, aged 44 (exactly Blair's age now), stressed how essential it was to modernise industrial relations and our relations with the trade unions i.e. supporting Barbara Castle over the White Paper 'In Place of Strife'. If it didn't happen, the report went on, Benn warned that Labour could be out of government for the rest of our lifetime and would be replaced by a government that would take more radical measures against the unions. That, of course, is a pure Blairite argument, I have to admit.

Thursday 18 April

I discovered that the three-line whip tonight on Ireland was to vote *for* the Government's Bill to set up elections in Northern Ireland. I couldn't believe my ears, so I went round and checked, and I wasn't prepared to do it. So I went into the House and leaned down next to the Chief Whip and said, 'By the way, I'm sure for reasons you'll understand, you won't expect me to vote tonight.' He said, 'Go home.' They kept fifty Labour MPs – 'a core vote' – to support the Government and other people just sloped off.

I had a word with Michael Brunson, who was in the House, and said, 'Really you ought to realise that the Labour Party is not all behind Blair.'

He said, 'Oh, he's doing very well.' And he added, 'We just report.'

I said, 'You don't just report, because you don't put difficult questions. I was amazed to see this morning in *The Independent* that the Parliamentary Labour Party was split fifty-fifty on the question of the single currency,' and Michael said he never knew that. 'Well, you could have found that out at any time,' I said. He gave me a sort of smug look, because these guys live in the warm glow of approval from Prime Ministers, Leaders of the Opposition, Ministers and Shadow Ministers.

Israel has been bombing the Lebanon to try and get rid of the Hizbollah and it bombed a UN refugee camp and killed ninety people. Even the Americans have been forced to demand a ceasefire.

Wednesday 24 April

Went into the House, and as I was voting on a free vote on reform of the divorce laws, I saw John Major. I said, 'I'm glad to see you here, John. Nice to think we're sticking together; bipartisanship on everything, you know.' He said, 'Except in my party!' And I said, 'And mine!'.

To the Campaign Group. Skinner gave a report of the National Executive meeting and said that the proposal to abolish child benefit for sixteen to nineteen-year-olds had caused a storm in the constituencies. Gordon Brown had said that the statement on child benefit was only a review and was being undertaken by himself, Chris Smith and David Blunkett – though Chris Smith didn't even know what had been announced.

Diana Jeuda had asked if they would please brief the Party when any of our values were being abandoned. Skinner had asked if there would be a ballot on the Manifesto and Blair didn't answer – apparently it will cost

£1 million to have a ballot. Alan Howarth, the Tory MP who defected to Labour, is not eligible to stand for a Labour constituency because he hasn't been in the Party for two years, but the NEC agreed to abandon the rule. Blair said he simply didn't understand the opposition to putting Howarth into a constituency.

Dennis also reported that Tom Sawyer had announced that a member of the Party's administrative staff had been appointed to the Prince of Wales's Trust and how proud we should be of her, because 'Years ago people who worked at Transport House were unemployable elsewhere.' An absolute cheek – they were committed and that's why they stayed.

Thursday 25 April

Mr Ibrahim came to see me; he does from time to time. He said the American policy now was such that Muslim fundamentalism was growing everywhere, and I asked whether he'd noticed the admission by the Americans that they had allowed Tehran to export arms to the Bosnian Muslims, even though there was an embargo. 'Oh,' he said, 'we knew that.'

The PLP is absolutely up in arms at Blair and the child benefit issue is really big; if he doesn't understand that, he doesn't understand anything. Chris Smith, the spokesman, wasn't told; Gordon Brown said it was a review; and Blair's office and his spin doctors put out the story that this was a firm decision. That annoyed Brown and Smith and everybody else.

Monday 29 April

Sat in the Tea Room. Audrey Wise took half an hour to describe what happened at the USDAW conference, an interminably long account. Then to my room and worked. Andrew Mackinlay told me that today Tony Blair was at Basildon, a seat we've got to win. The Labour candidate there is Angela Smith, who used to work for the League Against Cruel Sports. She had received a phone call, from an official at Labour Party HQ asking if she had replied to a questionnaire that *Tribune* had sent out. It shows that fifty parliamentary candidates out of 200 are overwhelmingly against Trident, the single currency, and so on. This woman cross-examined Angela – did she answer it? Well there was no reason why Angela Smith should have replied, because the questionnaire was anonymous, but she said she had. So this woman went through the questions, asking her what her answers had been and threatening that, if she didn't write a letter recanting, Blair might not come to Basildon. Angela stuck her ground and Blair did go. It's an indication of this enormously authoritarian dictatorship from the top.

Members are going in every day now to see Blair, and I suppose at some stage I might be invited, but I don't want to give my comments with a group of people there – I want to talk to him privately.

Friday 3 May
Labour landslide in the local government elections – Tories lost about 600 seats; Labour gained a lot.

Sunday 5 May
Walked down to Shepherd's Bush Road, where people were gathering for 'Urban Occupation' at an unnamed destination. George Monbiot, from The Land is Ours movement, had asked if I could go. There were the Newbury bypass protesters, people from the various environmental and green movements. I was the only MP there and I wandered round as an ordinary member of the group, talking to people.

Monday 6 May
Masses of telephone calls about The Land is Ours campaign, which took over the derelict Guinness site by Wandsworth Bridge, so tomorrow morning I'm going to get up at the crack of dawn and go to the site. The press coverage of the land issue in Wandsworth is really very sympathetic, and quite exciting.

Tuesday 7 May
Up at 5.45 and went to the derelict site in York Road; 500 people had turned up yesterday and worked very hard, building lavatories and a kitchen and putting up tents and a hut. Children had come and built little gardens, and there was a play area, and so on – very impressive.

I got paired for the last vote and got home at 10.45 – a very busy day. I'm pleased I've made contact with the green movement.

Wednesday 8 May
Roy Hattersley rang and told me some interesting things. He had complained to Blunkett about the report in the press of Blunkett's speech at the Social Market Foundation. Blunkett had apparently attacked comprehensive schools. So Blunkett sent him the full text of the speech, which, Roy said, wasn't too bad. Roy had discovered that Blair's office had circulated and highlighted the one sentence attacking comprehensive schools – that's the spin doctors' work.

Roy is afraid that Alan Howarth, the Tory MP who defected, might be imposed on his constituency.

Tam Dalyell was in the Members' Lobby with the parents of WPC Yvonne Fletcher, who was shot outside the Libyan Embassy twelve years ago. With them was the producer of the programme which established that she was shot not by the Libyans or from the Libyan Embassy, but from another building which at the time was occupied by British and American security forces. Very distressing for the parents. I asked them why they don't make a claim for compensation, because it would force the Government either to lie again or to grant something.

Thursday 9 May

Caroline and I caught a taxi to lunch with Peter Palumbo (Lord Palumbo), the very wealthy former Chairman of the Arts Council, and his wife, a beautiful Lebanese lady with no sense of humour. Peter Carter was there, and Sandy Wilson, the architect of the British Library. We had a very agreeable lunch there. Palumbo gave me a radio in the shape of the Stirling building in the City – the Prince of Wales had said that Stirling's design reminded him of a 1930s wireless set. So we've got this little wireless as a curiosity.

Andrew Mackinlay tried unsuccessfully to insert a new clause into the Armed Forces Bill that 300 soldiers executed for cowardice in the First World War should be pardoned. He made a powerful speech, but the Tories were whipped against it. Edwina Currie moved another amendment to say that gays should be allowed in the armed forces, and that was overwhelmingly defeated by a whipped Tory vote. John Reid, our spokesman, voted against. David Clark voted with us but, really, when you get the Labour leadership not willing to stand up for civil liberties, it is utterly disgraceful.

Sunday 12 May

The most interesting story in the papers this morning was in the *Observer* – a whole page devoted to relations between senior members of the Shadow Cabinet: how everybody hated Gordon Brown; the relationship of each person to Blair; what their prospects were; and so on. Mandelson said he regretted the breakdown with Gordon Brown, but hoped to make it up and looked forward to being Foreign Secretary in two years. Caroline, who is a lot shrewder than me, thought this was a Mandelson story – still trying to knife Brown, but at the same time making out that he's anxious to improve relations and indicating his ambitions.

George Monbiot rang and left a message that there was going to be a video shown tonight at the Guinness site in York Road, about the occupation. So I rang him on his mobile and he said that the video was off, because the solar energy wasn't working and 'Anyway I'm leaving the site at four, we're handing over the keys to local residents.' I was told that Monbiot had a close relationship with the media. Meanwhile, next Wednesday Guinness will go to court and get an injunction.

I heard about a meeting at Highgrove which had been called to discuss rural England and the relationship between the countryside and urban expansion. One of those there had been interested in the Guinness site project. And, believe it or not, the seminar that he attended was chaired by Jonathan Dimbleby. Apparently, the Prince was very confused, a tortured soul. Every time he spoke, his hands twisted and he looked away and he was very spooky – the earth is ours, we come from the earth, we must go back to the earth and we mustn't disturb the earth. I could see a strange alliance of genuine homeless people, and environmentalists who wanted to use the derelict sites to house homeless people which sounded very radical, with interested encouragement from rural people who would like the homeless to stay in the big towns so that they don't ruin the beauties of the English countryside. The media, the Prince, and this allegedly radical movement – were people being exploited by all this? It drew my attention to two things: that there is an environmentalist wing that doesn't really believe in anything, other than getting back to the land (particularly attractive if you've got several castles); and the powerlessness of groups in dealing with the Establishment, if something real is to be done.

The only organisation strong enough to deal with the accumulation of power from ownership of land is the trade union movement. You *must* have a trade union movement, a socialist perspective and a strong organisation in order to deal with the real problems of society.

It did also remind me of our lunch on Thursday with Lord Palumbo, who said that the Princess of Wales took people up and then dropped them – including him – and that she was totally self-obsessed, deserted by her mother and her husband and by everybody, just thinking about herself. According to one newspaper today she has allegedly been to the Queen and said that if she doesn't get a proper financial settlement she won't agree to a divorce by consent – she'll wait the full two years and then she'll sell her jewels in order to live, which would be a great embarrassment.

Wednesday 15 May

Simon Heffer – plump, with bright-red hair and a pin-striped suit, a Euro-sceptic Thatcherite – came to see me about his book on Enoch Powell. At the end I asked, 'Did Powell ever talk to you about the death of Mountbatten?'

'Oh yes,' he said. 'He thought the Americans killed him'.

I said, 'Powell had told me that but I thought it was so way out, I didn't want to mention it to you.'

'Oh yes,' Heffer said, 'he thinks the Americans killed Airey Neave as well, because they wanted to get a NATO base in Northern Ireland.'

I asked if Heffer thought it was related to Mountbatten's speech repudiating nuclear weapons. He said it might have been, but as far as Enoch was concerned, it was too professional.

Then, as he left, Heffer said, 'I don't think the party structure will survive the next election.' I agreed with him. I think the Conservatives will be beaten, there will be a Thatcherite Party and the Tory MPs who are wet will join the Liberals, and Labour will work with them. 'Oh no,' he said, 'the Tories think Paddy Ashdown is a nutter. They'll join the Labour Party.' Well, that really frightened me – he is a shrewd man because he knows the Tory MPs quite well and I think he has some indirect contact with Blair. Heffer said the Tories think Blair is a good and reliable Conservative. So maybe after the Election more Tories will join the Labour Party – that's why Blair wants to make it easy for Alan Howarth to get a seat. He'll have a Labour-Tory coalition at the core and he can let the left go. Interesting.

Tuesday 21 May

I had a talk to John McAllion, Irene Adams and Jimmy Wray. Wray had a famous Scottish boxer with him – don't know who he was, but he's won three gold medals. John and Irene had both been to an Oxford college on a training course for Labour Shadow Ministers; £900 each to go and they said it was absolute rubbish. Kaufman and Hattersley – ex-Ministers – spoke and some civil servants. Hattersley said there was no democracy in Government; what the Prime Minister says goes. One civil servant said you mustn't put unrealistic things in your Manifesto, because they can't be done and there's no pretending they can. Someone asked, 'Do you regard Labour MPs as stakeholders?' and was told, 'Oh, don't be ridiculous!' John and Irene said it was an awful waste of time and they learned nothing useful.

Sunday 2 June

Jack Straw is reported on the front page of the *Observer* as being in favour of a youth curfew to deal with youth crime, an idea that Clinton endorsed last week. Unbelievable.

Thursday 6 June

Went by taxi to address the London Diplomats Group, organised by the Quakers – they invite quite senior diplomats (though not ambassadors). I was asked to talk about the future of Europe. With the end of communism and the influence of the IMF all over the world, there was no politics in it at all: the development of the EU, the extension into Eastern Europe, acceptance of the single currency, the role of the IMF was all normal and natural to them.

Had a long talk to the Chinese First Secretary at the embassy – a very charming man called Liao Dong – and said how much I admired Mao Tse tung, or Zedong, the greatest man of the twentieth century. He said that I couldn't admire Mao more than he did. I asked him how Mao was viewed now. He said Mao was 70 per cent right and 30 per cent wrong; the Cultural Revolution didn't work. He said he had been named after Mao – it was amusing. Afterwards he asked if he or the Chinese Ambassador could come and see me, and I said I'd be absolutely delighted.

Monday 10 June
I'm very tired. I'm trying to lose weight, because I'm up to thirteen stone and I ought to be twelve. I have this great craving for chocolate. If I cut out chocolate and bread, I could pretty well manage.

Saturday 15 June
Caroline had severe back pain all day; she lay in bed hardly able to move.

There was a bomb in Manchester (the IRA presumably) which injured 200 people, so that really has changed the whole situation in Northern Ireland.

Monday 17 June
Our forty-seventh wedding anniversary. Caroline was a little bit better and she put on the red-and-white striped dress that she wore the day I met her on 2 August 1948. She lay in bed with her pearls on and it was just lovely; in the evening we had a meal together. I played her a compact disc that I'd bought on relaxation. She said the guy rabbited on.

Wednesday 19 June
I don't want to sound too pessimistic, because I'm not a pessimistic person, but you realise that a lot of things you'd like to do you'll never do. I'll never finish my archives, I'll probably never see another volume of the *Diaries* published. You have to come to terms with the fact that old age does get a grip of you, and any idea that anyone of my age might have of a comeback politically is utterly laid to rest by Thatcher, who's finished; by Heath who's considered an old bumbler; by Gorbachev, who got 0.5 per cent of the vote; and so on.

I had a message today from somebody who said that he and his wife had had their sixtieth wedding anniversary but hadn't received a telegram from the Queen. Well, it's too late to do anything about that. I told him he would have had to send the wedding certificate to the Palace in advance, and so on, so I sent him a telegram wishing him every happiness, congratulating him, and saying, 'A view I'm sure the Queen shares'!

Saturday 22 June
Went to go and get money from a cash machine and three young men were standing there and one of them said, 'There's Tony fucking Benn.' So I turned away and they called after me, 'Anthony fucking Wedgwood Benn.' I just walked away. People are a bit excited because England beat Spain in the Euro football thing; England won on a penalty in extra time, so there are a lot of drunken crowds in the street.

Sunday 23 June
Up at six o'clock, got three meals for Caroline (breakfast, lunch and

dinner) and covered them all in shrink-wrap stuff so that they keep fresh. Packed up to go to Chesterfield.

Monday 24 June
I took Caroline to Charing Cross Hospital today for a mammogram and there is a lump in her breast; they did a needle test and a biopsy, which we should know about at the end of the week, and it does look pretty gloomy.

Wednesday 26 June
Germany beat England in the European Cup.

Thursday 27 June
At eleven o'clock the surgeon phoned. He said nothing had actually been identified, but he wanted to do further tests, so we went in at twelve and Caroline had further biopsies and another X-ray.

Tony Blair's announcement that there would be a referendum in Scotland with two questions – 'Do you want a devolved assembly?' and 'Do you think it should have taxation powers?' – has killed it stone-dead. There's absolute fury in Scotland, and George Galloway was on television saying there'll be a revolution there about this. Brian Wilson, was saying, 'It's quite reasonable – you couldn't do it without consent.'

Blair came out earlier this week with a statement that we would keep nuclear weapons, and of course the Scottish Labour Party, the Scottish TUC and many of the Scottish churches are against nuclear weapons, so this will fan the flames of Scottish nationalism even more. They'll say, 'If you vote Labour, you'll have a Labour Government not only making a mockery of devolution, but insisting that you have nuclear weapons in Scotland.'

Tuesday 2 July
I rang early to see if they were going to give Caroline a bed in hospital and, to cut a long story short, I was able to take her in at two o'clock. Later she heard that her back problem was definitely osteoporosis, which is a very painful complaint of old people, but it's not bone cancer. That cheered her up a bit.

Wednesday 3 July
Caroline didn't have a very good night because there was a lot of noise in the ward.

The consultant surgeon removed the cancerous lump from her breast with a single incision, and I waited in the day room. I lay down on some cushions, because I was very tired, and the sister came in and said, 'We're hoping to admit you as soon as possible.' So I said, 'I wish you would.' She was very nice.

Then I sat by the lift where you can smoke, and there was a Ghanaian woman who was the supervisor of the domestic staff. She told me that her staff get £3.15 an hour and they work eleven hours a day, six days a week. 'I'm going home to Ghana. I'd rather be an old woman in Ghana than here.'

I asked, 'What did you think of Nkrumah?'

'Oh, a wonderful man, Nkrumah. But he was too much for the liking of the Americans, so the CIA had him removed while he was in China and everything's gone downhill ever since.'

I said, 'I knew Nkrumah.' We had a good talk.

Tuesday 9 July

Nelson Mandela arrived today, so the traffic is in chaos. There he was in a Rolls-Royce meeting the Queen, with the Irish Guards present and the whole pomp and panoply of a monarch. I found it a bit revolting, considering that the guy had been in prison for twenty-seven years when nobody was prepared to support him. I'm not blaming him, because he's got to get money from foreign investors and all that, but it isn't the Mandela cause that I supported, as such.

Saturday 13 July 1996

There was a bit in the *Sunday Telegraph* magazine by Cristina Odone saying how she fell in love with me when I went to the Christian Socialist Conference. She had it all wrong; she is a bit of a self-publicist.

Monday 15 July

I had a word with Derek Foster, who'd been at the Durham Miners' Gala over the weekend and I said, 'You know, it is extraordinary to me that Tony Blair could have addressed 20,000 of his devoted supporters and he didn't bother.'

'Well', said Derek, 'I spent a couple of hours trying to persuade him, but the Durham Miners' Gala is Old Labour, he doesn't want to be seen there.' And he continued 'I told him: you're not forming the SDP again you know!'

Margaret Beckett, who was standing there, said to Derek, 'If you said that to him, that's why you're no longer Chief Whip!'

Tuesday 16 July

Caroline is extremely tired and she's got these racking pains in her joints and muscles and her appetite's not good.

I went off early to drop my car at the House of Commons and went to see the Chinese Ambassador, Jiang Enzhu, in the embassy in Portland Place. When I arrived I was greeted at the door and was taken upstairs to the state rooms on the first floor.

A young man came towards me and I shook him by the hand and said, 'Do tell me, please, how long the Ambassador's got because I mustn't detain him, he's a very busy man.'

'Oh,' said this man, 'I am the Ambassador.'

I laughed and said, 'You look so young.'

We sat down and had nearly an hour's talk; very typical – some Chinese tea and nuts and raisins put in front of me. He sat in an armchair and I sat on a couch opposite him and in another armchair was his private secretary writing it all down.

He told me a bit about himself. He said he'd been in the Chinese diplomatic service for thirty years, so he must now be nearly sixty but not a grey hair in his head. He said he'd been at Harvard at one stage and his most recent appointment had been as Deputy Foreign Minister of China, a hugely important position considering the size of that country with 1.2 billion people.

I asked him about Hong Kong, and he said the British Government had failed to honour the commitment that had been entered into, and so on. So then I got talking to him more philosophically. I said, 'I'm a great admirer of Mao. He made mistakes, because everybody does, but it seems to me that the development of the countryside and so on was very sensible.' I put it to him that the disappearance of the Soviet Union and the defeat of socialism in many other parts of the world represented a great setback – not that I was ever a great supporter of the Stalin regime. Anyway he was charming.

At three o'clock Caroline and I went off to the hospital to hear the result of the tests. To put it plainly, it was a very big lump in the breast and they discovered cancer in eighteen of the twenty-five lymph nodes in the arm, so it is very serious. They haven't found it anywhere else, but they're going to do further tests.

Obviously I pressed as to what the prospects were, and the professor said to Caroline, 'Well, I think there's a better than fifty per cent chance that you'll be here in five years' time.' But it was about as gloomy a prognosis as you can imagine, considering the fact that a month ago we had no idea that this was the situation, and the cancer must have been growing for a year.

They put her on drugs; she's going to have more tests; she'll probably have radiotherapy.

I have clearly got to restructure my whole life to be of service to her, and cut out anything that I don't have to do. We'll see our way through the immediate period and then see how it settles down. I think morale is important and I'm not going to be pessimistic about it, but at the same time it is very, very sad. I think of all the times I could have spent with her and done things together with her, and now it's too late to go over all that. I haven't been a very good husband in those terms; I've put politics first.

She's had a full and happy and satisfying life as a writer and teacher and grandmother and friend, but I haven't really played the full role in enriching her life by my friendship as I should have done, I'm afraid.

Friday 19 July
I spoke to Joy Johnson, who was a BBC producer who moved over to work with Tony Blair and resigned earlier this year, I think. She was given redundancy pay with a gagging clause, so that nobody would be able to hear what happened, but she told me she kept a diary. She said that Blair had once said to her, 'Do you think I'm too hard on the unions?' And she said, 'Yes and I think you're too hard on the Party.' He said, 'I will know how to be Prime Minister and Leader, but I don't know how to handle the Party.' Well, that's an interesting comment.

Monday 22 July
There was absolutely massive arm-twisting going on by Blair and his henchmen to try and persuade people to vote for Harriet Harman in the Shadow Cabinet elections. Many people have been dissuaded from standing – for example, Dawn Primarolo, who I suspect (though I can't prove it) was told she'd lose her Front Bench job if she stood.

I had tea with Jeremy Corbyn, who said that he had been asked to appear on the *Midnight Hour*. Labour Party Headquarters evidently rang up and said, 'If you use Jeremy Corbyn you will never get another Shadow Cabinet Minister to appear.' So the TV producers pulled out. I can't say I'm surprised, but I'm disappointed with the Parliamentary Party; they gripe privately and then go along with what they're told to do by the Leader who is our boss.

Came home, found Caroline still on her computer since this morning.

David Heathcoat-Amory has resigned as Paymaster General because he disagrees with the Government on Europe, so that'll give another twist to that argument.

Tuesday 23 July
Sheila was in the office, tremendously supportive.

In the afternoon we went to Charing Cross Hospital. We had to wait for an hour maybe, then we went to see the doctor, whose name I've forgotten. I think I probably repressed it.

But he had the reports of the scan that was done last week at St Mary's, Paddington. When he said that the scan of the spine was very sinister, it was quite clear that Caroline has got cancer of the spine, which is terribly serious; it means it's adrift in the bloodstream and, not to put too fine a point on it, he made it clear how serious it was. He said that Tamoxifen, I think, did attack systemic cancer and that they were going to radiate the spine and not the breast (which implies they've sort of given up on the breast) starting next week for two weeks; and he said he had known of people living for ten years. But that was exceptional. Caroline was so brave.

Wednesday 24 July
Caroline was bearing up marvellously today, considering all the strain she's under, and she did manage to eat a few meals. She told Hilary and Melissa the state of play and I think they understand it.

Spoke to Dave two or three times. Did wonder if I should give up Parliament to look after Caroline, but I don't think she'd want that. We'll see how we get on.

We had the Labour Shadow Cabinet elections today. Jeremy Corbyn used my proxy vote and Harriet Harman plummeted to the bottom, just nineteenth or something.

Thursday 25 July
As I get further and further from daily politics, I become less and less excited by it all and wonder how you can actually make any change. The higher you get the more you're silenced by the Leader, and the more ambition takes over from commitment.

Friday 26 July, Chesterfield
Before my surgery I told Tom and Margaret about Caroline's illness and they were very sweet about it. I also passed on the money from the MPs' pay increase to the Party funds.

Then I went to my surgery, and it went on from twelve to seven.

The first one was a man who had been charged with a traffic offence that he said wasn't in the Highway Code. Then somebody came with an oxygen mask on because he'd got asbestosis. Then a man whose wife had left him and whose daughter wouldn't see him, and he'd lost his house, so in the end I wrote to his daughter. Then a man who came to thank me because I'd got his windows fixed. And so it went on. I didn't have time for lunch or dinner. Then I went to the General Committee.

Nobody referred to it at the GC, but one woman who had come to the surgery, an old Party member, gave me a kiss and said, 'I've been praying every day for Caroline.' I told Caroline that later and she was very moved, and so was I.

Saturday 27 July
A woman called Barbara, a graduate of Queen's University, who has a boy of eight, came this afternoon and agreed to come and help do the jobs that Caroline can't do.

Monday 29 July
I went out and did a bit of shopping, then our GP came to see us. She's a very nice woman; she stayed for about an hour and went over it with Caroline. I walked to the car with her.

I asked, 'What is it? Is it three months, six months or a year?'

She said, 'The worst case is three months and beyond that it might be longer, it could be more than a year.' But she said the important thing is to be comfortable and enjoy life and be together. Very sensible, so I decided that I'd cancel everything. I'll go through my September engagements tomorrow with Sheila.

Today Caroline said, 'I'll never be a pixie* jumping up and down again.' And she cried a bit, and I cried. Oh, dear, dear. She is such a lovely person.

Tuesday 30 July
At half-past twelve Caroline and I went over for her radiotherapy, and I went and sat outside for a smoke and who should come up but John Wells. He has been having radiotherapy for a growth on his neck for ten years, but he said, 'As an actor, I don't want people to know. Are you in for it?'

I said, 'No, Caroline is.' It was rather comforting to find somebody who'd been having treatment for ten years.

The most exciting news of the day is that the four women who did £1.5 million of damage to the Hawk aircraft at British Aircraft Corporation were acquitted by a jury on the grounds that it was the lesser of two evils. They were stopping these planes going to Indonesia to allow the Government there to suppress the people of East Timor. A most sensational judgement, comparable actually to the judgement that was reached when juries refused to convict for sheep stealing because it led to the death penalty.

Wednesday 31 July
Caroline was very, very ill this morning. She was dizzy, she had vertigo, she had palpitations, and I was so worried and she was so distressed that I rang our GP and she said that perhaps Caroline should go into hospital again.

But Caroline said, 'I don't want to go into hospital, I'll never come out.'

So I said, 'I promise you, darling, I won't let them do that.' We did go in, and they did blood pressure and blood tests and said that she should have a brain scan and possibly a blood transfusion; she's a bit anaemic, and all together they were very worried. They prescribed much stronger

* One of Caroline's nicknames from early in our marriage was Pixie; mine was Greensleeves.

drugs for the nausea and she has painkillers. Sheila was here, she's a tower of strength, a marvellous woman.

Barbara came today to do the cleaning and the shopping; she brought her little son Archie, of eight, and a little girlfriend of his called Tracy.

Thursday 1 August

When we got to the hospital there was only one other woman in the waiting room for radiotherapy and she and Caroline fell to talking. She had breast cancer too. She began crying and Caroline began crying and I began crying, and then people were beginning to fill the waiting room and there we all were, crying. Caroline was called away and I said to Rosemary (that was her name – I don't know her last name), 'Tomorrow is the forty-eighth anniversary of our meeting.' And then I began sobbing, and she came over and sat next to me and gave me a tissue to cry into, and I've put it in an envelope and kept it because it was such a loving thing to do.

The thing that comes out of all this is that the nurses, the doctors, the Macmillan nurses, the GP, the people you meet are just so loving, and it's got nothing to do with monetarism or profit, it's just natural love. I found it all very, very moving.

Thursday 8 August

Clare Short was interviewed by the *New Statesman* and attacked the spin doctors.

The spin doctors are dismissing it as the angry voice of a disappointed woman, but it's released into the public domain the power of the spin doctors and, with Blair on holiday in Tuscany, it's done him a lot of damage.

Wednesday 14 August

Colin Powell, the former Chairman of the American Joint Chiefs of Staff, gave a speech at the Republican Convention yesterday about the liberal traditions of America, about immigrants, about a woman's right to choose. It really sounded more progressive than Clinton; I suppose the right-wing Republicans – the Gingrich Republicans – realise that they'll never win unless they re-establish a broad humanistic approach. Clinton moves to the right to pick up the right-wing vote and the consolidation of the one-party state is really what's happening everywhere. But I am disconnecting very much from British politics now.

Thursday 15 August

About half an hour ago Marcia Williams rang me.

She had just watched the video of a programme about Harold Wilson and she said there was a really sinister reason behind Wilson's death; she said, 'I can't tell you on the phone.' But she did say that she felt that the destruction of Harold Wilson after his death was part of the security services' attempt to suggest that Labour Governments were untrustworthy in order to pave the way for a Tory victory. If you rubbish Labour Governments that have been there, and if you say that Blair has no experience, then you are actually getting rid of the Labour Party and helping a Tory victory. I thought it was very shrewd – an angle I hadn't thought of.

We went over it; we talked over everything, and what Harold had been through and what she'd been through, and how Mary would be very distressed by the programme if she'd watched it; and how brutal to do it after he's dead; and what rubbish to suggest that his mind was going when he resigned, because after that he did a whole series of television programmes, he chaired the commission on the City of London; the Alzheimer's didn't come until after the major bowel-cancer operation, and so on.

Marcia was so friendly and she said how fond Harold was of me. She said Blair and Mandelson are nothing to do with the Labour Party and she didn't think Blair would win. She said, 'I wouldn't put any money on a victory by Blair.'

The papers have been full of a story that the Queen and the Duke of Edinburgh and Prince Charles have been examining the role of the monarchy. They came up with all sorts of absurd ideas like giving up the Civil List and allowing members of the royal family to marry Catholics, giving up the title Head of the Church of England – a few little things of that character.

Saturday 31 August

At 6.30 Lissie rang to say that a baby girl had been born to her at St Mary's Hospital at 5.16, a baby she's going to call Sarah Caroline.

Went to see Melissa, who had put little Sarah in a cot, and Hannah greeted her mother and then said, 'Where's the baby?' And so Melissa said, 'Well, you look and see.' And Hannah went over to a little crib and looked over and said, 'Nice.' So sweet of her.

Monday 2 September

Roy Jenkins was on the radio, Apparently he is regularly consulted by Tony Blair. He said he didn't think there was much in the label Social Democrat; he hadn't called himself a socialist for many, many years, but he didn't think there was much in it.

Tuesday 3 September

Early this morning the Americans bombed Iraq, allegedly because Saddam had sent his troops north to support one faction of the Kurds against another faction, who had called in the Iranians.

Not a single critical word in the media. I decided to put out a press release criticising and attacking this and I faxed it round, not that I think anyone would really take much notice of it, but I thought I have to do it.

Wednesday 4 September

I should report that the hostility to American action is growing worldwide. The Chinese are against it, the Russians are against it, the Irish Prime Minister (who is also President of the European Commission) is against it, and Egypt and Jordan, and so on; so America has taken a terrible risk.

Friday 6 September

Got up at 5.45 to go to BBC Broadcasting House to do an interview with Jim Naughtie of the *Today* programme about Iraq. I got three minutes and made most of the points that I wanted to.

I came home, and from ten to eleven Mr Ibrahim who is looking after the Iraqi interests section from the Jordanian Embassy – a very old friend of mine – came to see me.

He said that Turkey wanted Iraqi oil and had made incursions into Iraq and had breached its sovereignty, just as Iran had.

He thought Saddam would be very cautious, and I think that is true because it would be foolish to provoke the Americans at this particular moment, even though on the question of legality there can be no question that the Americans have acted completely illegally.

When Ibrahim was on *Newsnight* the other night, Sir David Hannay, a former British Representative (I think) to the United Nations, said, 'Ah, it wasn't a breach of international law, because Saddam is a regime and Iraq is a territory.' A completely nonsensical argument, and afterwards, apparently, Hannay said to Ibrahim that he recognised that it was not the right thing to say.

I said, 'Perhaps we could get some sort of a dialogue going, a British-Iraqi dialogue?'

'Well,' said Ibrahim, 'there is a conference on oil in London, but the British wouldn't give an Iraqi representative a visa.'

'Well, perhaps the Royal Institute of International Affairs would organise it?'

'They're supposed to be independent but they're really under the thumb of the Foreign Office.'

'Why don't you transfer the dialogue to Paris, where the French have no such inhibitions, and have an Iraqi-European Union dialogue, in which Ted Heath might participate?'

Ibrahim was excited by that and said he would put the idea to Baghdad; he thanked me very much. He said, 'You're the only man I can really talk to in an open way.'

I had a sandwich, and then I got in the car and drove to the Eco-Village at Wandsworth to take part in a little film that is being made.

As we were filming, I turned around and there was an absolutely naked woman; she was about thirty, very attractive, had a wedding ring on one hand, and was hanging up her laundry. She was absolutely natural, quite unembarrassed, and I asked her about herself. She said she was a German teacher from Potsdam who had come over to work in England and learn a bit of English. She hadn't been very happy or made many friends, so she decided to come to the Eco-Village. I've never been to a nudist colony before, but I can see how, if everybody is naked, people walk about, you don't take much notice of them. But I told the cameraman that I didn't think that should be in the film because it would give a false impression of what it's all about. It was such a beautiful day that it was a sensible thing to do. I would have taken off my clothes, but there wouldn't have been much to show.

Wednesday 11 September

I rang Ted Heath in Salisbury and told him that I'd seen Ibrahim, and I said I thought it would be polite to let him know what I had suggested, and would he consider it?

And Heath was full of hurumph, hurumph and he said, 'I don't think they'd give a visa to anyone from Iraq.'

I said, 'Well, possibly not, but Paris might be a suitable place.'

Then Tam Dalyell rang and said that, as the Americans have today threatened that they will use disproportionate force against Iraq (because, apparently, a missile was fired at an American aircraft in the no-fly zone), he felt this was the time to go back to the Prime Minister and ask for a recall of Parliament. I said I'd support that.

Friday 13 September

Huge story today is that Stephen Byers had dinner with four journalists on Wednesday night and evidently suggested to them – they all printed the same story – that if there were strikes when Labour was in power, Blair might put a referendum to Party members suggesting that the links with the unions be broken.

It was so obviously a gross thing to say, particularly at the end of the TUC conference, that John Edmonds made a speech calling for Byers's replacement. Blair's office said that it was totally untrue; Stephen Byers denied that he said it.

Saturday 14 September

When I reflected on it, I realised that it isn't really a row about Labour's relations with the trade unions; it is a crisis of credibility.

I do not know whether to believe a word I read in the papers, I'm fed up with nudging and winking and briefing and denying – I want to *know*. I think that is what will destroy us in the end.

Sunday 22 September

Drove to Chesterfield for a meeting of the Party. There are 843 members of the Chesterfield Labour Party, and thirty-five were present; it was an all-members meeting.

The purpose of the meeting was to present *The Road to the Manifesto* and the aims and objectives of the Chesterfield Party, which we are relaunching. I had drafted a resolution that this meeting, open to all members of the Chesterfield Labour Party, pledge itself to work wholeheartedly for the election of a Labour Government on the basis of the Manifesto, which the Party will put before the nation, and to campaign for the aims and objectives adopted by the constituency party.

Anyway, Darryl Alvey, the Chairman, presented *The Road to the Manifesto* very clearly and plainly. Then I presented the aims and objectives.

Some members of the right were there: barristers, very pro-European, very Blairite and New Labour.

The first question was whether we could, in our aims and objectives, state that 'conscience is above the law'. Some members said I was arguing for people to do what they liked, but I said, 'No, we have to recognise that all our rights were won by struggle.'

Then there were other questions asked; it wasn't a bad discussion. At the end Jill Brunt moved an amendment, that instead of saying 'we will campaign for the aims and objectives adopted by the constituency party,' we would say 'on the basis of a Labour Government we would long-term' – or something like that – 'campaign for the aims and objectives . . . '

I didn't object to that, though it came from somebody who, I suspected, would have moved that we drop the aims and objectives altogether. But that didn't happen and her amendment was carried.

I didn't make a point about it, I accepted it; the members thought the aims and objectives were too bold and conflicted with the Party programme.

I dealt with the questions as best I could.

Wednesday 25 September

Gerry Adams was due to give a press conference at the House of Commons tomorrow to launch his book *Before the Dawn*. But later Jeremy Corbyn, who was organising the event, told me that officials at the House banned it on the grounds that you couldn't use the House of Commons for promoting a commercial publication – fair enough.

So Jeremy transferred the press conference to the Irish Centre in

Islington and said we'd have a meeting with Gerry Adams in the House at nine o'clock in the morning. I said I'd go to that.

Well, all hell broke loose. On the one o'clock news it was the top item. At two, the Chief Whip, Donald Dewar, issued a statement saying that disciplinary action would be taken against Jeremy Corbyn. I rang Dewar and said, 'Just to let you know I'm going to be there tomorrow.' That took him aback. I went on, 'I don't know what disciplinary action can be taken for meeting somebody in the House of Commons. Ceausescu, Khrushchev and Bulganin were all there. Anyway, Gerry Adams has already met President Clinton, Vice-President Gore, Senator Bob Dole, Ted Kennedy, Nelson Mandela, and John Bruton.' This took him even further aback.

Later on, the news bulletin said that the Chief Whip would actually move a resolution to withdraw the whip from Jeremy and me. So I rang Dewar back and I said, 'I'm told by *The Times*,' – who'd rung me – 'that the spin doctors are saying that you have decided to move a resolution at the next PLP meeting to withdraw the whip.'

Then he got really worried. I told him we should be issuing a press statement saying that we're searching for peace, and writing to Clinton, Major and Bruton asking them if they can help to get the peace process on its way, and also to call a round-table conference on the basis of a permanent ceasefire.

The withdrawal of the whip was widely discussed on the six o'clock news. Blair should have said nothing about it. 'It's a private initiative, nothing to do with me.' But he chose to make an issue of it and it's now being described as a test of his leadership. I have to be clear in my mind that I have taken a considerable risk, and Jeremy has too, but he's much weaker than me because to pick him off would be easier.

All in all, it was quite a day. The phone has rung absolutely continuously, but if anything it's somewhat stiffened my resolve. I wish I hadn't got into this, because I don't want a confrontation with anybody. It did frighten me in a deep way, and Jeremy said that ITN were camping outside his house.

Thursday 26 September

Got up at the crack of dawn and heard on the news that Gerry Adams himself had decided to call off the meeting at the House of Commons. The press was hysterical. The tabloids were full of abuse, and the heavies had built up the Mandelson story of 'Blair's fury' and the withdrawal of the whip, and so on.

I rang Donald Dewar in Scotland and said, 'Look, Donald, I read in the papers that I'm going to be expelled before the Conference; this is Mandelson again. I'm not blaming you, but the plain fact is that this is being done in your name.'

I think the row between him and Mandelson must be building up a bit.

I continued, 'I regard you as being somebody in the John Smith tradition, and I had a great respect for him.'

Dewar said, 'Well, I cannot claim to carry his mantle on my shoulders.'

'I'm not saying you do. I'm just saying that I greatly respect you; I wish we could cool it a bit.'

I think the truth is they are backing off.

Had a word with Jeremy, who said that Clare Short had rung him up. She'd said to him 'I know I'm not your favourite person' and Jeremy said, 'That's right,' but, said Clare, 'I just want to say how much I support you.'

Stephen was terribly worried. He thinks his dad's going to be expelled from the Party.

Monday 30 September, Labour Party Conference, Blackpool

Who should I see just a few feet away on the train but Tony Booth, Cherie Booth's father, a lovely guy; he had a tall, slim girl with him; she had on a little pass that said 'Leader's Office', and it was Cherie's sister, Lauren Booth. I had a lovely talk to Tony and I said to Lauren, 'Tell your sister not to be worried by what they say about her, because the media will create an image and then destroy it. And it's horrible until you realise that it's not you they're destroying – it's the image they've created. Then you go through the battlefield unharmed.'

Tuesday 1 October

I watched Blair's speech. It lasted for an hour and five minutes and began with a video (the whole conference centre is full of videos running all the time) – pictures of Blair, smiling, Blair, Blair, Blair. To have people come all the way to Conference just to watch a video is an outrage; at a critical moment after the video all the lights in the conference chamber went out and the spotlight went on some white doors and in came Blair smiling and smiling. A cold hand went round my chest. He made all sorts of carefully prepared jokes; he had his teleprompter – there was nothing natural about it; and then he went on, 'I vow to do this, I vow to do that.' And at the end, when he'd finished, a Union Jack was flashed onto the screen. It was the National Front, it was everything that I feared, and it made me absolutely sick.

Friday 4 October

We watched Rory Bremner. He is very clever. He took Blair's speech and cut into it with applause from the Tory Conference, so when Blair said, 'We will be strong on defence', you saw Portillo clapping and Major laughing and Heseltine nodding. Very clever. Then they had John Fortune and John Bird discussing how, when Labour loses the election, there is going to be a management buy-out and the Party will be turned into a publicly quoted company.

Tuesday 8 October

This morning, I got my Labour Party ballot paper to vote on *The Road to the Manifesto*. I noticed immediately that there was a number on every ballot paper, so the computer would be able to identify who had voted for and against, and who hadn't voted. Well, I am not voting for it or against it, and I suppose the fact that I don't vote will be on the computer; the next stage will be to get every candidate to register in writing their support for the Manifesto and I am not going to do that. By God, it is a police state in the Labour Party.

In the afternoon I went to Charing Cross with Caroline; they were very pleased with her progress and I think a bit surprised to see how well she was.

Friday 11 October

Tony and Cherie Blair sent Caroline a lovely bunch of flowers, which was very nice of them.

Wednesday 16 October

I went to the PLP meeting, which was a really nasty meeting. I must say, I didn't think it would be as bad as that. Donald Dewar made a long statement explaining why he had criticised Jeremy Corbyn and me.

There was a lot of bad feeling. Mo Mowlam said that the peace process has got to go on. She sort of smirks and smiles, and there is no substance at all.

Donald Dewar wound up and there was a lot of applause for him from the Labour MPs who were critical of us. It really was a warning of what the years ahead are going to be like.

Thursday 24 October

Caroline and I packed up and drove to Stansgate, where we found that the pargeting had been completed. Pargeting is a form of decoration on the outside of houses, very common in Essex, and we had commissioned a wall commemorating in bas-relief the death of Rosa Luxemburg and Karl Liebknecht who were shot in 1919 by the Social Democratic Government. It is a copy of the sculpture by Mies van der Rohe in 1926, the year Caroline was born.

Hitler had the sculpture, which was forty feet high, removed in 1934 when he came to power, but we have photographs of it, so I sent them to a young pargeter called Ian Warren to decorate the wall. Caroline was really thrilled with it.

Tuesday 5 November

The Manifesto results were announced today. The ballot must have cost nearly £1 million and apparently only 11 per cent voted against it,

200,000 in favour. When the BBC announced it at four, they said, 'This is the final end of Old Labour.'

Tony Blair said, 'This is New Labour. New Labour will be elected, and New Labour will govern with a mandate.' So it is quite threatening.

Friday 8 November

I caught the train to Nottingham and was met by Alan Simpson to take me to a meeting. He was one of those, along with Jeremy Corbyn and Ken Livingstone and others, who met Sinn Fein last week in the House of Commons. Every one of them had a letter from the Chief Whip, and Simpson was called in to see Donald Dewar. Alan said that he asked Dewar, 'While we are together, perhaps I can ask you why it is that the regional offices tell local parties not to allow me to address meetings?'

'Well,' said Dewar, 'you are seen as being anti-Labour. You are isolating yourself and, if you choose to go along this course, you could be in trouble.' It was a direct threat, not to mention a breach of privilege for threatening a Member of Parliament for meeting people in the House of Commons.

Dewar then said to Alan, 'You went into the Cafeteria at one twenty, and at one forty two of the Sinn Feiners went to the lavatory; then you stayed in the Cafeteria until seven minutes to three,' and so on. Apparently Sinn Fein were accompanied by undercover agents from MI5, and it was just as if Alan was a criminal being followed by the police. I found that very frightening.

Thursday 14 November

I had an invitation from Janet Anderson, a Labour MP, and Sir Graham Bright, a Tory MP, to a champagne reception in the House of Commons on behalf of Safeways foodstore. I thought it was a bit much, so I wrote to Sir Gordon Downey, the Parliamentary Commissioner for Standards. I also sent a copy to Donald Dewar, the Chief Whip.

Sunday 17 November

Gordon Brown is apparently going to announce that there will be a referendum before a Labour Government goes into the single currency. That is the first time Labour has agreed to that. I tried, I think in the summer of 1993, and it was deferred and they didn't want it. The Goldsmith campaign for the Referendum Party has clearly made a big impact, and the polls appear to suggest that more Labour voters are in favour of a referendum than Tory voters, so Blair has got to take account of that.

Also, Blair has been in Paris and there have been all these public-sector strikes in France against the cuts in public expenditure to prepare France for the single currency, and I dare say that alerted him. Thirdly, I think

Robin Cook, for whom I haven't got an awful lot of time, is more of a Euro-sceptic. The business community is not very keen on the Social Chapter, and Blair is prepared to move under pressure and that, in a way, is a good sign.

Tuesday 19 November

To the Labour Action for Peace meeting, where we had a report on a talk by Mo Mowlam who had impressed them enormously with her intellectual grasp of the Irish situation. She said she had been trying to get to see Sinn Fein for ages, but couldn't. She said Gerry Adams would see her only if he could have a photo-opportunity with Tony Blair, which I think is slightly unlikely to be true.

Thursday 21 November

The Independent today had a story about Donald Dewar, Sinn Fein and MI5. MI5 denied it on the lunchtime news programme, so it must have been the House of Commons security services.

Peter Hain came at 8.30 and we had a talk. He wanted to know what it was like to be a Minister. He thought the unions might well decide to put their money into their own campaigns and not into the Labour Party, which personally I think would be very sensible.

He said he had left the Tribune Group, which had defeated him as Secretary, and he is now in a group called 'What's Left', with Jean Corston and Roger Berry and one or two others.

At the House there was a marvellous demonstration by people from Tooting to save St George's Hospital. Outside the House of Commons they had assembled a little table and they had a mannequin lying on the table, with a wig on, and they covered it with a blanket and then a man with a John Major mask, in a white coat, operated on it and removed the heart out of the NHS. Terribly good, not costly and very imaginative.

Tuesday 26 November

While I was waiting at the BBC to go in for an interview, a very nervous-looking young man clutching a white, rather tatty bunny came up to me in tears. 'I just want to thank you for all you have done,' he said. He was obviously having a nervous breakdown. He said, 'I am a transsexual and I wanted to have an operation, but the psychiatrist recommended against it. So I had hormone treatment and the BBC made a programme about it and I have come to collect the tapes.' I had an interesting conversation with him about being a transsexual and the prejudices against it.

Thursday 28 November

I got a taxi and went to Welbeck Mansions in Welbeck Street for the unveiling of a plaque to the Hungarian cartoonist Vicky, whom I knew and much admired. Vicky killed himself thirty years ago, and Michael Foot made a powerful speech about him. 'Someone once said, "No one loses a night's sleep over world affairs", but it wasn't true for Vicky.' Foot described how he had committed suicide in the very block of flats where we were putting up the plaque. Nick Garland, who now does cartoons for the *Daily Telegraph* and whom I also much admire, came up and we went and had a cup of coffee in a café nearby.

It was interesting talking to Nick Garland. He put to me that the political climate had changed. The old idea that you could solve problems was out of date. Ideology was dead.

I said, 'Good heavens. We are in the grip of the most powerful ideology of all – capitalism.' It had never occurred to him that capitalism was an ideology.

He said he was reading the history of the White House, and how Roosevelt had to make up his mind whether he would take everything over and run the war, or call in the industrialists and persuade them what had to be done. He is a very talented cartoonist.

On Monday Tony Blair has invited the Central Group of MPs to a talk next week, and I might go and hear what he says.

Monday 2 December

I joined the Central Group of MPs meeting Blair in the Shadow Cabinet Room. Bruce Grocott, Paddy Tipping, John Heppell, Joe Ashton, Paul Boateng, Austin Mitchell and Dennis Skinner were there.

It was a very interesting meeting. Blair began by introducing a pollster who said that the East Midlands was a critical area – it was absolutely critical to win seventeen seats there.

I hadn't been in the Shadow Cabinet Room since I was a member of the NEC, I should think; we used to meet there. It was totally different, because in the old days there were trade union banners on the walls and no booze. Now there is booze and no banners.

I watched Blair and he seemed slightly uneasy.

It came to my turn and I made some points. I had my differences with Labour Governments, but I was very proud to be in them and, when I hear all previous Labour Governments being denounced for "tax and spend", who were they? Denis Healey? Callaghan? Roy Jenkins? Hugh Gaitskell? Philip Snowden? Were they always taxing and spending?

Blair dealt with all the minor points and then said, 'As to Tony's point, we had to be new, because we were not electable in 1983.'

It was quite jolly and friendly. Of course Blair has a wholly different project. Anyway, I am glad I said it.

I must report one thing. For two days running my answerphone hasn't had a single message, although I have been away for hours and hours. If I was saying what I really thought, I would have had a mass of calls. So I think that is one of the reasons I am a bit downhearted, but at the same time I think it is right to zip my lip and hold tight. And after this election is over – and it is only four or five months away – then one is absolutely free.

Wednesday 4 December

I went to the Commons and the Parliamentary Labour Party met to discuss the new Standing Orders, and the key to them all is that you can be suspended from the Party or have the whip withdrawn 'for action likely to bring the Party into disrepute'. There were one or two minor amendments. Jeremy Corbyn got one through.

I went on in a rather rambling way about attacking Old Labour; about the people in the past who had been expelled. It was a very bad speech, and the Party hacks had turned up to vote the changes through and didn't want to hear speeches. That's what Chris Mullin told me. But there was that same atmosphere, as in the Fifties, of intolerance – get on with it, vote, vote vote – it was really unpleasant. I loathed it and I came away sunk in gloom. Only twenty-eight people out of 270 Labour MPs were against this catch-all phrase of bringing the Party into disrepute.

Thursday 5 December

Still feeling a bit depressed. I did see Derek Foster at the House tonight and he said, 'I am so glad you spoke at the Party meeting yesterday. We do need people with experience of what all this expulsion business means.'

I said, 'Well, it was awful, and I think they would like to get rid of some MPs before the election.'

He said, 'I am sure they would.'

We talked about Mandelson and I said, 'I think he is a really bad influence.'

'I absolutely agree with you.'

Wednesday 11 December

I walked over to the studios at 4 Millbank to do *House to House*. I had a word with John Biffen and his wife, and with Michael Spicer who is passionately anti-Maastricht. I said, 'Well, who do you think will end up as Leader after the election?'

Michael Spicer said, 'I think it has to be a Euro-sceptic who is emollient. Michael Howard would be fine.'

He told me a story about Blair that I found very interesting. 'When I was a Minister at the Energy Department pushing through electricity privatisation, Tony Blair was leading for the Opposition and he came to me and said, "There are four things I am going to make a flaming big row about, and I want to make them early in the morning in order to catch the one o'clock news."'

So that told me something about Tony Blair and I suppose, from a career point of view, it is very effective. I asked, 'Does he frighten you in the House?'

'He's a good barrister,' said Spicer, who hadn't much time for Major.

Monday 16 December

I had a word with Roy Hattersley, who told me that he went to Slough recently to do a meeting and Margaret McDonagh sent a message to him saying, 'You are not to speak about comprehensive education. It is a big turn-off in the Home Counties.' Roy was absolutely gobsmacked by this and said to me, 'This is not the Party I joined.'

Thursday 7 January 1997

Blair, in an interview in the *Big Issue*, the newspaper of the homeless, said it is right to be intolerant of homeless people on the streets and came out with this zero-tolerance policy akin to the New York police force's, whereby the beggars, 'squeegee merchants' and homeless people have just been driven off the streets. The most illiberal comment you could possibly imagine.

The other thing is that John Major had his first presidential press conference. So the election campaign has begun.

Wednesday 8 January

Today the Labour Party launched its new election campaign with a presidential press conference.

Friday 10 January

A completely free day in the office.

Saturday 11 January

Caught the train to Newbury and was met by Peter Boyle and driven to his house, past the site of the Newbury bypass – huge razor-wire fences and police buses and everything I associate with the miners' strike of the 1980s.

I met John Vidal from the *Guardian*, Charles Secrett, the Chairman of Friends of the Earth, George Monbiot, Jill Eisler from Ploughshares, and two members of the Green Party. It was extremely cold and misty and foggy. We had a sandwich and a cup of tea.

Then we walked across the road to the paddock where there were 2000 or 3000 people. The loudspeaker system wasn't working but I shouted as loud as I could. John Vidal was very sympathetic – just finishing a book on 'Mclibel', the libel case brought by McDonald's against two people who criticised the company for its policies.

People had broken through the fence with wire-cutters and they all streamed in and surrounded a tree called Middle Oak, the one tree they had succeeded in saving. It is going to be the centre of a roundabout. At one stage the police were chasing them but so many came in, danced round Middle Oak and some of them climbed the tree, and the police evidently withdrew. Two vehicles were set on fire.

It was an interesting gathering. Charles Secrett, for example, made a speech about what a wicked thing the car was, whereas in my speech I said the wicked thing was worshipping profit. The Green Party speaker was keen to say that the Greens had been the only people who had opposed the Newbury bypass. There were Animal Liberation people there, all sorts of people the Government must absolutely detest. It was very inspiring. Yet the atmosphere was similar to the poll tax revolt or Wapping or the miners' strike (which of course was very much more explicitly political). But all these people, including Peter Boyle who was a businessman, had been radicalised by what they had seen.

I found it all very exciting, but I was frightfully cold.

Sunday 12 January

Bought the papers and there was a bit about Newbury, but not a great deal.

Monday 13 January

I worked on a critique of the Police Bill, about which I have been increasingly concerned, because it gives the police the power to bug and burgle anybody they like without any authority from magistrates or judges or Ministers. So I wrote to forty MPs with a draft Early Day Motion and a postcard for reply. It was very cautiously drafted: 'This House has grave anxieties about the provisions of the Bill, which would erode civil liberties', and so on. It was done like that because I didn't want to make it impossible for Tories to support it – not that I think any of them will.

When I got to the House, the first person I saw was Chris Mullin, so I told him what I had done. 'Oh, no,' he said, 'the Bill's perfectly all right.'

I said 'What do you mean?' He replied, 'They've always done that. This puts it on a statutory basis.'

'What about the bugging and burgling of the last Labour Government as described in Peter Wright's book *Spycatcher*?'

'That's quite different. You had better have a word with Jack Straw.'

'I don't think there is much point in that.'

Well who should come up at that moment but Jack Straw, and he said, 'It's perfectly all right.'

I was terribly discouraged, because I had still regarded Chris as a bit of a liberal. Later I looked at the *Guardian* and there was an article about it saying that Chris Mullin supported Jack Straw's approach and that Jim Callaghan was against it.

Wednesday 15 January
A woman called Amanda Hume from Speech Recognition Ltd came to install a voice-typing system on my computer. I sat with a headset on and began dictating while the system interpreted it onto the screen. The first results were absolutely hilarious.

When I said, 'This is a test of this machine . . .' It came out as, 'List is a test Mr Bishop.' Then I dictated something about the election, which came out as, 'Election decision ensures telex, prejudice, Bolshevik technology playback obsessional promotional Ashurst.' Then 'My name is Tony Benn and in my office works Sheila Hubacher' became, 'My name is Bogey Benn and in my office works Cheeky Biker.'

We just sat there giggling ourselves silly. I hope I can make it work because it is a big investment in money, but I will have to practise and practise until it becomes usable.

Sunday 19 January
Today there was big coverage about a woman called Nicola Horlick, a pension fund manager with Morgan Grenfell earning £1 million a year, who has been sacked. She has got PR people and lawyers working for her and she flew to Germany to see Deutsche Bank, who own Morgan Grenfell. Thousands of miners, steel-workers and car-workers are sacked, but her dismissal gets major coverage. She is claiming £1 million compensation and then, blow me down, today in the *Sunday Express* there was a headline: 'I want to be a Labour MP now,' says Nicola Horlick.

Mandelson is a friend of hers. She claims to advise the Labour Party on tax. It just makes your mind boggle with the implications.

Monday 20 January
Gordon Brown made a statement that he as Chancellor would not increase income tax – neither the standard rate nor the top rate – for the whole life of the next Parliament and that there would be a two-year freeze on public-sector pay. The combination of that with yesterday's story about Nicola Horlick shows that we are a party that has adopted Tory policies. I have said it many times, but it is crystal-clear that that is what has happened.

Jack Straw came up to me and said, 'I hope you noticed that I listened to you about the Police Bill', because he has done a U-turn about bugging being authorised by a judge.

Had a talk to Chris Mullin later. I must be careful not to pick a row with Chris whenever I see him, because it is a bit distressing. He wants to be Chairman of the Home Affairs Committee when the next Government is formed. He doesn't want to be a Minister and I think that is a perfectly legitimate ambition.

Tuesday 21 January
Caroline went to Charing Cross Hospital for a check-up. The results on the tests of the spine they had done last time were not too bad; she has got to go back in two months.

Saturday 1 February
I had been invited to go to an international conference against the Maastricht Treaty at Central Hall, Westminster and when I got there, there were eighteen nations represented – bus-loads of people from Germany, France, Italy and all over Europe. Even some people from Brazil. It was a marvellous rally and the great thing about it was that it was international. Nobody could say this was the British against Europe. This was the European working class against the bankers and the Commissioners. There was an item on the six o'clock news quoting what I had said quite fairly and then, at the end, making the point that 'the two MPs' (Jeremy Corbyn and me) were totally unrepresentative of the Party.

Monday 3 February
Up early, drove to the Commons and was taken to the Royal Naval College, Greenwich, to talk at the Joint Services Defence College. The college brings together the more senior officers of the Services and they asked me to present what they call an 'alternative view'. They have already had Nicholas Soames, Denis Healey, Sir Nicholas Bonsor and Norman Tebbit to speak.

Afterwards I had lunch in the Painted Hall – I was there fifty-two years ago as a young sub-lieutenant A in the Fleet Air Arm. I began by saying that when I was there in 1945 an old admiral had said that the Russian Revolution was caused by the abandonment of saluting in the Tsarist navy and that I had found that very helpful; it explained the Cold War and one or two other things – it was naval indiscipline that had caused all the trouble! They laughed a bit. They sort of laugh in spite of themselves. But the Painted Hall is so beautiful. It has been cleaned up. It took ninteen years to paint and the artist, James Thornhill, wasn't paid, so he painted himself into the picture holding his hand out. Now they are selling it off. I think it will go to Greenwich University.

Tuesday 4 February
I talked to Chris Mullin, who looks as if he is making progress with his campaign to get Freemasons to declare their allegiance.

Wednesday 5 February
Alan Simpson told an extraordinary story – he laughed about it, but it was an extraordinary story. There is always a briefing meeting for those Labour MPs who have got questions for Major during PMQs, to plan the

attack. He had got Question 2 for tomorrow so he went along to the meeting in the Shadow Cabinet rooms. Alastair Campbell was there. Everybody is handed a supplementary question to follow their main question and Alan said he was going to ask about Europe.

'Oh no, you can't do that,' he was told.

'Why not?' asked Alan.

They wanted him to ask, 'Is the Prime Minister aware that everyone in the Labour Party supports the Leader of the Opposition, whereas within the Tory Party, they are divided?'

Alan said, 'I can't say that because I don't believe it.'

'It would be good for your career,' Alastair Campbell said.

So Alan said, 'What career?'

And Campbell replied, 'It will get you through to the election.' That indicated that he would have to pay a price even to survive as a backbench MP.

Friday 7 February

David Blunkett has written an article for the *Daily Mail* saying that if, or when, he is Secretary of State for Education, he will take over the work of local education authorities that he believes have failed, to safeguard the interests of the students in their area. He will put in somebody from OFSTED, an educational expert, possibly a Chief Education Officer from another area; an appointed quango will replace democracy in local authorities. It is an outrageous idea, totally undemocratic, totally authoritarian.

Sunday 9 February

Melissa drove us to the Odeon at Marble Arch to see *Evita*. It was a very, very good film, a musical really without any dialogue to speak of. Madonna played the part of Eva Perón brilliantly. What frightened me was that Perón had a party called Labour linked to the unions, and then he repressed union opposition with great brutality, using the police. Eva Perón was clever and skilful in building up support, although she was phoney; Perón himself reminded me so much of American and British politicians, demagogues building up support. It was scary because fascism is very attractive, otherwise it wouldn't have been supported. Indeed, today a fascist candidate won the mayoralty of a town in the south of France. I think fascism is coming back.

Wednesday 12 February

Hannah, aged three, has always been frightened of men with beards, so I had sent a photograph of myself from 1969 with a beard, and I wondered how Hannah would react; so I rang Melissa, and Melissa said Hannah looked at it and flared her nostrils and said, 'Yes, but it was a very small beard.' So she wasn't going to be caught out!

Went into the House after lunch and the Police Bill debate began. Michael Howard, who has a permanent, fixed, insincere smile on his face, presented the Bill. I intervened on a number of matters during his speech. He had to give way to me though he didn't much like it. I intervened on what would be on the police computer, why it was that large numbers of people with a common purpose could be bugged. He said it could be used against neo-Nazis whipping up football violence, which was absolutely irrelevant.

Jack Straw, in all fairness, made a much better speech for the Bill than Howard. Straw is a very competent lawyer. He and Howard were absolutely hand-in-glove. Jack wants the Bill desperately, not just because he has been told by Blair that we have got to support it, but he wants it because it will give him the powers he wants.

Andrew Mackinlay was extremely good, Neil Gerrard was very good, Chris Mullin was a great disappointment. He sounded like a Permanent Secretary advising Jack Straw on what he should do; but still he knows an awful lot about it.

I saw Norman Tebbit just before I went into the debate. He was watching the little meteorological computer screen that has been installed near the Post Office. As I passed, I said, 'There is a lot of mist over Europe, I think.'

He said, 'More than mist. It is very, very foggy.'

'I think this whole business is beginning to come unravelled.'

'In the House of Lords, for the first time in either House, we carried a motion that would amend Section 2 of the European Communities Act,' Tebbit said.

'Well, I introduced a Bill to do that in 1979,' I said. 'I must admit, I have been very slow in taking up your lead,' he replied.

I said, 'Well, I am a libertarian, Norman; if only you would drop all this economic nonsense, I would be with you on all these things.' He was very friendly. He is a funny man, Tebbit; underneath he is really a rather decent guy and he is a libertarian.

Saturday 15 February

The Economist today had a picture of Straw and Howard under the heading 'Partners in Crime – The Threat to Britain's Liberties'.

Monday 17 February

I went into the Lobby and I had a chat to Ian Paisley. He made a very good speech last Wednesday on the Police Bill, and I told him my theory that the single currency and 'convergence' reminded me of Esau, who gave up his birthright for a mess of pottage. I said to Ian, 'No doubt Esau and his brother Jacob had convergence criteria which were approved by Isaac, and so Esau gave up his birthright and got some red lentil soup. I love the Bible.'

He said, 'So do I, especially the book of Genesis.'

'We have got to be careful, otherwise David Trimble will be worried if we are seen talking too much.'

Paisley is a very nice guy. He is a good constituency Member. He has got a good class sense. He is a demagogue and is anti-Catholic and all that, but he is an amusing guy.

Wednesday 19 February
Caroline went to the hospital for her relaxation class and said that many of the women there, much younger than herself, were on chemotherapy and were bald and had wigs. She really likes going and she is very practical about it. She doesn't know how long she will live, but she is very strong and clear. I wrote a poem for her today called 'The Tiger in my Tank'.

I went to the Commons and talked to Chris Mullin, who is tabling a motion attacking the *Daily Mail* for naming the so-called murderers of Stephen Lawrence.

Thursday 20 February
Had lunch, a snooze and then into the House for Prime Minister's Questions. Then, at 3.30, I presented my European Communities (Amendment) Bill which would allow the House of Commons to accept or reject European legislation. Had a word with the Speaker who called me over to the chair. I had written her a note last week saying, 'Dear Madam Speaker, I was touched and moved that you should have come in to hear me speak on the Police Bill. Your support and encouragement are welcome from all dissenters, including yours truly.'

She said today, 'I always enjoy your speeches. You always put it so clearly and so amusingly.' Well, that guaranteed, I might add, that I would be called this afternoon and she said, 'Of course I will call you.'

Friday 21 February
Had a phone call on the train to Chesterfield from Teletext, who said that this morning they had a phone-in opinion poll on the question: 'Mr Benn has introduced a Bill to give the House of Commons the last word on European legislation. Do you agree with it or not?' A total of 1900 people rang and 88 per cent agreed.

David Blunkett made a statement that the redistribution of wealth is no longer an objective of the Labour Party, and Frank Field welcomed it.

In the evening Caroline and I went to Melissa's fortieth birthday party, organised by Paul. The kids were all there, and Tim Owen and his wife, Gemma Redgrave, were there, Ruth Richardson and her husband, and their baby, Josh. I had a talk to Becky Swift, the daughter of Margaret Drabble, who was kneeling talking to Caroline. I liked her very much. She said she had kept a diary since she was fourteen. I said my diary was rather chronological. She said, 'Mine's all over the place. "Hey, ho," it will begin and then I'll say what I am thinking.'

I said, 'Well I think that would be much more interesting, truthfully.'

Tuesday 25 February

The Government have announced the privatisation of the London Underground, which is not very popular with anybody.

Thursday 27 February

Caroline went shopping with Melissa in Oxford Street and she really loved it. When they were having a cup of coffee, Melissa asked her something about her health and Caroline told her, and Melissa burst into tears and said, 'Don't leave me, Mum.' It was so sweet. We have had our tears, but now we are in a more practical approach to it all, although it doesn't alter that agony.

Tuesday 11 March

I was in the Chamber and Ted Heath beckoned me over, so I went and sat next to him on the green benches and we discussed briefly the *Question Time* we're doing together on Thursday.

In the evening there was a debate on the Finance Bill, with an amendment moved by Alan Simpson calling for a cut in VAT on energy-saving materials.

This amendment had been moved last year by Dawn Primarolo on behalf of the Shadow Cabinet; this year, because it involves some minor spending commitment, Gordon Brown has banned it and therefore Dawn Primarolo was put up again, really to humiliate her, to repudiate what she had said last year.

Alan Simpson had worked with local authorities and old people's organisations on this, and I was so angry that after he moved the motion, I got in – only for about ninety seconds, I should think. The whips have been very, very heavy in telling people not to vote.

Afterwards I had a brief chat in the Tea Room with Dawn and told her that she should have said, 'Look, if you want to reverse your policy, get somebody else to do it.' But they deliberately made her do it to humiliate her.

Thursday 13 March

Went to Birmingham in the afternoon for *Question Time* at Pebble Mill with Ted Heath, Liz Lynne and Frederick Forsyth. I must say Ted was very good and progressive; Liz Lynne is of course a progressive Liberal; Forsyth was awful on crime and trade unions and the Labour Party, but he wasn't bad on the privatisation of social services. I said there were two

Labour Parties. There was the Labour Party and New Labour, and they were in coalition and I worked very well with them.

Monday 17 March

Today a General Election for 1 May was announced, the longest election period this century. Major obviously calculates that he'll bore people into abstaining, and that Blair will be revealed as an empty head. But I desperately hope that we win and I desperately hope that we have a big majority.

This is my seventeenth election. I'm hopeful Chesterfield will be all right, but the Liberal appeal for more money for health, education and higher tax is actually very credible. I'm hoping I'm well enough known in Chesterfield to carry the vote, but you should take nothing for granted; if the Tory vote collapses and they vote Liberal, then I'm sunk.

Tuesday 18 March

The *Sun* came out in favour of Tony Blair, so that's the price we all have to pay for Blair capitulating to Murdoch.

Wednesday 19 March

When the election was announced I felt very frightened, I don't know why. I can't explain it, because I've fought sixteen parliamentary elections and won fifteen of them, but somehow I feel that I'm vulnerable. I think it's Caroline's illness: it's being away so much, and wondering whether I'm right to have taken Chesterfield for granted in the way that I have.

Went into the Commons because the Party meeting was to be addressed at three by Blair. He thanked the retiring members; he had an awful smirk on his face the whole time.

He said, 'We can't take anything for granted in the election. The Tories have lots of money; the media are not as unsympathetic as they have been in the past,' at which there was a lot of laughter, referring to the fact that Rupert Murdoch has come out in support of Blair. He went on, 'We have a supreme organisation in some marginal seats, and we have the telephone numbers of all the Tories who promised to switch to Labour, so we can ring them up before polling day.'

He continued, 'I hope all Labour candidates will be very careful what they say. We must be the party of unity, we must have confidence in our message; don't say we're the same as the Tories because, for example, we're going to get rid of the internal market in the NHS, we're going to end the assisted places and spend the money elsewhere, we're going to get young people into work. We've got to have a great deal of discipline. It's an exciting time, an opportunity for us to look after the people who rely on us.'

I talked to a few people. Had a long talk to Joan Lestor; I'm very fond of Joan, and she doesn't look too well.

I asked what she was going to do with her papers, and would she write her memoirs? We talked about love affairs and she said, 'In the old days, these things were sort of understood but not commented upon, and now the whole thing is scandal, scandal, scandal.'

Friday 21 March, Chesterfield

To the Town Hall to receive the Worcestershire & Sherwood Forest Regiment, which marched through the town with bands and banners and fixed bayonets and armoured personnel vehicles. Some of them were in nineteenth-century uniforms with black spiked helmets, red tunics and blue trousers. It was really, I think, a recruiting drive. I stood on the steps with Lady Hilton, the widow of a former Lord Lieutenant, the Duke of Devonshire, the Mayor and the bigwigs. The Mayor gave the regiment a little present, and the Colonel came up and spoke to me and then the Sergeant-Major came up in his red uniform. It was the class structure of Britain in microcosm.

Sunday 23 March

Stephen's wife, Nita, has got herself a job at Millbank Tower, starting tomorrow, working as a press officer for the period of the election campaign. She's very, very competent. I raised the question of the blind trusts – these are the trusts set up to fund Blair, Prescott and Beckett and one or two other Shadow Cabinet members, which are supposed to be all right because nobody knows who's contributed to them. I said I thought that was sleaze of the worst kind. But Nita said, 'No, no not at all, for example the trade unions poured millions of pounds into a blind trust.' I can't agree. What's to stop individual MPs having a blind trust?

Monday 24 March

Tony Blair passed through Chesterfield today with a film unit. He was filmed at Chesterfield station. He never let me know, and I suppose he didn't want to be filmed with me, and I don't know I'd want to be filmed with him. But I was a bit cheesed off about it, because I ought really to have been there.

Wednesday 26 March

We went to Hertfordshire, to a model village established by Fergus O'Connor, the radical Chartist MP and reformer. This village, Heronsgate, was set up in 1847 to provide housing and land for people from the poorer industrial towns in the north, but it's now the most fashionable little enclave of very rich people, with ponies trotting along the lanes and huge listed houses and old cottages.

We went first to the Church of St John, and there in the churchyard about thirty-five party members were gathered, and the Chairman of the local Party nominated Marc Wilson as the candidate, and he was duly selected. Every day Blair tells us Labour has changed, but when you see the local Labour parties they haven't changed at all. We walked from there to the house of Johnny Speight, the man who wrote *Till Death Us Do Part*. He's an old cockney from Canning Town, a very talented writer, and he had this lovely little cottage where we sat and had a cup of tea. From there I was driven all the way to Hemel Hempstead to Tesco supermarket, where about fifty or more Labour people had assembled.

It was the beginning of the campaign and it gave me a bit of confidence. I couldn't be in any other party but the Labour Party really. I know all sorts of things go wrong but the heart and spirit of the Party now are fine and nothing really has changed, despite Blair.

Friday 28 March, Stansgate

We had a meal with the family and then we went out into the garden and watched Hale-Bopp's comet, which was fantastic – this great big thing about four times the size of the stars, travelling at 100,000 miles an hour, two million miles away, I was told. It really was something worth seeing.

Saturday 29 March

The Labour Party dropped its commitment to publicly owned railways and they've also announced that the Labour candidate fighting Neil Hamilton in Tatton has decided he's going to withdraw from the election if the Liberals also withdraw, in favour of an anti-corruption candidate.

Wednesday 2 April

The Tory manifesto was issued and they did succeed in getting command of the election agenda. Major, who was interviewed by Jon Snow on the Channel 4 News, was very serious and calm and confident. But the really big news today is that Hilary rang to say that he had been shortlisted as one of five for the Pontefract and Castleford candidature – the MP Geoffrey Lofthouse retired at the last minute.

Thursday 3 April

One nice story that I heard a couple of days ago about Millbank Tower. They have set up batteries of young people – or it might be a contract company – telephoning Party members to get money out of them for the campaign. One young woman in her mid-twenties rang up Jim Callaghan and said to him on the phone, 'Have you ever thought of being a bit more active in politics?' So Callaghan said, 'Well, I was a Labour Prime Minister – what more could I do?'

Friday 4 April
Blair has said that there will be no increase in taxation in England or Scotland while he's Prime Minister, and he drew an unhappy parallel between the Scottish Parliament and a parish council, which has caused a sense of outrage in Scotland.

Saturday 5 April
Caroline told me when I got home tonight that Gore Vidal, the famous American writer, had been present at the launch of Labour's Manifesto and had thought Blair looked very frightened.

Sunday 6 April
Martin Bell from the BBC has agreed to be the anti-corruption candidate in Tatton.

It's interesting that in the Manifesto the word socialism isn't mentioned once and even the *new* Clause 4 has been removed. They used the new Clause 4 to get rid of the old one, but they didn't even want to use the new one, which had to be sounding radical in some respects to beat the old one; now that's dropped as well.

Monday 7 April
The sad news today, and I didn't hear it until half-past ten, was that Hilary did not get selected for Pontefract and Castleford. They chose Yvette Cooper, a twenty-eight year-old economics correspondent of *The Independent*, and partner of Ed Balls, who is special adviser to Gordon Brown. My heart goes out to Hilary.

The big political news today is that at a city conference Tony Blair came out in favour of the privatisation of air-traffic control, of government land, Channel 4, and so on.

Tuesday 8 April
Neil Hamilton was re-adopted as the Tory candidate for Tatton and I have a sort of feeling he might do well. I don't know, I think the whole idea of putting the BBC war correspondent in a white suit, Mr Clean and all that, is utterly ridiculous.

Wednesday 9 April
Today has been entirely devoted to a bitter slanging match between Major and Blair, each saying that the other is lying and can't be trusted.

Thursday 10 April
I heard a party political broadcast by the Labour Party – 'Labour Means Business' and so on – which is really designed to alienate every trade unionist there is; Major is carrying on with his attack on the Social

Chapter and Blair is in full retreat on it; there's a difference of opinion about what's going to be privatised and what isn't; and Ray Powell, the MP for Ogmore, has said publicly that he was offered a peerage if he would retire to make his seat available to somebody else, which Ron Davies denies. Major is making good use of the muddle, I must say. I think he's very clever.

Friday 11 April, Chesterfield

Bumped into the former Liberal Mayor of Chesterfield, and I asked him how he was. He said, 'My stomach's very bad, I won't be able to do anything in the election. But I shall be voting for Tony on 1 May.'

And I said, 'Well, I presumed so' (as Tony Rogers is the Liberal Democrat candidate).

And he replied, 'Ah, but I haven't told you which Tony! You're the only one against Europe.'

Angela Browning has said she will not accept the single currency because it would involve transferring our gold and dollar reserves to Frankfurt and 'that would be a breach of sovereignty, and I won't go along with it.' So of course the Labour Party immediately denounced Major for not sacking her and said that Labour was united, the Tories were divided; and Ashdown said the same. It was ridiculous.

Went down to the station, picked up Caroline, and we came back and did a little bit of folding of election addresses in the Labour Club.

The bungalow's a lovely place to be during an election, but this is my last parliament, there's no question about it. I'm totally out of sympathy with the politics of the Labour Party and maybe Blair will carry it all off, get massive media support, but we will see. And I have to look after Caroline, so I'm pretty sure this is my last campaign and a strange one it is. The polls show Labour 20 per cent ahead of the Tories. I can't believe that.

Saturday 12 April

Caroline was disturbed all night by my talking clock, which announces the hour every hour because I've forgotten how to switch it off. So I'm going to have to hide it in the bathroom at night.

Got in a cavalcade of about four cars and went to Poolsbrook and Duckmanton, old mining villages – only four miners left there now.The land has been open-casted and landscaped, so it looks all right, but it's the scorched earth policy of the Government, a wicked thing to do.Somebody asked, 'What is Labour going to do about pensions?' Well, I couldn't answer. I said, 'I'll be fighting for them.'

Really there is no policy directed at these people, and they are ignored and neglected and a lot of undecided people might come down in favour of the Liberals. I might even lose Chesterfield, it's a possibility; it's even a possibility that we might lose the election if the undecided people came to the conclusion they didn't like Blair and voted for Ashdown; it doesn't seem very likely, but it's not impossible. Yesterday David Butler said it would be a landslide, but I don't believe it.

Sunday 13 April, Chesterfield
This is the Labour Party daily briefing, by fax, to all Members today:

> The Tories claim that the motions submitted to next weekend's Scottish TUC conference, such as calling for the re-nationalisation of the railways and a £4.50 minimum wage, herald the return of trade union militancy under a Labour Government. They mean no such thing. The Scottish TUC conference is nothing to do with the Labour Party, it is separate even from the TUC; nothing that it says or does makes any difference to Labour's manifesto policy. We have made our position on industrial relations clear – Labour's relations with the unions will be based on fairness and not favours; the key elements of 1980 trade-union reforms on ballots, picketing and industrial action will stay; the firemen's dispute in Essex is similarly nothing to do with Labour. We've called on both sides to resolve their differences through independent arbitration; in our view industrial action would not be justified.

We drove to Manchester for the Chesterfield v Middlesbrough match; took us ages to get there because the whole of Chesterfield was going.We found our way into Old Trafford and bought some rosettes for the grandchildren. Anyway, we went into the directors' suite and they were sitting down to a meal, and we were seated at the table with the Football Association.

We went out and watched the game and it was a thrilling game. Just to set the record straight, Middlesbrough is a top-class club with tons of money and very valuable players and Chesterfield is a little small-town club. All the press said that Chesterfield dreams will end today.

Anyway the first goal was scored by Chesterfield; then the second goal was scored by Chesterfield. The Chesterfield supporters – who filled about two-thirds of the stadium, I would imagine – 24,000 people, just cheered to the echo. We were all in blue, of course. Middlesbrough fans opposite, in red, were much quieter, and didn't have so many flags.

So we were 2-0 up and then Middlesbrough scored once. Then Middlesbrough scored again, and at the end of the regular game it was a 2-2 draw. So there was extra time. In the first quarter of an hour of extra time Middlesbrough scored again, so they were leading 3-2 and we'd given up hope. And then literally fifty-five seconds before the final whistle blew, Chesterfield equalled 3-3.

So a very, happy day; the football game was a wild success; I suppose we've got a sporting chance of Chesterfield getting into the final at Wembley. But it's just lovely to see a little place like this, with such lovely people, get such a boost.

Monday 14 April, Chesterfield

I got up early as usual, went and bought the papers, then we had breakfast. Caroline packed up and I took her back to the station, knowing that the bungalow would be lonely without her for the next week or so.

I drove to Halifax. I got totally lost in Sheffield, going round in circles, and it finally took me two hours to get to Halifax.

Alice Mahon was waiting for me. Alice has got only a 500 majority and there is a strong Tory vote in Halifax. The Labour Party HQ seemed to be far better organised than we are in Chesterfield: all the literature ready to go out, all the maps on the wall.

Halifax Town Hall is beautiful. Built in 1863 by the architect who worked on the House of Commons a bit earlier and they said that he practised on the Palace of Westminster before he came to Halifax. When you saw the stained glass and the lovely murals in this beautiful building you realised that working-class councillors would be totally overawed – as MPs are when they come to Westminster.

The phenomenal success of Chesterfield football has taken politics completely off the agenda, certainly until the play-off, which is Tuesday week. Meanwhile people watch all this terrible negative campaigning, with no difference between Blair and Major.

Tonight Major attacked Blair for hypocrisy for sending his kid to a grant-maintained school. Blair said, 'We're not going to do anything about grant-maintained schools because they work.'

Wednesday 16 April

I went to the football club and for two hours we walked from the front to the back of both queues of people queuing to buy tickets for the match. There must have been 10-15,000 people in the street – there never has been such an event in the whole of my political life. I met everybody who was queuing. I will be at the game too.

Sunday 20 April

I went out this morning leafleting.

I had a flaming row with a man of seventy-four and his wife, both of whom said they'd always been Labour but were voting Conservative this time. I asked, 'Why?' And they said, 'Because we don't trust Tony Blair. If it was you or Dennis Skinner as Leader, it would be different.' So I said, 'It *is* me you're voting for, not Tony Blair!' Then the woman launched into a bitter attack on a single mother with six children who went to bingo every night; she was against a minimum wage and said some people didn't want to work; I said to them at the end, 'I don't believe you ever did vote Labour. Those are real Tory arguments,' and they got angry, but anyway I'm glad I said it. But it had an effect on me for the rest of the day. Rang Caroline.

Monday 21 April, Chesterfield

I did a house call on a woman whose little boy of four was beaten up in the area where she lived. He was cut and had petrol thrown over him; it was terrifying. I couldn't get him to say anything, he was so scared. I said I'd try and do something about it.

There was an IRA bomb alert this morning which closed Paddington, St Pancras, King's Cross, affected the underground, Gatwick and Luton; these attacks – whether bombs or hoaxes – are extremely effective.

Tuesday 22 April

Caught the staff coach from Chesterfield football club to Hillsborough. We had a lovely seat in a box right high up, and could see the whole game, but it was a disappointing game. Chesterfield weren't half as good as they had been last time; Middlesbrough were much, much better and Chesterfield lost by 3-0.

It was very discouraging, but the Chesterfield fans were phenomenal; they waved their flags and cheered, long after the final whistle had blown. This little town has really done so much to give confidence to the team.

Thursday 24 April

Canvassing in the evening – the sweetest moment of all was when one little girl of about five came up to me and said, 'Have you ever met Tony Benn?' So I said, 'Yes, I have, have you?" Yes, she said, I have met him. So I said, 'Well, I've met him too. *I'm* Tony Benn.' And she looked so surprised. All the older girls of seven and eight just giggled and said, 'Tony Benn, we're voting for Tony Benn.'

I stayed up and watched Blair doing a one-man question-and-answer session on *Question Time*. He was very good, very persuasive, very agreeable, very attractive; when Mandelson isn't round his neck he's much better.

Friday 25 April

I went out to a dinner organised by Ann Denman, Tom and Margaret Vallins and a lot of mates: Bob and Mary Burkitt, Colin Wainwright, Ian and Fran Street, old comrades of the Party who had got together and booked a table for thirty in the Santiago restaurant on the Sheffield Road. A cake had been made with 'Best of Luck, Tony' written on it and horseshoes and a red flag. It was just so sweet really.There was dancing and I went up and down the tables and talked to different people, and I really, really liked it. I got back to the bungalow and was absolutely exhausted. I think I went to bed without a cup of tea, which is almost unheard of.

Saturday 26 April

Alexandre Drobnan, the Russian professor, came to see me in Chesterfield. We had about an hour and a quarter together. He's a socialist, a very scholarly man, studied Lenin and thought he was brilliant. He had never, ever been to Britain before, but he'd read the six volumes of my *Diaries,* which is absolutely amazing. He was born in Russia in 1934 and his mother had starved to death when he was eight, because the Germans confiscated all the food. It made him very bitter and he hated Gorbachev, whom he felt had let him down; Yeltsin was loathed. Drobnan was furious about the extension of NATO, really passionate about that.

Sunday 27 April

Went to the station to pick up Caroline, who travelled up with Stephen and the children (Emily and Daniel). Daniel quite fearlessly went up to boys twice his age who were playing football and offered them Labour stickers and Emily distributed posters. It was a perfect afternoon's canvassing, which they'll never forget, I suppose. When they're seventy-five people won't believe that they canvassed with their old grandfather in 1997. Stephen videoed a lot of it so that's all on the record.

Monday 28 April

A woman had in her window a sticker saying, 'I'm not an OAP, I'm a recycled teenager', which I thought was rather nice. And one man whose door I knocked on, who had been a socialist all his life, said he was going to write a book when he retired called 'Born to Toil'. He pulled out of his wallet a little statement by Thomas Carlyle which he read to me: 'If a man has suffered a great injustice he may take a lesser injustice as if it was a favour.' Powerful stuff.

A Bengali came all the way from Liverpool to see me. He said he'd helped in Bristol in 1983 when I was beaten and was a great friend of Eric Heffer. He owns forty tandoori restaurants and said he was here to be sure that everyone knew who to vote for. Couldn't have been nicer. He gave me a big hug.

Tuesday 29 April

Went over to the Club at 9.30 and had a talk to Alexander Drobnan, this Russian professor who is still in Chesterfield and wants me to arrange for him to meet leading Conservative Euro-sceptics and Europhiles in the weekend following the election, which I can't possibly do. We tried to send him off to Newport but he said his ticket wasn't transferable. I told him to ring my brother Dave for a talk, as Dave is a great expert on Russia, and later I heard that he had asked Dave to put him up for Friday night. I feel sorry, but he lacks initiative.

Went to the Sheepbridge Estate and I talked to the girls as they came out of a factory; they earn £3.35 an hour. They produce the little bags they give you on airlines, with a toothbrush and a razor in. I had a chat to some of them.

Came home and Lissie rang, bless her heart, and she said that Hannah and Sarah had been out in the park and met Ken Livingstone. Livingstone spoke to her for a bit and when he left Hannah said, 'What a very silly man.' She's three and Ken Livingstone's the former Chairman of the GLC and a Member of Parliament.

Alan Simpson rang. He's been asked to write an article by several papers after the election. I think it's a little bit risky and I said, 'Whatever you do, don't give any hostages to fortune, because if there is a possibility of your getting office, you would ruin it if you said anything that was unhelpful in the eyes of Mandelson.'

Wednesday 30 April

The Russian, Drobnan, went to London to see Dave.

At ten o'clock I went out with Malcolm Gee, whom I dearly love. He was the Secretary of the Trades Council, and the AEU, in Chesterfield and has now got a bigger job in the AEU. We drove around and had a very interesting talk; he said that some union General Secretaries don't want the anti-union legislation repealed because it keeps their unions under control, and I think he's absolutely right. It explains why they don't like strikes, because strikes put them under pressure, whereas if there are no strikes and a bit of unemployment it keeps their members quiet. I thought that was a significant comment.

He asked me all about Herbert Morrison and all sorts of people whom I'd known in the past and then went on to discuss the difference between Methodism and Congregationalism, the Baptists and the Quakers. I'm really fond of Malc Gee.

Part Four
May 1997–May 2001

New Labour now found itself in a position of unchallenged political power, able to do almost everything it wanted with impunity, and certainly acting as if Parliament, Party and public were all in uncritical support of its policies and leadership.

Under the banner of modernisation many of the policies of the Conservative governments of the 1980s and 1990s reappeared – privatisation; the retention of severe restrictions on the trade unions; a refusal to raise taxes for the wealthy; continued enrichment of corporate 'fat cats' and, most significantly, the search for economic stability required of governments whether Tory or Labour, by the Maastricht Treaty, which delayed the necessary provision of funds for the public services. Public expenditure levels set by the Conservatives were maintained for the whole of the 1997–2001 Parliament.

Britain went along with the United States in again bombing Iraq, making war on Yugoslavia and giving apparently unquestioning backing to Clinton in his foreign policy and military strategy – even to continuing general support for Israel, though that country was denying the Palestinians the right to their own state.

The most optimistic progress came with the positive and imaginative policy pursued in Northern Ireland, which led to the Belfast Agreement and the establishment of an Assembly in Stormont that gave the Nationalists their place in the government of the province.

The record on constitutional change was impressive, with legislation set in motion for a Scottish Parliament, a Welsh Assembly, a Mayor of London, and the replacement of most hereditary peers, albeit by others appointed through patronage.

For the last six months of my fifty-one years in Parliament, I was engaged in various end-of-term activities, while remaining actively involved in political campaigns. I was particularly interested in the system for electing the Speaker: this was dictated by convention and, owing to the large number of candidates who put themselves forward this time, became a complex and unnecessary process, but ended with the right candidate in Michael Martin.

Caroline's health became my major concern from 1996 when her spinal cancer was first diagnosed and this is reflected in the diary increasingly from then until her death in November 2000.

She was determined that, despite her illness, I should continue to play as active a part as possible in my constituency, in the House of Commons and in the election campaign in 1997.

Indeed it was she who suggested that when I left parliament I should explain that it was 'to devote more time to politics', a phrase which has been widely understood and appreciated.

Thursday 1 May 1997, Chesterfield, General Election

I got up at six. Got to the polling station at twelve minutes to seven, and the polling clerk brought out the ballot box and showed it was empty before he locked it. I was the first in to vote: two votes, county council election and the parliamentary election.

The battle bus that was in the car park was burgled in the night and all the electronic equipment was stolen.

From nine to twelve Caroline and I went out to all the Committee Rooms. Tony Rogers, the Liberal candidate, was putting out last-minute leaflets on the Sinn Fein visit to try to undermine me, and Paddy Ashdown had done a 'personalised' letter to every elector about how important it was to keep out Tony Benn with his 'left-wing antics'. So my anxiety has returned a bit.

The polls closed at ten. It was really weird. It was a lovely evening and for the last four hours we did nothing. There was no canvassing done, which would allow us to know who hadn't voted and needed knocking up.

Polls closed, then we began watching television, waiting to go to the count, and it was quite clear from the exit polls that they anticipated a Labour majority of 159. In the event it was 179, and so it is the Labour landslide that was predicted. The Tory vote virtually halved; my vote fell by a few hundred and Tony Rogers's vote rose by a few hundred.

I realised fairly late that I was the target of an attack by Liberal HQ in London on Chesterfield, a systematic attack, and it's amazing they didn't do much, much better. The Club had been having a party from ten o'clock (there was one guy absolutely flat out, he fell over in the car park), and there was a huge cheer as Caroline and I went in. I made a speech, people hugged and waved and shouted, and then we sang the 'Red Flag'. Finally we got back to the bungalow and went to bed about half-past five in the morning and it was quite clear by then that there was a Labour landslide. Portillo out, masses of Tories out.

Friday 2 May

When we got home we watched pictures of Blair in Downing Street shaking hands, kissing; Cherie Blair waving; his children going into Number 10. It was a national celebration of a formidable kind and I got the feeling that the media was absolutely delighted not to have to discuss the electorate any more. They were just celebrating the return to personality politics, and who the new Cabinet would be. Major said he'd resign the Conservative leadership.

Of course Blair and Mandelson are celebrating this as a victory for New Labour. You just have to bite your tongue at the moment because it wouldn't help. You've got to think very carefully about the future and how you react.

It's now about twenty to twelve on the evening of 2 May, and since yesterday morning I've had two hours' sleep, so I am kind of tired, indeed I'm exhausted, and thank God the election is over.

Saturday 3 May

The news of the Labour Government dominates the papers, all over the place: new Ministers, everything sorted out, and so on. The whole place is still in a state of high excitement with pictures of people going to Number 10.

Sunday 4 May

I caught the 9.15 to Chesterfield, for a civic reception for Chesterfield Football Club in the Town Hall; it was absolutely packed with players and councillors and journalists. The Duke of Devonshire was there. Apparently he said he was in favour of people voting Labour, and I had a word with him about hereditary peers. He said he didn't mind them going, but he said he was a bit doubtful about a quango to appoint life peers, which I privately agree with.

Then I came back. It was a great celebration, with 5000 people outside the Town Hall in their blue shirts, waving.

I can't believe that in five years, when I'm seventy-seven, Chesterfield will want to re-elect me for a further five years till I was eighty-two so I think probably that is the end of Chesterfield. It's a sad thought, and what am I going to do when I'm seventy-seven?

Monday 5 May

Hilary's been offered a job as an education adviser by David Blunkett; he rang me up and I urged him strongly to take it, because I think it's of supreme importance that he gets that experience. He'd be seconded from MSF because he couldn't sacrifice his permanent job. He's already highly regarded by the Party and he'd be a good link between John Monks and David Blunkett; also he'd get to know Ministers, he'd read the Cabinet minutes and it would help him greatly. So I'm hoping that he will take it, but he hasn't made up his mind.

Wednesday 7 May

Overslept. Hardly had time to do anything before I went to the PLP meeting, which was held in Church House.

Nick Brown, the Chief Whip, was there. The television and media were in the gallery because the whole thing was really a rally: it wasn't a meeting of the parliamentary party. I saw lots of new people. It was a lovely meeting.

We had Nick Brown, then Prescott holding up the 'credit card' of pledges, Then he said, 'Now, the man who won the election,' and in came Blair, waving; he gave a very tough speech about discipline and authority, and so on and so on, and he got a standing ovation.

Then Dennis Skinner asked about the decision to give independence to the Bank of England. 'Who elected Eddie George?' Then Ken Livingstone made the same point, and then we had Donald Anderson and Dennis Canavan to talk about Scotland. Blair said, 'We handed over to the Bank of England because it was right.' No argument about it.

I went to the Campaign Group, and the Bank of England issue came up and we had a long discussion about what we're going to do about that. Should we put down an Early Day Motion? Issue a statement? It was agreed that we would play it fairly cautiously; explain what it means i.e. to prepare the way for a single currency. We agreed to invite Eddie George to the Campaign Group.

Thursday 8 May

I went to the Tea Room and who should I see there but Yvette Cooper talking to Jack Straw. Jack said to me, 'Well, one thing you'll be pleased about is that I'm bringing the prison service back under my control as Home Secretary.'

So I said, 'That's fine, because I get letters from a lot of prisoners. Why don't you take back the Bank of England? It's much better for it to be under the Home Office than on its own.' He gave me a slightly quizzical look.

Saturday 10 May

Melissa said today there should be a 'moratorium on carping', so I'm taking that on board.

Wednesday 14 May

The opening of the new Parliament. Wandered over and saw Clare Short and her long-lost son, the boy whom she had to give up for adoption as a baby.

Saw Albert Booth who said he'd been offered a peerage and I said, 'Well, do tell me how it was done.'

Well, he said, 'It was very discreet. Michael Foot came up to me and asked if I had thought of serving the party in a "new capacity."' Albert said to Michael, 'Certainly not.' Albert said to me, 'If I had accepted, then

I'm sure I would have been made a peer; but if I was to say I'd been offered a peerage it would be denied. That's how it's all done.'

The motion of address was moved by Gerald Kaufman, a very amusing speech; I can't stand the man, but it was very funny. And then Chris Mullin made another very good and funny speech. Then Major replied; it was quite reasonable, repeating some of the anxieties of the Tories in the election. Then Blair made a very confident speech – it was really a new President Kennedy, more so even than President Clinton. Kinnock, by the way, was in the Gallery.

Thursday 15 May

Tony Banks said he wanted to have a word with me. So we sat and he talked about his own position. He took the oath of allegiance with his fingers crossed and that's caused some comment; indeed, the Speaker said today that she would watch the behaviour of Members very carefully as a result of that; Tony's also made some statement about the possibility of a British football team, which has caused some upset in Scotland, and he's wondering how far he can go. But he's a very popular appointment as Sports Minister so I think it'll be all right.

Friday 16 May

Did my surgery which lasted from ten till two, the usual range of problems – I suppose there were seventeen cases. Slept on the way back. In the evening Caroline and I went to have dinner with Marion Miliband, Ralph's widow. Marion's been working for the European Commission and she seemed very happy.

The other guests were Tariq Ali and his partner Susan; Andrew Glyn, the Oxford economist who used to be with Militant and worked in the Treasury for a time, and his Australian wife; Edward Miliband, who is now Gordon Brown's adviser. We had a very amusing evening. Tariq gossiped about Benazir Bhutto's husband; Tariq told a story of how Enoch Powell had told him that when he'd first arrived in Delhi it was very early in the morning and he slept on the floor on a mat at the railway station, and the smell of India had excited him and he'd loved India ever since. Caroline remembered that when we went to see Enoch, he took her into his room and there was his old teddy bear, and how important the teddy bear was. It was a nice evening. The moments of tension, such as there were, related to our comments about the transfer of the control of interest rates to the Bank of England under Eddie George; Edward, being very loyal to Gordon Brown, looked a bit disapproving. But still he's a good lad, he's very friendly.

Saturday 17 May

Tony Blair was in Northern Ireland yesterday and said that he had authorised his officials to make contact with Sinn Fein, and the Irish Government had done the same at an official level, and if there was a ceasefire there'd be all-party talks within a week or two.

Monday 19 May

Rushed into the House and went to the Serjeant at Arms' office to meet Gerry Adams and Martin McGuinness, the Sinn Fein MPs, who are negotiating about the conditions laid down by the Speaker as to their use of the House. The Speaker won't allow them access to Members' facilities while they refuse to take the Oath to the Queen. They wanted a proper pass, a Member's pass, and the Serjeant said, 'I'll give you a day pass.' They didn't want that. We discussed it and what rights they'd have; could they sit beyond the bar of the House, and watch the debates? They were very serious about it; just wanted to make the point.

I took them up to my room and we discussed the options: for them just to accept the Speaker's ruling; to take the oath – which they won't do, although they did indicate that later Sinn Fein policy might alter; to try to speak from the bar; to take their seats without taking the oath, and be expelled and cause by-elections.

Then they went to see one of the clerks, whom I've never cared for much, who wasn't exactly helpful. But he said he thought a pass would be arranged and went over it all. The clerk said that the Speaker had allowed them to have House of Commons stationery.

After that I took them through the House of Commons (the House wasn't sitting at the time) and through the Members' Lobby, where there were lots of visitors. I took them and showed them the plaque to Countess Markiewicz, the first woman MP.

I sat through the whole of Parliamentary Questions and at 3.30 I raised a point of order with the Speaker about the rights of the constituents of Gerry Adams and Martin McGuinness. She didn't want me to raise it, because she said privilege shouldn't be raised in the House, but at the same time I really didn't want to let this one go. The House listened quite quietly. I don't know what they made of it, but the Speaker didn't give a proper answer.

Voted in the first vote of the new Parliament, which we won by 417 to 159.

Tuesday 20 May

Drove to the Commons for the votes on the Queen's Speech.

In the Lobby I went up to David Blunkett, put my hand on his shoulder from behind and said, 'This is the father of your new adviser.'

So he said, 'I'm so delighted. Hilary's such a marvellous guy and the nearest I could get to a Benn was him.'

So I said, 'Well, he's a great guy, he is.'

Then I walked past Prescott in the Lobby and he told me all about his struggles with the Permanent Secretaries. I had sent him a copy of my paper on the Civil Service before the election, which he found very useful. He told me how the whole Civil Service was permeated with the idea of privatisation; how he was told there was nothing he could do if British Airways sold off some of their lines to somebody else as a sweetener for their shareholders; how he discovered, or was told, that he had no power to do anything about the railway regulator. I got the impression he was really putting up a good old battle.

Thursday 22 May

Had a talk to Colin Brown of *The Independent* who was very jolly and friendly and said that Mandelson was absolutely loathed because he'd ring up editors to put pressure on particular correspondents. Interestingly, he said that Mandelson, as a Minister without Portfolio, does not receive any parliamentary questions, so it's not possible to get at him. Brown said that Mandelson terrified the journalists. 'Well,' I said, 'he doesn't bother us very much.'

Sinn Fein were talking at an official level yesterday with the Government in Belfast. Clinton is coming over. There is a lot going on, a new statement every day. Yesterday we had the new half-hour Prime Minister's Questions where they announced the ban of land mines. And it's all very popular and the euphoria is continuing.

Saturday 24 May, Stansgate

Had twelve hours' sleep. It was a cool but sunny day, and Caroline went to Southminster to do some shopping.

I talked to Lissie about the meaning of the phrase 'the new man'. She is of course a socialist feminist, and she thinks that the fact Blair presented himself as a new man i.e. shown with his children at home, playing football, and so on, was an indication that public opinion required political leaders to be like that.

She also said that she thought it was time I 'moved on'(this great phrase that young people use) and that I shouldn't outstay my welcome in Parliament, that I should think of some academic job that would carry me forward after I leave Parliament in 2002, by which time I'll be seventy-seven. Melissa is very interesting and encouraging.

Sunday 25 May

Thatcher had been to see Blair at Number 10 before his summit meeting in Amsterdam with the European Heads of State, and I had various telephone calls hoping that I would say 'How outrageous'. LEFT OUTRAGE is a headline they keep permanently in print. I said, 'Well, I think it's quite natural. Lots of people maintain contact with each other – the Prime Minister and Leader of the Opposition see each other very, very regularly.' That slightly disappointed them.

The other story in the paper today is that for the first time in 180 years an American President is to address a British Cabinet.

Well, I remembered that Nixon had come to the Cabinet in 1969 so, I looked it up in my diary and rang various papers, including *The Independent* and *Guardian,* to tell them this. It's all this Alastair Campbell stuff, putting out stories as if something is new, has never been done before.

For example, there was the story that for the first time Cabinet members were calling each other by their Christian names, whereas of course this was done in the 1974-9 government. Michael White said this had turned out to have come from Campbell and not from Blair.

Thursday 29 May

Clinton at Number 10 is being built up to an extraordinary degree. It's an opportunity for Blair to boost his reputation as a new young Leader. Clinton was limping with a stick because he's had a fall.

After being filmed in the Cabinet Room, they went into the garden and they had two little stands; Blair read a statement saying that the difference between left and right has gone, the difference between ideologies has disappeared and we are now at the radical centre. It was all crap.

Sunday 1 June

The Sunday papers had a story that Excalibur, the computer that Labour bought for the election, which had a record of every speech made by every Tory Minister over the last five years, is now being used to collect information about what every Labour MP says, for disciplinary purposes. I had a phone call from *The Independent* asking me whether I was going to look at my record and I said 'No'.

Tuesday 3 June

There was a vote at 6.30, then Caroline and I walked over together to a party at Number 10. We were invited with other Central England MPs.

We walked up the stairs, where all the photographs of the former Prime Ministers are, and went up to the State Rooms. The first time I'd been in those rooms was sixty-seven years ago, when I went to watch the Trooping of the Colour when father was Secretary of State for India.

I went again in 1945 when father was appointed Secretary of State for Air. He didn't have a car, so I went out into the street in my RAF uniform and just held up my hand and commandeered a car and said, 'You've got to take this man,' pointing to my father, 'to Downing Street.'

I had a funny feeling about the place. It was my place of work for eleven years and I knew it very well, but I didn't feel connected to it in any way. It was full of new MPs and there were Tony and Cherie Blair. I gave Cherie a hug and Tony gave Caroline a kiss.

Charles Clarke and Caroline and I had a nice talk. His father, Otto, was once my Permanent Secretary and Charles said, 'You know, my father believed that he and the Crosland/Wilson generation had solved the problems of the Thirties and my father never understood why in 1968 the students were so restive. I said to him, "Dad you're a member of the Establishment" and that made him more angry than anything else.'

Wednesday 4 June

I rushed into a meeting of the Central Group of Labour MPs. It was a huge meeting because the Central Group has grown enormously as a result of all the election victories. There was the regional press officer saying, 'I must warn everybody that if they're invited to do a broadcast, they must get on to me as the regional media officer; sometimes I really worry when I see a Member going on television unbriefed; sometimes you see them on *Newsnight* and they haven't been in touch beforehand.'

They're turning MPs into pawns in the machine game; that was going on during the election and it's just continuing. I suppose MPs will break out of it.

Patricia Hewitt, who was there, said how important it was – she's an old apparatchik of the Kinnock era.

Thursday 5 June

Little Daniel, who's five, said to his dad, 'Daddy, what is the biggest number in the world? Is it 168,000?' And Stephen said, 'Well, Daniel, there's 168,001'. 'Oh,' said Daniel, 'I got very close to it, didn't I, Dad.' Marvellous.

I went to the Speaker's party, a party to celebrate the fiftieth anniversary of the Marshall Plan. The Plan instigated a system under which the Americans gave us, I think, $3 billion, which at the time was a lot of money. I got there early and said to the Speaker, 'I'm looking forward to this because I hope to see a lot of the old boys.'

'Oh' she said, 'you'll see some young boys and girls too.' And indeed it was quite balanced.

There was Peter Shore, and I had a brief word with him. There was a man, I think called Sir Arthur Bryan, who was the Chairman of Wedgwood Pottery and said that my father and Josh Wedgwood had been great friends, which was true; and Ted. He's so old now, grey and bent and fat, and always gives me a funny look; he doesn't approve of me at all.

The American Ambassador, William Crowe, is a heavy man with heavy jowls. I learned later he was exactly my age, seventy-two. He said the Marshall Plan was the beginning of globalisation, the Americans wanted to stop the growth of communism in Europe and it was the first time that American troops and economic interests were firmly connected. A very candid explanation. But he stated it in a sort of informal, rather friendly way, like your grandfather might do. Afterwards I went up to him and said, 'Just to tell you how much I enjoyed your speech, Ambassador.'

He said, 'I've been fifty years in the service of the United States Government, forty-seven in the navy as an Admiral and now I'm Ambassador.'

I told him I'd been in Parliament for forty-seven years. I don't suppose he'd ever heard of me and it doesn't matter.

David Frost was there, buttering people up. And David and Debbie Owen. Thatcher was there; she was right in front of me, and I leaned over and said, 'Well, Maggie,' – I suppose I shouldn't have called her Maggie, but I did – 'well, Maggie, you certainly have some influence on the Bundesbank.' (The Bundesbank have wrecked the plan by the German Government to fiddle the Maastricht criteria to get into the single currency.)

She turned round and looked at me and said, 'What a scandal that whole thing is. They got us in by trickery.' Of course she opposed the referendum in 1975 and favoured British entry into the EEC then.

Then she went on to say, 'The Germans have caused all the trouble in Europe, always the Germans.' And, it seemed to me, a deep dislike of the Germans came out.

'And the French. It's always the Continent that's caused trouble. We've got to be British.'

So I said, 'Well, it's a bit difficult for me because my mother was a Scot, my wife's American with Irish-Scottish ancestry, one of my sons has married a woman who is half Indian, and another son lives with a Muslim. We're breeding a UN peace-keeping force.'

I thought she was slightly bonkers actually. And of course she's no longer Prime Minister so she can't overpower people. She didn't overpower me. I probably shouldn't have called her Maggie. Then she said, 'The communists killed ninety million people.'

I said, 'All wars kill people, you know.'

She was just sort of boiling with ideological frenzy, but I'm glad I spoke to her.

Friday 6 June

One exchange with Mrs Thatcher that I forgot to mention yesterday was that I said to her, 'You know this problem of Europe is not a new one. Julius Caesar arrived with the single currency in 55 BC; and the first Iron Lady, Boadicea, raised the men of Essex, the Icenae, and killed 7000 Roman soldiers.'

'Oh,' said Mrs Thatcher, 'I was the first Iron Lady, not her.'

I had a long talk to Melissa on the phone. She quoted Paul, who said, 'If an old man sits quietly by the river bank long enough, the bodies of all his old enemies will float by.' And that's a bit how I feel.

Monday 9 June

Went into the debate on Europe, a debate in anticipation of the Amsterdam summit on 17 June, opened by the Foreign Secretary, Robin Cook, whom I do find difficult to take, with his beard; he was looking round, so pleased with himself. I didn't get any sense that he faced real decisions he'd have to think about. He was followed by Major, who explained why he'd come out for a delay in the single currency and, indeed, the case for that is increasingly strong. It's obvious that Jospin doesn't intend to stick tightly within the Maastricht criteria.

I was called after John Major and was followed by Ted Heath, so I had absolute prime position and I made a speech that I'd thought about a bit.

There were a few interesting speeches. Denzil Davies made a brilliant speech because he's so analytical. Barry Sheerman explained why he'd gone from being anti to pro single currency because of globalisation. Ann Clwyd was in favour. David Davis wound up for the Tories and made many references to my speech. Then Alistair Darling, Chief Secretary of the Treasury, a very distinguished-looking man with his designer beard, made the winding-up speech.

What pleased me today was that in the first round of the Tory leadership election Michael Howard dropped to the bottom, so I think he has pulled out, so it's now between Clarke and Hague and Lilley or Redwood. We'll see what happens, but the opinion polls show that Clarke would be more popular, more likely to win support.

I've got to have three teeth out at 8.45 in the morning.

Wednesday 11 June

Got up early, walked to the dentist and had three roots removed from my upper jaw, leaving a great gap.

Friday 13 June

I went to the Chesterfield Executive Committee in the evening. Questions were raised as to whether two Party members, Mr and Mrs C, who had covered their house with Liberal posters, should be expelled from the Party and there was some discussion about this.

I gave my election report and there were a number of comments.

Steve Lismore thought my report was much too complacent and that it was a great mistake to suggest that people who came into the town and didn't share our values were beyond the pale; we should address their problems too (which, of course, I never denied). On the Irish issue, the charge that I was going to meet Sinn Fein did a great deal of damage –

the Liberals made a lot of use of it and Steve was absolutely shocked when he read afterwards that I'd shown the Sinn Fein MPs around the House of Commons.

Dave Walsh said it was a very subjective report, that the Liberal challenge had been underestimated, and he agreed that the Irish question had done a great deal of damage.

Then Darryl Alvey, the Chairman, said we'd better have a special meeting. I said I'd support the idea of a special meeting because I think we need to discuss all these things, but on the Irish question it was unpopular being in support of all-party talks, but that's what I believed in. The thing had a nasty flavour to it and Tom and Margaret had told me for some time that they thought the Chesterfield party was moving to the right.

Monday 16 June

Saw Jeffrey Archer who, blow me down, pulled me aside as I went by. He was talking to Peter Bottomley – no doubt about the Tory leadership. He said, 'That was a brilliant speech you made on the election of the Speaker, best speech I've ever heard. I'm speaking at the Oxford Union tonight, I'm going to refer to it.'

'Well,' I said, 'It was a bit more popular on your side of the House than it was on mine.'

Tuesday 17 June

Our forty-eighth wedding anniversary. I overslept. Caroline went into the garden and cut three lovely roses and put them on the stairs so that when I went down to get the breakfast I saw them. I had already bought a pot plant and some flowers, and so I took them up with the breakfast.

I'm hopeful that we'll see our golden wedding, which will be lovely.

Wednesday 18 June

Caroline wasn't feeling too well today after the anniversary dinner and she was tired and so she rested.

I went into the Commons for the meeting of the Central Region, to which Tom Sawyer, the General Secretary of the Party, had been invited to talk about the *Party into Power* document. He said that we can't go back to where we were under the old Labour Governments. *Party into Power* was to provide a partnership between the Government and the Party to deal with mistakes in the past; the stakeholder concept of the Party was that there would be representation of local government, the Parliamentary Labour Party and some constituency Labour Party seats in policy-making. The Party had been defective in the past, but we would have a two-year rolling policy discussion and we wanted a healthy party, open to the CLPs.

I was intending to say something, but I'm glad that didn't. I listened to the points made by Members. What was interesting about it was that the past is now written off as a failure. Well, I've sat in seven Parliaments as a Government Minister or Government backbencher and the Party's often been right, and not the Government. The new scheme doesn't provide for resolutions, doesn't allow constituencies to vote for the MPs they want because the Party will pre-select them. What they hadn't got clear at all today was that the Government is there to govern, but we're there to represent. It confirmed me in my view that this is just an attempt to control us, and I was interested that some of the MPs expressed doubts.

I saw Derek Foster in the Division Lobby. He used to be Chief Whip and then was promised that he'd be in the Cabinet in charge of machinery of the Government, but was robbed.

I asked, 'Why did Blair get rid of you?'

He said, 'I used to warn Blair about Mandelson. Mandelson's behaviour was quite intolerable. He'd come into Blair's office, take off his coat, put his feet up on the desk and behave as if he owned the place.' He went on, 'I think Mandelson will bring Blair down – not meaningfully, but I think he will.'

I said, 'I think Mandelson dominates Blair's mind.'

And Derek said, 'I think you're right. I think he'll crack up.'

Thursday 19 June

I caught the train to Chesterfield.

I got on the train (much more crowded that it usually is) and a man came and sat opposite me and I realised it was Steven Norris, the former Tory MP and Transport Minister. He's always been very agreeable and we talked for two hours; he did say some very interesting things. He's a passionate supporter of William Hague and he said that Ken Clarke is insulting and abusive and rides roughshod over people. The Clarke/Redwood pact uniting of opposites had been treated as utterly cynical by Tory MPs and he thought Hague would win.

We discussed, and agreed between us, that planning had to come back into the public domain, that public expenditure was not necessarily bad, that it was absolute nonsense to link investment with current expenditure, that the Treasury use of the PSBR was nonsense – nobody else used the PSBR.

Norris said he thought that the Tory Party under Hague would recover. We talked about cheap fares in London, about cheap fares in Sheffield, about the electric car, we talked about all sorts of things, because I was the Opposition Transport spokesman once.

He told me how ways could be found by which the electric car could be recharged from parking meters – an idea I talked about many, many years ago. Got back in time to watch *Newsnight* and there was Hague making his acceptance speech. Clarke won't serve under him, and

Redwood won't be offered a job, I wouldn't have thought.

They also had an item about a woman called Pauline Hanson who ran a fish-and-chip shop in Australia and set up her own party, called the One Nation Party, which is really a Le Pen-type party, saying stop Asian immigration, don't accept multiculturalism, don't give way to the Aborigines. In Australia Hawke and Keating destroyed the Labour Party by adopting Thatcherism and paved the way for Howard, who is now being outflanked by this woman who, within a year, has got 10 per cent of support in Australia.

Wednesday 25 June

The Campaign Group had an open meeting on pensions with Peter Townsend. There were eleven people present. Peter said there is now a two-tier Europe as far as pensions are concerned. In the Netherlands pensions are between £143 and £162 a week, which is more than twice the British figure. He said Denmark unemployment pay was 90 per cent of wages. He said that the privatisation of pensions in countries such as Chile had been a disaster, and in the United States people are increasingly realising that you've got to go back to proper social insurance. He said we should have a windfall tax on pension companies and we've got to get older people to recognise that they have a common interest with young people.

Thursday 26 June

I'm a bit low at the moment, I don't know why. Well, I do know why, I'm depressed. It's difficult to get old. I suppose making a contribution, when something comes up that you know something about, is useful. And I'm encouraging Members and talking to new Members.

Friday 27 June

We came back and I had a talk to Hilary, who had been in Luxembourg with David Blunkett on his first official visit; he went yesterday.

He said that COREPER, the Committee of Permanent Officials, had presented a very bland briefing note for David, and on one occasion Blunkett absolutely blew up because it looked as though our social security legislation was to be made subject to European control. He lost his temper and said, 'They'd have my balls if I went along with that,' and so on.

Saturday 28 June

Peter Mandelson has taken over responsibility for the millennium celebrations and it's going to be called the Millennium Experience. It's an absolute public relations stunt. One company is being paid £9 million to raise £150 million in sponsorship for a scheme which will cost £580 or

£600 million. It's a total waste of public money and a lot of people who don't like Mandelson hope it will fail, but I'm sure that with the Prime Minister behind him it won't.

Thursday 3 July

Anne Tyerman, senior producer at the BBC, told us this morning that last week she went to a meeting with Peter Mandelson of all the editors of BBC programmes. And Mandelson said that the object of this Government is to indicate clarity of purpose, and no backbench Labour Member was to be invited on any programme without his approval.

So here you have control of Ministers, by them not being able to submit papers to the Cabinet or inter-departmental memoranda, and the control of backbench Members. It is an absolute tyranny; of course it will completely break down.

Sunday 6 July

A beautiful sunny day. I spent the whole day trying to repair a serious leak in the tank at the top of the house, which poured onto the flat roof, came down through the ceiling into the back corridor on the ground floor, went through the carpet into the ceiling in the basement, brought down the ceiling, went all over the floor and soaked many of my photograph files.

First of all I had to climb out on the roof and clean all the muck off it and clear the drains; then I came in again and went upstairs to see if I could fix the tank. I unscrewed the ballcock and it was as heavy as if it was full of water, which it was, so I went out to buy a new ballcock, which didn't fit. So I drilled a hole in the old ballcock, emptied the water, covered the hole with sealant, put it on again and it seemed to work.

Then we had to dry the carpet, hanging it out over the back steps into the garden, clear all the muck on the basement floor and pull all the photographs out and put them in new boxes to dry. To cut a long story short, I was up and down the stairs twenty times, onto the roof four or five.

I remember the British Library saying to me, 'There are three hazards to archives. Fire, water and theft', and I dismissed all that, but actually water is the one that hit me in the end.

Monday 7 July

Up quite early.

Caroline went to the doctor to get her Tamoxifen. I must say, as a drug it seems to be doing her a bit of good, that and the radiation and the blood transfusion.

My eldest grandson, Michael, is doing work experience in my office and I took him to the launch of an exhibition in Westminster Hall of 500 years of parliamentary record keeping, opened by the Lord Chancellor, Derry Irvine, who had introduced Tony and Cherie Blair to each other. They were both in his chambers.

I introduced Michael to Betty Boothroyd who said, 'Oh, what's your task in life, young man?' And when she realised he was only fifteen she was amazed because he's much taller than I am.

Then we went to the Upper Waiting Hall where there was a parallel exhibition, attended by nobody, of electronic communication of information; masses of computers of different kinds. One allowed you to get access to Government information, another one allowed you to get through to local information, a third allowed you to be interactive. One actually enabled you to talk to your Member of Parliament – so that in principle you could have a surgery and talk to your constituents on-line.

Then we went to a final computer, where you could have a two-way conversation with somebody, with tiny little pictures of each person, and go through a document together that would be on both screens, amend it and then print it out. Absolutely dazzling technology – it's so totally different to anything that anybody even dreamed about when I was elected nearly fifty years ago.

David Blunkett made his big education statement today, concentrating on elite education, punishing teachers, sending highly paid teachers to go in as hit-squads to take over schools; the most ghastly *Daily Mail* Tory-type policy. It makes your flesh creep really, it really does.

Tuesday 8 July

Charlie the plumber came in (in his early fifties, I should think) and fixed the ballcock; but the roof still leaks, so we've got to have the roof done.

Michael arrived early with his shirt and his trousers all ironed, which he does very conscientiously. He opened the letters and spent the day with Sheila filing.

Wrote a letter to *The Independent* about Ireland, where there's a total return to violence.

Wednesday 9 July, Cambridge

Ruth and I got a taxi from the station to Churchill College and were received by the Master of Churchill, Sir John Boyd; by Dr Piers Brendon, the keeper of the archives, who is a writer and a fellow of the college and looks after the archives part-time, and by Alan Kucia, the principal archivist. They took us to see the conservator, who took all these papers that had been bent and damaged, covered them in fine silk, laminated them, bound them and indexed them.

Then we went to look at the database and into the great strong room, where Churchill's papers were all in archive boxes.

It was tremendously impressive, and Mrs Thatcher's files had just arrived – in cardboard boxes just like mine – and they've been stuffed into this humidity-controlled strong room. They've got five archivists working for five years on the Churchill papers alone, and they're only just halfway through; it's a huge job. They're taking each sheet of paper, making a summary of it, giving it a code number, and putting it on the database.

They showed me my letters to Churchill in 1955, 1961 and 1963 about the peerage case. They had his school reports saying that Winston doesn't know the meaning of work, he has no ambition and all that; it was great fun.

I think they would really love to have my papers at Cambridge. But they said Alice Prochaska at the British Library would never forgive them if they took my papers! But they couldn't have been kinder and they would have had us to lunch, but there wasn't time.

Got back and went to the Campaign Group, where there was an absolutely riveting discussion about the patenting of life forms, an issue that has become very important. The European Union has issued a directive about it and Lynne Jones was in favour of the directive, whereas Alan Simpson made a most passionate speech against it and I thought he won the argument hands down. I said if you could patent life, could I patent my sperm as a former hereditary peer? What about people in the Third World who had grown wheat for years and who then found it was patented and had to pay royalties to continue to grow the wheat? A really interesting moral and scientific argument.

Thursday 10 July

London was dislocated today by the Countryside Rally in Hyde Park where there were allegedly 100,000 people. Their campaign is that town folk don't understand country folk. They've managed to obscure the hunting question altogether.

The reporting of it seemed like an attempt to reverse political correctness based on the suggestion that thousands of hounds will be killed – a complete lie. I don't think it will alter opinion on this matter.

I heard more about attempts to control. First, the whips not only decided which Members went on the Select Committees, but then made their recommendations as to who should be the chairs; apparently there was objections to Harry Cohen being on the Defence Committee and Ken Livingstone being on the Northern Ireland Committee, and so on.

In the evening, I walked over from the House to a reception given by Carlton Television on College Green. They had put up a marquee, had an orchestra playing, there were limitless supplies of champagne and it was an indication of where power and money have gone. A hundred years ago it might have been a party in the garden of Lambeth Palace, given by the Archbishop of Canterbury, where everybody would want to be seen but now it's the media who have that sort of role.

Sunday 13 July

I came home and wrote a draft proposal for the British Library to apply for a grant from the Heritage Lottery fund to have my papers indexed before I die.

Monday 14 July

Had a cup of tea on the terrace at the House of Commons. I must say the House is totally dead. There's not a single speech worth reporting because the House is so constrained by its formalities.

Blair has killed politics really, and all the stuff about how focus groups are going to determine policy shuts the Party out even more.

I had a very nice, but slightly double-edged, anonymous postcard which I've clipped to my diary archives.

Dear Mr Benn

I am writing to thank you and express my admiration and respect for you. I've never written a fan letter before, but when I heard that Robert Mitchum, an American film star, had died and when the next day James Stewart, another American film star, had died, I thought I'd better get a move on. I'd rather experience the fear that I'm wasting your time than regret that I never contacted you.

Yours respectfully

A Brit Living in Japan.

I hope the postcard picture pleases you.

Tuesday 15 July

I went to the Labour Action for Peace meeting – there were all these old boys who really appreciate the opportunity to be in touch with Labour MPs. I raised the issue of sanctions against Iraq; the fact that the Indonesian authorities have been invited to Britain's arms fair this autumn; and the continuing Lockerbie business.

Tam said he'd got a question down to the Prime Minister tomorrow about the Lockerbie business; apparently Nelson Mandela spent forty minutes with Blair trying to persuade him to stop the sanctions against Libya. Tam heard this from Tiny Rowland.

In the evening I had a talk to Colin Brown, the political correspondent of *The Independent*, and I asked him whether he could confirm the story that there was an attempt to get rid of Andrew Marr. He said, 'Oh, yes.'

Had a chat to Chris Mullin, who has been elected Chairman of the Home Affairs Committee; he's very laid-back.

I went over to the Tate Gallery for a reception for Members given by the Tate Gallery Director, who said what a marvellous minister Chris Smith was. The department's name was changed today from the Department of National Heritage to the Department of Culture, Media and Sport.

Chris made an excellent speech and I said, 'That's the best speech I've heard made by a Labour Minister since the election.'

I think he was quite pleased, because I heard a rumour that Mandelson wanted that job, and that would be a catastrophe.

I wandered around and looked at paintings consisting of squares of solid colour – a square of red, a square of white, a block of red, a block of white, a block of blue, a curve of a single colour – there was nothing in it but colour. I can't say I was much struck, although the artist is obviously highly regarded.

Thursday 17 July
Michael was in, his last day of work experience, and he indexed all my press cuttings and also some of my speeches. He's a quiet, reliable, steady, accurate worker and it's been a pleasure to have him in the office.

Believe it or not, the Government has decided to continue the rate-capping of three local authorities (Warwickshire, Oxfordshire and Somerset), having spent the last eighteen years denouncing rate-capping as an infringement of local democracy.

A number of people, including myself, had spoken to the whips to express their uneasiness about this, and I said to the whips last night that I would probably not be able to vote for it.

When it came to it, I abstained, with Jeremy Corbyn, Ken Livingstone, John Austin and, I think, probably Dennis Skinner. I don't think anything will happen. It is the first time I have actually defied the Party whip since the election.

This morning I went to Black Rod's garden, at the Lords' end, where a long boat from Chesterfield had arrived carrying a piece of stone by canal. The boat had set off on 19 May and arrived today – about eight weeks by waterway. The stone had come from the same quarry as that used in the House of Commons, which was carried down the Chesterfield Canal between 1840 and 1844 for the rebuilding of the House. This piece of stone was brought down to commemorate the twenty-first anniversary of the founding of the Chesterfield Canal Society and the 150th anniversary of the first sitting of the House of Lords in their new Chamber, designed by Sir Charles Barry.

It was fun to go to Black Rod's garden, climb over a wall and down the steps, with the water lapping round.

We adjourned into one of the committee rooms and there was a gathering of MPs: Joe Ashton, Kevin Barron, Harry Barnes; Black Rod was there, and people from the quarry from which the stone had come. Terry Boston – Lord Boston – addressed us and said that when the House of Commons burned down in 1834, people gathered on the other side of the river and cheered because Parliament was very unpopular then. It did remind me that in 1834, just after the arguments about the Reform Bill and before the Chartists got going, people would have seen Parliament as an enemy and not a friend.

The people from the House of Lords refreshment department brought me a cup of tea, which was awfully sweet of them. I was very touched by that.

Yesterday, when I was walking to 4 Millbank to do a little broadcast, there were dozens of photographers perched on ladders down a side-street and they were there to film Jonathan Aitken, the disgraced minister who lost his libel case against the *Guardian* and is possibly going to be charged with perjury. He was doing a walkabout outside his house to get the press off his doorstep.

Friday 18 July, Chesterfield

The first thing I did was to go down to the Miners' Welfare Club for the Rotary Club – all men of course, a pretty tough audience to talk to.

Gerry Adams and Martin McGuinness have called for a ceasefire and are confident the IRA will respond and this has driven the Loyalists into an absolute panic. The last thing that the Unionists want is a ceasefire and they claim they've been betrayed, all the usual stuff.

Monday 21 July

At ten o'clock this morning Jean Hutchinson came to see me. Jean has been in prison eight times in Britain and twice in America for non-violent direct action and she said that if she was convicted this time, she'd get six months and be out in three months. She was a jolly, cheerful woman, about my age I should think, mid-to late sixties; she's been charged with using bolt cutters to cut through a wire fence at Greenham Common. She had asked me to give evidence in her favour. I had written her a short memorandum and she showed me what the Crown Prosecution Service had written about me, that 'Mr Benn is not an expert, all his evidence is hearsay and it can be disregarded, and he shouldn't be called,' which is amusing in view of the fact that I had ministerial responsibility for so many years for the nuclear industry.

Wednesday 23 July

Went into the House quite early to get a good place in the Chamber for Prime Minister's Questions. I asked Blair about the deal under which the Liberals had been given seats on a Cabinet consultative committee, and I got a pretty abrupt reply. The Tories appreciated what I was saying because it embarrassed the Liberals and, to some extent, embarrassed the Front Bench.

The Lib-Lab development is important. It's what I've always expected, that there would be a coalition, and the combination of that and the new Party disciplinary code means that if Labour Members vote against the Government they're in danger of being expelled, while if Liberals vote against the Government they're still on the Cabinet consultative committee.

Monday 28 July

Alex Falconer, a Member of the European Parliament, rang me up to say how much he'd agreed with my article in yesterday's *Observer* about New Labour. But he said, 'Tony, you're a fool to think the Labour Party's going to survive, because it won't; with proportional representation it's finished.'

I thought about that and I said, 'Maybe you're right Alex, there's no hope for the Labour Party. All I want is this; if the Labour Party splits, I want *them* to go not us.' Then I had a phone call from someone who had attended a meeting of local Labour parties with Mandelson and Tom Sawyer in the Grand Committee Room, and Mandelson had spoken for half an hour; his argument is that we've got to win the *next* election. So he is using the normal pre-electoral appeal for unity to silence us until the year 2002, when presumably we'll win and then we'll be silenced again for the election of 2007.

Thursday 31 July, America

Rang Sheila and she said hundreds of letters have arrived this week about my article in the *Observer*. Also a lot of letters from people absolutely furious at the news that the Government will not provide time for the Bill to ban fox hunting.

Saturday 2 August

Rang Dave in London, who read me the list of all the peers who've been appointed, including Michael Levy, who organised Tony Blair's blind fund, raised £1 million for Blair's office. That is reminiscent of the Lloyd George fund.

Also Dave told me that the new Questions of Procedure for Ministers has come out and Blair has laid down that, first of all, leaks from the Cabinet are absolutely prohibited; second, no Minister can give an interview to any journalist or broadcaster without seeking advance permission from Number 10 (which is Peter Mandelson, of course); and third, any minister who meets a journalist has got to put a written report in of his meeting to his own press officer (who no doubt has to send it to Number 10). There is really the tightest control there's ever been, although the press are still giving Blair a reasonable run.

Dave also said that the Lord Simon business is blowing up. He was the Chairman of British Petroleum and not a member of the Labour Party, was made a Minister in the Department of Industry, has two million shares in BP and, whereas the old Procedure for Ministers laid down that if you do have shares you have to dispose of them, the new *Ministerial Code* states that you have to consult your Permanent Secretary to see if there is a conflict of interest.

When I look at it from abroad and think about it, without being involved daily, I realise that this is really a completely corrupt system. It has all the appearance of a medieval court with the king, the power behind the throne, the courtiers, and the favourites.

Every time I come to America I get a new impression, not only of America but even more so of Western civilisation as it moves towards the year 2000. It is now entirely based upon international financial transactions and the gambling that lies behind them. China has applied to join the World Trade Organisation, but the *New York Times* said that the American Government was unlikely to agree because the Chinese, for their part, would not agree to American or foreign countries coming in and buying their companies.

You can see the discipline of the market extending everywhere and those who try and stand outside it or against it, for historical or other reasons, like North Korea, Libya, Iraq and Cuba, are punished either militarily or economically. It does mean that if a radical government was elected in Britain and tried to do anything about it there would be immediate consequences; investment would stop, money would stop coming in, we would be expelled from the World Trade Organisation, we would be condemned by the IMF, we'd be thrown out of the Common Market. In that sense the global economy is all-powerful.

The Labour Government is very popular with the British Establishment because it is supporting the system; it is a good Conservative Government.

On the other hand, the triumphalism about the American economic success is so great that you do wonder whether pride doesn't come before a fall.

Friday 8 August

Josh's son William, who is twelve, has passed the first Certified Netware Administrator exams. The questions were sent on the Internet from America and people could watch William working in his little examination room. He got 90 per cent, the youngest person ever to qualify for the exam, which is an international qualification that will get you a job anywhere.

Sunday 10 August

Wandered down to the shops to buy the Sunday papers, which are full of Princess Diana and Dodi Fayed, who's in love with Diana, and a lot of articles about Mandelson – he really has blotted his copy book with the media, just taking over everything.

He's only a Minister without Portfolio but he takes charge of press conferences, he bullies the media, and I think he's riding for a fall.

Tuesday 26 August, Stansgate

In the afternoon Roy Hattersley rang me and said the *Sunday Times* had suggested that he and I might do a joint discussion at Conference on the Sunday. And he's coming to see me next week. Washed the sheets, then I went over to see Dave and June.

Mandelson has been on television endlessly; under the new rules you can only broadcast with the consent of Number 10, and as he *is* Number 10 he always gives himself consent. He gave a Fabian lecture in which he announced the formation of a special committee, chaired by the Prime Minister, to look at poverty. The Millennium Dome at Greenwich is coming under violent attack and of course Mandelson's in charge of that.

John Prescott is supposed to be in charge in the absence of the Prime Minister, but Mandelson's had all the headlines.

Friday 29 August, Chesterfield

To the Town Hall for the meeting on the closure of Markham, the engineering company now owned by Kvaerner.

Markham's was absolutely supreme worldwide, had a massive role in developing mining equipment sold all over the world, but of course when the pits closed, it fell on very hard times. It got the contract for the tunnelling equipment for the Channel Tunnel, which was a huge contract. It was bought by Trafalgar House first, which was just an investment company, and then sold to Kvaerner, a Scandinavian company, which also bought another company in Sheffield. To cut a long story short, a couple of weeks ago they decided that business was so bad that they would combine the two companies, close Markham and move some of the skilled people and equipment to Sheffield.

They presented the case: about eighty jobs would be lost in Chesterfield, but highly skilled people would find it easy to get work, they said. I asked some questions, the sort you would put if you were Industry Secretary, and prefaced them by saying that I've been involved in this problem over many years.

But I felt that all the fight had gone out of people now – there is no national interest whatsoever in maintaining industry. Agriculture has to be preserved, quite properly, but globalisation means that you hand over the future of your economy to others.

A worker at Markham drove me back to the station and he was very upset because he said Markham was such a good company.

Fantastic clouds today – can't describe how beautiful they were. I can always see pictures in clouds; coming up to Chesterfield in the morning I saw a cloud that looked exactly like Hugh Gaitskell's face – his hair, nose and chin; then lots of elephants with long trunks; and people with Mr Punch's profile lying down.

Saturday 30 August, Stansgate

At 12.15 Chris Mullin and his wife Ngoc and her sister and the children,

Sarah and Emma, came to lunch. Chris is an old friend going way back; he edited *Arguments for Socialism* and *Arguments for Democracy* and he is now Chairman of the Home Affairs Select Committee of the House of Commons. He worked very hard on the Birmingham Six and got them released, and so on. He married Ngoc in Vietnam and after a lot of bureaucracy, brought her back here. Chris has become an Establishment figure and wants to stay in Parliament for another ten years till he is fifty-nine and then he'd like to retire and write. He adored Stansgate – he said it was the most beautiful place – and although the weather wasn't all that marvellous, he did think it was fantastic.

We walked around and went to the coastguard hut and looked in on the nature reserve; I took him round to look at all the archives, and his only comment was, 'I think there's an overload of information.'

I asked him about the Conference and he said there'd be a bit of a backlash about Blair's proposals, it will come late this year. He has sort of detached himself from politics. But it was nice having him there.

Sunday 31 August

Turned on the seven o'clock news and I heard, 'This is BBC Radio 4, Radio 5 Live, Radio 2 and 3. Diana, Princess of Wales, has been killed in a car crash in Paris this morning.' She and Dodi and a bodyguard and a chauffeur were driving a Mercedes through a tunnel in Paris followed by five paparazzi on motorbikes and they hit a wall. Dodi was killed at once, as was the driver, but Diana was resuscitated briefly on the site and taken to hospital and died two hours later. The bodyguard, I think, has survived. From then – five hours ago – there has been nothing but that on the radio; everybody has been interviewed: the Prime Minister, John Major, William Hague, David Mellor, Chris Smith, the Archbishop of Canterbury, the Chief Rabbi, the Moderator of the Christian Church in Northern Ireland. It's just blanket coverage. It is a very sad story – the Marilyn Monroe story – of a beautiful woman who had lots of lovers and never found happiness. Hardly any reference to Al Fayed, whose eldest son was killed, and no mention of the name of the chauffeur. Don't chauffeurs have names, don't they have families?

I refused requests to interview me because there is nothing whatever to be said really.

Roy Hattersley rang. He said the MEP Phillip Whitehead had been to see him and had told him that he'd heard from Mandelson that under the proportional representation system for electing our Members of the European Parliament, it would be on a list system and the Leader would decide the order of names on the list. That would provide, as Mandelson said, the opportunity to cull the number of MEPs who were unacceptable. Roy has always been against PR and I looked forward all the more to seeing him.

Monday 1 September

The *Guardian* had fourteen pages on Diana.

At ten Roy Hattersley arrived. I did an hour and forty-minute interview with him, which he will edit for the *Sunday Times*.

Roy is in a strange position. He is still himself – very pro-European and Euro-federalist, anti-trade union, doesn't believe in common ownership or Clause 4 – but he is a sort of Lord Bountiful. We went over the IMF crisis, the deputy leadership, the Falklands War, the SDP and so on. But what interests me is the power of global capital. He said that you can't beat it, you've just got to live with it – otherwise the economy would be ruined and confidence would collapse.

I said, 'I don't agree with that, but it would be as big a struggle as the anti-colonial movement.' I told Roy that if I ever left Parliament it would be because I wanted to devote more time to politics, and he laughed. That is going to be a joke of mine.

He said he thought he'd had more influence since he left Parliament than when he was in it. He sees Blair. I said I wouldn't vote for things I didn't believe in, and they probably will withdraw the whip from me. 'Oh no,' he said, 'they wouldn't dare withdraw the whip from high-profile people. They'd go for Alan Simpson, who is a really nice guy, or Ken Livingstone, but they wouldn't go for you.'

He is an honest Gaitskellite on the right of the Party – a European social democrat – and I am a socialist of a different kind. But we can both be perfectly happy in the Labour Party and that is what I care about.

He left and the One O'clock News was still 99 per cent about Princess Diana. Apparently the paparazzi who were there when the car crashed spent ten minutes taking photographs of the crash before they called an ambulance. If that is true it is an absolute scandal.

Later we heard that the driver had three times as much alcohol in him as the legal limit, and that has meant he has been named!

Tuesday 2 September

Had very good news from Jean Hutchinson, the grandmother charged with the offence of cutting the wire at Greenham Common. The Crown Prosecution Service decided not to prosecute and she was duly acquitted. Marvellous.

I drafted another statement for Helen John who, with Anne Lee, is charged with breaking the bylaws at Menwith Hill, which is the American Intelligence camp here, and faxed that through to her.

Thousands of people queued up last night to sign the books of condolence at Buckingham Palace and they'd discovered there were only six books and the Palace had to provide another ten. I hope by this time next week we will be able to re-enter the real world again, because there is something slightly sick about all this.

Wednesday 3 September

I went to St Pancras and caught the 9.30 to Chesterfield. Angela Eagle, the Parliamentary Secretary in John Prescott's super-ministry, was on the train, coming up to Chesterfield to open something. She confirmed what Roy Hattersley had told me: that Gordon Brown is telling everyone he is not responsible for the decision not to increase income tax or public expenditure – it was imposed on him by Blair.

I was told that there will be a service in Chesterfield on Friday evening in memory of Princess Diana. I can't go – I just can't. The whole thing is getting so ghoulish.

Tomorrow I go to York for Helen John. Vera Baird, the barrister who defended the Ploughshares Group who damaged the Hawk aircraft for Indonesia, will examine me on behalf of the defendants.

Thursday 4 September, York

I was met from the train by Helen John, who drove me to York Crown Court where her appeal over her conviction in the magistrates' court was being heard.

Helen's solicitor and barrister were there and we all talked. I gave them the fifteen-page document that I had prepared, with extracts from my diaries illuminating the fact that British security is subordinate to American security. They photocopied it and when we arrived in court and I was called, they handed out the documents to the judge and assessors and the prosecution lawyer.

I sat in the witness box and the judge said they'd have to consider it, so we had to withdraw. When we came back he said, 'This is hearsay. Mr Benn is not an expert, these are old recollections going back long before the by-laws had been introduced' (in January last year by Michael Portillo as Minister of Defence). 'Therefore the prosecution should comment.' So Timothy Stead commented, pleased that the judge had supported their case. Then Vera Baird made her statement and the judge said we'd have to adjourn again. When we came back he said he had taken account, and certainly hearsay was out of order, Mr Benn wasn't an expert and certainly this was old stuff. 'Still, I don't want to prevent him being heard.' So at 12.30 I got into the box and the interrogation began. I said no Minister was an expert, but I had been responsible acting under statute and answerable to Parliament and I had had security responsibilities.

Then Timothy Stead cross-examined me and he said, 'You've always been suspicious about this' – implying that I was subversive and therefore the security services didn't tell me anything. I said I was the Minister responsible for Aldermaston and could hardly have had a more responsible position.

Came back very tired. I'm so glad I went because I have huge admiration for Helen John.

I think I took a risk because the security services were present in court and so it will all go back to MI5 and the Americans.

People are angry with the royal family. Blair is trying to cash in on it and the Queen has had to agree that a flag will fly at half mast over the Palace, which has never happened before. They have sent Princes Andrew and Edward out among the crowd, desperately trying to recover their position. Earl Spencer, Diana's brother, has asked for the invitations to six newspaper editors to be withdrawn and that has been agreed. Elton John, the pop singer, is singing at the service.

Friday 5 September

Helen John and Anne Lee won their case. They won not because of my arguments, but because the military by-laws can only be used when the entire base is for military purposes, whereas there are sheep on the Menwith Hill base and there are those parts that are not used by the great big eavesdropping radar domes. So the judge said that it was not a legal use of the by-laws. An absolutely absurd point – none of my arguments about civil spying or commercial espionage or civil liberties had any part to play. But the judge said Mr Benn must have his full costs paid – his fare, his meals and his welfare for the day. So Vera Baird got up and said that Mr Benn travelled standard class day return on his pensioner's ticket and the whole court roared with laughter, so at least there was a happy recollection of my role.

I went to Chesterfield for the service for Diana in the end because I felt I just had to go. I sat in the churchyard and there were thousands of flowers.

The address was given by the Bishop of Repton and it really was totally inappropriate. He talked about an icon and the meaning of the word, about fantasy and what a fantastic life she led – fantasy was right. He then compared her to Jesus, who suffered and died very young, which I thought was a bit inappropriate. Then he said that in the next world we shall all be princes and princesses, which I thought was a bit crude. People just accept anything that's said on such occasions.

Saturday 6 September

Earl Spencer made a really remarkable speech at the funeral. He spoke with genuine love of his sister; how he and she had had to travel by train between her father's and her mother's home; he said her name is Diana, which means 'Huntress' and yet she became hunted; she didn't need to have a royal title to do good work, which was a direct swipe at the royal family for removing her HRH. The royal family have been totally sidelined. There were millions of people lining every route ten or fifteen deep. Absolutely quiet and absolutely genuine. Women crying, children crying, old men with their heads bowed, beautiful sunshine, and Hyde

Park with large TV screens to watch the service on. The applause after Elton John played his piece of music, and particularly after Earl Spencer gave his address, was heard in the Abbey from outside and spread into the Abbey; and I have never heard people clap in the Abbey or any church before (except maybe in 1976 in Burford). It was an amazing thing – sustained applause for Earl Spencer; that speech is worth really thinking about.

The coffin was put in a hearse and driven through London to the M1. People threw flowers on the windscreen of the car, and the windscreen wipers had to be used to clear the driver's view. The car stopped at the beginning of the M1 in order to allow the flowers to be removed. There were five motorbike outriders and on every bridge there were people watching. It would be a very insensitive person who didn't pick up all that emotion. Whether she had the merit that was claimed for her was hardly a matter of relevance – the fact is that she was seen to have those merits.

Tony Blair has come out of it very well because he is supposed to have told the Palace how to handle it. The Queen looked very uneasy and the Queen Mother looked even more uneasy. Prince Charles looked uncomfortable, but the cameras did not focus on the royal family at all during the service.

Tuesday 9 September

Sinn Fein have signed the Mitchell conditions renouncing violence.

Saturday 13 September

Rethinking Education and Democracy: A Socialist Alternative for the 21st Century, was published by Tuffnell Press today after three year's work by Clyde Chitty and Caroline.

Tuesday 16 September

On Sunday two days ago, the Greenham Common fence was knocked down at the airbase – the Americans have gone. The Greenham women and the people in the town were invited to join in a ceremonial knocking down of the fence. When they were there, in so far as they were mentioned at all, the women were always referred to as witches and lesbians and troublemakers and crypto-communists. I thought to myself, 'That is another victory from the bottom up that is never recognised.'

Wednesday 17 September

Caroline's back is painful today. She said she might contemplate taking painkillers. I must admit it is very worrying.

Thursday 18 September

Lew Adams, General Secretary of ASLEF, came to see me today. I've known him slightly, but he is of a newer generation than the guys I knew. He was on the footplate until 1989. He said that Blair had absolutely stunned the TUC conference by his hostility and that the General Secretaries – Bickerstaffe, Morris and Edmonds – were really frightened by him. John Edmonds had said that he shivered at the thought of a flexible labour market and Blair specifically attacked him for that during his speech.

Saturday 27 September

We caught the train to Brighton with six huge pieces of baggage and took our luggage to our flat in Ship Street. The taxi driver told us that the Labour Party had taken over the whole of the Metropole Hotel, and although the hotel had been compensated for the loss of its casino takings – £800,000 – the staff had been laid off without pay. I must say that is a really interesting reflection of the flexibility of Labour.

Monday 29 September

There was a police video camera videoing a demonstration in the streets, so I got my camera and went and videoed the policeman. I walked right in front of him and he said 'Get out of my way.' The campaigners were mainly women protesting against the export of live animals. They were lovely, but the thought that the police were videoing it was horrific. Police helicopters overhead, a hot-air balloon, a police ship off the coast – incredible security, all designed to make the New Labour Government seem powerful and strong.

We heard at 5.40 that Ken Livingstone had beaten Peter Mandelson for the NEC; it was under one member, one vote, marvellous!

Tuesday 30 September

Watched Tony Blair's speech on TV back at the flat. Extraordinary performance – I, I, I – *I* want modernisation, modernisation, this is the Britain *I* want. A mixture of Billy Graham and Prince Charles and it absolutely lacked substance. It didn't get a rapturous reception. Somebody said later that Blair wasn't very well, but it was more than that – it lacked substance.

One of the most remarkable passages of Blair's speech was that he felt his inheritance didn't just go back to Ernie Bevin and Nye Bevan and Clem Attlee, but to Beveridge, Keynes, and Lloyd George, of all people – Lloyd George, an absolute crook who also set up a coalition with the Tories. Very significant comment.

Got some more pictures of police activity – the air balloon and the patrol boat.

Caroline has been marvellous today – she must be frightfully tired and everybody asked after her.

Wednesday 1 October

Ruth and I went over to one of the BBC studios at the Conference centre and began editing all the film, for an insert into *Newsnight* – an alternative view of the Conference. We had the help of John Hinckley, a very nice guy. We've got about eighteen minutes of material to edit down to about ten.

Friday 3 October

From 8.45 a.m. right through till five we put the whole programme into shape. It is the most complicated job – editing – phenomenally complicated. We got the thing in good shape at about nine minutes and twenty seconds. We were off the editing machine for an hour at lunchtime because they were editing Jeremy Paxman's interview with Tony Blair. I never really went to Conference at all today. The skill of the editors John Hinckley and Clive Edwards and another photographer who had taken some shots, was incredible.

Amazing week – I've hardly had time to record my impressions of it. The woman who ran the buffet trolley on the train had once been a policewoman in Brighton and she had friends in the police who said that the security cost £2 million. It was unnecessary and very off-putting. Secondly, the whole thing was stage-managed to a phenomenal degree – it really was an outrage that delegates should come from all over the country and sit in the hall and watch videos of Blair's triumphs, shown several times.

Then there was the practice of bringing guest speakers onto the platform – one boy was brought on during the education debate to say that he had read four books instead of one thanks to David Blunkett's reading programme. A woman came on and said that after Jack Straw's visit to her housing estate, crime had disappeared. The only effective contribution of that kind was a middle-aged doctor who talked about land mines and the damage they did. He held a butterfly mine, in his hands – that was electric. But Conference is not the place where you put on a display; it is a place where people discuss alternatives and I felt strongly the total repudiation of any serious discussion about the future.

Incidentally, Andrew Morton, who wrote the book *Diana: Her True Story* has now republished it, and Diana's comments on tape about Prince Charles will do great damage to the monarchy. But we've got a new monarch – Tony Blair.

Tuesday 7 October

The Tory Conference met today. Major said goodbye and Hague took over. Hague is modelling himself entirely on Tony Blair – an Electoral College, consulting the Members, discipline among the Tory MPs, action on sleaze, and so on.

At a fringe meeting Alan Clark, when asked about the IRA, said that if you killed 600 people overnight it would probably give you peace in Ireland for the next twenty years – incredible advocacy of terrorism. It is difficult to take Clark seriously.

Sunday 12 October
Caroline wrote to all the children and I worked in the office.

Monday 13 October
Caroline was seventy-one. A year back we'd have never believed she would be alive, but she is just absolutely amazing. I took her flowers and gifts and in the evening Hilary turned up with more flowers and all the children phoned.

Thursday 16 October
I had a call from the *Jimmy Young Show* – I do like Jimmy Young – about the decision to spend another £170 million on more warheads for Trident, the Government having said that public expenditure would be tightly restricted. I did a little item with him; he gets through to a huge audience.

Saturday 18 October
Big news is that Gordon Brown has said in *The Times* that the single currency would not be brought in in this Parliament, apparently as a result of some deal with Blair. Blair's anxiety is that Rupert Murdoch will not support Labour if we go for the single currency. I don't believe it, but that is the big news story today.

Monday 20 October
The stock market fell by sixty points and the pound rose because of the new statement issued by the Government that we wouldn't join the single currency in the present Parliament (having briefed two weeks ago that we would, which had sent the stock market soaring and the pound falling). For the first time on Channel 4 News, tonight the spin doctors have been attacked by name: Charles Whelan, Gordon Brown's press officer, and Alastair Campbell. Campbell was quoted saying that something was 'crap' and another thing was 'bollocks'. The journalists loathe it and the editors hate it, and the honeymoon with the City is nearly over. After Black Wednesday today is known as Brown Monday.

Tuesday 21 October
Josh came in and spent the morning dealing with all the technical problems that have developed recently. The cable coming into the basement still received Sky News despite having it disconnected so he

wired that onto the computer in the office and you can watch TV – all five channels and Sky. He is a brilliant lad.

Wednesday 22 October

At three I did an interview with Radio 5 Live about Ken Coates and the row in Europe. The European Parliamentary Labour Party have had imposed on them this code of conduct, which they haven't accepted, which would make it an offence to discuss in public the new proportional representation regional list system. Under the system the Leader picks the list. A very important democratic issue. I defended Ken vigorously. He rang me later to say that he had been suspended, along with Hugh Kerr, Michael Hindley and Alex Falconer, but they did it wrongly so it may not be valid. He is trying to make it into a question of privilege.

Went by taxi to London University, where Melissa gave her lecture on the Politics of Motherhood. Her book is coming out shortly. She was amusing, confident, humane, analytical – very, very good and I was frightfully proud of her.

Thursday 23 October

Tony Blair was booed in the City of London when he visited the floor of the Stock Exchange yesterday. Although the spin doctors said the story was untrue, and one of the people asked for his autograph, his main allies are disenchanted with him. But much more significantly, Hong Kong lost 30 per cent of the value off its stock market and this spread around the world; the tiger economies are in serious trouble.

The Ken Coates story still runs and there is a lot of support for the MEPs affected, although Glenys Kinnock says they are a lot of wreckers.

Sunday 26 October

Caroline and I got up at 5.30, had breakfast and caught a taxi to Waterloo. We were the first to arrive, and then Hilary came with his four childrren, then Lissie and Paul and their girls, and then Josh and Naz and William and Nahal, and Stephen and Nita and their two. We boarded the 8.23 Eurostar. As we passed Ruth's house she waved a red handkerchief from her balcony and I filmed her waving it.

It was a perfect autumn day and a marvellous trip. We were going to do it last year but Caroline was too ill so we did it this year. I can't tell you how marvellous it was. I took a video of it.

Monday 27 October

Caroline rested all day – her cough was still there.

I went off to the Commons and Gordon Brown made a statement on the single currency. He committed us in principle as a government to going in – he just said the conditions had to be right.

Kenneth Clarke said this was the policy he had always advocated. When I was called I said that this was a most important statement and could the Chancellor confirm that everyone would be allowed to speak out and that there would be no attempt to gag anyone on any aspect of Britain's relationship with Europe. The Tories liked it and our people didn't cheer – you couldn't expect them to, sitting there and enjoying the humiliation of the Tories. But it is a historic statement and it also explains the cuts that are being made in legal aid and education fees, and lone parents and the new pension scheme – it is all about preparing us for membership of the single currency. It is a fundamentally undemocratic statement and a sticking point, and nobody could possibly go along with it who believed in democracy or the rights of the people in Britain, France and Germany to have any say. The great propaganda machine has started gearing into place. Later today we heard the New York stock market had fallen 500 points, which is the largest fall since 1987. The capitalist economy is in huge crisis at the very moment that we endorse international capitalism and abandon democratic safeguards. The Tories are against it for nationalist reasons but Kenneth Clarke could well be in the Cabinet with Paddy Ashdown – it is the Establishment fighting the people on democratic and economic questions.

After the long recess, I'm looking forward to this session of Parliament.

Tuesday 28 October

Saw Alan Clark in the Tea Room. He said, 'Your question yesterday in the House was very effective. This is like 1938,' meaning a general coalition around appeasement. I said, 'I think the Commons are committing suicide while the balance of the mind is disturbed.' I said that he must be glad to be back. He said this was why he wanted to come back.

Wednesday 29 October

A parcel arrived containing a 200-million-year-old fossil which was so heavy I could hardly carry it. It was presented to me by the Petroleum Geologists following a dinner last night. When you look at something 200 million years old it does give you a historical perspective!

Ruth said to me that in the Louise Woodward case in America, the English nanny who has been convicted of second-degree murder had said that she 'popped the baby on the bed', and the prosecutor asked her, 'What did you mean when you said you "popped" the baby?' It is apparently a verb they don't use in America. So we thought about the word 'pop' and how many uses it has:

popped him on the bed – placed him on the bed
popped off – left the room, unexpectedly
popped in – came into the room unexpectedly

popped over – went over to the shops
popped under – pop under the covers in bed if it was very cold
pop out – to do one or two jobs
pop up – to appear unexpectedly
pop through – for example, the window
pop the question
pop down – to the shops
pop on – for example, the kettle
pop away – to do a job
pop back, pop round, pop along

Very funny word – pop – it means a sudden and somewhat unexpected clear movement relating to what people do. We did have fun.

Friday 31 October, Matlock
Met Dr Margaret O'Sullivan, who is the county and diocesan archivist for Derbyshire. The reason for the visit was that the NUM archives for Derbyshire have finally been released. Margaret was a huge enthusiast and said that Derbyshire had the best miners' records of any county; Northumberland had let theirs go and Durham didn't have any, and Barnsley's were all being held by Arthur Scargill. The records we saw were in an extremely good state – lists of union members, what they were paid, minutes of lodge meetings held in local pubs, historical press cuttings covering the whole range of interests of miners – that is to say, coal prices abroad, the coal trade internationally, relations between the Government and the mine owners, and subsequently with the NCB. She was hoping to get a grant from the National Lottery Heritage Board.

Back to Chesterfield for a surgery. Mr Hall, of Hall the Gun Maker, and his son came to see me. They have been making guns since the 1880s, a high-precision company employing five people and selling very high-quality rifle and gun barrels and guns, and of course they have been completely knocked out by the firearms legislation. Unlike some at my surgery, who complain bitterly and shout at you, Mr Hall just asked for help, so I dictated a letter, which he could send to the bank or the Government, as he felt fit, to try and raise funds to allow him to diversify, because that high-precision engineering could be applied anywhere. He was very appreciative. I liked him very much.

Monday 3 November
I went to see the Chief Whip, Nick Brown, at 6.30 and admired his red box. He was very friendly and said 'you must have lots of them.'

I said, 'I know how busy you are and it is nice of you to see me, but I came to tell you about some anxieties I have about Government policy. My problems are in respect of tuition fees for students, cuts in lone-parent benefit and legal aid, giving the Bank of England control over the interest rates, the proposal for European elections using PR on a regional list system, and the single currency.'

He said, 'That's a lot.'

'I know, but part of your job is to pass comments from MPs up to the top and I thought I'd just tell you.'

He said, 'Tommy McAvoy, your whip, says you're always very responsible – you always let him know what you're going to do.' He went on, 'Well, other Members are coming to see me.' He was very jolly. He locked both doors! I think the important thing is to maintain good relations with the whips.

Thursday 6 November

Interest rates have been put up by another quarter of one per cent by the Bank of England, the fifth increase since Labour came into power.

Monday 10 November

I had to go the House because there was a Private Notice Question on Iraq by David Winnick, who is an absolute fanatic. Derek Fatchett was put up to answer and it was very unsatisfactory and he didn't look comfortable. The Tories and the Lib Dems gave support and other Labour members – Dale Campbell-Savours, Tam Dalyell, myself, Jeremy Corbyn and Harry Barnes – raised doubts. The public are not at all keen on another war with Iraq and yet Blair is making the most militant statements, and the media are full of pictures of Tornadoes and Cruise missiles and God knows what.

We had a vote on the Greater London Authority Referendum Bill, which will provide for a refendum in May on whether to have an elected mayor for London. I am opposed to it, with lots of other people. But I'm not raising my head above the parapet. Ken Livingstone wasn't even in the House.

On the second vote, John Major came up and asked how Caroline was. We talked about tuition fees and he said the policy was put to him three times and he refused to have anything to do with it. 'I'm in the wrong party!'

Wednesday 12 November

To the Queen Elizabeth II Conference Centre and, just as I was going in, who should I see but Rupert Murdoch. I was very surprised because it was like meeting the Queen at a bus queue; so I said, 'Oh we haven't met for twenty-five years.' (I was dead right because I checked it later in the day –it was 7 April 1972 when I went to see him about the referendum on the Common Market.) The *Sun* then denounced me as wanting to set up an Eastern European state, I reminded him.

Murdoch said, 'Oh that was Larry Lamb, the editor. Will there be a referendum on the single currency?'

I said there would have to be. We went up in the lift and I got out at the second floor but I decided later in the day that I would ring the editor of the *Sun* to see if he could spare half an hour to talk about the referendum. Murdoch is only in London till Friday – he is seeing the PM tomorrow. The editor suggested that I write a letter.

Walked over to Central Hall to address a sixth-form conference and found William Hague making a speech to the pupils, so I crept in the back and took pictures of him.

Walked back to the Commons and went into Prime Minister's Questions. Tony Blair was answering questions about the Formula One story – Bernie Ecclestone having given the Party £1 million, and the Party announcing that it wouldn't impose a tobacco-advertising ban on Formula One racing. Blair protested too much and it didn't come across well. Martin Bell asked, 'Now we've dealt with one sort of sleaze, have we got a new dragon with a red rose?'

I said to a few journalists in the House that it worried me that for the rest of my life every penny I gave to the Labour Party would be going to pay off Formula One, which I never watched.

Talked to Chris Mullin and he is very active in the struggle to defeat the reduction of the single-parent family benefit. A lot of Members are saying this is the one occasion when they will vote against the Government, but we will try to stop it going ahead before that. The lead is now being taken in the Campaign Group by Diane Abbott and Lynne Jones, Ken Livingstone, Jeremy Corbyn – all bright and able people – so I'm seeing my role as a much more reflective one, encouraging and helping.

Caroline is writing a marvellous review of Patricia Hollis's book on Jennie Lee.

Thursday 13 November

The Formula One story is even more incredible, because it turns out that when Blair wrote to Lord Neill, who has replaced Lord Nolan as Chairman of the Committee on Standards in Public Life, it wasn't about the contribution of £1 million pounds to the Labour Party (as we had been led to believe); it was about the fact that Bernie Ecclestone had offered more money. Blair wasn't altogether open with the House. Also, a study has shown that young people who watch Formula One racing are more likely to smoke than anybody else, so it is an awful mess.

Sunday 16 November

I forgot to mention that I watched Tony Blair on TV doing an interview with John Humphrys. Blair said that they couldn't rule out the use of force against Iraq, and Madeleine Albright, the American Secretary of

State, is touring the Arab world to get support for the Americans if they did decide to bomb Iraq over the removal of the weapons inspectors. Britain does everything Washington tells us to. Tony Blair particularly does everything Bill Clinton asks him to do. As for the Bernie Ecclestone business, Blair just gave long explanations and in the end said 'I'm still the man you voted for and you can trust me, I can change Britain' – totally egocentric.

Wednesday 19 November

I was taken at 7.45 by car to do the *Today* programme with Boris Johnson about the publication today of a survey on public attitudes to politicians and journalists. Johnson talked about how MPs didn't count, they were just marriage-guidance counsellors on a Friday. I just went for him. I shouldn't lose my temper, but actually it was quite good.

At six, I went to the Campaign Group, which was being addressed by Eddie George, the Governor of the Bank of England. It was a tremendous coup for the Campaign Group to get George to come, and it was very decent of him because we are generally known as the hard-left group. I introduced myself to George before the meeting and I said, 'Do you mind if I video it.' 'Not at all,' he replied. People are totally relaxed about videos now.

Eddie George was charming, couldn't have been more friendly. He is a sort of bank manager to the nation. He described the economic environment, talked about inflation being important, but said that growth and investment were also important; very shrewd because he knew the audience he was addressing. He said that the independence of the Bank gave him the opportunity to deal with interest rates, but he was working within the limits set by the Chancellor, and if the Chancellor raised the inflation limit, he would have to adjust. He said, 'The interest-rate increases we have announced will reduce demand and will prevent unemployment from falling further. Our main interest is in growth and sustainable employment.' He said that leaving the ERM had helped; inflation was going up a bit, demand will slow down sharply, but will be enough. He also said something about the EMU, on which he was a bit more doubtful.

He answered all questions politely. I asked, 'But what do we do if we want to change the policy? What about the economic and monetary union, where we won't even be able to influence decisions? If you can't change the policy by means of the ballot box, there will be a very low turnout at elections.' He answered that quite courteously.

The experience that had burned into his mind was the Thatcher boom-and-bust, and the damage it did – the fluctuations, high interest rates, unemployment going up and down and short-termism. Everyone's life is shaped by their own experience and his experience was what happened ten years ago.

Thursday 20 November

The revolt over the lone-parents benefit developed at yesterday's parliamentary party meeting; on *Newsnight*, they had Ann Cryer and Alan Simpson speaking against it, with Patricia Hewitt saying, 'Oh, the Campaign Group are just oppositionists. Everything the government does, they oppose.'

Monday 24 November

Talked to a few people in the Tea Room – Audrey Wise, Chris Mullin and others are determined to vote against attacking lone-parent benefits and, if they won't let the vote take place on the relevant clause in the Social Security Bill, we shall vote against the third reading of the whole Bill. That will put Tony Blair in much greater difficulty than us.

The important thing is how to respond afterwards if the whip is withdrawn. I shall say I am naturally very disappointed, never thought a Labour Government could do such a thing and will apply for the whip to be restored every month and force them to say 'No, No' continually.

Tuesday 25 November

Had a sandwich and a fruit salad and then went to the lobby of miners in the Jubilee Room; it is quite clear that the Government have decided to kill the remainder of the mining industry: 5000 jobs in mining and another 50,000 in associated manufacturing industries. They are doing nothing. They say, 'We can't. It's privately owned. We can't intervene, it's market forces, cheap imports,' and so on. The anger was very great. There were two members of the British Association of Colliery Managers, who said, 'We have just given up our contributions to the Labour Party.'

Wednesday 26 November

We rang Hilary, who is forty-four today, bless him.

To the National Portrait Gallery for the reception to celebrate the portrait of me by Humphrey Ocean. It was a jolly occasion. I thought it would be very formal but it was extremely jolly. I had invited the family and friends: Stephen was there filming, Josh and Naz and William, Ralph and Ann Gibson, Peter Carter, Humphrey and Miranda Ocean and his two daughters, and Joanna Lumley who is a friend of Humphrey's.

The only MPs' portraits in the whole gallery, other than me and Douglas Hurd, were Prime Ministers – Callaghan, Wilson, Macmillan, Douglas-Home, Mrs Thatcher. There were also pictures of the Queen, Arthur Scargill, Joe Gormley, Tom Jackson, Sid Weighell. It was a nice day. When you get to my age, the final corruption is that you are treated with respect, as a celebrity, a kindly old gentleman; you get honorary doctorates and busts and portraits. I told Ralph that I was seen as a harmless old gentleman and he said, 'Until you open your mouth.'

Back at the House John Battle had been put up, in effect, to say that the Government would do nothing whatever to save the mining industry – It's a level playing field . . . market forces . . . European conventions . . . privatisation – every excuse under the sun. It just makes your blood boil. This is not a government with which I have any sympathy whatever.

Came home and transferred the video and sent a copy off for Humphrey Ocean.

Friday 28 November

I went to the Commons because Mike Foster's Private Member's Bill to ban hunting with dogs was being debated and I didn't want to miss it. I heard a few of the speeches. To cut a long story short, it was carried by 411 to 151. An overwhelming majority. The Government is now the only obstacle to getting it on the statute book. When you look at the abstentions, very few members of the Cabinet seem to have voted. Blair and Cook were away, Straw abstained, Blunkett abstained, Mandelson abstained. It is quite obvious they didn't want the Bill, which I learned when I had a word with Mike Foster after he had won the ballot for the bill. But it was a tremendous victory and I saw people on both sides outside demonstrating.

I went to Chesterfield by train and there was a circuit court judge on the train, Judge David Pugsley. We talked all the way to Derby. He is the son of a Methodist minister. He stood as a Labour candidate in March 1974. He has written a paper called 'The collapse of non-conformity' and we talked about the relationship between dissent and politics and religion. He described how the First World War had drawn Methodist ministers into the army as chaplains, and after that they had ceased to be progressive; it was an interesting discussion, absolutely up my street. He had been to hear me speak at a Conference in 1973, knew Ralph Gibson, knew of Caroline. I found him very agreeable.

The political situation is thrilling. The Government, having made a huge mistake on Formula One tobacco advertising has now let the mining industry down. It is not going to help the anti-hunting lobby, and I think, bit by bit, the public is waking up to what sort of a Government it is.

Tuesday 2 December

Went to St Thomas' Hospital to see Professor Tom Pearson, the consultant haematologist. Pearson arrived and, as the nurses hadn't arrived, he walked along the corridor and took my blood himself. We had a talk, as we always do, about the Health Service. He said, 'It's just running down. And I'll tell you something else, three professors of the King's College Medical School have been sacked after an assessment of their work. I said to one of them, "I hear you are leaving the service. When are you going?' He said, "I've been told to clear my desk by tonight."'

Apparently they are merging all the medical schools, so they are having to get rid of people.

To Number 10 at two, for a meeting of Members for a pep talk from Tony Blair. We were ushered into the Cabinet Room. I took a few pictures and everybody was very friendly. I saw David Miliband walking by. I filmed Tony Blair as he came in. He is always charming and he gave a beaming smile, so I zoomed in on him. Then I put the camera away. I would have loved to film the whole thing.

It began about 2.07 and ended about 3.02. Tony Blair began by saying, 'I am sorry. I am rather pressed for time, I am between the state visit of the President of Brazil and the Moderator of the Church of Scotland.

'We are going through a difficult phase now. The important thing to remember' – which is a phrase he always uses, – 'is why we won, the importance of winning the next election; our job is to get the economy going and make an impact on the world and do it together. It will take time. As for spending, there are difficult choices to be made. As to the constituencies, the little things will be the difficult ones. We have got to decide on the big things. We mustn't be complacent about the Tories. The important thing is to keep the whole Party together, keep the Party united. That's the hard part, and if you forget, it's your difficulty.'

After he had finished, we were all invited to comment.

One MP said, 'There is too much secrecy. We don't know what Ministers are doing.'

Joe Ashton, as usual, made a long speech about how Wilson would have solved the problem of timetabling the hunting bill by sitting on a Thursday night.

Hazel Blears said something about there being too much detail of the minutiae. 'What is the big picture?'

Joe Benton said, 'We must go to a second term but as to single parents, I am really very worried.'

I realised that everybody there only had a minute, so I said I only wanted to make one point. 'I am voting against the Social Security Bill on Wednesday. You cannot justify taking money off the poorest to fight inflation. You can't ring-fence the rich and tax the poor. These are the poorest children of all. I won't encourage anybody else to vote against the Bill because I don't want them to get into trouble. If we had a free vote, you wouldn't carry the lone-parents cut in the PLP.'

Hilton Dawson said, 'On single parents, I haven't been in any way influenced by what Tony Benn said but I am going to vote against it too.'

Blair answered the various points that had been raised. 'On single parents, we are doing a fine job for single parents.This is much more an issue in the Party than it is with the public, and we will monitor it all. People want more public expenditure, but we should be in balance at this stage in the cycle and we must be tough on spending against borrowing and later cuts.'

Then he said, 'On the single parents, if you vote against it, that vote will become the issue. Tory spending limits were actually too slack. We won, despite our tough manifesto. The Liberals can argue for spending anything. On the Euro-elections, we have got to condition people to accept some defeats we may get as a result of proportional representation (because some people had raised the European elections under PR). And on fox hunting, we shall review the matter for future sessions.'

Somebody said, 'I am worried about single parents. Cutbacks are contrary to our policy on social exclusion and these are problems for real people. What are we going to do about the Child Support Act? Are we going to reform that?'

Tony Blair came back again. He said, 'The reform of the Child Support system would be very expensive. We have got to be firm on spending. As to lone parents, we have got to persuade people. Pensioners – we did that for pensioners in the winter.'

Another MP said, 'People are really happy in my constituency. Single parents are no problem at all and to vote against the Government – it would be breathtaking, how could anybody be so disloyal.'

Maria Eagle said, 'Ministerial letters to MPs read just like letters we used to receive from Tory Ministers.'

Tony Blair also responded to points about tuition fees. 'There will be trouble until it happens, but then it will all be forgotten. One third of students will be exempt. It will be okay on the day. Students take out loans anyway and, if we don't have them, we will never get the money we want in education.

'Attlee was crippled by Bevan in the Fifties, we were crippled in the Seventies and the public aren't interested in all these things. I need the Party to support me and it is up to us.'

He then went on to say there were two types of criticism – genuine doubts about single parents and 'destructive criticism, people who go to the media and attack the Party. We need a sense of unity and purpose. We won on 1 May because we were modernising and because we believe in justice; and the critics now are the same critics who said before the election, "If you do this, you will never win the election." They didn't believe in New Labour, but they were wrong. Westminster issues don't matter very much. If we win again, in the second term, greater changes will be possible.'

I went outside and had a job finding my coat, so I had to come back to the ante-room and there was the Moderator of the Church of Scotland and, I think, the President of the Baptist Federation, so I had a friendly chat to them. Tony Blair came out and he pointed at me and said, 'I'm going to promote him, you know. You realise that, don't you?'

Had a bite to eat later in the Cafeteria, talking to Maria Eagle and Clive Soley, the Chairman of the Parliamentary Labour Party. He said, 'I hope you will consider not voting against the Social Security Bill, because the Government have promised to review it.'

Well, I am not voting for a Bill that gives the Government the power to do it.

However smooth and chic Blair may be, he seems to me to be a frightened man. He doesn't want to take action against the Left of the Labour Party, and he said that if we were divided, that would do us damage, but for God's sake he has attacked Old Labour for years now. I am proud of Old Labour because I was a part of it and it did a lot of good things.

Tuesday 9 December

I had a note asking me to go and see one of the whips, Graham Allen, about the vote tomorrow. I went in and said I was voting against and I hoped they weren't going to take action against anybody. He said, 'We might ask them to do more campaigning in the country.'

I said, 'That would be fine. It would be difficult for anyone to do more meetings than I do.'

Later I saw Nick Brown in the Lobby and he said, 'You have always played it square with me, Tony, you always tell me.'

Wednesday 10 December

I did about eight local-radio station interviews on the lone-parent benefit and it is really worth doing them, because although each one addresses only a fairly limited audience, you are reaching all over the country and, from the questions asked, you sort of sharpen up your response.

A man called David Cooper came to see me at eleven. He looked like a little Santa Claus. He is sixty-seven and makes clay pipes, and had made me one. He is interested in morris dancing and told me there is a dance called the 'Baccy Pipe Gig', where you jump over churchwarden pipes, which were designed so that you could smoke in church, the smell mixing with the incense. Wooden pipes, he said, only came from France in 1860 and before that they were all clay.

I went into the House for the remaining stages of the Social Security Bill. Nobody knew how many Labour MPs would actually vote against the Government by voting for the amendment to delete the offending Clause 70, and how many would abstain. There was a marvellous debate. Audrey Wise, Alice Mahon, and Ken Livingstone spoke and Patricia Hewitt made a vicious little speech, and so did Lorna Fitzsimons, in favour of the Government. Harriet Harman was pathetic, although I had sympathy with her in one sense. Not a single member of the Cabinet sat with her when she was really under fire. Blair didn't come, neither did Gordon Brown or Cook so she was left isolated with junior Ministers. It was so obvious that we had won the argument.

In the course of the day, I spoke to various people about it. Malcolm Wicks said, 'I am going to vote with the Government with a heavy heart.' And I saw Tom Sawyer and he said, 'Tony Blair has bunkered himself in and we have got to help him.' Well that wasn't a good reason really.

On the vote, 47 voted against and 63 abstained, possibly more. In the Government lobby there was William Hague side-by-side with Tony Blair. I was told that a couple of Labour MPs were weeping. I doubt that but they were really, really sickened by it and we did very well.

When we had dealt with all the amendments, it came to the third reading and I spoke after Kevin McNamara and before Alan Simpson. I spoke for four minutes only. I said I was against the Bill, gave the reasons why, and said I intended to vote against the third reading. Most people on the Labour side thought one vote against was enough but I was angry at the way the Government had behaved, and during the day Denis Healey and the *Guardian* had come out against; and I was angry at the way Patricia Hewitt taunted Ken Livingstone. Dennis Skinner hadn't been keen on a second vote but when I did call it, he came in the Lobby and there was Paddy Ashdown and some of the Liberals. I said to Paddy Ashdown, 'The trouble is, Paddy, you joined the wrong end of the Labour Party. Come in with us. It would be a much better, more radical party. If I get expelled from the Party for voting with you, you will still be in the Cabinet Committee. My only hope with the leadership now may be to join the Liberal Party and be put on a Cabinet Committee!' Everybody did laugh. I must say, it was quite jolly. But it was interesting that on one side you had the Tory and Labour Front Benches, and on the other side, the Liberals and the Campaign Group.

What really happened today was that politics re-entered the House of Commons. The Chamber was crowded; the Press Gallery came to see who was abstaining, and covered it very widely in the media; there were demonstrations outside. MPs quoted in their speeches how many single parents there were in their constituencies, what the unemployment rate was. I felt as if the Labour Representation Committee had been reformed. I don't know what the whips will do, but I went to bed happier than I have been since Tony Blair became Leader.

Thursday 11 December

Alan Clark told me that he had refused to vote against the lone parents, and when I told that in the Tea Room, Labour MPs said, 'That's because he's responsible for so many of them!'

If they do try and pick off Brian Sedgemore, John Marek and Bob Wareing as bringing the Party into disrepute, it will be impossible to sustain; it is the Government that brought forward this proposal.

Yesterday in *The Times* there was a cartoon that was really quite funny: Dennis Skinner, Ken Livingstone and me standing outside Number 10 with Mandelson looking through the window, and on the door of Number 10, it said, 'Socialism Exclusion Unit'.

Friday 12 December

Did a surgery from eleven to three.

The response to the cuts in lone-parent benefit was phenomenal. People in the surgery mentioned it and I had messages on the telephone. There is no doubt that this has been Blair's biggest mistake so far.

At my surgery there were two people whose disability benefits had been held up for almost a year and one was weeping in my surgery. Then there was a man who had come originally as a Child Support Agency case and sat there with scribbled bits of paper with bizarre messages saying 'The Abbey National is controlled by the Mafia, the Lord Chancellor's Department is corrupt, the CSA are run by murderers.'

I said, 'All I can do is to advise you.'

He said, 'Will you put down a parliamentary question about my case.'

I said, 'I don't think it would help at the moment.' So then he said, 'You're well paid. You're not fit to represent people in Chesterfield.'

'I am advising you. I am giving you the best help I can.' He looked slightly murderous and you do get a few people like that.

Tuesday 16 December

The whips are seeing a few people. Audrey Wise had a thirty-second talk to George Mudie. Some of the new Members are being told, 'Two strikes and you're out,' which is a bit threatening.

Tomorrow there is the party meeting. Voted on the minimum wage and came home.

Wednesday 17 December

I got to the Parliamentary Party meeting early because I wanted to video people arriving. I knew I couldn't video the meeting itself, but I got a sort of feeling of it and filmed Tony Blair, Mandelson, Prescott, Nick Brown and Clive Soley.

Soley said, 'This is a private meeting and it is essential that we are able to talk to each other in absolute confidence, and we will put out a press briefing, afterwards, but it will be absolutely fair.'

At 11.33 Tony Blair in his shirt sleeves got up smiling broadly; he smiled throughout his two speeches, smiling so vacantly that it didn't seem very serious, though I later picked up what he said from Channel 4, because Number 10 put out a press release of his speech. So much for confidentiality. He listed all the achievements and said, 'Life will get harder. We are bound to anger some people. There are choices to be made. It is a test of our nerve. The Welfare State has got to be reformed. We said we would save money and modernise the Welfare State. We have got to change benefits in the right way in order to finance our education and welfare reforms. We wouldn't leave people without help. More is being spent on benefits than on education and defence. We have got to create opportunities. There are two types of criticism – constructive criticism and the sort of criticism that mouths the Tory stories that we are dismantling the Welfare State. It is up to us. We listen, of course. We must deliver our pledges and remember what unites us.'

There was then a discussion about the cut. A lot of Members spoke against it, then Tony Blair replied to the points raised.

'We must have long-term reform. Some will lose, but do not say this is dismantling the Welfare State. It is said that we are doing the Tories' job for them; it's not true. These are not tough times. The real crisis will be in three years if we haven't delivered.

'MPs may find it hard to go back to their General Committees, but you will have to tell your activists to accept what we are doing. Things will get a lot rougher, as they did between 1976 and 1979.

'We have all done a good job. Everybody has done a good job. We must be united – modern, moderate and united.

'The big picture is what matters and we will win.'

There was a round of applause as there had been after his first speech, but it was fairly muted.

Outside the Committee Room I saw David Hill, the Party press officer, briefing all the journalists about what had happened. I filmed him with John Sergeant and Michael Brunson picking up the story.

Standing in the Members' Lobby with Alan Simpson, the Chief Whip Nick Brown came up and he said, 'Alan, you have already been severely reprimanded. Tony, you are now being severely reprimanded,' and he gave me a big smile.

We had a lovely talk. I said, 'I think you are a very good Chief Whip.'

He said, 'I have no complaints about you.'

'Well, I am sorry for writing you so many letters.'

'No, you go on writing when you feel you can't vote.'

I think he was sympathetic because he was brought up by a lone parent.

Thursday 18 December

I came home and set up the Christmas tree, tidied up. Caroline's back is beginning to hurt her a bit. She gets very tired. She thinks she will be lucky to last another year. I hope to God that isn't true. I am afraid that I won't be as good as I should in being of assistance at that moment.

Saturday 20 December
I went to Piers's party. My brother Dave and June were there; their son, Piers's book *Ethics* is to be published in the New Year.

This benefits row is developing quite interestingly. Some militant disabled people turned up at Number 10, turned over their wheelchairs, sprayed red paint on the ground and threw it on the railings, then lay in the paint and were arrested. Blair was at Durham Cathedral talking about the urgent need for Benefit reform. In the papers it said Blunkett was against it and was worried, but today they said that wasn't true. They are getting into a muddle about it. The support for the opposition to benefit cuts is very strong.

Tuesday 23 December
The Benefit row is continuing, with Blair doing a whole series of interviews. There is no doubt whatever that he is in deep trouble.

Wednesday 24 December
A Cabinet Minister's son has been entrapped by a *Daily Mirror* journalist into selling him £10 worth of cannabis. Nobody knows who it is, but it looks as if it is the Home Secretary's son, which is difficult for Jack. I know the lad because I carried him in my arms at Blackheath in 1981 at the celebration of the Peasants' Revolt and he is now at Pimlico School where Patricia Moberly teaches him. Whoever it is, it's a terrible thing to happen.

Thursday 25 December
Christmas Day. We exchanged presents in the bedroom after breakfast, as we always do. I got some lovely clothes and a wind-up clockwork radio. I gave Caroline some books, perfumes, aromatherapy, outfits, a mixer. I had a bath and when I got out, I put my foot down and got a sharp pain in my foot. I thought I had stood on a safety pin, but when I looked, a wasp had stung me. Fourteen hours later, it still hurts.

The whole family arrived at about one. Peter Carter made a speech celebrating the twenty-first anniversary of his first Christmas lunch with us all.

It is amazing when I think that, eighteen months ago, we weren't sure Caroline would be here last Christmas, and then we weren't sure she would be here this Christmas. She does have backache and obviously has a very serious complaint of spinal cancer, but she is alive and enjoying life and I have much to thank God for.

Saturday 27 December, Stansgate
Did a bit of shopping. Got the papers. Jack Straw's son is the one who has been arrested on the drugs charge.

Ken Coates confirmed this and I think everybody knows.

Sunday 28 December
My laptop computer has gone on the blink so I am completely flummoxed for the whole week.

I heard that Robert Andrews died on Christmas day. He must have been in his mid-seventies. Mr Andrews served in the Royal Air-Force during the war, and for the last twenty-five to thirty years he has slept on the Embankment every night, gone to St Martin-in-the-Fields to wash and shave and dress, and come to the House of Commons and sat on one of the benches in the Central Lobby – sometimes sleeping, sometimes writing out a petition to the Queen. I have tried to talk to him, but he has become totally confused. He said what he was writing must be kept out of the hands of the Russians and Americans and it was very important. The vicar of St Martin-in-the-Fields asked if I would try and get him a pension, so I asked for some particulars and wrote, but he didn't want one. Andrews always looked tidy, a bit dishevelled, but never like a vagrant and the police in the Central Lobby were always kind to him.

Just before Christmas the police in the Central Lobby gave me a card to sign, which they had all signed to Andrews. Apparently, he went to the service at St Martin-in-the-Fields on Christmas Day, wandered out and collapsed in Piccadilly Circus and was taken to hospital. So I was told by the social worker from Westminster City Council. Somebody there told me that the City Council would probably pay for the funeral, and the family would be notified and there would be a service in St Martin-in-the-Fields.

Friday 2 January 1998, Stansgate
Jack Straw's name finally came out in the cannabis story because the injunction hadn't been sought in the Scottish courts, so it was published in the Scottish papers and leaked into England. Everyone knew anyway.

Ken Coates has transferred from the European Parliamentary Socialist Group to become an honorary member of the Green Group; and that means he will be expelled from the Labour Party. It wasn't very sensible and I did tell him, but he is set on his own course.

Saturday 3 January
Very high gales, although not as bad as in the West Country, where they rose to 70 mph and caused very serious damage.

Some of the children threw muddy tennis balls at the Rosa Luxemburg sculpture and we were so angry that we made them clear it all off. And they were very sorry.

It is nice to have the children but it is also nice to have peace and quiet and get on with work.

I sent off forty-four replies to people who had written to me about lone parents and benefits.

Sunday 4 January
The *Sunday Telegraph* had almost a whole-page profile of Melissa – a superb account of her arguments – and it has moved her head and shoulders above anyone else in her generation. She has reintroduced the idea that motherhood is worth doing and, though the difficulties of it are great, motherhood itself is satisfying. So many feminists in the past have seemed rather hard and anti-maternal, probably quite wrongly, but they have given that impression. Melissa has swung the pendulum back again.

Monday 5 January
Melissa was mentioned in the *Guardian* as one of the leading British feminists today, which is marvellous.

Thursday 8 January
I forgot to mention that when Caroline and I came out of the cinema last night after watching *Wilde*, we walked through Leicester Square – I haven't done that for years and it has all been pedestrianised now. It was milling with people, mainly young, probably half of them from abroad. It was really weird. I felt as if I was abroad myself. I felt a stranger in London for the first time. I realised that the life I have led – just Parliament, constituency, public meetings and the family – is a very narrow life.

It reminded me that fifty-four years ago this month, in 1944, I was in London and I went and sat on a park bench in Leicester Square. It was dark, in the blackout, and I felt I would just like to breathe in the London I was leaving, not knowing whether I would come back – because of course in the war nobody knows what is going to happen. A man came and sat next to me. It was one of those wartime meetings when you are like ships passing in the night. I remember him, and the immediate intimacy there is when you meet somebody you have never met before and will never meet again, rather like meeting somebody on a train. That has stuck in my mind though it was half a century ago. An extraordinary feeling it was.

Friday 9 January
Up at six and caught the train to Chesterfield. The Midland Mainline, which is the private company that has bought the Midland line of British Rail, has now established a new class. There used to be first class and standard; then it became first class, business class and standard; and now they have got a premier class, where you pay £2 more and the table is covered with crockery, and people come round and give you free

sandwiches and tea. In order just to sit there, you would have to clear all the crockery away that had been carefully laid out and would disappoint the women who come round and who are really stewardesses now. So I went in the standard part, where there is one smoker – because you can't smoke in first class now.

Did my surgery from eleven until three. A Mr W. and his wife came; they had been desperate before Christmas and I had given them £100 to tide them over because they had no money. Their doctor has registered them as sick, so at least they have got a month's money, although there was an attempt to stop that. The Benefits Agency wouldn't give her a crisis loan because it said she had no money to pay it back. It wouldn't give her any money because it said it had averaged out her income and 'you have a theoretical income'; so that couple and their two children would literally have starved. I am sure this is the first of many similar cases that will come to me and something will have to be done about that. The Tories introduced this law and the Labour Party won't repeal it.

Came home and watched a programme called *Euro Trash* which was an extraordinary programme – all sex and naked people. You wouldn't have believed this could appear on television. There has been such a change in public standards. There is a whiff of decadence about it, rather nasty: tight law and order and complete libertarianism. I can't say I disapprove of it. I just note it because cultural characteristics do go with certain political situations.

Blair has apparently taken the initiative and tabled a paper for power-sharing in Northern Ireland, in which there would be another forum involving Dublin, Scotland, England and Wales. That slightly irritated some people in Northern Ireland. But, at the moment, Blair walks on water as far as the media is concerned.

Tuesday 13 January

I talked to Ken Purchase, Robin Cook's PPS, in the Tea Room. I had the first ideological discussion about socialism with anyone for a long time. He said Cook had been forced by Blair to sell aircraft to Indonesia. He also said Cook was looking very carefully at how he could break this terrible control of British foreign policy by the US.

Talked to Chris Mullin and said I thought we were moving towards a coalition. He said he doubted that. He is very measured now, is Chris.

Then I talked to Julian Brazier, a man I have never talked to before, the MP for Canterbury; indeed, the first ever Catholic MP for Canterbury. He is a scholarly man and is a descendant of Bishop Stubbs of Oxford, the great constitutional historian. I told him father's couplet about Stubbs and Freeman: 'Ladling butter from their mutual tubs, Stubbs butters Freeman, Freeman butters Stubbs.' He enjoyed that. He said he was basically a Burkeian, had some doubts about democracy, thought the constitution was more important and was very much against the lawyers controlling a Bill of Rights, which I agree with.

Wednesday 14 January

Walked up from the House to St Martin-in-the-Fields for the funeral of Robert Andrews. He was an extraordinary man. He was an electronics expert, had lectured at Loughborough College and for the Pakistan air force. But from 1963 onwards his life had changed and he would sit in the Central Lobby of the House writing his petition to the Queen. He had made many friends there as a result.

I was asked to say a few words at his funeral. It was a huge event – a lot of Members, including Jack Weatherill, Michael Alison, Peter Bottomley, Gwyneth Dunwoody. Then PC Roger King, who knew him best from the Central Lobby; homeless people; and staff from the House in large numbers. It was lovely. At the end the vicar asked anyone who would like to say something about him to come forward. I learned more about him from that.

Friday 16 January, Chesterfield

Executive Committee of the Chesterfield Labour Party. The real lesson from the meeting was, first of all, how angry most members were with the Government's policies; secondly, this tremendous feeling of loyalty to the Party. Anyone who threatens to stand against the Party or gets expelled or leaves is treated with the utmost severity. Not that I have ever thought it would be an easy thing to do, but it was a reminder.

Saturday 17 January

Watched *Casualty*, which was depressing because Charlie and Bas have broken up. Spoke to Ken Coates who, I think, is a bit lonely now that he has been thrown out of the Party.

Sunday 18 January

Up at six and caught the nine o'clock train to Edinburgh. Read all the papers. What rubbish! Is Brown psychologically flawed? Did Blair cheat to get the leadership? What was the role of Mandelson? Cook and his marriage breakdown. Robinson and his offshore trust. Absolute waste of time! You have to glance at it, because it sort of makes you curious.

Got a cab to the Festival Theatre for the performance of *Writings on the Wall* with Roy Bailey. Tam Dalyell and his wife Kathleen had come, which was extremely sweet of them. His son and daughter-in-law were there, and so were Ron Brown and my old friend Fred Edwards from Dumfries, who always sends me boxes of tea. One very dour old Scot came up before the show and said, 'Mr Benn, I hope this is a concert about political dissent, and not pop music and a few soundbites from you.'

Tuesday 20 January

Today *The Times* published my article comparing Tony Blair to Ramsay MacDonald, but I think the truth is that nobody now has ever heard of Ramsay MacDonald. It's a bit like comparing Blair to Gladstone or Disraeli or Herbert Asquith. It seems that the betrayal by MacDonald has been forgotten.

At the House, Tom Baldwin of the *Daily Telegraph* wanted to talk to me in an informal briefing way. He said, 'Mandelson says to people, "We are going to hoover up the Liberals into our vacuum cleaner and then we'll hoover up the Europhiles and then it won't be the Labour party, it will be a new party."'

I think that is what will happen and it was an interesting confirmation from somebody who knows the spin doctors.

Thursday 22 January

Real crisis in the Northern Ireland peace talks. President Clinton appears to be in really big trouble. Dave, who had been to the Foreign Office this afternoon for a seminar on the Cold War with Jim Callaghan and Denis Healey, said that one or two people had said to him, 'This is the end of Clinton.' A woman who works in the White House told a friend that she had had a short affair with the President and that he had told her to lie if she was cross-examined. For a President to have an affair while President is one thing, but to tell somebody to lie on oath is a more serious thing. Dave told me that one or two people there thought he might be impeached. That would take the shine off the Blair story, and we would end up with President Gore, the present Vice-President, who is always regarded as a heroic figure on the left.

Monday 26 January

Jeremy Corbyn asked me to support him in his nomination of Mordecai Vanunu for the Nobel Peace Prize. Vanunu is the Israeli scientist who has been held in solitary confinement for years because he told the *Sunday Times* that Israel had nuclear weapons. God, what a world!

I heard the Liverpool dockers had ended their dispute today. A nice woman called Sally from Radio Merseyside rang me and said, 'I can't get any of the Liverpool dockers to say anything on the radio because they are so upset and so distressed. Will you say something?' So tomorrow morning I will say something on Radio Merseyside. But that is a classic struggle, betrayed by the Transport and General Workers' Union, by the Labour movement when the Tories were in office, and doubly betrayed when we came into power and applied the same Tory legislation against our people who were sacked for not crossing a picket line. Apparently, Blair told trade union leaders at a meeting at Number10 that marches by trade unions were as out of date as Orange Order marches. That has infuriated the trade unions, who don't like to be compared to the Orange Order, and has infuriated the Orange Order, because they don't like to be compared to trade unions.

Tuesday 27 January

I got up at 6.45 and did an interview with BBC Radio Merseyside about the dockers. I gave a very strong defence of them and said they had been let down by the Labour movement.

Sheila was in. She doesn't work on Mondays and it's always nice to see her on a Tuesday and we spend a lot of time discussing what is happening.

I left just after 6.15 in the evening and went to Number 11 Downing Street because Gordon Brown had invited Central Region MPs to a party. Brown was circulating and I put my camera on the mantelpiece and caught the general atmosphere. Then I filmed his speech. I think the sound is pretty good.

Looking back on it, Gordon Brown is obviously trying to build up his position as the alternative leader of the Party in case Blair fails.

If I were Blair, I would be a bit worried about Brown – not that I have any time for him but Brown is really determined to get that leadership. And he talks about the Labour movement and the trade unions and the constituencies, while Blair is busy talking to businessmen. So it is a clever campaign but, frankly, after the public expenditure cuts and the lone parents, I really don't think Brown would be able to get it. Cook is discredited, Beckett has disappeared, Prescott is nothing.

Jean Corston, the Member for Bristol East, David Blunkett's PPS, asked me in the Lobby if I was going to vote against the fees for students, and I said I was. So that will get through to Blunkett and that is one reason I wanted to say it. She said, 'Well, nothing will happen to you, you know that.'

I said, 'Well maybe, and I am not asking anyone else to do the same, but I think fees are absolutely wrong.'

Wednesday 28 January

Alan Simpson told me that, before the election, he had had a word with Gordon Brown about economic policy and Brown had said, 'Talk to Charlie Whelan', who is his spin doctor. So Alan approached Charlie and Whelan jokingly said, 'Look, the fact is this. You do what we say or we'll break your fucking legs.' That is the way he behaves.

At 1.30 I went to a meeting between the Central Region Group of Labour MPs and Harriet Harman.

Harriet began with an explanation of the costs of social security and fraud and abuse, and the need to discriminate between the rich and the poor receiving benefit. Why should my child get the same benefits as a poor child? and so on.

Graham Allen said, 'We have got somehow to manage the Party' – i.e. bully people into accepting this – 'and we should have all-member gatherings such as we had for the referendum on the Manifesto.'

I said, 'It is a very dangerous argument to say that the rich shouldn't enjoy the same benefits, because the whole principle of the Welfare State was that we all pay according to our wealth and get it according to our need. The affluence test is just a means test.'

Harriet said, 'All-member meetings would be a good idea' and, referring to my comment, 'The Welfare State is old-fashioned and we said in the election that we would deal with the Tories' social and economic failures, and that is what it meant.'

Alan Simpson said, 'Deflation is the problem now, not inflation, and Roosevelt in the Thirties went for industrial investment. The means test should be a last resort and never a general basis for the receipt of benefit.'

Saturday 31 January

Ibrahim arrived at 9.15 and we had a long talk. I asked how he saw the situation and he described it. He said, 'Why does America want to attack a small country like Iraq?' and so on. Well, that is standard diplomatic language. I asked what would happen. He said, 'I don't know, but the Iraqi Parliament is meeting tomorrow and they might recommend that Saddam concedes to the inspection of presidential palaces. As a matter of fact, the presidential palaces never came up before. Previously they said there were secret stores of biological weapons, and we said they could inspect them, but now this touches on our sovereignty.'

I said, 'Of course, it would always be open to you to say that if there are inspectors accompanied by Iraqi officials, that would be fine. But I presume it is all an American intelligence attempt to find out where they are likely to find the President.'

I went on, 'The reason I wanted to see you was to ask if there is any suggestion that might be helpful. The only idea I had that might be sensible is that King Hussein might possibly take an initiative and ask the European Union (of which Britain is now the President) to inspect or mediate, or something. And if that offer was made and Saddam agreed – because it couldn't come from Saddam, it would have to come from an independent country – then it would drive a bit of a wedge between Blair and Clinton and would delay it a bit.'

Ibrahim said, 'The trouble about King Hussein is that we think he has agreed with the Americans and given his consent for American planes to be based in Israel for the attack on Iraq.'

That is a terribly serious situation. First of all, it compromises Hussein vis-à-vis Iraq and vis-à-vis the rest of the Arab world. But if Israel is the base, then it opens up the whole question.

Ibrahim said that Butler, the former American Head of the Commission of Inspection, had actually spoken to a Jewish audience in the Middle East and said to them that Iraq has the capacity to wipe out Israel with chemical weapons, and the President of the Arab League had denounced this as an irresponsible statement. But if that were to happen, and if Iraq were to respond in any way against Israel, then the balloon would go up and everything would end in a great bloody battle.

I talked to Ibrahim about the possibility of any sort of settlement and he said, 'The Saudis and the Kuwaitis are financing this new bombing attack, as well as the Gulf War, because they have bought all these weapons from America and they need the money,' and so on.

I raised with him what had happened in 1990 when the American Ambassador in Baghdad had hinted to Saddam that, if Iraq went into Kuwait, it would be seen as an Arab problem. Ibrahim confirmed that. He said, 'I have seen the minutes of that meeting and that is what actually happened.' But he said that, as a matter of fact, there was a much longer-term plan to invade that the American Ambassador might not have known about because Schwarzkopf, the American general in charge of the operation, was actually training American troops in the United States in anticipation. So that put a new perspective on that.

The general impression I got was that not much could really be done and that this war was imminent, although the possibility of the Iraqi Parliament suggesting a withdrawal of position by Saddam might make things a bit easier. But Ibrahim didn't really think it would.

Sunday 1 February

This morning I was at Sky TV and talked to the make-up woman, a rather blowsy creature with lots of blonde hair, about forty-five. I asked what time she got up and she said 2.30. 'I live in Wiltshire, drive to Osterley Park, where Sky have their headquarters, and do the make-up there. It is absolutely insecure. You never know if you will be wanted. They have told me to come to Millbank one day a week and I have to pay twenty-six pounds a day to park my car.' She continued, ' I can't manage. I'm a lone parent. I have got my boy at a public school.'

I said, 'What about a trade union?'

'Sky won't have trade unions.'

So here you have everything. A woman who really found life hard, with great job insecurity, thought it desperately important to send her son to a public school and couldn't get into a trade union. That's Britain in 1998.

Monday 2 February

I went into the House for a meeting in the Terrace Bar for what was called 'a celebration', organised by the Department for Education and Employment i.e. a celebration of those schools that had been branded as failing schools and now have been 'acquitted'. Absolutely revolting.

Stephen Byers made a speech. I went round talking. I was there because Staveley Junior in Chesterfield had been branded a failure in 1995. I just said to everybody, 'I am absolutely opposed to this idea of branding schools as failing: naming and shaming.' Of course, they all agreed with me. I said, 'If you are going to name anybody as having failed, what about naming Chris Woodhead?'

Saturday 7 February

The situation in America is getting even more complicated. It has had a profound effect on the whole of Blair's visit, because he went over there to get world-statesmanship reputation side-by-side with Clinton, and ended up defending a lame President at the moment when the American press is not interested in Blair, but only in Clinton's sex life.

The Iraq thing has been going wrong in a big way because the opposition to military force is so strong.

Monday 9 February

I rang the BBC's *Midnight Hour* to see if they would let me off tonight's discussion about Enoch Powell, who has just died. I said I am not ill, just extremely tired. But they wouldn't so I got a taxi two hours later and went and did it. David Mellor was the chairman; and there was Hugo Young, the political columnist from the *Guardian*; Gisela Stuart, who is the Labour MP for Edgbaston, and Edward Leigh, an old Thatcherite Euro-sceptic.

We had a discussion about extremism and demagogues, and Hugo Young has a way of just dismissing people he doesn't like, as he did with Enoch Powell. Edward Leigh gave a spirited defence of Powell. Then we discussed Mosley and whether we are moving towards a coalition. I said I thought we were. I was aggressive and kept chipping in. I did find Hugo Young intolerably pompous. Gisela said afterwards that she agreed with me about Blair's language. She said, 'When the leader becomes the people, it is dangerous.'

I said, 'Ein Reich, ein Volk, ein Führer.'

She said, 'Well, you said that to me and I would have said it to you, but not to anybody else.' She was very sweet. I like her. Edward Leigh was just Edward Leigh – a real Thatcherite Tory.

It is now 1.30 and I must go to bed. News today: Turkey has criticised America for not consulting over the proposed attack on Iraq. King Hussein of Jordan has come out against the use of force. So the whole bloody thing is crumbling. I will be very interested to see what happens. I am going to put a question to Blair in the Commons tomorrow when he makes a statement and I think his position is getting weaker and weaker.

Tuesday 10 February

At eleven I went to do *Power House* and just as I was leaving the studio I saw Neil Kinnock. I asked, 'What do you make of this Iraq business?'

He said, 'I thought we should have polished off Saddam Hussein in 1990, but now I am very doubtful.'

'Well, the European Union hasn't been consulted.'

'I know that. There will be a lot of trouble there.' So that was quite interesting and Kinnock was friendly.

Wednesday 11 February

A hundred letters today about Iraq, not one of them critical. I think Blair must be very worried, because British opinion will turn against him immediately the casualty figures are shown on television, and he is alone. Jordan, Saudi Arabia, Turkey, France and Russia are against it and, although the Canadians have said they would send a few troops and the Australians have been asked, that is no world back-up.

Friday 13 February

Tomorrow is St Valentine's Day and I went out to buy Caroline two chocolate bunnies and some flowers.

Monday 16 February

Did Talk Radio with Kirsty Young and they had a telephone poll in which 7000 people had phoned in, of whom 80 per cent were against another war.

Spent most of the morning opening letters. One was from a man who said he was a squadron leader who had flattened Dresden and that now we had to flatten Baghdad.

Tuesday 17 February

Debate on Iraq. Robin Cook began with a speech that was very familiar, followed by Michael Howard, who supported him completely of course, except that the Tories had a little amendment about clarity of objectives, which the Government accepted.

Gerald Kaufman made a nasty speech, followed by Menzies Campbell, who made one of his right-wing speeches dressed up as a Liberal. I had prepared my notes very carefully. At the end when I read the Charter of the United Nations preamble – 'We, the people of the United Nations determined to save succeeding generations from the scourge of war, which twice in our lifetime has caused untold suffering to mankind . . .' – I was near to tears, and when I sat down they ran down my cheeks. One or two people afterwards said it was the best speech I have ever made.

Listened to other bits of the debate. George Galloway made a powerful and passionate speech. Tam Dalyell made a very scholarly speech. Harry Barnes talked about the economic conditions of the people of Iraq. From our point of view, it was brilliant. I didn't expect more than half a dozen in the Lobby, but when the vote came, Tam and I were tellers, and we got twenty-seven votes – including us. One of the whips was writing down all the names, no doubt with a view to disciplinary action. But the government only got 493 votes out of 650 MPs, so it was a staggeringly successful result from that point of view. Everyone who spoke, in fairness, was anxious about what might happen, but for the first time the House of Commons specifically endorsed the use of force.

After the debate I had a word with Ted Heath and I said, 'I wondered if you would speak,' and he shook his head. I said, 'You didn't mind my making a reference to you', which I had done once or twice. He shook his head. I said, 'I am right, aren't I, in saying that Blair has thrown away the leadership of Europe?'

He said, 'Yes.'

I said, 'Well, I greatly appreciate the *sense* of your encouragement, Ted!' And I left it at that, but I felt I sort of established a bond with the man and, of course, the reason he is pro-European is that he hates being bossed about by America.

Waiting for the results, I saw John Major and said, 'I must tell you this, John. The day you became Prime Minister, I was meeting Saddam in Baghdad, and Tariq Aziz, the Foreign Minister, was present and he asked me . . . 'What do you think of John Major? . . .' I said, 'I don't know him very well. . . .' He said, 'I have met him. He is a very charming man."'

John Major laughed and said, 'I did get to know Tariq and I liked him very much. We were on some UN commission or another.'

Then at the very end of the day, I saw Alan Clark who made fun of my false predictions over the Falklands. I said, 'Well, you made some pretty clear predictions tonight about this spreading but you are a historian and we need more historians in the House.' I do believe in having friendly relations.

Wednesday 18 February

I went to Whitehall for one of these vigils outside Downing Street and it was huge, bigger than last Saturday's. It was candlelit, very moving. Marion Miliband was there, Tariq Ali, Harold Pinter, a well-known actress whose name I have forgotten, Jeremy Corbyn and George Galloway. We made speeches and did lots of interviews and then went and presented a letter. Three guys tried to manacle themselves to the gates of Downing Street.

Friday 20 February

I forgot to mention last night that I had a discussion with John Nichols for

World in Action, and he told me that he was a pilot based at a Turkish airfield policing the no-fly zone over northern Iraq; at the same airfield were Turkish aircraft, literally side-by-side with his own, which would take off into Iraq and bomb the Kurds. Very interesting.

Went to the Chesterfield Party Executive Committee. Steve Lismore was the first to speak and as usual he was doubtful about what I should do on Iraq. He wasn't too critical, but doubtful. Paul Vaughan said, 'I admire Tony's consistency on foreign policy.' Mick Caulfield said, 'How do you deal with dictators?' and was a bit doubtful. Jill Brunt was absolutely opposed to the war, and said how disappointed she was by the new women MPs; her children were very worried about the war. Terry Gilby said there were no objectives in this proposed bombardment and that the young didn't want a war. Steve Brunt came in and he said, 'The MPs at the moment are programmed to follow what Blair says, and what we need is a dialogue. America just want to test the bombs.' Geoff Waddoups said that UK forces will be controlled by Clinton and, anyway, our regiments are overstretched. It was put to the vote and they unanimously supported what I had done. I suggested we might have vigils in Chesterfield schools and churches and that was agreed.

Saturday 21 February

Mrs Mac came back from New Zealand and brought pictures of her great-grandchild, Abigail. She was so happy to be back and Lottie cried when she saw her. She had been in a cats' home.

Friday 27 February

The good news today for Caroline was that she got her pension. She didn't retire until she was seventy. But to her horror, she discovered that all her National Insurance deductions from her wages as a teacher had gone to another person. I was very happy to take it up, but she went through the accountant, who threatened the Ombudsman and now she has got a refund back to her seventieth birthday. It is just the sort of case I would take up for a constituent.

I got to Chesterfield a bit late. Did my surgery from twelve to five, including seven cases about the Child Support Agency which is, without a doubt, the worst piece of legislation I have come across. I don't blame the people in Belfast, where the Agency is based, because how can one organisation know who is married, who is divorced, whose partner is who, whether they are in work, whether they have moved, etc. I wrote to the Prime Minister expressing my view that radical change was needed and I shall show that to anybody who comes to see me in the future.

Slept for two hours on the train and got home absolutely exhausted. These last three weeks, with the Iraq thing and the mail, have been too much to cope with.

Tuesday 3 March

Julian May came to do an interview for a BBC Radio 4 discussion. He told me what a nightmare the BBC is. John Birt is trying to economise, so television and radio programmes are presented by the same people, and the idea of a radio culture of its own has completely broken down. All the news is standardised – everyone is competing on a freelance basis.

He gave one example. He was going to do an interview next Friday and the studio was booked, then the interviewee had to go to a funeral. So this guy, Julian, rang BBC Resources – who book the studios – and they said, 'You can cancel it, but we will have to charge you £300 against your programme budget.' So when Julian said he wanted another studio, they said that would be another £300. Public service and common sense have just been abandoned in favour of managers planning all this income-raising. It is an absolute tribute to the Thatcher years.

Friday 6 March

Went in early this morning for the first day of the Report stage of the Wild Mammals (Hunting with Dogs) Bill. All the Tories turned up in force and they just talked it out. The whole thing was occupied with Heseltine, Hogg, Nicholas Winterton and all the fox hunters talking the Bill out. I thought, 'What a bloody fraud!' Here is the Labour Party saying they promised a free vote on hunting, with the clear implication that if the House wanted a Bill, they would find time for the Bill to go through. But what they now say is 'All they promised was a free vote and there has been a free vote'. It is like saying you will have a General Election but that you will take no notice of the outcome. The Labour Party briefing I had on 5 February said that the Government was 'neutral' on the issue of hunting with hounds and that the free vote fulfilled the Government's commitment; there are flaws in the Bill; no amendments were brought forward that addressed these concerns; more detailed drafting will be needed. And the Chief Whip has outlined the problems that this will cause in the Lords – there is not enough room in the Lords' timetable for a controversial Bill in this session, and it may be possible to bring back the measure under a future Government Bill, but no promises were being made. So really, many people who voted Labour, and the animal-welfare people who put £1 million into the campaign, have been betrayed. The whole debate today was a complete fraud.

I had a word with Tony Banks in the Lobby and he is as sick as a dog. Went to the Tea Room, where Chris Mullin and Elliot Morley, the Minister responsible for animal welfare, were looking terribly depressed. I said to Chris, 'The Government has capitulated to the country landowners.'

He said, 'I wouldn't say that. Why don't you have a word with the Minister,' gesturing towards Elliot.

So I said, 'Well, I am having a word with the Minister. What the fucking hell is the use of that?'

Chris said, 'I have never heard you swear before.'

'Well, I feel utterly betrayed. What do people have to do to get rid of hunting? How does the parliamentary system make it possible? It is no good asking voters to vote for me, even though I would always support a Bill, because I know the Government will do nothing about it.'

I think it registered. I am tempted not to vote for anything the Government does until they clear that up, but of course you can't.

Got home very, very angry.

Monday 9 March

I have had some nasty letters about going to Enoch's funeral and I don't want to upset the black community. The Bishop of Croydon, a black bishop, wrote me a hostile letter saying, 'I suppose it was just because of the parliamentary club.' So I rang his secretary, who is also a black woman, I think. I said, 'Look, I did denounce Powell for what he said, and if Archbishop Tutu can forgive apartheid, I must be able to forgive a friend who made a mistake.' I think it registered with her.

Friday 13 March

The *National Music Express* (*NME*), which is the very popular rock-and-pop magazine for young people, had a cover with a picture of Blair saying 'Betrayed' and inside six young pop stars were denouncing New Labour on the grounds that they had been absolutely betrayed by Blair, who cosied up to them. They hated three things: Welfare to Work, which is really workfare or compulsory conscription; secondly, tuition fees; and thirdly, the failure to have an inquiry into cannabis. I don't say it is significant in terms of the British Establishment, but it is interesting.

Monday 16 March

The *Guardian* this morning had a report by its correspondent in Bonn, quoting Peter Mandelson's speech of 3 March in Bonn, in which he had said (among other things) that democracy had passed its sell-by date. So I rang the *Guardian* and they faxed through the speech.

Tuesday 17 March

Walked back to the House and found a message saying, 'Call in at the Whips' Office about your unauthorised absence last night.' So I photocopied my letter to Nick Brown, the Chief Whip, which I had sent yesterday saying that I wouldn't vote on the Education Bill.

It is now about 5.30 and the House is empty, as it always is on Budget night. I remember my dad used to say to me that as soon as the

Chancellor and the Leader of the Opposition sat down, the House absolutely emptied and a Tory MP, who never normally spoke, would get up and say to an empty House, 'Mr Speaker, all over the country tonight, people will be turning to each other and saying, "Well, what do you think about the Budget?"' It was known as Cads' Night and, as a matter of fact, even when I first arrived, the House adjourned just after the speeches of the Chancellor and the Leader of the Opposition.

I find Budgets very difficult to understand, with all the tax changes, but I did watch Brown's speech, which was very conservative. It was a Budget to satisfy the world's investors, a Budget that Philip Snowden might have drafted.

My pager came up with a message saying, 'When the Chancellor sits down, a personalised press release will be available for you.' I went and picked up the press release from the PLP office and it described the effect of the Budget on *people in Chesterfield*. For example, it said, 'Tax cuts for employees paying National Insurance will make *36,292 people in Chesterfield* better off by £65 a year.' And then, 'The Chancellor has decided to help *2143 businesses in Chesterfield*.' And 'Child benefit for the eldest child will make *12,600 families in Chesterfield* £130 a year better off.'

It also said, 'Tony Benn welcomes the Budget to turn people's ambitions into achievements.' You have got to give them credit for professionalism.

Thursday 19 March

When I came out of the BBC this evening, a black guy jumped out of a car and shook me warmly by the hand. I asked, 'What do you do?'

He said, 'I'm a luvvie, I'm an actor.'

I said, 'Have I seen you in anything?'

'*The Full Monty*.'

I said, 'Gosh! I didn't recognise you.'

He was so friendly and he had another black guy with him and said, 'This is my mate.' I loved that film.

Caroline and Melissa went to tea with Ruth Fainlight and her husband, Alan Sillitoe, the writer. They had a lovely time and they know about Caroline's illness. Caroline went to one of Ruth's poetry readings recently, and Ruth was very touched.

Tuesday 24 March

To the lobby against the Child Support Agency which was really ghastly, I must say. I mean they've got a case, but they were largely men who had left their wives, with their second wives, and they were shouting and aggressive. I think the law should be changed, but I didn't care for the audience very much.

Caroline went to the hospital this afternoon and the check-up that she had suggested that her cancer is quiescent. There doesn't seem to be any change.

Thursday 26 March

I was working in my room at the Commons and I rang Caroline and she was delirious. I was so worried that I said to the whip, 'I'm off', came home and put an ice pack on her head, gave her a paracetamol, a little bit of food, which she didn't eat, and cooled her off.

Unfortunately she missed the Holland Park School governors' meeting, the last meeting before her time expires. She first got on in 1966, and has probably served longer than any other school governor in Britain. She cried a little bit at the thought that she'd missed it, just as she said that the last time she breast-fed Joshua she cried at the thought that she'd never feed another baby again. These are human touches.

Friday 27 March

Carol was a bit better thank goodness, her temperature was down.

Saturday 28 March

Coming back from Chesterfield last night I heard that Joan Lestor had died and then that Joan Maynard had died. Two remarkable women.

Joan Lestor I'd known from the time she got into Parliament in 1966. She was brought up in the old Socialist Party of Great Britain, very good on race matters, on homosexuality, civil rights; she resigned from the Government because of cuts. She was attached to Kinnock. Always got on well with people. She resigned from the Front Bench a couple of years ago on the grounds of ill health; she had been getting terribly thin.

Joan Maynard I met when she was first elected to the National Executive in 1972, before she got into Parliament. She was a remarkable woman – fought with the agricultural workers, campaigned against the tied cottage; a highly principled woman, always spoke about the bosses and the workers in such a clear way that people understood. Marvellous on Ireland, marvellous on the left, marvellous on civil liberties, a formidable woman. Chris Mullin went to see her pretty well every week, I think, in recent weeks.

So there we are are. Life goes on, and you do come to the end of life, and I've a feeling I'm coming to the end of mine.

Sunday 29 March

I must record, as a man for whom life depends entirely on the clock, that I absolutely forgot to put the clocks forward today. I always wait for the moment when we come to British Summer Time. I love it, but I hadn't noticed it, I was so busy and tired and exhausted. And that really shook me.

Monday 30 March

Found a long fax from the solicitor Gareth Peirce, who has been asked by Sinn Fein to advise on how they should respond to the proposed changes that have been offered by the Government, who have suggested amending the Act of Union and the Government of Ireland Act and various other Acts – including the Irish Government dropping their claim to Northern Ireland. Gerry Adams wanted to know in effect: is there enough in this for me to be able to persuade people that it's halfway towards a united Ireland?

I said, 'Well, it's a terrible responsibility to give advice; a future government could legislate any way it likes – you can't bind future governments. It looks to me as if what's being done is that the sovereignty that's claimed by the British Crown is being transferred to the people of Northern Ireland, and the Irish Government is being brought in as part of a condominium of the North; therefore it is a significant change and I think probably the Unionists will reject it.'

I hope it's the right advice, because Gerry Adams and Martin McGuinness might both be murdered by the IRA if they go along with it. On the other hand, nobody wants to return to violence. Anyway we shall see.

Wednesday 1 April

The Campaign Group had invited Jack Straw to a discussion about asylum seekers; he talked about the delays and the backlog, about European Union membership, about ID cards, about gangs at work. He said we need clear criteria; there is a problem of benefit entitlement because the UK is more generous with benefit than other countries. The Home Office might possibly pay cash in lieu to asylum seekers.

I'm afraid I went to sleep during a lot of Straw's speech, I was so frightfully tired.

Thursday 2 April

Alan Simpson phoned. He told me that the whips had said he could not be released to go to a meeting in Nuneaton that he had arranged unless he gave an assurance that he would not say anything against the Government.

So he had a discussion with Tommy McAvoy and with Nick Brown and they said, 'Well, we've got to keep the Government going. What about people who are kept here to allow you to speak against the Government?'

Alan got very upset about it and quite properly so. I suggested that he wrote to Tommy McAvoy and asked him a few questions. Is everybody asked what they're going to say at meetings? What is the form of words you wish me to use? Where is this requirement written down? They are putting the pressure on, there's no doubt about that.

Friday 3 April

Went to Chesterfield and did a surgery. Then I was driven to Sowerby in Yorkshire for Joan Maynard's funeral. I went over to Joan's house and there were various members of her family and Chris Mullin, who'd had an operation this week for gallstones and looked a bit frail. Tam Dalyell and his wife Kathleen had driven four and a half hours down from Scotland to be there and had a four-and-a-half-hour drive back. Lots of MPs were there and Michael Jopling, the former Conservative Minister of Agriculture,

Chris took me into the garden; he was one of Joan Maynard's closest friends and visited her every week. His children knew her. He showed me everything; took me to her desk. We walked behind the coffin and it was a very moving ceremony.

The church was packed with MPs and local people, and trade unionists from the Agricultural Workers' Union. They had loudspeakers outside for people who couldn't get into the church, and the police were there to control the traffic.

All the speeches were just so typical of Joan. Chris could hardly continue, he was so upset, but it was a lovely service. Reg and Mandy Race dropped me back to York and I came home.

What was important about Joan Maynard was the character of the woman, and the breadth of her interest – in football, in cricket, in the local community, in the campaign against electricity pylons; she was terribly actively involved and everybody there knew her and that's why they'd turned up. And character is what counts in the end, character and service.

Joan Lestor was also buried today.

Monday 6 April

I saw Dennis Canavan in the evening and he told me that he had just been cross-examined by the panel set up by the Scottish Labour Party to decide who were suitable candidates for the Scottish Parliament. Ernie Ross had been in the chair, Maggie Jones, and a couple of other people. He said it was the most aggressive interview he'd ever had. 'Have you ever voted against the Government? Have you ever kept your mouth shut so as not to embarrass the Government? Have you ever said anything critical of the Government?' Canavan said he felt that he was on trial for his life. One shouldn't underestimate the extent to which this absolute centralised tyranny is getting hold of the Party.

Friday 10 April

I saw Roy Hattersley on the train yesterday, and he said he thought that the Blair regime, the Blair politics, might last for thirty years; he didn't take the view I sometimes take that it's crumbling. He thought that

Scotland might be the weak link – the SNP might win there, or the Scottish Party might go to the left. He told me that Adair Turner of the CBI and John Monks of the TUC were working on trade union rights and recognition personally with Blair, and it was not going to go to the Cabinet at all; the cabinet wouldn't have any role in the matter.

Hattersley said he thought it was just like a court, with the courtiers around the king.

The big political news today, which really ought to occupy the whole of the diary, is that the peace talks in Stormont reached a successful conclusion. There was due to be a deadline at midnight; it was going wrong, and the Ulster Unionists were opposed to too-great powers for the cross-border authorities. Blair and Ahern, the Irish Prime Minister, flew to Belfast, sat through the night and rang Clinton. Blair saw Trimble and some concession was made; it was a very important day.

Senator George Mitchell, who was in charge of negotiations, said to the Plenary Session, 'When this little exchange is over – because I think we've more or less finished – the media will be brought in.' What he didn't know was that the television was already covering it, so you actually saw the authentic exchanges. Trimble wasn't too aggressive and Gerry Adams was very generous, and so on. There are a lot of pitfalls, because there will be shootings by the extremists. Ian Paisley was shouted down by his own supporters as an old dinosaur; quite why I don't know, I think they blamed him for not going in and stopping it. I think he is a completely discredited figure now.

Monday 20 April

Had lunch. Went to the Commons. There was a statement by Mo Mowlam on the Northern Ireland agreement, the so-called Belfast Agreement. Absolute unity across the floor of the House, although there was only one Ulster Unionist there, David Trimble; none of the others, including Paisley, came.

I asked whether the pledge of office required from the Northern Ireland Assembly would entitle elected members to sit in the House of Commons, because I wanted to make the point about Adams and McGuinness being eligible. But Mo Mowlam said that was a matter for the House and I got a bit of a brush-off. I had hoped to make more progress, but I think the truth of the matter is that, if there is a Northern Ireland elected assembly with Adams and McGuinness, it would be ludicrous if they couldn't sit in the House of Commons. So perhaps this isn't the moment to raise it. I'm not sure.

Tuesday 21 April

In the course of the evening I spoke to two Ministers who are threatened with the sack. One is David Clark, who is Mandelson's boss, and I said to him, 'Why don't you say something clear about trade union rights, or whatever, and then a) it would make it more difficult for you to be sacked, and b) if you are sacked, it'll be clearer why you've been sacked.'

He said, 'I take your point.'

Then I tried to speak to Gavin Strang. I said, 'Oh, Gavin, I read in the papers you're going to be sacked.' So he just walked down the steps. I said, 'Hang on a minute, I'm speaking to you.' So he turned round rather gruffly and I made the same point to him. He just turned away. So he knows what's going to happen to him and he's not prepared to do anything about it. I suppose he hopes that if he keeps his trap shut he might be saved, but he won't be.

Wednesday 22 April

Sat in the Tea Room with Alan Simpson and Llew Smith, and Llew told me that in Wales the people who'd been picked for the list of candidates for the Welsh Assembly were being psychometrically tested to see if they were suitable. Well, those tests, which are completely phoney, are used to appoint managers to see if they're responsible and all that; but to have vetting of candidates based on their psychological state and their political loyalty is incredible.

In that connection, later in the day when we had some votes on the Wales Bill, I said to the Chief Whip, 'Last night there was no vote on the European convergence criteria, and I told you I was going to abstain, so in effect everybody abstained.'

He said, 'Well, that means it won't go down on your record.'

So I said, 'I suppose you've got me on Excalibur,' that's Millbank's great computer which supposedly has all MPs' details, speeches etc on it.

'No, no, no,' he said, 'I have my own completely objective record and you're not the leading rebel.'

So I said, 'I'm not a rebel at all.'

He said, 'Dennis Canavan is a leading rebel.'

'It doesn't worry me, because I'm not trying stand for the Scottish Parliament, which Dennis Canavan is.'

'Oh,' he said, 'Dennis Canavan won't be.'

I don't think any of us on the left will survive. If you're going to have vetting of candidates for the Mayor of London, for the European elections, for the Scottish and Welsh Assembly, you're going to have it for MPs, and so we'll all be knocked out.

Sunday 26 April

Caroline and I went to Hilary's house to help canvass in Walpole ward where he's standing again for Ealing Council.

We canvassed on an old estate that is really run-down, covered in graffiti, lots of rubbish problems, drugs and crime. Very depressing, although when it was built it was an absolute model, because the slums it replaced didn't have bathrooms and these lovely flats with their verandas were so marvellous. A very high percentage of tenants were Asian and African. There was one Indian woman who looked at me through the window and said, 'Couldn't somebody clean the place up?'

Hilary said that you do have to have some sense of ownership if you want to keep it clean and tidy, and who owns the staircase? Who owns the open concrete spaces? It was a very shrewd point. The response was extremely friendly. The people who are discouraged are the Party workers because they feel that their philosophy has been set aside.

Monday 27 April

I got something marvellous yesterday from the Labour Party, intended for all candidates in local elections – *How to Campaign in the Local Elections:*

> Ideas for Photo Opportunities. Here are some suggestions of the kind of photos you can set up to get Labour's message across in the local media. MP pictured reading favourite book to small circle of children to illustrate reading hour, showing how Labour is introducing measures to improve literacy. All you need is children and a book. If you can get access to a school, arrange for the photo to be taken in the reading corner with bookshelves as your backdrop; arrange the children in a semi-circle and sit on a small chair at the front with an open book. Choose a large hardback book with a bold cover and children to either side, or sit amongst the children and let them read to you.

Wednesday 29 April

Had lunch at home, went to the House of Commons and looked in at the lobby of Hull trawlermen who have been denied any compensation when the long-distance trawler fleet was closed down, because of an agreement reached with the Icelandic Government. The Americans wanted to keep a base in Iceland so, by way of compensation, Britain gave the Icelandic Government a 200-mile fishing limit which knocked out our long-distance trawling industry; the owners got compensated with £30 million, but the trawler men got nothing. Alan Johnson, the MP for Hull, was very friendly, asked me if I'd like to say a word and I said, 'No, I've just come to express my solidarity.'

I saw Ted Heath in the corridor. I asked, 'Ted, when are your memoirs coming out?'

He said, 'In September but they're very, very expensive.'

So I said, 'That's because of the quality of book – and possibly because they don't think there'll be a huge sale.' So he laughed and his shoulders shook, as they do.

I went to the Campaign Group meeting, where we discussed the London Mayor because Ken Livingstone is certain they won't let him do it; there's a rumour going round that he'll be offered Glenda Jackson's job in the reshuffle, as Minister for London Transport, if he keeps out of the running for the Mayor's job. And Ken said, 'Well, I'd do it, except that I'm not privatising the Tube.' That was interesting.

Tuesday 5 May

The *Financial Times* had a front-page story that the Labour leadership was going to weed out left-wing MPs by interrogating them before agreeing that they could stand again as parliamentary candidates; I rang up Andrew Parker, who wrote the story, and he wouldn't tell me who it came from, but he said it was a senior Government source. I said, 'Well, that doesn't necessarily mean a Cabinet Minister i.e. it could have been Mandelson.'

And he said, 'Well, I can't reveal my source, but I tell you, it's an authentic story.'

Wednesday 6 May

At a quarter-past ten Jonathan Freedland of the *Guardian* came to see me.

He worked at the BBC for a time, he was in Northern Ireland, he was a general reporter, he went to America as Washington correspondent, he came back, and he's now a leader writer. He told me that the *Guardian* was divided between the left – Seumas Milne and one or two others – the centre, Hugo Young, former head boy at Ampleforth, and the economics -pages writers, who are very much committed to Gordon Brown, whom they think is a real socialist and will one day emerge.

Freedland told me that Blair had been to the *Guardian* and talked to everybody and it was very friendly until it came to the *Guardian*'s editorial policy, when he absolutely blew his top at them. Mandelson comes every six months and talks to all the staff and has lunch with the editorial board. He just tries to keep them in line. Jonathan said that the *Guardian* is seen as the main opposition paper to the Government – they can't abide it.

Thursday 7 May

During conversation in the Tea Room with Tony Banks he told me how he had moved into the political works-of-art field. He's always kept memorabilia, plates and things, now he's decided to make some serious investments. For example, he picked up a painting of Lord North from America which he will have made a bit on. He said that when he leaves Parliament he'll have this political art business to carry on.

Told me how he had a flaming row with Alastair Campbell over the time he was criticised publicly for describing William Hague as a foetus.

He said, 'I simply poured my abuse on Alastair Campbell, who since then has been all sweetness and light.' It was an interesting story.

Saturday 9 May

Caroline went to a conference of about 300 people on Education Action Zones, to which teachers, parents and governors had come from all over the country to describe the horror of these zones. The Government picks an area with an LEA, puts money in, and the money then goes to private companies to provide computers, rebuild the school, and so on. In effect, it's just a form of privatisation. There was a guy there from Ealing who was Chairman of the school governors, and a company had got the contract to repair the school and had put in a bill for £400,000 to put a new roof on the school. Being a chartered surveyor, he said that nobody would charge more than £200,000 for that. So the EAZs are a rip-off, very comparable to what was done by the last government when they closed the local-authority old people's homes and privatised them, and poured money into these private nursing homes – the death factories.

Sunday 10 May

Caroline and I went over to Marion Miliband's and it was a simply lovely evening. There were her sons, Edward, who works for Gordon Brown in the Treasury, and David, who is the head of the Policy Unit at Number 10. Also there was Sam, a Canadian trade unionist, Leo Panitch, Colin Leys and a friend of his.

We just sat and talked, and I did make a few jokes about the Third Way and modernisation. David was quite interested in the idea that possibly the Irish settlement might lead to a change in the oath of allegiance. He said he'd raise it when he got back to Number 10 tomorrow.

David is responsible for all domestic and European matters at Number 10, and they cover a very wide span, and of course Hilary sees David when he goes across for the meeting of advisers in the Cabinet Office.

Monday 11 May

Lunch at the Commons with a girlfriend of Caroline's. Her present husband is an American in his late sixties, perhaps turned seventy, who for twenty-one years was in American Intelligence as a warrant officer, a very senior operative. He said some fascinating things.

He said, 'We bankrupted the Russians by Star Wars, which they couldn't keep up. And in the end it bankrupted them and we contained them, because they could only survive if they extended their territory.' I don't think that was true at all.

I talked to him about his special expertise, which was in lie-detectors or polygraphs. He described how the polygraph worked: it measured your heartbeat, it measured your moisture, it measured your temperature. And he said, 'When you're very tense, it comes out in a different formation. It doesn't prove anything, but it gives you an indication.'

I said, 'There must be ways around it.'

'Oh, yes, you just work yourself up in a sweat when you're saying something absolutely true, or put a drawing pin in your shoe so that it hurts and you can confuse the operator.'

He did a lot of interrogation in Vietnam and what he told me absolutely horrified me.

I said it must have been very frightening for people to be interrogated on the lie-detector if they thought they'd be tortured. 'Well,' he said, 'we just shot 'em.'

He described one woman who came. He wired her up to a polygraph and she died. He said, 'Of course, what we didn't know was that she had been hung up by her thumbs by the South Vietnamese Government, and that was what did it.' He said that her death was very unfairly blamed on the polygraph. He described how they chained Vietcong suspects together and then asked each of them whether they were members of the Vietcong. He gave the impression that they were all shot – I don't know if they were.

Then he said, 'Also, I was engaged in counter-intelligence there. I ran a brothel in Saigon. We recruited prostitutes – young girls – at a better-than-usual rate and what we discovered was that the girls who worked with the madam, whom I knew very well – the ones who were double agents – would always say after a couple of years, "My mother's sick, I'm going home." The Vietcong wanted to debrief them. So I had to find out which were the double agents. There was a little boy of six who was the madam's son, who was in the brothel, and he knew all the girls and he loved riding in a jeep. So I used to give him a ride in my jeep and I'd ask him about them and he'd say, "Oh Katie's going home now", or, "Yong is going home now."' So he learned from this little six-year-old boy which girls were suspected double agents.

Then one or two other things that he said were interesting. He said that when he was in Washington he was a member of a health club and used to go in the morning for a sauna, and there were White House security people who lay in the sauna talking quite openly about what was going on in the White House in the 60s. One would say to the other, 'Whadya think of last night – they were all nude-bathing again, and then Jackie came in and we had to divert her. But of course Jackie, well, she likes boys too, and when she wants a boy she just grabs him. She had one lad, a bellboy, and took him up to her bedroom and that bellboy wasn't even cleared for security.'

Wednesday 13 May

Bernie Ecclestone gave evidence to the Neill Committee, apparently saying he'd given money to the Labour Party by a post-dated cheque because he wanted to be sure that taxation on the upper ranges didn't increase, and that possibly he'd done it also to woo the Labour Party away from the trade unions.

Thursday 14 May

Went into the House, and had a bite to eat; there was a statement by Robin Cook on the Indian nuclear tests. He made a most pompous statement, attacking the decision by India to have nuclear weapons on the grounds of proliferation and said that the money should be devoted to deal with poverty. He said it would be wrong to call for sanctions because it was a decision of the Indian Government and not the Indian people.

So I got in and I said, 'The whole world was shocked by the tests and I was glad to hear the Foreign Secretary say that the decision made by leaders shouldn't lead to punishment of the people – which is the argument we put forward on Iraq – but every argument against India having nuclear tests applies with equal force to Britain's nuclear weapons programme.' The House didn't respond in any way. But it is a clear case of double standards.

Tuesday 19 May

I went to a meeting that had been organised by Harry Barnes – a special briefing on education in Derbyshire. Rachel Squire, who is the PPS to Stephen Byers, the Education Minister, was there, and officials from the Derbyshire NUT.

We were told that eight years of cuts had had a catastrophic effect in Derbyshire, and on the health of teachers; one teacher said there were thirty-five to thirty-nine in her class, and sometimes more, of whom 35 per cent had special needs. She produced pictures of the children, lovely photographs, and said, 'Now this child can't punctuate, writes marvellously, but doesn't understand punctuation. If I could take this boy away and help him to punctuate, it would be marvellous.

'Now this one says, "Oh, school's so boring", but of course if I could spend a bit of time with him, he'd realise it wasn't boring because he's very, very talented.'

Then she said, 'These two students' (showing other pictures) 'are really quite good, but I haven't got the time to let them develop their talents to the full.' She was a young married woman, I suppose in her thirties, and she spoke with tremendous passion. She said, 'Eight years ago we had the smallest classes in the country and now we have the largest.'

Then somebody else, another teacher from a primary school, said,

'There's a shortage of space, there's overcrowding, we're using the library as a classroom, and only a quarter of the children can actually see the blackboard.'

Rachel Squire, a nice woman, said, 'I am very impressed. These are shocking stories, and I'll see the Minister.' But the idea that this is how you get things done is really contrary to the way this system works; you've got to have pressure, pressure, pressure.

Mark Seddon rang me up and said, 'Do you know that the Labour Party is harnessing volunteers to work in the Millbank Tower to ring up Party members to persuade them to vote for the members of the National Executive that they want.' Now that is evil.

Wednesday 20 May

At ten o'clock the Cuban Ambassador, Dr Lopez, came to see me. As it was such lovely weather we sat in the back garden. I asked him if he minded if I videoed our discussion and he said, 'Not at all.' But the noise from aircraft and an electric drill in the building next door virtually obliterated his voice.

He said, 'As far as Britain was concerned, there was absolutely no change in the policy between the Major Government and the Labour Government.' He went on, 'Italy, France and Spain traded very actively, sent Ministers, but Britain never sent a Minister,' though he said he thought Baroness Symons might go to the International Trade Fair in the autumn. He'd seen Robin Cook at a couple of receptions at the Board of Trade, who should have taken an interest from a trading point of view, but took no interest whatever. Lopez said the European Union are much better than the British at negotiating with the Americans, but they're doing it on the principle of free trade, not out of sympathy for Cuba.

Having said that, he thought pressure in the United States to change the policy was growing. Jesse Helms had suggested $100 million worth of humanitarian aid channelled through the churches in Cuba; the leader of the Cuban exiles in Florida had died, and things were a little bit easier. He said that Cuba is surviving and will survive.

The problem from an American point of view was allegedly human rights. On the compensation for nationalised assets, Lopez said that Cuba had reached an arrangement with all the companies, but the Americans would not accept compensation.

I suggested that Fidel should come to London, perhaps invited by a group such as Cardinal Hume, the President of the CBI, and Rodney Bickerstaffe. But he wasn't terribly impressed by that.

Then at 11.30 Michelle Gildernew from the Sinn Fein Foreign Office came to see me, a young girl of twenty-eight, an awfully nice creature. She's been going round seeing Members of Parliament to brief them.

Her comments were interesting. She said that women were very much in favour of peace; that Sinn Fein was trying hard to get on with the Unionists; that she'd had friends as a child who recognised that there would be unity in Ireland. When she was at Number 10 with Gerry Adams and Martin McGuinness, she spoke to Alastair Campbell. Blair had said, 'There won't be Irish unity in my lifetime' and Campbell had confirmed that. So apparently Michelle said, 'Well, who would have thought ten years ago that Tony Blair would have been Prime Minister?' And that rather took him aback.

She said that, whatever happened, neither Gerry nor Martin would sit in the House of Commons. They'll sit in the Assembly because it's in Ireland, but not in Britain. So all my efforts are in a way marginal really.

She confirmed that the legislation against guns that was passed after Dunblane did not apply in Northern Ireland, so if we're talking about demilitarisation we've got to talk about the extension of the gun law to Northern Ireland.

Thursday 21 May

In the afternoon I went to the Millbank Tower, where Tom Sawyer, the General Secretary of the Labour Party, had agreed I could film.

Tom was very friendly. He said, 'Would you like to look round the office?' So we walked round this open-plan office, with about 150 people there working on computers. He pointed in a general direction and said, 'That's the marketing department; that's the finance department; that's the constitutional department; those are the policy people.'

Then I asked, 'Where's Excalibur?' So they showed me this huge computer and I said, 'What have you got on it?'

'Oh, it's all published material,' said Tom, 'there's nothing secret on it.'

I asked to find my file, and they couldn't find it, they said. First of all they said there were 5000 entries and they couldn't find it. But they tried a second computer and the other machine found it. They had a scanned photocopy of my letter to John Major as Prime Minister about a Tory MP who was apparently also working for MI5 and they'd actually taken it off the paper, scanned it in and indexed it. It was a dossier, however you look at it. If ever they wanted to get me out of the Party, they'd just go through the file and dig out everything damaging, highly selectively, some of which would be press reports that might not be accurate.

For example, they had a transcript of an interview with David Frost earlier this year about Iraq. I haven't got a transcript, yet there was the thing, with very critical comments about Government policy on Iraq.

We wandered round the first floor – just about the same height as my bedroom when I had lived on the same site as a child.

Then a guy who I didn't know, the senior press officer, came in and said, 'We do not allow anybody to film – no media allowed to film in Millbank

Tower.'

I said, 'Well, it's not exactly the media, you know. I am a very senior member of the Party, the longest-serving Labour MP, thirty-four years on the Executive, former Chairman of the Party.'

'Oh no, no question of it.'

So Tom, who's the bloody General Secretary after all, said, 'I shouldn't have agreed to this. I'm sorry, you can't do it.'

Some of the staff – they are all very young – didn't look particularly politically committed. They looked at me curiously in a strange way.

Tom's secretary told me that she had worked for Harry Nicholas, Ron Hayward, Jim Mortimer, Larry Whitty and now Tom Sawyer, and she said nobody made any reference to the fact that she had been there twenty-eight years last Tuesday.

I got the feeling it was an organisation of an entirely managerial character, with lots of young people in their shirt sleeves; it might have been a bank, an insurance company, Tory Central Office – it might have been anywhere. There were posters everywhere, pictures of Blair, New Britain, New Labour, No Increase in Taxation, all over the place; it was really weird. It was interesting and certainly professional, but professionalism turned to what purpose?

As I was walking back to my the car, I saw a very old lady with a walking frame accompanied by a young black nurse. And as I stopped at the car she said to me, 'Tony.' And I looked at her and her face was familiar, though she was very old. She's eighty-four now – it was Rosamund John, the actress who was married to John Silkin.

So I stood and talked to her for quite a bit about her films *Green for Danger* and *The Way To the Stars*, and she said she was still mourning the loss of John. She was very touched I think, and was very gentle and sweet and at the end I said, 'Can I give you a kiss – something I've always wanted to do.'

Then she said, 'I must go now, I must go on walking.'

And I said to the nurse, 'She's a very, very famous actress.' The nurse had no idea.

Friday 22 May Chesterfield

A very distressed woman came to my surgery because her dog had been stolen and when she rang the Town Hall, they said, 'Oh, we've got your dog. You have to pay thirty-one pounds to get her back, as she was a stray dog.' Then they tried to charge her £6 for kennel fees. When she went the following day the dog had slept in its urine all night and was terrified. I said, 'Well, this is a theft. If the police had found the dog and brought it back, they wouldn't have charged you thirty-one pounds.' So I wrote to the Town Hall. But they are very unimaginative.

Wednesday 27 May
Guto Harri from the *World at One* came to do an interview with me about 'the cult of personality' and I had prepared some thoughts, which I put down.

Afterwards he told me how the spin doctors worked. He said that when he was appointed to a job in the BBC, he had a phone call from Tim Allen at Number 10 (who has now moved on to something else) saying, 'Congratulations, I'm so pleased that you've been appointed, please let us know if ever we can help. By the way, I've got your office number, but what's your pager number and your home number. And do you have a mobile?'

From then on there was an absolute barrage of criticism, advice and comment from Number 10. On one occasion Harri had decided to lead on a story that Kim Howells had made a speech saying that socialism was really dead. They blew him up – how they knew he was going to lead on it, he didn't know. 'You're not going to do that bollocks, are you?'

Charlie Whelan who is very abusive, Gordon Brown's press officer, continually pressed Harri, and he just felt under threat all the time.

Thursday 28 May
About lunchtime James turned up at the basement door, hair cropped, looking very grown-up and within half an inch of me in height; he'd cycled up with his friend Michael and thought they'd come and see me.

Melissa rang and asked if I'd come to tea, but I couldn't this afternoon. But the article by her in the *Guardian* this morning was absolutely magnificent. She got the front page, the next two pages and a bit of the fourth page all around her article on working mothers – really, really good.

Monday 1 June
I got up early because I had been booked to make a comment on Radio 5 Live about the Pakistan nuclear explosions, but they cancelled it because Paul Gascoigne has been dropped from the English World Cup team.

There was a little item in *The Independent* describing my visit to Millbank and saying that, knowing I was coming, they cleaned the whole place up and removed revisionist literature. It was quite a funny story.

Wednesday 3 June
I didn't go to the Party meeting this morning about the reselection of Members, but I'm told John McAllion made an absolutely brilliant speech about the way in which the committee interrogated MPs who might be selected as candidates for the Scottish Parliament. He and Ian Davidson and Dennis Canavan will probably be ruled out as unsuitable. The media are beginning to discover themselves what's going on.

I'm told Andrew Mackinlay got in a brilliant question to Blair at Prime

Minister's Questions. He asked, 'When we were in opposition we used to groan at the fawning, obsequious, softball, well-rehearsed and planted questions asked by Conservative Members . . . Will my Rt. Hon Friend distinguish his period in office by discouraging such practices?' It completely floored Blair, because when it was known that he had been put down to ask the first question, Andrew had been approached by Bruce Grocott, Blair's PPS, who said, 'I'd like to have a talk. Would you like to put down a question about the minimum wage?' And Andrew, who said he'd been thinking of his question for two weeks, just fobbed Bruce off and said he hadn't made up his mind.

So not only are the questions planted, but the PPS tries to get them arranged to help the Prime Minister or the Minister concerned. It has completely destroyed the vitality of Prime Minister's Questions.

Friday 5 June

The Dounreay nuclear plant in Scotland is to be closed. A few days ago it was announced that the Government had accepted nuclear waste from Georgia, 'to protect the world' from it being wrongly handled, and had sent it to Dounreay for reprocessing. Blair had said there was no cause for anxiety of any sort – it was all scaremongering. And today they've announced they're closing it down.

It is an example of how dishonest the Government is. Governments have never admitted the truth about Dounreay. I was much criticised for not going ahead with the fast-breeder reactor but I held back and in the end I turned out to be right. It will cost, I think, £5 billion and 100 years to clean up the mess and decontamination of the site. Nuclear power is finished and I'm glad I saw it; I saw it late, but I'm glad I saw it in time.

Saturday 6 June

Caroline and I left at two to go to Frances Benn's wedding to Michael Nestor at St Matthew's Church in Great Peter Street.

We got there in plenty of time, and there was Dave in a tail-coat with a yellow tie and a white shirt and a beautifully embroidered waistcoat; and there was Michael Nestor's father, dressed identically; and Piers in a tail-coat.

The reception was at the Royal Geographical Society. About forty of Michael's relatives from Ireland had come across for the wedding and we were put at a table with some of them: a builder, a retired farmer and his wife, and two marvellous nuns, Sister Marion and Sister Attracta, who both taught Gaelic. They said that what the Catholic Church needs is more feminine influence, and I asked them about the ordination of women, and so on.

It was such fun, and we were at their table and then we wandered round and took pictures. Dave made a very amusing speech, in which he said that when Frances was a little girl she said she'd have eight babies by eight different husbands, and everybody laughed.

I noticed that Naz was wearing an engagement ring and a wedding ring. I'd never seen them before, so I asked Caroline whether I should refer to them and apparently last Friday Josh bought her an engagement ring and a wedding ring. So they're engaged, and that was a smashing event.

Monday 8 June

We agreed at the Campaign Group to focus all our attention on Dennis Canavan's amendment tonight that maintenance grants should be continued.

When we had the vote thirty-one Labour MPs voted against the Government; the votes were widely spread across the Party – not all of the Campaign Group by any manner or means.

When I look at it, the speech I made this evening was absolutely minor in importance compared to the five, six, seven broadcasts that I have done in recent days, when I got through to millions of people. You can see why Ministers don't bother with the House of Commons.

Friday 12 June, Chesterfield

On the train was a lawyer, Vernon Colquhoun, who lives in Bakewell. He was dressed in a dinner jacket, having been last night at a party of doctors. We talked all the way up to Chesterfield, which made the journey more agreeable.

He told me one or two interesting things. He said the first animal rights legislation was introduced by somebody called Richard Smith in Ireland, known as Humanity Dick, in about 1829. He also told me the origin of the word 'indenture': originally lawyers would write out a contract on vellum, and then with a pair of scissors cut the contract in an uneven way so that the two bits of the indenture fitted together. He couldn't have been more friendly. He gave me a lift to the Labour Club.

Sunday 14 June

Watched a programme called *Pennies from Bevan* about the foundation of the National Health Service and it was really thrilling. Ian Hislop, who I've never taken very seriously, did present a lovely programme.

It was very well done. They interviewed Sir Richard Doll, doctors, matrons, nurses, patients, and it was just terribly good. Actually it made me cry, at the thought that after the war we had actually built up a Health Service for everybody, free at the point of use. It made me so angry that a rich country now claimed it couldn't afford it and kept putting on charges, prescription charges and all the rest. I thought the programme was salutary.

I read today that Dennis Canavan and Ian Davidson, who are both in Parliament, are not to be allowed to stand for the Scottish Parliament. This will enormously increase the attractiveness of the Scottish National Party, the SNP, in Scotland.

Ken Livingstone's also getting a very good press – we hardly open a paper today without 'dear old Ken' 'Ken says he'd like to be a gardener.' I don't think Blair quite realises what he's up to.

Wednesday 17 June

Our forty-ninth wedding anniversary. Caroline gave me a hug when I woke up. I had bought some flowers for her and brought them up with the breakfast. Forty-nine years is a long, long time. We've known each other fifty years, come 2 August: half a century, what a time. Ups and downs, as you'd expect, but great affection and mutual respect.

Saturday 20 June

At 7.30 I went to dinner with Ralph and Ann Gibson and Morris Abram and his new third wife. Morris was eighty yesterday and his wife is fifty-eight, tall, elegant, and obviously a very competent Italian lawyer who was working on human rights under Mary Robinson in Geneva. We had a long discussion over dinner – lovely dinner as always. Ann Gibson looked absolutely perfect; she looked as if she'd just won the Miss World contest, as I told her.

Going round the ages: Morris is eighty, Ann Gibson is seventy-eight which you would never believe, Ralph is seventy-four or five and I'm seventy-three.

I hadn't seen Morris Abram for fifty years; he left Oxford in 1948. He was then a very liberal Jewish lawyer, a good left-wing democrat. Last night it was quite clear to me that he has become right-wing. He's associated with the UN Watch, I think he's been President of the American Jewish Federation or something, and he was violently anti-Saddam.

Sunday 21 June

This evening we went to the fortieth wedding anniversary of Sir Christopher and Lady Foster, who live three doors up from us. They've got a lovely house, and the garden has a pond in the middle and a beautiful balcony; there were about 100 people there and the evening was perfect. I saw Samuel Brittan, Leon's brother, the old monetarist, and Val Arnold-Forster, who said her mother was 100. She's very devoted to her mother, but a parent heading for 101 can be a bit of a problem. Shirley Williams, Tam Dalyell and Calum Macdonald went to her 100th birthday. Eric Hobsbawm, the famous Marxist historian, was there and I went up and had a word with him. I said to him, 'What do you make of it all?'

'Well,' he said, 'Blair has no connection with socialism at all; he doesn't know what it means, he's just interested in power.'

Tuesday 23 June

Caroline and I got to the Grand Committee Room for Stephen's 'Links' Day. As Parliamentary Officer of the Royal Society of Chemistry, Stephen organises a day at the Commons for scientists to meet up with Members of Parliament. It was obviously a great success and lunch was laid on for everybody; we were put at the table with Tam Dalyell and Baroness Strange who is the sixteenth holder of the peerage founded by Charles I; her name is Cherry Strange, born in 1928, Conservative of course.

Quite a lot of people came up and Stephen was over the moon at the success of it all. He'd drafted the messages from the Speaker, from Michael Meacher, from John Battle. It was a really, really nice occasion.

Went back to my room, and was so tired I had a sleep. Then I hung about; there was a vote at eight; stayed in my room, wrote a few letters, really wasted my time. Caroline said to me today, which I absolutely agree with, 'This place has nothing whatever to do with democracy. It's just a club with a sort of royal ritual to amuse the middle class, and a lot of complicated procedure to confuse the working class, but Parliament has lost such power as it ever had. There was a time when it took control of things and improved people's lot, but now it's just an absolutely dead organisation. The media and the multinationals, the money men, have taken over the world.'

Sunday 28 June

I lost my pager today, the little Motorola mechanism that allows people to telephone me and leave a short message, which comes up as a script. You keep it in your pocket and it vibrates whenever it has a message.

I looked everywhere and couldn't find it, then I had this funny idea that it might have fallen in the trash bag with all the old newspapers and letters. So I brought the bags in from the front garden, rang British Telecom and asked them to send me various messages, and I crept round like a sniffer dog with my hearing aid on. Finally, as I crawled on my hands and knees from black sack to black sack, I heard one black sack make a rather pathetic little noise. So I ripped it open and there was my pager, all wet with teabags and ash from my pipe.

There's nothing like finding something you've lost – it gives you more pleasure than anything else.

David Trimble is obviously set to be the First Minister in Northern Ireland; he has still not talked to Sinn Fein or shaken Gerry Adams by the hand, and he's making a big thing about the question of decommissioning. The problems aren't solved, but at least there is some mechanism for dealing with them.

Thursday 2 July

To Kensington College where Caroline taught for twenty-five years.

Lesley Croome, who was the Director of Studies in Caroline's field, was there. Wandered round and looked at the fashion show and one or two other things, then went into the room and the Deputy Principal spoke. Then Caroline made a passionate speech about further education and its importance and congratulated them all and said, 'Believe in yourself.' They gave her tumultuous applause, and then I spoke, and then we jointly presented the prizes. Caroline was given a little package of essays, dedicated to her.

Friday 3 July, Chesterfield

To the Spire Church for a service to commemorate the fiftieth anniversary of the NHS. The service had been arranged by the Hospital Trust, and the order of service was printed as if it were a sort of advertising prospectus. There were various people asked to do readings, but not a single trade union was invited. Unison wasn't there, the Royal College of Nursing wasn't there, the Medical Practitioners' Union wasn't asked; it was a management function.

I preached from the pulpit, and told the boat-race story; people don't like to laugh in church, but they did laugh a bit, and afterwards I talked outside to a few people.

Tuesday 7 July

Nick Brown had agreed that I could interview him about being Chief Whip, and film it, so I went to Number 12 Downing Street and waited for Nick to arrive. There was a woman called Doris who had been there for eighteen years; she made us a cup of tea and we sat and talked. Then Nick arrived and we set up two cameras; he talked very openly about the job of Chief Whip, and about New Labour, which he thought was a generational question more than anything else. He's a great supporter of Gordon Brown and not a great supporter of Peter Mandelson, who is seen to be a Blair man. Nick said he didn't quite know what the Third Way meant; he was in favour of constructive discussion with other parties. The Tories couldn't get used to being in Opposition, but the Liberals were all right.

He told me the Cabinet only met for about an hour a week, which I thought was very interesting.

I asked him whether it was true that you had to submit papers to Number 10 in advance of submitting them to Cabinet and he said he didn't know, but he thought that was probably true.

Compared to the long Cabinet meetings we used to have in the old days, that is amazing; it just obliterates all serious discussion at every level. He said everything is sorted out bilaterally before it comes to Cabinet.

Saturday 11 July

What I haven't done yesterday and today is report the fantastic press coverage of this lobby business involving Mandelson and Derek Draper. The papers are full of 'Mandelson and his poodles'; 'Was Brown's budget leaked?' The whole thing is a mess, and I actually do feel that it is now beginning to unravel.

Monday 13 July

I went to the Amnesty dinner. There were about 150 people there at City University and I was asked to talk about the role of activism in the future.

Amnesty has got one million members worldwide; it received the UN Human Rights Award, it's had a Nobel Peace Prize, and it does motivate lots of people, many of them young. It has a staff of 300 in London, half of whom were there today. I was introduced as Tony Benn, a prisoner of conscience in the new Labour Party, which I thought was a very appropriate joke.

Got home about half-past eleven which was much earlier than I expected.

Tuesday 14 July

I had a chat to Mike Ambrose, the *Morning Star*'s political correspondent, and he said to me that there were people in the Lobby who thought Blair wasn't enjoying being Prime Minister very much and that he might go before the election.

He also said that Mandelson was very ambitious indeed and he thought that he might settle for being a commissioner in Europe, because he was so unpopular at home.

We talked a little bit about it. I don't go in much for this gossip, but it is interesting that the Brownites are so strong.

Anyway, at 3.30 Gordon Brown introduced a spending review with £40 billion more expenditure. I was too ignorant to ask anyone whether the figures he gave included private finance or just Government spending. We'll see.

But Dennis Turner, a solid old trade unionist from Coventry, said to me afterwards in the Lobby, 'Listening to Gordon Brown, that was real Labour.' And I think there probably is a body of opinion that believes that Gordon would be a better Leader than Blair.

I went on to a meeting of the committee composed of those councils that are worse funded in education, including Derbyshire, which was represented, and on to a trade union meeting in which they were talking about the Low Pay Commission, its future and its recommendations, which was quite well attended.

Thursday 16 July

We went to film people arriving at the press lobby briefing in the little room at the top of a long flight of winding stairs in the House of Commons.

We stood at the top and saw journalists coming up the stairs, and Alastair Campbell looked up and said, 'Oh, hello, Tony, what are you doing?'

I said, 'I'm filming this for my website: tonybenn.oldlabour.ok.'

So he laughed and said, 'Come on in,' which slightly took me by surprise.

Ruth filmed and I just sat at the back, although Alastair Campbell asked me to the front. I don't think the lobby briefing in that room has ever been filmed. Michael White was there, John Sergeant was there, and people from the other daily newspapers.

I rang Alastair Campbell later to thank him very much indeed for having let me come to the lobby and he said, 'Well, you know, I'm much more open than the press.'

And I said, 'I think that's true, I'm sure that's true.' I went on, 'Let me run an idea past you. I've interviewed Tom Sawyer and Nick Brown, and so on, and I'd love to perhaps be allowed to have a camera in Cabinet for just a moment.'

He said, 'Well, I'll put it to Tony.' So it may be that that'll come off, and that would be another coup.

Saturday 18 July

The Czar was buried yesterday in St Petersburg, or Leningrad as I call it, and Yeltsin was there. For this great royal oppressor of the Russian people to be commemorated by the former secretary of the Moscow Communist Party didn't seem to me very attractive, although I'm against murdering anybody, including the royal family of Russia or anywhere else; but it's just rather strange. The Orthodox church wouldn't participate and there was some question of whether they really were the remains of the Czar and his family. But Yeltsin's problems are economic and can't be solved by having a ritual celebration of a dead king 80 years after he was killed.

Monday 20 July

Ruth and I went to Pimlico School because there was to be a parents' meeting to discuss the private finance initiative under which the existing school in the middle of a square in Pimlico would be replaced by a building, losing much of its playground, and the remaining land would be used for very expensive private housing. And Jack Straw is the chairman of the governors, and his children are at the school.

I talked to some of the governors outside the school; there was a rainstorm so we hid under a bus shelter and they were absolutely explosive about the arrangement. Very opposed to it. Then we waited in a little restaurant just opposite the school under a canopy and had a cup of tea. At about 20 past nine the parents were streaming out absolutely hopping mad; apparently they'd voted against the private finance initiative, I think by 185 to 5; and yet two of the three parent governors had voted for it. So at the meeting today – by 78 to 5, I think – they voted no confidence in the parent governors , who included Jack Straw, who was taking the meeting. Jack's two police bodyguards spotted us with a camera and came out and talked, and we tried to see if we could get an interview with Jack, but he slipped away in the end. So I talked to the parents, and played football with some children.

Wednesday 22 July

Michael arrived for what I think is his last day; he's done a marvellous job in the office, always bang on time; he's opened the letters, and he's now indexing my speeches. It's nice to get to know your grandson in a working environment.

Thursday 23 July

Talked to Dave. If Caroline becomes very ill and incapacitated, I'll have to give up Parliament to look after her; but if the worst happened and Caroline were to die, I might only be able to cope by throwing myself into my work. It's a subject that occupies a lot of my thoughts and attention at the moment, and maybe I should be sensible and recognise that seventy-seven is the end of a very full parliamentary life, after fifty years in the Commons.

Monday 27 July

Caroline went to Holland Park School today because, although she's retired after thirty-four years as a governor and twelve as Chairman, she's decided to take on the responsibility of the old students and old staff association.

I went to the House of Lords for Hugh Jenkins's ninetieth birthday party. There was a huge crowd there in the Cholmondeley Room; Michael Foot was there in the corner, looking terribly old, and blind in one eye; Frank Judd, Lord Judd, was there; Clive Dunn was there, because of course Hugh Jenkins was Arts Minister; Peter Shore was there, looking terribly old – he has osteoporosis and emphysema and he's got a stick.

The first reshuffle announcements were made this morning. Four Cabinet Ministers sacked: Harriet Harman, Gavin Strang, David Clark and Ivor Richard; Frank Field resigned in a huff because he wasn't given the top job; he'll be praised to the sky for his integrity by the Tory press, but I think it is a victory for the revolt over lone parents. Mandelson has replaced Beckett, which is a terrible kick in the teeth for her. Nick Brown was moved from Chief Whip and goes to Agriculture.

Tuesday 28 July
Sat in the Tea Room, and talked to Chris Mullin, Jeremy Corbyn and David Clark, the Chancellor of the Duchy of Lancaster who was sacked yesterday. He was obviously upset to be sacked, but he did tell me some very interesting things.

He said that the Cabinet now meets for between twenty and fifty minutes, and there are no Cabinet papers whatsoever submitted by Ministers. He said, 'Well, no Cabinet papers have ever been submitted. The agenda is "parliamentary affairs, home affairs and foreign affairs" and we sit there and are told things.' He said that from the moment he went to see Blair on his appointment, to the moment when he went to see Blair to be sacked, he never once had a private talk with Blair. And when he had a point he wanted to make, Jonathan Powell, Blair's Chief of Staff, would come and see him. He saw quite a bit of Richard Wilson, the Cabinet Secretary. Wilson had said to him that all Prime Ministers had a power base either in Parliament or in the Party, and in most cases in both, but Blair took no interest in the Party or in Parliament and simply addressed the nation over the heads of the Cabinet, Parliament and the Party. Wilson found that very worrying.

Wednesday 29 July
I went into the House at three o'clock and heard Prime Minister's Questions from my seat in the House, which I don't normally do. Hague was terribly effective, just listing all the things that had gone wrong, and Blair was so smirky and bland. He looks about ten years older now than he did a year ago; of course, being Prime Minister's a stressful job.

Hague taunted him with the resignation of Frank Field and I thought, 'Well, I'll ask him a question.' So I stood up, and to my amazement, the Speaker called me and I said, 'The Prime Minister knows that everybody recognises his sole right to appoint people to the Cabinet, but would he give a categorical assurance that he wouldn't appoint the Liberal Leader Paddy Ashdown to the Cabinet, for which he's been queuing up for so long.'

The Tories exploded with laughter. Ashdown laughed but was embarrassed. Labour MPs went 'Oh' and all Blair said was, 'I can't go beyond what I've said already, namely that I'm in charge of Cabinet appointments.'

At five o'clock I went by taxi to the corner of Green Park, Constitution Hill and Buckingham Palace, where I met Don Jordan and Roy Hattersley with his dog Buster. The light wasn't frightfully good, but the sound was clear, and Roy said to camera everything I wanted to say – it's a new party, no links with the past; socialism is about planning the economy and/or greater equality; this government is about neither.

Caroline, Hilary and Michael came and we had dinner in the Strangers' Dining Room and we sat on the terrace and talked.

Michael is so mature now, he's almost seventeen. Carol looked absolutely marvellous, looked about fifty. I saw Mark Fisher today and said, 'I'm so glad you survived the reshuffle.' Well, he didn't; he was sacked by Blair. And I was so sorry about that because he's such a good Minister for the Arts. It shows I haven't followed things very carefully. Mark was very relaxed about it.

Saturday 1 August, Chesterfield

My surgery was burdensome. I had Mr N again, who is engaged in a huge row with the Child Support Agency, with the courts, with the Abbey National; he comes and plonks himself down and tells me how everybody is corrupt.

Then somebody else came, a man who said that his incapacity benefit had been cut. I said, 'What's wrong?'

'Oh, I've got bad nerves.'

I asked, 'Have you seen a doctor?'

'Oh, no, I haven't seen a doctor.'

'You can't just say you've got bad nerves and expect to be put on incapacity.' The surgery is now becoming just a sort of psychiatric surgery, with a doctor with no psychiatric qualifications.

The whole New Labour business is so unattractive, and I don't like the House of Commons; and the surgeries and correspondence are so burdensome that I really decided I would retire from Parliament at the end of this parliament.

It was really quite a serious and conscious decision to retire and spend my time more sensibly. Anyway, that's my thought at the moment.

Came back on the 2.37, got home about half-past five, packed up and drove to Stansgate. It was a lovely evening, the tide was high and our holiday began.

Wednesday 12 August

I got up early, picked up Ruth and we went to the British Library for breakfast with Dr Brian Lang, the Chief Executive of the British Library, a very cheerful, jolly Scot; Alice Prochaska, head of Special Collections; Ann Payne who is the director of manuscripts; and Stephen Johnson from the Heritage Lottery Fund. We were there to discuss the deposition of my archives and a bid for a grant from the Fund. Over breakfast they told us about the Queen's visit to the British Library and how Brian Lang had to negotiate with the Queen's private secretary as to what the Queen would say when she came. 'Would she say the British Library was a magnificent building?'

'Oh, quite out of the question.'

'Well, would she perhaps say it was a beautiful building?'

So it was settled that she would say it was a remarkable building.

Then they described the visit of Prince Charles, who'd been bitterly critical of the library design. And when he got there they said, 'You didn't inspect the designs, you never visited it, you always attacked it.'

'Well,' he said, 'it wasn't a proper library.'

'What do you mean?' 'Well, it wasn't symmetrical and it didn't have a proper portico,' he said to them.

I said, 'Well, I wonder whether if it had been thatched, it would have been better.' And we laughed. We had a very jolly breakfast.

Stephen Johnson, representing the Heritage Lottery Fund, said two things. First of all he asked, 'What is special about this collection? We don't normally support appeals for material less than twenty years old; this goes back sixty years but does include the last twenty years. And,' he continued, 'we don't support the archives et cetera of people who are still alive.'

I said, 'Asking me to die is a bit much. Could you not say I am politically dead?'

So they all laughed. They were very jolly and I think actually, in the light of this, Alice and the Heritage Lottery Fund will succeed. But Brian Lang, Alice and Stephen Johnson said they'd all like to come and see the archives, so I think in September we'll try and arrange a trip.

Caroline had a scan today. Apparently the result is pretty negative, which is good news.

Thursday 13 August

The plans for the Labour Party Conference were revealed at a press conference organised by Tom Sawyer who said there was a left-wing plot to take over the party. I went to bed at 8.30 and went out like a light. I am emotionally exhausted.

Friday 14 August

The whole of the morning was devoted to television and radio interviews. I managed to develop a fairly clear case about the Conference – it would be a case of 'management' versus 'representation'.

Well, I watched the interviews and all they used was twenty seconds of me saying that in future Conference will be like American conventions, where you don't have resolutions but balloons. Both BBC and ITV introduced me as 'a left-winger'. So I rang the BBC and they subsequently changed it to 'a former Cabinet Minister' – the BBC is back to its old tricks.

Did *The World Tonight*. I said, 'How long do you want?' They said, 'One minute' and so I did exactly one minute.

I recorded the various news bulletins and they are still using the 'left-wing' line and it is very unattractive. I have got to find a way round this and I don't know quite how to do it.

They had Derek Draper arguing with Ken Livingstone on the Channel 4 News. Well, Derek Draper is a nobody – has never been elected to anything, was appointed by Mandelson. He said the Party didn't want Liz Davies on the National Executive. Ken was very good and quiet and he is a formidable figure now on the left, and carries a lot of support.

Caroline rang and said she was coming home from the hospital, so I drove over there and brought her back. She was sick because she had her first radiotherapy today and is on radiotherapy for the whole of August.

Tuesday 18 August

The papers are full of Clinton's evidence and his broadcast admitting that he had had an 'inappropriate relationship' with Monica Lewinsky.

Melissa took Caroline to the hospital today.

Wednesday 19 August

The Real IRA have apologised for the bombing of Omagh and said they are ceasing military operations.

I suppose something may emerge to compensate for the terrible grief.*

We went to the hospital and while Caroline had her radiotherapy, I went to the hearing-aid unit. The technician reduced the ear mould so that they didn't hurt as much. He said, 'Your ears are full of debris, you had better go and have them suctioned.' Instead of using a syringe they now use a suction pump. So what with that and the new hearing aid and more comfortable moulds, my life has been transformed.

I have had nice correspondence, which I have put in my files, from a woman called Frances from North Yorkshire. She corresponded with me and I sent her my mum's book *My Exit Visa*. Finally she wrote and said she had decided to take her orders as a priest in the Catholic Church and that two bishops had agreed to ordain her. She is sixty-seven, very determined, and knows that it won't be valid, but the bishops are valid bishops; she feels it has got to be done and she is going to take on a parish in Northern Ireland. She thinks that when the Pope goes, this will all change. I have had a nice discussion with her and sent her a letter for her ordination on 14 September. So she has got all the guts that go with being a pioneer. I liked her very much and it is a principled stand. My mum would be so pleased.

Thursday 20 August

All of a sudden, on the six or seven o'clock news, it was announced that

*On Saturday 15 August 1998, the 'Real IRA' exploded a car bomb in the centre of Omagh, Co. Tyrone, killing 29 people. The group had split in 1997 from the Provisional IRA over the peace negotiations.

America had bombed Afghanistan and the Sudan, apparently using Cruise missiles. And a bit later we heard that Blair had supported it.

Friday 21 August
The media are much more critical about what the Americans have done than I would have expected. Robert Fisk had an excellent article in *The Independent* pointing out that Osama Bin Laden, who is a Saudi multimillionaire, leader of the World Islamic Fundamentalist Movement, was funded and supported by – and the base that was bombed yesterday was built by – the Americans, who used him to engage in terrorist attacks against the Russians when they were in Afghanistan; then, of course, he was a freedom fighter. I said very crudely tonight in an interview that the reason Britain followed the US was because they lend us nuclear bombs and, in return, we have to do everything they tell us.

I also wrote to the Speaker, and sent a copy to the Prime Minister, asking for the recall of Parliament. I have a feeling that opposition to this attack will be as strong over the next few days as it was to Iraq.

Saturday 22 August
The INLA in Ireland has called a permanent ceasefire and the Real IRA, I think, have announced a cessation of hostilities, so it looks as if the Irish thing is going well.

I heard on the news that some people had stoned the British Embassy in Khartoum because of British support for the American bombing, and there are big demonstrations against the Americans. Two UN officials have been killed. The more you think about this, the more horrific and unwise it was for the Government to support what the Americans have done. *The Independent* and the *Guardian* were very critical today, although when they talk about 'Labour opposition', it is always left-wing opposition.

Monday 24 August
There are millions of programmes about cancer on television and Caroline watches them all; she is very sensible about it.

Tuesday 25 August
A very troubled night. I have slept badly for the last three nights, having nightmares and waking every hour.

We went off to the hospital for Caroline's radiotherapy.

While I was sitting outside the hospital, a very attractive thirty-year-old African woman came and sat down, and I asked if she was a patient. She said, 'No, I am a medical interpreter for the Sudanese Embassy and I am here interpreting for a patient from Qatar who has come here for treatment.' I asked what the Sudanese Government was like and she said,

'We have had military governments, right-wing governments, labour governments linked in some way to the unions.' I asked if they were honest and she said, 'All governments are corrupt.' But she was charming and modest.

At six, the Sudanese Ambassador, Omer Yousef Beeredo, came to see me, a very distinguished diplomat aged fifty-nine, served in Britain 1963–9, has been the UN representative in Geneva, New York, Saudi Arabia, and Permanent Under-Secretary at the Ministry of Foreign Affairs. He is a highly skilled, cultured, experienced diplomat. He said the American attack was quite unjustified. The World Health Organisation supported the factory that had been bombed; it provided pharmaceuticals for Sudan. The Americans had had it on the global list of terrorists since 1993, although ex-President Jimmy Carter had said this was quite unjustified. He pointed out that the Sudanese had got rid of Bin Laden.

Then Beeredo reminded me that 100 years ago General Gordon was killed at Khartoum by the Mahdi who was treated as a Muslim fundamentalist. So nothing really changes.

I asked, 'What could be done?'

He said, 'We would like an inspection, but as the UN won't send one, the Arab League are supporting us.' He said the only real support in the European Union came from Italy. Spain wasn't really interested, but in fact Blair's response probably did represent European opinion.

I asked about the Israelis and Beeredo said he thought it was possible that they had stirred the Americans into bombing Sudan because they hate the Islamic movement. We talked about the anxiety of a new Cold War with Islam.

The Russian economy has completely collapsed: shops are closed, and the rouble has lost half its value.

Thursday 27 August

In the afternoon, the phone rang and somebody said to Sheila, 'Can I speak to Tony Benn. It's Mo Mowlam.'

So I picked up the phone and said, 'Mo, I hope you have had my message, via Ann Taylor, saying I couldn't support the anti-terrorist legislation.'

She said, 'No, I haven't, but I rang to have a word with you about it.'

I said, 'Well, I'll tell you what my concerns are. The policy on Northern Ireland has been absolutely magnificent and the wisdom shown has been so great. But I am concerned about three things. First of all, that peace is secured by getting the public to want an end to violence, which you have achieved by having talks. Secondly, there is a danger of this legislation producing injustice that will encourage violence among some groups. Thirdly, there is the civil liberties aspect of it.'

Top: From war to peace: Gerry Adams and Martin McGuinness of Sinn Fein approaching the House of Commons

Bottom: Campaigners for international justice: John Pilger and Alan Simpson with Tony Benn

Left: 'Didi': Bible scholar, Congregationalist and mother of Tony and David Benn

Bottom: The Benn extended family: *Top row*: Stephen, Joshua, Naz, Michael, Nita, Paul (with Sarah) and Hilary (in strip); *Middle row*: William, Melissa (with Hannah and Bunny on lap), James (behind Tony), Caroline, Emily and Caroline (Carrie); *Kneeling*: Sally, Jonathan and Daniel (Spiderman)

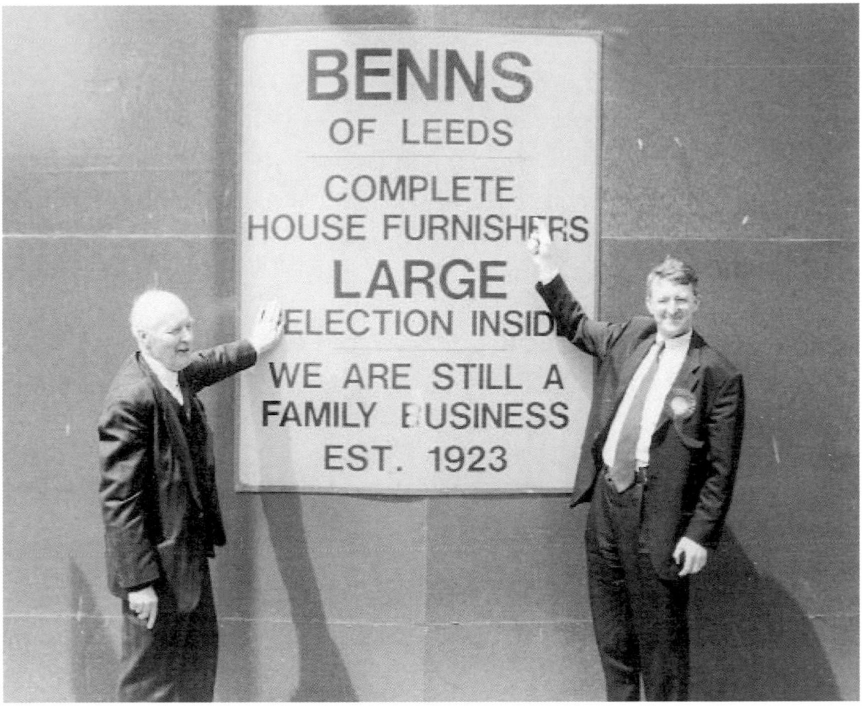

Top: Campaigning for Hilary in June 1999: two family firms in Leeds

Bottom: Last day in Parliament with
(left to right) brother David, Melissa, Joshua and Stephen

Top: The Chesterfield connection: my good friends Tom and Margaret Vallins

Bottom: The TEABAGS Summer School at Stansgate:
(left to right standing) Charlie Crowe,
Simon Fletcher, Sean Arnold, Rachel Thomson,
Ruth Winstone, Laura Rohde, Catherine Hood;
(left to right seated) Jennie Walsh, Caroline Benn, William Benn, TB, Andrew Hood

Left; Tony Banks, former Sports Minister, animal lover and close friend

Below: TB campaigning with Alice Mahon, the consistently principled MP for Halifax

Below: Tony Benn films 'Boom and Bust': Tony Blair with sculpture of Harold Wilson (flanked by Michael Martin, Lady Wilson and sculptor Ian Walters) in Speaker's House

Speaker Boothroyd – the
first woman Speaker, in procession

Speaker Martin – the
first Catholic Speaker
since Sir Thomas More

Top: Three faces of Socialism, the political, the religious and the industrial: Tony Benn with Donald Soper and Jack Jones.

Right: TB's retirement party for Commons' staff with parliamentary cake catching the Speaker's eye

Bottom: Retiring Members of Parliament in 2001: the Speaker flanked by Ted Heath and TB, with among others, Norman Fowler, John Morris, Judith Church, Bob Sheldon, Ken Livingstone, Jeff Rooker, Robert Maclennan, Giles Radice, Tom King and John MacGregor

'Well, I hear what you say. Jack Straw is in charge of the legislation, which hasn't been finally drafted yet.'

'Also,' I said, 'this business about legislation might affect issues abroad. I mean, I supported the ANC, which was a terrorist organisation.'

I got the impression she was distancing herself a little bit from Jack Straw and Tony Blair.

I said, 'I think you have done a marvellous job, Mo. I think it is the one real success of the Government, and I am Chairman of the Committee for Mo for Number 10.' She laughed. I said, 'I am speaking from the office where you worked many years ago.'

Sheila said afterwards, 'You are an old flatterer.'

But I am serious. I do think she has done well; anyway, I was flattered that a Secretary of State should ring me up at home.

We came down to Stansgate and Caroline went pretty well straight to bed.

Sunday 30 August

I went to Southminster to get the papers, which are full of the Russian crisis.

Also, the papers announced the wealthy and showbiz people who gave money to the Labour Party; Melvyn Bragg has been made a peer, and David Sainsbury, who was a trustee of the SDP, is made a peer and is now Minister in charge of science at the DTI.

Monday 31 August

I am very worried tonight. I am due in Parliament on Wednesday, but I just don't think I can leave Caroline. I will ring the Chief Whip. They won't mind a bit – they'll be delighted. But it is the first time I have an absolutely clear choice. Do you look after your beloved wife or do you go and pursue your parliamentary business when it is of no consequence whatsoever whether or not you are there?

Tuesday 1 September

Caroline and I walked in the garden, which was a good sign. I think she will be well enough for me to leave her for a day.

Gerry Adams said today that violence is over and done with and finished. That isn't quite the same as saying the war is over, but on that basis Trimble has invited all the party leaders to meet next Monday; and Clinton is arriving on Thursday. So the whole thing is moving and that makes the anti-terrorist legislation even less necessary.

Clinton is in Moscow, and really it is a couple of old flops talking to each other – Clinton hasn't got any money to give to Russia, and Yeltsin hasn't got any power to pursue any policy. So it is just a sort of photo opportunity that convinces nobody.

Wednesday 2 September

I got up at five. Dave appeared and drove me to Southminster for the train to London. It was the first time he had driven for about three years.

The House had been recalled and Blair began with a statement about Omagh and about the American bombing of the Sudan. I got in a question to him about the historical background to all this and he dismissed it. Then there was the procedure motion for getting the Bill through.

Well, up popped Richard Shepherd, the Tory MP, obviously considerably moved and agitated, to complain about the way the Bill was being handled and the way Parliament was being manipulated. He got support from Gwyneth Dunwoody and then she got support from Ian Paisley.

So I joined in and said we were like the Supreme Soviet being told what to do by Brezhnev. Eighty-five people voted against the government's handling of it. It was a real shock for the Government. I found myself in the Lobby with Ian Paisley and told him about the Catholic nun who was going to be ordained as a priest and said, 'How on earth will she manage in Northern Ireland?' He is always very friendly towards me. I said, 'What the House of Commons is doing today is roughly like what the Duma is trying to do to Yeltsin.'

Jack Straw then introduced the Bill itself, which he did very well. He responded to every sort of question. Quite a lot of good speeches were made, which will all be recorded in Hansard.

I was finally called at about 9.58 and I spoke for sixteen minutes, which was longer than I meant. A number of Tories came up and congratulated me.

Finally, at about twenty minutes past midnight we had a vote on Kevin McNamara's amendment declining to give a Second Reading to the Bill. I voted and there were seventeen people in the Lobby, which was really impressive because it took a lot of guts to vote against the Bill in the present atmosphere. I took my video camera into the Lobby, where the light wasn't very good but I just got a snap of Members sitting there laughing.

There was so much concern about Caroline. Tam Dalyell and Dennis Skinner and Jeremy Corbyn said, 'You must go home', so I did.

Tuesday 8 September

At 9.30 a twenty-two-year-old Harvard student called Jonathan Finer came to interview me for something he is writing on the New Labour

Government. He was an intelligent lad, had worked with an American senator and last year was an intern at the Labour HQ at Millbank. In a straightforward, somewhat naive way, he described exactly what happened: how he briefed Ministers and MPs, and checked out what was said on every programme. He said that MPs seem to accept everything they are told, unlike American Congressmen, who would wonder how it would 'play' in their own district. He said, 'We had to get the message across.' I asked where the message came from and he said, 'From Number 10 and the advisers. I worked for the Policy Officer.' I asked how old the Policy Officer was and he said, 'Twenty-two. He has been there for two years since he left college.'

After lunch, Caroline and I went to see Dr Lowdell, the consultant oncologist. He said they were going to put her on another drug, because the Tamoxifen has probably done its work. He did confirm that the radiotherapy was the cause of her nausea, depression, pain and everything else.

Monday 14 September, Chesterfield

I had promised to go to the Carers' Forum of Social Services. There were seven women and five men, including representatives of the health authority, social services, voluntary organisations and some carers. It was a very practical meeting and impressive in that way, but I felt they were flitting about on the margins. They asked, 'Could we get a bit more information out? Could we coordinate better? There are 6.8 million carers in Britain, 100,000 of them are over seventy-five, they are under terrible stress and they don't get a break unless they can prove they are breaking down themselves.' According to the Prince of Wales Trust report, the value to the community of the work done by carers is £34 billion a year. So I talked to them and they were all very friendly, but they just didn't connect their problems with the political process at all.

I have been thinking further about retirement and Caroline and I have talked about it. I have decided to jump the gun and issue a statement at the time of reselection in Chesterfield, saying that I want more political freedom. 'I have done fifty years in Parliament and it is quite clear to me now that most work needs to be done outside Parliament. I intend to spend the next twenty-five years on that. I shall stay a loyal member of the Labour Party, but I shall vote and speak entirely according to my conscience because that is what needs to be done.'

Friday 18 September

To the Demaglass factory, which produces very high-quality glassware; they have just laid off ninety people because of the slump in exports caused by the strong pound and high interest rates.

I was met by Don Greaves, who is the tough, decent managing director, and Trevor Finch, the regional organiser of the GMB. Ruth filmed us while we talked.

Don Greaves said that whereas his exports to Germany had amounted to £7 million a year they had now dropped to £0.5 million and he blamed the Government sharply for this, saying that they were just relying on interest-rate manipulation when there were many other mechanisms, including higher taxation on the wealthy, which he favoured, that would help to control inflation. Trevor Finch agreed. Very useful discussion.

We wandered round and looked at the work being done – the beautiful hand-decorated glassware.

Caught the 5.30 home.

Stephen came over and took Caroline to the Pharmacy, a fancy new restaurant in Notting Hill Gate, which is now almost world-famous, designed and owned by Damien Hirst, the artist. The food was marvellous and the service great, and it cost £25 for each meal – £100 for four without drinks or dessert. That's a pensioner's income for a week.

Sunday 27 September, Labour Party Conference, Blackpool

This morning *The Independent* had a story that Tony Blair and Dennis Skinner were very close and that Tony would be happy if Dennis remained on the NEC. It isn't that Dennis is moving to the right, but as you get older you want to be respected and he hasn't been keen on the recent revolts. We had the results of the NEC constituency section and Mark Seddon came top, Liz Davies third, and four of the six on our list got on – I couldn't believe it, because there had been such a lot of attacks, particularly on Liz who was cheated of a parliamentary seat by the smear that she was a Trotskyite.

Andrew Hood was at the *New Statesman* party; he wrote the book *Common Sense* with me and now advises Robin Cook. He said he'd like a talk. Apparently, the Foreign Office did not know about the American bombing of the Sudan until Blair had already publicly supported it, and there was obviously a lot of resentment at the FO about that.

Monday 28 September

Mandelson spoke today and got a rough passage – I've hardly taken any notice of the Conference, but tomorrow morning I might take my camera into the private session, as the press are excluded. I don't think they'd stop me.

Tuesday 29 September

At 2.30 Tony Blair made his speech – there was the usual build-up – he came on and smiled. Then he told a joke about how, when he met Jospin and addressed a public meeting, instead of saying, 'How much I admire Lionel Jospin in many ways', he said, 'I desire him in many positions', which I thought was a very crude joke. He is still talking about how amazing it is to be Prime Minister. Then he launched into a speech which, it was put to me later by an old trade unionist, was a moral rearmament speech. And it was. No reference to full employment. The globalised economy was hailed as being the great achievement, and the fact that trillions of dollars cross the exchange rates every day was something you boasted about.

He said he would sack bad teachers, close bad schools and bring in super-teachers; what was wrong with paying headmasters £60–70,000? We would betray our children if we didn't. As for the reform of the Welfare State and the NHS, the money available should go on modernisation. He got a two-minute standing ovation. Cherie Booth came up onto the platform and hugged and admired him, and then Prescott and Mrs Prescott joined them and they walked through the conference hall.

Dashed to the last meeting of the day, the Tribune Rally in the Opera House. Robin Cook had pulled out and I had been put on, and I was very pleased because I hadn't spoken at a Tribune meeting for some time. I looked ahead at the problems and then drew on the inheritance of the past to see how it could help us tackle the problems of the future – a philosophical speech. I told the story about the boat race, which always goes down well. John Edmonds made a very personal speech about 'greedy bastards' and Alan Simpson talked about the corporate Welfare State, which was thoughtful. Then Ken Livingstone made a very good speech, as he always does. Then Barbara Castle was brought on – very frail, but she made a passionate speech and bitterly attacked Gordon Brown for the way pensioners had been treated.

Finally onto the platform came Gerry Adams – I shook him warmly by the hand and he made a powerful speech about Irish unity and the union, and appealed to the Labour Party to help to bring about justice for Ireland.

Wednesday 30 September

An Asian man from the north-west came up to me today asking if I could advise him on getting a peerage. He said, 'I know Jack Straw' and he'd written to the Prime Minister asking for a peerage and made the point that he was a very active member of CND. Somebody said to me that the trouble with this Conference is that there are too many people on the make. There was a guy who worked for Leonard Cheshire Homes and said that he was leaving Conference because he was disgusted by all the people there to get something.

Friday 2 October

Carol is better every day. She has more energy and has put on weight, and by the time she goes to see the consultant next week there will be a bit of progress after the devastating effects of the radiotherapy.

Monday 12 October

At 11.30 Mr Paic from the Yugoslav Embassy came to the office – he is the Minister Counsellor. He is forty-nine, and was head of the American department in the Yugoslav Foreign Office. We had a long talk. He said that the Germans have undoubtedly armed the Kosovo Liberation Army and he thought the Americans had as well. He said his side had in fact withdrawn forces from Kosovo some time ago, but nobody believed it. The media was terribly biased.

He thought Britain was trying to assert its influence as a world power again, and I put to him that I thought we did whatever we were told by the Americans. For this month Britain has the presidency of the Security Council, so of course that is another platform on which Blair can parade. I said that on the whole people are sympathetic to Yugoslavia and remember the war and Tito; he said the sticking point is that NATO insists on putting in an army of occupation to monitor and verify the Dayton agreement. He said Yugoslavia will not accept NATO. He said, 'We have been occupied by the Turks and the Austro-Hungarians and the Nazis, and we won't have it.'

I said, 'Have you thought of trying to get independent people?

He said, 'Oh, yes: Japan, Brazil, Ireland, India, but not NATO.' He put a slightly different perspective on it all.

I stood out in the street with him afterwards waiting for his car to come and pick him up.

Tuesday 13 October

Caroline's seventy-second birthday and what a fantastic pleasure that she should still be here when three years ago she thought she had six months; two years ago we thought she had three months; and she is still here and feeling better today.

I bought her flowers and took her breakfast as usual and a heater, a shopping bag and a few little things for her toilette.

Sheila arrived and I hadn't seen her since last Thursday – it is always lovely when she enters the office.

Wednesday 14 October

Ted Heath published his memoirs today; at the very moment he publishes them there is a lot of discontent in the Tory Party and in his own constituency of Bexley and old Sidcup, over whether he should retire. Well, he will be eighty-five at the next election and he'd like to stay – he doesn't want to be in the Lords with Thatcher. But the pressure to go builds up and I don't want that to happen to me.

I spoke to Rory Bremner to say how much I enjoyed his show and put a few thoughts in his mind, and he suggested that I ring John Bird tomorrow, which I would be happy to do.

Thursday 15 October

I drafted an amendment to the Defence White Paper coming up on Wednesday and worked on a Bill to abolish the Lords, based on Cromwell's original bill. BBC Scotland rang about the monarchy. Carol had Kay Foster, the wife of Sir Christopher Foster, who lives near us, to tea. I had a letter today from the Prime Minister on the way the Royal Assent works – i.e. it was quite in order for the Queen to give the Royal Assent before a Bill has been passed. Well, I certainly learned something from that.

Hattersley has written a marvellous article about Blunkett and selection in schools. The first comprehensive school to be 'named and shamed' has been handed over to a private company to run – my God, what a government!

Had a word with John Bird from the Rory Bremner programme. He and John Fortune do these discussions known as the two Johns, and I briefed him on education.

Friday 16 October

Caught the 7.30 train to Chesterfield and did my surgery from ten till one.

Today David Trimble and John Hume got the Nobel Peace Prize, which infuriated Ian Paisley and left Gerry Adams out, though he congratulated them very skilfully on their award.

I'm very depressed – very, very depressed.

Sunday 18 October

Did a fifteen-minute discussion on reform of the Lords with Bernard Weatherill and Lord Winston: the discussion just goes on and on and on, and the one question they're all determined to avoid is: why shouldn't we elect a second chamber? The amazing thing about Britain is that people should have been persuaded that they are not fit and worthy to elect a second chamber – they just accept it and they accept that power should rest in the hands of one man, the PM, who is the only person who can make peers.

Caroline has some new drugs and they don't seem to be helping at all.

I forgot to mention that General Pinochet, former Chilean dictator who came to England for medical treatment, has been arrested. The Spanish Government issued a warrant and, presumably because we're in the EU, we had to respond. I think something will happen. He is a war criminal.

Tuesday 20 October

Went with Caroline to get her injection of this new drug, which apparently costs £75 a shot. The nurse said to her, having looked at her notes, that it was amazing how well she looked, considering how ill she was. Her response to cancer has been phenomenal.

After I dropped her off, I went to the Commons and left a message with Ann Taylor, the Chief Whip about Caroline, asking if it would be possible for me to have a letter, signed by Ann, that I could photocopy and use with the whips when necessary, and I'm sure she will agree.

Wednesday 21 October

Went into the House and drafted, and got some support for, a motion congratulating Peter Mandelson on the fact that he had said Pinochet was a brutal dictator, and if he was given diplomatic immunity from arrest, it would be gut-wrenching – for which according to the *Sun*, Mandelson has been rebuked today.

I had a brief word with Ann Taylor, who said that if it's an emergency I must stay at home with Caroline, but 'I hope you don't give the impression that you're only going to vote when it is *against* the Government'.

I said, 'Not at all, I've got a very good record, but there are some things I can't vote for.' She may be a bit tougher than Nick Brown.

Saturday 24 October

Caroline and I went to the University of London Institute of Education meeting on comprehensive schools. The referenda or ballots on the retention of grammar schools are to be held shortly. Roy Hattersley and Michael Mansfield both spoke; Dimitri Coryton, of the Conservative Education Association, made an excellent speech. Roy paid tribute to Caroline's work, which was very pleasing, and she got a great round of applause.

Then we went down to Leighton House – which was once Frederic Leighton's studio – in Kensington. Believe it or not, I have never been there before, though it is so close. A most elaborate house, with all sorts of works of art and ceramic panelling and masses of pictures. We went for the benefit for Mordecai Vanunu, who has been in prison for twelve years in Israel after he was kidnapped, gagged and left in solitary confinement because he revealed the fact that Israel had nuclear weapons. An extraordinary evening, with lots of people there. Susannah York introduced the evening; she has been to Israel and seen Vanunu, and she is very good on the nuclear question. Julie Christie, who was one of Caroline's pupils, read some letters from Vanunu. The Velvet Fist sang a couple of songs and I was asked to speak. Paul Foot turned up and we stayed till 8.15.

Eddie George has made a statement to the effect that unemployment in the north was a price worth paying to deal with inflation – that got him into a lot of trouble.

Monday 26 October

Ruth arrived and she told me that Helen and Bertie Leigh, who are friends of hers, had been to some occasion that had been addressed by Tony Blair, and Blair had said how the Labour Party had prepared very carefully for office. 'Of course,' he said, 'we had all read Tony Benn's diaries and heard about how the Civil Service had obstructed Ministers, which in his case of course was perfectly justified.' Well, that was an interesting comment.

Later on I saw Brian Sedgemore in the Lobby and he confirmed from his own experience that in 1981 Tony Blair was rushing round trying to get people to support me for the Deputy Leadership – that's how you get to the top.

There is a book by Penny Junor setting out to justify the Prince of Wales by saying that Diana committed adultery first, and issued death threats to Camilla Parker-Bowles. The Palace denies any responsibility for it, but I think this story will run and run.

Tuesday 27 October

Ron Davies, the Welsh Secretary, has resigned – an extraordinary scandal that I don't understand. He went for a walk on Clapham Common and apparently picked up two men, then went back to their flat, where they robbed him and stole his car. I don't know what he was doing, but obviously there is a scandal – and he has just resigned. The first sex scandal, if it is a sex scandal, for the Government.

Wednesday 28 October

Pinochet was cleared by the courts today on the grounds, according to the Lord Chief Justice, that he was Head of State at the time when the crimes occurred and therefore was exempt from extradition. So if Hitler or Mussolini or Franco or Saddam or Milošević came to London, they would be free to come and stay – amazing, but that is the British court system for you.

Thursday 29 October

The Jenkins Report on PR has come out – much trailed. Roy has recommended 500 MPs elected on a constituency basis and 15–20 per cent elected on regional lists from the parties. It's a move towards PR, but not the full system that the Liberals want, and Paddy Ashdown's whole future depends on securing something. We would lose sixty-nine Labour MPs under this system and the Tories much the same, and the Liberals would have a huge increase; so not surprisingly Roy Jenkins has come up with this proposal. Blair is a bit scared and nothing will happen until after the election; but certainly the next Parliament would be so different from this one that, just as when I left the NEC in 1994 the Executive was finally strangled, so as I leave Parliament in 2001/2 there won't be a House of Commons left in any meaningful way.

Monday 2 November
At 10.30 Zuhair Ibrahim came to see me for about forty-five minutes. He's now a very old friend and he is going back to Baghdad. He's had a bad back, which required an urgent operation, and he has been very poorly. He said when he goes home he is going to leave his son and daughter here, because his wife's grandparents live in England.

He is a professional diplomat, sixty-two years old, and has had a most fascinating life. His first appointment out of Baghdad was in Athens and then he went to the Yemen; then to Sweden and then to Tokyo. He said that relations between America and Iraq were absolutely at their peak in January 1989, when the heads of fourteen American corporations came to Baghdad. And Ibrahim was told by the American Ambassador, 'This is your greatest triumph, because these are the people to whom President Bush listens.' Then something went wrong. There was a conference of the Arab leaders in Amman, attended by Iraq, Egypt, Jordan and possibly Saudi Arabia, and Saddam made a statement saying that America must withdraw from the Gulf. Mubarak, the Egyptian President, stormed out of the conference at the end of the first day, and Ibrahim thought that was when the Americans decided they had to bring down Saddam. Apparently, at the same time there was a big military parade in Baghdad on Army Day with a huge display of armed force. An Irish man who was there – a diplomat – said, 'This is not going to be acceptable to Washington.' So Ibrahim thinks that was the turning point.

The man has enormous experience.

We had a marvellous talk and he was sitting in Keir Hardie's chair, because his back was so bad and he wanted to sit upright. He told me I was his best friend here, although Edward Heath has been very friendly. Derek Fatchett, the Foreign Office Minister, won't see him.

I'm glad I've been able to put this down because I've enjoyed my relations with Ibrahim. He said George Robertson had talked about using force again. I think Robertson is a little twit.

Wednesday 4 November
I went to the trade-union meeting in Committee Room 10, which Peter Mandelson was to address. He floated in looking frightfully self-satisfied, smirking and oily. He began by saying there had been rumours about the

new Bill, 'but I'm totally opposed to spin doctors' – a very poor joke. He said that improved industrial relations were central to New Labour and that flexibility of labour was the key. You had to have minimum standards and proper rights for workers. He mentioned the Working Time Directive and a national minimum wage.

Then someone noticed that up on the wall there was a light that said 'Broadcasting' – so the whole thing was being broadcast or recorded. So they discovered the switch and switched it off, don't think anybody heard it, but that was amusing. Mandelson went on to say that the balance of power between management and the workforce has got to be maintained; Partnership at Work had been agreed by the CBI and we had to reassure the CBI. There was a lot of CBI pressure.

I had a bite in the Tea Room and saw Jean Corston, who had led a parliamentary delegation to Chile and was anxious about Pinochet being extradited for fear it might undermine democracy in Chile.

Friday 6 November

Maurice Chittenden of the *Sunday Times* rang to tell me that when Carlos the Jackal, who had lived in Notting Hill Gate for a time, left his flat, they found my name among many others of people he wanted to kill. He is now in prison in France for life. Carlos has written to the *Sunday Times* saying he was sorry that he included me in the list! Interesting – I remembered it well, of course.

Monday 9 November

Went into the Commons and walked across with Gerry Bermingham to Number 10, for the meeting of MPs with Tony Blair. I did it about a year ago; this year it is Members with surnames beginning A and B.

We all trooped in and Blair began by saying that we must keep our eye on the big picture; the economy is what matters; we need stability; and in public expenditure, investment must go hand-in-hand with reform.

Joe Ashton said, 'I've never known a Government being in power for eighteen months and still being so popular, but don't take on the trade union movement because it was *In Place of Strife* and prices-and-incomes policy that got us defeated in 1970 and 1979 . . . Don't give way to the CBI or Murdoch – we don't need him. We don't have to cater to him on economic and monetary union, which we must get into – we must have EMU.'

Candy Atherton said, 'I hope you'll come to Cornwall for the total eclipse of the sun next year.'

Roger Berry and other Members made some points about the Post Office, public expenditure and welfare, trade unions and fat cats, and Blair replied to them. He said, 'We need a sensible policy with regard to the trade unions, and we're never going back – we do need the support of the business community and they are accepting lots of things: the Working Time Directive, the Social Chapter and the minimum wage.' On Murdoch he said that we would decide the question of the single currency ourselves. It is sensible to be cautious. He made some comment about Candy Atherton, saying that he'd come to the eclipse if he could.

'If you're going to have a market economy, you are going to have fat cats. On Welfare, the changes are justified and the expenditure is up front and the savings are long-term. On the Post Office, we have said we are going to keep it public, but it has got to be competitive and within the European Union rules, and of course there will be scope for private investment.'

Anne Begg made jokes about the SNP and said that there are two parties in Scotland – the loyal Labour Party and the beleaguered councils and unions, who feel left out. Then Harry Barnes said, 'I'd like to ask about the Third Way – free enterprise and social justice simply don't go together, and is what you're doing just transitional or is it a permanent change? What is your attitude to democratic socialism?'

I said that in my constituency the pits are closed; the company that cut the Channel Tunnel has been taken over and closed; a little glass company in Chesterfield, which had exports of £7 million to Germany, has found them cut to £0.5 million because of high interest rates. And I said, 'I just wonder what our attitude is to manufacturing industry? It is absolutely essential. I am sure you're thinking about these things, because it is very worrying, and buying and selling companies abroad and inward investment aren't the answer – look at Siemens, who have closed, look at Rover, look at Ford. Younger members will be concerned about this.' 'And,' I added, 'I look forward to the day when you take your seat as Lord Sedgefield.'

To Anne Begg, Blair said that nationalism is a cultural question and solidarity is the key between the Scottish and English people – I thought that was amazing. He said the Labour Party in Scotland is sympathetic to the SNP and what we had to do was modernise the Scottish Labour Party, because they are often the obstacle. He said we must make an ideological challenge to the SNP.

To Harry Barnes, he said, 'Look, what I'm doing is not transitional. We have to have a long-term commitment to the market economy, and this idea that you have a Labour Party in support of Labour and a Tory Party in support of capital is completely out of date. The Liberals had the right idea in the 1970s and we have got to redefine our values as part of a competitive world. As for the Third Way, it is not like the old left or the old right – because there is a role for government and the values are unchanged.'

When he came to me, Blair said there are two things to remember – one is that there has got to be economic stability, and we can't go back to boom-and-bust, we need more productivity. The Japanese have shown us. Then he said something about schools: schools have a lot to do with our decline – no sort of an answer.

Anyway it was useful and it was all very jolly. I left, and who should be standing there but Gerry Adams – I never thought I'd see Gerry Adams inside Number 10.

Caroline cut my hair, bless her heart. She said yesterday, 'I'm not afraid of the future' and I thought that was amazing. She had heard about cannabis being suitable as a painkiller, so when we saw the doctor last week she was prescribed it, but of course will not get it.

Wednesday 11 November

Ken Livingstone is reported in the *Evening Standard* as saying that he will stand as an independent, which is quite untrue.

Clinton is threatening war in Iraq at the same time as celebrating the Armistice – my God!

Saturday 14 November

I started work on my income tax – which I detest. The sight of the tax return almost drives me to the point of a nervous breakdown.

Late tonight we heard that Saddam Hussein has announced that he will resume UN arms inspections, and so America and Britain have been left out in the cold. A pleasing end to the thing, but it hasn't really ended because the Americans are talking about wiping out Saddam.

Monday 16 November

I jumped in a taxi and went to lunch with Rory Bremner and John Fortune and the team on the show. We had a good old talk. Rory is a serious person and he was making notes. I said, 'You have to anticipate the full Coalition that is coming, with Ken Clarke and Heseltine around the Cabinet table.' I also made suggestions about a debate between Old Labour and New Labour showing that in many respects they are identical. And I suggested that Bremner dramatise the eight telephone calls that occurred last Sunday night between Clinton and Blair – where Blair kept getting totally contradictory instructions: put the aircraft on alert, take them off alert; ending up with Clinton saying to Blair, 'Why don't we bomb the Sudan again!'

Dashed back to the Commons and there was a statement on Iraq. I put a question about the illegality of it all, particularly the aim to topple Saddam, which is the new American objective. They have put $100 million into toppling Saddam, which is about ten times as much as they have put into saving the homeless people in the Nicaraguan and Honduran hurricanes. I got the usual reply from Blair.

Then I went up to my room and the European Elections Bill came up, changing the system for electing MEPs from first-past-the-post to a closed list, which will only allow voters to vote for a party and not for candidates. So Mike Elliott who has been an MEP for fifteen years, has been put at the bottom of the list in the London region and will never get elected unless everybody voted Labour. I spoke on that. Jack Straw is pathetic. Austin Mitchell, Gwyneth Dunwoody and I all spoke against the closed list system, but of course we are tied by the Party and it has to go back to the Lords tomorrow.

Tuesday 17 November

I went to the Central Hall, Westminster to give a lecture on New Labour to about 200 students. Paddy Ashdown spoke first, followed by William Hague and then me. In the room behind the platform, before William Hague came up, I spoke to his assistant, a very well-dressed young man, who said, 'I work with William Hague.'

And I asked, 'What did you do before – were you a civil servant?'

He said, 'No, I was a Member of Parliament.' I think it was Sebastian Coe, the runner, who was defeated in May 1997, so I was a bit embarrassed.

Wednesday 18 November

My pager said, 'If Members would like to go home, see the whips.' I did, but they said, 'Oh, we're only giving time to people who are supporting the Government.' I said I did, I supported the spirit of the Government – the Third Way between the Lords and the Commons. Tommy McAvoy, the Deputy Chief Whip who is a bit of a thug, said, 'The Third Way is out.' So I had to stay and I didn't get home till one. I was really angry with them, but I don't want nastiness with the whips. But they are the machine people who convert Blair's determination into bullying.

Sunday 22 November

Another great build-up of hostility to Iraq, and now the UN inspectors say the Iraqi Government will not allow them to see the documents they want. Significantly, a couple of days ago in Japan, Clinton was asked why he hadn't bombed Iraq and he said it was because 10,000 civilians would have been killed, so that implied a certain stepping back from the brink.

Tam Dalyell has spoken to Tariq Aziz, Foreign Minister in Iraq, who says that the documents they want do not exist.

Monday 23 November

Had a bite to eat and went into the Commons in the afternoon to get a book by Anthony Giddens on the Third Way, because I'm interviewing him tomorrow morning. It is absolutely high-table chit-chat – nothing of any substance whatever in it – but I'm glad I read it, and I'll try and get him to explain it in a way that will be meaningful. I think he'll find it a bit difficult because it is pure waffle.

Tuesday 24 November

Troubled night – didn't sleep very well. Went by taxi to the London School of Economics to see Anthony Giddens, the Director of the LSE, about the Third Way. I'd had a great argument with him at Conference, where I had harangued him when he was signing his book, and he said, 'Come and see me.' We had an hour's discussion and he was very polite and friendly, and very nervous. He really did give it all away. He spoke as if globalisation was something that had just been discovered, the idea of the financial community – I know it's a bit new, but it's been going for a long time. He said that globalisation is inevitable; social democrats with the values of the left have got to appeal to the centre and the right; the centre is more interesting than it's ever been; we have got to have relations with the US; and the social democratic parties in Europe had made all these adjustments. He went on to say that capitalism was the only way forward and questioned why people should have pensions; 'people don't want to retire and they shouldn't retire'; we should be flexible – just academic waffle.

He kept talking about 'democratising democracy' and the 'democratic family' and it was just a load of philosophical nonsense. It tells you much about Blair's position.

Wednesday 25 November

When I got to the Commons somebody from the Press Association came up and said, 'What do you think? The House of Lords have voted by three to two to overturn the High Court decision and have ruled that Pinochet could not enjoy immunity.' Tremendous victory and the people outside Parliament were cheering; the Chileans who have been out there in the cold for a month were just holding up their placards. Unbelievable, really important.

Thursday 26 November

I asked Chris Mullin if he knew that the Liberals had the Queen's Speech read to them the night before it was delivered, and he gave me a look of incredible superiority and said, 'I hear what you say.'

I said, 'I don't want you to hear what I say. I want you to bloody well do something about it!'

I asked Ann Taylor why they got it and she said, 'The Opposition always get it; we did in Opposition in the Shadow Cabinet.'

I said, 'I don't remember that, but it's quite a different thing reading it to your own party.'

'Oh,' she said, 'that's a matter for Paddy Ashdown.'

I was so incensed that after lunch when we got to the end of Business Questions I asked the Speaker about it. She listened respectfully and of course the Tories cheered like anything. I made it clear that it was her job to see that there wasn't any blurring of the two responsibilities of the legislature and executive. I'm glad I did that – the House was empty, but it doesn't matter.

I saw Chris Patten as I was getting into a taxi, former Chairman of the Tory Party and Governor of Hong Kong. I asked him, 'Are you going to be Governor of London?'

He said, 'I wouldn't want to stand between Ken Livingstone and his destiny.'

I said, 'If you did, you'd have the full support of Tony Blair. How are you getting on in Northern Ireland? When I was over there I told them Chris Patten was in Hong Kong and that was given back to China, and now he's come to Northern Ireland . . .'

He said, 'That's exactly what Ian Paisley said!'

I haven't seen Patten for six years since his defeat in 1992.

Saturday 28 November

There is a bit in the papers that there is a great plan for the Government to call the House of Lords back on Boxing Day to force through the European Elections Bill, and Blair and Ashdown will appoint fifty more peers. It is so crude now – we won the election, Ashdown was defeated in the election, and the Liberals are being treated as if they were partners – they are not partners. It is horrible.

Tuesday 1 December

Up at 5.15 and made breakfast and got a taxi at 6.10. The cab driver said, 'I know where you're going – you're going as a character witness for Peter Tatchell.'

I said, 'How do you know that?' He said it was on the news this morning.*

Had a cup of tea and a doughnut at Victoria and got on the train which took two hours to get to Canterbury East. I had bought an £8.50 standard-class pensioner's ticket, but I had to pay £3 more to go into first class to smoke. I got to Canterbury and walked to the magistrates' court. There was Peter Tatchell and we had a chat. Then his barrister arrived and I

* The gay rights campaign Outrage! interrupted the Archbishop of Canterbury during a sermon in Canterbury Cathedral to draw attention to his perceived discrimination against gay men and women. Peter Tatchell of Outrage! was tried for 'indecent behaviour in a church' under Section 2 of the Ecclesiastical Courts Jurisdiction Act 1860 (formerly part of the Brawling Act 1551).

went over some areas that might be touched upon in my examination and cross-examination. Peter said, 'Come and meet the press.' I put my bag down and a woman who was with him said, 'Don't leave your bag – my handbag was stolen in court yesterday, and when I rang the police they didn't even know where the Canterbury magistrates' court was.' That was very funny.

I affirmed, and was then examined by Peter's lawyer and brought out some interesting points about conscience, the law and how it has changed, and various other issues. I was cross-examined by the prosecuting counsel, who was very mild with me, and I was honest in responding and said that the bishop was a law-maker as well as a bishop and it was in that capacity that Peter Tatchell was campaigning against him.

The prosecuting counsel wound up with a lot of legal argument about the meaning of brawling under the 1551 Act. Then the defence counsel began to sum up, but I had to leave to come back to London.

Wednesday 2 December

The Independent printed the whole of my statement to the magistrates' court and there was a lot about Tatchell. I realise now why the magistrate fined him £18.60, because that was the date of the Ecclesiastical Courts Jurisdiction Act; that was an amusing thing to do.

Drifted into the House and heard the end of PM's Questions and it was clear that some huge news had emerged – I didn't understand the exchanges between Blair and Hague, but later discovered that Lord Cranborne, the leader of the Tories in the Lords and son of the Marquess of Salisbury, had entered into private negotiations with Margaret Jay and Jack Weatherill, the former Speaker, and Dick Marsh of all people; and they had cooked up a scheme under which the hereditary peers would be allowed to elect seventy-five peers from among their number as representative peers and fourteen others would be elected by everybody with two peers 'ex-officio'; and on this basis the Tories would facilitate the Government's legislation. It is a terribly clever move by Blair; he has split the Tory Party. Hague has sacked Lord Cranborne as leader of the Tories, although I think a lot of peers will probably agree with Cranborne. So Blair has split the Tories, opened the way for his legislation, and absolutely disregarded his election manifesto that he would get rid of hereditary peers, because there will be ninety-one of them left. No move whatever towards a democratic second chamber.

Today is the day the European Elections Bill is being rushed through. I wrote to the Chief Whip saying I wouldn't vote on it.

Chris Mullin, who is on Labour's Parliamentary Committee which meets weekly with Blair, wrote to say he had raised with the PM the question of the Liberals seeing an advance copy of the Queen's speech. Blair had said, 'Paddy Ashdown shouldn't have done it and the Speaker was very angry.' He put a PS: 'I hope you'll record this in your diary.' So I've done that for him.

Monday 7 December

Big news today is that Peter Mandelson has been forced to keep the Post Office in the public service, though he very much wanted to privatise huge chunks of it; to reverse what Rowland Hill did in the 1840s and Charles II did in 1660 would have been more right-wing than you could imagine and more than any Labour Government could get away with – though nothing would surprise me.

Ken Livingstone asked me the other day if I had noticed that the one way of getting into Parliament without going through an NEC vetting committee is by Blair making you a peer – absolutely no check on you, no questions asked about your suitability or record in the Party – you're just put there for life. And we are told that no one can expect a job for life!

Tuesday 8 December

Caroline very sweetly watched the first cut of the ITN programme I've been filming in recent months about New Labour and she had a lot of criticisms – I was a stumbling old man; there was too much of me; too much band music; it wasn't clear. It depressed me very much because I haven't really got control of it. Later Sheila watched it and agreed with everything Caroline had said.

There is this terrible case of the electronic engineers in Chechnya, who went there to work on a mobile-phone network and were captured by terrorists, and their bodies were found today. They had all been beheaded. Ghastly story. What a bloody awful world we live in.

Wednesday 9 December

Sheila was in, working on the Christmas cards, and the computer failed and there was absolute panic, but she checked it at the back and got it to work. Caroline went all by herself – by cab to Victoria, train to Croydon, and back by train and cab – to see Daniel in his school Christmas play. Amazing achievement, because she hadn't taken a painkiller – it's hard not to believe that she isn't going back to the state of reasonable normality that she was in six months ago.

After ten, as there was expected to be a vote at midnight, Alan Simpson and Audrey Wise came to the Viewing Room and watched the rough assembly of the ITN programme. They liked it very much – it gave me a huge boost.

Thursday 10 December

Chris Mullin is not looking very well – I wonder what's wrong. He's going to have some tests tomorrow. He has lost a lot of weight.

Saturday 12 December
I stuck labels on the Christmas cards – a terribly time-consuming job. We're only sending a few hundred this year.

Tuesday 15 December
To Central Hall for a Sixth-Form Conference on religion and politics. When I was there I met Professor Ted Wragg, who told me that David Blunkett was being steadily undermined by Chris Woodhead, the OFSTED Inspector, who has been imposed on Blunkett by Blair. Ted Wragg said Woodhead is close to Blair and Prince Charles – and, I added, the *Daily Mail*.

So later in the day, when I saw David Blunkett in the Lobby, I said, 'I think you ought to go and see Blair and say, "If you want Woodhead, I accept that, but he should not be allowed to undermine the Secretary of State for Education, whom you appointed."' I think Blunkett took that point.

Caroline went shopping in her wheelchair with Barbara and then went to have her injection this afternoon. At three I was picked up and taken to the BBC in Wood Lane and I was told the Spice Girls – a very popular group of young women – were there.

Wednesday 16 December
There were air raids in Baghdad just before ten. I went off to *Newsnight* and there were Menzies Campbell and Michael Howard, and it was treated as a sort of spectacle – over to Baghdad to see the fires burning. I got very angry and I said, 'Look, people are being killed as we are talking, and we are discussing it as if it were a spectator sport' – it quite shook the panel. Then, after one or two exchanges, they tried to take my microphone off me and I said, 'I'm not leaving the studio', so the discussion continued. I was unbelievably angry.

After that I went and did News 24 and then Radio 5 Live. When I got home at one there were twenty messages on my answering machine – every broadcasting organisation in the world seemed to have rung.

Thursday 17 December
Into the Commons and saw Ted Heath and asked him if he was going to speak today. He said, 'No. It's easier for you.'

I said, 'What do you make of a government that believes it's at the heart of Europe and does everything Clinton wants?' and Ted gave me a friendly smile. I said, 'I greatly value my friendship with you.'

I was called and had some doubts about my speech because I was a bit steamed up. I made a ten-minute speech, which was a bit over-the-top, but I felt very strongly.

I moved the vote at 9.59 and Tam and I were to be tellers, but the Government didn't put in any tellers themselves, so we had to adjourn without a vote, which was a Government trick to deny us the opportunity of getting twenty-five people into the Lobby against the Government, including Martin Bell.

Bill Clinton goes on smiling, but the impeachment vote is likely to take place in the next couple of days and it may be that this will blow up in his face.

Friday 18 December, Chesterfield

Caught the early train to Chesterfield. The first thing I had to do was take part in a long interview for Radio Sheffield with a poet called Ian Macmillan. I have never been interviewed by a poet before and his questions were totally different from the political questions – very deep and interesting, and touching on all sorts of moral choices and political opinions, though they didn't deal with day-to-day politics. I thought it was great fun. They asked me to pick four pieces of music, so I picked the music from *Brassed Off*, 'Vincent' by Don Maclean, the Trumpet Voluntary and 'Winter Turns to Spring' by Roy Bailey. I really enjoyed it.

Saturday 19 December

To Whitehall where about a thousand people had gathered. Christian CND, Labour CND, London CND, the Green Party, the Spartacists, the Muslim Communities . One Iraqi woman came up and just wept bitterly on my shoulder and I was so moved that I was crying. Then a BBC woman came to interview me and she was crying. It was really something.

The Russian Duma have voted to suspend sanctions against Iraq unilaterally.

Big demonstration in Paris, and George Galloway flew over there to address it. Things are going very well indeed from the point of view of the anti-war movement. I think a lot of people will resign from the Labour Party in utter disgust and disappointment.

On the midnight news Clinton and Blair, in almost identical statements, have announced that the bombing of Iraq has stopped, both claiming huge credit for having dealt with Saddam and so on. That is the end of a four-day war in which apparently more Cruise missiles were dropped on Iraq than throughout the whole of the Gulf War in 1990.

Sunday 20 December

Caroline went to the Christmas Carol Service in the Albert Hall with the grandchildren. Daniel, Emily and Jonathan went onto the platform and for the third year running a Benn won a prize. Daniel, who is just seven, put his hand up immediately when the audience was asked to give the words of a carol – I think it was 'Once in Royal David's City'. He put his hand up and he half-remembered the second line, so Jonathan and Emily pushed him forward and Daniel went on to the podium and sang 'was a lowly cattle shed', and the whole audience of thousands applauded him. It was absolutely thrilling.

Monday 21 December

Tony Blair was on the radio saying, 'We've put Iraq back into the cage', and hinting that we might go to war again. He has sent the *Invincible* out there.

As the war is over now and people can look at it differently, opposition is building up on a huge scale. Dennis Halliday, in charge of the humanitarian mission in Iraq, has resigned in disgust.

Tuesday 22 December

It turns out that Mandelson borrowed £373,000 from Geoffrey Robinson to buy a house in Notting Hill Gate. As Mandelson is not a well-liked figure, it has caused a huge stir. Nothing wrong with borrowing money, but when two Ministers lend each other money it does create a relationship. It is more likely among the Tories than within the Labour Party. If Mandelson were to be in trouble, then Blair would be alone. Blair goes on blathering away, to try and pick up support for the bombing, which he cannot get. The French are angry. It is an extraordinary situation we're in.

Wednesday 23 December

Banner headlines denouncing Mandelson: 'Mandelson the Deceiver', 'Mandelson Must Go', 'Blair in Trouble', and so on. It was very interesting and the media dislike him – the journalists because he has manipulated and bullied them.

Caroline's helper, Barbara, and her son Archie came and helped peel the potatoes. Archie opened all my mail: 99.9 per cent sympathetic; only two or three abusive letters.

The director of my film about New Labour had asked me what we would do if Mandelson resigned, because he features in the film, and I said, 'There is no question of him resigning.' Well, he did! When I got to the Commons I was told that Mandelson had resigned. I didn't believe it, but it was confirmed and later Geoffrey Robinson also resigned. So Blair has lost his main adviser. I'm sure Mandelson still will advise him, but it will be difficult for him to be privy to Cabinet secrets in the way he was as a Cabinet Minister. I think Blair is terribly weakened and Clinton, his one prop, is also weakened. Blair is beginning to get into serious trouble.

I had about twelve invitations to broadcast on the Mandelson resignation but I declined. Mandelson himself appeared on all the programmes as if it were a great triumph to have resigned. That is his spin on it.

I got a taxi to ITN and when I got there they were anxious about how we modify the programme in the light of Mandelson's resignation. So I redid the commentary because I'm determined that we use him. It is now a very important programme. It has Mandelson, Nick Brown, Geoffrey Robinson, the Iraq War – I am pleased with it.

Thursday 24 December

One thing that is clear is how the journalists hated Mandelson, because they are really putting the knife in. I think it is the end of New Labour, because Blair without Mandelson is lost. I know Alastair Campbell is competent, but he hasn't got anything like Mandelson's idea of 'the project', as they call it, and the *Sun* had a picture of a turkey with Mandelson's face – stuffed!

Friday 25 December

Dickens's *Scrooge* was on – the 1951 version with Alastair Sim as Scrooge, in a star-studded cast. When you look at *Scrooge* now you realise that Dickens has come back. Blair is taking us back to Victorian liberalism with an authoritarian touch to it. But this is not a day for politics.

We had twenty for lunch and the kids had brought some of the food, so it took the responsibility off Caroline. But she and Josh, bless his heart, did the guts of the washing-up. The forty-fifth Christmas lunch that Caroline had given here, and we've been married forty-nine years. She gets tired, but she was lively and worked like a beaver.

Saturday 26 December

I had a strange dream last night. I dreamed that I was parking my car round the corner and Tony Blair came up and said, 'You can't park here – the parking restrictions apply on Saturday.'

I said, 'It's a public holiday – Boxing Day.'

And he said, 'I'm sorry, but the parking restrictions apply because it is Saturday – anyway we've got to generate the income to keep the traffic wardens paid.'

I thought nothing of it until later, when I went to the car. There was a police van and a police car, and the police were arresting somebody. I asked what it was about. The policeman said, 'You can't park here, you know – it's Saturday restrictions.' I said, 'It's a public holiday.' So my dream was actually repeated, only instead of Tony Blair it was a black policeman. You have to put that down when it's Christmas and there's no news.

We went to Croydon to visit Stephen and his family. Emily and Daniel played bass and violin and Stephen accompanied them. Then we drove to Ralph and Ann Gibson's. He was my best man – they got married on 10 December 1949 and we were married on 17 June 1949, so we're a bit ahead of them.

Monday 4 January, 1999
Went by underground to St Pancras for the opening of the Manuscript Room in the new British Library. Alice Prochaska had invited me and there was a huge crowd of the literary and academic establishment. Carol's contemporary from University College, Professor (now Lord) Randolph Quirk and his wife were there, Harold Pinter and Antonia Fraser, Michael Holroyd. I had a long talk to Stephen Green, who is the Chief Executive of the National Heritage Lottery Fund – used to work in the British Library. He said 'Your application' – I said not mine, the British Library application – 'Ah yes! It is coming up this month for a preliminary examination and it's got more red flags on it than any application I've ever seen.' Then he said perhaps I had lost a few points by saying that if charges were introduced to the British Library, I wouldn't give them my papers. I said that I had never said that – I had said that the purpose of giving them was so that everyone would have free access.

I don't know what will happen. I'm getting very discouraged about it. But if it doesn't come off, well, there you are. They will just be left at Stansgate in a trust to be put on permanent loan.

Wednesday 6 January
Hottest 6 January in London since 1841 – 61°F – could have been a spring day or an early October day.

I never thought Mandelson would go. I used to know Geoffrey Robinson quite well when he was Managing Director of Jaguar and I liked him, but he did nothing politically – just went into business when we were in Opposition and made himself a multi-millionaire. It doesn't matter at all to him whether he's a Minister.

Who leaked the story about the loan? Was it Charles Whelan, Gordon Brown's press officer? Steve Byers has gone to Mandelson's job, and Dawn Primarolo of all people has been made Paymaster General – rewarded for her absolute total obedience to all the instructions (however contradictory) from the top. Barbara Roche promoted. It is all looking very nasty and I was tempted to say something about it all, but I've kept my mouth shut because the Party hasn't liked what's happened, and they certainly wouldn't like it if they thought the so-called left or Old Labour was taking advantage of it. I have to recognise that I'm not a very significant figure any more – not a significant figure at all. I'm just glad I have nothing whatever to do with it.

Sunday 10 January
Tony Blair did an interview with David Frost this morning and I gather he said that he had no real differences with the Liberals. He is facing quite a substantial revolt in the Cabinet – Prescott allegedly, and Jack

Straw and others, are revolting against the strong Liberal links, but Blair is determined to push it.

Monday 11 January

Tam Dalyell raised the story in *The Times* today, written by 'our political correspondents', that Betty Boothroyd might retire early and that the Government was unhappy about the opportunity she gave to Tony Benn and George Galloway on Iraq. He raised it as an attack on the chair and the Speaker, and I followed it up saying it was very important that the primacy of Parliament should be reasserted. The Speaker was quite pleased and said she had no intention whatever of resigning.

Tuesday 12 January

Sheila came back from her holiday in Goa and had a marvellous time. There was a pile of mail and she was so calm about it. I told her I was depressed and I think I'm old and I've got eczema, and I'm beginning to think I might have prostate trouble. She is a homeopath and she laughed and went through all my symptoms. She said it's lovely to be back, but she does so much more work when I'm not here.

Caught the train to Kent for Ron Huzzard's funeral. It was lovely. Ron was a Quaker and a socialist, and apparently a great Duke Ellington fan. So a very severe-looking man said, 'We're here to give thanks for the life of Ron Huzzard and now we're going to have ten minutes silence. Then anyone can speak who wants to.' Then the curtains drew in front of the coffin and we had another three minutes' silence and walked out to Duke Ellington. Lots of jokes and laughter. Frank Allaun had come all the way down from Manchester. Tam and Bruce Kent and some others came back in the train and we talked all the way back to Victoria and came to the House.

In the Tea Room were Chris Mullin and Jean Corston, Andrew Mackinlay and Audrey Wise and Derek Foster and the atmosphere was very jolly. People are so pleased that Mandelson has gone; it is just like a release from prison. Later on Stuart Bell, a senior backbencher, said that Mandelson could not come back in the present Parliament to any ministerial position, so Blair has got a problem on his hands.

Thursday 14 January

At Caroline's suggestion, I wrote a paper for the Campaign Group proposing that we should launch a discussion about whether all votes in the Commons should be free votes. It may be that in this way we can restate the democratic case against presidential government by saying that there have got to be checks and balances, and there are none.

Charlie Whelan, Gordon Brown's disgraced spin doctor, has now been taken on by the BBC to do Radio 5 Live. When you look at it, the media and the spin doctors are the same. John Sergeant, Robin Oakley, both at the BBC, Michael Brunson at ITN, Michael White at the *Guardian*, could perfectly well be Government press officers, and the press officers – spin doctors – could perfectly well be journalists. They are all doing the same thing: perpetuating the idea that the Government is marvellous.

Friday 15 January, Chesterfield

To the Executive Committee where Walter Burrows said, 'I just want to raise one question. Tony spoke on Iraq, but he didn't make it clear that he was speaking for himself and not for the Chesterfield Labour Party.' Walter always has a go at me. I replied that I thought I was speaking for the Chesterfield Labour Party because the Aims and Objectives make it clear what our position is on treaties and peace; and the new Clause 4 of the Party Constitution says that the Labour Party is committed to the United Nations and democracy and peace; and the Charter of the UN says you can't use force without the authority of the Security Council. I said I'd had a couple of thousand letters – only four of them critical. But I just felt that I was on the defensive. They had a long discussion afterwards about how to revitalise the Party because only about three people turn up at ward meetings.

Saturday 16 January

I did have a very interesting phone call from Riad Al Tahir, an Iraqi businessman who said that the bombing had frightened people terribly because of the noise and the explosions, and that the hatred of Britain was now very evident – before, if you came from Britain, people were nice to you, but not now. Saddam Hussein is absolutely the super-hero of the Middle East – the new Saladin, who was the great Muslim leader at the time of the Crusades. We are going to have to pay a very heavy price for that policy in the future.

Wednesday 20 January

Paddy Ashdown has announced that he is resigning as Leader of the Liberal Party in the Commons from June. Very puzzling because nobody knew why. There were the usual rumours – were there skeletons in the cupboard? Was Blair going to make him a Cabinet Minister? Was he going to be made a Commissioner in Brussels? Or Secretary General of NATO? But with Mandelson and Ashdown both having gone within a month, the Lib-Lab project is in difficulties and the left is slowly growing in strength – very slowly, but it is.

Thursday 21 January

Melissa's partner Paul had a launch party for his book, *Face to Face: Therapy as Ethics*. Robin Cooper, who apparently is Paul's psychotherapist, made a long speech, mainly about the Philadelphia Society. Paul made a very good speech indeed and it was widely applauded. The launch party was a late Christmas present to Paul from Caroline.

Monday 25 January
I decided to draft a statement announcing that I wouldn't be standing for Parliament. I have talked about it for so long and thought I'd try and set down the arguments. Showed the draft to Caroline and, as usual, her advice was very sensible – don't gripe at New Labour, just make it clear that you're going to work in politics, but not in Parliament. But when I looked at it it frightened me a bit – I thought, 'These are the last words of a man just about to jump over the Clifton Suspension Bridge or off the top of Big Ben.' I thought, 'What do you do if you're not in Parliament?' But the reality is I can't go on. Everyone has to face this fact. We'll see, anyway. I won't announce it until I have to, and probably September would be the right time to do it. I did also include a reference to the fact that Carol had cancer and I had leukaemia, but I don't know whether that is sensible.

In the Members' Lobby later I saw Ted Heath and said, 'Oh, Ted, are you standing for Parliament in the next election?'

'Why do you ask?'

'I've got to make up my mind and, as we were elected the same year, I couldn't bear the thought that you were there and I wasn't, or I was there and you weren't. Although that same concern will not worry you so much.'

He shook with laughter and said, 'I haven't made up my mind – I'll let you know.'

After the last vote Tam Dalyell had an adjournment debate on Iraq and made a very quiet powerful speech, at the heart of which was Denis Halliday's contention that 6–7000 children under five years of age were dying every month because of the sanctions. Tony Lloyd, the Minister, replied in a speech that was so disreputable – I couldn't believe that any Labour Minister could speak like that.

Wednesday 27 January
Had a long talk to Alan Simpson about genetically modified food. He said that Monsanto was the main company and it also produced Agent Orange, which had a catastrophic effect on soldiers in Vietnam where they used it as a chemical defoliant. He gave me a copy of a memorandum Monsanto have written saying that the only group in Britain they have persuaded to support GM food were Members of Parliament – who have actually banned it in their own restaurants in the House.

Who should float by but John Major, so I said, 'You're looking very well, very happy. I think I should nominate you for one of the People's Peers.' And he said, 'Oh, I don't want that.'

I said 'You are entitled, as a former PM, to a peerage.'

He said, 'No!'

Major is such a nice guy. Dennis Skinner once said of John – when he was heard to say there were four bastards in the Cabinet – that he couldn't count!

Sunday 7 February

I rang the Save the Children Fund in Chesterfield to say I couldn't come to their service next Sunday because I don't like to be away from Caroline; the woman who is organising it was very understanding. She said her husband died of cancer ten years ago. He was seventy-seven when he died . He was a theatre organist, who rose up and down out of the floor in the cinemas in the old days.

I sent £20 for the service to put into the Save the Children Fund collection. The Duke of Devonshire and all sorts of bigwigs are going to be there in the parish church. I just can't make it, it wouldn't be fair to Caroline. I'm definitely not going to be a Member next Election.

Monday 8 February

We went to 1 Parliament Street for the unveiling of my portrait by Andrew Tift, the portrait painter. Very agreeable little ceremony. Andrew Tift and his family were there.

The BBC have been pursuing me to do something on Dickens and *Great Expectations*, which I would be happy to do, except that I don't know much about *Great Expectations* or Dickens! But they want to talk about class in the nineteenth century.

Wednesday 10 February

Caroline and I went by taxi at 11.50 to Channel 4 Headquarters in Horseferry Road for the Parliamentary Awards, organised by Channel Four and the House Magazine. Ann Widdecombe and Richard Shepherd and I sat together, and Ted Heath was there. The 'rising star' award was given to Oona King; Chris Mullin was questioner of the year; political humourist of the year was Rory Bremner, who is a great friend; peer of the year was Lord MacKay; journalist of the year, Matthew Parris; political book of the year, Ted Heath; speechmaker of the year, me; Channel 4 News award, Mo Mowlam. Caroline said what she didn't like was that she was a non-person again, just my wife. Of course when she goes to her own events, she is the star and I am the spouse.

Later at a union meeting in the House we heard the RMT deputy General Secretary, Bob Crow, a member of the Socialist Labour Party, say that on Sunday there is to be a strike of Tube workers against privatisation. The House of Commons Transport Select Committee has come out against the privatisation and what the unions want is support and MPs to back them up. Bob Crow said they may want to remove the sponsorship by the RMT of some MPs.

Friday 12 February, Chesterfield

A Mr A. came to see me who hears voices all the time – he believes he is controlled by technology and wanted me to put it right. I said, 'I can't,' And he said, 'Well, perhaps *you're* being controlled by technology.' I said, 'If I am, it doesn't worry me – you should try and forget it.' He is only thirty – obviously a deeply worried man.

Big row over genetically engineered food; the Government has come out strongly in favour of experiments into GMOs, which is really Monsanto in control of Government policy. No doubt Clinton had a word with Blair.

Sunday 14 February

To the Virgin cinema in Haymarket to see *Bulworth*, starring Warren Beatty as an old Democratic Senator who in his last primary election realised that everything he said was rubbish, and, so he switched from being an absolute deadbeat Clinton-Blairite-New Democrat to being a socialist. I must say it was marvellous – amusing and very radical indeed. We enjoyed it greatly.

Monday 15 February

At ten, three cameramen came to do an interview with a guy called Ali G., which was the most extraordinary political interview I have ever done.

He was wholly cynical and wholly ignorant. He said socialism is dead now – who wants socialism; the unemployed are just lazy; women get pregnant just to get benefit. When I mentioned the fact the miners were sacked by Margaret Thatcher, he said Thatcher was a communist, wasn't she? I said no. 'Well, she was a socialist.' It was an interview with an intelligent guy who believed everything he read in the *Sun*, hated the unions and said we should nuke Saddam Hussein. No knowledge of history at all, but it was an interesting interview – he was an intelligent guy and he had about a hundred questions.

Jack Straw made a statement on putting people with personality disorders into custody – really it was internment without trial. The argument was that these people may not have committed offences and are not classified under the Mental Health Act as being ill and treatable, so you had to have a new way of dealing with them. I nearly said – but I'm glad I didn't – that it sounded like a desperate attempt to prevent Ken Livingstone from becoming Mayor of London. Paul Boateng had written a bitter attack on Ken in the *Evening Standard*, but this evening Ken had a meeting in the Central Hall, Westminister and it was attended by 1000 people in support of his candidature. It is going to be very hard for Blair to stop him now.

Thursday 25 February

I had a meal in the Commons with Mark Marlesford. Mark was very interesting – he used to be Mark Schreiber before he was made a peer by John Major. He told me the inside story of the so-called compromise plan for the House of Lords, which led to the dismissal of Lord Cranborne as Tory leader in the Lords. Apparently the discussions had been going on for some time, possibly even since before the 1997 election, between Derry Irvine and Lord Cranborne. Ivor Richard, the leader in the Lords, was very resistant to them and perhaps that is why he was sacked. Margaret Jay became Leader after the summer. Cranborne put the idea to his colleagues in the Shadow Cabinet twice and they turned it down; then he went and negotiated it finally with Irvine. Blair and Alastair Campbell approved it, and a meeting was held of Tory peers in the House of Lords. When Hague heard about it he exploded, there was a violent row in the presence of the Tory peers and then Hague sprung it in the House of Commons on Blair. That was what Marlesford said.

Sunday 28 February

The Life and Death of Colonel Blimp was on TV – a marvellous Powell and Pressburger film made in 1943. I saw it for about the fourth time.

Monday 1 March

Clive Efford, the MP for Eltham, took me to a fundraising dinner in his constituency, held in the Tudor barn built by William Roper, Sir Thomas More's son-in-law, a beautiful building that is now a pub. Clive is the MP for Stephen Lawrence's family and he has had a hell of a job to cope with all this. He has been a councillor for fourteen years and is a taxi driver by profession. He took me to the place where Stephen Lawrence was murdered; the plaque to commemorate him was defaced over the weekend. The police had a video camera overlooking the site of the plaque, but it was a dummy camera. Clive had to protect the family, but also had to prevent the tabloids from suggesting that his whole constituency is racist, which he says it is not. He says the people who killed Stephen Lawrence were actually local thugs who had stabbed white boys in the area.

Sunday 7 March

Caroline and I sit and talk a lot of the time. We were considering what it was that made possible the great reforms of 1945. It was the Russian Revolution, which created an anti-capitalist superpower and forced the Western establishments to make concessions to the working class, and end colonialism; and then it was the Second World War, which took the working class out of their environment. There was greater equality because you had to ration food to see that the nation survived. Everybody, at home and abroad in the services, realised that if you did plan, you could produce a much better society away from profit. And even though the dominating objective was winning the war, it showed that these techniques were possible.

I am still struggling in my mind with the problems of my retirement. I had pretty well decided to go, and I realise that when I do go I will have no access to the outlets that I have as a Member of Parliament. I think the thing is to go when you are ahead, and if I was by any chance reselected and then re-elected, I would regret it because I probably wouldn't have the strength or energy, particularly if Caroline isn't with me, to do it.

Frost, the brilliant detective series, was on tonight. Caroline loves police films. I must say *Frost* and *Morse* and *Taggart* are really good.

Monday 8 March

My preoccupation at the moment is with retirement. I had a lovely talk to Alan Simpson. I asked what he thought and he said, 'Stay, because you provide a shield for us all on the left. If you weren't there, we would be more vulnerable. Also, you are a great explainer of things.' So I am torn really. I am actually in quite a state about it. John Major said, 'You must stay.' People assume I will stay but I know I can't and I am frightened really that, if I am not in Parliament and Caroline isn't here, I will go into a steep decline.

Tuesday 9 March

I was absolutely exhausted and had awful dreams. I dreamed of cats and birds glued to bits of foam rubber so that they couldn't escape.

Sheila came in; the overload of mail and phone calls led her to describe the office as a factory, which it is.

Caroline and I went to the hospital and we were there for two hours. She is making progress and was told she wouldn't need further treatment for a year. So that was marvellous.

Wednesday 10 March

My friend Bernie Wooder has named a star after Caroline and me. There are thousands and thousands of stars and an enterprising company has set up a Universal Star Register, which will name one of the unnamed stars after you – for a fee – and register it in a book that is kept at the British Library. It is a lovely gift. You get a certificate and a map of the constellations showing where your star is. So I rang Bernie to thank him. He said, 'Don't leave Parliament. You give people hope.' But I am so out of sympathy with the Government.

Thursday 11 March

Nicholas Soames, a former Tory Defence Minister, came up and said he thought we must now have a debate about the attacks on Iraq. So he and Tam joined up and he was asked to go on Channel 4 television.

I was having a cup of tea in the Tea Room and Major said, 'Have you heard that Oskar Lafontaine, the German Finance Minister, has resigned?' He had only heard two minutes ago.

I said, 'Lafontaine earned the reputation of being Red Oskar, the most dangerous man in Europe, as the *Sun* called him, because he is a Keynesian!'

I came home and I listed to the bulletins and the attacks on Oskar Lafontaine. He has paid the price for daring to challenge the Central Bank about interest rates and for saying, 'If you don't do that, we'll reflate the economy by wage increases and public expenditure.'

Sunday 14 March

Stephen rang to say that Emily has been elected by secret ballot to the School Council to represent her schoolmates, so he is as chuffed as anything.

I discovered that Budget Resolution 17 was to cut income tax. So I wrote a note to the Chief Whip saying, 'I cannot vote for the Budget Resolutions on income tax because, in the election, I argued for redistributive taxation and for money to go to the public services, which need the money now.' I just left it on the letter board for her. I feel that I have that freedom now.

I saw Ted Heath and he said in a very grumpy way, 'I see Mohamed Al Fayed has announced in the *Evening Standard* that he is doing *Any Questions?* with us. I thought we had agreed not to do it with him. He probably wants to do it to give himself credibility with us.'

I said, 'Well, he must have a low level of expectation if he thinks appearing with you and me would do any good.'

I will get onto the BBC and confirm the position, but it may be that Al Fayed himself put out that statement to the press.

I also said to Ted, 'I am so pleased John is writing his memoirs.'

He said, 'What has he got to say?'

I said, 'Well, I think if you have held high office, you have an obligation to the future to describe what you did.' Ted grunted.

John by contrast is so happy . There is no doubt that this realignment is producing a greater sense of agreement among people who are straightforward.

The whole European Commission has resigned because the Five Wise Men have exposed such sleaze, corruption and cronyism that they felt they had no alternative. It gives me an opportunity to write to the Prime Minister demanding that the new British Commissioners should be interviewed by a House of Commons Select Committee and approved by the House before they are appointed, and to try and get some accountability back that way.

Tuesday 16 March

Went into the House at 2.30 and asked a question of the Foreign Office about Iraq. David Winnick said that bombing wouldn't get rid of Saddam. Menzies Campbell said it was wrong to bomb installations. Nicholas Soames got in. So there is a bit of a mood building up.

At 3.30 the Prime Minister made a statement on the European Commission. I was called fairly low down the list, and I asked whether he would allow the House of Commons to elect the Commissioners. He turned that down.

Later John Major came up and said, 'I heard your question to the Prime Minister. Let's make a little bit of mischief and put down an Early Day Motion together.'

I said, 'By all means, yes.'

He said, 'I'll get six Tory MPs' and I said I would get six Labour MPs.

Wednesday 17 March

I came into the House. There was a gathering round the statue of George V, facing Old Palace Yard, of the Alliance for Regional Aid, covering the steel, coal and textile areas including all the Coalfield Community people. The meeting was addressed by Stephen Byers, the Secretary of State for Trade and Industry. It was absolute crap. He said, 'We are considering, discussing, hoping, planning, thinking, the Commission are doing everything . . .' Of course the Commission doesn't exist any more.

At four, I went to the Members' Dining Room where Stephen had organised a reception to launch a book, published by the Royal Society for Chemistry, called *The Age of the Molecule.*

A professor of chemistry began by saying, 'This book is completely non-political, doesn't deal with issues about genetically modified food or pollution. It is written by people who are at the cutting edge of chemistry and, to make it readable, we had it edited by a science editor.'

So I went up to him afterwards and said, 'Supposing I had made a speech to a lot of scientists about my work and said, "I must tell you that my book is completely non-scientific. It doesn't deal with any of the main problems facing society but it does get contributions from the cutting edge of Parliament – that is to say, the ones who are climbing up the ladder and in order to make it readable, I got the editor of the *Sun* to edit it." ' He laughed in an embarrassed sort of way. I said, 'When you say a thing is non-political, it is an insult to my profession just as when I say it is non-scientific, it is an insult to yours.' Scientists will do almost anything rather than get involved in the affairs of society.

At 3.30 William Hague asked the Prime Minister if he agreed that Commissioners should be elected by the House of Commons. I was frightfully chuffed. I wish I could have the same success in the Labour Party!

Thursday 18 March, Chesterfield

David Blunkett was visiting a school in Chesterfield today, so I was up at 5.30 and went up on the train. Had a talk to Margaret Vallins about what I should do about Parliament, and she said, 'Why do you have to decide now? Leave it until the last minute and make a decision then.' I am not going to agonise about it any more.

Went to the new Brimington Junior School. It is a marvellous bungalow building around a courtyard with rocks and fountains, and there is a mound outside that can turn into an amphitheatre for performances. The old school was a Victorian building in an old street, terribly cramped.

David Blunkett arrived with I think, his private secretary, and his dog Lucy. David marched in and the children sang and some played violins. He made a lovely speech in which he paid tribute to Hilary and to me. It was all very good-natured. Then he unveiled the plaque and there were lots of photographs.

Friday 19 March

NATO has ordered the peace monitors out of Serbia and Kosovo and there is no doubt they are just about to bomb Serbia. It is all about the credibility of NATO; it is quite illegal, they will kill a lot of people and I think it will precipitate the most frightful crisis.

Tuesday 23 March

I went into the House of Commons and at 3.30 the Prime Minister made a statement, in effect announcing that NATO would be bombing Yugoslavia. Blair said it would take 100,000 troops to invade Yugoslavia, and that wasn't on the cards.

I bought a lovely toy for Hannah. A jumping tiger, which you press and it jumps up and down and talks. It is simply heavenly.

Wednesday 24 March

I went to the Commons in the afternoon and took the cuddly toy tiger with me. I took it to the Whips' Office and said, 'This is a model mascot for New Labour' and I took it to the Library and the Campaign Group.

The bombing began today and I told the whips that I felt so strongly – and I thumped my heart – that I would not allow a three-line whip, or any whip, to interfere with me. Tommy McAvoy, the Deputy Chief Whip, seemed to accept that.

Did *Newsnight*, *News 24*, BBC World Television, Breakfast Television, BBC World Radio and finished with Radio 5 Live.

Got home absolutely exhausted. But since the Government is reluctant to put up Ministers and I am one of the very few people opposed to the war, I got the opportunity of doing a lot of broadcasts.

Thursday 25 March

I went to the Commons through a terrible traffic jam and got there in time for the debate on Serbia, opened by Robin Cook. Cook and George Robertson just repeated the standard routine; no depth of understanding of any kind by either of them. But several MPs, including Alan Clark, came out against the war. On our side, Harry Barnes regretted it, but said it was necessary and so did Harry Cohen. Ken Livingstone was gung-ho and said Milošević was a fascist and had to be dealt with. Alice Mahon and George Galloway made good speeches. I spoke for eighteen minutes – longer than a speech should last. The *Daily Express* correspondent came up afterwards and said how much he had enjoyed it, and so did Edward Leigh, a very right-wing Tory MP, who said, 'I agree with everything you say now.'

Something is happening in politics. I think that with the class analysis, the socialist analysis, virtually eliminated now from politics, it has all just become individuals putting their case.

Then I walked over to Number 10 with Alice Mahon and Jeremy Corbyn, with a letter about the situation in Yugoslavia. The Serbs who were waiting outside were so affectionate. So many Serb women came over and gave me hugs, with tears in their eyes, because their country is being attacked and they were so grateful because they had seen me on *Newsnight* and other programmes.

Saturday 27 March

I had a call from a man in Belfast whose wife was Serbian; she came to the phone and burst into tears because the Americans had bombed her sister's house, and her sister was so traumatised that she couldn't speak for an hour, and there are two little children there – could I get them refugee status? I said I would try.

At 1.30 we went to Hannah's house for her birthday and I gave her the jumping tiger Tygger, made in China, I might add.

Monday 29 March

I had a chat to Stephen, who said I must not be a George Lansbury – i.e. 'Hawking my conscience from Conference to Conference' – which was the phrase used by Ernie Bevin when he got rid of George Lansbury as Leader of the Labour Party.

Friday 2 April, Stansgate

The grandchildren played violent computer games with lots of shooting, and so on. Looking at these little children with buttons that can kill people confirmed the validity of the argument I used on Iraq last year, that many young people think war is just a computer game.

I had a phone call from a Dr Harvey, a sixty-two-year-old GP who has been visiting Barry Horne who is on hunger strike in prison. Horne has got an eighteen-year sentence, allegedly for arson against an animal-experimentation centre. Harvey said Horne was on his fourth hunger strike and, without breaching medical confidentiality, it was clear he was going to die, and would I send a message to him.

I said, 'Well, it is very difficult to send a message that would be meaningful.'

Anyway, between us, we negotiated a message and I rang the prison hospital where Horne is. And the message I gave was: 'I greatly value what you have done and want you to live to help advance the cause we share. Tony Benn.'

I think he probably will kill himself and that was the impression the doctor gave.

The news from Yugoslavia is tragic. There is a massive humanitarian catastrophe which the Red Cross can't cope with and neither can the UN High Commission for Refugees. Macedonia won't take any more refugees. It is alleged that there has been a coup in Montenegro, and a pro-Milošević general has been charged. But according to a Yugoslav whom I spoke to on the phone tonight, the Americans have now appointed somebody to replace Rugova to represent the Albanians.

Saturday 10 April

Today was the day that the Heritage Lottery Fund people came to visit Stansgate to look at my archives: Anne Summers from the British Library, Tim Wheatley, Stephen Green, Mike Smethurst.

We walked round and looked at all the papers. I thought they were singularly unimpressed. I am not suggesting they should be over the moon, but they might have said it was interesting. Not at all. We came back to the house and Caroline had produced a fabulous lunch, which she was working at for hours.

Afterwards we talked for a bit. They put all sorts of things, such as the question of 'additionality' i.e. why should the British Library receive extra funds for the archives? They raised questions about 'the balance of the archives' between old and new material, how much of it was less than twenty years old, etc. Ann Summers was extremely good at putting the Library's case.

I washed up and and put the examples we had prepared for them away. Caroline was just exhausted.

Sunday 11 April

Demonstration in Trafalgar Square against the war in Yugoslavia. The line-up on the platform was dazzling: Tam Dalyell, John Pilger, Bruce Kent, Alice Mahon, David Wright who is Chairman of CND, and Mark Steel, the *Guardian* columnist. John Randall, the Tory MP, spoke. Alice Mahon spoke. Carol Turner had organised it all. While I was speaking, I was so tired and I wasn't absolutely sure I wasn't going to fall down. I had a pain in my left side and I did wonder whether I was going to collapse, but I managed it all right. Had a sip of cold tea in the car and drove home. There were between 10,000 and 15,000 people there, with representatives of three political parties and a message from Rowan Williams, the Archbishop of Wales. The BBC News at six never mentioned it. I am sure Alastair Campbell just rings up John Birt and says, 'We don't want any news of demonstrations against war', whereas on every bulletin there is George Robertson or Tony Blair or Robin Cook yattering away; pictures of refugees – a little girl of two looking very plaintive and lost.

I rang the BBC News Editor to speak to her about it but she was in the studio and she hasn't yet rung back. I will register my protest and leave it at that.

Yesterday, when Caroline and I were talking at Stansgate, she said that she saw death as a great adventure. She said, 'I am not afraid of pain because they can deal with it. It is a big adventure that lies ahead of us.' I thought that was very bold and positive. She and I have agreed a gravestone that is going to be prepared for both of us, in black marble at an angle by the pond at Stansgate, and we are going to have a bench where the kids can sit. Our ashes will be put under the gravestone. So having collected a thousand or more boxes with all our writings and papers, there will be one last box where we go ourselves.

Monday 12 April

Blair has said that those who are opposing the war are appeasers.

I caught the train to Chesterfield and slept and read the papers on the way. *The Independent*, *The Times* and the *Financial Times* and, of course, the *Morning Star* had photographs of the rally, but not one word in the *Guardian*. It is permanently on-message from Millbank Tower. Still, it doesn't matter.

Wednesday 14 April

A NATO plane appears to have bombed an ethnic Albanian refugee column and killed forty or fifty people.

Went to the Commons in the afternoon and we had the Campaign Group entirely devoted to Kosovo. John McDonnell is an excellent Chairman and everybody wants to hang together. Harold Best began the discussion, very firm on all this and saying that good Samaritans came in early. I said I thought it would be a long war, with depleted uranium being used; Russia might come in and NATO might split; the choice really was a peace settlement or a Vietnam War. I talked about the refugees and said the British media were terrible. Harry Barnes, who favours the war, gave a long convoluted story about being in a better position to criticise the Government because he supported the war. He is a very muddled man. Audrey Wise was concerned. She said she didn't believe in the sovereignty of nations; you had to care for refugees, but at the same time she felt we should have limited objectives, oppose the use of cluster bombs and call for no depleted-uranium bullets.

Ann Cryer was more doubtful. Lynne Jones said her view was known which, I think, is in favour of the bombing.

It was rather strange, but a useful discussion and the Campaign Group is divided on that, and on Europe.

Friday 16 April

Who should be on the train but Alice Mahon, and I had a lovely talk to her all the way to London. She is a very imaginative and able Member of Parliament. The *Daily Mirror* has arranged for her to go to Belgrade for the weekend with an interpreter and a journalist, and when she takes part in the debate on Monday, she will be able to give some account of the damage done in Belgrade. That will be a powerful contribution. She has been in Parliament since 1987. She is really formidable and much underrated.

Monday 19 April

The debate on Kosovo began at 3.30. Cook made a speech that I thought was odious, just repeating the insults to Milošević personally and the war-crimes question. Menzies Campbell said he agreed with me that the House should have a vote on it. Alan Clark denounced the Government and so did Peter Tapsell. Roger Gale intervened and said, 'If we are not at war, how can there be war criminals?' The general impression I got was that the tide was turning. Alice Mahon made a marvellous speech. So did George Galloway.

Tess Kingham, whom I like very much, came out in favour of the bombing. I heard later that she is a gypsy, her parents were gypsies; and were hounded all over Europe. She is a very nice woman.

The vote fell in the end, because of the whips' tactics, but we made the point. I think it is most important for Parliament to reflect the anxieties that exist on all sides of the House.

The atmosphere in the House is quite serious.

Thursday 22 April

I had an interview with a Yugoslav writer, and at the end I made some reference to Crown Prince Paul who, in 1941, offered to do a deal with Hitler. She said, 'He was absolutely right. It would have saved our country. You see, I am Jewish.' She is violently anti-socialist, a Yugoslav monarchist. For a Jew to advocate a deal with Hitler that would have saved the Jews – and indeed Yugoslavia – from Nazi bombing was shattering.

The Heritage Lottery Fund board has turned down the archive project flat and said it was for the British Library to do; it would have nothing to do with it. This process all began in 1993 and the whole thing has come to nothing. It is terribly disappointing, but in a funny way a relief.

Friday 23 April

NATO have attacked not only Milošević's residence – like bombing 10 Downing Street – in the grounds of which Tito's body is buried, but also the headquarters of the Socialist Party and a television station. Apparently two people died. The attack on the TV station has really stirred up the media.

Monday 26 April

Went to the Commons and Blair made a very hawkish statement. Tam Dalyell said he was absolutely appalled that the Prime Minister was so hawkish. The questions were critical, but Blair is just on a high at the moment; you can't get anywhere near him.

There was a nail bomb in Brick Lane. And today Jill Dando was murdered, shot in the head, outside her house in Fulham. She was a terribly popular TV presenter. Who did it, I don't know, though apparently a well-dressed, dark-haired man was seen running away from the scene.

There was a bomb in Moscow today. There are repercussions from a school massacre in America.

Meanwhile, the Americans say that British technology isn't really good enough for the war, and RAF Harriers have been written off as being less technologically effective than the Americans' planes; so they have carried out 70 per cent of the air strikes themselves and ours have been held back by bad weather.

Wednesday 28 April

I went into the Commons for Prime Minister's Questions and, much to my surprise, I was called by the Speaker. So, in view of further accidental bombings of civilians in Belgrade, I asked, 'Is the Prime Minister aware that, although the House and the whole world is united in opposition to the cleansing and brutality by Milošević in Kosovo, the indiscriminate destruction of the infrastructure in Yugoslavia and the killing of innocent citizens, many of whom have long been opposed to President Milošević, does nothing in the short run to help the refugees? And that in the view of many people, including me, that destruction and killing amount to a war crime in themselves.' The whole House was absolutely frozen with horror. Blair gave a long reply about the number of people who had been murdered and killed and raped, and so on. I felt it had to be said.

Thursday 29 April

I went to the meeting of the Trade Union Group of Labour MPs, with John Monks talking about fairness at work, and listened to this middle-aged man in a sharp suit talking about trade unionism and saying, 'We have made a bit of progress, but there are some people in the CBI who might possibly be trying to reverse it, and we hope that you who have done so much to help will continue. Of course, we take the view that it would be better if both sides of industry, the social partners, negotiated these things in advance.'

There was no sense or awareness that there was any conflict or contradiction of economic interest between the owners of industry and the workers in industry. And that abandonment reminded me, in a strange way, of photographs of Victorian trade union leaders in their suits and gold watches trying to look respectable.

Friday 30 April

I discovered today that last night at eleven on Channel 4 they broadcast my interview with this guy Ali G, who had claimed to be speaking for young people; the whole thing was a complete hoax, but I treated him reasonably respectfully and I gather from one or two people that it was all right. But it was a fraud to write and say you want to do an interview about young people and politics, then bring this chap along who is an actor and makes you look a proper charlie.

I went to Swindon for *Any Questions?* I heard on the news that there had been a big bomb in the gay pub *The Admiral Duncan* in Soho and it is thought to be the same perpetrator responsible for Brick Lane and Brixton, so this is getting quite serious.

Nick Clarke was in the chair and on the panel were Ted Heath, Max Hastings of the *Evening Standard* and Roger Scruton, a very right-wing philosopher who taught my nephew, Piers. I had guessed most of the questions except one about the monarchy and one about our greatest achievements.

I was driven home and at midnight, it being the full moon, Caroline went into the garden and planted half a potato, keeping the other half in order to cure the little wart on her face. For someone who is so academic and so scholarly to have such faith in what is really witchcraft is amazing, but last time she did it, it worked.

Sunday 2 May, Chesterfield
Walked over to the Club and watched Rory Bremner. There were a couple of drunks in the Club and they kept talking to me while I was trying to watch it. There weren't many people there, and it's not the old Labour Club of years ago when people talked about politics.

Monday 3 May
The bombing of Serbia continues; the electricity supply and the water supply have been hit and Serbia is just being destroyed before our very eyes. Blair is fanatical and obsessive, Cook is so pompous, and Robertson is just an automaton repeating insults to Milošević all the time. I can't believe it is happening.

I had a talk to Caroline about when I will go, and she wants me to say I am giving up Parliament to spend more time on politics.

Wednesday 5 May
Voted at ten on the third reading of the Greater London Authority Bill. Just as I was going in to vote, Nicholas Soames, a former Defence Secretary, came up and said, 'Tony, just to let you know, last night I had dinner with George Bush [the former American President], and the journalist with *Newsweek*, who has just interviewed Milošević in Belgrade. It is clear that there is no question of the Serbs giving way.'

So I said to Soames, 'Well, that means troops will have to go in, but the Americans won't have it.'

He said, 'Well, that is their problem.' He is very sympathetic towards me on all this.

Thursday 6 May, Chesterfield
The day of the Scottish parliamentary elections, the Welsh Assembly elections and local-government elections. Really a turning point in British politics.

Caught the 7.30 train and slept part of the way to Chesterfield. I had a list of all the Labour local-council candidates and I telephoned all forty-five of them and left messages where I could.

In the afternoon Bob Pont drove me round with the loudspeaker and I was doing the announcements. 'Today is polling day. Vote early. Vote Labour.' I got so sleepy, I began saying, 'This is Tony Benn, the Labour candidate,' so he took the microphone away from me.

Friday 7 May
We lost nine council seats – eight in my constituency – all to the Liberals. I rang the defeated candidates, who all agreed that the Liberal vote hadn't really increased, but that the Labour vote had collapsed. Blair is destroying what he calls Old Labour by taking away their motivation to

vote. In Scotland there is a hung Parliament, so there will be a coalition with the Liberals. Dennis Canavan was elected as an independent. In Wales it was a hung Assembly and there will be a coalition there. And Blair is absolutely thrilled. He must be the first Party Leader we have ever had who doesn't want Labour to win. I think that is permeating through to people.

I was so thrilled about Dennis Canavan that I wrote a letter to the Chief Whip and copied it to the Prime Minister, and to Clive Soley, the Secretary of the Labour Party, calling for the restoration of his whip. I cited S. O. Davies from Merthyr Tydfil, who was de-selected in 1970, stood as an independent, was re-elected, came back to Parliament and got the Labour whip back. I also said that if you can work with the Liberals, you can work with Dennis Canavan.

My new battery-operated letter opener arrived. The last two have broken.

The new Scottish and Welsh Parliaments do detract considerably from the House of Commons.

My brother Dave was at Chatham House yesterday and everyone on the platform – generals and diplomats – was against the war. I think the opposition to war is growing strongly and Clinton simply can't get the Senate to organise an army to go there. So I think Clinton will betray Blair and leave him as the one squawking hawk with no troops, because Blair hasn't got enough of an army to do any damage to anybody; hardly enough to capture the Channel Isles, I would think.

Saturday 8 May

A bomb landed on the Chinese Embassy in Belgrade, killing three and injuring twenty. That has created a completely new situation. The Chinese Government has issued a statement saying it is a war crime and violent barbarism. The UN Security Council was meeting in an emergency session last night. Of course Robin Cook said this was regrettable. The Russian Minister announced that he would not come to London. So all of a sudden, with all the other examples of error, the situation is absolutely critical.

Got a taxi to the Embankment where there was an enormous crowd gathering. I estimated between 25,000 and 30,000 people were on the march to Hyde Park. The Serbs are awfully friendly and all the women come and give you a kiss on both cheeks and some of the men do too, and you feel a very warm feeling. Altogether it was a good meeting and, despite the rain, people stuck it out.

Monday 10 May

I got up at 4.45. I heard on the news that Derek Fatchett, Minister of State at the Foreign Office, died last night.

Did an interview, and in the cab coming home I asked the cab driver what he did before he became a cab driver and he said, 'I worked with ladies of the night.'

I said, 'What do you mean.'

He said, 'I worked for prostitutes, varying from twenty to fifty years old. I used to sit with them in a car until a message came through, then I would drive them to a hotel and one of them would go in. She would get two hundred pounds, of which her pimp or organiser got thirty pounds and I got thirty pounds. And I would wait for her to come back to the car again. Sometimes we would have five a night, from ten o'clock until 5 am. The women who did it were mainly in debt and sometimes earning a thousand pounds a night, five nights a week. They often got into the habit of big spending and usually got into debt again. But most of them left the profession.'

I asked if they were attacked. He said, 'No, not really; of course in a hotel, you knew the room number and you would know who it was.' He spoke of them with some affection and said he had kept in touch with two of them. 'Of course, quite well-known people used the prostitutes and we knew who they were – but I am never going to write a book.' It gave me an insight into the system.

I thought about Hilary being considered for the by-election which will be created in Leeds. Hilary has a very strong claim for consideration.

At 3.30 we had the statement that lasted until 4.15. Then Tam Dalyell, Alice Mahon, Carol Turner and George Galloway and I got in a taxi and went to the Chinese Embassy. The Chinese were very courteous. Alice made the opening statement and said, 'We want to extend our condolences for the loss of lives in the Chinese Embassy that was bombed.'

The Chinese Minister said, 'The Chinese regard it as a barbaric act, and the war was an act of aggression and must be stopped.'

I spoke next and I said, 'I repeat what has been said, because I know China and have very great admiration for your ancient civilisations,' and so on. 'But I do think that now you have a unique opportunity of influencing the outcome.' Apparently, the Chinese have said they will not support any peace arrangement that doesn't include as a pre-condition the ending of the bombing. They were courteous.

After the Kosovo statement, Tam Dalyell raised with the Speaker the right of Parliament to decide anything. I added that there is a crisis in the House of Commons now, which has no rights in questions of war.

As the Speaker left the chair, she said, 'Come into the little room behind the Chair' – a room used for 'the usual channels' – and we had a word with her. She said, 'Don't press me, don't press me. I have got to be absolutely impartial.'

I said, 'You are, you are fine. But this is a parliamentary issue.'

She said, 'Well, I am seeing the Leader of the House at the end of the week, leave it with me.'

So I thought I would draft a Humble Address to Her Majesty praying that the Royal Prerogative of war-making be transferred to the House of Commons. I spoke to Menzies Campbell, the Liberal Democrats' Defence spokesman, and he said he would look at that; if I could get some heavyweights, I think we might make some progress, because it is a scandal that the House of Commons has no powers in these situations.

Today my brother Dave became a grandfather for the first time: Frances and Michael Nestor had a boy. So that is lovely

Wednesday 12 May
The Government is boxed into a corner. The air bombardment isn't working. The Americans won't use ground troops and the UN diplomatic option using the Russians seems to have collapsed; so they are totally in a corner.

Thursday 13 May
I drafted the Humble Address to Her Majesty praying that the Royal Prerogative of war-making be transferred to the Commons, to allow us to vote on the war. Then I wrote to a number of Privy Councillors asking if they would support it.

At the House of Commons there was a meeting with foundry workers from Derbyshire whose firm had gone bust. They had no redundancy pay and no Job Seekers' Allowance.

Friday 14 May
Scotland has gone in for a coalition with the Liberals. So whereas Dennis Canavan, the Labour Member, was thrown off the list as unsuitable, Jim Wallace, the Scottish Liberal leader, is Deputy First Minister in the Scottish Parliament. I think the impact of this on the Labour Party in London is going to be tremendous. The Liberals don't like it because they feel they have been captured by Labour. Labour don't like it because it is clear that New Labour would rather work with the Liberals than with the Labour Party.

Monday 17 May
I lay on the chair in my room at the Commons, my mother's old Parker-Knoll. Tonight is the big rebellion by seventy Labour MPs against cuts in incapacity benefit as part of the Welfare Reform Bill. I woke up at about 3 a.m. and thought to myself, 'What am I doing? I am the last surviving Member of the post-war Labour Government that introduced the Welfare State on the basis of universal benefits, and here I am being kept up by the whips at night to dismantle the fucking thing. What am I doing?

Why am I here?' I was so angry, and I went and said that to one or two people. Barry Jones, whom I like very much, said, 'Well, put that in your diary,' so I have done.

We had votes and filibustering by the Tories. I left the House at about five, when it was already light, and got to bed at 5.30.

Tuesday 18 May

Today George Robertson made the worst speech I think I have ever heard in my life from a serious Minister, comparing the bombing of Yugoslavia with the Berlin airlift. But the tide of opinion is shifting strongly in our favour, in the sense that nobody now thinks it is going to work without ground troops. The Americans won't have it, the Germans won't, the Italians won't, the French and the Dutch. So it is all crumbling before our eyes.

Wednesday 19 May

I talked to Barry Jones and Stuart Bell, both of whom are on the right of the party, and we were saying how awful the New Labour MPs were.

Thursday 20 May

We came to the Welfare Reform Bill and we had expected forty-seven to vote with us, but we got sixty-five Labour MPs voting against the Government, another thirty-nine abstaining; the Government won by 310 to 270. So it was a triumph.

Saturday 22 May

Hilary phoned to say he had been shortlisted for Leeds. I must say, I think Hilary has got a reasonable chance. The selection conference is on Monday.

Monday 24 May

The only news worth recording – and it absorbed the whole day – is that Hilary was selected as the Labour candidate for Leeds Central, one of the safest seats in Britain. The dear old boy on the first ballot was ahead by 63 to 57 against Maggie, the chair of the local party. On the second ballot, it went up to 80 to 70. He rang to say he got it and we just screamed. Caroline's stomach has been churning all day. I think it is one of the worst weekends I have had, because I wanted it so much and the uncertainty was so great, but he pulled it off, bless his heart.

So the rest of the evening was spent just ringing up the family and talking about it. Sally and the children had mixed feelings. If ever anyone deserves it, it is Hilary. He joined the Labour Party in 1971, was elected a councillor soon after his first wife Rosalind died in 1979, was Deputy Leader of Ealing Council, has worked for MSF for nearly twenty-five years as Head of Research, was appointed as Blunkett's adviser on lifelong education two years ago and as Chairman of 'Unions 21', which brings him together with all the union people.

At the end of May Caroline and I went back to Cincinnati, her home town, to celebrate our golden wedding with her American family and friends. Stephen and Nita, and their two children, Emily and Daniel, were there too. We visited her old home, and the Church of the Advent where we were married, but which was boarded up.

We discovered very interesting aspects of American society; one friend of Caroline's said that Congress was 'completely bought' by corporate business and therefore Congressmen didn't speak on some of the big environmental issues that were worrying Europe, such as genetically modified food and the use of depleted uranium.

While I was there I had breakfast with the World Affairs Council in Cincinnati and met an old friend, Jack Gilligan, who had been Democratic Governor of Ohio. He told me that the prison population had grown tenfold in fifteen years, and that 40 per cent of prisoners were black.

Meanwhile, Hilary was busy in Leeds campaigning in the by-election to be held on 10 June. We arrived back in London on 7 June.

Tuesday 8 June
John Major wrote to me today saying he couldn't sign my motion on a debate on the Royal Prerogative of war-making, in the House of Commons, but adding a note: 'The House of Commons is becoming a family affair. You must be thrilled about Hilary', which was very sweet of him.

Wednesday 9 June
Caroline and I got up very early and went by taxi to King's Cross, and got to Leeds at 11.30 for the eve-of-poll campaigning. We were met by local MPs, Kevin Barron, Gerry Sutcliffe, Laurie Quinn and by Hilary.

Caroline was taken to the Queen's Hotel, Room 504, which reminded me of that old wartime song:

> 'In Room five-hundred-and-four
> I didn't stop to ask a price,
> That kind of thrill don't happen twice,
> Not even if you're in paradise,
> Room five-hundred-and-four,
> I turned the key in the door . . .'

Anyway, I went off with Hilary. It was all laid on to the last detail, every minute of the day. We went to Benn's furniture store (no relation!), where Mr McBride sat us on the sofa and described his wonderful products. We went to a sports and social club for a lovely gathering; it was

Old Labour to a T. Maggie, the chair of the local party whom Hilary had defeated at the selection conference, was very generous and, after talking to people, she called us to order. Tomorrow the old boy must surely be an MP.

Thursday 10 June

Came home and had a word with Hilary, who is very worried that the turnout could be the lowest ever in a by-election. He asked what he should say in his speech at the count. I said, 'Look, first of all you must mention Derek Fatchett – not to use that as an excuse for the turnout, but to say the constituency is still stung by the death of its previous Member. Secondly, you must say that a lower turnout is bad for democracy.' He had wanted to say it was 'bad for all parties', but it is not for him to speak for other parties. I said, 'Say "Labour has done well, but we have got to do more." ' I think he will take that.

Well, we got the result at about 12.25.

So this day Thursday, 10 June 1999, ends as Hilary Benn becomes the MP for Leeds Central.

Saturday 12 June

Our golden wedding party in the Churchill Room at the Commons; I gave Archie, Barbara's son, my video camera and asked him to film it.

It was a lovely party, just lovely. The children played like anything and the video became increasingly of the children filming each other. At the end, I took a group into the Chamber of the House. The Doorkeeper opened it specially for us and shut it behind us, so we turned the House of Commons Chamber into a sort of children's playground. We rehearsed Hilary taking his seat. Jonathan made a passionate speech against genetically modified food, first from the Opposition Despatch Box and then from the Prime Minister's Despatch Box. Carrie sat in the Speaker's chair and acted the part, and I managed to get a picture of Archie. It was just such fun.

Caroline and I were totally exhausted, but it was a lovely day, ahead of the exact date next week. Caroline made a marvellous speech.

Monday 14 June

At one we all had lunch in the Strangers' Dining Room – Caroline and I and Kevin Barron, Laurie Quinn and Phil Hope – and later we went for a photo-call with all the Yorkshire MPs. Kevin Barron is looking after Hilary and he doesn't need his daddy there at all.

Stephen, Josh and Melissa arrived and I took them up to the Strangers' Gallery. The House was crowded. Of course the Tories are absolutely cock-a-hoop about the European election results. They have done brilliantly.

At about 4.15 the Speaker said, 'Members desirous of taking their seats will now come to the Table.' So in a very ragged way Kevin, Hilary and I walked into the Chamber, bowed, walked five paces, bowed, walked five paces and went to the Table; and there was a thunder of cheers from the Labour benches. It was too much for me. I felt my face crumbling and I walked back to my seat. And when Hilary took the Oath, then signed the Nominal Roll and walked past the Front Bench, with people patting him on the back, to shake hands with the Speaker, I just burst into tears. I didn't want to take out my handkerchief, but I was overwhelmed by it. It was heavenly. I was so proud, absolutely as proud as can be.

Then we went and had a cup of tea on the Terrace. I can't count the number of people who came up. Many of them I didn't know, but Hilary is very, very highly respected, a modest guy.

In the Lobby Peter Mandelson went up to congratulate him, and I felt I really ought to keep away, because although people congratulated me too, it was nothing to do with me. I was just so proud.

I think politically it was the most exciting day since I took my seat in 1963 after the peerage battle.

But I did feel very strongly – even more than before – that this is the time to go. You can't have two Benns competing for the attention of the House. I remember my dad saying to me when I was in Parliament, 'I am fed up with people saying to me, "I heard your son speak, your son this and that." ' I know what he meant. He was joking, but it is real.

All the staff were so friendly. They really were so nice – the Badge Messengers, the cleaners, the cafeteria staff.

Tuesday 15 June

At 10.30 William Rees-Mogg came to have a talk; he was the Editor of *The Times*, and is now a businessman. I couldn't quite make out why he had come, so we talked in a jolly way for an hour about everything. He was very candid about Hague. He said he thought Hague wasn't as right-wing as he makes out; he's a sort of mainstream Tory. He thinks Blair is an authoritarian of the worst kind. I was very candid with him because I have known him for so long.

In effect, what he had come to tell me was that he agreed strongly with the line I had taken on the war against Serbia over Kosovo, and he agreed with me entirely about Europe. We discussed the nature of politics and he said there would have to be a party representing labour interests and it will reappear. He was very hostile to the pro-European Tories, the Heseltine–Clarke Tories, and they, of course, have been ruined by two things – the massive defeat of the Tory pro-Europe party and the success of the UK Independence Party.

The 'dangerous old Benn' had disappeared. I asked about Rupert Murdoch who, Rees-Mogg said, was very relaxed. He let *The Times* run itself, and was mainly interested in the tabloids.

It all helps me to plan a life beyond those magic words 'MP'. I was so tired that I dozed in my room, and Hilary was in and out because he is using my office. Then there was a vote at midnight and I took Hilary home.

Wednesday 16 June

Blair had a very bad Prime Minister's Questions. There are rumours now that Mandelson is going to be brought in to replace Beckett. If that happened, there would be one hell of a row.

There was a little note from Caroline in the fridge saying, 'I have got my tipple' – a glass of water with a little lemon in it – and 'Happy anniversary'. And at one minute past twelve, it was by then our golden wedding.

Monday 21 June

I heard from one of the policeman at the Commons, who lives in police quarters in Ladbroke Road just behind our house, that his quarters were to be privatised by the Metropolitan Police and their two-bedroom flat would be offered to him to buy, but he can't possibly afford £190,000. So in effect he is being evicted by the Met as a result of privatisation.

Wednesday 23 June

I got seats for Hilary's secretary, and Sal and three of the children – Michael, Jonathan and Carrie – in the Gallery, and Hilary made his Maiden Speech at about five. It was a triumph. I sat just in front of him, looking up and watching him, and he towered over the House. He was confident, clear, with a touch of humour, very sincere about Fatchett and very strong about Leeds Central and its problems. Though I say it myself, it was one of the best Maiden Speeches I have heard in the House. There was a mass of praise afterwards. Robert MacLennan said it was a marvellous speech, Patrick Cormack said, 'The House is united on one thing – the brilliance of the speech made by the Member for Leeds Central.' Jack Straw had listened to the speech and smiled at me.

I just cried.

Friday 25 June, Chesterfield

I had a talk to Tom and Margaret Vallins. I said, 'Look, I have now got to decide quite quickly what I am going to do about standing again.'

Well, they said, 'Tony, there is a big campaign to get rid of you in Chesterfield. It is not personal, but it is all these people who want the seat. We are not at all sure we could get you re-selected. Anyway, we could not bear the thought that you were defeated as a result of not being re-selected.' So that really settled it.

Saturday 26 June

I drafted the statement giving my reasons why I was leaving Parliament at the next election. Caroline cut it down to a tiny fraction of what it was and made it clearer.

Sunday 27 June

I sat down and wrote three pages for the Neill Committee on Standards in Public Life to which I am giving evidence tomorrow. I should have put the papers in days ago.

I think it may be that I have established the idea that this is not a retirement, but a new stage in my life and in my political work, so I am very happy.

Monday 28 June

I got up at about six and bought all the papers, and there was blanket coverage of the statement I made yesterday. Sunday was obviously a quiet news day – apart from Northern Ireland – and the political correspondents had read their cuttings and wrote all these 'obituaries', with pictures of the family and of me, and so on.

I did six broadcasts and then went off to the Royal United Service Institution in Whitehall to give evidence to the Committee on Standards in Public Life. A notice said: 'No photography, no recording', but there was a television camera there. So I said to Lord Neill (I had actually asked in advance), 'Do you mind if, as an archivist, I video-record this session?' He said, 'Not at all.' So I put my camera on the table and videoed the panel. I was asked a lot of questions about corruption, and I tried to make a point about the purchase of political parties, rather than individual rotten apples, and I emphasised the register of Members' interests, disclosure, disqualification, criminality and impropriety. It is a subject I have thought about very carefully – I do know all about it and I felt it was quite good.

When I went into the Whips' Office to get permission to come home tonight, Tommy McAvoy said, 'What are you doing now? Fighting the Government somewhere else?'

I said, 'No, Tommy, but when we stayed up all night in order to impose a means test, it did tip me over.' They laughed a bit and they are a bit uneasy.

Knowing that I don't have to go before the electors again, I don't have that sort of built-in monitor which says, 'Should you say that? Might it upset people?' For example, I was thinking about the legalisation of cannabis and, in my heart of hearts, I have always thought that the law should be relaxed, but I didn't want to alienate people. So there is a freedom from electoral accountability.

Also, I smoke my pipe everywhere now. I went to the BBC, which is strictly non-smoking, and I just smoked. The staff of the House are extremely friendly.

Thursday 1 July

At 8 a.m. a nice woman called Nicci Gerrard from the *Observer* arrived to do an interview. She lives in Suffolk and had to get up at 5.15, caught the train to Liverpool Street and cycled here from Liverpool Street. She has got four children, from eleven down to about five. She was a very sympathetic woman and I liked her enormously. Because she was so sympathetic, I probably said more than I should have done. I think she understood what I was saying.

Just as she was leaving, there was a knock at the door and and there was a lady who said, 'I am the photographer.' I asked her name and she said, 'I am Jane Bown.' Now Jane Bown is one of the most famous photographers in Britain. She is three weeks older than me, born in March 1925. This lady with her little cameras came with no fuss. I sat in the front garden on the bench, she took about fifteen pictures and went off. It was really a great honour.

Tuesday 6 July

We had a bite to eat in the Cafeteria, went on to the Terrace and sat with Alice Mahon and her husband, and Kelvin Hopkins and his wife. I went and had a word with George Galloway, who has written me a really lovely letter about my retirement. Kevin Barron was there, Mike Connarty and his wife; Hilary turned up later. It was just a perfect summer evening on the Terrace. It might have been any time in history over the last 200 years, I should think. Members were there with their friends and their partners and their political allies. People were drinking quietly.

Thursday 8 July

Stephen Byers, the Secretary of State for Trade and Industry, announced the Government's decision to turn the Post Office into a public limited company with shares, all of which at the moment the Government will hold. Of course, the Tories just lapped it up. They were laughing themselves silly, because this was Tory policy.

I had a word with Alan Johnson, who used to be General Secretary of the Communication Workers, and he said, 'Oh well, it's all right because the Government have given us an assurance that they won't sell off the shares.'

But later in the day Blair made a statement saying he would give no guarantee whatever that they wouldn't sell off the shares, and I am sure they would.

Saturday 10 July

I worked on my letters and Caroline worked on her speech about Keir Hardie for the Socialist Workers' Party annual Marxism Conference.

The conference was extremely full, and I set up two cameras to get Caroline's speech. The first was unfortunately stuck on the photo setting, but I did get a bit of her speech.

The difference between her speaking style and mine was that hers was well researched, clear, analytical, historically accurate, illuminating, delivered from a sitting position, and listened to intently by everyone.

At the end of the meeting the chairwoman, a very nice young woman, said, 'Paul Foot has arrived,' and in a wheelchair pushed by his partner Clare was Paul, looking very old and grey. The whole meeting gave him a standing ovation. We had a word with him and said, 'We never believed in the second coming until you appeared.' His mind is fine despite his stroke. His legs are shaky. He is at home for the weekend and is having physiotherapy. It was just lovely. You don't realise how fond you are of somebody until they arc ill. I remember when I was ill, he sent me his book *Red Shelley*.

Tuesday 14 July

Caroline went to the hospital on her own, and the cancer activity rates were down to sixty (normal is fifty). A few years ago it was 350.

Thursday 15 July

The Northern Ireland Assembly met today, and David Trimble and the Unionists did not appear, did not nominate anybody to attend, so it was a farce really. There were their empty seats. Seamus Mallon is Deputy First Minister and Martin McGuinness was nominated as Minister of Education. Then the whole thing came to an end. That was the dominant news today.

There was a statement on Northern Ireland. I put my grandson James in the Gallery and Mo Mowlam made a statement about the breakdown of the talks. Afterwards James and I did a tour. I took him to the Hansard Room; introduced him to Tommy McAvoy, the Pairing Whip; took him into the Whips' Office; introduced him to Judy Mallaber, who is the MP for the Amber Valley; introduced him to lots of Members and he really did have a very nice time.

On the Terrace I had a chat to Richard Burgon, who is the nephew of Colin Burgon, the MP for Elmet, just outside Leeds. He was a young lad of about sixteen or so, a good socialist, had written a thesis on 'Tony Benn's Influence on the Labour Party' and had on a T-shirt which said 'Socialism is the Flame of Anger and the Flame of Hope'. He had had it specially made.

Thursday 22 July

James stayed and did filing and watched the test match on TV, and he was so tired he had a sleep. This is the end of his two weeks' work experience and he has been a huge help.

I went to the Commons and had tea in the Tea Room with Don Dixon and Geoffrey Lofthouse, both former MPs, now peers. Don is such an interesting man. He was a shipyard worker and writes, or wrote, in the name of Ripyard Cuddling; he recorded a collection of his poetry called *Shipyard Muddling by Ripyard Cuddling*. He is a very amusing, shrewd guy. It was lovely to talk to him and Geoffrey and we just had a good old gripe about New Labour.

I went to a meeting at three in Room 7, where Martin McGuinness was talking. He said at one point that he thought Tony Blair and Mo Mowlam were quite decent. He said, 'As an Irish Republican, I am not in favour of a British Prime Minister appointing a Secretary of State for Northern Ireland, but Mo Mowlam must stay. She is really good and, if she is sacrificed, it would be appalling.'

Went down to photocopy my report for Chesterfield to the floor where all the secretaries – mainly Tory secretaries – are. They said, 'Oh, we do like your suit' (because I was wearing my seersucker suit). They all gathered round and said what a lovely suit.

Saturday 24 July

Mrs Mac came in. She's got bad arthritis in her neck and she's worried she may have to give up working for us which is very distressing. She is going to New Zealand for the Millennium and is very excited, but she is poorly.

Monday 26 July

I had a word with Martin Bell, the MP who took over from Neil Hamilton; he was wearing his light suit and I was wearing my light-blue seersucker. I said, 'I wear this suit as Labour's answer to Martin Bell.' He said he'd love to stand again, but he had given a pledge that he wouldn't and 'I can't break my word or they'll say that all politicians are the same.' We had a bit of a chat.

Then Caroline arrived at the Commons and we went onto the Terrace.

I went to get Caroline some cheese and biscuits and saw John Major in the corridor. I said to him, 'Oh, John, how's your boy?' because his son James has had a pacemaker fitted at the age of twenty-four.

He said, 'Well I'm a bit worried about him. How's Caroline?'

I said, 'Oh, she's just here, come along.' So I took John up to Caroline and he gave her a big kiss. I went and got some cheese and biscuits and apparently John asked Caroline, 'How's Hilary getting on?'

And she said, 'He's very sensible, but that won't last for ever because you don't get anywhere if you're just sensible – as you know, John. You don't leave any footprints in the sands of time if you're always sensible. I know that from Tony and you.'

Major said, 'Well, the footprints I left are on quicksand, owing to my party.' So he's obviously still sore about that. By the time I got back he was still talking and a lot of Labour MPs looked at me in a funny sort of way.

Tuesday 27 July

There was a statement made by Helen Liddell on the sell-off of 51 per cent of the National Air Traffic Service. A question had been put down to find out the Government's intentions, and the written answer was due to be released yesterday, but they held it over in the hope that nobody would discover it until after the House had risen for the summer recess. But Bernard Jenkin, from the Opposition Front Bench, got the Speaker's permission to put down an emergency Private Notice Question asking about it, as Helen Liddell had been on the radio this morning. So Liddell made a long and involved statement about private-public partnerships and moving into the modern age, and safety, and so on. All the Labour MPs – Gwyneth Dunwoody, Martin Salter, John McDonnell were highly critical. The Tories were just laughing themselves sick.

I said that the statement owed more to Mrs Thatcher than to the Labour Manifesto and reflected the Government's deep hostility to the public sector. It would be no comfort to know that the policy of sell-offs was created by the Maastricht criteria, and that money would go to the Balkan war and to protect the rich from income-tax rises – the one pledge that had been kept.

Later Bob Marshall-Andrews and I sat down for about half an hour and he said he'd been talking to Stephen Byers, the Secretary of State for Industry, and that he and Stephen were thinking of writing a book about how Labour had reached the point it had reached. Bob, who's an old mate of mine, was very angry at me for having retired. I can't change my mind on that. But it's an interesting idea to write a joint book with a right-wing Labour guy, although I hope it doesn't reflect a conviction by Bob Marshall-Andrews that all is lost.

Thursday 29 July

I had a very nice letter from Jennifer Tanfield, the retiring Librarian from the House of Commons, a charming woman, about my retirement.

Reshuffle today: lot of people sacked. Glenda Jackson has gone, Alan Meale has gone, Tony Banks has gone, Doug Henderson has gone. Chris Mullin has got a job in the Government – junior Minister in Environment, Transport and the Regions. I am pleased about that, but it is sort of 'take your partners for the next dance'.

I don't think the people brought in are any more competent than the people thrown out. I am absolutely certain that Mo Mowlam, Margaret Beckett, and Cunningham simply said to Blair, 'We are not going. Sack us if you like, but we are not going.'

Friday 30 July

Up at 5.30, caught the 7.25 to Chesterfield for a meeting at the NUM with Harry Barnes, Dennis Skinner and the solicitors, Graysons. We discussed two things. First of all, there is a need for a testing centre for miners' chest and hand complaints because there are 3000 cases in Chesterfield, but there is no testing centre, so they have to go to Sheffield or Nottingham. Second, there is a discrepancy between the DSS assessment for disability and the Health-Call assessment, and Government compensation is based on the Health-Call system, which is less accurate.

We had a long discussion.

Then I went to do my surgery. Somebody came to complain about a solicitor. A teacher who lives in a listed house can't get insurance on it unless some trees are cut down, but the trees are also listed. So I wrote to the local authority to sort that one out. Some residents from Brampton came to complain about a club that has a licence for 2000 people and makes an intolerable noise; and a girl of sixteen was murdered there last Saturday.

Saturday 31 July

Tony Blair, Clinton, and other Western leaders are in Sarajevo, allegedly to launch a Balkan Recovery Plan but, having bombed the hell out of Serbia and refused to help to rebuild it until Milošević has gone, it isn't exactly very positive. But it provides plenty of photo-opportunities for Blair and Clinton to be seen being cheered by Kosovar refugees.

Tuesday 3 August

A very, very hot night. I was tossing and turning and coughing all night.

Caroline and Barbara went out together, with Caroline in the wheelchair, and did some shopping – tons of food, because we are going to Stansgate.

I rang Chris Mullin about his job at the Department of the Environment. He said he was reluctant to go because he was giving up a lot, which indeed he is as Chairman of the Home Affairs Select Committee. Chris told me that he is the Minister in charge of the privatisation of the National Air Traffic Service. So that's why Blair twisted his arm, because he wanted somebody who once had a left-wing reputation to carry that through.

But he goes in at the age of fifty-two or fifty-three and I said, 'Go for a time and then you can come out and take over another committee – the Privilege Committee, or something of that kind.' Chris is a respected parliamentary figure now.

Wednesday 11 August, Stansgate

Cloudy, dark and cold.

Caroline and I watched the eclipse; it was a total eclipse in the south, although where we were it was only 97 per cent. It was very, very cloudy and we sat in the front garden with a bucket of water so that if the eclipse was too bright we could watch its reflection.

It got a bit dark and a bit cold, and the birds stopped singing; an eclipse is a great sort of religious global experience and everybody was very excited by it.

Tuesday 17 August

A tragic earthquake in Turkey. Originally they thought 500 people had died but by the end of the day they were talking about 5000 or 10,000 people killed. The British Government has put aside £0.5 million in relief.

When you think that £8 billion was spent on killing 2000 Serbs and half a million pounds is going on trying to rescue up to 10,000, it just confirms how disgraceful war is.

Tuesday 24 August

I wrote a letter to *The Times* linking together the bombing of Iraq, the inadequate help given for the Turkish earthquake and the continued support for the KLA in the Balkans. I wrote that I couldn't recall a government pursuing such an unethical and immoral foreign and defence policy. *The Times* rang to make sure I hadn't sent it to any other paper.

There was a programme on TV called *What Granny Did in the War*: interviews with old ladies in their seventies and eighties describing their sex lives during the war. It was exhibitionist, in a way, in the new exhibitionist tendency of saying everything on television to everybody. Younger people watching it would have been amazed to discover that their grandmother or even great-grandmother had sex with an American soldier in a doorway. Of course, I remember it all!

It removed the idea that the Sixties were the beginning of permissiveness because during the war all these things broke down.

Sunday 29 August, Stansgate

The *Observer* printed my letter, this time on transport – the case for publicly owned transport. That was the fifth letter published this week.

There are eighteen of us here now. While Hilary was climbing the treehouse to do some sawing, he fell off the ladder and we were terrified that he'd broken his back, but he was all right, thank God; he'd just bruised it.

Wednesday 1 September

The Irish settlement is just getting terrible.The Unionists are in effect demanding the resignation of Mo Mowlam, because there've been some punishment beatings and death threats by the IRA – mainly directed at their own community, a sort of disciplinary action – and although it's happening on the Loyalist side, Trimble takes no responsibility for that.

Blair has just come back from holiday yesterday, 31 August, and he's got that on his plate; he's also got to find a new Defence Secretary and a candidate for Hamilton, because George Robertson has gone to NATO.

I feel the New Labour period is passing to its end now; can't quite describe it. And just as all the right-wingers called themselves modernisers when they wanted to get rid of socialist ideas, so I'm a post-moderniser. I feel the pendulum beginning to swing back.

Friday 3 September

Carolyn Djanogly called this morning to give me her book, *The Centurions*. She is a photographer, and has taken photographs of a hundred people she thinks have shaped the twentieth century. She asked me to sign a copy so that it can be auctioned for charity.

Saturday 4 September

I caught the 7.33 to Southminster, where Caroline met me and we went back to Stansgate together for our last day there.

It was beautiful: there wasn't a cloud in the sky, there wasn't a ripple on the river, the sun was shining brightly, the flowers were blossoming. Caroline gardened for a bit and watered the flowers.

We had an evening meal and watched the most exquisite sunset; it really was beautiful. Stansgate sunsets are always lovely, but this, somehow, was the best I remember. You could see the sun as a great red ball, descending slowly behind Osea Island, and the clouds went absolutely red, they hardly seemed to be moving. We left Stansgate with some regret at about eleven minutes past eight.

Stopped at a shop in Steeple to pick up the bottle of sherry that Carrie had won by winning the darts competition at the Steeple Country Fair last Monday.

Monday 6 September

Watched *Newsnight*; they had a discussion on child poverty, quite extraordinary. They showed pictures of horrible housing estates with boarded-up windows; dirty little children with filthy faces, smoking cigarettes, five and six. One boy said, 'I go out and nick money, the only way I can manage.' Then they showed distraught-looking lone parents.

They had three people representing children's charities, pressure groups with middle-class representatives, Alistair Darling, the Social Security Secretary, and David Willetts, the Shadow Social Security Secretary. Alistair Darling said, 'Well, of course the reason for this is that there are families that had no experience of work for years.' And Willets said, 'The real problem of course is that this is the break-up of family life.' So neither of them took any economic responsibility for unemployment or for low pay. Nobody in the whole programme made any reference whatever to the fact that the gap between rich and poor has widened; there were statistics showing that children in poverty are now one in three of the population. Absolute scandal! But it was a completely non-political Victorian bit of media slumming, and I found it very interesting.

Tuesday 7 September

Mrs Mac came in with a collar round her neck. She's determined not to let the osteo-arthritis stop her coming to clean for us. She knows all the family, she comes to our parties, and she's got a cat called Lottie, named after the National Lottery, that she loves very much.

In the afternoon, after lunch, I had a phone call saying that Alan Clark, the local MP for Kensington and Chelsea, had died.

Some of the things he said were outrageous, but on the Balkan war he and I were totally opposed to it and he spoke out very strongly.

He was a serious historian; his study of one of the disastrous battles of the First World War, called *The Donkeys*, is very famous. He was a diarist of course, although his diaries didn't say much about politics; less well known is the fact that he was a vegetarian, against hunting and, as a Minister, tried to stop the import of fur from animals that had been trapped, though that policy was vetoed by the Tory Government because the Canadians depended on it.

He was very kindly. I've never forgotten the speech he gave at Bob Cryer's memorial meeting in the Jubilee Room of the House.

BBC Television and Channel 4 came to my house and I did a brief comment for each of them, and I think they were probably shown.

Wednesday 8 September

My first visit this morning was with four members of the Garvaghy Road Residents' Association who came to discuss how to handle their meeting with the Prime Minister at eleven o'clock.

I listened to their account. I think there have now been 200 attempts by the Orange Order to march along the Catholic Garvaghy Road since the march was banned in 1998, and the residents are under terrible pressure.

I put three points to them, which they seemed to accept. First of all, to ask Blair quite bluntly, 'Why is it that the law is different in England and Northern Ireland? Why isn't the Public Order Act applied in Northern Ireland, which would give the Minister the right to ban marches, as we've done in Dover?'

Secondly, 'Is he aware of the human suffering caused by this type of harassment?' I gave them my plastic bullet, which I was given in Derry about a month ago, to show the Prime Minister in case he'd never seen one before. If there is a tragedy there and one of their people is killed as a result of police action or whatever, this would act as a recruiting sergeant for violence. They don't want incidents returning that might lead to violence.

Thirdly, relate all this to the peace process.

They told me one quite extraordinary story: that Jonathan Powell, the Prime Minister's Chief of Staff, had been over to see them and had said to them that they had had the idea that Tony Blair himself would lead the Orange Order march down the Garvaghy Road, and Cherie Blair would lead a parallel march of Catholics.

I said, 'I can't believe that suggestion was seriously put forward.'

'Oh, yes, indeed,' they said, 'and it's in writing.'

So I said, 'Well, send me a copy.'

But it gave an insight into the idea that Blair has only got to descend from the clouds and all historical problems and social tensions will disappear. It was just incredible – it was a gimmick of the first order.

The other news is that Lord Sainsbury has given £2 million to the Labour Party. He's a Minister in the Government; £2 million represents 10 per cent of our total income, and I think it represents about three-quarters of our income from individual membership subscriptions.

Thursday 9 September

Portillo announced this morning that he had had some 'gay experiences' when he was a student and also that he was going to go for Alan Clark's seat. As Alan has been dead only three days, I thought it was indecent haste. The fact that Portillo's a potential challenger to Hague will amuse the correspondents, because they think Hague's no good and they would like a strong Tory Party.

Friday 10 September

This morning there was a very interesting news story about an old lady of eighty-seven who had worked for a company that produced components for nuclear weapons and had supplied information to the Russians. The Home Secretary has decided not to prosecute, and what was interesting about it was that she said she didn't regret it. She said, 'I didn't take a penny– no money; but I wanted to help Russia because I admired their education system and their health system and I was in favour of peace and socialism.' She was reported as saying that she didn't like Stalin very much, but she thought Lenin had good ideas; she couldn't bear Chamberlain, but she did subscribe to Churchill's Aid to Russia Fund. In a world where nobody acts on principle any more, I thought that was very interesting.

Monday 13 September

At eight o'clock this morning, before I was even properly dressed, Des the builder arrived and, to cut a long story short, he and two of his mates knocked down the office kitchen at the back of the house, which was subsiding into the ground. It was unbelievable – one minute it was there, and then I looked out and it had been knocked down. I did manage to take one picture of them while they were working at it.

Then at nine o'clock a couple of very nice lads from Cambridge University came to do an interview. I'm always a bit suspicious of Oxbridge students, but they were good socialists.

One of them had brought with him a little bit of equipment, one-third of the size of a mobile phone, which was a tape recorder and it transcribes everything direct onto a computer. Well, as there was hammering and an electric drill going on outside, I should think the whole recording is a failure. Still, I'm going to enquire and see whether it works. They promised to send me the particulars.

Went to Brighton for the TUC conference; coming back on the train, it was a lovely evening, and there was one absolutely incredible cloud formation which I couldn't believe: it was a skeleton of a fish, the main bone in dark cloud and then all the little rib bones perfectly set; it could have been a salmon after people had eaten it. I found that fascinating and it didn't move, because there wasn't much wind.

The train was a disgrace. Connex get, I think, £80 million subsidy a year and make a loss, so that the subsidy goes to pay the dividends for the company; but when I went to the lavatory, the light had been stolen or broken, the door didn't lock, the lavatory didn't flush and the sink was blocked. I thought, 'My God, no wonder people would like public services publicly owned.'

Wednesday 15 September

Des was at work; he's now dug a hole nine feet deep where the old kitchen used to be.

The big political news today is that the Government has subsidised, through the export credit guarantee department, the sales of arms to Indonesia to the extent of £130 million. Indonesia is bankrupt and we give Hawk aircraft and guns to the Indonesian Government to repress the people of East Timor. The UN has passed a resolution calling for a peacekeeping force to work under the supervision of the Indonesian army, which will be responsible for security. Compared to the Kosovo story, it's a complete disgrace. Utterly hypocritical and disgusting.

Saturday 18 September
I wasn't down to speak, but I thought I'd go to the National Pensioners' Convention demonstration, out of solidarity; Jack Jones, who is eighty-six and marched from the Embankment down to Big Ben and then up Whitehall, is quite remarkable. There was one man of ninety-one who said to me, 'We've been marching together for sixty-five years, Tony.' Well, I don't think I go back quite as far as that.

As we passed Number 10 Downing Street there was a crowd of people demonstrating against Government policy towards Indonesia and East Timor, so we gave them a wave.

Ken Livingstone was at Trafalgar Square; also Trevor Phillips who is another candidate for the Mayor of London. Barbara Castle came on and made a speech. Will Hutton was there.

Jack is very loyal to the Government, Barbara is a bit more critical; and although Jack and Barbara are the two leaders of the movement, I think there's a little bit of tension between them, going back to *In Place of Strife* in 1969.

Came home. *Casualty* was on television, Caroline's favourite programme. It is so emotionally stressing and so many people are injured, that I find it difficult to watch.

Tuesday 21 September
Caroline went to the hospital for her visit to the cancer specialist at Charing Cross; and it was the best result she's had in three years. The activity rate had dropped to forty-nine and normally it is fifty and the blood count had remained steady so she doesn't need a transfusion, bless her. It's absolute will power, diet, determination, intellectual interest, optimism and courage. An amazing woman!

Any news, particularly world news? Well, the militia is still making life impossible for the so-called UN peacekeeping force. I don't know, I mustn't sound too grumpy because I'm busier and happier than I've been for a long time, because I'm free to defend all the things I believe in.

Monday 27 September, Labour Party Conference, Bournemouth
The Conference is totally different now; they really have obliterated any function of decision-making and the media just hover around trying to find a bit of trouble. But the press may get bored with Jesus Christ taking responsibility for all our sins.

Tuesday 28 September
I was invited to the Channel 4 breakfast – God knows why I was asked. It

was held in a huge dining room with a top table at which were sitting Chris Smith, Vanni Treves, who is the Chairman of Channel 4, Tessa Blackstone and Jeremy Isaacs. Then at my table were Elinor Goodman and Chris Mullin.

Vanni Treves welcomed us, as if somehow Channel 4 was running the Conference at Bournemouth and we were his invited guests. Then he did a long commercial about Channel 4 and his programmes; then Chris Smith got up and said he'd cut the levy on Channel 4 if they made more domestic investment.

There's no question about it, the media have taken the whole thing over. As I left I was given a T-shirt and a little rubber television set (a toy) to press in my hands for stress.

When Vanni Treves said, 'We are very glad our masters' – referring to the Government – 'have conceded some reduction in taxation,' I thought, 'our masters' indeed. It's the other way around.

I'm glad I went; it was nice of them to ask me.

We tried to get to Hilary's lunchtime meeting, but were prevented by a pro-hunting demonstration, allegedly with 16,000 people. There are far fewer people who hunt than there are against genetically modified food or on the Pensioners' Convention, but this is a good story for the media, because it embarrasses Blair.

Took Caroline to the station because she is going back to London, and a very nice woman said she would help Caroline off at Waterloo. Turned out that she was a pro-hunting person, so that was funny.

At about eight I went down to the Tribune meeting in the Winter Gardens. I would be surprised if there were 200 people there; last year it was 1200. It was a terribly disappointing meeting, to be truthful.

After Bill Morris, Margaret Beckett, and Stephen Pound, Rhodri Morgan and Ken Livingstone both spoke. Then Tony Booth. Then they had an auction of a Harrods hamper for £200. It went on for so long that people were drifting out, and by the time I was called at about ten to ten, the audience had dropped to about two-thirds of what it was when I arrived. Too many speakers, too long.

I entirely forgot to mention that after I got back from the station I watched the Blair speech on television.

The first and overwhelming impression is of a man absolutely inflated with his own role – '*I'm* doing this, *I'm* doing that, only four other people have ever experienced it, *I'm* under pressure.' It really frightened me.

On the other hand, he played all the right notes about the Health Service, dentistry and drugs, equality of opportunity and how the class war's over. Everybody cheered him; he got a standing ovation.

I thought the PM had gone right over the top.

Wednesday 29 September

There were 250 people at the Campaign Group rally at the Wessex Hotel – bigger, I think than the Tribune Rally. I said that after the class war has been abolished by Tony Blair, he's going to announce that Darwin was wrong, that the world was made in seven days – and you know by whom; that Galileo was wrong, the Earth does rotate around the Millbank Tower.

Then we had Jeremy Corbyn talking passionately about the arms trade; Alan Simpson talking about genetically modified food; Ken Livingstone making his campaign speech for his bid as Mayor of London. It had real substance.

Thursday 30 September

Who should get on the train with me but Edward Miliband. Edward used to work in my office, as a teenager. He's a nice lad, and I know him quite well. He is now part of Gordon Brown's team.

He is very modest; I asked about Charlie Whelan, and Edward said he was a bit difficult and so in the end he had to go. Peter Mandelson was very sensitive and desperately wanted to be loved, but wasn't a great thinker; Blair depended on him very much as a spin doctor.

I asked about Europe, and he said at one stage Gordon Brown was supposed to be keen and Blair reluctant; now they say the opposite, but it does critically depend on the economic circumstances.

I feel like a weekend in bed. The flat we were in in Bournemouth was very damp and cold and I think I must have picked up bronchitis there.

Wednesday 6 October

The rail crash at Ladbroke Grove has turned out to be much more serious than people realised. A complete coach, the first-class coach at the front of the train coming in from Cheltenham, caught fire and they said the death toll was anything from six to twenty-six. They haven't even got into the coach yet and the identification of bodies will be almost impossible.

It has raised the question of rail safety and privatisation, and ASLEF, the train drivers' union, has said they will ballot for industrial action if automatic train protection is not introduced.

Friday 8 October

Terrible pain in my back. I took a painkiller, which I don't normally do; I've only had a couple in the last week or two and I can't remember when I had one previously.

Sunday 10 October

The only vaguely interesting political news is that Frank Dobson has decided to give up his job as Health Secretary and run for Mayor of

London. As he's fifty-nine I'm sure it was obvious to him that he wouldn't be long in the Cabinet.

Thursday 14 October
To Wesley's Chapel in City Road for a 'dialogue' with Dr Leslie Griffiths, who is the President of the Methodist Conference.

He and I sat in front of the congregation and he put very searching, difficult questions about compromise, about nuclear power, about Europe, and so on.

It was a model interview and afterwards I went to unveil the bust of Donald Soper by Ian Walters, with all Donald's family present. A beautiful bust, absolutely lovely.

Met Simon Fletcher at the House of Commons. Simon was a Teabag and is now principal researcher and adviser to Ken Livingstone. He wanted to have a talk about the Mayor of London, because the Party has worked out a system under which they think they can exclude Ken. What they've done is to revitalise the idea of an Electoral College so that the individual members in London would be reduced to one-third of the total, another third will be made up of trade unions, and the final third will be made up of MEPs, MPs and candidates for the London Assembly. Simon wanted to go over with me what Ken should do.

I said, 'Obviously you do have to consider, if Ken is excluded by one means or another, whether he'd stand as an independent.'

Simon wanted to explore that a bit.

I said, 'I don't want to see Ken expelled from the Party, which he would be immediately. On the other hand, there'll have to be a break made one day, and maybe Ken standing independently in London would be the moment to break the power and reputation and standing of New Labour.'

What came out of it really was that Simon thought that if Ken won the individual members' ballot and won the trade union ballot, but a combination of MPs' and MEPs' votes excluded him, that would be a fiddle and he would possibly stand as an Independent.

Sunday 17 October
At 11.30 Caroline and I set off for Oxford for David Butler's seventy-fifth birthday party, which was held in the Rector's lodgings of Exeter College, because of course his wife, Marilyn, is the Rector there.

A beautiful buffet. David and Marilyn's three children, Daniel, Gareth and Edmond, were there with their wives and children; Vernon Bogdanor and Lord Holme, who is a passionate supporter of proportional representation, a Liberal Democrat; Hugh Berrington whom I hadn't seen for years, an old research assistant and Andrew Adonis, a young man at Number 10 responsible for education policy, who is writing a life of Roy Jenkins.

I was asked to speak, so I spoke very briefly and then I played a recording that was made on the 19 June 1946 by Peter Blaker, David Butler, John Turner (who's now dead) and Humphrey Richardson. Peter Blaker was saying he thought David Butler would never marry, but would be surrounded by feminine admirers and foolish women. That caused a bit of amusement. My speech wasn't very good, but I was told to keep it brief. David was in an embroidered waistcoat, open-necked shirt, looking like a waiter; it was all very jolly. I think Andrew Tyrie, a Tory MP, was there. I was the only Labour person there.

Wednesday 20 October

John McDonnell raised the case of Ricky Reel, the black kid who was attacked by a white racist gang and thrown into the Thames. He made a powerful speech; he's an excellent Member of Parliament, John is. The Metropolitan Police, or the Home Secretary, will not release the Police Complaints Authority report, which revealed terrible weaknesses in police handling of it.

As I left the House after John had spoken, Geoffrey Robinson came by. He's an old friend.

I said, 'I see you're getting a lot of flak, and I've had my share of it. What do you think's going to happen? We must have a talk.'

He had to rush off, but he said, 'I tell you, Blair will win the next election and then the whole thing will collapse.'

I didn't quite know what he meant, but I will try and have a word with him. Mo must be as sick as a dog to have been replaced by Mandelson.

Friday 22 October

I heard from Jeremy Corbyn in the House of Commons yesterday that the alleged cancellation of the world debt was a complete fraud, because a condition has been imposed that any country that had its debt cancelled had to privatise its assets; so that's where the money will be made.

I mean, if ever the Marxist critique of capitalism was correct, it's on this. Somebody wrote in the *New Yorker* the other day, 'Marx may have been wrong about communism, but he was certainly right about capitalism.'

Saturday 23 October

I went to Conway Hall for the Mordecai Vanunu benefit concert. They won't let him into a Christian prison, even though he has converted to Christianity. Every year they have this benefit concert for him, and Susannah York and Julie Christie have played a part in it. Bruce Kent acted as compère and Benjamin Zephaniah read some marvellous poems: 'What's it got to do with me?' 'Dream for the Future' in which black people would go to Hampstead Heath with poodles, and 'The

Turkey is My Friend', inviting the Turkey in for Christmas. Velvet Fist sang a song.

Monday 25 October
I was sitting in my room and who should pop in but Hilary – so we had a meal in the cafeteria downstairs. He wanted advice about Select Committees, standing committees and about procedure, so I gave him the best advice. Fabian Hamilton came up with another Member for Leeds and said what a fine speech Hilary had made when he opened the sewage plant. Hilary is so happy.

I got back and watched the last episode of *The Major Years*. All the usual stuff was blown up – the rows and the sleaze, and the sex and everything; I thought Major came out of it very well. But they tried to mock him, and he is somebody who has been air-brushed out of history because the Establishment has got to prove to itself that it was right to transfer its loyalty from the Tory Party to New Labour; and in order to do that, they have to rubbish Major.

Tuesday 26 October
There was a little bit in the *Guardian* about Ministers trying to get rid of Betty Boothroyd because she was obstructing the Government in its plans to modernise Parliament; I was so incensed by this that I rang the Speaker's Office and arranged to see the Speaker this afternoon.

She said, 'I'm not worried about it, because I'll go when I want to.' I think probably she is going to retire some time next year, but I raised with her the constitutional question of relations between the executive and the legislature. Later I raised it in the House, with tremendous support from the Tories.

When I went to have a cup of tea and a bun, I found I didn't have my purse, so Nicholas Soames, who was standing next to me, said, 'That was such a magnificent question I'll pay for your tea,' so he paid 95p.

I said, 'Tea for questions!'

He told me he had been at Churchill College and that, 'They desperately wish they could have your archives, because they think they are the most comprehensive record of this part of the century, but they haven't got room for them.' Very matey.

But when I sat down with Dennis Skinner, he said, 'You shouldn't have raised that point with the Speaker – you got excited; nobody's interested.'

The Earl of Burford, heir to the Duke of St Albans, jumped on the Woolsack today and called out 'Treason' – it was really rather pathetic, because the Labour Party has betrayed its Manifesto pledge to get rid of all the hereditary peers, but the hereditary peers have gone along with the process of retaining some hereditary element because they think this is the best way of preserving a presence. I've no sympathy for them at all.

Wednesday 27 October

I met Angie Zelter of the Ploughshares Group, who attacked the Trident base in Scotland and was acquitted by a Scottish sheriffs' court by a judge who said that the nuclear weapons programme was illegal and criminal. Amazing judgement from a court – I couldn't believe it. Anyway, I had been in touch with the Ploughshares Group over the years and I took her to the Campaign Group. She was keen that the issue of nuclear weapons should be pursued in the Commons on an all-party basis and I understand that. Of course the verdict was hardly mentioned in the English press.

Ken reported on the London mayoral election. Frank Dobson has simply been told that he is going to have to leave the Department of Health, and he will be given a bit of a push for Mayor. He doesn't want the job, and it's all been taken over by the Millbank spin doctors. Every London Labour Party member has had three letters from Dobson already. Where the money comes from nobody knows. Very pessimistic about the outcome. Ken is doing well. The big problem is that if he does stand as an independent, as he is likely to do if he doesn't get adopted as the Labour candidate, Londoners will have real difficulty in supporting him.

Sunday 31 October

The wife of Ivor Richard, who was sacked by Blair last year as Leader of the House of Lords, has published a very bitter diary in which she says that John Prescott was furious with Blair for freezing Cabinet pay, and Blair annoyed Callaghan by describing the Lords as bastards, and so on. Absolute gossip, but interesting.

There was also an item in the *Sunday Times* to say that the team sent into Kosovo to examine the 100,000 allegedly killed by the Serbs had only found 1000 bodies. The propaganda in wartime is terrifying.

Monday 1 November

I rang Gloria Redfern, who was in Rhodesia during the war; she worked in the Service Club and I had a bit of a crush on her. She married Ron Redfern, who was a colleague and comrade of mine when I was training as a pilot in Rhodesia; he died in 1971 at the age of forty-six. Her sister-in-law told me Gloria had cancer. She is seventy-two now and I haven't seen her for fifty years. I think she was pleased.

Tam Dalyell had the adjournment debate and he used it to raise the question of Yugoslavia. He did it brilliantly – to an empty House. There was a vote on whether public records should be kept on vellum or on archival paper and Brian White, MP for Milton Keynes, where the factory that does the printing on vellum will be closed, asked me to vote against, which I did.

Tuesday 2 November

A mad woman rang three or four times today. Her first call said that Tony Worthington, an MP, was posing as a surgeon in a hospital and his wife was posing as a professor at a college, and would I take this up? Sheila reminded me that she had rung up some time ago and said that the Prince of Wales had gone to Scotland to molest John Major. These are the people who make your telephone line a little bit more interesting.

Wednesday 3 November

There was a story in the paper today that the Prime Minister had offered life peerages to the Duke of Edinburgh, the Prince of Wales, the Duke of York and the Earl of Snowdon. All but the Earl of Snowdon had refused. It's just such an amazing story – the fount of honour is obviously now gushing from Number 10 rather than the Palace, and the idea that such an offer could have been made without the Queen's consent, and that if she gave her consent they should have refused, is the world turned upside down. It made me laugh.

Drove Hilary home. On the way he told me an interesting story. He said that Peter Mandelson had come up to him and said, 'I hope you won't think me cheeky or rude, but your gestures are so like your father's that you'll be mocked by people. You ought to try and change them.' It didn't upset Hilary because he's a tough cookie, but it's an astonishing thing for Peter Mandelson to say. I cannot imagine anyone saying that to a new Member. But it is true that he does sound like me, and Bob Marshall-Andrews said, 'Close your eyes and it might be you.'

Thursday 4 November

Heard from the Speaker's Office that I have got an adjournment debate on Tuesday on the relations between the Executive and the Legislature.

I sat in the Tea Room most of the time while the Greater London Authority Bill was going through. Jim Marshall from Leicester – very decent guy – is utterly depressed by what has happened. George Mudie said the whole thing will collapse. They may go along with the Government out of loyalty and so on, but people are very candid and I don't think there is much support for Blair really. A Liberal MP said the situation has now been reached where we ought to consider separating the Executive from the Legislature, because the real Government (and he is right) is the hundred advisers at Whitehall who decide everything, and then decisions are fed out to Cabinet Ministers, who are really sort of figureheads. And Party discipline is used to enforce it on the rest of us.

Came home and had a meal, which was lovely, and to bed early.

Saturday 6 November

With the minutes of the Parliamentary Committee and the details of the

Whip for the coming week there was a little note saying, 'The Committee noted that if colleagues were determined to table motions at the PLP meeting, they had the right to do so, but were agreed this would be an unwelcome return to past practices and one to be discouraged where possible.' So the Parliamentary Committee (which is the elected committee of Labour MPs who meet Blair every week) does not think there should be any motions or debate or decisions by the PLP. It is the extinction of democracy in the PLP, just as they are trying to extinguish it in the Conference and policy forums and branch meetings and General Committee meetings of the Labour Party. Everybody must take their instructions from the top.

Tuesday 9 November

Mo Mowlam came up to me in the corridor. She said to me, 'It is very important what you are doing and it must be put on the record,' so she was indicating her support for my criticism of the presidential style of government. She must be as sick as a dog that she was taken away from Northern Ireland when she had really saved the day.

I voted against the Government on the Welfare Reform Bill three times. Then at quarter to one in the morning my adjournment debate on the legislature's relationship with the executive came up. I had worked very hard on my speech, and written to all the editors of the broadsheets and sent a note to all the lobby correspondents. There were about fifty people there, and it went down very well – about twenty-three minutes. Graham Stringer replied – it wasn't very consequential. Afterwards lots of people came up. A policewoman who had heard me from the Gallery said she found it very interesting. I'm sure the whips will be furious.

Wednesday 10 November

We had the Lords Bill back from the Lords with amendments, and the big one was the Weatherill clause that allows hereditary peers to elect ninety-one of their number to sit as 'elected hereditaries' alongside the life peers. Most people in the Labour Party are absolutely thrilled that the project is being carried forward and that the hereditaries are going, but in effect it is the transformation of historical patronage into contemporary patronage – i.e. the patronage of the PM. He has appointed 170 peers in two and a half years, which is quite incredible – and there will never be a second stage of reform. You'll never get rid of a single peer who is there now. I found the whole thing very depressing.

At the end I saw Mo Mowlam and she said, 'You suggested we might have a talk,' and so we went up to my room. She had a whisky and said she shouldn't have drunk it.

She said George Mitchell was very good and McGuinness was very good but she believed that Trimble and Adams had lost the historic opportunity to take the lead. She was clearly very sorry to go and I said, 'I assume you were threatened with the sack.'

And she said, 'Oh no, I was offered some other job, and I pointed out to the PM that someone else was doing that job, and what was wrong with the way he was doing it?'

She has been moved to the Cabinet Office as Cabinet Enforcer, which is a non-job. She said that Blair only talked to two or three people – Philip Gould and Alastair Campbell, and probably David Miliband and Jonathan Powell – but he didn't consult anybody. She had had no idea that Mandelson was to be put jointly in charge of running the next election and she was quite bitter.

Blair must have been shaken that when he mentioned Mo Mowlam's name at the Labour Conference in 1998, she got a standing ovation during his speech. She was very friendly.

Thursday 11 November

House of Lords absolutely packed. It is a historic day – the hereditary peers to be excluded from the Lords. There was Lord Irvine on the Woolsack – a rather arrogant man, from what I can gather. Mrs Thatcher was sitting on the Front Bench on the Opposition side and next to her Lord Cranborne, sacked by Hague for doing a deal with Blair and then rewarded with a life peerage a day or two ago; quite a few Ministers – Lady Jay, Andrew McIntosh and Baroness Scotland, who is a very distinguished lawyer and highly competent in answering questions. I didn't see any of the ex-Ministers I knew, but I wanted to get a glimpse of it all.

Sunday 14 November

At home there was a little note from the Tories: 'Michael Portillo is your candidate' and 'Sorry to miss you'. On the reverse side it said: 'Greetings, Michael'. I wetted my finger and rubbed it and it was a message he had written himself. I think he probably planned a photo-opportunity to arrive at my house with a camera unit. I'm very glad I was out.

Wednesday 17 November

Mitchel McLaughlin, the Sinn Fein representative, and others came to the House to brief a group of Members on what was happening. The IRA issued a statement today saying that they would talk about decommissioning as soon as the Executive was set up. And Trimble is apparently trying to argue for that in the Unionist group, though of course there is no guarantee that Gerry Adams will be able to carry the IRA with him.

There is a real feeling now of a breakthrough – really significant – and what they said about Mandelson, which I thought was interesting, was,

'At least when we talk to Mandelson we know we're talking to Blair.' That is true. Mandelson would never be overturned by Blair, and Mandelson is committed to try and make a success of it all.

I asked Helen Jackson, who was there, about the possibility that McGuinness and Adams might take their seats. And Helen, who is Mandelson's PPS, said, 'Well, we suggested that they have the facilities of the House at their disposal, although they won't take the Oath.' That was what I suggested to Betty Boothroyd, but now I think it is the right time to rethink the whole thing. Mandelson will put that to Blair, and Blair will put it to Betty Boothroyd. I asked how we could build up support in Britain, because the damage done by violence over the years to the nationalist cause had been very great, and Mitchel responded to that.

Ken Livingstone went to the committee that was supposed to pick the shortlist and they obviously tried to trip him, but he did very well and they didn't know what to do. So they met and met and met, and decided to have another meeting on Thursday. This threw Number 10 into chaos because Jeremy Paxman from *Newsnight* and Elinor Goodman from Channel 4 were ready to interview Blair about whatever he was going to say to explain how Livingstone was unacceptable, but he cancelled it all; while they were waiting outside Number 10, they could hear a great party going on upstairs for the 'eve of Queen's Speech'. Livingstone is very clever, saying he will go along with the Manifesto so long as it doesn't include anti-semitism! A very light way of dealing with it. I think they probably will put him on the list now because he will make some concession, and later will probably go his own way. Dobson has apparently said that if Livingstone is not on the list, he (Dobson) will withdraw and that will throw the whole Number 10 strategy into total chaos. It is such an astonishing situation.

Had a letter from the Secretary of the Chesterfield Party saying there is an Executive Committee on Friday. They never warned me and I already have a meeting arranged in Sheffield; but I'll be at the General Committee next week. I just don't want a row with Chesterfield at the end – I'll just leave it. I'm too old for that sort of a row.

Thursday 18 November

Senator George Mitchell has completed his review of the Belfast Agreement. Trimble's got to keep his Unionists in line, many of whom are highly critical of the Belfast Agreement, and Adams does not control the IRA, but the statement made by the IRA yesterday that they would begin decommissioning has provided a key to it. Sinn Fein are very sensitive to the problems that Trimble faces and think he wants to try.

Blair launched into a violent personal attack on Livingstone, actually naming him and saying it's back to the bad old days of Old Labour, and so on; it was quite unnecessary and very stupid, because it's building up a bigger sympathy vote for Livingstone.

I saw Ken later in the day. He was fairly chirpy but rather tired; he seemed quite happy with the line I was taking, which is that he has been the pioneer of New Labour policy on Ireland and transport, on racism and women's rights and gay rights. Now he is on the shortlist it would be difficult for him to run as an independent.

Melissa was on *Dispatches* at midnight. She reviewed the papers at the beginning and the end of the programme and she was marvellous: very attractive, slim, confident, relaxed, clear – a real professional. I'm awfully proud of her.

Saturday 20 November

I came home, parked the car outside (thinking it was safe) and when I went out again I had a penalty notice, because apparently you can't park in that spot on a Saturday afternoon. My only compensation was that it gave me the idea to enlarge the notice on a photocopier and attach it to the Speaker's coach, which is currently parked in a corner of Westminster Hall.

Jeffrey Archer, the Tory candidate for Mayor of London, has had to withdraw because tomorrow the *News of the World* is alleging that he lied to cover up his visit to a prostitute; that means that there is no Labour candidate, and won't be till the middle of February. There is a Liberal candidate, Susan Kramer, whom I met the other day, but there is no Tory candidate; and so the whole mayoral election has been turned into a farce.

That will dominate the news – along with Cherie Blair's new baby.

Looking at the general political scene, Glenda Jackson may turn out to be quite a powerful candidate because Dobson isn't doing very well. And Number 10 blames everybody but themselves and so, if Dobson doesn't do well, they will switch their support to Jackson, and he will be as bitter as hell at having been forced to stand as Mayor and lose his job at Health.

It's all so dirty and boring – court politics of the worst possible kind.

I discovered that the Cabinet Office had commissioned a paper on globalisation, describing in some detail all the strains it would produce. That explains why, when I saw Sir Richard Wilson, the Cabinet Secretary, at the Speaker's party, he said, 'Your mind and the Cabinet Office mind are converging.' He must have read my speech about the WTO.

Monday 22 November

Caroline spent most of the day resting in bed. She does have to take it very easy now. I think she might need a few painkillers because her back aches; having said that, she did the laundry, she got me lunch, she worked on her Christmas shopping, she wrote some letters. She's terribly busy.

I blew up the penalty notice that I had found on my car to A4-size and stuck it on the Speaker's coach at Westminster Hall and took a couple of photographs.

Tuesday 23 November
Well, the Archer story runs and runs and runs, and everybody is attacking him.

I saw the Speaker passing through Westminster Hall, so I pointed out to her that I had put this penalty notice on her coach. I said it was no good her thinking that she could go on coming to work every day in a big vehicle like that; she should come in by bus, as John Prescott does. Peter Jennings, the Serjeant at Arms, was standing there laughing. It is nice being my age; you can really do what you like. Betty Boothroyd was very jolly and said how pleased she was that Caroline was better; she'd seen her at her party. She's asked me to dinner on 2 March to celebrate the fiftieth anniversary of Ted Heath's election to Parliament – Ted had asked for me specially to be invited.

Wednesday 24 November
I had to slip out of the Coalfields Community Campaign meeting because I was due at the Remploy meeting; these factories were set up after the war, highly subsidised, to allow disabled ex-soldiers to get work. Now they have been handed over by the previous Government to a private company, working along commercial lines and closing down many of them and sacking hundreds and hundreds of workers. A group of MPs is trying to get the Managing Director sacked. Well, I didn't think that helped very much. What you have to do is get the Remploy factories brought back as a public service for disabled people. The Government is always saying it wants to get disabled people back to work and here is an opportunity to do it – and they have left it to the market.

Thursday 25 November
I got up very early and went to the polling station at Pembridge library for Portillo's by-election, I sat there for an hour taking numbers; then I went and voted myself. I came home, made a cup of tea and as I was coming downstairs to the basement, with things in each hand, I went absolutely flat on my face. It's about the third or fourth time I've fallen this year. My dad died after falling down the stairs and fracturing his rib, which gave him pneumonia, so I have got to be careful.

Portillo won with a 4 per cent swing to the Tories, which wasn't bad considering all the scandal about Lord Archer this week.

Sunday 28 November
The *Sunday Telegraph* printed extracts from Paddy Ashdown's diary, in which he reveals his coalition plans with Labour. Apparently there was a

dinner party with himself and Mandelson, Roy Jenkins and Blair, which in effect planned the coalition; he said Blair had offered Cabinet jobs to Menzies Campbell and Ashdown before the election. I'm particularly anxious to keep out of it because it is so personal.

Tuesday 30 November

Went into the Commons and had tea in the Tea Room and a chat. George Howarth, who is a Northern Ireland Minister, told me that Paisley had brought a delegation to protest about Sunday trading in Northern Ireland. Behind him was a group of Democratic Unionist politicians. Paisley said to George, 'What you are doing is destroying the last remnants of Puritanism in Northern Ireland,' and he gave a huge wink. It's an interesting insight into Paisley.

Brian Sedgemore, who is campaigning passionately for Frank Dobson to get the Labour candidacy for Mayor, said that Blair had called a meeting of London MPs behind the Speaker's chair – presumably in his own office – and blamed him (Brian) for not doing enough for Dobson.

Brian did confirm that Blair had campaigned for me for the deputy leadership in 1981 and was a member of CND.

As a result of the implementation of the Belfast Agreement and the establishment of the Executive, tomorrow night (1 December) power will be transferred to Stormont.

Martin McGuinness, the chief negotiator for Sinn Fein, is Minister of Education and this has caused fury among the Tories; he failed the eleven-plus and said that he was in favour of comprehensive education, which will make him even more controversial than being a former member of the IRA Army Council.

Wednesday 1 December

I did a little LBC broadcast about the riots at the World Trade Organisation in Seattle. Seattle has shaken the British Establishment completely, because it thought it had blanked out all protest for ever; even Clinton has had to say that people are entitled to protest. And this is a popular protest. So I was quite pleased about that.

Friday 3 December

The Seattle Conference seems to have ended in a complete disaster. There is no agreement; the Third World countries have decided to stand up against dictation by the multinationals backed by America and Europe; it's the best thing that could have happened and people everywhere are discussing capitalism. Caroline thinks there is a parallel with 1906: after the Liberals were elected in a landslide, disillusion spread and the trouble began.

Saturday 4 December

I do want to say something about the World Trade Organisation. It's very, very important and there is an opportunity there for a really thoughtful speech that will read well in fifty years' time, even though it won't go down well with my colleagues; to explain why politicians come together at the top and are all committed to market forces – globalisation – with a few marginal differences between them. People outside feel unrepresented, excluded, angry, and the more we open British politics to international business, the more we have to clamp down on the British people. I think that's an argument that will make a bit of sense.

Thursday 9 December

We had the big debate on the World Trade Organisation. Stephen Byers opened the speech with incredible, uncritical support of world capitalism. I had worked very hard on my speech – I don't usually work very hard, but I had prepared well.

Then in the evening I looked in briefly at the Speaker's party for Jenny Tanfield, the retiring Librarian. Betty is very sociable. There was a lot of booze there. I had a word with the Speaker and said to her, 'Couldn't you arrange for ex-members, who do not become peers, but who have served for a long time, to have the same facilities as the MPs who become peers?' Because, currently, former Members have no rights in the place, except to visit the Members' Lobby. She wasn't exactly enthusiastic, but I planted the thought.

Friday 10 December

Les and Ricky were working on the wiring for the kitchen. I went to the bank and got out £3000 in cash, just in case there is any problem with the banking system due to the millennium bug. I dare say a lot of other people have done that. I came home and put it under the mattress – it may be unnecessary.

Got a taxi to the Middle Temple Hall for Ralph and Ann Gibson's fiftieth wedding anniversary. Caroline and I and Ralph and Ann had a meal together in Chicago some time in the spring or early summer of 1949, and so the four of us have 200 years of married experience between us. Our kids and their kids were there. There were lots of people whom I knew, but the awful thing was that my memory began to let me down. I had to ask people who others were. There was Lord Wigoder, a very distinguished judge, Louis Blom-Cooper, who has spent all his life campaigning for us to adhere to the European Convention on Human Rights, which we have done; and a man called John Wedgwood came up – his grandfather was Josiah Wedgwood – an eminent physician. The Gibson twins Mary and Elizabeth made a speech about how much they loved their mummy and daddy; Lissie was boohooing like anything. She is so sentimental, it made me cry.

Left to get a taxi in Fleet Street; it was pouring with rain, quite cold, and there were no taxis. After about half an hour I had almost given up hope but a taxi that didn't have its light on, going westwards, saw me did a U-turn and the driver opened the window. 'Are you Tony Benn?'

So I said, 'Yes.'

'Pop in,' he said. 'Oh, I can't believe I have seen you. My dad is eighty-five and such an admirer of yours. What can I do for you?'

So to cut a long story short, this chap, Raymond McCullough, drove me to Middle Temple Hall, picked up Caroline and Neville Labovitch, and Ralph and Ann, who had a bit of a job getting into the cab. She is eighty, and her daughter Mary said that she thought Ann was a tiny bit tipsy. And we all drove back. Mr McCullough gave me the name and address of his father, who is coming back from Florida tomorrow. He saved my life!

Louis Blom-Cooper said that he thought Jack Straw was the most reactionary Home Secretary we have had.

Sunday 12 December

A late lie-in; read the papers. John Prescott has been stripped of responsibility for transport; it's gone to Gus Macdonald, who used to be a Trot on Clydeside and then was head of Scottish Television; a charming man, but of course a terrible kick in the teeth for Prescott. Steven Norris has been rejected by the Tories as their candidate for London.

This is the most important news of all: Mo authorised the bugging of Gerry Adams's car. Now, I have never known the name of a Minister used in connection with a bugging; when asked, they always say that this is a matter Ministers never discuss. The only conclusion I can reach is that Tony Blair was putting that story out in order to discredit Mo Mowlam with her friends in Sinn Fein and to discredit her with the left. I will see Mo and talk to her about it some time this week if I have a chance.

Monday 13 December

In the Lobby I went up to Mo Mowlam, who was surrounded by admirers, and said within the hearing of everyone around her, 'I have had a talk to Julia Langdon who wants to write a biography of you'.

And she said, 'Well, five people are queuing up, but Julia Langdon seems all right.'

Then I said, 'By the way, I notice – it was released, I think, over the weekend – that you authorised the bugging of Gerry Adams and Martin McGuinness and of a Sinn Fein car during the negotiations on the peace process.' I went on, 'I don't know whether you did or didn't, but all I do know is that never in fifty years have I heard it said, with authority, that a named Minister had ordered the interception of a named person. And that could only have come from Number 10 Downing Street.'

Mo said, 'I know.' So she realises now that the Prime Minister is trying to destroy her; partly, I think, because she was too popular, and partly because the Ulster Unionists hated her anyway.

If Livingstone does emerge as an independent candidate, which I think he almost certainly will, I shall support him. I am not going to let Livingstone be isolated. I shall simply go round saying that he's overwhelmingly the best candidate; the problem was caused by the fact that the Prime Minister, quite wrongly, sacked Frank Dobson. Obviously I don't want to be expelled from the Labour Party, but I am not going to let Blair get away with this; looking back on my life, I have always concluded that I never went far enough.

Tuesday 14 December

I went into the House and heard Douglas Hogg, Lord Hailsham's son, make a marvellous speech on the Anti-Terrorism Bill; the Liberals are not voting against the Bill, both Front Benches are supporting it. I spoke – but it wasn't what my dad used to call an A-class speech. I told the Chief Whip I couldn't support it.

I had a letter from Blair today in response to the one I sent him about the Liberals. All he said was, ' Dear Tony, thanks for your letter; the Liberal Democrat membership of the Cabinet Co-ordinating Committee is working well. All the best, Tony.'

Wednesday 15 December

I went to the BBC for a twelve-minute interview with Patricia Hollis (Baroness Hollis) about the centenary of the Labour Party; the BBC woman didn't know that Labour had ever won a working majority before Blair won, so it was easy to deal with her. But the argument between Patricia Hollis and myself was an interesting one. I asked her about New Labour as a new political party, and she did what all New Labour people do: she talked about poverty, and the need to deal with inequality of opportunity, and so on, which is radical language associated with Conservative policies. Very clever.

There was a huge traffic jam tonight – the Spice Girls are appearing at Earls Court. Got home very late.

Friday 17 December

On the train to Chesterfield I read the *New Statesman* which had a two-page story on the 'Dream Cabinet of the Century'; they had asked readers to nominate it. Tony Blair got only one more vote than I did, so he was made Minister of Agriculture, and the *New Statesman* staff allocated the job of Leader of the House of Commons to me. Churchill was Minister of Defence; Lloyd George, Social Security; Thatcher, Cabinet Enforcer; Jenkins, Home Secretary; Attlee, Prime Minister; Barbara Castle, the Environment; and so on. Caroline said she thought only 123 people had voted! Still, that was better than nothing. So that entertained me on the journey.

I rang Jean Corston, who is on the Parliamentary Committee that meets with Tony Blair, to ask her a couple of things and she told me that Blair had an enormous affection and respect for Chris Mullin. I said, 'Well, it was a bit rough to appoint Chris to look after the air traffic control issue.'

And she said, 'Oh, Tony Blair didn't know he was going to get that job; he put him in the Department of the Environment and the Regions and Prescott put him in charge of air traffic control.' She was sure Chris would get promotion.

The United Nations have offered a suspension of sanctions if the Iraqis will allow inspectors in. And the Iraqis have turned it down, on the grounds that the inspectors are simply identifying targets for the next rounds of bombing. The French are against the proposal; I think they abstained, with the Russians and the Chinese. Britain as usual does everything it's told.

Did an interview for Radio 5 Live about it with a man called Terry Taylor, a professor at Stanford University. He knew all about chemical and biological warfare, so I asked him, 'What about the bombing of the Sudan?'

'Oh well,' he said, 'We know that some years ago that factory, which is partly owned by Osama Bin Laden, was producing a precursor for chemical weapons'.

And I said, 'Well, the Americans have never given any evidence for this, and the British Government have never said they agree with it; they simply said we support it because the Americans told us this.' I also put to him the question of whether the inspectors in Iraq were spies for Israel and America, and he said, 'Well, of course, all the things they discovered they shared with the other members of the UN.'

I can understand why Saddam says he doesn't want the inspectors back, and I think he is in a strong position because the Western front on this is cracking; it's just America followed by its little dog, Britain, with nobody else in favour.

Saturday 25 December

I had a word with Dave and wished him a Happy Christmas and he said, 'I wonder whether Ken Livingstone has thought of asking Glenda Jackson to run as his Deputy Mayor?'

So I rang Ken and he said, 'Oh yes, yes, Glenda and I are giving a joint press conference on Wednesday to complain about the way the ballot is being fixed, and I'm certainly thinking of asking her to run'.

I said, 'Well, it will be much better than Trevor Phillips, who is running with Dobson'. Ken also said, 'Mo Mowlam is coming to a meal shortly'. Well, that is a very important bit of information, because if Mo came out for Ken, or Mo ran with Ken (which I'm sure she won't), it would be a sensation.

Friday 31 December

The most important thing of all has been that Caroline is still alive and very active, although she is in pain and she has got to go and have further scans; but she is an amazing woman – still has time to plan Christmas, thinking of everybody, buying all the presents and organising everything; and although she has to rest a lot because of the discomfort in her spine and take painkillers, who would have thought three and a half years ago that she would still be here.

We have been married for half a century, which is one-fortieth of the whole Christian era. So we have had a long stint and, although I hope it doesn't end, we have really had a marvellous time and we have got a marvellous family; marvellous opportunities throughout our lives. And Caroline has been an absolute tower of strength – I can't tell you what a tower of strength she has been.

Thursday 6 January, 2000

Tony Blair has gone cool on proportional representation. I don't think you could get it through Conference myself, or the Cabinet for that matter; he is supposed to have gone cool on it because of the experience of the Scottish Government, which is a coalition and already has trouble over tuition fees. Also, Blair is supposed to have realised that the European elections under proportional representation produced a catastrophic fall in turnout.

The Transport and General Workers' Union ballot for the Labour candidate for Mayor of London was 85 per cent for Ken Livingstone, 7 per cent for Glenda Jackson and 6 per cent for Frank Dobson, which is an astonishing result. If that were to take place across all the trade unions, of course he'd win despite the MPs who have got to vote for Dobson or risk their careers.

Monday 10 January

The big news today is that the flu epidemic has knocked the Health Service sideways; and what's so interesting is that it has established a real weakness in the Health Service. It can't cope with emergencies, but the cleverness of the Government's spin doctors is to make the big story 'A Flu Epidemic'. Saw a bit of *Newsnight* with John Denham, the Health Minister, and he was just batting on, the way Ministers do now; they just talk through questions, go on repeating the same points, look very confident. And in terms of the skill of its presentation, you simply can't beat the Government. Harry Barnes said to me, 'Why did we spend so much on the millennium bug and so little on the flu bug?'

Tuesday 11 January

Shaun Woodward, the Tory MP who has defected to Labour, saw me and chased me in the Lobby. He came up and said, 'I first met you when I worked for *Newsnight.*'

So I said to him, 'Well you know you should resign your seat.'

He said, 'Ah yes, but I feel I'm in the same party – individual liberty is what matters.'

Rubbish! He obviously wanted to say that he had spoken to me.

The Home Secretary seems to have accepted that General Pinochet, who was due to be extradited to Spain for trial on basic human-rights and torture allegations, should be released on the grounds that his health wouldn't allow him to stand trial. That's exactly what I thought would happen, but there will be one hell of a row. I saw Robin Cook in the Lobby and I told him. He hadn't heard, and I said, 'If you let that happen, you will totally undermine all of the arguments about war criminals.' He looked a bit shaken.

Wednesday 12 January

At 3.30 we had a statement by Jack Straw explaining why he was going to let Pinochet go. I got in a question comparing the wars against Iraq and Yugoslavia, when innocent people were killed and it was justified on humanitarian grounds, with the release of a torturer on humanitarian grounds. The ethical foreign policy is finished. I was the only one who spoke against it. Bob Marshall-Andrews was very respectful of Straw because, from a lawyer's point of view, you had to take account of these considerations. And Tam Dalyell, who had apparently seen the Chilean Ambassador, was persuaded that this was the right decision. Jeremy Corbyn and Ann Clwyd, who were both much involved, were not called at all and they complained to the Speaker. I think the Speaker was a bit anxious about it.

The more I think about the Pinochet thing, the more utterly disgraceful it is. There is a man who unquestionably ordered the killing and torture of a lot of people. Three or four Governments (I think Spain, Norway, France and Switzerland) have all got extradition appeals for him and, on the grounds that he is not very well, he is being let off. I think anyone who had been tortured is entitled to know that the person responsible for it is properly examined. The more I think about Jack Straw, the more frightened I am by him; he has got all the right-wing thought processes. He is also trying to get rid of juries for certain trials and calling it modernisation.

Thursday 13 January

Took Caroline to the hospital to have her injection in advance of her full scan, and it is now about a quarter to twelve and I am just going to take her back again.

I sat in the room where the scan was done by a very senior and experienced technician and, as the scan was done, I talked to him about it: what does this mean? What does that mean? He didn't seem very worried by the pictures that he took and I came away quite relieved.

Friday 14 January

While I was in Chesterfield I had a message on my pager to ring Sally Morgan at Number 10. Well, Sally Morgan is the Prime Minister's closest political assistant really. So I rang Number 10 and there was a great deal of embarrassment. 'We're awfully sorry, but I'm afraid we want to get on to your son,' so I sent a pager message to Hilary. They wanted him to find out whether Stephen Pound, the member for Ealing North, was going to be supporting Frank Dobson; and the reason for that was that Stephen had said at an earlier meeting with Blair, 'Won't it be counter-productive?' and apparently Blair had turned on him. The fact that the Prime Minister spends so much time trying to stop Ken Livingstone is highly significant. Ministers and MPs have been really bullied to do more and more to get Dobson in, and of course it's not helping Dobson at all.

Today Lord Winston, who is a doctor and has been made a life peer by Blair, made a statement saying that the Government was deceiving people about the NHS and it needed much more money, and that the reforms the Tories had introduced had not been changed; he also said something very indiscreet: that Cherie Blair was going to have a Caesarean operation when her baby is due in the summer. Well, he knew he had no business to say that, but it has created a huge uproar and already by tonight the spin doctors had forced him to retract. The Blair miracle is beginning to evaporate.

Monday 17 January

At long last, and after about three months of chaos in the office, the carpet-fitters came to put a new carpet in the two rooms.

It was Jill Craigie's memorial service today. Jon Snow, who made a very touching speech, is such a nice guy, and Paul Foot made a brilliant, moving speech about how he had been brought up as a public schoolboy never to discuss anything difficult, and how Jill would probe until the real issues came out. He was able to stand, even though he was very shaky on his legs. While we were sitting there Cherie Blair arrived and sat next to Caroline.

Caroline told her that we know Tim Owen very well – he used to go out with Melissa and is going into new chambers with Cherie. Cherie and Caroline had a long talk while I went and had a word with Alastair Campbell. I told him about Sally Morgan ringing me on Friday and I said, 'When I rang back, I thought at least I was going to be offered a peerage!'

He said, 'You really ought to come and film a Lobby briefing at Number 10 and see how the press behaves.'

So I said, 'I would love to do that.'

Caroline thinks he is a bit nervous of me. I don't know whether that's true, but still, I'm strongly in favour of getting on well with everybody. It was a huge gathering; we spoke to Michael Foot briefly.

Tuesday 18 January

Went over to the House. Then, just after half-past three, I raised with the Speaker the question of Ian Paisley's letter to a constituent describing Martin McGuinness as a terrorist. I did rather hope the Speaker would say that she deplored the use of such language, but she said, 'I'm not commenting on the private correspondence of Members of Parliament,' so I half-achieved what I wanted by putting it on the record. I saw her later in the corridor in plain clothes (she must have been to a tea party or something) and so I said, 'I hope I didn't embarrass you.'

'No, not at all,' she said, 'but I couldn't say any more than that.' She went on, 'What I'm really nervous of is that when we have the debate about allowing McGuinness and Gerry Adams to use the facilities of the House, which is what Peter Mandelson's going to propose in a week or two, the word terrorism will be thrown across the floor all the time.'

So I said, 'Well, I understand that.' Then, as I had the opportunity, I said to her, 'By the way, Betty, I see you took part in the hundredth anniversary of the first car to come to the House of Commons. Well, on Monday 31 January I shall be the first to bring an electric car in; it is called the Sparrow. If you have got nothing better to do . . .' So maybe Betty will come out and drive it round the block, which would be very nice.

I had a note from Portillo saying that he was intending during the health debate to quote my diary on the resignation of Bevan, so I saw him in the corridor and said, 'Which bit are you quoting?' he said, 'When you say that the idea of a free Health Service was not a matter of principle but a matter of practice.'

I rushed back to my room and found the diary entry, and it is true that at that time I was a sort of New Labour man and I supported Gaitskell against Nye on the question of prescription charges. But when I turned the page it said that I would be in favour of increasing income tax to meet the costs. So when Portillo got up to speak and made the point referring to me, I got up, thanked him for telling me and said, 'If he reads on a line or two he will find that I was in favour of increasing income tax.' So at least I saved my reputation.

Then in the corridor I saw Ann Taylor and Clive Soley. 'Ah, just the two I want to speak to,' I said, pointing to the messages I get regularly on my pager telling us that WE DO NOT RESPOND TO MEDIA SURVEYS, WHICH CAN BE UNHELPFUL. I asked, 'Why do you send us these?' 'They *can* be unhelpful,' they said.

'We are all free men and women, you know. We are not going to say anything damaging, but if somebody rings me up and says we are doing a survey asking, "Do you think that the House of Lords should be elected", why shouldn't I say yes? Alastair Campbell answers media questions every day.'

'Well, that's quite different. Anyway,' Clive said, 'You don't have to obey the message.'

'I know that, because I make up my own mind.'

Ann Taylor must be very angry with me because I just vote according to my conscience. And there is something funny about Clive Soley. He used to be very progressive and left-wing, but he has gone the other way.

I had tea with Mark Fisher in the Tea Room – very nice lad is Mark. He said Caroline was just as lovely as ever. Then, when we had the vote, I went up to Mo in the Lobby and she said, 'Oh, Hilary speaks with such clarity; he must be fed up with people comparing him to you.' Then she said, 'I'm busy on drugs.'

So I said, 'I hope you put the whole case for cannabis, not just for recreational use, but above all for medical use. You know Caroline has got cancer and if she needs cannabis, she should have it.'

'Oh, I'm working on that, but they are very resistant to anything.'

I drove Hilary home and he told me that Mo had said to him that she thought cannabis should be legalised, and with the tax revenue they should fund the problems associated with alcoholism etc., which I entirely agree with.

Wednesday 19 January

Sheila arrived and we sorted things. She is so efficient, she has got everything organised, tidy; at the moment she is engaged in a tussle to throw more things out.

I met Helena Kennedy, a top New Labour QC, just outside the House of Lords. She said, 'Will you look at these amendments on the Bill relating to jury service?'

So I told her, 'Helena, you don't have to persuade me!'

Thursday 20 January

Sky Television came to interview me about the Wakeham Report on the Lords, which is the most undemocratic proposal you could imagine. There was a tall black guy with dreadlocks working on the camera, and I introduced myself.

So he said, '*I'm* Tony Benn.'

I couldn't believe it, but he showed me his pass and there it was: Tony Benn, with his photograph. We had a good old talk and it turned out that his parents had named him Tony after me; and his brother is Nigel Benn, the boxer. Really funny. Very nice guy and he wrote a little note saying 'Nice to meet another one', signed Tony Benn.

Thursday 27 January
Stephen has just come back from Stormont, where he had been talking to some of the members of the Northern Ireland Assembly on behalf of the Royal Society of Chemistry. He's very imaginative, I must say; but he was absolutely hilarious about Northern Ireland. He said he met some members of the Assembly and they assumed that he wanted money. 'How much do you want?'

Well he said, 'I don't want any money. I just want to try and help and cooperate.' They didn't really understand that. Then he said he listened to a debate on education, peppered by accusations shouted across the Chamber. 'You're a member of the Army Council of the IRA' or 'You're a terrorist'. He was also shown what's called the Strong Room, where members of the Assembly hand in their guns when they arrive and they are locked in the Strong Room until the debate is over. He said, 'When Clinton came over he couldn't believe this.' Apparently they were persuaded to leave their guns at home when Clinton was there, but a fully armed Assembly discussing decommissioning is rather comic, I must say.

Fiona Mactaggart, the MP for Slough, had offered to lend me a book by John O'Farrell – which she did yesterday – about the Labour Party and I flipped through it; it was so contemptuous of the Eighties that it really made me angry. So I got extremely cross in the Lobby with Fiona yesterday. I thought I would find her and have a word with her and apologise, which I did, and every time I tried to say something she said, 'Oh, don't reopen it.' Jenny Jones and Hazel Blears were sitting there with her, and Caroline Flint opposite, so there were four women and me and every time I tried to raise the subject, she said, 'Oh, don't start that again.' I said, 'Well, that book pressed my ejector seat,' and Fiona said, 'We knew that.'

Later I was sitting with a table of Tories. Nicholas Soames opposite did a marvellous imitation of Ali G. when he said to Teddy Taylor, 'Is Jamaica in the European Union?' And when Teddy Taylor said 'No', Ali G. asked, 'Is that racism, man?' He was very jolly; I do like Nicholas.

Friday 28 January, Chesterfield
Went and did my surgery from two to six.

Talking of surgeries, today Nigel Jones, the Liberal Democrat MP for Cheltenham, and his assistant, who was a local councillor, were attacked by a man with a sword; this killed his assistant and seriously injured Nigel. It's amazing it's never happened to me in fifty years. I've had one or two sort of nasty people come, but no one has ever threatened to injure me. But it's just a warning.

Then I went to the meeting at the Winding Wheel centre about the WTO in Seattle, organised as usual by the Socialist Workers' Party. An SWP journalist who had been at Seattle gave a most vivid account of what had happened – how the police had used plastic bullets and tear gas on students; how 40,000 trade unionists joined the students; how the Mayor of Seattle had said that the protesters had won. He linked it all to the general political situation in Britain.

Monday 31 January

I got up very early this morning and Wayne Mitchell arrived at about half-past seven with a friend and a little three-wheeled brightly painted Sparrow electric car. His company produces electric vehicles and has imported this little one from Los Angeles. I promised them I would take it to the House of Commons to give it a bit of publicity. I had cleared it with the Speaker, with the Serjeant at Arms, and told the police at the House.

I'd never been in an electric vehicle before. It has a little switch that says 'reverse', 'forward' and 'off' and an accelerator and brake. It was just a pleasure to drive and everybody waves at you – you really feel as if you are a racing driver doing a lap of honour. Got to the House and it was a tremendous success. What they didn't tell me was that they had arranged for five other Sparrow vehicles to go in, so there they all were: canary-yellow and pink with green spots.

The Serjeant at Arms was there; the Speaker turned up and did a circuit round New Palace Yard with it; then all six cars did a circuit. It was huge fun; I haven't had as much fun since I learned to fly. TV and press photographers were there and it was a boost for electric cars and for the possibility of jobs.

Caroline went to the Chelsea and Westminster Hospital to see Dr Costello, a haematologist; and she had a mass of blood tests and Dr Costello said that she had pernicious anaemia – that's to say, vitamin B_{12} is not getting through. She is going to have injections every day.

Had a talk to Jeremy Corbyn, who told me that somebody has leaked the correspondence between the Home Office and General Pinochet's legal team. Straw's making a great thing about not being able to release the medical report.

Tuesday 1 February

Northern Ireland is in a tremendous state of crisis. Trimble had set a deadline for the end of January for decommissioning. General de Chastelain, a Canadian general in charge of links with the IRA, had to report that no weapons had been handed in.

Trimble wants the Assembly and the Executive suspended and direct rule reintroduced; Gerry Adams says deadlines are not necessary. The truth is that Trimble is being told: if you don't produce results we are going to scupper you.

Today Haider, the far-right Austrian Leader, has negotiated to enter his country's coalition government, and the Americans and the European Union are talking about taking sanctions against Austria. I'm very much opposed to Haider, but once the European Union takes sanctions against governments it doesn't like, it really is like Mrs Thatcher suspending Liverpool City Council. I mean, it is a move against democratic control; of course it's quite ineffective anyway, because all it does is strengthen the Leader concerned – as we know in Yugoslavia and Iraq. It is a sinister development but it would be very unpopular to oppose this because people would say you're soft on fascists. That isn't the issue.

Thursday 3 February

I was so tired in the House that I had a snooze and, believe it or not, there was a Disney film called *The Sword and the Rose* with James Robertson Justice and I just watched it in my room (I'm really ashamed, it's the first time I've ever done it).

At seven o'clock there was a statement on Northern Ireland by Mandelson, in which he described the crisis there and said the Government intended to introduce legislation next week that would allow direct rule to return. Mandelson did handle it very well, so I waited just behind the Speaker's chair and when I saw him I said, 'I think that was the best statement I have heard made by a Secretary of State in a very difficult situation.'

He said, 'I appreciate that.'

Monday 7 February

The telephone rang all morning. One man rang and said, 'I'm a businessman and I'm trying to get on to the Chesterfield Borough Council, and I ring them and they simply won't pick up the phone.' To begin with I thought he was a London businessman, so I said, 'Well, I can't help you.'

Then he said, 'Why? I thought you were my MP.'

So I said, 'Yes, I am, for Chesterfield.'

'Well, I'm a constituent and I am trying to get on to Chesterfield Borough Council.'

Anyway I told him to hang on, then I picked up another phone, rang Chesterfield Borough Council and they answered. Then I put both phones together and he made contact with them.

Wednesday 9 February

This afternoon was the debate in the Welsh Assembly on a vote of no confidence in Alun Michael, who Blair imposed on the Welsh party as First Secretary last year, preventing Rhodri Morgan from being elected. Rhodri is not a left-winger by any means; he is a retired former DTI civil servant. Just before today's vote in the Welsh Assembly was due, Alun

Michael resigned because he knew he was finished. So Morgan has become acting First Secretary, and of course now has to be elected as the Labour Party leader in Wales. So I went round saying to everybody, 'You have heard the news, haven't you?'

And they said, 'What's that?'

'Peter Mandelson has suspended the Welsh Assembly because Alun Michael, like Trimble, has resigned.'

'You can't be right!'

I had this exchange with Mark Fisher and when I said, 'No, I was joking!' he said, 'I wish you wouldn't make such realistic jokes.' I might add that Blair has now given his support to Morgan and said he was a very loyal member of the Party.

Well at 4.30 I was conscripted to go on to the Committee on Delegated Legislation to discuss a statutory instrument, introduced by David Blunkett, which would allow some change in the policy on foreign-language teaching but would also allow citizenship to go on the National Curriculum. Professor Bernard Crick, whom I've known for nearly fifty years, had written an advisory committee report and sat through the debate; and the Labour Minister spoke, followed by James Clappison, who put a lot of legitimate questions. Then of course nobody wanted to speak except the Liberals and Eric Forth. So I was called and I made a joke about languages and the complication for people who were trying to translate *manãna* the Spanish word for 'tomorrow' into Irish; how they didn't have a word in Irish conveying that degree of urgency. At the end of my speech I said that I hoped Chris Woodhead, the head of OFSTED, isn't brought in, because he's had a catastrophic effect on teachers' morale and he'll start having a league table of Ministers, naming and shaming them. I said, 'My view, I feel sure, is shared at a high level in the Department of Education.'

Thursday 10 February

The hijack at Stansted has ended – I think the truth is that these Afghanistani guys hijacked a plane with a lot of passengers in order to get political asylum here; and I don't think the passengers were really under any threat at all. They kept sending messages to the press saying, 'We'll kill them if you don't do what we want,' but they never said what they wanted. It's quite a difficult problem for the Home Secretary, I have to give him credit for that.

Sunday 13 February

We caught the Jubilee Line to the Greenwich Dome and there all the family turned up, as arranged, at 10.30.

I was very much opposed to all the money wasted on the Dome, but whatever you think of the wisdom of doing it, Richard Rogers's great structure is terribly impressive. The people running the various exhibits were all extremely friendly. One, for example, in the Talk Zone (run by British Telecom) had a British Telecom engineer training people; he was coming up to retirement and thought he would spend the last month in the Dome. Then he's going to train at university and become a primary-school teacher. There was a picture of me in the People Zone.

Saw Alistair Darling, whom I'd never spoken to in my life, but did today, with his wife and children having an ice-cream cornet. We saw a marvellous gymnastic display. The Faith Zone had all sorts of faiths but no socialist faith. The Mind Zone was a sort of exploration of people's minds. The Talk Zone was mainly about new technology, and another BT engineer showed us a wireless application project whereby you could surf the Internet on a mobile phone and do almost anything you wanted; that obviously is the future. It was actually a thoroughly enjoyable day.

Monday 14 February
St Valentine's day and I had a lovely present from Pixie this morning; and I took her a rose on her breakfast tray.

Tuesday 15 February
After a campaign by Gordon Prentice, the Government has decided it will put up the minimum wage this year, by ten pence an hour. The Government had said it wouldn't, but because of the fear that there might be a vote forced tomorrow morning at the Parliamentary Party meeting, it has decided to capitulate, so it shows it is worth putting the pressure on.

The Parliamentary Committee report – that is the committee of Labour Members that meets Tony Blair each week – tells you so much about New Labour. The report for Wednesday 9 February, said:

> Item 4 The Committee noted that a motion had been submitted by a number of colleagues for discussion at the PLP on the subject of the National Minimum Wage. It was agreed this be taken at the next meeting. Concern was expressed at the possibility there could be a proliferation of motions at PLP meetings, with damaging consequences. The main concern was that meetings would increasingly become a focus for media speculation about personalities and potential divisions in the Party, undermining the present format, which encourages Ministers to be open and available to colleagues. The Chair said that he was giving active consideration to developing a mechanism by which backbench colleagues could have a greater degree of determination of the matters discussed at PLP meetings, but preferably on a basis which did not involve decisive votes.

Well, that is modern Labour: we don't want any votes, we don't want any decisions; we just have 'doors always open to Ministers'. I think that tells you a great deal.

Sunday 20 February
In the afternoon the results for the candidacy for Mayor of London were announced. Predictably, Ken Livingstone won 60 per cent of the votes of all the individual members and the majority of votes from those unions that were balloted; of the eighty-eight MPs and Greater London Authority candidates, only eight voted for him. So Dobson won by 1.5 per cent. An absolutely fiddled system. I'll just go back over it quickly.

First of all, nobody but Blair wanted an elected Mayor; but when it was announced, Ken Livingstone indicated from the beginning that he would be a candidate. Blair tried to get Glenda Jackson to run then he forced Dobson to resign from the Cabinet to run and withdrew his support from Glenda, which made her very angry. We were told there was going to be a One Member One Vote system for London Labour Party members, then they introduced an Electoral College and all the Greater London Authority candidates who had been selected were given a vote, even though none of them had ever been elected to anything. The AEEU, under Sir Ken Jackson, wouldn't have a ballot; the South London Co-op wouldn't have a ballot; there was telephone voting, which was open to abuse; there was no scrutiny of any kind of the votes. And thus a predictable result was produced. Ken Livingstone understandably did look very disappointed and said that it was a tainted procedure and Frank Dobson should retire. That's going to be the big story.

Monday 21 February
No Labour MP can risk expulsion by supporting Ken, but it is a terrible tragedy for the Labour Party. I had a row with Dennis Skinner and Brian Sedgemore, who is a total cynic. Brian said, 'Well, it was the same system that you had when you fought the deputy leadership.'

'Tony Blair is becoming a Mussolini,' I said.

'Oh no, he's not,' said Sedgemore. 'He can't make the trains run on time.' That was quite funny.

Tuesday 22 February
This morning the story in the *Guardian* was that maybe Dobson would retire and the National Executive would have a special meeting and propose Mo Mowlam as a candidate. Quite an incredible story; could do damage to Dobson. I know Mo doesn't want the job, and if they did ditch Dobson, it would really be the end.

Saturday 26 February

Caroline had a tummy ache and in the afternoon the pain had become so acute that she cried out; she had a very high temperature of 103°, and she was shaking like a leaf and her pulse was racing and I got really frightened. She said I had better ring for an ambulance to take her into hospital, and Jane Pettifer, our local doctor, called for one – to my amazement within about twenty minutes a very senior paramedic arrived with a young man. The young man turned out to be a doctor – I've never known a doctor to come out with a paramedic before. Anyway, he examined her and said he didn't quite know what it was. Then a few minutes later an ambulance with four people arrived, packed Caroline up and took her to the Accident and Emergency department at Charing Cross Hospital. By then she was virtually unconscious; she doesn't remember going to the hospital at all. They examined her and brought down a consultant called Mr Hafez, a very distinguished Egyptian who was on duty overnight. They decided to take her in, which was a great relief because I didn't think I would be able to cope. Just before I called the doctor, she had gone into the bathroom on her own and fallen and I found it very difficult to lift her.

The odd thing was that in the early hours of the morning I went to the loo and heard a bang downstairs. I didn't know what it was but when I went downstairs I discovered that the star chart with details of the star that had been named after Caroline (which had been given to me by Bernie Wooder) had fallen off the wall, and that seemed like a bad omen.

Wednesday 1 March

Caroline's in a sort of semi-intensive care unit, where they keep a very close eye on you and are popping in and out all the time, taking blood pressure and temperature.

In the ward there's a wide variation and turnover of people. When she first arrived there was one old man in the corner opposite her; he has been replaced by somebody who has just had a major operation, absolutely wired up like anything; next to her was an elderly woman who disappeared and was replaced by an Iraqi man. Dead opposite her was an old man who was waiting to have his legs amputated because he has diabetes; but at the end of today a man of about sixty-five turned up, who's got prostate cancer.

The porters here are employed by a private company who got a contract with the hospital. A young lad told me that they don't get London weighting and are not represented by a trade union. Tonight an agency nurse came in from Nightingale Nursing Services.

Thursday 2 March

Caroline has been moved to another ward, this time an all-women's ward.

There was a very tall, elegant woman of about thirty and I asked her where she was from, and she said that she was from Kosovo. I assumed she was a Serb, but she said, 'No, I'm an Albanian and we will never forget what you did for us.' Well, I suppose she must have assumed that I supported the war.

Came home and changed into my dinner jacket, which still fits after fifty years. I went into the House and then went over to the Speaker's dinner for Ted Heath. As I arrived, Tony Blair was coming up the stairs with someone from Number 10, one of his political advisers, and he said, 'I'm only coming for drinks.' Anyway the two of us arrived earlier than anyone else; he said that he couldn't wait to get out of his business clothes and into jeans and an open-necked shirt and I said I was just the same; we had a discussion about whether we could wear open-necked shirts in the House. He said, 'I couldn't do it,' and I said, 'Honestly, you're wrong. Jimmy Carter was the first American President to look informal. If you turned up with an open-necked shirt, as long as you were respectable, you would absolutely change the culture of the House – everyone would follow you. You'd set the fashion.' He laughed.

Austin Mitchell was there taking a few photographs. I was put between Lord Carr, who used to be Minister of Labour, and Lord Hurd, who used to be Foreign Secretary. Talked mainly to Douglas Hurd, who is frightfully friendly; he is only seventy. Carr was elected along with Enoch Powell and Iain Macleod and Ted Heath in 1950. Betty got up and made a very gracious speech about Ted. Ted was sitting there in a white dinner jacket with a cummerbund holding in his large girth. He made a very amusing speech, without notes, in which he talked about his early days in the House.

Tam Dalyell was there; everybody was congratulating him on the obituaries he writes for *The Independent*, and he said that he dare not ring the home of MPs in case their wives think he is ringing to get details for their forthcoming obituary. Jim Callaghan was there with a stick, looking rather thin I thought. I greeted him as he came in and he gave me a sort of watery warm smile.

Next to him was Clarissa Eden, the Countess of Avon, Anthony Eden's second wife; she must be in her eighties now. At the very end, looking terribly frail and shaky, and almost inaudible, was Jeremy Thorpe; he has got Parkinson's disease and really is very ill. When you get near him he's almost like a ghost. Then across the table was Lady Soames, Nicholas Soames's mother and Churchill's daughter; she gave me a kiss on both cheeks and couldn't have been friendlier. She is very nice, is Mary Soames, and I said to her how kind Churchill had been to me.

I saw Mary Wilson and said how much I had loved Ian Walters's statue of Harold in Huddersfield. She said, 'Oh, it's lovely. People said, "Where is his pipe?", but if you look he's putting his hand in his pocket to pull it out.' Next to her was John Major, always very cheerful, and then Lady Thatcher. After the dinner I went up to her and said, 'May I pay my respects' and she couldn't have been more friendly. She and Hurd agreed that I shouldn't leave Parliament.

I said, 'It was very nice of you to come to Ted's party'.

And Thatcher said, 'Oh well, you know, as you get older you get mellow.'

It's hard to believe, and I said, 'I often talk about you as somebody who says what they mean and mean what they say – and do it. And what they now treat with contempt is a conviction politician.'

She became very animated, and at one stage when I said to her, 'The European thing's going wrong, isn't it?' she said, 'And I'm absolutely delighted.'

It was very interesting – it was like going to Madame Tussaud's, with the waxworks being able to speak. I should think the average age was well over seventy.

Oh, Charles Kennedy was there, but I didn't speak to him.

I forgot: of course, the political news today is that at eight o'clock this morning Jack Straw announced that he had decided to let Pinochet return; a Chilean military aircraft had already been brought to Brize Norton, and Pinochet was driven at high speed to the airport and was off by a quarter-past eight. Of course Thatcher made a comment saying that it was marvellous. It's a tragic error. Straw has totally undermined the ethical foreign policy; the principle that people are responsible for their actions; the criticism of Milošević and Saddam. So, in a sense, it helps the left's cause, but what a disgraceful thing to do. There is some talk of Pinochet being prosecuted in Chile, but they can't do that because he has life immunity as a Senator.

Friday 3 March

Rather lazy start. Went off to the hospital and Caroline is going to be discharged on Monday; she has been disconnected from everything. The neurological man is going to look at the problem of her legs, because that's the thing that would matter most to her. At any rate they have done nothing, but they have not discovered anything.

Saturday 4 March

I happened to switch on the television and there was a programme, using detailed archive material and interviews, about the shooting down of the Iranian Airbus by the Americans in the Persian Gulf on 3 July 1988. Everyone had known that it was shot down 'by accident'; but it wasn't just that they failed to recognise that it was a civilian plane and killed as many people as died at Lockerbie. There is no doubt whatsoever that Iran saw it as part of an undeclared war on themselves, and at the end they linked it to Lockerbie and left no doubt that the Iranians did the Lockerbie bombing as retribution for what happened to the Iranian Airbus.

Monday 6 March

Ken Livingstone announced today that he was standing as an independent and Dobson immediately denounced him, saying that he wasn't a socialist or a left-winger – really abusive language, the kind of language Thatcher used against Livingstone in the 1980s. Blair was on television saying much the same.

I walked over the bridge to County Hall, which was of course the headquarters of the GLC, and I was last there in 1986 when the GLC was abolished. Now it's all been done up as a hotel. There was an ITN party to celebrate the retirement of Michael Brunson and the appointment of John Sergeant from the BBC. While I was there my pager went off; I normally get a message from the whips saying, 'Adjournment Debate will begin at eight', but this arrived on my pager as 'A German Debate will begin at eight'. So I said to Alastair Campbell, 'You know, they get a bit muddled at Millbank Tower' and showed him the message, and Alastair, who has a good sense of humour, saluted me, 'Ja wohl.' I just wandered round, as I did really at the dinner for Ted Heath, talking to a few people.

Tuesday 7 March

I went to the House of Commons and left a little envelope with £100 in it for Ken Livingstone's campaign. I'm sure he needs support.

Wednesday 8 March

Went to the Commons. Had a meeting of the Campaign Group, which was really interesting. We thanked Bob Marshall-Andrews for the brilliant work on the Jury Trials Bill. Jeremy Corbyn reported on Pinochet, and said that there was going to be a Pinochet-watch in Chile keeping us posted, and that he thought the real reason Pinochet had been sent home was that the Americans put pressure on Blair, because they knew that if he came to trial Henry Kissinger's role would be exposed.

Just as I was coming home to get Caroline a meal, I saw Peter Kilfoyle in New Palace Yard and I said to him, 'How are things going?'

He kept me talking for about twenty minutes and his comments were absolutely to the point. He said, 'Blair reminds me of Peter Sellers in the film *Being There*. He's completely out of touch with the Party, he has a completely different agenda. I'll tell you in confidence that David Clark, who was a Minister in the Cabinet Office for fifteen months, never had a face-to-face with Blair.'

And I said, 'Well, I knew that because David told me.'

Kilfoyle said, 'The Cabinet never discussed anything; the minutes were so boring, just noting that "the Prime Minister said" and "Gordon Brown said."' And he went on, 'Blair simply doesn't understand the movement. There is real poverty in the North; some in London, but there is more in the North, but he won't understand it.' Peter Kilfoyle is right-wing but he does believe in the movement. He said that he didn't believe in charismatic leaders; in that connection he compared Tony Blair with Ken Livingstone.

So I came home, and I have got to go back in a few minutes' time to vote at ten o'clock.

Thursday 9 March
The replacement part for the Dyson vacuum cleaner arrived. Mrs Mac couldn't use the Dyson because a key component has got lost, but I rang them up and they sent it to me at no extra cost; I think it would cost fifteen or twenty quid to buy. So that increased my respect for them.

Then somebody from the Dolphin Stair Lift Company arrived and I decided to go plonk – for nearly £5000 I have ordered a stair lift so that Caroline will in future be able to get downstairs from the bedroom without any strain or effort or risk of falling.

Decided to cancel my surgery tomorrow. I'm going to cancel almost everything next week that I possibly can.

Friday 10 March
After fifty-one years of putting my work above Caroline and the family, I've decided to reverse the whole proceedings. It's an easy thing to do because somebody else can do the surgeries, and meetings; they will always get other speakers, and the whips are very understanding.

Barbara discovered that there is no hot water going into the washing machine. So I tried to turn the hot tap, which was stuck. I used a spanner and broke the tap, so now I've got to get a plumber in to do that job. The Macmillan nurse is coming next and she had prescribed some pills, which I collected for Caroline today. So that's the new domestic Tony Benn, and I must say I'm enjoying it.

Sunday 12 March
Newspapers full of rubbish. There was an article saying Frank Dobson would have to shave his beard off if he wanted to win – and, believe it or not, on Channel 4 tonight Anthony Howard was interviewed about bearded Prime Ministers, and there was a mock-up of Dobson without a beard and of Blair with a beard. I have never heard such nonsense in my life. Then an article about Steven Norris's sex life; he is the Tory candidate. Livingstone is doing very well wooing everybody.

Will Hutton said that he thought the boom would collapse, because it was just like the South Sea bubble, or Japan two years ago; and there is a sort of general feeling, which I agree with, that the rise in share prices is just out of this world.

Caroline has been in considerable pain and there is not a lot I can do, but I take her up ice packs for her leg and take her meals and drinks.

Monday 13 March
I said to Alan Simpson, 'I cannot come to Manchester on Saturday.'

'I would never have forgiven you if you had come. Lots of people are ready to give you advice as to how to be a good socialist MP, but there are very few people who can advise on how to be a loving partner.' I thought that was so sweet; he always gives me a hug. I saw Tam, and people were very supportive and I appreciated it.

Tuesday 14 March
I came home and gave Caroline a meal. Actually I left the potatoes on in a saucepan with the heat on. It was a non-stick pan, which I thought was ruined, but it wasn't; the potatoes were just resting in a red-hot pan. It must have been on for about four hours.

Wednesday 15 March
Melissa had a marvellous article today in the *Guardian* attacking the Government's plan to make marriage the preferred option advocated by schools; this is to fend off the criticism that's arisen over the proposal to repeal Section 28, which made it illegal for schools to promote homosexuality (something they never did). Melissa's article was very sharp. And I would hope it would embarrass Blunkett and Chris Woodhead; Melissa is happily in a partnership and not married, and other people don't want to marry at all.

I went over to the House, having done the diary, and sat and listened to some of the debate on the Terrorism Bill and I must say my blood ran cold. I heard Charles Clarke, the Minister, saying that these powers to declare people as terrorists were very unlikely to apply to genetically-modified-food campaigners and hunt saboteurs and other people who engage in demonstrations. Well, of course an assurance by a Minister has no validity at all; we are handing over the most repressive powers ever to a future Government, which will say they were introduced by the Labour Government. To my mind it is an indication of two things: first of all, that the security services want something else to do; the level of terrorism in Britain is absolutely minimal now, with the Northern Ireland peace holding and the Cold War over. So almost any form of activity that could threaten property has been defined as terrorism. Douglas Hogg intervened several times; I tried to intervene on Clarke, but he said, 'The Right Honourable Gentleman hasn't been here during the debate.'

Thursday 16 March
Sheila was in the office doing the best she can in the most difficult

circumstances, because I am hardly here and I'm dashing about doing my domestic duties. Josh gave me the most beautiful present, a Philips phone into which you could just say 'Office' and it dialled Sheila automatically, or 'Mum' and it dialled home.

Then the new Macmillan nurse arrived; her name is Vanessa, and I thought she was about nineteen. She had a long talk to Caroline, and then I went in to get to know her and I noticed that she was married and I said, 'Is your old man in nursing?'

And she said, 'Oh no, I'm a widow, my husband died six years ago.' She is in fact thirty-one years old and she has two children (an eight-year-old and a three-year-old), so she must have become pregnant after her husband had died, but she is an awfully nice woman. These Macmillan nurses look after the patients and not the disease; that's what is so marvellous.

I went into the House just before four o'clock. The second debate, which I went in to hear, was on Rover. The Tories had quite properly put down a motion because BMW have decided to 'cherry-pick' the Mini and the Land Rover from Rover and let the main Rover plant just close. As I was sitting up in my room and turned on the monitor, I saw that Geoffrey Robinson was speaking; he and I of course worked very closely on the British Leyland case in the 1970s and he became Paymaster General in 1997, until his resignation. I have always retained a certain feeling for him and he has always been personally friendly, so I went and sat in on the debate. He said, 'I'm glad My Right Honourable friend is here.' He argued that ownership does matter, and that globalisation shouldn't interfere with national interests; we have an interest in manufacturing. It was the real Geoffrey Robinson, the industrialist and interventionist whom I'd known in my ministerial days. Some New Labour MPs were laughing at him and mocking him because he has been so associated with New Labour; so afterwards I congratulated Geoffrey and said that he had spoken very boldly, that he knew what he was talking about, that he said what he thought. In his speech he did point out that wages in Britain are 30 per cent lower than in Germany, but that it was more expensive to sack people in Germany. Anyway BMW is based in Munich and isn't interested in Longbridge. It was a good speech.

Friday 17 March

I got in a taxi and went to the chemist John Bell & Croyden in Wigmore Street, and I went into the disabled section and bought everything I could see that might be useful: two lavatory seats that raised the height of the loo; a bath handle for the side of the bath to help you in and out; a bath mat; something that allows you to pick things up from the floor without leaning over; a comfortable pillow; a blow-up circular cushion to sit on. I just bought everything I could think of. It came to £350, but I thought it would make life a bit easier for Caroline.

Saturday 18 March

Blair is reported to be furious with BMW. Stephen Byers's reputation has gone through the floor, quite properly, and he is now asking BMW to compensate for the loss of jobs at Longbridge; but of course, though it's politically embarrassing at home, Ministers have no will to intervene when it involves a serious conflict with a big multinational company. If I were in Byers's position, I would call in BMW and say, 'Just to let you know we are no longer ordering any more BMW motorbikes for the Police and BMW trucks for the army, BMW buses for local authorities,' and put a bit of a pistol to their head and insist on taking over the company ourselves. There is no desire to do that; indeed, if you did it, that would be regarded as Old Labour at its worst.

Monday 20 March

I had a very nice letter today from two doctors in America, who sent me a cheque for £750, payable to the Chesterfield Labour Party, to celebrate my seventy-fifth birthday and in thanks for my speech on the World Trade Organisation. I wrote to them immediately and sent the cheque, their letter and a copy of my reply to the Treasurer of the Chesterfield Labour Party.

A young couple – the Reverend Andrew Morris and his wife, the Reverend Nicola Morris – who run a centre in Kingston for outcasts, heroin addicts and unemployed people, came to see me; they are both radical Baptists and wanted to come and interview me about the Nonconformist tradition. He had been a window cleaner and she had been a social worker; he was twenty-five and she was twenty-eight.

Then I had a phone call from the Cabinet Office saying, 'I know it is short notice, but could you go to Fleet in Hampshire tomorrow to address a top-level management conference because Lord Marshall, the Chairman of British Airways, can't go?' Well, I couldn't.

I went into the House for a vote. Went to the Tea Room and Diane Abbott was there, and I said to her, 'We must get Ken back into the Labour Party as soon as the election is over.'

She said, 'Certainly if Shaun Woodward, the Tory MP, could join the Parliamentary Party after standing against a Labour candidate, so could Ken Livingstone.' So that's the argument and I think it's one that might be properly launched at an appropriate stage.

There was a vote and I took Hilary home.

Wednesday 22 March

Went to Millbank for *Power House* with Norman Lamont and Jamie Shea, the NATO spokesman appointed at the insistence of Blair when the Kosovo war coverage was getting a bit rough. What he did (which is the technique they now use) was that he simply never stopped talking; he never came to the end of a sentence, just went on and on. In the end the only way they could deal with him was to fade the sound down and come to me. Lamont asked me whether I thought Kosovo was against the UN charter, and I said that it was; then he went back to Shea and he had another go at it. Finally they faded him out again. As Sheila was saying today, it's all advertising and marketing now – there is no ideological content, there is no appeal to anyone else to do anything, just to accept the product as presented.

Blair made a statement about more money for the National Health Service, but it's got to go hand-in-hand with modernisation. So he denied the Secretary of State, Alan Milburn, the opportunity; he picks all the glamour jobs and offloads all the failures onto his Ministers.

In the Commons today I felt for the first time that I was a visitor to the House of Commons; I'm disconnecting from the Parliamentary Labour Party. I am also becoming disconnected from Chesterfield, because all the political meetings have been cancelled until May.

Saturday 25 March
There was an awful programme this evening on BBC2 on the USSR – it just rubbished anyone who had ever been sympathetic to any part of the Soviet period. They used Robert Conquest, a real Cold War man, to rubbish Ken Gill and they rubbished John Kenneth Galbraith, Barbara Castle, Bernard Shaw; you would think nothing was achieved in Russia in those years.

Later we watched *Casualty* – the last one of the series – and Charlie had a heart attack at the very end.

Monday 27 March
Stephen looked in; had a lovely talk. He's off to New York and Washington for about eight days, addressing the American Chemical Society.

In the evening I intended to go and see David Butler's book, *British Political Facts 1900–2000*, launched at Politico's bookshop and I got in a taxi because I couldn't bear the thought of driving through the traffic myself. At Politico's I went in and saw Neil Hamilton in the corner, and then I saw Silvia Rodgers, Bill Rodgers's wife, so I asked, 'Where's David?'

And she said, 'Oh, he won't come.'

So I said, 'What do you mean, he won't come – it's his book.'

She said, 'Oh, I thought you meant David Owen – he's refused to come.'

So I said, 'Well, what is this, then?' and I discovered that it was the launch of Bill Rodgers's book *Fourth Among Equals*. So when I heard that I just turned on my heels and walked out. I did not want to be photographed with Bill Rodgers or Shirley Williams or Neil Hamilton. I was in the shop for about forty-five seconds, came home and had a meal. Caroline and I watched a marvellous programme about the search for Sodom and Gomorrah under the Dead Sea.

George Galloway told me today that one of the distinguished doctors who is accompanying him to Iraq had been approached by Thames Valley Police, who said, 'We just want to warn you that you will be used by Saddam Hussein to promote his own politics.' Well, that really is the sign of a police state!

Tuesday 28 March

Walked to Number 10 from the Commons for the MPs' annual meeting with Blair. There was a nice Irish lady who gave us all a cup of tea and I said, 'How long have you been here?'

She said, 'Nine years.'

And I said, 'I first came here seventy years ago and I was given a chocolate biscuit.' So she rushed away and brought me back a chocolate biscuit, which was very sweet of her.

I sat in my usual seat and Blair had a big smile.

We went round the table and David Chaytor said that Chris Woodhead is an electoral liability and is demoralising teachers. Well, that was a plain enough point. One Member said that we must end hunting if we are going to win the election. Piara Khabra, who is actually a bit older than me, said that we had to do something about pensioners.

Tony Blair answered some of the points that had been made. He said that schools are a problem, funding is a problem, but Woodhead was misrepresented and is very credible. On the NHS we must get good services and we don't want to waste cash. The hold-up on hunting is the Lords' fault (which was quite untrue). To Khabra he said that some pensioners have huge incomes; there are rich pensioners and poor pensioners and you can't give a big increase to all of them, and therefore it is better to concentrate on the poorest. That is the case for the means test rather than taxing rich pensioners.

Then we had the next round and I was first to be asked to speak. I had thought hard about what I wanted to say. 'I can tell you that governments eventually get unpopular, and when you get unpopular and run into difficulties, you will need the Party; you will need us.' I said, 'New Labour was an interesting slogan, but to call it a new party was a mistake, the same mistake as Arthur Scargill made when he set up the Socialist Labour Party. When you take over a defeated army you don't say, "Your uniforms are scruffy, your weapons are no good, your discipline has gone to hell", you say, "You are a marvellous army and we are going to win." As for the big-tent philosophy, people simply don't understand how you can prefer to be in a party with Shaun Woodward rather than Ken Livingstone, or with Heseltine rather than Dennis Canavan.'

I went on, 'The Cabinet meets for twenty minutes, if you haven't got a photo opportunity. In January 1968 we had eight full-day meetings in the Cabinet – we really discussed, things, had marvellous discussions and at the end you felt committed to the decisions that were taken.

'I had a phone call the other day. I'm a bit deaf, and a man rang me to talk about electric cars, but I thought he said "elected Tsars". So I thought we were making some improvement if we elect them.

'Really it's motivation that matters – you've got to motivate people and we can't just be spectators of your personal achievements. You have got to recognise you need us.' I wondered how it would go down, but I put it as nicely as I could.

Maria Fyfe raised Section 28, which is a huge issue in Scotland. John Austin said that Section 28 does cause homophobia; and he said that the NHS would not show the progress we need by the election, and that the incomes-link for pensioners is a very important issue. Tony Wright talked about the north–south divide and the hostilities towards refugees. Some very valid points were put. Then Rudi Vis said, 'In my constituency we're all lawyers and accountants and we like New Labour very much,' which is a powerful way of putting the point.

Tony Blair replied to various points made by Members round the table. On asylum, we must sort it out quickly; he reiterated the point about pensions, that the cost is too great because there are rich pensioners and they don't need support; on the NHS, we would meet the target but efficiency is the key. He said that in Scotland Section 28 is a big issue, and we must be smart about it. Then he came to my points; he didn't really answer me, but he did say concerning the Cabinet that the thought of eight full-day Cabinet meetings in a month – God! 'We are more united ideologically than we have ever been. We're always told we've forgotten the core vote but when we stuck to the core vote, we lost in the past.'

Monday 3 April

My seventy-fifth birthday. Dear old Stephen rang this morning from Washington at nine o'clock (four o'clock Washington time) and later I had a pager message from Hilary, who was in Leeds; I had phone calls from Josh and from Melissa; my grandson Jonathan phoned me personally; and Sally sent a message, so it was lovely.

I went to the House of Commons. I had put a note in to the Speaker saying that I'd like to ask a question about pensions during Social Security questions, and obligingly she called me. I made a strong point about linking pensions to earnings, and in reply Alistair Darling, the Social Security Secretary, wished me a happy birthday and said that he was sure I was looking forward to my free television licence – which really was an insulting response.

Wednesday 5 April
There was the debate on the disclosure of Government information and Tony Wright moved an amendment. He has formed a little all-party coalition with Simon Hughes, the Liberal, and Tories David Davis and Richard Shepherd, and Mark Fisher on our side, to get a decent Freedom of Information Bill.

Thursday 6 April
Lazy start – I'm getting very lazy. It was Sheila's birthday and I gave her a bottle of whisky and some mints.

I walked to Action Bikes, just next to Scotland Yard, and bought myself a little electric-battery motor scooter – a Micro City Bug. It cost me nearly £600. I thought I might be able to use it in London. So when I left the shop, I got on it and tried to go down Victoria Street, but I was so wobbly and, what with these bloody great buses and cars, I thought, 'I'll be killed.' So although I had my helmet on, I walked up to the House of Commons with it. Later in the day, after the vote, a lot of people turned up and tried it. Alan Simpson, Jean Corston, John Sergeant – it just was a wild success! Mind you, we tried in a little courtyard where there was nobody about. Still, I thought, if you're seventy-five you can have a bit of a gamble.

Then we had a vote, and I changed into evening dress and walked to the Banqueting Hall for the Rowland Hill Post Office Awards. I'd been asked to present a Lifetime of Achievement Award to David Gentleman, with whom of course I'd worked in 1964 when I was Postmaster General and had asked him to design some stamps. It was a beautiful event and I sat between the Managing Director of Royal Mail Stamps & Collectibles and the Managing Director of Postal Services. Opposite, around the table, was the chairman of the stamp company Stanley Gibbons, and I could see, out of the corner of my eye, David Gentleman. Jonathan Dimbleby introduced the scene. He went on for about three-quarters of an hour, listing the shortlisted people and the people who'd won, and a lot of speeches were made. Finally it came to my turn. I mentioned that the Banqueting Hall was where Charles I was led out to be executed, mentioned the Post Office, mentioned Rowland Hill as a great nineteenth-century reformer.

What interested me was the enormous scale of the philately business: the people who sell stamps at post offices, the people who promote stamps, the distributors of stamps, the stamp auction companies, the designers of stamps, the people who've done research on stamps; indeed, one of the other awards was a Journalistic Achievement Award given to two people who'd made the programme *Benn's Gallery* in January, which I had narrated, about stamp design. Afterwards, people came up and asked for my signature. I didn't want to stay too long because I had to walk back to the Commons, put my little Micro City Bug in the boot of my car and come home.

Friday 7 April

The Wild Mammals Bill was the second item of business, and the Bill came on early. I was there in time, thank God, and at a quarter past two, having had the whole day on the Bill, somebody moved the closure; but only seventy-four people voted for the closure and it takes a hundred people for a closure motion to work, so in effect Labour MPs, by their abstention, killed the hunting Bill. I was told that Labour Ministers had had a pager message saying, 'Don't vote.' So the net effect of all this is that those constituents of ours who are committed to animal welfare will leave the Labour Party in droves.

Sunday 9 April, Stansgate

I drove the Micro City Bug to Steeple; it took me twelve minutes. I must say, apart from bumps going through the farmyard, it was a very easy run. Then when I got there and turned round to come back, I saw Josh's car, so he drove the Bug back and I drove his car; it was an extraordinary spectacle because he was wearing this bright yellow jacket that I had bought and a crash helmet, and you saw this absolutely erect figure, mainly yellow, moving about like those figures that you have on computer games, at which you fire a gun and knock them over.

Monday 10 April

To the BBC meeting organised by Greg Dyke, the new Director General, for MPs and members of the House of Lords, to explain the policies he was pursuing. I shook him by the hand, and said, 'I'm so pleased you've been appointed. Everyone welcomes the disappearance of John Birt, but you mustn't let it go to your head.'

He laughed and said, 'I came to see you when you were Secretary of State for Energy and you explained all about the Labour Party.' So I said, 'Oh well, I was wrong about that!' He was very jolly. Then I went and sat in the audience, next to John Biffen.

Dyke said, 'We now spend twenty-five per cent of the licence fee on administration, and we want to cut it down to fifteen per cent.' He had been on the record saying the BBC was over-managed and under-led, which I thought was a very good phrase. When I spoke to Dave about it later this evening, he said he thought it was a phrase that could apply to the Soviet Union!

Dyke certainly is imaginative, and he's very open to people. Peter Shore had written to him about the bias against the Euro-sceptics.

A lot of questions were asked. He responded quite reasonably, but they weren't very interesting, I didn't think: about repeat programmes, about relations with Parliament, and so on.

Thursday 13 April
The bath machine for Caroline has been delivered on loan from Kensington Borough Council. You put it in the bath and press a button and a chair takes you down into the water and brings you up again.

Saturday 15 April
The news from Washington is that they're preparing for a huge rerun of Seattle, the anti-capitalist campaigns; the police made a raid on the headquarters of the campaigners to pre-empt them, but these young campaigners are on the Internet and they've got their computers and cameras and are busy photographing the police, so the balance of power is shifting a little bit, as far as technology is concerned.

Saturday 22 April, Stansgate
Up very early. A whole crowd of us went to the Imperial War Museum in Duxford as my birthday present from Joshua. A man of about fifty-five (he'd been an engineer with the Coal Board, then with Rolls-Royce) took us round. He showed us the Avro Anson, the Mosquito, and took us to the American Air Museum, a beautiful building designed by Norman Foster – much the best part of it all. At the end I put on my RAF jacket with my wings and ribbons, and photographs were taken of that. Then, after lunch, we went to look at Concorde and the VC-10, and we left at about four o'clock and came home. It was a really, really nice day.

Friday 28 April
Michael Heseltine announced yesterday, or the day before, that he was going to give up Parliament to devote more time to his publishing house. Well, he must be ten years younger than me; I think he's in his sixties. He missed being Prime Minister, which was all he cared about, and became Deputy Prime Minister, which doesn't amount to a row of beans, but he has had huge coverage in the papers.

He's passionately keen on our going into the euro, but there is great discontent in the euro-zone about the way the euro is being handled. The fact that the euro is down and the pound is high because of Gordon Brown's conservative economic policy, means that our manufacturing industry is being hammered into the ground, which is one of the problems of the Rover company. It all looks a bit shaky.

Monday 1 May, May Day, Chesterfield
A man opposite me on the train started talking, and it turned out that he was a member of the Labour Party and had read everything – lives of MacDonald, of Snowden, of Cripps, of Bevin, of Bevan, of Gaitskell, Dalton, and all my diaries. He said, 'You can't go back to '83 again, but at the same time, the Labour Party is in a bad way,' which is what everybody says.

I didn't feel too grand. I had an abscess on my gum. I've had it before, and my face was blowing up and it made me feel lousy.

I saw Anne Scargill, whom I hadn't seen for ages. She and Arthur have parted – I don't know why – so I gave her a big hug and she asked warmly after Caroline.

Later I ran to the station and caught the 1.40. I was so tired I just sat there in a sort of frozen way, and got home about 4.30, very, very tired.

There now is a lot of pressure on the Government to do something about Rover. BMW have agreed to talk to the Phoenix Group, which is headed up by a former Chief Executive of Rover.

Tuesday 2 May

There was a statement today by Jack Straw about the demonstration in London yesterday, which I should have reported. At the TUC May Day demonstration, 15,000 people marched on Trafalgar Square (there was not a word on the BBC about that). The news concentrated on two or three incidents that occurred in the anti-capitalist demonstration. First of all, the statue of Churchill in Parliament Square was daubed and someone put a slice of turf on his head so that it looked like a Mohican haircut; and then the Cenotaph was daubed with graffiti. And somebody smashed McDonald's in Victoria Street. Of course, that's what the television cameras were waiting for – they just covered it and covered it and covered it.

The BBC is not remotely interested in an argument about globalisation or capitalism; they're only interested in trouble, and of course that means that if you want coverage you make trouble. So they have a heavy responsibility.

Jack Straw made his statement, and Livingstone was blamed for it – it was his support for direct action that led to all this, as if he personally had daubed the Cenotaph and smashed McDonald's! It just shows they'd do anything to destroy the man.

Incidentally, it won't do any good.

Wednesday 3 May

Two men arrived and, within about five hours, they installed the stair lift, which has absolutely revolutionised life for Caroline. She can go up and down between the kitchen and the bedroom whenever she wants, and she absolutely loves it.

I took Caroline to her hairdresser's. I think next time we'll get the hairdresser to come and do her hair at home. Having her hair done at the same time was a woman who turned round and said, 'My husband is a great admirer of yours.' It was the wife of Donald Bruce, Lord Bruce of Donington. He must be ninety now. He was Aneurin Bevan's PPS. It was nice to talk to her.

Then I went in to the Commons and went to the Campaign Group, where we had a discussion about selling off air-traffic control – there's going to be a huge revolt next week; unbelievable. Dennis Skinner said to me that the Prime Minister was in a race between economic crisis and polling day, because if unemployment began rising, he'd be in difficulty. I think there are problems other than that. I had a long talk to Jeremy Corbyn about Ken Livingstone who is standing for Mayor in the election tomorrow. I said, 'Well, what I feel about it is this. I'm a Labour man. I joined in '42. Everything I've ever had in my life I owe to the Labour Party.'

He said, 'Well, let me put it to you like this. This is the one chance of saving the Labour Party.'

I must say, it was persuasive.

Friday 5 May

Ken Livingstone overwhelmingly won the election as Mayor of London. Norris came second, and Frank Dobson came third, just 1 per cent above Sue Kramer, the Liberal Democrat. It is a tremendous success for Ken, because Thatcher abolished the GLC in 1984 to get rid of him and he's come back as Mayor of London. Not only did he defeat Thatcher, but he defeated Blair, who tried desperately to stop him getting it. Ken was expelled from the Labour Party, and he's built a very broadly based coalition of people who backed him.

His first words as Mayor were, 'As I was saying before I was rudely interrupted . . .' Then he went on to say that he wanted to cooperate with the people who'd fought in the campaign and to work with the Prime Minister, and so on.

It establishes that following Blair is not the only way to win. So it sort of exorcises that bogey.

Then, of course, the local elections. The Tories won nearly 600 seats, we lost 580, and obviously there were mass abstentions. Hague is proving that his crude nationalism and xenophobia, and so on, are capable of mobilising the real Tory vote, the right-wing Tory vote.

It's a warning to Blair, and yet, in the back of my mind, I wonder whether he cares very much. In Scotland he has created a coalition in which the Liberals are necessary to hold up the Labour administration; the Labour majority in Wales depends upon other parties' support. He's now introduced a scheme in London that leaves no party in overall control; actually the Liberals or the Greens hold the balance in the Greater London Authority. The last stage would be for Labour MPs to be defeated in the next election, and then Blair could carry on with the Liberals and some Tories in the House of Commons.

Wednesday 10 May

I went to St Thomas' to see Professor Pearson, and he said to me today, 'I don't think there's any question of the leukaemia affecting the rest of your life.' He's now been made head of the pathology unit at Guy's and St Thomas' Hospital and was being required to cut £1 million out of the £15 million budget for pathology. I later heard from Patricia Moberly, the Chairman of St Thomas', who happened to be at the House in the evening, that the hospital has to put in a bid for new NHS money. So the idea of properly funding the Health Service has gone by the board, and it's now a sort of lottery again.

I heard this morning that my adjournment debate on Socialism has been picked by the Speaker for Tuesday 16th, in the new debating chamber in Westminster Hall. The subject is not called 'Socialism' because there is no ministerial responsibility for Socialism. So it's been called 'Wealth and Poverty in the Economic System', and the Treasury will have responsibility for responding.

I saw John Major later and I said, 'John, here's your chance – Tuesday's debate on Socialism. As you're well to the left of Tony Blair, I'm sure you'd like to take part.'

Thursday 11 May

Alice Mahon told me that she, Tam Dalyell and Bob Marshall-Andrews went to see the Prime Minister about sanctions against Yugoslavia; he gave them half an hour, which I think is quite interesting. I would be humiliated to go and plead with Blair. But they're keen and active, and they're very good Members of Parliament.

Friday 12 May

My cousin Glanvill Benn died a couple of days ago. He was ninety-four, a very nice man indeed. He married Catherine, a beautiful secretary at Benn Brothers, in about 1931. She's nearly ninety. I've rung him up occasionally, and he has always been very encouraging and extremely kind. I just don't think I'm going to be able to make the funeral because I've got such a lot on, but I shall send some flowers and write.

Sunday 14 May

Caroline fell twice today. I didn't hear her call, and so she crawled back into the bedroom and managed to get up, but it is a real source of anxiety and I've got to think carefully about whether we have somebody in all the time when I'm not here. It is really distressing for her, and terribly worrying for me.

Anyway, Melissa came with her girls Hannah and Sarah, just after twelve. We had lunch together, then I took Hannah and Sarah out shopping to buy a few things from the local food store. Melissa insisted that I held their hands all the time, so I told them that they had to watch me because I sometimes wanted to run under a bus! So every few minutes

I said, 'Oh, I'm going to run under a bus,' and they tugged me and said, 'No, no!' So they learned a bit of road safety the other way round. We went into Gap and looked at the clothes, and then they walked me back. When they'd gone, after lunch, I went to sleep for three hours in bed. I was just so tired.

Tuesday 16 May

I got up at 6.30 a.m. and went off to the House of Commons for this hour-and-a-half debate on socialism held in the new Westminster Hall chamber. I'd never spoken in Westminster Hall before. It was opened last autumn.

I made a special point of paying tribute to the Liberals in the nineteenth century, with municipal socialism or municipal democracy, and to the old Tories, Churchill and Macmillan and Heath, who were caring Conservatives. I spoke for about twenty-four minutes, followed by Bob Wareing, Ann Cryer, Jeremy Corbyn and Alan Simpson; they were all really good speeches and we were all confident. We weren't aggressive. Professor Steve Webb, who is a Liberal Democrat, spoke for the Liberals for a few minutes and could not have been more supportive and sympathetic. Then Howard Flight, a Tory Front Bench minister, I presume, spoke and he couldn't have been more friendly. Then Melanie Johnson, who is a junior Treasury Minister, replied for the Government. I felt that socialists were no longer on the defensive. The case is reasonable, the arguments are sensible, the support for these ideas widespread.

Thursday 18 May

Caroline was in hospital for a scan on her legs. She's very happy in the ward and told me later in the day that she had a long talk to a young Colombian of about twenty-five, who is working as a cleaner. She said he was immensely well read, tremendously interested in politics, and wanted to go home and save his country. He said to her, 'Nobody talks to me, and it's so nice to talk to you.'

Saturday 20 May

Tony Blair's little baby boy, Leo, was born in the middle of the night.

Monday 22 May

I had a word with Tessa Kingham. She was elected in 1997, and announced last week that she was giving up Parliament because the conditions were so awful for a young mother. She's got a girl of five and twins of about four months old. So I said to her, 'Now look, I will make an offer. I will put five hundred pounds up to buy necessary play-school equipment if you will get the women Members to occupy Annie's Bar (which is the drinking den where journalists meet MPs) and set up a crèche there and just stop the drinking – drive the boozers out.' Well, Tessa was very excited, and Oona King, to whom I mentioned it later, was equally excited. Whether the women will do it or not, I don't know, but I sat down and worked out a poster that you could put on the door, saying, 'House of Commons Crèche and Play School. Only children and families admitted. The bar has been closed. No smoking.' If they do it, I'll stick it up. But people are very unimaginative. They wait for the modernisation committee to make a recommendation, and the Speaker to assess it, and the House to debate it, and nothing will be done in this Parliament.

Wednesday 24 May

Friends of Caroline's – Marjorie and Les Applegate – came to lunch. It was their fifty-third wedding anniversary, and Caroline has known Marje . . . oh, since she (Caroline) was about ten: about sixty-five years. Marje is a very beautiful woman, she's a talented sculptor of renown and she married Les Applegate, who was her old steady. I helped a little bit to get the lunch, and Carol came downstairs, wearing a beautiful red dress, and they had a lovely talk. I stayed for lunch and then I went off, because I had to go into the House for a meeting about the Patten Report.

The position is this: that Chris Patten, who was a former Tory MP and former Governor of Hong Kong, was asked to look at policing in Northern Ireland, and made some very constructive recommendations: that the RUC change its name from the Royal Ulster Constabulary to the Police Service of Northern Ireland; that there be an oath of commitment to human rights; that plastic bullets be restricted; that an ombudsman be appointed; and so on. In order to woo the Unionists, who are meeting this Saturday, Mandelson has made a lot of concessions, including that the title RUC (which is highly provocative) should remain. Of course, Sinn Fein are slightly anxious that if these concessions are made, the IRA might withdraw their offer to put their weapons beyond use. I mean, put crudely, Sinn Fein want the RUC decommissioned, and the Unionists want the IRA decommissioned. There's a sort of rough parallel. It's very important that the Unionists get the blame for the breakdown because they are the ones who do not want this to succeed. There's no question that that is the actual situation. But it was an interesting meeting. I'm dictating this the following morning, Thursday morning, and the banner headline in the *Guardian* says, 'Clinton is not prepared to go along with what Blair wants.' So that's a good thing.

Thursday 25 May

Mr Ibrahim, my Iraqi contact, came and we had a long chat. He stayed for about an hour and a quarter and we had a really interesting talk. He is 65 now, and has a very bad back, leaving him in continual pain. His wife has wisely used her time here in London to get a PhD at City University, and they have a son in computing, and a daughter who is working here.

He described the break-up of Yugoslavia, and thought this was a German plan to set up an Adriatica, stretching right through the Balkans down to the Adriatic, to be controlled by Europe. China, he said, was reluctant to confront America because it wasn't strong enough; of course, yesterday they did actually get admitted to the World Trade Organisation and had 'most-favoured nation treatment'. He thought that in forty or fifty years' time China will be the dominant power in the world, without any doubt.

Caroline had been asked to launch the North Kensington Community Archive Appeal. We took her in her wheelchair and there were lots of people she knew – many of them our children's friends and contemporaries! Carol had worked very hard on her speech; of course she knows the area very well.

Saturday 27 May

> Hello, this is Daniel Benn, Tony Benn's grandson, I think, and I'm in his office and I'm feeling a bit weird because this is the first time I've ever been speaking on a microphone before. My grandfather's a bit of a nincompoop, that's Tony Benn, in other words. My dad's a nincompoop. All my family are nincompoops; well, most people are.

Well, that was Daniel, who came down to the office on Saturday 27 May and recorded on to my diary cassette.

By a majority of 53 per cent to 47 per cent, Trimble persuaded the Ulster Unionist Council to go along with the restitution of the institutions in Northern Ireland, the Executive and the Assembly, on the basis of the IRA offer to put their guns beyond use and open them to inspection. So that was a good move. Mandelson will now feel free to come home and get another job in a reshuffle. That fills me with gloom: that he will get the credit for having pulled it all off, and poor old Mo Mowlam, who did all the work, is being briefed against by Number 10.

Monday 29 May

This morning I had a rather interesting exchange on the telephone with Jack Straw, the Home Secretary. The background is that I've had letters for a long time from a prisoner who was charged with armed robbery and the attempted murder of a policeman. To begin with he denied all the charges, although he had had various convictions for armed robbery, but finally he confessed to the armed robbery, but said that he did not intend to fire at a policeman. He fired a bullet at a car to disable it, and the bullet ricocheted off and grazed the policeman's shoulder, although it didn't even require hospital treatment. At any rate, the man had been kept in prison for twenty-seven years, and it's a tremendously long time to be kept in; and he's always been refused parole.

I've been writing about his case to the Home Office, and I had the help of a woman who is a *Daily Telegraph* reporter with whom he is in correspondence. He wrote to me a few weeks ago and said that if he didn't get parole this time, he was going to go on hunger strike and die. She was very worried about it. Anyway, I wrote to the Home Secretary about parole, which was refused, and the Home Secretary wrote back and said, 'Oh, it's nothing to do with me. The Parole Board decides. The Home Secretary has no discretion at all in the matter.' But the woman had been at the Parole Board hearing, and it opened with a statement from the Home Secretary saying that he did not want the man released.

I was so incensed about this that I rang up the Home Secretary a couple of weeks ago – the first time I've ever rung up a Home Secretary about a case, but I felt this was utter deception. I spoke to Jack and he just reiterated, 'It's nothing to do with me.'

I said, 'Half a minute, Jack. There was somebody at the Parole Board who told me that a letter from you had been read out, saying you didn't want him released.'

Straw was absolutely knocked back. He said, 'Oh well, I'll let you know about it. I'll ring you back.' He never did. All that happened was that I had a whole series of letters from the Prison Service describing the man's medical condition.

So I wrote another letter to Jack, saying that I felt utterly let down that he'd never rung me back. Then yesterday morning I had a message, 'When can the Home Secretary speak to you?' I gave him my home number. They'd also rung Hilary because they seem to find it impossible to distinguish between Hilary and me.

Anyway, at about twelve o'clock Jack did ring me and he was very, very concerned. He said, 'I've gone into all this very carefully. It is undoubtedly true that a letter was sent in my name which had never come to me. I am reviewing all that.'

Anyway, to cut a long story short, Jack did say that he was looking into it carefully. So after I'd spoken to Jack and to the prisoner's probation officer for the third time, I rang the prison and spoke to the Duty Governor about his medical condition.

I felt I had done as much as could be done. I had contacted the Home Secretary, spoken to him twice, spoken to the former probation officer three times, spoken to the woman who was interested in the case, and ultimately sent a letter to the guy saying, 'You've got to make up your mind what you do, but you're such a talented and determined man that I'd be sorry if it ended, so keep at it.' They promised that when I faxed that through to the prison, they'd take it to him.

The man is not a constituent, not important politically if you like, but his case highlighted a number of things: the tremendously long prison sentences that people get; the way that parole can be refused because a guy won't plead guilty, which isn't fair; the danger of violence building up in a prison; and the limited role that an MP can play if he really wants to.

Monday 5 June

I saw Nicholas Soames and Richard Shepherd and David Davis having a cup of tea, so I said, 'Can I join your big tent?' That's the great phrase about Blair. I asked, 'What would you think about putting down a resolution that nobody should be nominated for the House of Lords unless their names have been put on a list and approved by the House of Commons?' So they all bought it immediately. David Davis was a bit cautious: Nicholas Soames said he's got 'other fish to fry', slightly confirming the theory I have that Davis would like to be Leader of the Tory Party. That would be, I must say, a very good development. Anyway, I took Hilary home, and that was the end of Monday 5 June.

Tuesday 6 June

In the afternoon I went to the Commons and I circulated my motion on the scrutiny of names of potential peers by the House of Commons. Nicholas Soames and Richard Shepherd and David Davis supported it. I spoke to Paddy Ashdown about it in the Lobby. 'Oh,' he said, 'it sounds a good idea to me, but I don't know what the Liberal policy is.'

I said, 'You're a free man, like me.'

He said, 'You've always been free.'

I said, 'Not always. I was in the Cabinet and I was given parole', so he laughed.

Then I saw Charles Kennedy later. He said, 'Well, it sounds like a good idea. Let me have a look at it.' It would be nice if it worked.

Wednesday 7 June

I can't remember whether I recorded that this morning Tony Blair addressed the Women's Institute national conference and was received with a slow hand-clap, jeers and heckling. It made Sheila laugh louder than I can remember for a long time, because here's the man whose whole appeal is to middle England, to middle-class women. Apparently what they objected to were two things: first of all, that it was a political speech, because Blair attacked the forces of conservatism, although apparently they'd asked him not to make a political speech. Second, he patronised them. There was a lot of comment during the day, including comment from the editor of *Cosmopolitan*, I think, who said that women really didn't like him.

Caroline and I had lunch together. She got the lunch on her own. I shouldn't let her do it but, using the little electric wheelchair, she managed to get backwards and forwards in the kitchen.

I think Wednesday 7 June might possibly be remembered as a turning point, because the New Labour balloon is going down with a sort of hiss. It isn't a bubble that's burst – it's just expiring.

Thursday 8 June

Twenty-four people signed my Early Day Motion on the nomination of peers, which wasn't bad, and I told the press about it.

Friday 9 June

I did an interview with Sue MacGregor for Radio 4 about the Early Day Motion that the House of Commons should have the power to vet nominations for peerages. It was fun. Then, about an hour and a half later, Trevor Kavanagh, the lobby correspondent of the *Sun* and this year's chairman of the press lobby, rang up and said he'd heard the interview and would I write 500 words by mid-afternoon? Well, I wasn't going to Chesterfield until later, so I sat down and wrote an article and faxed it through to him. He asked, 'Would you like to write regularly for the *Sun*?' Well, I don't want to be known as a *Sun* columnist, but I wouldn't mind writing occasionally if there is something to say, because you are getting through to a working-class audience that is potentially Thatcherite but should be socialist. I'll think about it anyway.

I left an hour to get to St Pancras, but the traffic was absolutely solid and I missed the train by five minutes. I got to the meeting in Chesterfield at about quarter to seven, left at about quarter past seven, and somebody dropped me back at the station and I came home. I was actually in Chesterfield for one hour and eight minutes, and I had done five or six hours' travelling to do it. It's mad, but I'd said I'd do it and I did do it.

Sunday 11 June

Melissa came with Hannah and Sarah. Lissie helped Caroline upstairs in the bedroom, and I got the lunch. Then after lunch Josh arrived, bless his old heart, and helped her with her computer.

I took the little girls out in Caroline's little motorised vehicle, which she can sit and go shopping in. We went round the block, all the way up towards the shops, turned left, turned left again, down past the police station, left again and got home. I said to the girls, 'Now you get off and I'll bring it up the ramp.' I began driving it up the ramp, into the house, and all of a sudden it toppled – the whole thing crashed backwards and I hit my head hard on the path and hurt my arm. The children just stood there and looked, didn't know what to say; and a very kind man saw what had happened and came in from the road and helped me to my feet. Josh meanwhile had gone out to look for us. He didn't know where we were.

When he came back, he was very, very angry with me, and quite rightly, because if I had disabled myself there would have been two disabled people in the house. So I got a real verbal beating-up from him and Melissa, and from Caroline, and I just lay on the bed for about three hours and had a rest.

There is an unbelievable story in the *Sunday Times* that they're going to advertise for peers i.e. individuals can apply for consideration for appointment to the House of Lords. It's going to be done by a company on behalf of a commission appointed by the Prime Minister, and they are expected to make it representative (young, ethnic, women); and so Parliament, or at least a tiny section of it, is going to be appointed on the basis of civil servants. It's just laughable, and dangerous, but typical of the way they approach it. So my resolution on the House of Commons vetting all possible candidates could not have come at a better time.

Wednesday 14 June

The prisoner who was on hunger strike has decided to take food again, which I was pleased about because it would have been a wasted life.

In the course of the day I had a talk to Peter Tapsell in the Tea Room. He told me he had seen Lady Avon, Anthony Eden's widow, who said how charming I'd been at the dinner for Ted Heath and how all the Tories had absolutely ignored her and cold-shouldered her; the only two people who were nice to her were Tam Dalyell and me. Well, she was very nice to me, and I wheeled her in her wheelchair back to the lift. Peter Tapsell said, 'The trouble with the Tory Party now is they're run by guttersnipes.' That really was the snob's view of his own party!

I saw Peter Kilfoyle in the back corridor between the divisions and had a talk to him. He told me what the Lord Chancellor, Derry Irvine, had said last summer: that Tony Blair had always wanted to be Prime Minister, but never wanted to be Leader of the Labour Party. He thought that threw a great deal of light on Blair's position – that he could be all things to all men. Kilfoyle is very academic, a formidable man.

Thursday 15 June

At eight o'clock Caroline and I went off to the hospital. It really is a big struggle now, getting her down the steps, into the wheelchair, from the wheelchair into the car, put the wheelchair away, drive to the hospital, into the wheelchair, into the hospital. And when she got there, bless her heart, the registrar tried three times to inject the chemotherapy drugs into her spine and failed – hit the bone, hit the nerve, and poor darling Caroline had to wait for another doctor, who succeeded. So she's got six more after today and it depresses her very much.

Saturday 17 June

I got the electric vehicle down the ramp and managed to get Carol in, and she drove it to Holland Park. It was absolutely packed with people, but very few children. When we were young, it was stuffed with local children, but now people can't afford to live in Notting Hill Gate any more; today the park was full of yuppie couples. We went to the open-air restaurant and got some soup and a roll and a banana, and I got ice cream. After I got her back upstairs and into bed, I went out in the vehicle on my own to see how easy it would be for her to get to the restaurant where we're going to have lunch on Tuesday. I tried the back streets: the pavements are very narrow, and there are lamp-posts, which mean you have a job squeezing by. So the only way of getting to that restaurant is on the main road, and that's what we'll probably do. In the end, I gave up. It took me half an hour and I never got anywhere near the restaurant, but it was worth a try.

Sunday 18 June

Was travelling up to Doncaster on the train and I decided to go into a first-class compartment and pay a weekend supplement, and who should I see sitting there but John Reid, the Secretary of State for Scotland. Now, of course, Scotland is really run by Donald Dewar, but there has to be some coordinating London Minister and John Reid has a very small department at the Scotland Office, as it is now called.

He was quite ready to talk and I had nothing better to do, and it was the first serious discussion I've had with a Cabinet minister since the election. Reid used to work with Neil Kinnock, was very left-wing at one time and did his PhD on a Marxist analysis of the economy of Dahomey in West Africa, he told me. So I was talking to somebody who was probably ideologically one of the very few genuine intellectuals of New Labour.

First of all, we discussed the relationship between him as Secretary of State and Donald Dewar, who is First Minister, in Scotland. He said that the devolution had worked quite well institutionally, but the problem was that the political life of the Labour Party in Scotland had been subsumed and there was a danger of it going nationalist. And so he and Brian Wilson, who is with him in the Scottish Office in London, had done fifty-five party meetings in Scotland to try and build up the strength of the Party there. He did admit that the Government had made a big mistake and was out of touch on things like the Alun Michael appointment and old-age pensions.

I asked about the Cabinet and Reid said, 'Well, we meet for perhaps up to an hour once a week, and it's pretty well a discussion of current affairs, but twice a year we have a strategic meeting.' I got the impression the Cabinet didn't have a real life. He said that no papers were submitted by Cabinet Ministers. It is all done by Blair. He didn't really deny that.

Then I said to him that I thought Tony Blair really wanted a coalition. John Reid was very sensitive about it. He said, 'Oh no, I don't think so. He's very keen to have another Labour Government. He believes in community and solidarity and he's a Christian socialist, remember.' It all sounded wobbly and Liberal to me, but I think I planted in his mind the thought that Blair wouldn't really care if the Labour Party was cut and the Liberals came in. 'Well,' he said, 'we do have to heal the historic link with the Liberals, which was broken when the Labour Party was set up.' He was a real New Labour man, but he spoke with some suspicion of people he called 'Nouvelle Labour' – that is to say, people who wanted to go even further. He thought Charles Kennedy would stay independent, but that we should cooperate on some issues.

Then he said that he had made a speech in which he argued that colonialism had been a progressive force because it transferred technology, and he said that was based on Marx's analysis that capitalism was progressive. Well, that's true in the sense that capitalism precedes socialism; but he said it had got him into a lot of trouble.

At the end Reid said, 'You know, I never thought of you as hard left. You're an old Liberal of Christian extraction.' And he made me out to seem a bit harmless!

I said, 'I'll tell you one person for whom I have a very high regard, and that is Tommy Sheridan' – the Scottish Socialist Party member of the Scottish Parliament.

Reid said, 'Well, so have I; a very fine man.'

I should add that Tommy Sheridan got married yesterday, on the 17th, which was our fifty-first wedding anniversary. He asked Caroline and me to the wedding, which we couldn't make, obviously.

But the insight from John Reid confirmed my judgement that he's a formidable figure. I found him very agreeable. He's like many ex-Marxists; said we've all become consumers now, not producers, and that the knowledge economy has replaced the class system – and all that rubbish.

Wednesday 21 June

I looked in briefly at the disability tea party organised by Mencap. Alan Haselhurst, the Chairman of Ways and Means, was there and I said to him, 'Did you see in the paper at the weekend that Blair wants Menzies Campbell to be the next Speaker?'

'Yes, I did. Every week it goes on.'

Obviously Haselhurst feels that he ought to be the next Speaker and that the Number 10 machine is trying to bypass him. So it was probably more useful to talk to him than to raise it with the Parliamentary Labour Party, because when I raised it with Chris Mullin the other day, he said, 'Well, what's wrong with the Prime Minister having an idea as to who he wants to be Speaker?' Well, of course, when the Prime Minister has an idea, it doesn't help to make a free vote possible.

Thursday 22 June
Oh no, I totally forgot! Quite hilarious! Roy Jenkins, the Chancellor of Oxford University, gave an interview to the *Spectator*, and he was asked whether Tony Blair would be given an honorary degree. He said, 'No, not now.' The reason he gave was because of this farcical attack upon elitism at Oxford. Then he went on to say that Tony Blair had a second-class mind that was giving weak leadership on Europe. Well, since Tony has absolutely depended on Roy Jenkins, I thought it was terribly funny! Also very arrogant of Roy, but terribly funny, and this is splashed all over the evening bulletins. It's just another of the pillars of Blair's support that is being eroded.

Saturday 24 June
To a park near the Imperial War Museum for a demonstration in support of asylum seekers. It was organised by the SWP and I'd put my name down, so they described it as a demonstration called by me. And when I got there, there were hundreds and thousands of Kurds – because the Kurds and the SWP march decided to converge on this particular park. When I got there, a bit ahead of the asylum seekers, they poured in. I don't know how many there were – 2000, 3000, 5000 – a very, very big meeting. I was asked to speak, which I did. It was all right (about seven or eight minutes) and then I wended my way home.

Monday 26 June
The world news today is that scientists in Britain and America have cracked the human genetic code. I believe they said it would take something like three-quarters of a million pages of A4 to describe it, but the significance of it is absolutely enormous. They've been working on it for ten years, but it means they can really identify the make-up of every human being by studying their DNA code in detail. No doubt it will provide opportunities for replacing old organs when they wear out, for dealing with cancer and a whole range of other illnesses, but of course it also raises other questions: that if you have a genetic code which 'inclines towards criminality' they might lock you up without bothering to try you; or if you are 'educationally subnormal' they wouldn't bother to test you, they just wouldn't let you go to a good school; or indeed, if your code indicates defects, it might be harder to get life insurance.

Caroline keeps talking about where she wants to buried, which I find very distressing. On the other hand, she wants to talk about it. It's hard to be familiar about death in the family, with the one you love most; it is very, very hard, but it has to be done. You have to be sensible about it.

We've got used now to discussing sex in society, and now we've got to get used to discussing death.

Tuesday 27 June

This morning it was reported in the papers that Mo Mowlam had said that the Queen should move out of Buckingham Palace into modern accommodation, in order to modernise the monarchy. A ridiculous idea! I mean, the one case for having the Queen is that she *is* in Buckingham Palace, they do change the guard, and it's a tourist attraction. It was absolutely offbeat.

I went onto the Terrace, and there was David Lammy, the black twenty-seven-year-old MP who's won Bernie Grant's old seat. I shook him by the hand, met his mother and his sister. I said to him, 'The one thing you've got to be careful of is being described as a future Prime Minister. The place is absolutely riddled with ex-future Prime Ministers.' He was very friendly and nice. I said, 'Anyway, you are lucky to have been educated at Harvard and not at Oxford. No one would go near Oxbridge. My kids wouldn't look at it.' Of course Lammy's the baby of the House.

I told the Whips' Office that I was going home and Caroline was poorly. I made her a meal and took it up to her in the bedroom, and she sat there. Oh, when she's ill, I get so worried. It's just so sad to see the one you love in pain. But she's got amazing powers of recovery.

Wednesday 28 June

I jumped in a taxi that the BBC had provided and went to Radio 4 to do *The Moral Maze*. I did it once before, but David Starkey, the historian, was so rude to me that I had refused to do it again. But they keep ringing me up, and this programme was about religion and politics, in which I had an interest, so I agreed. Starkey was pretty well as rude as ever. I must say I gave as good as I got, and I made them laugh and argued my case.

Caroline is ready to go for her chemo tomorrow.

I should have mentioned that yesterday the Government made an announcement about compensation for vaccine-damaged children. Twenty years ago, when I was a Bristol MP, there was a woman called Enid Needs who brought her disabled son to see me. He was in effect poisoned by vaccination, so it is a subject I have been interested in for years. They offered him £10,000, and I think the Government yesterday announced a substantial increase; that is the product of a lot of pressure.

Saturday 1 July

Today was a really big day, because Josh and Naz got married. Carol and I got ready in our best outfits, and we went in a chauffeur-driven car to Chelsea Register Office. We had to go all the way round to the disabled entrance, up little lifts, down little lifts, round through the library. Then at about four o'clock we went into the Marriage Room, where the registrar went through it all, and William and Nahal were the witnesses, which was lovely. Naz looked dazzlingly beautiful, and her family were there – Parvis, her father, and Homa, her mother, and her sisters and her brother and their families. There were other friends and it was just great. We needed a bit of help to get Caroline out of the car, then she went upstairs utterly exhausted and went to sleep.

Then at seven o'clock, or soon after, we set off for Pinner for the reception: the weather was perfect. Piers Corbyn, who runs a weather-forecasting service, couldn't have been more right. Emily played her violin; Daniel and Jonathan played on their cellos; Carrie played the electric organ; then James sang a couple of songs with his guitar. It was just fantastic really. The family couldn't have been nicer, and after short speeches dancing began.

By midnight it was time to take Caroline home.

Tuesday 4 July

Blair, having been clobbered by the police chiefs over the idea of police constables having the right to fine people on the spot for hooliganism, has now come out with a new idea that the Home Secretary can take away people's passports if they're suspected of being football hooligans.* This is a desperate ploy to try to get the World Cup brought to Britain in the year 2006 – which I don't think there's any chance of.

Wednesday 5 July

Dave rang today in connection with the proposal that football hooligans should have their passports withdrawn, even if they haven't committed an offence. He remembered that in 1955, four years after Burgess and Maclean defected, Anthony Eden had made a speech saying that he would not be prepared to preside over a government that would remove people's passports without a trial. Dave identified the date of the debate and I rang up the House of Commons library. They produced Hansard – for 7 November 1955 – and I photocopied the relevant passages and took them to the Campaign Group. It is a scandalous piece of legislation, it is just as though the *Daily Mail* or the *Sun* writes our Manifesto now.

Saturday 8 July, Durham Miners' Gala

I got on the balcony of the County Hotel at about half-past nine and we didn't leave until about half-past one, so in the bright sunshine, which

*The Football (Disorder) Bill was widely criticised for being incompatible with European Community law on the free movement of persons in the European Union, and with the Human Rights Act.

gave me sunburn, I saw all the banners go by: the Durham miners; the Yorkshire miners; UNISON; a couple of lads who just had a big red handkerchief that said 'People not profit'; asylum seekers; the Aged Miners' Homes banner. There were children dancing, and I stood there and I wept and wept. I thought to myself that if Caroline goes, I shall be left to spend the rest of my life alone, and I shall miss her so much if anything happens. So I wept for her, and I wept for the miners, and I wept for myself, and I wept for the problems in society, but it was deeply moving. I saw Don Dixon, I saw Giles Radice marching with his banner; it was terrific.

I saw Arthur Scargill go by, just an isolated figure, holding a banner about pensions – didn't even march for the Yorkshire miners or the Socialist Labour Party.

Ken Cameron was there, just retired from the Fire Brigades' Union. He's been awarded the Che Guevera prize in Cuba, the third one ever – Che got the first one, Nelson Mandela got the second, and Ken Cameron got the third. I think all the north-east Members of Parliament were at the Gala, except of course Blair and Mandelson.

Blair was at the National Policy Conference. The unions are beginning to be accused of bullying the Government.

Sunday 9 July

I drove Caroline to the University of London for the Marxism 2000 conference, to take part in a discussion about the prospects of socialism in the twenty-first century. I must say she made a beautiful speech. It was historical, it was analytical, it was what my dad used to call 'class', and it received very warm applause.

The Marxism conference is a useful exercise. It brings about 7000 people to London every year, and it is a sort of university of socialism with a marvellous programme of talks; it is organised by the Socialist Workers' Party.

Monday 10 July

In the afternoon, some amendments had been tabled to the Terrorism Bill to try and redefine terrorism away from the Government definition that anyone who is politically motivated and damages property is a terrorist, which is an outrageous definition. The harsh authoritarianism that has crept into our politics now is really quite alarming. It was all discussed in an empty House with very little serious debate and no vote. I think there was a party at Buckingham Palace for Members of Parliament; so the House adjourned at six, before allocated time was up.

Everything confirms my decision that it just isn't worth staying on.

Tuesday 11 July

At five o'clock a cab arrived, which Stephen had booked to take Caroline and me and her sister Nance to the London Eye, this fabulous wheel across the Thames from the Houses of Parliament. We got there and the weather was absolutely lovely. We got out of the cab and I pushed Caroline's wheelchair towards a sort of open-air restaurant, and who should I see there but Zuhair Ibrahim, whom I first met ten years ago. He's now an old friend. He has retired from the Iraqi foreign service, and he was there with his wife and a friend.

Anyway, the entire family gathered. Because we were a big group they let us have a pod of our own, and the wheel stopped for a second so that the wheelchair could get on, and I pushed Caroline over to the other side, facing the House of Commons. It was an absolutely fabulous view. I knew it would be good, but I didn't know it would be as good as that. At the very top, the wheel paused for five minutes, which was slightly worrying, and the noise of the kids all laughing and joking in the pod was tremendous. There was a young woman employee in the pod with a mobile phone. She told me that she worked five days a week and did twelve circuits every day, so she does sixty circuits of the wheel every week. It's far taller than Big Ben; I hadn't appreciated that. It was just such a great day.

Then Caroline and I went home in a taxi. I decided not to go into the House because I still have this awful flu. It was the Northern Ireland Police Bill, and Hilary said there was only one Ulster Unionist in the Lobby because their MPs are all over in Northern Ireland, where the Orange Order disturbances following the Parades Commission's decision to ban the Drumcree march has created a certain amount of instability.

Clinton, Barak and Arafat are at Camp David trying to hammer out a peace deal. I must say Arafat does look a most insubstantial leader of the PLO compared to what he once was. Prime Minister Barak has been deserted by his coalition partners in the Israeli Government, so it's all very shaky and I'm not sure what will come of it.

Wednesday 12 July

When I got to the House of Commons at about twenty to four, I discovered that Betty Boothroyd had announced that she intended to retire. She received an extremely warm reception from the House, and I went and thanked her very much indeed. I did two or three little television interviews about it.

I then went to the Campaign Group, where this awful football-hooligans Bill was discussed. It is, I think, in some respects the biggest restriction of civil liberties to deal with the smallest problem. I mean, they don't apply the same principle to murder or rape or paedophilia, only to football hooligans. I told Graham Allen, one of the whips, that I couldn't vote for it. Anyway, I've got flu.

Thursday 13 July

Michael Meacher came and sat next to me at tea; we had half an hour together. He's always very friendly. He said he'd never had a one-to-one talk with Blair. Once a fortnight Prescott has a meeting in his department, which has got eight Ministers in it, at which Prescott takes up 90 per cent of the time, and then asks, 'Does anyone want to add anything?' And that's about all. There's no collectivism; the extinction of Cabinet government is very significant.

Anyway, tonight was the Football (Disorder) Bill and I was not prepared to listen to the debate, or vote for it. It went on, I think, until about 1.15 in the morning, but I told the whips I was going home.

Friday 14 July

Up at five o'clock. I met Derek Ezra on the train to Chesterfield, and had a long talk to him. The train was held up because a Virgin train had broken down on the line. There was an awful delay. Derek is eighty-one now. He was Chairman of the National Coal Board in the Seventies and said that he supported the miners in each case when there were strikes during his tenure; and he had very good relations with Joe Gormley, the old NUM President – which I think is an aspect of corporatism that people on the left tend to forget. He said, 'We must go back to coal; the Government is not remotely interested in coal or manufacturing. There's no industrial strategy, no energy policy, nothing.' He was very critical of the Government. He's a Liberal himself; said he joined in the Thirties when the Labour Party was very left-wing and the Tories were engaged in appeasement of the Germans. He stuck to it. He's in the House of Lords. He said, 'You must come to the House of Lords.' I said I couldn't really do that.

Monday 17 July

The papers this morning are full of a leaked memorandum by Tony Blair, called 'Touchstone Issues', in which he says that the Labour Government is out of touch with the gut instincts of the British people on, of all things, crime, family values and defence. Reading the memorandum, which is printed in full, it becomes clear that he thinks the public want more money spent on defence; consider us weak on the family and soft on crime; and, he says, something must be done to jail muggers. And then he adds, unbelievably, 'And when initiatives of this kind are worked out, I wish personally to be associated with them.' No consideration of the real nature of the problems, no analysis of the choices; just a request for gimmick responses to tabloid pressure, which have got to give him a boost. It was an incredible memorandum. I've never known a Prime Minister send a memorandum like that, but he may be doing it all the time. Anyway, that is a big, big story, and William Hague exploited it quite sensibly and properly.

Caroline's feeling a bit better, a little bit better every day.

I went up to Hyde Park and was met by Tom Corby, who's the press officer for the Royal Parks Authority, and by the new Chief Executive of the Parks Authority, in a lovely house overlooking the park, right in the depths of it. I didn't know it existed. We walked over to the new sculpture of the Reformers' Tree. The story of the tree is that it was torn down, or burned down, during riots in 1866–7, when the Home Secretary tried to ban demonstrations in Hyde Park. In 1977 Jim Callaghan planted another tree there, but nobody knows where it is. This new tree was a sort of mosaic in pebbles, black on white, with an inscription round the circumference. Tom Corby is a good old leftie and had asked me to dedicate the tree. The sculptor, Harry Graham, and his wife Catherine were there, and their little girl, called Georgia, who ran all over the sculpture and tried to pick the pebbles up. I met Ruth's brother Neil, who was responsible for painting the sculpture with some anti-graffiti substance so that nobody could wreck it.

Went on to the Commons and had a bite to eat with David Davis and Richard Shepherd, two Tory MPs whom I very much like, in the Tea Room. They both said they'd support Gwyneth Dunwoody for the Speakership. If they do that, I think she'll get it against Menzies Campbell, whom Blair seems to want. It was very interesting.

After that, I wrote a note to the whips and said I wasn't proposing to stay because they're going to be up late tonight passing this awful Football (Disorder) Bill, which Richard Shepherd, David Davis and Jeremy Corbyn voted against on the second reading. I can't be bothered to do that now. I want to be home.

I came home and had a meal with Caroline, which was lovely.

Tuesday 18 July

Gordon Brown made a long statement about the comprehensive spending review, in which he announced enormous increases. But people are so sceptical now, they really don't quite know what to make of it all. I feel the same, but of course Labour MPs cheered him to the echo.

As I was going into the Members' Lobby, John Major said to me, 'Well, what about the Speakership?'

So I said, 'I've only ever said I'm not standing as a *Labour* candidate, you know,' because the Speaker stands as Speaker, and not for a party, at a general election – so he laughed. But this little mini-mini-mini-ground swell of support for the idea of me as Speaker is growing. I've got to be careful. I cannot lead people along when I don't really want to be Speaker, but I certainly do intend to make a speech after the Recess about the future of the House of Commons.

Wednesday 19 July

I had a word with Bruce Grocott, the Prime Minister's PPS, today. 'Bruce, why do we never see Tony at any Labour gatherings?'

'Oh,' he said, 'he does meetings with Labour Party members regularly.'

'Yes,' I said, 'but I didn't mean that. When I was at the Durham Miners' Gala, where 65,000 people had gathered, people asked "Why does he go to the Women's Institute where he gets shouted at, rather than here?"'

Bruce said, 'Well, you see, in the old days, he would be exposed to criticism there.'

'Well,' I said, 'maybe, but they'd have given him a warm welcome.'

Thursday 20 July

Sheila was a bit cross with me today, A pigeon was dying in the back garden and she thought I should have rung up the RSPCA or the RSPB. By the time we got on the phone, the bird was dead.

Anyway, I decided to draft a memorandum from Professor Philip Gould, Medical Director of the Millbank Clinic, to the Prime Minister, saying that he'd completed the diagnosis on the patient and New Labour was suffering from BSE (Bogus Spin Excess), which can lead to CJD (Contaminated Jargon Disorder) and can prove fatal in political parties; and added, 'Please keep this entirely to yourself.' I thought it was quite amusing.

No political news other than the fact that the much-heralded ten-year transport plan was launched today with billions of pounds for everything. But it all covers up, of course, the privatisation of our transport system.

Saturday 22 July

I had a talk to a few people in the House about the Speakership. One Tory MP said that the system under which the Speaker was chosen was highly defective, because if you had more than two candidates there was no way of sorting it out. There are a lot of candidates – Alan Haselhurst, Michael Martin, Mike Lord, Nick Winterton, Richard Shepherd, who sent me a letter this morning enclosing a photocopy of a leading article in *The Independent* saying that he'd be the best Speaker; there's Gwyneth Dunwoody, and I suspect they will certainly bring Frank Dobson forward. I had a good old talk to people about it.

Then I saw Tony Banks in the Lobby in one of the divisions, and I said, 'We haven't had a chance of talking.'

He said, 'I'm taking soundings to see. I'm just taking soundings . . .' A reference to this idea that I might be a candidate.

Tuesday 25 July

Caroline and I left after lunch to see her cancer consultant.

When I was there, somebody told me that a Concorde had crashed in Paris, and subsequently I learned what had happened. It appears that its engine caught fire on take-off and it crashed and killed everybody in it, and killed a few people on the ground near a hotel: the first time Concorde has ever had a crash of that seriousness. Only yesterday they announced that there were some hairline cracks in the wings, which they were dealing with. It's very, very sad.

Caroline got a lovely meal. I'm absolutely exhausted – morally, physically and politically.

Wednesday 26 July

I got up at half-past six today, and to cut a long story short, I did eleven broadcasts about the Concorde tragedy.

I had dug out the film I took when I went up in the fourth supersonic flight in the spring of 1970; I made copies of it and gave it to everybody. I think it was used by one or two programmes. I was very pleased about that. The line I generally took was that this was a beautiful aircraft; we were well ahead of anybody else; a quarter of a million jobs depended on it; the technology had been advanced in all sorts of other directions; and it was a major defence of British industry against de-industrialisation. I particularly developed that line of argument whenever I had a little bit of time to do so.

Richard Shepherd, whom I like very much, would like me to sponsor him for the Speakership. He is hoping for support, particularly from the Labour side. Patrick Cormack, who's a very nice guy, would also like support. Nick Winterton has put his name into the ring. Who else? There's Gwyneth Dunwoody of course. There's Mick Martin, the Deputy Speaker. As I say, there are a lot of candidates, but nobody quite knows how to deal with the matter.

One little item I think I forgot to report. As I was going over to 4 Millbank, I saw Greg Dyke, the Director General of the BBC, who's a very friendly chap, talking to somebody just outside St Stephen's entrance. So I went back and had a chat, and I told him the story of the boat race between the BBC and a Japanese crew: how the Japanese won, and Birt reorganised the BBC crew and it lost again, and so on. The BBC finally won by having a steering committee and one man rowing the boat. Dyke nearly doubled up with laughter. He'd never heard it before, and it absolutely sums up what he felt about Birt. He said, 'What do you think Birt's going to do about crime?' because Birt has been made Blair's adviser on crime.

So I said, 'I'll tell you what he's going to do about crime. There will be a boat race between the Metropolitan Police and a Japanese crew.'

He laughed again, and it was very jolly; I'm glad to get on with the Director General of the BBC because for the last few years there's just been such hostility.

Thursday 27 July

I walked up from the House to the Cabinet Office to see Mo Mowlam, because she'd invited me to tea. I was taken through the great cavernous building, which I hadn't been in for twenty-one years, into her office, which overlooked Horse Guards Parade. I looked out and said, 'Oh, you must have seen the Queen Mother's birthday rehearsals.'

'Oh,' she said, 'I've got a flat in Admiralty House [just the other side of Horse Guards Parade] and we've had the rehearsals for the Tattoo, we've had the Trooping of the Colour, we've got the Queen Mother's birthday.'

So I said, 'It's enough to make you into a monarchist.'

'Oh no, quite the opposite,' she said.

She didn't have any shoes on, her hair was all over the place, and she was in a simple blue dress and put her feet on the table. I got a cup of tea and two lumps of sugar and a biscuit, and we chatted for about twenty minutes.

Caroline had said to me, 'let her do the talking', so I asked about Ireland and Mo said, 'Oh well, we did very well. The chemistry was right. Bill [that's Clinton], Bertie [that's Ahern, the Irish Prime Minister] and Tony got on very well together.' She said, 'The problems aren't over yet, you know; they aren't over yet.'

I said, 'No, but I thought when you visited the prisoners in the Maze Prison that was very significant.'

'Well, I had to take a risk, but I asked people, "Why shouldn't I do it?" and they couldn't think of any reason.' I said I presumed it was a collective decision. 'No,' she said, 'I took the risk myself.'

If that's the case, it was very impressive.

She said Paisley was quite a human figure. She described how he had fumed at all the people in drag who'd marched in front of Edward Carson's statue, calling for equal rights for gays. 'All these sodomites,' he had thundered.

Anyway, I asked, 'Do you think Peter Mandelson wants to come back to Government?'

'No, no, no.'

Then we moved on a little bit. She said, 'Well, on drugs, I mean the Americans are spraying the fields from the air, killing the poppies (or whatever the drugs come from), and I think they should be more sensible. I think they should compensate farmers for tearing up the fields. Indeed, I do sometimes think,' she went on, 'that the legalisation of drugs and using the money to help drug addicts would be best, but you can't say that. It's not on at the moment.' It's a view I sort of half-share.

Anyway, at 2.22 p.m., a little message came on my pager saying, 'Vote expected shortly', so I said I'd better go. Mo said, 'Take my car and go through Downing Street and wave at the crowds, and they'll think there's been a reshuffle.' So she took me down, introduced me to her driver, and he took me along Downing Street, through the gates and into the Commons. I don't think there was a vote actually.

Monday 31 July

Vanessa, the Macmillan nurse, came. She did say she thought it was possible that Caroline's paralysis in her legs might have nothing to do with the cancer. It might be caused by the pernicious anaemia. She's very nice, and very understanding; the Macmillan nurses are marvellous.

I rang Steve today, and he had been to see this 5000-year-old man who was frozen in the Alps. When they first found him, they thought he was a climber; then an old climber; and then they did a test and found he was 5000 years old and had a spear and an axe. They keep him in an ice box, in a deep-freeze, and you can see him. That is something.

Ruth rang me up to tell me that her sister Jill went on holiday and arranged to have a man live in and feed and exercise the dog. No one is sure what happened exactly, but it seems that he had a heart attack and collapsed, and he was in the house for three days with the dog barking continually until the neighbours came in and found him dead on the floor. Her other sister Jo had to sort everything out. These are grim things, but they're part of the human condition, which is as interesting as the political news at the moment, of which there is none.

I received today a copy of *The Truth at Last*, which is the fascist paper in America that has produced a special commemorative edition about Mosley. The centre pages are devoted to a picture of his huge gathering, held at an indoor venue in London on 16 July 1939, and you realise that the Nuremberg Rally is the basis on which all modern political conventions – Conservative and Labour, Democratic and Republican – are based. The Führer goes forward and there's tremendous cheering; everything is focused on the Leader rather than on the people. Democratic assemblies are much more collective. There's a platform, a committee, and people can speak from the floor, but it's just not like that now. I find it really quite frightening. I had felt this in the past, but it was interesting that an American fascist paper should not only have published a special edition all about Oswald Mosley, but also made his speeches available on cassette.

Sunday 6 August

The *Observer* had an article this morning by a guy called Martin Bright about my being considered for the Speakership. I should have mentioned that last Thursday the *Daily Mail* had a mock-up picture of me in the

Speaker's dress, and an article by Mark Seddon saying that I'd be the best Speaker to save democracy. It's not that I'm a serious candidate, but I'm glad that my name's mentioned because it gives me more leverage in arguing about the process for selecting the Speaker.

Wednesday 9 August
There's been an attack by John Bercow, a Conservative MP, on Cherie Blair as Lady Macbeth, which is a thing they used to say about Caroline.

Thursday 10 August, Stansgate
We brought down from London the bench on which I had proposed to Caroline in 1948 and put it by the pond, and there we're going to have our ashes put in a little grave. It sounds slightly morbid, but we don't want to go through all the hassle of church, because interring my mother's ashes was so complicated. It will be nice to have the grave at Stansgate, and if it's all swamped by the sea in the future, it doesn't terribly matter.

The stair lift has been installed here, a very complex one, and carries Caroline up and down stairs, as in London; and here, we have a bath bubble, which you put in the bath and it lifts you up and lowers you. So Caroline can have a bath, which she otherwise couldn't have done. This mobility through new technology does make a hell of a difference.

Tuesday 5 September
Mo Mowlam has decided to stand down from Parliament.

Tam Dalyell wrote a beautiful obituary of Audrey Wise.

In the mail this morning, a postcard arrived from Jim Callaghan:

> Dear Tony,
>
> Unlike some, you and I have been fortunate in our wives and our long partnerships with them, so I was very sad to learn of Caroline's illness and send my best wishes to her and to you in your care for her.
>
> Ever,
> Jim Callaghan

Well, I was touched! I mean, really tearful, so I rang him up at once and I said, 'Oh Jim, it's Tony Benn. I got your card this morning, a few minutes ago. I was so touched by it.' I went on, 'We've had, over the years, one or two marginal differences of emphasis.'

He said, 'Oh, that's the greatest understatement of your life!'

So I said, 'Well, I remember you once said to me, "I'm not as nice as I look", and I said, "Neither am I." The great thing about you, Jim, was that you had your roots in the movement, and you had a little bird on your shoulder telling you what the movement would and wouldn't put up with.'

He said, 'Absolutely right.'

I didn't take it further on the question of New Labour. He said that Audrey was eighty-seven, and he's eighty-eight. 'If we went together, we'd be very happy.' Anyway, it was lovely.

Wednesday 6 September

Barbara, who's been helping Caroline for four years now, said she would come in every day. Well, that is a tremendous asset. While she was here, we tested the button for the emergency service to which I have subscribed for Caroline. It went 'beep-beep-beep-beep-beep' and then a voice came through the loudspeaker 'Caroline Benn, how are you?' So I answered, and the voice asked, 'Who's that? Is that Tony Benn?' The details were on their computer screen. I said it was just a test and she said that was fine.

I had a bath this morning and, I must report it, a wasp stung my private parts; it's been stinging all day. I could feel this thing flying around in my pants, and I tried to swat it and I probably did succeed, and it responded by stinging me.

Anyway, I went to the Commons at half-past eleven to see Bill Mckay, the Clerk of the House of Commons, an awfully nice man. I presented him with a memorandum which I'd drafted suggesting that the Speaker be elected by a ballot of Members and then a vote in the Division Lobby between the two candidates with the top votes. To my surprise, he wasn't unsympathetic. I'd worked it out very carefully, and it was quite a good memorandum. I left it with him and he said he'd think about it.

Monday 11 September

There's a fuel crisis in Britain because this blockade of the refineries by truck drivers, taxi drivers and farmers has really created a major petrol shortage, so I thought I'd better go out and see if I could get some petrol because I've got to take Caroline to the hospital. I found one garage where the pumps did have a little, so I filled the car up and bought a spare can and filled that.

But the general impression of a breakdown of law and order is going to damage the Government. First of all, there is the absurd policy of having the highest level in Europe of tax on fuel, while at the same time complaining about increased OPEC prices. The threat that if the Government does cut fuel tax (which it should do), it will hit health and education spending is untrue. It could have come out of the Dome, or nuclear weapons, or excursions into Sierra Leone, so that's not a credible argument. Of course, the reason they don't want to cut the revenue is because one of the options open to them would be to increase income tax on the wealthy, and they don't want to do that, either. In a way, although I don't support this type of action, it is a popular movement – if the word 'popular' is used in its proper sense – against a high level of tax.

Monday 18 September
Ian Walters came in and did a couple of hours' work on the sculpture of Caroline which, I must say, really is good.

Wednesday 20 September
Lord Melchett, the Executive Director of Greenpeace, and the Greenpeace protestors were released after being acquitted in court for criminal damage against a genetically modified crop, which they said might pollute neighbouring fields. Michael Meacher was asked to comment. He said, 'Oh, I'm not commenting on the courts, but if we didn't allow these tests, the country would be flooded with genetically modified seed,' implying (a) that the Government intends to take no more notice of the courts than it does of protesters, and (b) that the real bully boys, namely the genetically modified seed companies, can get away with anything because the Government couldn't stop them. Even the media is beginning to notice the fact that politics is now the politics of the streets. That's where all political ideas begin and they end up in Parliament, so there's nothing very strange about it. *Any Questions?* which I am doing this week, should be interesting.

Thursday 21 September
As we were getting a meal in the evening, the phone rang and it was Don Brind, who is a press officer at Labour Party HQ, who used to be a TV journalist. He said, 'Have you a moment?'

So I said, 'Yes.'

He said, 'About *Any Questions?* tomorrow. We offered them Andrew Smith, and the BBC picked you, and we don't want a spin put on it to the effect that Labour Ministers are afraid of appearing on programmes.'

'Well, I was asked a long time ago and I accepted.'

'You appreciate what I'm saying?'

'Are you in fact saying that you'd like me to cancel my acceptance and give it over to Andrew Smith?'

'Well, not exactly,' said Brind.

I said, 'But you would be pleased if I did?'

'Well, you can understand the reasons.'

I said, 'Look, I am the most senior Labour MP, probably the longest-serving ever. I've been in Parliament for fifty years. I've been in the Cabinet for eleven years, on the Executive for thirty-three, Chairman of the Party, and I've done *Any Questions?* since 1951. It really is a bit insulting, you know, to say to me that you think I should stand down.'

'Oh, well, I didn't mean that.'

I said, 'If this is control freakery, it's a very vivid example.'

'You said that. I didn't!' replied Brind. Then he said, 'All right then, let's move on to the next point. You saw what Portillo said about cutting fuel taxes?'

I said, 'Yes.'

'You realise his connection with the oil industry?'

'I didn't actually.'

'Well,' Brind said, 'Portillo is connected with the oil industry, and it's a point you might make.'

So I said, 'Look, Lord Simon, who was chairman of BP, was a member of the Government and, as far as I know, is not even a member of the Labour Party.'

After about ten minutes, Brind rang off.

Years ago, when Neil Kinnock was Leader of the Party, I used to sit on the platform at Conference with the other members of the National Executive. Little marks would be put alongside the text of Kinnock's speeches – for example, when he said, 'We want to look forward with confidence', the cameras would be told to turn to Gerald Kaufman or someone; and when he said, 'And we're fed up with party rows', the marks would indicate that the camera should focus on me looking glum. So one year I went up in the gallery and who should I see wandering around with a roving camera but Don Brind, trying to find me. He was looking everywhere. I put up a newspaper so that he didn't catch my face.

At the end of September Caroline went into the Pembridge Centre for Palliative Care, attached to St Charles Hospital, for a week, so that I could go to Chesterfield and then on to the Labour Party Conference in Brighton. Although I was reluctant, she insisted that I should go to my last Conference as a Member of Parliament. The Conference itself was uneventful, although it did vote against the Government's policy in supporting the restoration of old-age pensions linked to earnings. I had hoped to speak on the subject but, in the event, was not called to the rostrum. During the course of the week I came back to London to see Caroline, though she was cross that I did so.

Friday 22 September

I overslept and had to rush for the Chesterfield train, but I had time to get Caroline her breakfast and put out the things she needed. I did a surgery from 10 a.m. to 3 p.m., enormously long and exhausting, but I got through it.

Lissie said, when I rang her later, that she and Mum had a bit of weep together in the car as she left home to go to the hospice. Lissie was wonderful, and stayed for a bit. Mum has a room with a window and greenery beyond. Joshua went in the evening. I expect Stephen will go on Sunday. I just don't want to go to the Labour Conference. I don't want to do anything really.

Saturday 23 September
I went to see Caroline at the hospice from half-past eight until about half-past eleven. She's settling in, and they're very nice to her there. The weather was lovely and the door was open, and I can sit outside and smoke through the French windows, and she can see into the garden and she's got everything she needs. It is awfully hard for her, but she just thinks of other people all the time. She's determined that I go to Brighton so that I will be able to enjoy myself and she'll be looked after. She's just a completely selfless person.

Thursday 28 September
In the afternoon I went and collected Caroline in a cab. Lovely to have her home! Then I went up to Dr Pettifer's surgery to collect some drugs for her, and Caroline got the meal. She watched *Taggart* on TV.

The big news today of course was that Denmark voted substantially against the euro single currency. The opinion polls had been rather contradictory, and it is a real hammer-blow for the euro-enthusiasts in Britain. I hadn't quite realised, until somebody brought it to my attention, that not a single country in Europe, in the euro, has ever been allowed to vote as to whether they wanted to go into it or not, so there is no popular support for the euro at all. Especially interesting for me was that the political leaders in Denmark are generally in favour, as are the main political parties, the bankers, the media, business leaders and trade union leaders, but the people turned it down. It's the people versus the Government.

At the end of the Labour Conference in Brighton today, Nelson Mandela spoke and said, 'I know you've come out of curiosity to hear the views of an old-age pensioner from the colonies', and everybody laughed. But it was a lovely speech, and he hugged Tony Blair and it was great.

Sunday 1 October
Over in Denmark, where the referendum on the single currency went the 'wrong' way, Prodi, the President of the European Commission, demands that there should be another referendum. There's no logic in this at all! Demonstrations in Belgrade against the authorities are good and the police are brutal. Demonstrations in Prague against capitalism are bad and the police are wonderful. One day, people are going to wake up to this! I don't know when, but they will.

Monday 2 October
Lissie told us that Hannah, who is six, said, 'I want to watch Jon Snow interviewing Gordon Brown on Channel 4.'

So Sarah, who is four, said, 'Who's Gordon Brown?'

Hannah replied, 'He's the Chancellor of the Exchequer, and he's in charge of our money.'

So Sarah said, 'I thought that *you* were in charge of our bunny,' and burst into tears.

That is a lovely story of a six-year-old discussing with a four-year-old the role of the Chancellor of the Exchequer on Channel 4. Bunny is much the biggest figure in that household.

Forty or fifty people have been killed in conflicts between the Palestinians and the Israeli forces. The Israelis have used helicopter gunships to shoot at the crowd. I think a thousand people have been injured. The whole thing is breaking down all over again. I must say, if I were Arafat (for whom I haven't a lot of time), I would simply declare a Palestinian state here and now, because the American offer to mediate and head up an inquiry is simply not good enough. Israel is a client state of the United States.

Friday 6 October

The big political news today is that Milošević has conceded defeat in the presidential elections. He went on television, congratulated the new President and everyone welcomed it, but of course now they're demanding that the new President hands over Milošević to The Hague to be tried, and he says he won't. I think if he did, there would be a lot of trouble.

Michael Lord, one of the Deputy Speakers, rang me up about his candidature, having received my letter about the possibility of having hustings and a ballot to elect the new Speaker. He was quite interested in it. He felt if there was a hustings meeting he should go, but the really interesting thing he told me was that, down in Bournemouth at the Tory Conference, the word had gone round that a deal had been done between Blair and Hague that Sir George Young would be the new Speaker, and that Labour MPs would be whipped to support him. If that's really true, that will kill off the House of Commons stone dead as a legislative assembly.

Blair's made a big speech in Poland, in which he says the European Union must be a superpower but not a super-state, which is a typical spin doctor's phrase. What the hell does it mean? A superpower has nuclear weapons. Is Europe going to have nuclear weapons?

He wants to enlarge the EU within four years to include Eastern Europe, and that will no doubt mean Serbia; it's quite obvious that a development is in progress that will obliterate democracy.

Wednesday 11 October

I sort of realised with a blaze of the obvious today that I am entirely dependent on women. I've always been dependent on Caroline. I'm dependent on Sheila in the office in London, and on Margaret Vallins in the office in Chesterfield. I'm dependent on Barbara, who is marvellous. I'm dependent on the district nurses; that is to say, Hilary, Irene,

Beverley, Dixie and Cynthia, who come in so regularly. I'm dependent on Dr Jane Pettifer. The realisation that I'm being carried by all these people in trying to look after Caroline was a real eye-opener to me.

I went in to the House of Commons and had a bite to eat in the Lords cafeteria. I saw Sir George Young, who is Blair's favoured candidate as Speaker. So I went up to him and said, 'Did you get my letter?' – I had sent every candidate my plan for hustings and a ballot to choose the Speaker.

He said, 'Yes, I did.'

'What do you think of it?'

'Well,' he said, 'it's not a bad idea, if it can be done.' He wasn't critical of it. He's a very gentle, tall, elegant man, and I could just imagine Mr Speaker Young without any difficulty at all. But he said, 'Did you see the piece in the *Express* today? It's reported that you said it had all been fixed for me.'

I replied, 'Well, I heard that from the rumours going round at the Tory Conference in Bournemouth.' Young looked a little bit embarrassed. I said, 'I hope it hasn't done you any damage.'

On the Speakership, *The Independent* had a page listing thirteen candidates. It never mentioned the proposal for a ballot; it was just the usual 'Who's going to get the cushiest job in Parliament?' type of story.

I have cancelled my surgery for tomorrow. I have to be in London for Caroline.

Friday 13 October

Caroline's seventy-fourth birthday.

She had a very, very bad night indeed, stomach distended, tossing and turning; the district nurses came this morning.

More support for my plan on the Speakership: from Andrew Robathan, Jonathan Sayeed, Gillian Shephard, and David Davis, the Tory Chairman of the Public Accounts Committee; Julie Morgan; John Butterfill, who is himself one of the candidates – and said he'd prefer it if it was an alternative vote, and I'm not against that – Phyllis Starkey; Roger Berry; Alan Simpson, and Kelvin Hopkins.

Tuesday 17 October

I went to the Commons and saw Bill McKay, the Clerk of the House. I asked him, 'In your view, would it be in order for Ted Heath to accept a manuscript amendment, on the process of selecting the Speaker, from me?'

He said, 'Yes, it would. I'm bound to advise him,' he continued, 'that the existing procedure is probably preferable, but it would be in order.'

So Ted, as Father of the House, when he chairs the proceedings for Speaker, has absolute discretion. I then photocopied a note for Members of Parliament, with the amendment attached, and took copies up to the Press Gallery and distributed them around the House; put it up on noticeboards in the Members' Lobby, in the Whips' Office, in the library, in the Smoking Room and in the Tea Room.

Sunday 22 October
I went first of all to the Parliamentary Labour Party meeting. It was a crowded meeting and I got up straight away and asked the Front Bench if they could give some indication of their view about the procedure. I said, 'We don't know the names of the candidates. We don't know the procedure, until Ted tells us. We don't know anything; it is ridiculous and we should have a ballot.' Margaret Beckett jumped on this straight away: 'Oh no, you can't change it now. We've got to go ahead.' So that is the Ted Heath/Tony Blair (and, I dare say, William Hague) view.

Anyway, we also discovered that Clive Soley and Margaret Beckett and others were pushing for Labour MPs to vote for Sir George Young. They did not want Michael Martin. So Blair wants Ashdown in the Cabinet and a Tory in the chair of the Chamber. It's so clear and so apparent. I put it to a Member and he said, 'Oh, we know that.'

I went to the hustings meeting, with about 150 people there, where some of the candidates spoke. I filmed a little bit of the PLP and a little bit of the hustings on my video camera, and I made the same point. There was a lot of support for a ballot. Except for the Tory MP Eric Forth, everybody there voted for a ballot. So that gave me a lot of strength.

Then I went to the Clerk's Office. I couldn't get to see Bill McKay, the Clerk himself, but George Cubie made it absolutely clear, without actually telling me, that Ted was not going to accept my amendment, and he handed me a form of words that I could use to put the case and said I would be heard.

Dear old Tam Dalyell had already reserved a seat for me in the Chamber next to his own.

So I went into the House at 2.30 p.m. Hilary was sitting just behind me. The place was absolutely packed, certainly on the Labour side. Tony Blair announced that the Queen wanted us to elect a Speaker, and then Ted made a statement saying how he was going to handle everything. Then I got up on a Point of Order, and I was able to read the whole of my manuscript amendment so that it will appear in Hansard. So that was an achievement. Ted said he couldn't accept my proposal; he was bound by the standing orders. Then a mass of Members got up to support me! David Davis, Tam Dalyell, Gordon Prentice, Andrew Tyrie and Paul Tyler got up – it really was a bombardment. Hilary said to me later, 'Why didn't you get them all to put up their hands, like a factory-gate strike meeting, because you'd have got a shower of hands?'

Anyway, Ted would not budge, and I decided that, as he wouldn't budge, the House would not welcome a procedural wrangle about adjourning the House, or moving him out of the chair or anything. I don't think it would have been popular. So then we began, and the first person to be moved was Michael Martin, and we had the two speeches in support.

Then before the debate really got going, I got up and made my second speech about the role of the Speaker, and in support of Michael Martin. The first speech that I had made was very widely acclaimed, particularly on the Tory benches. The second one was more political, about the House of Commons being in decline. 'Take tomorrow's parliamentary business. We're discussing the Insolvency Bill (Lords). Perhaps we should be discussing the Bankruptcy Bill (Commons).' People appreciated my point, so it was quite okay. But Hilary thought I went a bit over the top, and of course the House of Commons doesn't really want to hear political arguments. They don't mind little parliamentary jokes.

David Davis had spoken just ahead of me, and then, to cut a long story short, we went through all the speeches, both by candidates and their proposers, and the Division. I voted for Mick Martin consistently, except for a couple of divisions that I missed. I didn't hear George Young, but he was bitterly disappointed to be defeated, because he had the support of the Labour Front Bench and his own Front Bench. Nick Winterton made a strong speech. Richard Shepherd made a very good speech. I didn't think much of Menzies Campbell, who was put up, but the debate went on and finally, at about a quarter to ten, we finished.

Just after Mick Martin had been elected, I got up and congratulated him and said that this was an election of international importance, because Members who had heard the nine o'clock news would know that Iraq, Libya, China and North Korea had decided to adopt this method of electing their own Leader. People sort of tittered! And then I came home.

Tony Blair made a bold statement declaring himself to be an environmentalist. He invited business people and environmental groups to hear it, but didn't invite the trade unions.

Wednesday 25 October

I went into the House and I went to the Speaker's Office and there was Mick Martin himself, the new Speaker. He wasn't wearing a wig. He wasn't wearing silk stockings and knee breeches. He was wearing a suit and a gown with Geneva bands. Well, considering he's a Catholic, he looked exactly like the Moderator of the Church of Scotland, and I teased him about that. But it's a great thing to be the first Catholic Speaker since Sir Thomas More. It is amazing. He said that he'd been invited to go to Rome to celebrate the canonisation of More, who I think is now St Thomas More, but he said he thought that might be a bit difficult. I thought that was very amusing.

Friday 3 November

Caroline was in great distress today. The district nurse decided it was necessary to call the doctor. Dr Mok turned up, because Jane is on holiday, and she immediately called an ambulance, and Caroline and I went to the Pembridge Centre for Palliative Care at St Charles Hospital.

A very nice young doctor came to see her, and Heather, the nurse, and others who knew her welcomed her as an old friend.

I rang the family on the mobile phone and told them the news, and then I went back and had a word with the doctor. He said, 'Look, this is very serious. It may require an operation. I can't of course do it at the hospice. I think I'm going to move her to St Mary's, Paddington.' The thought of a second ambulance trip, particularly feeling as poorly as she was, was very difficult for Caroline, but she did agree to go.

This time we had a St John Ambulance Brigade ambulance; two of them were volunteers. I told them I'd been in the St John Ambulance Brigade during the war, and I still had their little black first-aid book. They said, 'Oh, my goodness me, we don't think there's a copy of that, even in the archives of St John Ambulance!' So that amused me.

Anyway, we got to St Mary's and the surgeon had a look at her and Caroline was immediately put in a little cubicle. Well, I left at that stage and Stephen, bless his heart, without telling me, arrived and stayed all night, right through until six o'clock in the morning.

Saturday 4 November

The doctors saw Caroline today and helped to relieve her pain. I was there when they came and they decided to keep her in until tomorrow or maybe Monday, to be sure there wasn't an infection.

There are floods all over the place; so far the news at Stansgate is good, for the Blackwater is tidal.

The railways are in a state of total crisis because they've now examined the track and found dozens, if not hundreds, of bits of track that must be replaced. So of course the railway service is in chaos.

The Director General of the CBI said that Britain is becoming a banana republic. You can't blame Blair for all this, but somehow to have kept back money for so long that could have been used to reinvest and re-equip shows that you do have to have national planning. You can't leave these things to market forces.

But I can't say politics is my main interest at the moment. What I have learned recently is the tremendous importance of personal relations.

I have also realised what an international world we live in. Beatrice, who comes in the morning as a district nurse, is from Nigeria, and there's another nurse from Australia. Irene Chan is a Malaysian Chinese. When Caroline went in last time to hospital, George Lee, the surgeon, was himself a Chinese from Singapore. His boss, the consultant, is Mr Patel, who's an Indian. We've had carers from the Philippines, from St Vincent, from Kenya, from Hungary. We are part of a world community. If some of these people had come as asylum seekers, they would have been kept out; but when an industrialised country needs them it uses its wealth to buy highly skilled people who should really be in their own countries.

Sunday 5 November

Well, Caroline was much better and she waited in hospital all morning to come home. It was a private ambulance, and they didn't have any uniform on. One of the crew had only been in the ambulance service for a month and previously she'd been a chef. So I felt this was an example of privatisation.

Wednesday 8 November

I asked Caroline today, because one or two people have suggested it, 'Do you think you should have a permanent nurse? Would you rather have a nurse?' And she said, 'No, I'd rather you looked after me,' and that was such a sweet thing to say. I was really touched by that, and it gave me a big boost.

The American presidential election is apparently hung. Gore has got a bigger popular vote than Bush, but it all hinges on Florida, where the American media first of all said Gore had won, then Bush had won, then Gore had won. Actually it was all based on exit polls, and the result depends on postal votes; and there's a recount in Florida. So neither of the candidates can say very much. Ralph Nader got about 3 per cent, which probably contributed to the defeat of Gore and will make people angry with him, but as he said on television, 'Well, this is the end of the two-party system and corporate finance' and I agree with him.

Thursday 9 November

I attended today, at the invitation of the *Guardian*'s editorial board, a discussion that the *Guardian* might declare itself a republican newspaper.

When I got to the Soho club in Greek Street, I found them in a little room, and round the table were Professor Vernon Bogdanor, a right-wing academic; Michael White, the political correspondent of the *Guardian*; Polly Toynbee, a Labour loyalist; Alan Rusbridger, the Editor; two women I didn't know; and senior journalists Jonathan Freedland and David McKie. Geoffrey Robertson, the QC, left early.

As I arrived, Vernon Bogdanor was arguing that the left used the monarchy as a scapegoat, so I said to him, 'Well, let me just put one point to you. Why should I have to tell a lie to get into Parliament?' I developed the argument about the Oath of Allegiance, the Privy Councillor's Oath, the nonsense of it, and the fact that bishops had to pay homage.

The other line of argument about not removing the Queen is that, if you transfer all of the Crown prerogatives to the House of Commons, why worry about the Crown or the Queen? I said, 'Well, the existence of the

Crown has of course a huge cultural effect on us. We're trained to believe we are inferior, and our social history is obliterated by the history of kings and queens.'

They put the case that the Monarchy is irrelevant, and the really important things are health and education. They asked whether any of my constituents had ever raised the Crown with me.

I said, 'Well, the link between the Crown and people's experience is not explained very well. People don't realise that the laws made in Brussels are made by Royal Prerogative. We don't discuss it, and when people ask, "Why have we got troops in Sierra Leone?" I have to say, Don't ask me, I can't do anything about it.'

I wasn't really friendly to them. I said, 'Well, I'm not sure that the *Guardian* should become a republican paper, because you are an Establishment paper and the establishment desperately needs the monarchy.'

Michael White said, 'If you had proportional representation and a federal Europe, then that would surely deal with people's disenchantment with the House of Commons?'

I said, 'The fact is that in a federal Europe we don't have any democracy at all, because the Central Bank has got the power to make our economic policy without anyone being consulted. That's why people are switched off.'

I've privately dubbed White 'the Millbank professor of political theory and modern government'.

I said, 'Today's discussion will be fully recorded.'

They said, 'Can we see it before it's published?'

I said, 'No!'

Gore, who apparently has the majority of the popular vote, feels that this gives him the moral authority to challenge the results in Florida. Bush is confident that he will win.

I did talk to Joshua, who was here tonight (as I have done to Stephen and Hilary, and I spoke to Melissa this morning), to make it clear that I thought Caroline, Mum, probably did have liver cancer and therefore we were on the last lap. Lissie said she wanted to see more of her and talk to her, and so do I. I put Caroline to bed, very carefully, and do all the necessary things, but she is in acute pain.

I gave Caroline a little food and then, as I dictate this at eight o'clock, her great friend Phyllis Lambert from Canada is due for three days. She insisted on coming; as Barbara said, Phyllis has come to say goodbye to one of her very best friends, and I think that is true.

Monday 13 November

Lazy start, and Phyllis Lambert left today. She's been here since Friday. She's a very old friend of Caroline's. They were at Vassar College together. After I had proposed to Caroline, and she had returned to America, Phyllis came to Oxford and telegraphed back, 'Nuptials must be.' She's used her wealth to establish the Centre for Contemporary Architecture in Montreal. She was very sweet today and we had a little bit of a talk.

Wednesday 15 November

I had a brief word earlier in the afternoon with Ken Livingstone. I'd asked him to sign my Early Day Motion about the House of Commons controlling the executive. 'Well,' he said, 'you know I'm pro-Europe.'

I said, 'I know that, Ken, but this is the fiftieth anniversary of my election and I'd quite like to include that.'

'Oh, all right,' he said, 'just because it's the fiftieth anniversary!' So that was very nice.

I came home and gave Caroline a meal. She ate practically nothing. The last *Morse* is on television tonight, a programme she has adored, but tonight Morse is to die. So it is the genuine end of an era. Caroline's brother and sister, Graydon and Nance, and Graydon's wife, Sherri, arrive next week.

I was thinking the other day that it is like a honeymoon again. We're together, with no interruptions, and I'm at home all the time, and that's lovely. There's a sweetness about it because it brings out such lovely qualities in people. I've cancelled my surgery. I've cancelled everything really.

Nothing more about the American presidential elections. There's a big row about Europe because Joschka Fischer, the German Foreign Minister, who is a Green, called for the election of the President of the Commission, which would be a super-super-state. There was an exchange between Blair and Hague in the Commons about a super-state and a superpower. It's all rubbish!

Thursday 16 November

Caroline was in very great pain today. In the end I called Dr Pettifer and she arranged for an ambulance. At 1.30 the ambulance arrived and took Caroline to Charing Cross Hospital; two young women had to struggle to get her into the wheelchair, onto the stair lift, down onto a stretcher. It was terribly painful and she was immensely brave. We got to the hospital at about half-past two, with the appointment with Dr Lowdell fixed for four, but actually he saw her straight away, with his new registrar. He examined her. He didn't say very much except that the cancer activity rate, when normal, is forty, but was now 389.

Saturday 18 November

I rang the children. I left the hospital about six in the morning because Caroline was sleeping and quite rested. I came back and had a huge breakfast of orange juice and cornflakes with a banana and honey, and two eggs and toast and lots of marmalade and tea. I had a bath and got fresh clothes, then I got back to the hospital by nine, and I stayed all day until about 4.30 in the afternoon.

Caroline very much wants to come home. In effect, she knows the score and she wants really to die at home.

I was home at 5.30 and preparing for another night in the hospital. It's immeasurably sad, but we are a mutally supportive family. We all hugged each other no end, and cried and laughed and joked. It was just beautiful. I can't describe it in any other way, and Caroline was marvellous, although she's terribly weak and very grey. She's determined to hang on for her sister, Nance, and her brother, Graydon, who are arriving on Tuesday. The Thanksgiving dinner, I think, should go ahead.

Thursday 23 November

Well, this diary jumps to 3.15 on the morning of 23 November. I want to do it now because five hours ago – just over five hours ago – my beloved Caroline died in Ward 6 North at Charing Cross Hospital.

I don't quite know how to start this diary, because I haven't kept notes over the last few days because it just wasn't possible. I haven't slept at home for a week. I've just tried to get a rest on the couch there. But at any rate, Caroline went in on Thursday 16 November. Originally it was just to get drained again, but then it was clear that it was much more serious.

All the children came to see her – I forget which day. Every one of the grandchildren came. Michael came down from Leeds. She was failing fast, and it was obvious that she couldn't get home on Monday as I'd hoped. She didn't want to be in hospital at the end. She wanted to be at home, but I was very, very anxious that it would be impossible to care for her at home. So they kept her in hospital, and absolutely rightly so.

Gradually, over the last four days, she lost – well, life just ebbed away from her. She found it very difficult to speak, although she recognised people. Right up to yesterday, the day before she died (or should I say Tuesday), right up to then she could respond if you said something to her and she squeezed your hand. The greatest pleasure of all was that the day before she died (that's Tuesday, because it's now Thursday morning) her sister Nancy arrived from Cincinnati, and her brother Graydon and his wife Sherri. Stephen met Nancy, and Graydon came on his own. Caroline was so pleased to see them. And her friends Fleury and Patsy arrived, I think on Monday, and she recognised them. And PC (Peter Carter) came and she recognised him. So we were all there, and it was a mixture of laughter and tears. Tears because we love her so much, laughter because there was so much about her life we could joke about.

At any rate, last night (that's Wednesday night), we were all gathered there; all four children, Stephen and Hilary and Melissa, with her partner Paul, and Joshua, and myself. We were gathered round the bed. The sister came in and said, 'She's very strong. She's hanging on.' I'd asked everybody: her consultant, the house doctor, the Macmillan nurse, the oncologist who heads the Macmillan team, Columbia Quigley, the head of the hospice. They all came. Sarah, the ward sister, said, 'Sometimes, you know, it helps if you say, 'you can let go now if you like.'

I had a kip from about a quarter to six to quarter past seven. Stephen said, 'I think her breathing is getting shallower,' because her mouth was open and she was getting cold. Caroline's breathing was very shallow and intense.

So we all gathered round her bed, and at about a quarter to ten I leaned over and I said, 'Darling, we're all here. You can let go now, if you want to. If you want to go, you can let go.' I gave her a kiss on her brow, and it was very, very, cold, and at six minutes past ten on Wednesday 22 November, she gave her last breath. There had been gaps between the breathing, and she just quietly stopped breathing. Then a second later there was an exhalation of breath, and I wondered somehow if it was coming back; but it was what we had hoped, that she should be released.

So we were all in tears. We kissed her, one by one. Michael, her eldest grandson, was there for the death, and earlier in the day we'd had Nita and Daniel and Carrie. Carrie said to me, 'You must come and live in our house now.' It was just so moving. The people there were so kind – all the doctors, all the nurses, all the other patients who had cancer.

The children helped me to get the stuff home. Lissie sat next to me. She wasn't sure I could drive properly.

My dear children were such a source of strength, not only to me personally, forcing me to sleep and hugging me when I was crying, but also on Tuesday night, when the Political Studies Association was making a series of awards. Ted Heath, Margaret Thatcher and I were to be given an award as outstanding parliamentarians, and Stephen went for me and made a little speech. Then yesterday Hilary went to the Savoy Hotel, where I was being given another award as an outstanding parliamentarian of the year, and he made a speech there. So they carried the load for me.

When I look back on Caroline's life, she was the finest person I ever met in the whole of my life. She just absolutely radiated goodness. She had a capacity for love and interest in other people that was unparalleled. She had a most formidable intellect, a tremendously powerful character. She said the other day, 'This illness is really a test of character', because she was totally paralysed and depended on others to do everything for her: pick up a pen she'd dropped, move her legs, turn her in bed. But Barbara, who's been invaluable, sent a note saying, 'I've moved all the equipment out of the bedroom because it was a torture chamber,' and that's right.

Stephen has been wonderful. He's made all the arrangements, been to Kenyon's, negotiated with Golders Green Crematorium.

We had a discussion about the funeral and decided on the list of friends we wanted to invite. The children played and drew drawings. It was lovely. There was a beautiful obituary in the *Evening Standard*, drawing heavily on the announcement that I had made in the middle of the night, stressing all Mum's own work. I didn't want her to be overshadowed by me.

Friday 24 November

Marvellous obituaries of Caroline – absolutely fabulous ones! The *Guardian* had a lovely one by Julia Langdon, with a comment by Clyde Chitty. Tam Dalyell did a wonderful one in *The Independent*. The *Daily Telegraph* had three-quarters of a page of news story and then an obituary. *The Times* had an obituary. And truthfully, she got the obituaries you'd expect from a major political figure. She would have been amazed to see it. Even the *Daily Mail* had an article by Simon Heffer. It hadn't much to do with Mum, but he wrote it. Who else wrote? There was a bit by Paul Routledge in the *Mirror*; the *Morning Star* described hers as a good life. The photograph of Mum in the *Guardian* was lovely.

Saturday 25 November

Mrs Mac came in. She had known Caroline for many years. Masses of letters and flowers, and members of the public ringing up and saying, 'You don't know me, but I want to tell you how much I admired Caroline.' Joan Horrocks had put an advertisement in the *Morning Star* saluting Caroline. I feel absolutely overwhelmed by it. The letters: Arthur Scargill, Lady Wilson, right-wing Tories, communists.

Monday 27 November

I got up very early, and just before nine o'clock Caroline was brought back by the funeral director, Kenyon's, and she lay on a trestle in the front room, with lots of flowers. She lay there until half-past twelve: over three and a half hours. All the children arrived and the grandchildren, and the guests began arriving, and they all went in; almost all of them went in to see Caroline, who looked so beautiful. I kissed her, and dropped tears on her cold, cold face.

Then, at half-past twelve, the bus arrived for all the guests to get to Golders Green, and Caroline went out into the hearse with lots and lots of flowers, and the bus followed. We went up Golders Green Crematorium and got there at about quarter to two.

Graydon, Hilary, Stephen and Joshua carried Mum's coffin into the chapel and laid it to rest, very careful. Richard Moberly took the service, and the chapel was full. There must have been eighty people there, I should think. The organ voluntary was 'Sheep may safely graze' and before that 'Tears of grief' from Bach's *Passion*. We sang the Battle Hymn of the Republic, a tribute to Caroline's American roots.

Then after that I gave my address. I had to read it; I broke down three times, but I tried to do credit to her. The children had made many useful amendments because collective effort is better than personal writing. I read it to Caroline yesterday at Kenyon's and she didn't object – the first time she hasn't improved my text herself!

Then we sang 'Jerusalem' and Richard read some prayers, and then came the committal and I saw the coffin disappearing, and then the blessing. And then we all went out into the gardens and the music that was played was 'The Internationale', which is lovely, sung by a chorus. There were many, many tears, and I hugged everybody who came by. Then we put the flowers back in the bus, and we drove back home. And then people stayed and stayed and stayed. It was half-past ten before I got to bed. I was absolutely exhausted.

Tuesday 28 November

After lunch, I got in the car and I took all the flowers to distribute. I started at Charing Cross Hospital, and took some flowers to the radiotherapy department. Then I took some more up to the oncology clinic, and I burst into tears there. Then I went down to the car again and I took some more flowers. I left some on the eighth-floor ward, where she was before, and went to Ward 6 North, where she was when she died.

Then I drove up to the hospice, and I took some flowers there. So that's the end of Tuesday 28 November.

Wednesday 29 November

There were hundreds more letters about Pixie – absolutely amazing. Teachers who remembered the support that she gave in the Seventies on comprehensive education, one of whom is now the headmaster of a successful comprehensive school. A letter from Tony Blair; a letter from Jack Straw; a letter from Paul Foot.

Anyway, Josh arrived and took me to the House of Commons. Then we got Gallery tickets for the family: Lissie, Stephen, and Nita and Sally. Hilary had a question to the Prime Minster.

After Prime Minister's Questions, at 3.30 p.m. exactly I was called by the Speaker, and I made my little personal statement. Hilary had suggested that I cut it down, which was very sensible, and Ruth suggested that I included a reference to my two constituencies. It only lasted fifty-five seconds.

'Mr Speaker, as tomorrow is the fiftieth anniversary of my first election to the House of Commons, may I take this opportunity of expressing my sincere thanks to many Members, past and present, from all sides of the House, for the kindnesses shown to me and my family, and especially in the last few days following the death of my wife, Caroline.

'Those of us who work here will know of the strong bond of friendship and warmth between Members and staff who work with us in the building, and I am proud to have been a member of that wider parliamentary family, first as a representative for Bristol South-East and now Chesterfield, from whom I have learned and gained a very great deal during my half-century in this place.'

There were masses of condolences from MPs, who came up from all sides of the House, stopped me, and so on.

Thursday 30 November

Just before I went to bed, Josh phoned, and he said that Alan Simpson, backed by David Davis and 205 MPs, had tabled an Early Day Motion congratulating me on my anniversary. This is what they signed:

> This House celebrates the fiftieth anniversary of the Right Honourable Member for Chesterfield, who first entered Parliament on 30 November 1950 as the then Member for Bristol South-East; recognises the unique contribution he has made to the defence of parliamentary democracy and the constitutional importance of the House of Commons; respects his own lifetime commitment to the causes of peace, democracy and socialism; and wishes him well following his decision to leave Parliament at the next election in order to devote more time to politics.

Among the Tories who signed it were John Bercow, Julian Brazier, Kenneth Clarke, David Davis, Alan Duncan, Iain Duncan Smith, Gerald Howarth, Julian Lewis, Patrick McLoughlin, Gillian Shephard, David Tredinnick, John Whittingdale and Nicholas Winterton. And the Liberals were: John Burnett, Paul Burstow, Don Foster, Simon Hughes, Paul Keetch, Robert Maclennan, Lembit Öpik, David Rendel, Bob Russell, Andrew Stunell, Jenny Tonge, Paul Tyler and Phil Willis. And Alec Salmond from the Scot Nats and William Ross from the Ulster Unionist Party. Well, that is something. I'm going to have that framed. I think that's a lovely memento.

Monday 4 December

Barbara was in, and she is going to come three days a week in future: Monday, Wednesday and Friday.

After lunch I took a taxi up to the health centre and returned all the equipment that the district nurses had been using. Then I took the drugs to the chemist, who will destroy them.

I can manage physically on my own. I can feed myself and do all that has to be done, but what I miss is some hugs and the companionship of Pixie. She would have been thrilled with all the letters that came in, amused by the mail.

Wednesday 6 December

I thought as it was the last opening of Parliament, I would go – the last one I shall attend as an MP. The *Guardian* this morning came out in favour of a republic in a rather woolly series of articles, but still.

I went to the Commons, and Black Rod came in and demanded that 'the House attend Her Majesty', and Dennis Skinner called out, 'Tell her to read the *Guardian*,' which was amusing. I pushed my way near to the front as we trooped into the Lords.

I noticed one thing, and that was that the peeresses were still sitting in their tiaras in the House of Lords. Well, I can understand the peeresses being there when there was a hereditary chamber, because it was a sort of stud farm, but now it's all life peers I don't know what they were doing there. I pointed this out to Ian Paisley, who laughed.

I went to the Speaker's party. Michael Martin was awfully friendly. I thanked him for letting me make the personal statement, and he clutched me and said, 'Oh, I'm so sorry about Caroline. Isn't Hilary doing well?'

I said, 'Well, you are doing very well,' because there have been some poisonous attacks on him.

I had a talk to Jack Jones, who had a pint of beer – the first time they've ever had a pint of beer at the Speaker's party. But Michael Martin is a working-class lad, and he had his relatives from Scotland there, who were just dear old Labour people.

I saw Cherie Blair, who had such a big hat on that I couldn't kiss her, but she took it off and gave me a nice kiss and said how much she'd appreciated Caroline, and how she was going to write. I said Caroline liked her.

A very nice American woman came up and clutched me in a warm way and said, 'I lost my husband that way.' It turned out she was now married to Eric Forth. She couldn't have been nicer, so sensitive, and was really very affectionate. Anyone who's had this experience knows what it's like.

Thursday 7 December

An awful night, with coughing and nightmares, and I got up at about half-past five and went to Chesterfield for my surgery.

When I arrived, I got a taxi to the Labour Club, and as I walked to the bungalow, I just burst into tears. I spent so many happy times with Caroline there, and I realised I couldn't do my surgery. I just went in, looked round, sat down and wept, so I rang Margaret and told her. She came over from the office and gave me a hug. I just sat there and wept and wept and wept. She was so kind. She said she didn't think I should have come today, but I felt I had to go back there.

Anyway, I was in a very tearful mood and I slumped in the train, got back and came home, feeling absolutely awful. So I forced myself to have a meal, and then I had a hot bath and went to bed.

Saturday 9 December

Josh and William looked in. I heard on the phone that Reg Race has been selected for Chesterfield as the candidate to replace me. Having been an MP before, Reg is a very competent and experienced parliamentarian. He'll know exactly what has to be done. He also knows Chesterfield well, because he lives not far away in Derbyshire.

I'm a bit low tonight. I'm shivering again. Josh and William got me a meal, and I sat down and ate it with them. They're so sweet. Lissie phoned from Bristol, and she was on the phone when Stephen rang, so Josh held the phone so that she could talk to Stephen.

Sunday 10 December

Hilary picked me up and we went to Marion Miliband's for dinner with David and Edward Miliband. David is still at Number 10, and Edward is at Number 11. Marion has now been a widow for six and a half years. We had a very amusing dinner. I was keen not to be provocative in any way, and it wouldn't have been possible anyway. The boys live entirely in the world of the Prime Minister's advisers. They see policy as something they work out, push through the policy forums, push through the Conference and then, having had an election victory, they push it through the Cabinet and the Commons. There's no real participatory element in it. They're both in their thirties, I think, and I was treated as a sort of kindly old gentleman.

I had this terrible cold and I've got a bloodshot eye, which makes me look utterly grotesque, and Marion insisted on putting a cold teabag on my eyelid.

I just felt that this was a part of my own Party that saw itself as being absolutely separate from, and superior to, anyone else. I asked a few questions about various things, and said that in the old days we had flaming rows but we got on all right, but nowadays there seemed to be some personality conflicts without a political content. I didn't want to row with them because they're very sweet. They both wrote lovely letters about Caroline, and Marion is a great friend.

So anyway, at about half-past ten, Hilary said, 'I must take my dad home.'

Monday 11 December

On the American presidency, the Supreme Court is giving a ruling at any moment – I think tonight or tomorrow. I think it will be Bush. I may be entirely wrong. But even if they gave a decision that appeared to favour Gore, they'd have to count the votes again. It's all very, very shaky.

Tuesday 12 December
A letter arrived in the mail this morning to Caroline Benn; it was a letter from Millbank Tower, signed by a senior Labour peer. I knew perfectly well of course that the letter had been printed to all Labour Party members – I'll probably get one soon; it was an appeal for money, and was asking 'Ms Benn' if she would like to remember the Party in her will.

It is really a silly thing to do, because a lot of Party members are old and in the course of the year quite a number of their spouses will die. Many could find it upsetting. I didn't want to make a row about it, but later in the day I did mention it to one or two MPs.

I went to the House of Commons and then I walked over to Portcullis House – this new parliamentary building – which I've never been into before, and up to the Grimond Room. I gave evidence to a Select Committee with Peter Bradley, Sir Peter Emery, and Alan Keen, about the election of the Speaker. Nick Winterton was in the chair. Eric Forth was there and said absolutely nothing. Afterwards I looked round Portcullis House, and who should I see sitting having tea but Andrew Tyrie, the Tory MP for Chichester. He was having tea with Donald Macintyre the *Independent* correspondent, and they said, 'Oh, come and join us.' Andrew Tyrie was trying to interest Macintyre in his plan for defining which items should come back to the nation states in Europe – the subsidiarity rules – and to try and persuade his own party to go for an elected House of Lords. Tyrie is a very clever man. He was a research assistant, working with John Major and Nigel Lawson. If they had won the election, he would obviously have had a job. They were both very friendly.

I came back to the House, went to the Tea Room, and Harold Best came up and sat down with me. Harold is a Leeds Member and he said how well Hilary was doing. He said that we need some new ideas to reconnect with young people. I should add that Sheila, one of the Tea Room staff, came and sat next to me. It was so sweet, and she said, 'Oh, we're so concerned about you. All of us are so concerned about you.' It was just lovely.

Wednesday 13 December
I went into the Commons because there was a 'deferred vote'. This is the new system that has been introduced whereby you vote on a ballot paper on particular issues that have been considered in the House earlier in the week. The Whip was sitting there ticking Members' names off. It was extraordinary! If you could have a ballot for that, you could have a ballot for the Speaker.

At six o'clock both the Campaign Group and the left trade unions were meeting at the same time, in adjacent rooms, so we merged the meetings.

It was really useful because it brought the parliamentary and the trade-union left together – a thing we've been trying to do for years. I'm a sort of liaison officer between them. We agreed that we would have some structure of cooperation in the future. I hope it isn't too bureaucratic.

We discussed the closure of Vauxhall at Luton, and how we could use the trade unions, who are now becoming increasingly uneasy about what's happening, to introduce some really big and important points into the Manifesto, such as the repeal of some trade union laws, the public ownership of the railways, the link between pensions and earnings, and so on. And to have campaigns on these issues during the election. My idea is to have 'Labour Plus', where you promote Labour plus certain other things.

I walked over to Great George Street, where the BBC Christmas party was going on, and I saw Bill Morris, the General Secretary of the Transport and General Workers' Union; he told me that Stephen Byers did know about the closure of the Vauxhall plant before the workers knew and he did nothing about it. The department just washed its hands of the plant. It's as if you had a war going on and your own Ministry of Defence had only one facility – namely an ambulance brigade – to pick up the wounded, without any system to actually prevent the enemy from destroying things.

Well, a whole clutch of BBC producers came up and were so friendly. It was really rather nice. I did feel this extraordinary goodwill that Father used to complain of.

Gore, in about an hour, is expected to concede the American presidency to Bush. Clinton has been in Ireland, and I think is spending the night at Chequers.

Walking to the dentist today, I felt very defenceless. It's funny, I can imagine a widow feeling defenceless if her husband dies, but for a man to feel defenceless if his wife dies is an indication of how much I depended on Caroline: the intellectual rigour of her comments on my press releases and speeches; how she bought all my clothes, cut my hair, looked beautiful herself and always checked me over to see if I looked respectable when I went out and didn't have burn-holes in my sweater. She was just a friend, a dear, dear, dear friend.

Thursday 14 December

I went and had a cup of tea in the Commons, and then I drove to Arkwright Road in Hampstead for the ASLEF party. I got lost and in the end I was just going round in circles, but I happened to see a cab driver, who said, 'Turn right and then left.' It really scared me – the traffic is so heavy and you can't see the street names. But anyway, I got to Arkwright Road and there was a party going on in the ballroom.

I was seized by a woman who said, 'Come and have a word in the office.'

So I went in and there was my dear old friend Ken Gill, and a couple of trade union officials in ASLEF. We had a real 'hair let-down' talk about what we had to do now; how we should still continue to campaign for policies that we had failed to get in the Manifesto. I was really excited by this, and then in came Mick Rix, the General Secretary, who is a very nice lad. I should think he's in his early thirties. He said how well Hilary was doing, and that gave me a big boost.

Anyway, what the RMT and ASLEF have decided to do is to come together; they're going to issue a set of very tough safety demands on the London tube, and if they're refused, they're going to go on strike in January. They're going to strike on Mondays and Fridays, so office workers will have a longer weekend, which they hope will be popular.

My idea about campaigning inside and outside the Manifesto – the Labour Plus idea – is one that I think really does have resonance. I'm really pleased about that.

Anyway, I was then picked up by Tony West, who is retiring in a few days' time, and he took me to another room crammed with people and sat me down and I was asked to say something there. We discussed how we could reawaken radicalism in the trade union movement. I found it very stimulating.

Towards the end, Glenda Jackson, the local Member, was asked to say a word. All she said was how there weren't enough women or ethnic minorities in the London fire brigade. Well, it was a fair point but, you know, they're facing all these terrible cuts and hardship, and just putting the feminist case without relating it to the other problems was a bit off-putting; anyway we've got an answer to that.

Then I had to slip off. So I enjoyed it very much, and I felt reaffirmed in a strange way. It is my other family really, the left trade union movement.

I left and drove back to the Commons, which didn't take long, and went to the Attlee Room in Portcullis House for the Iraq-Great Britain Society; as I arrived George Galloway was speaking. Then he asked me to say something and so I congratulated him and the Society and the work he'd done (the Miriam Appeal, the Red Bus to Baghdad, and so on), and mentioned the double standards of Clinton, the man of peace in Northern Ireland and the man of war in Iraq; and I mentioned the Palestinians.

Friday 15 December

At four I went to the Pugin Room at the House, where the *Breakfast with Frost* team had set up a studio for a joint interview with Ted Heath, as we are both leaving Parliament. I've never known the Pugin Room made available as a studio – it's normally where Members take guests for coffee and drinks – but the media completely occupy everything. I went out of my way to be courteous about Ted, and said I agreed with him about Europe, in that it was political and nothing to do with economics. He said he thought Parliament was in terrible decline, that nobody took any notice of it, the Prime Minister never turned up, there were no public meetings, the media had taken over everything.

I thought I would try my luck by asking him about the Lords. 'Ted, I hear you don't want to be a peer, but what would happen if the House of Commons made you a peer?'

He said, 'What do you mean?'

'Well,' I said, 'the Commons makes former Speakers peers by resolution. Why can't we make you a peer?'

'Oh, I don't know about that.'

So I said, 'All that would happen is that we pass a resolution and you'd be an elected member of the House of Lords.' I thought that might appeal to him because he is in favour of election. He said 'No!', but the point was that I planted the idea and, I must say, it was rather fun.

Saturday 16 December, Chesterfield

The Annual General Meeting of the Chesterfield Labour Party was at 11 a.m. It was a very crowded meeting, there must have been fifty or sixty people. I saw all my old mates there.

The officers were elected and at the very beginning Joe Murphy, who was in the chair, said, 'Let's stand for a moment for Caroline,' so I stood and, of course, found myself crying. It's sympathy and respect that are so unbearable.

Anyway I sat down, and when we came to the MP's report, I thanked them particularly for Caroline and referred to the last years in Chesterfield and the struggle ahead. I spoke briefly about the impact of Bush and the possible slump, and how public opinion was shifting. Then Reg Race talked about campaigning, and by that time there was no particular reason to stay so I slipped off, because Reg has taken complete charge of the constituency now, as I expected he would. Mandy, his wife, drove me to the station.

Later, I watched the programme that Michael Cockerell had made about Betty Boothroyd. Here is a woman who had had a very long period of service, was on the National Executive of the Labour Party, Speaker of the House of Commons, and the whole thing was presented as if she were a pop star. It was the *Hello* or *OK* account of her life, probing her about why she'd never married, and so on. I'm so glad I didn't agree to take part.

So anyway, that's it. It's five past ten, and I'm going to have a quick bath and go to bed, so that is the end of Saturday 16 December 2000. I'm just a bit low and lonely and miserable at the moment – I am.

Sunday 17 December

Lissie and the girls arrived for lunch, and after lunch the four of us went in a taxi to the Albert Hall for the annual carol concert. The grandchildren were all there. It was great.

We all came back home in two taxis. That was Stephen and Emily, Hilary, Michael, James, Jonathan and Carrie, Lissie and her two girls, and Josh, Naz and William. We went and got pizzas, or Stephen did.

Thursday 21 December

I was walking along the corridor outside the Smoking Room when I saw Jack Weatherill (Lord Weatherill), the former Speaker. 'Oh,' he said, 'I've been looking for you. I've been up to your room. I want to have a talk.'

So I said, 'Let's go into the Smoking Room.'

'Well, it'll have to be private.' So we looked round and there was nobody there, so he said, 'I understand you're thinking of joining us.'

So I said, 'You've been talking to Lord Marlesford.' He clasped my hand and I said, 'I'm not looking for anything. The reason I'm so happy now is that I don't want anything. I couldn't accept patronage anyway, but if the House of Commons decided to *elect* me, that would be different.'

'Ah,' he said, 'leave it with me.' Then he went on to describe in great detail the background to the reform of the Lords. He said, 'I'm the convenor of the independent peers, and I have set up a little working party of my own. I didn't ask the Liberals along because they were involved with the Government, but I did ask Dick Marsh, and we came up with the idea of elected peers. So I put it to Ivor Richard, who was then the Labour leader of the Lords, but he wasn't very interested. Then I put it to Lady Jay, Margaret Jay, when she took over, and she said, "Yes, I think I'll do that."'

I said, 'What about Cranborne?'

'Oh, Cranborne knew about it.'

I said, 'Why didn't he tell Hague?'

'Oh well, he did,' Jack said. 'Remember it was all done under Privy Councillor terms.'

So you saw how the Establishment works – all-party, Privy Councillor terms. Not that I was in any way surprised.

Sunday 24 December

Christmas Eve. I didn't get up very quickly. I went to Josh and Naz for the family breakfast, which has been going on among our children for twenty-two years. We had a lovely breakfast, with champagne and scrambled eggs, croissants, and cereal. They've got a new scheme now, under which each family buys the present that their children want, and then the members of the other families subscribe to it.

I came home on my own, and I began preparing for tomorrow and realised that I couldn't find Caroline's silver cutlery from Cincinnati, which is always kept in the same place. I looked absolutely everywhere, but I couldn't find it anywhere. So I got really, really worried. We wondered if it had been stolen.

Monday 25 December

Christmas Day. Truthfully, I was dreading today, but Josh and Naz came last night and that helped, and I did sleep. Josh and Naz, who were cooking all morning, had the idea of looking at the files on Caroline's laptop, and Josh found a note saying where the silver had been hidden. It was a miracle! Mum sent us a message on Christmas Day from the next world, telling us where to find the silver – just astonishing!

Well, everybody arrived: Stephen and Nita, and Emily and Daniel; Hilary and Sally, and Michael, James, Jonathan and Carrie; Lissie and Paul, with Hannah and Sarah; and Josh and Naz, who were here anyway; and PC. The kids all brought food. I did absolutely nothing. They carried the whole day. I just wandered round as if I were a guest. The table had been laid, and everything was laid exactly as it always was.

All the kids left, except for Paul and Lissie and the little girls. I sat and talked a bit to Paul and Lissie. They love talking about other members of the family. The girls were very excited to be in our bed, and I'm sleeping in the little bed in the front room.

Thursday 28 December

I rang Alice Prochaska about the archives to talk to her about the indexing of them, now that the funding has been killed by the National Lottery Heritage Fund. She said that the British Library was in acute financial difficulties; they were making people redundant in the Library; they had lost a lot of the money that they used to get from making books available to other libraries, because of the Internet; and although her job is safe, some of her staff might go. So that is the end of that, and if I do want those archives to go to the British Library, I shall either have to find alternative funding or I will have to pay for it myself. But I do want to get rid of them now, so I have an incentive for the indexing. I must have spent a quarter of a million pounds, or £300,000, on my diaries and archives – if not more – and that would be a very substantial gift.

Monday 1 January, 2001

The first day of a new year and of a new life.

Thursday 4 January

I was asked today to do about five broadcasts on the million-pound donations to the Labour Party by Paul Hamlyn, Lord Sainsbury and Christopher Ondaatje. I had thought about this very carefully and my argument is clear: that this is the Americanisation of politics: big business buys both parties. Politics has become a question of marketing and high-pressure salesmanship instead of discussion and debate; it switches people off and they don't vote. I believe that every elector should get a note about what income all the major parties are getting; all candidates should have to declare their interests on the ballot paper; and no company should be allowed to donate to a party unless there has been a ballot of shareholders.

In early January Melissa and I went to Caroline's home town to attend a service to remember Caroline, to which many of her American family were able to come and pay tributes to her.

Sunday 7 January, Cincinnati

Lissie and I went into the Church of Our Saviour, and Mother Paula Jackson was there, a very colourful, very charismatic person.

Anyway we went in and met lots of Caroline's friends and of course her family.

Very High Church service, lots of incense, very beautiful. And at a certain point Graydon went up and gave an address; it was very measured and calm and clear and plain. Then I spoke and at the end I just bowed my head and came back; it all came from the heart, and it was a marvellous thing for Caroline to be celebrated there. Afterwards we had family photographs in front of the altar.

Later Mother Paula told me that she knew John Robinson, who was a Bishop of Woolwich, the one who wrote *Honest to God.* And she said, after a lot of drink had been consumed, that he consecrated her as a bishop – although at the time she was a southern Baptist. It's a lovely bit of gossip to put down.

Melissa has been the star of the show; everybody wanted to see her and she reminded everybody of Caroline. She has been so good and cheerful and gets on with everybody so well. I'm just the old man now.

Monday 8 January

Caroline's nephew, Johnny Mitchell, came and collected us and drove us to the airport. We were told to get there early if we wanted to sit together. We got there about three hours early, got to the gate ahead of anybody else and, to cut a long story short, they 'dumped us' i.e. they had over-booked and we were told that we would be rerouted to Paris and would catch a British Airways plane to London from there. We waited and waited, and Johnny Mitchell stayed with us; it was very sweet of him. And finally we were put on the plane for Paris. It was just infuriating and there was no one high-level that we could talk to. The Delta agent told us they did it to maximise their revenues.

Wednesday 10 January
I put a question about the House of Lords to the Prime Minister during Prime Minister's Questions. 'As we now have a fully elected Parliament in Scotland, elected Assemblies in Northern Ireland and Wales and London, why can't *we* have a fully elected Parliament?' I got a totally negative answer from him, but the more I think about the idea that I might be made a peer, the more utterly ridiculous it is; I couldn't possibly touch it.

Thursday 11 January
I rang Dennis Turner, Chairman of the Catering Committee, because I have asked for the Speaker to give me the right to use the Tea Room and the Library; and he referred it to Richard Allan of the Information Committee, whom I phoned yesterday. They both said they didn't see why, if I have been here fifty years, I shouldn't be allowed to. I have been saying to people that I can't afford a peerage – it costs £2 million now to get one.

But I did also hear from Hilary that Chris Mullin had approached the Speaker about electing me as a peer, in the same way that a Speaker is elected to the Lords; but I really think it would be very difficult, unless it was absolutely as clear as a bell that I was not the beneficiary of patronage. And in the House of Lords even a dead duck has to take a title.

Tuesday 16 January
Walked to my bank and back across Parliament Square, where there was a demonstration against Iraqi sanctions. I must say I have never seen such heavy-handed police; there were perhaps 100 or 200 demonstrators, but there must have been 600 police and about six police trucks. On the pavement of Parliament Square there was also a demonstration in favour of hunting, which the police didn't disturb at all. When I tried to leave, I was told that we were all to be bottled in in Parliament Square, so I said to the policeman, 'I want to speak to the Inspector.'

He said, 'I am the Inspector.'

I said, 'Well, we want to leave.'

'Well, I can't let you leave.'

'I'm a Member of Parliament.'

'I can let you leave, but I can't let anyone else leave.'

I said, 'Well, I'll stay here until you do.'

So I rang the Police Superintendent at the House of Commons and later he did come over. And finally they let the protestors trickle out but it was so stupid. At one stage the policeman said to me, 'Will you vouch for the fact that they won't sit down?'

So I said, 'I don't know, I can only ask them, "Are you going home?"'

Later I rang the Home Secretary's office and told them.

I saw Chris Mullin and had a cup of tea with him. He said that he had had a word with the Speaker and with Margaret Beckett about my election to the Lords. Chris really wanted to know what I wanted to do and I said, 'I'm very ambivalent about it, Chris.'

He said, 'Well, you will have to make up your mind and stop fudging.'

Anyway I am coming round to the idea of a Writ of Attendance, which I've been looking into, whereby non-peers could, in years past, be summoned to the Lords without being ennobled.

In the Lobby I had a word with Richard Allan about my request to use the Library and he said it had been agreed in principle by the Committee, but it was put to the Committee that I shouldn't use research facilities or borrow any books. The Librarian was worried that an understanding that retired Members of over fifty years' service could use it would reduce to forty years, then twenty years – a typically bureaucratic attitude.

I said, 'Well, I don't want to do more than just sit in the Library, read the papers and have somewhere I can work if I do come to the House.'

Tuesday 23 January

The Speaker's Chaplain, Robert Wright, wrote in his own hand to say that the Speaker had offered his house for the reception after the memorial service to be held for Caroline. That's a very sweet gesture, and of course I shall take it up.

Wednesday 24 January

I stayed up till about one o'clock this morning listening to a BBC Knowledge programme; it was on the development of capitalism under Thatcher; the way that privatisation had occurred; the transfer of power from government to the market; interviews with Mohamed Al Fayed, Tiny Rowland, Sir James Goldsmith: it was an absolutely riveting programme.

I rang Daniel this morning and I said, 'Break a leg', because he is in *South Pacific* at the Churchill Theatre, Bromley.

Blair summoned Mandelson to Number 10 yesterday. Blair must have been shaken at this latest business about Mandelson's alleged intervention to get a British passport for this Indian businessman, Srichand Hinduja, who'd given £1 million towards the cost of a 'faith zone' at the Millennium Dome.

To the Central Hall, Westminster, to support a demonstration against council house privatisation, which only took five minutes.

I sat up in my room and watched Prime Minister's Questions, and of course by then Mandelson had resigned; but he took Northern Ireland questions himself, having made it plain that his resignation took effect after Prime Minister's Questions.

Then I walked to Victoria Station and met Melissa and we just caught the 6.41 to Bromley South, and walked up to the Churchill Theatre for *South Pacific*. There were Nita and Emily and Nita's mother, Pratima. Stephen turned up later.

The show opened with Daniel and a little girl singing this song, which sounded like 'Deta moi dah dah dah dah dah dah', and Daniel was tremendously good. I videoed it, quite illegally. It was part of that post-war optimism of American musicals, where everybody was nice and there was only one death. Terribly professional, marvellous sets, and I really enjoyed it.

I suppose I should comment on Mandelson. There is no question about it, he was the architect of New Labour; his real impact on the Labour Party was to convert it formally and completely from socialism to a liberal party; he had a project which meant that the Liberal and even Tory wets would come into Government, form a coalition, and the Labour Party could in effect be disbanded. You'd make a few compassionate gestures in favour of the poor. He was a thoroughly bad influence on British politics. I suspect Campbell said to Blair that it was either Mandelson or him; Campbell was not prepared to go on defending Mandelson.

Friday 26 January

The Mandelson story still goes on and on and on.

A huge earthquake in India has killed perhaps 13,000 people there.

That was the end of Friday, 26 January 2001.

Sunday 28 January

I got up fairly early and I went to Sky television to do an interview with Adam Bolton about the Mandelson business.

When I came out of the studio I saw Bob Kiley, whom Ken Livingstone is recruiting from the United States as a transport adviser to revitalise London Underground, having saved the New York system. He said, 'Oh, I did enjoy your broadcast.'

And I said, 'Well, I heard you on *Any Questions?*' which I had yesterday and he was extremely good. I asked him if he knew Jack Gilligan, the former Governor of Ohio, who once said to me that there would never be democracy in America if big business buys both parties and expects a pay-off, whoever wins.

'I know Jack very well,' Kiley said. So it was a sort of real meeting of minds.

Monday 29 January

To the Jerusalem Chamber in Westminster Abbey for a huge meeting about Caroline's memorial service. Canon Wright was there, and the Director of Music, the press officer, people from the Receiver General's

Office; it's all got to be finalised by 6 February, so I have got a lot of work to do. The Director of Music said that he didn't know the music for the 'Red Flag' or 'The Internationale', so I said that I would get it. So later I rang up Chappell's, but they didn't have it; I rang the *Morning Star* and they said, 'Try the Marx Memorial Library', which did have it. If Blair does come, he will have a bit of a shock.

Tuesday 30 January

Melissa had a fabulous article on comprehensive education in the Education supplement of the *Guardian*, with a picture of her on her first day at Holland Park School. I know Caroline would have been over the moon.

Went to a meeting at seven o'clock in Room 10, to hear a major in the United States Army describe how he was sent to the Gulf just after the Gulf War to check on the depleted uranium that had been used, and he discovered that no warnings had been given, no preparations had been made, vehicles were polluted, the ammunition was polluted, the air was polluted; he has got cancer himself.

I had a message yesterday from Robert Redfern, the son of Gloria Redfern, whom I had known in Rhodesia fifty-five years ago and on whom I had a great crush; the last time I spoke to her was about two or three weeks ago, and her son rang to say she had died. So I rang him tonight and had a nice talk to him.

Saturday 3 February

Stephen rang to say that Nita had been appointed by Tony Blair to be his industrial adviser during the election year; it's a very big thing for her.

Sunday 4 February

There is an anti-globalisation conference in London this weekend, organised in effect by the Socialist Workers' Party. The more I think of the SWP, the more I realise how important that element is in any successful political movement. Liz Davies told me she had left the Labour Party; I was sorry, but I understand.

There were 1300 people at the conference, and around the corner were tons of police buses; the anti-globalisation movement is now treated as a terrorist threat. It's quite extraordinary because it's perfectly peaceful – lots of young people.

None of these people think New Labour is worth a row of beans. Boris Kagarlitsky, the Russian socialist writer whom I met in Moscow years ago, is campaigning against globilisation and came up to have a word.

Monday 5 February

Jonathan was fourteen today and I gave him a call. He is such a sweetheart, so serious and thoughtful and kind.

Tuesday 6 February

Into the House for a meeting addressed by a retired American admiral called Gene Carroll, who is the President of the Center for Defense Information in Washington; he'd come over specially to help with the campaign against the proposed US National Missile Defense System.

Harold Best said there is evidence that Fylingdales and Menwith Hill, the two stations that would be needed for this Star Wars programme, had already been refurbished and strengthened. The Admiral said that the Star Wars programme was unnecessary and costly. There was no enemy; it was easy to deliver weapons to the United States, and you could attack New York using a Panamanian ship with a bomb in the hold. He said that the American policy was now 'layered defence' – that's to say, defence at every level – and that laser weapons could be in permanent orbit, which could shoot down other missiles and satellites and could pinpoint and destroy Earth targets; if this happened, the United States would totally dominate space, and indeed would dominate the world.

He also said that NMDS would violate all the arms-control agreements that had been reached; it would frustrate the reduction in nuclear arms that had already been agreed; and that when this process began there had been 25,000 nuclear weapons in the world; they had hoped to get it down to 3000, but that would be lost if Star Wars went ahead. He said that we need a new generation of Greenham Common women to protest. Fylingdales is, in effect, a US base, and I think Britain pays only 25 per cent of the cost of modernising it.

Well, it was very strong stuff for an American admiral; he was thoughtful, academic and quiet and was listened to in intense silence. There were a few questions about it, and he said that Bush was absolutely committed to National Missile Defense.

I said that it seemed to me that one way of warning the American administration would be that our support for American policy, which had been consistent over the years, might be withdrawn.

The Admiral said, 'Well, the best way to deal with that, you know, is to back the Rapid Reaction Force, which would indicate that Europe is losing confidence in NATO.'

And I said, 'I am not very keen on that, either.'

He did also say that fear of China was a dominant consideration. 'There is no enemy facing the United States but fear of China is a real fear.' There were huge profits to be made by Boeing, Lockheed and Raytheon and that was really what it was about.

Monday 12 February

I was in the House and saw that defence questions were coming up, so I went into the Chamber and I asked a question of Geoff Hoon, based on what Admiral Carroll had told us about Star Wars. I got a totally unsatisfactory answer, but I registered that this was an attempt at world domination.

Then at 3.30 Blunkett made an announcement which, not to put too fine a point on it, is the end of comprehensive education as Labour Party policy. Blair apparently made a speech earlier in the day about what he called post-comprehensive education. Alastair Campbell referred to bog-standard comprehensive schools in cities and the whole thing was not only ignorant and an insult, but a total, absolute betrayal; Roy Hattersley was on the five o'clock news and I think it will create a tremendous row. I feel that Caroline's legacy has been betrayed. I really feel that very strongly.

At seven o'clock Mrs Mac, Ruth, Sheila, Barbara and Archie came in for a sort of farewell dinner in the Strangers' Dining Room.

The European Union has warned Gordon Brown that his public-expenditure plan exceeded the limit set by the EU, and has reprimanded Ireland, which is in the euro-zone, for their level of public expenditure. So it's absolutely explicit and plain to everybody that if you go into the European Union, they will cut your pensions, they will cut your health expenditure, cut your education spending, and apparently they are talking about a £12 billion cut in Britain.

Wednesday 14 February
To the Attlee Suite for Stephen's seminar on science and the election. He has worked ceaselessly on this, to get all these scientific organisations together. He managed this morning to get the heads of the scientific societies to go to Number 10, where they were photographed with Tony Blair; so it has been a triumph for him.

They had four or five speakers and then questions. The contributions made subsequently by Lord Sainsbury, and by the Liberal Democrat MP Evan Harris and others, were extremely good. Stephen had been terribly anxious about it.

Thursday 15 February
I went over to my old DTI office at 1 Victoria Street, now completely refurbished; I wouldn't have recognised any of it. I had gone there with Dennis Skinner, David Winnick, and representatives from Stirling Tubes from Wolverhampton and Chesterfield for a meeting. The story is very simple: Sandvik, which bought Stirling Tubes in 1987 has decided to close it and sack everybody and move all the removable equipment back to Sweden.

We were received by Alan Johnson, the former General Secretary of the Union of Communications Workers, who is now Minister of State in the Department of Trade and Industry. The case was made, and all Johnson offered to do was write to the president of the company himself. So I made as powerful a point as I could. I said, 'Look, this is just accepting that it's going to happen,' and made my usual argument about Britain's industrial base.

Alan Johnson, who is a very nice lad, said, 'Oh well, the days of intervention are over,' although actually if they are going to apply Common Market law, which he implied was a restraint, why don't they enforce the law that says you have got to consult before closing a factory?

Johnson was so cautious that when, at the end, David Winnick said, 'Can I tell the press that you are going to write to the company,' he said, 'I will have to speak to the Secretary of State,' so he didn't even want that to be known. I find it terribly discouraging.

Sunday 18 February

Well, the whole world has condemned the bombing of Baghdad by American and British forces last Friday. It's really quite astonishing; the French were not consulted or told, although they are a very important country in NATO; Turkey made it clear that its own air bases were not to be used for the purpose; the Arab League has condemned it; and Britain and America are completely isolated. The Prime Minister made statements saying that we were protecting our pilots, and so on, but it simply isn't credible. One paper suggested that Blair had taken the initiative, which is not inconceivable, but in fact he couldn't have moved Bush if Bush didn't want to move; it's all in preparation for his visit to Bush next week to establish his credentials as a loyal puppet.

Friday 23 February

Up at 6.15, caught the 8.25 train to Chesterfield for a meeting with DYNAH – 'Do You Need a Hand' – a volunteer group that helps old people to cope with simple repairs of one kind and another.

They have helped about 20,000 people, they have sixty volunteers, and need £86,000 a year for overheads and about another £100,000 for employment. They are a marvellous group. They really wanted me to come along and meet them and I was very impressed, I must admit, by the quality of the people.

Executive Committee meeting tonight and Reg Race, the Labour candidate, is putting in a huge effort to win Chesterfield. There is thousands of pounds' worth of the most expensive equipment being installed by Millbank and they have allocated a full-time organiser to Reg.

I sat there and chatted to my mates, because I know them all very well, but I felt increasingly like Banquo's ghost at the feast. At the end of next month I'll clear my bungalow and take my possessions down to Stansgate, and that will be the end of the Chesterfield connection.

My final farewell in Chesterfield will be at the May Day rally on Monday 7 May. By then the election will be over.

Monday 26 February
Stephen and Nita and their children came into the House and we put Nita, Emily and Daniel in the Lords' Gallery. As the eldest son of a peer, Stephen was entitled to sit on the steps of the throne. He hadn't done it since they removed hereditary peers from the Chamber, and I thought I'd go and sit next to him, so I went round and I was just sitting there laughing myself silly. There were Stephen and I on the steps, observing the Lords from one end; Hilary at the other end, where MPs are allowed to stand; and two grandchildren and Nita sitting in the Gallery. Then Stephen and family went off in a taxi back to Croydon.

Thursday 1 March
The rumours at the moment are that the election will be postponed because of foot-and-mouth, which is spreading all over the place. It's in Scotland, it's in Northern Ireland, it's all over England, and cattle are being slaughtered by the thousand; you see pictures of a dead cow being picked up by its leg by a crane and being dropped on to a pyre to burn. It really is a holocaust of animals, a ghastly thing. All this export of animals for slaughter, the global trade in food, and so on, is bringing health hazards; it would be better to have local farmers growing local food and feeding local people from local markets. I think they are the lessons to learn from this.

Tuesday 6 March
I got up at a quarter to six because I wanted to be well prepared for the memorial service. To St Margaret's at about a quarter to ten, I guess.

Gradually the officials there turned up, the two church wardens and senior officials, who were dressed up almost like colonels and generals – you realised that it was run as a military event. Hilary turned up early and began marking out where everyone would sit and I wandered around. It's very difficult to remember everyone who came to the service. I might have missed some. The Speaker was there of course; Cherie Blair, Jack Straw, Dawn Primarolo, Clare Short, Peter Hain, Chris Mullin. Then of course we had the whole extended family; David and Marilyn Butler; the Gibsons; June Battye; everyone from the office.

I stood and received everybody: Labour MPs Ann Cryer, Alice Mahon, Bill Michie, Alan Simpson, Dennis Skinner, Ann Clwyd. Some Tories came: Peter Walker, John Biffen, Richard Shepherd, David Davis. Then the SEA (Socialist Education Association) people, and a delegation from Holland Park. Then there was Vanessa, the Macmillan nurse. I just hugged absolutely everybody; it was very moving really. I suppose about 500 people turned up. Lots of peers; and John Platts-Mills, Jim Mortimer, Gordon McLennan, Peter Shore, Michael Foot; the Chesterfield people. The left was well represented.

Anyway, we went in and the service began; we had the lovely Order of Service cards. It was handled with military precision. The Speaker was there, flanked by Nicolas Bevan, his Private Secretary.

The service went through beautifully and I was in fairly good control. We had hymns, followed by Stephen, who made a marvellous speech from the pulpit; it went on for about eight minutes, which was twice as long as had been agreed! Authoritative and very sensitive. Then Clyde Chitty described his recollections of Caroline as an educationalist. Then prayers, and Melissa and I walked up to the front. Melissa went to the lectern and I went to the pulpit, and Melissa spoke for about eight minutes, the sort of thing only she could do as well as she did – informal, conversational, humorous, tender; then she stood there while I spoke. I had prepared it with great care; it was timed for about four and a half minutes, and I made jokes and people laughed. Then at the end what I meant to say was, 'She taught us how to live and she taught us how to die, and you can't ask any more of anyone than that,' but at that point I was in tears, so I just said, 'You can't ask any more than that.' And I came out of the pulpit and darling Melissa held my hand as we went back to the pews.

The readings were by the Speaker (the Sermon on the Mount) and Jane Shallice, from *Keir Hardie*. Then we poured out into the sunshine, to the tune of the 'Internationale'. It was a beautiful spring day. Then about 120–30 people, whom I had asked especially, walked to the Speaker's House for the reception. Dear old Michael Martin had made the Speaker's House available for us.

Jonathan said after the service, 'We learned so much about Grandma that we didn't know.' And at the party everybody talked to everyone else. It was lovely, just lovely; lots of people came up and lots more hugs.

Later I went to the Tea Room for a moment and there was the Speaker – in my lifetime the Speaker had never been seen in the Tea Room or on the Terrace or in the cafeteria; but Michael is different. I really never will be able to thank him enough for his kindness. He said how the service had meant a lot to him. As a Catholic, he had never been allowed to read the Gospel in church; it was always done by priests. He said how good Melissa was. He was lovely.

Friday 9 March

I was collected and driven to the Ernie Bevin School, Tooting, where I was met by Lisa Jenkinson, the producer of *Any Questions?*, whom I adore; she is about thirty, I guess. This was my fiftieth-anniversary programme. The rest of the panel turned up: Michael Heseltine floated in as if he was the Prince of Wales; Teresa Gorman; and David Steel, who is now the Presiding Officer, or Speaker, in the Scottish Parliament – he said that he wasn't political any more and couldn't comment on political questions!

At the very end (and I have never known this to happen), after the programme had gone off the air, they gave me a standing ovation. Well, that was really something; it was a good left audience, of course.

Then we got into a car and at about ten o'clock we got back to the Pharmacy restaurant – Damien Hirst's very fashionable place – where the BBC had laid on dinner. I had assumed it would be with Heseltine and the panellists, but it was just with the senior BBC people and the family. We had a lovely meal for over two and a half hours; it must have been terribly expensive – I think each meal was £37, plus the wine. Jonathan Dimbleby made a little speech at the end about the programmes that I had done, and all sorts of things he remembered about me, and on behalf of the BBC he presented me with a beautiful Roberts radio, revival issue, one of the best radios you could buy – a sort of 1930s portable. I was thrilled and I thanked them all. We just had lots of fun; the only people who weren't there were Hilary and Sal. I think I can honestly say that it was the happiest evening I have had since Caroline died; indeed, probably for much longer, because I was always worrying about her. I felt like a thirty-year-old again, and downstairs there were all these twenty-five- and thirty-year-olds dancing their way round the bar.

Monday 12 March

At half-past twelve in the Speaker's House Tony Blair unveiled the bust of Harold Wilson by Ian Walters, which had been commissioned by the Chairman of the Works of Art Committee. It was a very strange gathering, absolutely full of middle-aged men. Robert Armstrong, former Cabinet Secretary, was there and I had a chat to him; his comment, 'economical with the truth', during the *Spycatcher* trial must have put him in every book of quotations. Mary Wilson was there, and very, very sweet; Marcia Williams, Barbara Castle, Lena Jeger, Peter Shore. Very few other Labour MPs or Labour people. Tony Banks, now the chairman of the committee, made a little speech, and I took a picture of Blair with Harold's bust; I said I wanted to get a picture of Boom and Bust (that's the great slogan that Blair always uses).

Tuesday 13 March

The huge funeral pyres of cattle are just so distressing, and the disease has spread to France. There is some anxiety or question now as to whether the election can be held on 3 May, which is what everybody expects.

Wednesday 14 March

I went into the Commons after lunch and heard that Jack Straw was the man instrumental in Mandelson's departure; apparently a week before Mandelson made the statement saying that he hadn't remembered talking to Mike O'Brien about the Hinduja passport case, Jack Straw had raised it with him and had reminded him; and Jack was the one who put his foot down, so that is very interesting.

Had a word with Angela Smith, who told me later that the Parliamentary Committee have decided to have a full discussion next week about my request for 'visiting status' at PLP meetings in future. Also Jean Corston said that her husband, Peter Townsend, had had a word with Anthony Giddens of the LSE, who would be delighted at the idea of my being a visiting professor. I must say I think it would be quite fun.

Saturday 17 March

Went to Speakers' Corner, from where the Palestine solidarity march had just left. I caught up with them and we went up Parliament Street to take a letter to Number 10.

It was terribly cold, terribly wet, and I was dressed up in all my woollies. Like all these great events, they're organised by the Socialist Workers' Party. The Labour Party organises absolutely nothing in support of any campaign; it just says, 'vote for us and hear the marvellous things we're doing'. The Socialist Workers' Party organises, and it has decided to put up candidates in the General Election as part of the Socialist Alliance. Number 10 was very polite, of course. Got to Trafalgar Square and had to be hauled up on to the plinth, because there was no ladder and only a hand-held loud-hailer. I spoke very briefly and then was dropped off the plinth, and I bought a sandwich on the way back to the House of Commons.

The farmers are now beginning to get up in arms about the slaughtering of sheep and cows that are not themselves infected, or are not in an infected herd but are within three kilometres of an infected herd.

Tuesday 20 March

It appears that Number 10 is absolutely adamant that they want the election on 3 May, but the pictures of troops on the news and of weeping farmers, and of the collapse of local hotels and shops, is creating a sense of crisis. And if the Government does go ahead, I think people may say, 'Why are you doing it? You have got another year, you have got a huge majority – what is the point? You are trying to cash in in some way before the world slump hits you.' So it is very difficult. I talked to a lot of people about it, but most people seem to be certain that the Prime Minister will go ahead.

I had tea with Tess Kingham. Tess is the MP for Gloucester, who after four years has decided to give it up; she has got twins and a little child of five and she is writing a book. She wanted to expose New Labour and how difficult it was to be an MP, with the whips and all the rest of it; I think it could be quite a good book coming out at a good time. So I encouraged her as best I could.

Friday 23 March

Foot-and-mouth could rise from 400 cases to 4000 and Blair was shouted at in Cumbria last night; I think he will defer the election now. That'll leave me in an impossible position, having made my last speech in the Commons. I've got to decide what I can do and I haven't any energy left; I'm exhausted today.

Tuesday 27 March

Rang Hannah on her seventh birthday.

Channel 4 had laid on a discussion with Ted Heath on Thursday and they rang to say that they had arranged for the talk to be filmed over lunch at the Savoy. So I said, 'Well, I'm awfully sorry, but I won't do it there.'

'What do you mean?' they asked.

'It's in the middle of an election, and Ted is asking people to vote Tory and I am asking people to vote Labour. And with the farmers' livelihoods at stake, the idea that these two gentlemen will be having lunch at the Savoy in a lordly way, discussing the election, just isn't on. I haven't been to the Savoy for lunch for perhaps fifty years.' They were shocked.

Anyway, I then went to the Lobby party for retiring MPs, and I saw Ted sitting in the corner dressed up in a summer suit. And I said, 'Ted, I can't do this programme over lunch at the Savoy. You know, the farmers will be losing their livelihood, and I represent a Labour constituency.'

'Oh, just like you,' he said, 'to raise a moral question.'

I am not doing it.

Wednesday 28 March

I saw Clive Soley in the corridor and he said that the Parliamentary Committee had considered my request to be allowed to attend PLP meetings as a visitor and that, although he had approached it with an open mind, the committee thought that was not possible. I am not surprised one bit; I never thought they would.

Thursday 29 March

I had a phone call and a letter from a farmer called Malcolm Sutton in Belper in Derbyshire. I am not his MP, but he wanted to tell me that he thought food imports should be stopped; we should stop killing healthy animals; we should vaccinate where necessary; we should let the disease run its course, slaughter the very sick animals on welfare grounds, and let British farmers produce British meat. What he said to me was, 'You know, the Ministry of Agriculture is just working with the big agribusiness companies; they are ignoring the small farmers.' Then later, on Channel 4 news, I saw how they handled foot-and-mouth in Thailand, where they don't kill animals; they treat them and they get better. It's another insight into the effects of globalisation. Later I had another phone call from a farmer in Devon who said much the same. I am not an agricultural expert, but it was flattering that they thought it was worth ringing me.

I had a letter from John Haylett, the Editor of the *Morning Star*, enclosing a note from the Avon company. The *Morning Star* had quoted what I had said about the Labour Party making me feel like an Avon lady, and the company wrote to him and protested. So John wrote, 'Dear Tony, obviously ruffled a few feathers! I see no point in giving Avon free publicity but now you can keep it for your "Capitalists I have upset" file. Keep it up, all the best, John.'

Saturday 31 March

I had a word with Hilary, and with Stephen and my brother Dave and it does now look as if there will be another five weeks of Parliament, with a two-week recess; so in effect I have got another three weeks in Parliament, instead of three days.

Sunday 1 April

Well, all the papers confirm today that it will be a 7 June election. It was leaked to the *Sun*, so that Murdoch can claim that they played some part in the decision.

Tuesday 3 April

There was a vote at10.45 and I went into the Tea Room where Tommy McAvoy was sitting, and I said, 'Tommy, it's my birthday today, so will you let me go home?'

'Yes,' he said, 'there is a handful of Members very bored with having to stay.'

And I asked, 'Can I take my boy home?'

So they all said, 'Aaah', and sang 'Happy Birthday'. I took Hilary home and I got back at midnight.

This American spy plane, which collided with a Chinese fighter and was forced down on the island of Hainan, has resulted in Bush making the most aggressive demands that all the crew and plane be returned at once. Of course the plane is full of hyper-super-equipment, and I have no doubt the Chinese have emptied the whole plane and have studied the contents very carefully; they will have some clever scientists working on it. Bush claims that the aircraft is 'American sovereign territory' and you can see how all these wars in the Middle Ages built up; an incident becomes a major confrontation. And of course the American threat is that they will equip Taiwan with the latest radar in order to threaten China.

On television there was an American Congressman justifying what Bush had done. 'Well, China is rearming, it's rearming all the time.' Of course the United States is about to spend $60 billion on Star Wars. It is dangerous and frightening, and you can see how it might develop.

Sunday 8 April
I went out early to Punjani's, the local newsagent, and I bought the *News of the World*, which had about ten pages of the full transcript of Prince Edward's wife, Sophie, the Countess of Wessex, who was duped into being indiscreet about the royals and politicians to a fake sheikh who pretended to be a businessman.

I was asked to appear on the *Today* programme tomorrow morning to discuss it, and I said, 'I'll talk about the monarchy, but not about the Countess of Wessex.' But they didn't want that; they just wanted comments about modernising the monarchy and scrutinising the Civil List. The Prime Minister has issued a statement from Number 10 saying how important it is that the monarchy be maintained; every Prime Minister depends entirely on the Crown for the powers they exercise of patronage and peace and war and treaty-making, and the one thing they don't want to discuss is whether we should have a monarchy or not.

I cancelled *The Independent*, which I bought for years, and decided to shift to *The Times*. *The Independent* pretends to be independent but actually it is as Tory as they come. Its leading articles are written by people of twenty-five with headings saying, 'Don't forget the need for Peace, Mr Bush' or 'Work for the Future, Mr Arafat'. I think I would rather read Murdoch, who is openly right-wing though he supports Labour, than read *The Independent*. I may move on to the *Daily Telegraph*.

Monday 9 April
A car drove me at 5.45 a.m. to Radio 4 for an interview about Sophie and the Queen. I had prepared it very carefully, because I knew I'd only have three and a half minutes, and I said that the Crown and the royal family were quite separate and that it was ridiculous to attack the royal family. The real question was: why couldn't we elect our Head of State and be citizens? Why should the Prime Minister have so much power? When I got back the phone rang continuously, so obviously the point did get across.

Wednesday 11 April
Up at seven and dozed on the train to Chesterfield. I walked down to the Winding Wheel centre for Fred Westacott's funeral. Fred's coffin was draped with the Communist Party banner, and just before the coffin was removed, the Clarion Choir came in and did something I've never heard before – they hummed the 'Internationale', a beautiful soft humming. And as the coffin was taken out, the choir burst into song: 'Arise ye starvelings from your slumber, arise ye criminals of want'. I was quite

overwhelmed. I said to Barry Johnston, who organised it, 'thanks for asking me to do it.'

He said, 'Oh, it wasn't me, it was Fred. He wanted you to speak.'

The small farmers are beginning to wake up to the fact that the Ministry of Agriculture is doing a deal with the big agri-businesses and the small farmers are going to be shut down and paid off. Also Cammell Laird in Birkenhead is closing and Motorola is sacking 3000 people in Tam Dalyell's constituency. Whenever you open the page of a paper there are closures, or huge bonuses being paid to the directors of banks. The socialist case is so easy to make now, but the opportunity to make it is almost zero – in the media, that is.

Alan Simpson has given me a copy of *The Times* for the day I was born – 3 April 1925 – in a beautiful leather-bound case. He is so generous; he's undoubtedly the leader of the left now. He has got vision and he integrates all the different causes: the environmental movement, the peace movement, the trade-union movement.

Wednesday 18 April

Today I had a letter from Ali G., the man who interviewed me in that hoax programme two years ago. He said that he had greatly enjoyed the interview – I was the only one who had dealt seriously with his loud, sexist, materialist image of youth. He thanked me for defending his work, which I did in an article in the *Guardian*. He was writing to ask if I would take part in his new film about getting elected to Parliament; I wrote and said I couldn't. You can't be a comedian and a serious politician. At the end of my reply I said, 'You're my main man', because at the end of his letter he said 'Respect' – and those are the phrases he uses the whole time.

Friday 20 April

I had an anguished phone call from a teacher in Chesterfield. He said, 'I am going to find it difficult to say this, because I can't control my distress.'

So I said, 'Well, take it steady, then.'

'In Duckmanton' – which is a mining village in my constituency – 'the Ministry of Agriculture is dumping the unburned carcasses of dead animals that have been culled, in a landfill site. Not only is the stench terrible, but rats are eating the flesh of the dead animals, and badgers as well, and running all over the place. The disease could spread, but also they are being put on top of a disused mine where there is a build-up of methane gas, and it could easily explode and blow the carcasses into the air.'

I rang Nick Brown's private office and told them this, but they are so punch-drunk there that I don't know if they took it on board.

Monday 23 April

Today I started distributing tickets for my farewell party. I have decided to ask a few staff from every department of the House; it will have to be very discriminatory because I am only allowed 120 people.

Harry Barnes raised in the House this issue about the carcasses at Duckmanton. Whether the handling of foot-and-mouth will have an effect on the election, I do not know. The Tories are divided, and there's talk about Portillo standing against Hague after the election.

Wednesday 25 April

Stephen met me at Victoria and we went by train to Croydon, and then by tram – Croydon now has trams! – to Woodside School, the school where Emily and Daniel are. It is a lovely school. I love primary schools; I had a cup of tea with the head and then went to talk to 240 children.

They had their questions ready – 'How old were you when you became an MP?', 'What does an MP do?' and so on.

Then I said 'Now I want to ask you some questions. How many of you are vegetarians?' About 5 per cent put their hands up. 'How many of you eat meat?' The rest put their hands up. 'If, in order to eat the meat, you had to kill the animal yourself, would you be ready to do it?'

'Oooh.' Only three hands went up.

'If you had to go into the garden to kill a chicken before you could have lunch, what would you think of that?'

'OOOh!' That really made them think.

They were sweet, lovely kids.

Then Daniel and Emily, who are on the school council, took me round and I met the teachers. Then a steel band played. I must say, I never realised until I looked into the drums that the metal is beaten in such a way that you get exactly the right note, and you have to play with great precision.

I was asked to talk to all the staff, and I presented the Investors in People award.

Thursday 26 April

The first people's peers were announced today. It was absolutely ludicrous: there were five knights and three professors. Not a single socialist or trade unionist. It is just the Establishment re-creating itself. Talk about reform of the House of Lords!

Friday 27 April, Chesterfield

My last surgery – after fifty years.

Mr K. wanted proper redundancy after being off sick. Mr S. wanted me to refer his case to the Ombudsman. Mr C. complained about pigeons. Mr W. who lost a leg and was picked up for drink-driving, came to say that he thinks he has won his case. I was really pleased. Mrs H. had a housing problem. Mr G. was a Child Support Agency case. Mr S. had trouble with neighbours. Mrs C. wanted to bring her relations over from India.

I've summarised, but it is very complicated. You have to listen carefully and understand the problem. All the files will be handed over to my successor, Reg Race. These are the things that the British Library are really interested in because they are social history.

Went on to a meeting of Chesterfield Football Club because the Football League has fined the club for some irregularity, and this has created an outcry in Chesterfield. There were a thousand people at a meeting two nights ago.

Then to the Executive Committee of Chesterfield Labour Party, which wasn't quorate.

I went back to the bungalow and Josh was there. He had come all the way from London to help me clear the bungalow of boxes of files and the bed. We had a lovely talk and lots of tea. He is such a friend.

Tuesday 1 May

The May Day anti-capitalist rally was today. It had been built up by the press as a thousand violent anarchists who were going to destroy London. The police were . . . I wouldn't exactly say heavy handed, but what they did was to squeeze everyone into Oxford Circus. I had two calls about it from people there who couldn't get out, and I rang the Home Secretary's office and made the point to them. I might add that there was no coverage of the arguments against globalisation.

Thursday 3 May

I saw that there was a Private Notice Question by Francis Maude to Robin Cook about the Star Wars scheme. Yesterday the Prime Minister had been very vague about it, whereas Alastair Campbell had said it was a good idea, and the Tories were exploiting the difference between the two. Cook was fumbling and bumbling about how sensitive it was. Menzies Campbell was very much against the scheme, and so was Donald Anderson. I got in with a devastating question – though I say it myself. Probably the last time my voice will be heard in the House. I said that I could well understand why the Government was cautious before polling day, because Star Wars was unpopular; the truth was that we depended entirely on the Americans for our so-called independent deterrent and use of their satellite system, and that is why historically Britain has followed the policy dictated by Washington. I referred to Admiral Carroll, who said that there would be a lot more Greenham Commons if Star Wars went ahead, which he (Robin Cook) would well understand as a passionate and articulate member of CND. The Tories roared with laughter. Cook thanked me for my helpful remarks and so on. I remember hearing him at Labour Conferences years ago arguing for CND; and more recently talking about an ethical foreign policy. And now he has carried through the policy of sanctions against Iraq, the bombing of Kosovo and is now coming out for Star Wars.

Saturday 5 May, Edinburgh

Was met by Jim Swann, who came on behalf of Tam Dalyell, who has torn his Achilles tendon. Jim was a perfect Scottish trade unionist and he took me to his home, a beautifully decorated council house, which I presume they bought; everything was immaculate and welcoming. I had half an hour's kip before he drove me to the May Day march. David Thomas, a property developer who had bought the Leith Liberal Club for development, had gone through all the stuff in the club and found a bell given to my father by the Leith Liberal Party women, with the election results for 1918 engraved on it. He brought it all the way to the march for me. Very sweet of him.

Ann Henderson, an old friend, and her dad brought me some sandwiches, and then Jim took me back to his house. I was pretty tired and had another kip, and then we had a lovely meal of salmon, potatoes and broccoli, beautifully cooked by Chrissie Swann.

I am so happy in Scotland.

Tuesday 8 May

Dissolution of Parliament announced; the election is on 7 June.

Went into the Commons at six for the farewell party for the staff, held in the Speaker's House. Ruth had commissioned from Dominique, one of the chefs, a cake in the shape of the House of Commons Chamber, with a little figure standing there with a pipe in one hand and a miniature Hansard in the other. Chris Pond, the head of the Members' Library, made an amusing and friendly speech, very radical in character, and I spoke about my family memories of the House. Then Michael Martin made a lovely speech; he said he remembered that when he was a new Member, I had asked him if I could help him.

The police were represented, the cleaners, the Speaker's office, the doorkeepers, and Library staff; lots of photographs, including ones of me, Stephen and Hilary with the Speaker.

Wednesday 9 May

I went to the Parliamentary Labour Party meeting. I had written to Clive Soley, the Chairman, and said I'd like to say a word – a reasonable enough request, as it would be my last PLP meeting. He came up to me as I was sitting there, next to Bob Sheldon, and said, 'I can't call you because I'd have to call every other retiring Member.'

'Well,' I said, 'it's up to you, Clive, but if you're looking for a reason to call me, I'm the longest-serving Labour MP there has ever been in the Labour Party, and it would be nice to say something.'

'Oh well, I can't do it.'

Anyway, Tony Blair came in, immaculate in a light-blue shirt and a pink tie, and lectured us about the election, about apathy and all the rest of it. It was a sales manager's pep-talk to the regional sales directors. Then, as soon as he sat down, Clive Soley adjourned the meeting. I thought it was very ungracious and discourteous.

Then I decided I'd sit in for Prime Minister's Questions – the Speaker had indicated that he would give priority to retiring Members. So when I was called, having thought about it a great deal, I said, 'May I thank the Prime Minister for all his very hard work during the past four years, and the Leader of the Opposition for the help that he has given during that time? May I also express the hope that on 7 June people realise that many thousands sacrificed their lives to give us the vote, and that if people do not use it, they betray that inheritance. Finally, will he believe me when I say that this is not a coded request for a peerage? I do not believe that in the second Chamber – however reformed – it would be possible to pursue an interest in democratic politics.'

They didn't quite understand that, but still.

William Hague had said earlier that the Right Honourable Gentleman, the Member for Old Bexley and Sidcup (Heath) would be missed across the House, and I would be missed only on his side of the House. It was a bit ungenerous, but I got my own back for that. Then Ted Heath made his statement, about eleven minutes, in the form of a personal statement, his farewell as Father of the House, which was very nice, and he made a friendly reference to me. Tony Blair, in answering, also made a friendly reference. So there's all this mass of goodwill at the moment.

Stephen was in the gallery, bless his heart, for my last question.

The Speaker had a party for retiring Members. There was quite a crowd – there are eighty-five retiring Members, and their spouses came. I was hoping to get away as I didn't want to stay very long, but the Speaker said, 'We've got to have a photograph.' So we all went into the Queen's Bedroom, where there's a huge bed that the Queen used to sleep in, on the night before her coronation (I think to be sure that she wasn't violated – I don't know, there's some history to it). Ted and I were in the front with the Speaker, and all these people stood up and were photographed by a man on top of a ladder.

Then Mick Martin said, 'Oh, we want you to make a speech.' So we stood in front of the fireplace and he said a few words about Ted and me. I was next, and I thanked him and said he was the people's Speaker, very much one of us. I quoted Grandfather Holmes's poem – he was known as the Poet Laureate of the House of Commons: 'Though politicians dream of fame and hope to win a deathless name, Time strews upon them when they've gone, The poppy of oblivion.' Then Ted made a short speech, thank God, and I crept away.

Friday 11 May

I got up at six. It was a beautiful day. I went to the House of Commons for the last time as a Member of Parliament. I sat outside the gate in the sunshine, waiting for my brother and the kids. I got them in the Gallery, but it was quite impossible for them to smuggle the video camera in. I slipped it to Stephen, but they searched him and took it away.

In the House was Mark Fisher, and he told me that he had actually been offered a peerage by a senior officer of the Labour Party, in order to remove him from the Commons. That really was absolutely corrupt; that patronage should no longer even be through Number 10, but through the Party machine. Mark was incensed by it!

Anyway, John Bercow had the debate, and made his speech on diabetes – a very serious speech, and he paid a tribute to me. So I got up and thanked him and said that his speech, which was scholarly and important and entirely without crude party points, was an indication of the work of Parliament, and you could be absolutely sure that not a word of it would be reported!

The Speaker paid tribute to Caroline and her book on Keir Hardie, and he made a terribly funny speech about how, when he went on a parliamentary delegation to China with Peter Emery, they saw terrible working conditions in a factory and photographed them. He said to Emery, 'I'll put that in my election address and say, "This is Thatcher's Britain."' Everybody laughed – he'd broken all the rules, because Speakers don't make speeches!

Other Members were very friendly, and at the end I had my little Sony Ruvi camera on my lap, covered with a handkerchief, and filmed the very, very end of the Parliament when the Speaker reads the Royal Assents and then says, 'Order! Order!' and puts the question that 'The House do now adjourn. If any are of that opinion, say Aye, contrary No.' Nobody said 'No', so he simply moved out of the chair. Then, by arrangement, I handed the camera to Mark Fisher and Andrew Mackinlay and Tony Banks who filmed me lighting my pipe.

Then I went to the Speaker's Office to thank Mick Martin and Nicolas Bevan said, 'He's *still* in the Tea Room.' Speakers 'don't go' to the Tea Room. And when I got there, there was Mick with his wife, Mary, a beautiful woman. He told me that his father-in-law, I think (that's Mary's father), had gone in the pits when he was fourteen, and his first job was to bring up the bodies of miners who'd been killed in a fire. The other miners said, 'Oh no, he can't do that. We'll do that.' I gave a big hug, two big hugs, to the Speaker and kissed his wife – another precedent.

Monday 14 May

Up at 7.15 a.m. and had my first hot bath upstairs for ages, because Josh had fixed the broken hot-water heater. I had a banana, a bit of cheese, and a cup of tea for lunch. Then I drove to the House of Commons. When I got there, it must have been about 4.15, I think, who should I see but Stephen, who had come to help me pack. We went up to my room and we cleared the whole room. At five o'clock, which is the time Parliament was dissolved by Royal Proclamation, we sat there in an empty room; and as Big Ben struck five, my parliamentary life came to an end. I felt very relaxed about it. At about half-past five we went downstairs and began packing up the car.

Oh, and I got a pager message just after five, from a close friend, saying, 'There is life after Parliament.'

On the seventh of June 2001, Labour was returned to power for a second term with a majority of 167.

Chesterfield fell to the Liberal Democrats.

When the membership of the new Government was announced, Hilary was appointed as a Minister, and I was Free at Last.

Principal Persons

ADAMS, Gerry. President of Sinn Fein. MP for Belfast West 1983–92 and since 1997. Sinn Fein Member for Belfast West in the Northern Ireland Assembly since 1998. Leading participant in the peace negotiations for Northern Ireland.

AHERN, Bertie. Prime Minister of Ireland since 1997. Lord Mayor of Dublin 1986–7.

ALI, Tariq. Historian, novelist, film maker and socialist commentator.

ASHDOWN, Lord (Paddy Ashdown). Leader of the Liberal Democrats 1988–99. Liberal, then Liberal Democrat MP for Yeovil 1983–2001. High Representative for Bosnia and Hercegovina since 2002.

BANKS, Tony. Minister at the Department for Culture, Media and Sport 1997–9. Chairman, of the House of Commons Works of Art Committee since 2001. Last Chairman of the Greater London Council 1985–6. Labour MP for Newham North West, then West Ham, since 1983.

BECKETT, Margaret. Leader of the House of Commons 1998–2001. Secretary of State for the Environment, Food and Rural Affairs since 2001. Labour MP for Lincoln 1974–9, and for Derby South since 1983.

BENN, Caroline (1926–2000) Also known to the family as Carol and to Tony Benn as Pixie. An American citizen, born in Cincinnati, 13 October 1926. Graduate of Vassar, of the University of Cincinnati and of University College London. Married 17 June 1949. Author of several books including a novel; three education books on comprehensive education (with others); and a biography, *Keir Hardie.* Chair of the Governors of Holland Park School and Governor of Imperial College; a co-opted member of the Inner London Education Authority. Tutor at the Open University and lecturer at Kensington and Hammersmith Further Education College. A founding member of the Campaign for Comprehensive Education and President of the Socialist Education Association. Mother of Stephen, Hilary, Melissa and Joshua and grandmother of ten grandchildren (see family tree). Opera lover and keen gardener.

BICKERSTAFFE, Rodney. NUPE General Secretary 1982. General Secretary of UNISON 1995–2001. President of the National Pensioners' Convention since 2001.

BLAIR, Cherie (Cherie Booth), QC. Chancellor of John Moores University. Contested Thanet North for Labour in 1983. Married to Tony Blair.

BLAIR, Tony. Prime Minister since 1997. Leader of the Labour Party since 1994. Labour MP for Sedgefield since 1983. Barrister.

BLUNKETT, David. Secretary of State for Education and Employment 1997–2001. Home Secretary since 2001. Labour MP for Sheffield Brightside since 1987. Leader of Sheffield City Council 1980–7.

BOATENG, Paul. Minister of State at the Home Office 1998–2001. Financial Secretary to the Treasury 2001–2. Chief Secretary since 2002. Labour MP for Brent South since 1987. Member of the Greater London Council 1981–6.

BOOTHROYD, Baroness (Betty Boothroyd). Speaker of the House of Commons 1992–2000. Labour MP for West Bromwich, then West Bromwich West, 1973–2000. Chancellor of the Open University.

BROWN, Gordon. Chancellor of the Exchequer since 1997. Biographer of *John Maxton* and editor (with James Naughtie) of *John Smith: Life and Soul of the Party*. Labour MP for Dunfermline East since 1983.

BUTLER, David. Political scientist and broadcaster. Co-author of *British Political Facts 1900–2000* and other political reference books. Married to Professor Marilyn Butler, Rector of Exeter College, Oxford, since 1998. Close family friends.

BYERS, Stephen. Secretary of State for Transport, Local Government and the Regions 2001–2. Secretary of State for Trade and Industry 1998–2001. Minister responsible for school standards 1997–8. Chief Secretary to the Treasury 1998. Labour MP for Wallsend, then Tyneside North, since 1992.

CALLAGHAN, Lord (Jim Callaghan). Prime Minister 1976–9, and Leader of the Labour Party 1976–80. Chancellor of the Exchequer 1964–7. Home Secretary 1967–70. Foreign Secretary, 1974–6. Chairman of the Labour Party 1973–4. Labour MP for South, South East and again South Cardiff, 1945–87. Father of the House 1983–7. Made a Knight of the Garter in 1987. Married to Audrey Callaghan.

CAMPBELL, Alastair. Press Secretary to the Leader of the Opposition

(Tony Blair) 1994–7. Press Secretary and Official Spokesman to the Prime Minister 1997–2000. Head of Strategic Communications Unit, Prime Minister's Office, since 2000. Political Editor of the *Daily Mirror* 1989–93.

CAMPBELL, Menzies, QC (Scotland). Liberal, then Liberal Democrat MP for Fife North East since 1987. Chief spokesman on defence and foreign affairs 1997–2003.

CARTER, Peter. Architect, and close family friend.

CASTLE, Baroness (Barbara Castle) (1910–2002). Leader of the British Labour Group in the European Parliament 1979–85. Secretary of State for Social Services 1974–6. Minister of Overseas Development 1964–5. Minister of Transport 1965–8. First Secretary of State at the Department of Employment and Productivity 1968–70. Chairman of the Labour Party, 1958–9. Labour MP for Blackburn 1945–79.

CLARK, Alan (1928–99). Conservative MP for Kensington and Chelsea 1997–9, and for Plymouth Sutton 1974–92. Minister for Defence 1989–92. Historian and diarist.

COATES, Ken. Member of the European Parliament 1989–99 (Independent Labour 1998–9). Author of numerous works on socialism and industrial democracy.

COOK, Robin. Foreign Secretary 1997–2001. Leader of the House 2001–03. Labour MP for Edinburgh Central 1974–83, and for Livingston since 1983. Chairman of the Labour Party 1996–7.

CORBYN, Jeremy. Labour MP for Islington North since 1983. Vice-Chairman of the All-Party Parliamentary Human Rights Group.

CUNNINGHAM, John (Jack). Minister of Agriculture, Fisheries and Food 1997–8. Minister for the Cabinet Office and Chancellor of the Duchy of Lancaster 1998–9. Labour MP for Whitehaven 1970–83, and for Copeland since 1983.

DALYELL, Tam. Father of the House of Commons since 2001. Labour MP for West Lothian, then Linlithgow, since 1962. PPS to Richard Crossman 1964–70.

DEWAR, Donald (1937–2000). Secretary of State for Scotland 1997–9 and first First Minister of the Scottish Parliament 1999–2000. Labour MP for South Aberdeen 1966–70, and for Glasgow Carscadden, then Glasgow Anniesland, 1978–2000.

EDMONDS, John. General Secretary of the GMB since 1986. President of the TUC 1997–8. Member of the Labour Government Skills Task Force.

FALKENDER, Lady (Marcia Williams). Private and Political Secretary to Harold Wilson 1956–83. Journalist and political columnist.

FOOT, Michael. Deputy Leader of the Labour Party 1979–80, and Leader 1980–3. Lord President of the Council and Leader of the House of Commons 1976–9. Secretary of State for Employment 1974–6. Labour MP for Devonport 1945–55, Ebbw Vale, 1960–83 and Blaenau Gwent 1983–92. Biographer of Aneurin Bevan. Married to Jill Craigie.

FOOT, Paul. Journalist, author and political campaigner. Winner of the George Orwell Prize for Journalism in 1994. Columnist for the *Daily Mirror* and *Guardian*.

FOSTER, Derek. Labour MP for Bishop Auckland since 1979. Labour Chief Whip 1985–95.

GOULD, Bryan. Labour MP for Southampton Test 1974–9, and for Dagenham 1983–94. Retired in 1994 and became Vice-Chancellor of Waikato University, New Zealand.

HAGUE, William. Leader of the Conservative Party 1997–2001. Secretary of State for Wales 1995–7. Minister in the Department of Social Security 1993–5. Conservative MP for Richmond (Yorks) since 1989.

HARMAN, Harriet. Secretary of State for Social Security and Minister for Women, 1997–8. Solicitor General since 2001 (and appointed a QC). Labour MP for Peckham, then Camberwell and Peckham, since 1982.

HATTERSLEY, Lord (Roy Hattersley). Deputy Leader of the Labour Party 1983–92. Secretary of State for Prices and Consumer Protection 1976–9. Minister of State at the Foreign and Commonwealth Office 1974–6. Labour MP for Birmingham Sparkbrook 1964–2001.

HEATH, Sir Edward. Leader of the Conservative Party 1965–75. Prime Minister 1970–4. Secretary of State for Industry and Trade, and President of the Board of Trade, 1963–4. Chief Whip 1955–9. Conservative MP for Bexley, then Old Bexley and Sidcup, 1950–2001.

HESELTINE, Lord (Michael Heseltine). Deputy Prime Minister and First Secretary of State 1995–7. President of the Board of Trade 1992–5. Secretary of State for the Environment 1979–83 and 1990–2. Secretary of State for Defence 1983–6. Minister in the 1970–4 Government. Conservative MP for Tavistock 1966–74, and Henley 1974–2001 Contested the party leadership in 1990.

HUBACHER, Sheila. Private secretary to Tony Benn for most of the 1990s. Practitioner of homeopathy.

IRVINE, Lord (Derry Irvine). Lord Chancellor since 1997. Shadow Lord

Chancellor 1992–7. Contested Hendon North for Labour in 1970.

JACKSON, Glenda. Under-Secretary of State for the Environment and Transport, responsible for transport in London, 1997–9. Actress with the Royal Shakespeare Company.

JENKINS, Lord (Roy Jenkins) (1920–2003). Chairman of the Independent Commission on the Voting System 1997–8. President of the European Commission 1977–81. Home Secretary 1965–7. Chancellor of the Exchequer 1967–70. Home Secretary 1974–6. Deputy Leader of the Labour Party 1970–2. Labour MP for Central Southwark 1948–50, and for Stechford 1950–76. Leader of the SDP 1981–3, and SDP MP for Glasgow Hillhead 1982–7. Biographer of Churchill, Gladstone, Asquith and other political figures.

KAUFMAN, Gerald. Shadow Foreign Secretary 1987–92. Chairman of the Culture, Media and Sport Select Committee since 1997. Minister of State, Department of Industry, 1975–9. Labour Party press officer 1965–70. Labour MP for Manchester Ardwick 1970–83, and for Manchester Gorton since 1983.

KINNOCK, Neil. Leader of the Labour Party 1983–92, and Chairman 1987–8. European Commissioner since 1995. Vice-President of the Commission since 1999. Labour MP for Bedwellty, 1970–83, and for Islwyn 1983–95.

LESTOR, Baroness (Joan Lestor) (1931–98). Chairman of the Labour Party, 1977–8. Labour MP for Eton and Slough 1966–83, and for Eccles 1987–97. Under-Secretary of State at the Foreign and Commonwealth Office 1974–5, and at the Department of Education and Science 1975–6.

LIVINGSTONE, Ken. Mayor of London since 2000. Labour MP for Brent East 1987–2001. Leader of the Greater London Council from 1981 until its abolition in 1986.

McAVOY, Tommy. Senior Government Whip (Comptroller of HM Household) since 1997. Labour MP for Glasgow Rutherglen since 1987.

McGAHEY, Mick. (1925–99). Vice-President of the National Union of Mineworkers, 1973–87. President of the Scottish Area of the NUM 1967–87. Chairman of the Communist Party of Great Britain 1974–8.

McGUINNESS, Martin. Sinn Fein MP for Ulster Mid since 1997. Member of the Northern Ireland Assembly since 1998, and Minister of Education since 1999. Chief Negotiator for Sinn Fein in the Northern Ireland peace process.

MACKINLAY, Andrew. Member of the Foreign Affairs Select Committee since 1997. Labour MP for Thurrock since 1992.

McNAMARA, Kevin. Opposition spokesman on Northern Ireland 1987–94. Founder Member of the Friends of the Good Friday Agreement. Labour MP for Kingston-upon-Hull North, then Central, then Hull North and again Kingston-upon-Hull North, since 1966.

MAHON, Alice. PPS to Chris Smith, Secretary of State for Culture, Media and Sport, 1997 (resigned over government policy on lone-parent benefits). Labour MP for Halifax since 1987.

MAJOR, John. Prime Minister and Leader of the Conservative Party 1990–7 (resigned and re-elected as Leader in 1995). Chancellor of the Exchequer 1989–90. Foreign Secretary 1989. Chief Secretary to the Treasury 1987–9. Minister in the Department of Social Security 1985–7. Conservative MP for Huntingdonshire 1979–83, and for Huntingdon 1983–2001.

MANDELSON, Peter. Minister without Portfolio, Cabinet Office, 1997–8. Secretary of State for Trade and Industry 1998 (resigned December). Secretary of State for Northern Ireland 1999–2001 (resigned January). Labour Party's Director of Campaigns and Communications 1985–90. Labour MP for Hartlepool since 1992.

MARTIN, Michael. Speaker of the House of Commons since 2000. Deputy Speaker 1997–2000. Chairman of the House of Commons Administration and Finance and Services Committees 1992–7. PPS to Denis Healey 1981–3. Labour MP for Glasgow Springburn since 1979.

MAYNARD, Joan (1921–98). Labour MP for Sheffield Brightside 1974–87. Vice-Chairman of the Labour Party 1980–1. Secretary/Chairman of the Yorkshire area of the National Union of Agricultural and Allied Workers from 1956.

MEACHER, Michael. Minister for the Environment since 1997. Member of the Shadow Cabinet and Opposition spokesman 1983–97. Parliamentary Under-Secretary of State for Industry 1974–5, Health and Social Security 1975–6, and Trade 1976–9. Labour MP for Oldham West, then Oldham West and Royston, since 1970.

MILIBAND, David. Schools Minister in the Department for Education and Skills since 2002. Head of the Prime Minister's Policy Unit 1997–2001. Head of Policy to Tony Blair 1994–7. Secretary of the Commission on Social Justice 1992–4. Labour MP for South Shields since 2001. Son of Ralph Miliband (see below) and older brother to Edward (see below)

MILIBAND, Edward. Special Adviser to Gordon Brown, Shadow Chancellor and Chancellor of the Exchequer, since 1994. Original Teabag (see below).

MILIBAND, Ralph (1924–94). Professor of Politics, Leeds University, 1972–7, and visiting Professor of the Graduate School, City University of New York. Author of *The State in Capitalist Society* and other seminal works of analysis of capitalism.

MOWLAM, Marjorie (Mo). Secretary of State for Northern Ireland 1997–9. Minister for the Cabinet Office and Chancellor of the Duchy of Lancaster 1999–2001. Labour MP for Redcar 1987–2001.

MULLIN, Chris. Parliamentary Under-Secretary of State at the Department of the Environment, Transport and the Regions 1999–2001, and at International Development 2001. Chairman of the Home Affairs Select Committee 1997–9 and since 2001. Editor of *Tribune* 1982–4. Author of *A Very British Coup* and other political novels, and of *Error of Judgement*. Labour MP for Sunderland South since 1987.

PAISLEY, Ian. Protestant Unionist, then Democratic Unionist MP for North Antrim since 1970 (resigned and re-elected December 1985/January 1986). Democratic Unionist Member of the Northern Ireland Assembly since 1998. Member of the European Parliament for Northern Ireland since 1979.

PORTILLO, Michael. Chief Secretary to the Treasury 1992–4. Secretary of State for Employment 1994–5 and for Defence 1995–7. Conservative MP for Enfield, Southgate, 1984–97 and for Kensington and Chelsea since 1999.

PRESCOTT, John. Deputy Leader of the Labour Party since 1994. Deputy Prime Minister and Secretary of State for the Environment, Transport and the Regions 1997–2001. First Secretary of State since 2001, with responsibility for the regions, housing and urban affairs since 2002. Labour MP for Hull East since 1970. Member of the European Parliament 1975–9. Contested the deputy leadership in 1988.

PRIMAROLO, Dawn. Secretary to the Treasury 1997–9. Paymaster General since 1999. Opposition spokeswoman on health and treasury matters 1992–7. Secretary of Bristol South East Labour Party 1979–83. Labour MP for Bristol South since 1987.

RACE, Reg. Labour MP for Wood Green 1979–83. Labour candidate for Chesterfield in the 2001 General Election.

REID, John. Health Secretary since 2003. Secretary of State for Scotland 1999–2001. Secretary of State for Northern Ireland 2001–03. Defence Spokesman 1990–7. Labour MP for Motherwell North, then Hamilton North and Bellshill since 1987.

ROBERTSON, Lord (George Robertson). Secretary of State for Defence

1997–9. Secretary General of NATO since 1999. Labour MP for Hamilton, then Hamilton South, 1978–99. Full-time GMB official 1968–78.

ROBINSON, Geoffrey. Paymaster General 1997–8. Owner of *New Statesman* magazine. Industrialist: Chief Executive of Jaguar Cars 1973–5. Author of *The Unconventional Minister.* Labour MP for Coventry North West since 1976.

SAWYER, Lord (Tom Sawyer). Chairman of the Labour Party 1990–1. Deputy Secretary of NUPE (UNISON) 1981–94. General Secretary of the Labour Party 1994–8.

SCARGILL, Arthur. President of the NUM 1981–2002. Member of the TUC General Council 1986–8. Founder of the Socialist Labour Party 1996.

SHEPHERD, Richard. *Spectator* Parliamentarian of the Year 1995. Candidate for the Speakership in 2000. Conservative MP for Aldridge-Brownhills since 1979.

SHORE, Lord (Peter Shore) (1924–2001) Secretary of State for the Environment 1976–9. Secretary of State for Trade 1974–6, and for Economic Affairs 1967–9. PPS to Harold Wilson 1965–6. Labour MP for Stepney, then Stepney and Poplar, and then Bethnal Green and Stepney, 1964–97. President of the Labour Euro Safeguards Campaign. Married to Liz Shore, Deputy Chief Medical Officer, DHSS, 1977–85.

SHORT, Clare. Secretary of State for International Development since 1997. Member of the Labour Party NEC 1988–98. Labour MP for Birmingham Ladywood since 1983.

SIMPSON, Alan. Secretary of the Socialist Campaign Group of Labour MPs. Keen environmentalist and contributor to *Localisation – a Global Manifesto* by Colin Hines. Labour MP for Nottingham South since 1992.

SKINNER, Dennis. Chairman of the Labour Party 1988–9. Member of the Labour Party NEC 1978–93 and since 1994. President of the Derbyshire NUM 1966–70. Labour MP for Bolsover since 1970.

SMITH, John, QC (Scotland) (1938–94). Leader of the Labour Party 1992–4. Shadow Chancellor 1987–92. Parliamentary Under-Secretary of State, then Minister of State, at the Department of Energy 1974–6. Minister of State in the Privy Council Office, with responsibility for devolution, 1976–8. Secretary of State for Trade 1978–9. Labour MP for Lanarkshire North, then Monklands East, 1970–94.

SOAMES, Nicholas. Conservative MP for Crawley, then Mid Sussex, since 1983. Minister for the Armed Forces 1994–7. Parliamentary

Secretary at the Ministry of Agriculture, Fisheries and Food 1992–4. Son of Mary Soames; grandson of Winston Churchill.

STEEL, Lord (David Steel). Liberal Democrat Member for Lothians in the Scottish Parliament, and Presiding Officer, since 1999. Leader of the Liberal Party, 1976–88, and then joint Leader of the Liberal and Social Democratic Alliance during 1987. Liberal MP for Roxburgh, Selkirk and Peebles, then Tweeddale, Ettrick and Lauderdale, 1965–97.

STRAW, John (Jack). Home Secretary 1997–2001. Foreign Secretary since 2001. Shadow Home Secretary 1994–7. Adviser to Barbara Castle and Peter Shore, as Secretaries of State for Social Services and for the Environment respectively, 1974–7. Labour MP for Blackburn since 1979.

TAYLOR, Ann. Leader of the House of Commons and Lord President of the Council 1997–8. Chief Whip 1998–2001. Shadow Leader of House of Commons 1994–7. Labour MP for Bolton West 1974–83, and for Dewsbury since 1987.

TEABAGS CLUB (The Eminent Association of Benn Archive Graduates). Students and other young people who worked in Tony Benn's office for work experience, or as a labour of love, during the late 1980s and 1990s. The original Teabags were Edward Miliband, William Whyte, Hugh Scott, Hwyel Jarman, Andrew Hood, Charlie Crowe, Sean Arnold, Simon Fletcher, Saumiya Bhavsar, Martha Wharlley, Sarah Clancy, Laura Rohde, Assad Khan, Sara Lauchlan, Clare Smith, Kenny Seth, Paul Fisher, Sam; honorary Teabags include Ruth Hobson, Jennie Walsh, Dr Catherine Hood, Rachel Thomson, Clare Bonnin, Helena Cullen.

THATCHER, Baroness (Margaret Thatcher). Leader of the Conservative Party 1975–90. Prime Minister 1979–90. Secretary of State for Education and Science 1970–4. Junior Minister in the Ministry of Pensions and National Insurance 1961–4. Conservative MP for Finchley 1959–92.

TRIMBLE, David. First Minister of the Northern Ireland Executive since 1998 (resigned and re-elected 2001). Leader of the Ulster Unionist Party since 1995. Awarded the Nobel Peace Prize in 1998. UUP MP for Upper Bann since 1990, and UUP Member of the Northern Ireland Assembly since 1998.

VALLINS, Margaret. Chesterfield District Councillor 1987–91. Constituency Secretary to Tony Benn 1984–2001.

VALLINS, Tom. Former Secretary of the Chesterfield Labour Party. Election agent to Tony Benn 1987–2001.

WEATHERILL, Lord (Bernard [Jack] Weatherill). Speaker of the House of Commons 1983–92. Conservative MP for Croydon North East 1964–83, and MP (Speaker) for Croydon North East 1983–92.

WHITTY, Lord (Larry Whitty). General Secretary of the Labour Party 1985–94. European Coordinator for the Labour Party 1994–7. Minister in the Department for the Environment, Food and Rural Affairs 2001.

WINSTONE, Ruth. Editor of Tony Benn's *Diaries*. Associate editor of *The Times Guide to the House of Commons*, and editor of several political biographies and other works. Research Library Clerk of the House of Commons.

WISE, Audrey (1935–2000). Labour MP for Coventry South West 1974–9, and for Preston 1987–2000. Member of the Labour Party NEC 1982–7.

Appendix 1

Members of the Cabinet

The Cabinet, November 1990

Prime Minister, First Lord of the Treasury and Minister for the Civil Service	John Major
Lord Chancellor	Lord Mackay of Clashfern
Secretary of State for Foreign and Commonwealth Affairs	Douglas Hurd
Chancellor of the Exchequer	Norman Lamont
Home Secretary	Kenneth Baker
Secretary of State for Trade	Peter Lilley
Secretary of State for Transport	Malcolm Rifkind
Secretary of State for Defence	Tom King
Lord Privy Seal and Leader of the House of Lords	Lord Waddington
Lord President of the Council and Leader of the House of Commons	John MacGregor
Minister of Agriculture, Fisheries and Food	John Gummer
Secretary of State for the Environment	Michael Heseltine
Secretary of State for Energy	John Wakeham
Secretary of State for Wales	David Hunt
Secretary of State for Social Security	Tony Newton
Chancellor of the Duchy of Lancaster and Minister for Citizen's Charter	Chris Patten
Secretary of State for Scotland	Ian Lang
Secretary of State for Northern Ireland	Peter Brooke
Secretary of State for Education and Science	Kenneth Clarke

Secretary of State for Health	William Waldegrave
Secretary of State for Employment	Michael Howard
Chief Secretary to the Treasury	David Mellor

The Cabinet, April 1992

Prime Minister, First Lord of the Treasury and Minister for the Civil Service	John Major
Lord Chancellor	Lord Mackay of Clashfern
Secretary of State for Foreign and Commonwealth Affairs	Douglas Hurd
Chancellor of the Exchequer	Norman Lamont
Home Secretary	Kenneth Clarke
President of the Board of Trade	Michael Heseltine
Secretary of State for Transport	John MacGregor
Secretary of State for Defence	Malcolm Rifkind
Lord Privy Seal and Leader of the House of Lords	Lord Wakeham
Lord President of the Council and Leader of the House of Commons	Tony Newton
Minister of Agriculture, Fisheries and Food	John Gummer
Secretary of State for the Environment	Michael Howard
Secretary of State for Wales	David Hunt
Secretary of State for Social Security	Peter Lilley
Chancellor of the Duchy of Lancaster and Minister for Citizen's Charter	William Waldegrave
Secretary of State for Scotland	Ian Lang
Secretary of State for National Heritage	David Mellor
Secretary of State for Northern Ireland	Sir Patrick Mayhew
Secretary of State for Education	John Patten
Secretary of State for Health	Virginia Bottomley
Secretary of State for Employment	Gillian Shephard
Chief Secretary to the Treasury	Michael Portillo

The Cabinet, May 1997

Prime Minister, First Lord of the Treasury and Minister for the Civil Service	Tony Blair
Deputy Prime Minister and Secretary of State for Environment, Transport and the Regions	John Prescott
Lord Chancellor	Lord Irvine of Lairg
Secretary of State for Foreign and Commonwealth Affairs	Robin Cook
Chancellor of the Exchequer	Gordon Brown
Home Secretary	Jack Straw
President of the Board of Trade and Secretary of State for Trade and Industry	Margaret Beckett
Secretary of State for Defence	George Robertson
Lord Privy Seal and Leader of the House of Lords	Lord Richard
President of the Council and Leader of the House of Commons	Ann Taylor
Secretary of State for Culture, Media and Sport	Chris Smith
Secretary of State for Education and Employment	David Blunkett
Secretary of State for Social Security and Minister for Women	Harriet Harman
Secretary of State for Wales	Ron Davies
Chancellor of the Duchy of Lancaster	David Clark
Secretary of State for Scotland	Donald Dewar
Secretary of State for Northern Ireland	Marjorie (Mo) Mowlam
Secretary of State for Health	Frank Dobson
Secretary of State for International Development	Clare Short
Minister of Agriculture, Fisheries and Food	Jack Cunningham
Chief Secretary to the Treasury	Alistair Darling
Minister for Transport	Gavin Strang

Appendix 2

National Executive Committee of the Labour Party, 1991

Tom Sawyer (Chair and NUPE representative)
John Evans, MP (Vice-Chair)
Sam McCluskie (Treasurer)
Neil Kinnock, MP (Leader of the Labour Party)
Roy Hattersley, MP (Deputy Leader of the Labour Party)

Trade Union representatives:
Tom Burlison (GMB)
Peter Burns (AEU)
Tony Clarke (UCW)
Gordon Colling (NGA)
Bill Connor (USDAW)
Andy Dodds (RMT)
Eddie Haigh (TGWU)
Ted O'Brien (General Media and Paper Union)
Colm O'Kane (COHSE)
Jack Rogers (UCATT)
Richard Rosser (TSSA)
Barbara Switzer (MSF)

Socialist, Cooperative and other organisations:
John Evans, MP (National Union of Labour and Socialist Clubs)

Constituency Labour Party representatives:
Tony Benn, MP (Chesterfield)
David Blunkett, MP (Sheffield Brightside)
Robin Cook, MP (Livingston)
Bryan Gould, MP (Dagenham)
John Prescott, MP (Hull East)
Jo Richardson, MP (Barking)
Dennis Skinner, MP (Bolsover)

Women members:
Margaret Beckett, MP
Anne Davis (National Union of Labour and Socialist Clubs)
Diana Jeuda (USDAW)
Joan Lestor, MP
Clare Short, MP

Youth representative:
Alun Parry

General Secretary:
Larry Whitty

National Executive Committee of the Labour Party, 1993

Tony Clarke (Chair)
David Blunkett, MP (Vice-Chair)
Tom Burlison, (Treasurer)
John Smith, MP (Leader of the Labour Party)
Margaret Beckett, MP (Deputy Leader of the Labour Party)

Trade Union representatives:
Judith Church (GMB)
Tony Clarke (UCW)
Gordon Colling (Graphical Paper and Media Union)
Bill Connor (USDAW)
Dan Duffy (TGWU)
Nigel Harris (AEU)
Vernon Hince (RMT)
Charles Kelly (UCATT)
Colm O'Kane (COHSE)
Richard Rosser (TSSA)
Tom Sawyer (NUPE)
David Ward (NCU)

Socialist, Cooperative and other organisations:
John Evans, MP (National Union of Labour and Socialist Clubs)

Constituency Labour Party representatives:
Tony Benn, MP (Chesterfield)

Tony Blair, MP (Sedgefield)
David Blunkett, MP (Sheffield Brightside)
Gordon Brown, MP (Dunfermline East)
Robin Cook, MP (Livingston)
Neil Kinnock, MP (Islwyn)
John Prescott, MP (Hull East)

Women members:
Hilary Armstrong, MP
Brenda Etchells
Diana Jeuda (USDAW)
Joan Lestor, MP
Clare Short, MP

Youth representative:
Claire Ward

General Secretary:
Larry Whitty

Appendix 3

Campaign Group of Labour MPs: active Members in the 1990s

Diane Abbott
John Austin
Harry Barnes
Tony Benn
Dennis Canavan
Jeremy Corbyn
Ann Cryer
Bob Cryer
John Cryer
Bob Etherington
Maria Fyfe
Bernie Grant
Neil Gerrard
Lynne Jones
Ken Livingstone
John McAllion
Alice Mahon
Alan Meale
Bill Michie
Dawn Primarolo
Alan Simpson
Dennis Skinner
Llew Smith
Bob Wareing
Audrey Wise

Appendix 4

Abbreviations

AEEU	Amalgamated Engineering and Electrical Union
AMICUS	Union of manufacturing, finance, science and engineering workers
ASLEF	Associated Society of Locomotive Engineers and Firemen
AUT	Association of University Teachers
BECTU	Broadcasting, Entertainment, Cinematograph and Theatre Union
BFAWU	Bakers Food and Allied Workers Union
CASE	Campaign for the Advancement of State Education
CBI	Confederation of British Industry
CLPD	Campaign for Labour Party Democracy
COI	Central Office of Information
CP	Communist Party
CPAG	Child Poverty Action Group
CRE	Commission for Racial Equality
CSC	Cuba Solidarity Campaign
CSC	Comprehensive Schools Committee
CWU	Communication Workers' Union
EC	Executive Committee
EDM	Early Day Motion
EQUITY	British Actors Equity Association
EU	European Union
FDA	First Division Association of Civil Servants
FOE	Friends of the Earth
GC	General Committee (of a constituency Labour Party)
GMB	(Union for) General, Municipal, Boilermakers
GPMU	Graphical, Paper and Media Union
HoC	House of Commons
HSE	Health and Safety Executive
ILO	International Labour Office
IOD	Institute of Directors
IPPR	Institute for Public Policy Research

ISTC	Iron and Steel Trades Confederation
Lab	Labour Party
LAP	Labour Action for Peace
MSF	(Union for) Manufacturing, Science, Finance
NACODS	National Association of Colliery Overmen, Deputies and Shotfirers
NATFHE	National Association of Teachers in Further and Higher Education
NEC	National Executive Committee (of the Labour Party)
NUJ	National Union of Journalists
NUM	National Union of Mineworkers
NUT	National Union of Teachers
OFSTED	Office for Standards in Education
PLP	Parliamentary Labour Party
PMQs	Prime Minister's Questions
PNQ	Private Notice Question (a procedure for raising an urgent issue)
RMT	Rail Maritime and Transport Union
RSC	Royal Society of Chemistry
SEA	Socialist Education Association
SERA	Socialist Environmental and Resources Association
SWP	Socialist Workers' Party
TGWU	Transport and General Workers' Union
TUC	Trades Union Congress
UDM	Union of Democratic Mineworkers
UN	United Nations
UNA	United Nations Association
UNISON	The public service union
USDAW	Union of Shop Distributive and Allied Workers
WBAI	American public service radio network
WEA	Workers' Educational Association

Benn Family Tree

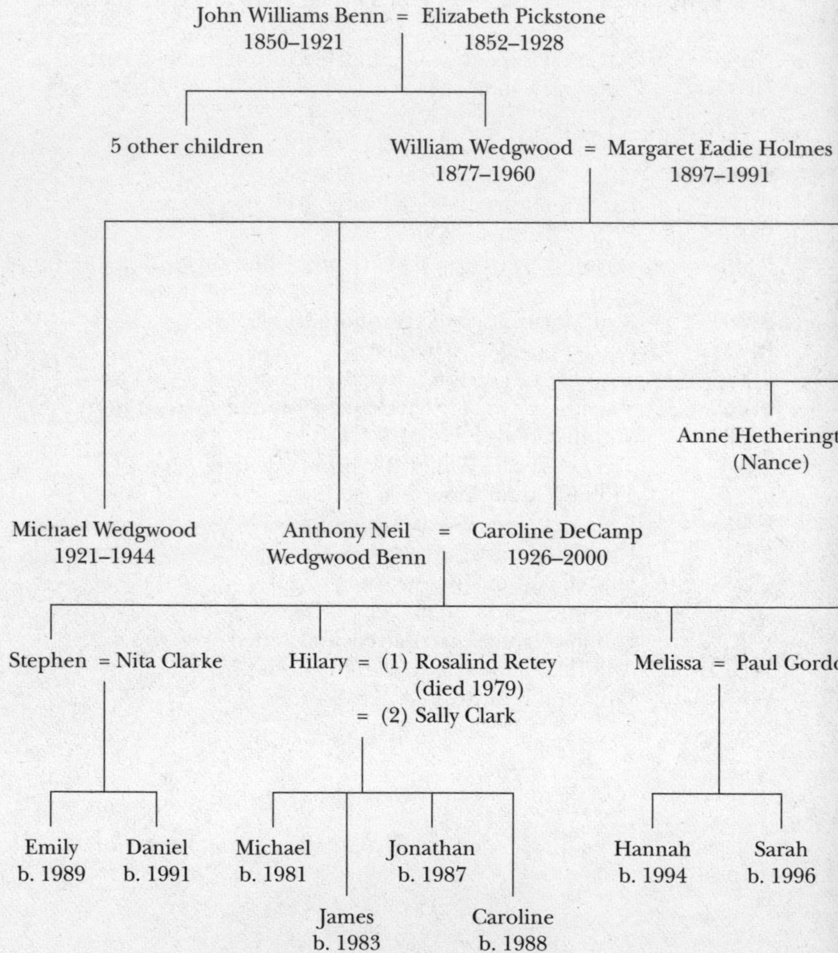

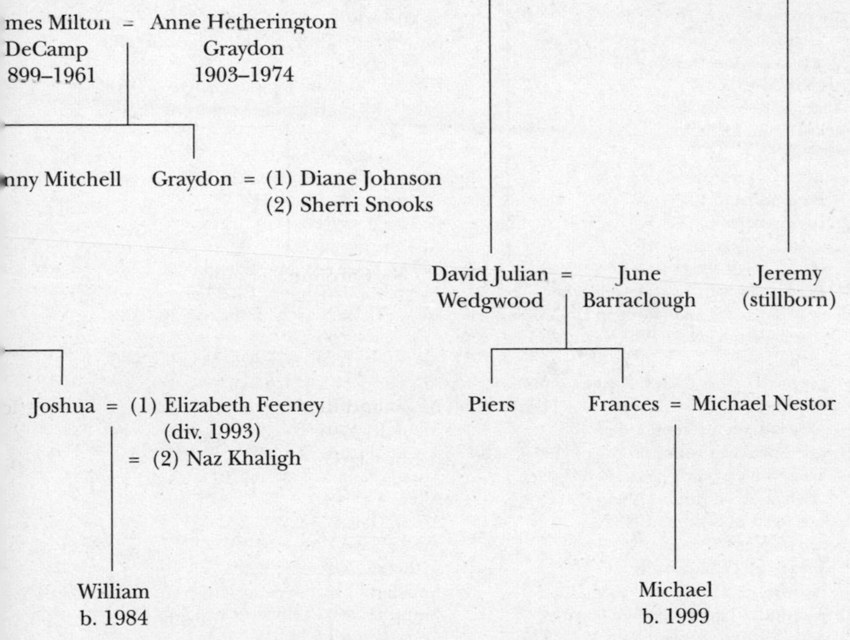
mes Milton = Anne Hetherington
DeCamp
899–1961
Graydon
1903–1974
nny Mitchell
Graydon = (1) Diane Johnson
(2) Sherri Snooks
David Julian = June
Wedgwood
Barraclough
Jeremy
(stillborn)
Joshua = (1) Elizabeth Feeney
(div. 1993)
= (2) Naz Khaligh
Piers
Frances = Michael Nestor
William
b. 1984
Michael
b. 1999

Index